If All the World Were Paper

Awarded the

EDWARD CAMERON DIMOCK, JR. PRIZE
IN THE INDIAN HUMANITIES

by the American Institute of Indian Studies and
published with the Institute's generous support.

AIIS Publication Committee:

Sarah Lamb, Co-Chair
Anand A. Yang, Co-Chair
Chanchal Dadlani
Sonal Khullar
Preeta Mani
Tulasi Srinivas
Tariq Thachil

If All the World Were Paper

A History of Writing in Hindi

Tyler W. Williams

Columbia University Press

New York

Columbia University Press wishes to express its appreciation for assistance given by the Wm. Theodore de Bary Fund in the publication of this book.

Columbia University Press
Publishers Since 1893
New York Chichester, West Sussex
cup.columbia.edu

Library of Congress Cataloging-in-Publication Data
Names: Williams, Tyler Walker, author.
Title: If all the world were paper : a history of writing in Hindi / Tyler W. Williams.
Description: New York : Columbia University Press, 2024. |
Includes bibliographical references and index.
Identifiers: LCCN 2024009700 (print) | LCCN 2024009701 (ebook) |
ISBN 9780231211123 (hardback) | ISBN 9780231211130 (trade paperback) |
ISBN 9780231558754 (ebook)
Subjects: LCSH: Hindi literature—To 1500—History and criticism—Theory, etc. |
Hindi literature—1500-1800—History and criticism—Theory, etc. |
Hindi literature—Manuscripts. | Material culture in literature. |
LCGFT: Literary criticism.
Classification: LCC PK2035 .W55 2024 (print) | LCC PK2035 (ebook) |
DDC891.4/309— dc23/eng/20240325

Cover design: Chang Jae Lee
Cover image: *Candāyan* of Maulana Daud. Manuscript copied circa 1570, Hindustani Ms. 1, Folios 82v and 83r, John Rylands Library, Manchester.

This work is dedicated to
Allison Busch (1969–2019),
teacher, mentor, and friend.

Yā Kabīkaj

Contents

Acknowledgments ix

Prologue: Into the Archive xiii

Introduction: Writing a History of Writing in the Vernacular 1

1. Storytellers and Storybooks 26

2. Saints, Singers, and Songbooks 74

3. *Pothīs*, Pandits, and Princes 119

4. The Guru's Voice and the Sacred Book 154

Conclusion: Building an Archive for Hindi 205

……

Notes 229

Bibliography 271

Index 291

Acknowledgments

If the following pages demonstrate but one thing, it is the fact that *every* book is the work of multiple hands. From the paper, bindings, ink, and paint to the page numbering, typesetting, hand copying, and—of course—the composition of the work of literature itself, every book is an object produced through multiple, intertwined, and collaborative forms of labor. The book that you now hold in your hands (or read from a digital device) is no different: it is the product of many people's labor, and I appeal to the reader to take the time to become acquainted with some of these people over the next few paragraphs. They have been, in material as well as intellectual ways, just as critical to the creation of this book as its putative author (who takes full responsibility for any shortcomings).

To begin, Rosa at Foster Hall, University of Chicago, and Irina and Barbara at Knox Hall, Columbia University, are the people who maintain the spaces in which we work. Tracy Davis, Emily Kort, Alicia Czaplewski, and Alyssa M. Padilla at the Department of South Asian Languages and Civilizations and Jessica Rechtschaffer, Leah Smith, Jill Kitchen, and Michael Fishman at the Department of Middle Eastern, South Asian, and African Studies performed the labor that made research and teaching possible for me in those departments.

Manpreet Kaur provided assistance and encouragement throughout the research and writing of this book. Her research and expertise in Punjabi and South Asian literature and religions have been a source of both knowledge and inspiration over the past several years. I will be forever grateful for her willingness to discuss and give feedback on iterations of the manuscript and for our shared experiences working in the field.

This project received financial and logistical support from the United States Fulbright-Hays Doctoral Dissertation Research Abroad program, the National Endowment for the Humanities, the American Institute of Indian Studies, and the Committee on Southern Asian Studies at the University of Chicago.

The following institutions graciously allowed me to consult their manuscript collections: the Nagari Pracharini Sabha, Banaras; Bharat Kala Bhavan, Banaras Hindu University; Hindi Sahitya Sammelan, Allahabad; Vrindavan Research Institute, Vrindavan; Rajasthan Oriental Research Institute, Jodhpur; Mansingh Pustak Prakash, Jodhpur; Rajasthani Shodh Sansthan, Chaupasani; Abhay Jain Granthalay, Bikaner; Anup Sanskrit Library, Bikaner; Rajasthan Oriental Research Institute, Jaipur; Royal Pothikhana of the Maharaja Sawai Man Singh II Museum, Jaipur; Oriental Institute, Maharaja Sayajirao University of Baroda; Lalbhai Dalpatbhai Museum, Ahmedabad; Shri Hemachandracharya Jain Library, Patan; Shree Mahavir Jain Aradhana Kedra, Koba; Chhatrapati Shivaji Maharaj Vastu Sangrahalaya, Mumbai; Asiatic Society of Mumbai, Mumbai; Bhandarkar Oriental Research Institute, Pune; Government Museum and Art Gallery, Chandigarh; A.C. Joshi Library, Punjab University, Chandigarh; Bhai Kahn Singh Nabha Library, Punjabi University, Patiala; Asiatic Society, Kolkata; Bibliotheque nationale de France, Paris; British Library, London; John Rylands Library, University of Manchester; Kislak Center for Special Collections, Rare Books and Manuscripts, University of Pennsylvania, Philadelphia; Asian Art Museum, San Francisco; Metropolitan Museum of Art, New York; and the Art Institute of Chicago. Without the assistance of their knowledgeable and helpful staff, this project would never have been possible. Special thanks are due to Kamal Kishore Sankhla, Mahendra Singh Tanwar, Vikram Singh Bhatti, Vandana Prapanna, Reema Hooja, Sweta Prajapati, Yatin Jain, Seema Gera, Qamar Adamjee, Jérôme Petit, Deepak Bharatan, Madhuvanti Ghosh, Mritunjay Kumar, Benjamin Flemming, Shreenand Bapat, and Amruta Natu.

The communities of the Niranjani Sampraday and Dadu Panth have been gracious, welcoming, and helpful to me over the past sixteen years of research. Within the Niranjani Sampraday, Swami Samvardas Shastri and his family, as well as the Parik family, have extended enormous help and kindness and shared much knowledge over the years. Within the Dadu Panth, Acharya Gopaldas Ji made much work possible through his blessing.

Purushottam Agrawal, professor emeritus of Jawaharlal Nehru University, deserves the credit for setting me on the path of studying precolonial Hindi literature and working with manuscripts. My sincere thanks to Akshara Ravishankar Parmeswaran, with whom I read manuscripts of vernacular commentaries on the *Bhagavadgītā*; Zoë High, who included me in her readings of Dakkani literature; and Anna Lee White, who procured important materials from India on my behalf. My gratitude to Rita and Christopher Williams for their constant support and encouragement. Special thanks are due to Magnus Berglund, who told me that I should write for a living.

This book has benefited from the feedback, suggestions, and assistance of numerous readers and interlocuters: my colleagues at the Department of South Asian Languages and Civilizations, especially Ulrike Stark, Andrew Ollett, Whitney Cox, and Thibaut d'Hubert; the participants in the 2014 American Institute of Indian Studies Dissertation to Book Workshop, especially David Boyk; the Mellon Fellows at the Interdisciplinary Center for Innovative Theory and Empirics, Columbia University; colleagues Monika Horstmann, Dalpat Rajpurohit, Imre Bangha, John Cort, Winand Callewaert, Ramya Sreenivasan, Carl Ernst, Gurinder Singh Mann, Pashaura Singh, Linda Hess, Raman Prasad Sinha, Devendra Kumar Singh Gautam, Divya Cherian, Joel Lee, and Patton Burchett. I am also grateful for having had the opportunity to learn and receive assistance from three colleagues who left us far too early: Sunil Kumar, Kavita Singh, and Aditya Behl.

I would especially like to thank all three anonymous reviewers for Columbia University Press; their criticisms and suggestions helped to make this a better book. I am grateful for Leslie Kriesel's careful editing, which greatly improved the clarity and flow of the book. My heartfelt thanks to Christine Dunbar and the staff of Columbia University Press for their help and support in seeing the project to completion.

This book is the product of research carried out in the Department of Middle Eastern, South Asian, and African Studies at Columbia University. I am heavily indebted to the close reading and feedback of Sheldon Pollock, Sudipta Kaviraj, John Stratton Hawley, and Francesca Orsini. Jack, as John S. Hawley is popularly known, provided particular encouragement and insight throughout the process.

Finally, and most importantly, if the reader finds anything valuable in the pages that follow, then I strongly encourage them to read the work of Allison Busch (much of which is freely accessible online), whose original thinking and fresh approach to reading precolonial Hindi literature and writing about its history were a source of inspiration for this study. Allison oversaw the research and writing of the manuscript that eventually became this book, and her engagement with and encouragement of the project helped me to follow through with it. She gave me a copy of her first monograph inscribed with the words, "To Tyler: proof that dissertations do become books!" This is for you, Allison—we proved it again.

Prologue

INTO THE ARCHIVE

Material culture is best understood as the history and philosophy of objects. It proceeds from the idea that objects, tangible and imagined, locate the entirety of human experience and understanding. We are simply creatures that know and make sense of the world and our places within it through things.

—Bernard Herman, "On Southern Things"

Near the heart of old Banaras, tucked behind an unassuming gate near the main post office, stands a three-story building of red brick (fig. 0.1). This elegant but forlorn structure is perhaps the most hallowed institution of modern Hindi literature: the Nagari Pracharini Sabha, or Committee for the Promulgation of Nagari. Founded in 1893 by college students, including several individuals who would go on to become prominent scholars of Hindi, the Sabha quickly developed its program around three main goals: to promote the use of Hindi in the Nāgarī script as the language of government and civil society, to recover the literary history of Hindi by searching for copies of premodern works, and to publish selected premodern texts as well as new works of criticism, literary history, and lexicons. The Sabha had been active for eleven years and had achieved a considerable degree of success in these endeavors when it inaugurated its new headquarters at this site in 1904.

Entering through the front door of the building, one comes to a dimly lit vestibule, the left wall of which is adorned with a battered and rusted metal sign hanging askew. The sign reads: *hindī hamārī rāṣṭrabhāṣā hai / nāgarī hamārī rāṣṭralipi hai / sarvatra hindī kā hī vyavahār kījiye* (Hindi is our national language. Nāgarī is our national script. Please use Hindi at all times). Passing this poignant metaphor for the current state of Hindi's aspirations, one enters the main reading room of the Sabha, an impressive two-story hall with arcades on the ground floor and galleries on the upper floor. In the center of the room stand long reading tables; the upper galleries are decorated with portraits of the Sabha's founders, leaders, and luminaries, including Shyamsundar Das, founding Sabha member and pioneering literary critic; Ayodhya Singh Upadhyay "Harioudh," poet, essayist, novelist, and chairman of the Hindi Sahitya Sammelan; Ramchandra Shukla, a towering figure in the disciplines of literary history and criticism and author of several of the Nagari Pracarini Sabha's critical editions of Hindi works from the 1920s through 1940s; and Mahavirprasad Dwivedi, periodical editor and ideological beacon of the Hindi movement in the first quarter of the twentieth century. Premchand is here, as well as Bhartendu Harishchandra, Raja Shivprasad "Sitar-i Hind," and Maithalisharan Gupta. They and other doyens of Hindi literature look down at the library patrons below, as if monitoring the progress of contemporary Hindi scholarship.

On most days, the library is nearly empty. Other than the occasional postgraduate student who has come to read one of the Sabha's printed publications or study for civil service exams, the only regular visitors are a few locals who come to read the newspaper. The library's handwritten register, which records every consultation of the materials, reveals that few scholars visit in search of the thing that the library is most famous for: its large and invaluable collection of precolonial manuscripts, which sit in metal cabinets on the second floor. These manuscripts are sometimes loose, sometimes bound assemblages of handwritten folios, recording everything from religious hymns and epics to scientific treatises and riddles composed in a variety of idioms related to, but distinct from, "standard" or *mānak* Hindi as it is spoken and written today.

This unique and irreplaceable resource of precolonial and colonial-era manuscripts has suffered significant harm and depredation over the past few decades. The Sabha has neither the resources nor the expertise to properly conserve the manuscripts, resulting in the damage or destruction of many valuable items. Even worse, manuscripts occasionally disappear entirely, being stolen or, more often, misplaced. The Sabha has consequently become wary of granting visitors access, a measure that further discourages the already small group of research students and scholars in India and from abroad curious and patient enough to work on unpublished precolonial material.[1]

Confronted with the library's rapidly disintegrating collection and the administrative inertia that seems to affect not only the Nagari Pracharini Sabha but also many similar institutions in contemporary India, some scholars throw up their hands, abandon any hope of working on such materials, and chalk the situation up to the myriad problems faced by a postcolonial society. Others find it increasingly difficult to see a role for such institutions in India as the country focuses more and more of its aspirations and resources on competing in global markets dominated by science and technology. "What use are old books," I have often heard asked, "when information about the whole world is available through a computer or even your phone?"[2]

A simple rebuttal to this argument could perhaps be made on the basis of the (in)availability of the collection's content: in fact, the majority of works in the Nagari Pracharini Sabha's manuscript collection, like that of most other manuscript archives in India, is *not* available in print, much less in digital form.[3] Most of the manuscripts have never been closely studied, and many contain works that have never been published or of which there are no other known copies. As many literary historians, philologists, and historians of South Asia know, many if not most of the region's manuscript libraries hold similarly unique and valuable collections. The total number of manuscripts in South Asia is estimated to be around thirty million; yet even the Government of India's attempt to create a comprehensive catalogue under the National Mission for Manuscripts has, to date, been able to catalogue only a little over four million items (a nevertheless impressive accomplishment).[4]

Yet I would argue that there is another, equally important reason to devote time and thought to the manuscript archives of South Asia and the institutions that preserve them: aside from the manuscripts' textual content, their material qualities tell us much about the literary, intellectual, and religious culture and history of the subcontinent that we could not learn through other means. Just as it would be impossible to understand our present-day social networks without studying the digital technologies of the internet, World Wide Web, audiovisual recording, and handheld devices, it is impossible to understand the textual and performance cultures of precolonial South Asia and the networks of people and institutions that created them without paying close attention to the material technologies utilized, including writing on paper, palm leaf, cloth, wood, stone, and numerous other materials.

Thinking critically about the materiality of the archive also draws attention to the historical, political, and cultural processes that shaped the modern institutions that now preserve that archive—indeed, that *produced* it as both a concrete object and an object of knowledge. This includes libraries like that of the Nagari Pracharini Sabha but also museums, educational institutions, and cultural organizations.

If we truly want to understand why these institutions sometimes seem so "dysfunctional" and the precolonial archive of literature and scholarship remains largely neglected, then we must study their logic and how the archive was constructed during the colonial and postindependence periods. In doing so, we may better understand how the construction of the precolonial literary archive contained the seeds of its own decline and how its treatment has coalesced with broader trends such as linguistic nationalism, print capitalism, and the collapse of local intellectual networks so as to render the archive ostensibly redundant.

Although the antiquarian might see value in preserving objects for their own sake, it is not easy to convince the scholarly community, let alone the public, of the need to conserve manuscripts without showing their utility. And it is impossible to convince others of that utility without identifying manuscripts' unique attributes and demonstrating their *significance*. There is a relatively small but dedicated and growing community of scholars, librarians, and conservationists in India and other South Asian countries demonstrating *why* and *how* the manuscript archive possesses value.[5] In consonance with this broader movement, this book is an argument for the unique importance of manuscripts to the history of Hindi (and to the history of South Asian languages more generally) and thus for their utility to scholars of language, literature, history, and religion. At another level, this book is an argument for changing the ways we *interact* with those manuscripts and with the archive in general. I deliberately use the term "interact" because written documents are not simply inert objects upon which human agents act but rather "things" or "agents" in their own right, in the sense suggested by Bruno Latour: they can affect human agents emotionally and cognitively, shape their action and behavior, and these effects themselves can vary depending upon time, place, and social and political context.[6] To take a ready example, a copy of the Bible may affect an individual's emotions and shape their actions in very different ways depending upon the individual's religious and cultural habitus and upon whether they encounter the Bible in a church, in a courtroom, or in a museum.

FROM "BOOKS" TO "MANUSCRIPTS" AND FROM "OBJECTS" TO "THINGS"

One might frame the paradox posed by the Nagari Pracharini Sabha in the following way: its deteriorating state is mirrored in the conditions of many other archives and libraries in India, and every so often a scholar or political leader will make a plea to "save" and "conserve" these manuscripts because they are part of the Indian nation's historical, cultural, and/or artistic "heritage" (*virāsat* in Hindi). Despite these appeals, conservation initiatives are consistently difficult to start and even more difficult to sustain. I would argue that the primary and paradoxical reason is evident in the empty chairs of the Nagari Pracharini Sabha's reading room: scholars do not come to consult the manuscripts because they simply see no use for them. Appeals that cite the "value" of manuscripts as "heritage" fall flat precisely because "heritage" has no inherent relationship with "utility." In fact, a bid to "save" a piece of material heritage, whether it be a book or a building, is often a call to remove that object from use or circulation, to place it behind ropes or behind glass, to protect it from the supposedly deleterious effects of human contact.[7] In short, to "save" books is to make them useless *as books*. There is another paradox here: those who "use" manuscripts by mining them for textual information, including those who call for their preservation and conservation, often forget that it was precisely by rendering them useless as "books" that these "manuscripts" were brought into being in the first place. To put it another way: the Nagari Pracharini Sabha and its sister archives and libraries brought into being the very "manuscripts" (*hastalikhit granth*) and "historical documents" (*aitihāsik dastāvez*) that they collected and archived by destroying these artifacts' identities as "books" (*pustak, pothī, kitāb, guṭakā*, et cetera).

The distinction between "books" and "manuscripts" is reified and enshrined in the organization, catalogues, policies, and architecture of the Nagari Pracharini Sabha itself. The Sabha's collection of printed books and its collection of manuscripts are recorded in separate catalogues, kept in separate parts of the building, placed in different types of storage units (wooden, glass-faced bookshelves for printed books; metal cabinets for manuscripts), requisitioned through different processes and policies, and catalogued according to different schemata. Yet the predominance of this distinction effectively flattens all other distinctions, particularly those between different types of handwritten materials. The manuscript holdings of the library include bound volumes of beautifully calligraphed poetry, illustrated narratives of high artistic quality, loose collections of folios containing liturgical songs, and personal notebooks containing everything from recipes and spells to astrological charts and doodles, and more. These inscribed objects, made of paper, palm leaf, wood, cardboard, cloth, and other materials, assume a dizzying variety of dimensions and formats. From their form and signs of usage we can deduce that they were used by pedagogues as teaching aids, by preachers as liturgical scripts and sermon notes, by singers as *aide-mémoire*, by astrologers as reference guides, by merchants as account ledgers, and by some individuals as handy containers for any textual material that might be of possible future importance, interest, or use, much like the commonplace books of Renaissance England.[8]

The variegated texture or topography of this textual archive has been largely obscured by the modern philological, historical, and literary practices upon which the Nagari Pracharini Sabha and similar institutions were built and that they have continued from the late nineteenth century into the beginning of the twenty-first. These practices of collecting, editing, printing, and interpretating treat manuscripts and their contents as a raw material to be harvested, processed, and reformed into critical editions, scholarly criticism, and literary histories. Rarely have those involved recognized the material artifacts that we call manuscripts as objects worthy of scholarly attention in their own right.

There is a certain irony in speaking of "manuscripts" in precolonial South Asia. In English, usage of the term "manuscript" (a borrowing from Latin *manuscriptus*) to mean a document written by hand began only at the turn of the seventeenth century, roughly a century and a half after Johannes Gutenberg introduced movable type to Europe. (The same is true of other terms used in paleography and codicology, such as "colophon.") Indeed, a "manuscript" could only be imagined as a distinct object once an alternative to it existed. Thus manuscripts became a distinct class of textual artifact in Europe only after printed books had not only arrived but also begun to displace handwritten books. Similarly, in South Asia before the spread of print technology in the eighteenth century, all documents were written by hand and thus were "manuscripts" by our modern definition; however, the people who copied, illustrated, bought, sold, and read them never thought of them as such or referred to them by any term that referenced their quality of being written by hand.

Instead, they referred to different types of handwritten documents by a variety of names that reflected the religious formations, literary traditions, genres, or performance contexts with which they were associated. The terms for "manuscript" in Hindi, including *hastalikhita granth* "handwritten document" and *pāṇḍulipi* "yellow writing," came into use only in the late nineteenth century as the rapid spread of printing in Hindi was radically transforming the landscape of Hindi language and literature. At this moment, the Nagari Pracharini Sabha and its library came into being, in part because its founders and early administrators felt an urgent need to collect and preserve the precolonial literary heritage before it was eclipsed by the prose literary traditions of modern print culture.

The term *nuskẖah* ("copy," from Arabic) is also sometimes used in modern Hindi and Urdu to refer to handwritten books, but its etymology and precolonial usage show that its sense has less to do with writing by hand than with copying. That *nus̱ḵẖah* referred to copying by hand would have been assumed in a world in which copying was *only* done by hand. The term formerly indexed a whole practice and process of written transmission carried out through the labor of human bodies and enacted through human social networks; only after the introduction of printing technology, with its mechanized means of reproduction and anonymous modes of distribution, could *nus̱ḵẖah* take on the connotation of a *handwritten* (as opposed to a printed) copy of a work.

The various peoples of South Asia that wrote, copied, bought, sold, read, studied, and enjoyed books made their own distinctions between types of written artifacts that made sense within the literary culture and media ecology they inhabited. These distinctions appear now and then in documentary sources from the period. For example, in 1637 CE, when the Mughal state notarized the transfer of famed Vaishnava scholars Rupa and Sanantana Gosvami's library to their nephew Jiva Gosvami in Vrindavan, the scribe, writing in Persian, used various terms from Indic languages and Persian (such as *postak-hā* for loose-leaf books and *tamassuk-hā* for receipts and bonds) to describe the contents.[9] Paying close attention to the terms that writers and audiences used for different types of "books" in early modern India can alert us to distinctions that these people made regarding genre, material format, and reading or performance protocols.

One of the primary arguments put forward in this book is that we should recognize and study handwritten books as "things" in the rich sense proposed by Bruno Latour and theorized in recent explorations of "thing theory."[10] By calling them "things," we acknowledge that they are not simply "objects" upon which human subjects act but rather agents in their own right that shape and respond to human behaviors and human perceptions. Consider a simple, commonplace example from contemporary South Asia: in many places in the subcontinent, should an individual accidentally drop a book on the ground or touch it with their feet, they will immediately pick up the book and touch it to their head or heart in a performance of contrition for any inadvertent disrespect they may have paid it. When asked about this practice, different individuals may give different reasons for their behavior, which can vary based on religious, caste, and class background. Yet one thing is clear: a book is not simply an inert object that we treat with indifference but rather a thing that can cause us—or even compel us—to perform certain actions and feel certain emotions. This reckoning with the material "thing-ness" of the literary archive is well overdue: as Bill Brown writes, "objects" suddenly appear to us as "things" at the moment that they stop working for us, when they cease to be so easily used as mediums for seeing something else.[11] Manuscripts gradually ceased to be transparent mediums of knowledge in the nineteenth and early twentieth centuries as printing slowly penetrated every social and institutional space in northern India: this was the moment at which manuscripts became visible as things taking up space on shelves, in trunks, and in cloth-wrapped bundles at *kabāṛīvālā* (salvage dealer) shops in Indian bazaars. This new visibility reflected Marshall McLuhan's observation that the nature and form of a given medium become truly perceptible only at the moment when that medium, at its very peak, is beginning to be superseded by another.[12]

THE LIBRARY OF THE PAST IS A FOREIGN COUNTRY

As a consequence, using terms and concepts inherited from a postprint (or post-digital) world to understand written textuality in a time and place in which all documents were written by hand is bound to lead to confusion. For example, today we easily make a distinction between a printed book of famous quotations and an individual's handwritten notebook of quotations (a thing that many diligent and inspired young students in India still keep today); the former is a "published" *book*, the latter a "private" *notebook*. Such a distinction is not so easily made between textual artifacts from a period in which all documents were handwritten and the institution of publishing—with agents, editors, payments, royalties, printing, editions, and sales—did not exist. Nevertheless, I argue in this book that we *can* make distinctions between artifacts copied for individual or "private" use and those intended for circulation among multiple individuals and groups; we simply have to learn to recognize the relevant markers and distinctions when we look at the written page.

Working with literary (or religious or scholastic) materials from a society that did not use print technology requires us to recognize certain kinds of epistemological difference, including differences in what Ronald Deibert has termed "social epistemology."[13] Put succinctly, any given medium—be it writing, painting, radio, television, "the digital," or others—suggests, figures within, and reifies certain ideas regarding how we can know the world. From Plato's paradoxical use of writing as a metaphor for memory in the fourth century to contemporary understandings of the human brain as a computer, we use media and indeed "think through" media in order to understand how it is possible to know (and in order to hypothesize the locus of knowledge).[14] We must therefore approach the study of written materials created in nonprint societies with a sensitivity and awareness of our own epistemological difference, for as the following chapters will demonstrate, composers and audiences in precolonial South Asia (whether they were literate or not) used the practice and artifact of writing to critically think through questions of knowledge and its transmission in ways often different from our own.

By the same token, media change always occurs in a dialectical relationship with intellectual and social change: the introduction of print technology to Europe in the fifteenth century brought about far-reaching intellectual, social, and cultural changes that could not have been anticipated and that did not, in their totality, follow a clear teleology or causal logic. To explain how media change simultaneously "restructures consciousness" (to borrow the words of Walter Ong) and reorders society, Deibert suggests the metaphor of a qualified Darwinism: "Changes in the mode of communication will 'favor' or allow for the selection among the extant symbolic forms and biases of a society, thus giving rise to a new social epistemology—rethreading the webs of significance, in other words."[15] Certain ideas, institutions, and communities—for example, the monastic order of the Niranjani religious community discussed in chapters 3, 4, and 5—will gain advantage by embracing that technology in certain ways while other ideas, institutions, and communities will diminish in influence.

What follows is an exploration of what happens when a "vernacular" language—*deśa-bhāṣā* or *deśī bhāṣā*, the language of a particular region or people—is first committed to writing and enters the realm of book culture. Writing had been practiced in South Asia for roughly fifteen centuries before the first literary works in Hindi were written down in the fourteenth century. Nevertheless, the transformation of the spoken, "quotidian" language of north India into a written, refined, and, most importantly, *material* textual object during the dynamic period of the early Indian sultanates transformed not only Hindi but also South Asian book culture as a whole, producing new book formats, page layouts, paratextual elements, and orthographic practices. The precolonial, handwritten book in Hindi was part of a multilingual book culture even while it retained features that marked it as distinctly vernacular in character. There existed considerable heterogeneity among Hindi "books," with terms like *bayāẓ*, *safīnah*, *guṭakā*, *pustak*, *pothī*, *granth*, and *vāṇī* referring to different types of text artifacts both bound and unbound—but again, their collective use in performative, liturgical, and pedagogical practices associated with vernacular literary, religious, and scholastic genres gave them specific features that in turn help us to identify a distinct and vibrant vernacular book culture.

FIGURE 0.1 The Nagari Pracharini Sabha of Banaras

Photo by author

If All the World Were Paper

Introduction

Writing a History of Writing in the Vernacular

kara kaṭa grīvā naina mukha tana dukha sahata sujāṁna
līkhyo jāta māhākaṣṭa suṁ saṭha jāṁnata āsāna
kaṭhinnū bīkaḍa begāḍī nīcā mukha aru naina
yaha saṁkaṭa pothī likhī tuma nīkā rakhīyau saina

Hands, buttocks, neck, eyes, face—
The wise endure these bodily pains.
A book is copied with great labor,
[But] the base think it's easy.

The jeweler [endures] fierce straining,
His face and eyes [cast] downward.
In such hardship I copied this book;
Keep it carefully, my friend.

—Scribal colophon, *Paramānand Prabodh* of Anandram (Ms. 16699, Rajasthan Oriental Research Institute, Jodhpur)

Completing his (or possibly her) 1863 CE copy of Anandram's *Paramānand Prabodh* ("The Apprehension of Ultimate Bliss," a Hindi commentary on the *Bhagavadgītā*), an anonymous scribe left a vivid description of the bodily labor that made nonprint book culture possible in South Asia. The scribe exhorts the reader to recognize this labor as such (by comparing it to a type of artisanal labor, that of the jeweler) and to honor it with devotion and care for the object produced, the book itself. By virtue of this request, the scribe establishes a relationship with not only the immediate patron of the manuscript but also any and all anonymous, future readers: the object of the book connects these persons across time and space. The colophon thus foregrounds the embodied practices and social relationships that undergirded the literary world of precolonial Hindi and other South Asian languages before the consolidation of print technology's hegemony in the Indian subcontinent.

This book is an investigation of how such embodied practices, social relationships, and material textual artifacts constituted one another in a dialectical manner in the literary world of precolonial Hindi, from the late fourteenth century to the middle of the eighteenth. These practices, relationships, and artifacts have been largely absent from contemporary discussions about precolonial literature in South Asia, especially in Hindi. While working in the Rajasthan Oriental Research Institute in Jodhpur in 2009, I was struck by the preponderance of manuscripts in the collection either authored or copied by monks of the Niranjani Sampraday, a religious community that emerged in the region of Rajasthan at the turn of the seventeenth century. The Niranjani Sampraday and its authors find almost no mention in histories of Hindi literature or in modern academic literature generally. Yet here were hundreds of hand-copied books containing everything from hymns and hagiographies to metaphysical treatises and astrological charts. This made me wonder how different the history of Hindi literature—and with it the history of religion in north India—might look if the written archive were our point of entry into reconstructing the textual world of the early modern period, rather than the received canon of literary "greats" that was delineated by nationalist literary critics during the early twentieth century.[1]

A second observation that occasioned this research came while reading Sheldon Pollock's sweeping study, *The Language of the Gods in the World of Men: Sanskrit, Culture, and Power in Premodern India*. Pollock's provocative thesis regarding the origins and trajectory of vernacularization—the process through which "languages of place" came to be used alongside and sometimes even supplant Sanskrit as mediums of literary and intellectual discourse—has initiated a productive debate among scholars of vernacular languages like Hindi. Perhaps his book's most interesting argument regards the connection between writing, the definition or identity of literature (*kāvya*), and the status of a language as a "literary" or "workly" language. At the risk of oversimplification, Pollock's argument may be summarized as follows: beginning with the invention of literature proper in Sanskrit, i.e., *kāvya*, as a distinct form of textual and cultural production in the early centuries of the Common Era, literature was in part defined, and indeed made possible, by the technology of writing and by its existence as a material text artifact that could circulate across geographical and temporal distances. Sanskrit was one of only three such "cosmopolitan" languages (the others being Prakrit and Apabhramsha) in which one could credibly compose literature during the first millennium; vernacular languages, including premodern forms of Hindi, were excluded from both the sphere of literature and the sphere of writing and written textuality. Consequently, during the second millennium, vernacular languages had to be, in Pollock's terminology, "literized" (committed to writing) and "literarized" (refashioned according to the discursive, literary, generic, and aesthetic codes and conventions of the superposed language of Sanskrit) before they could be regarded as mediums for literary and intellectual thought.[2]

Because Pollock's narrative is explicitly concerned with the *intellectual* history of language and literature, I was left wondering about the material and social history of this process of literizing and literarizing the vernacular. Who first transcribed the vernacular in writing, how, and for whom? How were the customs and conventions of writing the vernacular worked out? How did the material "nuts and bolts" of literary inscription, circulation, and performance work? In contrast to Pollock's model of a two-stage process in which the vernacular is inscribed first for documentary purposes by courtly elites and only later for literary purposes (and later still for devotional or religious purposes), the history of writing in Hindi is intractably messy: mundane and privileged forms of literacy and inscription overlap and crisscross; distinctions between genres and indeed between entire discursive spheres like literature and scripture appear to have been unstable and shifting. I wondered if starting from the material archive might lead us to reconstruct a history of vernacularization in northern India that looks different from that presented by Pollock as a story of the "great works" of Sanskrit and vernacular literatures. How might that history change if told from the point of view of, say, a rural monk inhabiting the discursive lowlands of popular devotional lyrics in Hindi, as opposed to the point of view of a court poet inhabiting the lofty heights of Sanskrit *kāvya*?

This book then is a close study of the various types of material text artifacts that contain works in the Hindi language, including everything from individuals' personal notebooks to lavishly illustrated codices. I use these artifacts to reconstruct the types of intellectual and physical labor that produced them and the social relationships—including those within and among pedagogical, religious, and literary institutions—through which they circulated and were employed in different types of oral performance. In doing so, I sketch a provisional history of the processes through which Hindi was discursively and materially fashioned into a literary language—a history of vernacularization constructed "from the ground up."

JUDGING THIS BOOK BY ITS COVER: "A HISTORY OF WRITING IN HINDI"

Unpacking the subtitle may help to clarify this book's theoretical orientation, goals, and methodological program. I call this "a" history of writing in Hindi because I do not intend for it to supersede or displace existing histories or believe that it can provide an exhaustive account of even one of the several literary traditions upon which it touches—including the Sufi romance, the devotional hymn, the scholastic treatise, and the sacred scripture—let alone the entirety of Hindi's rich linguistic and literary past. Such a comprehensive history would be a gargantuan task—for example, the Nagari Pracharini Sabha's *Hindī Sāhitya Kā Bṛhat Itihās* (Comprehensive History of Hindi Literature, 1957) spans more than seven thousand pages in sixteen volumes—and the history of the language now known as Hindi and the galaxy of literature composed in it is so rich and complex that no single approach could ever sufficiently describe, let alone explain, the multiple and knotted trajectories of its development. I have tried to present a new and different approach to writing the history of Hindi that *supplements* existing accounts and enriches their insights.

Only a dialogue between multiple approaches to literary historiography—at points argumentative but often complementary and collaborative—can reconstruct the world of early Hindi literature in all of its color and detail. To give just a few examples, the nationalist school of Hindi literary history inaugurated by Ramchandra Shukla in the 1920s understood literary history as the expression of the people's ethos (*jantā kī cittavṛtti*) and was thus able to shine a light on Hindi's past that illuminated some of its important contours; in the 1940s and 1950s, Hazariprasad Dvivedi's approach, writing that same history as a history of ideas, illuminated another set of outlines; Francesca Orsini's recent writing about Hindi's development as part of a broader multilingual literary history of South Asia has revealed yet another set of intersecting currents and regions. Shining a light from the angle of the material and social history of writing will illuminate another set of contours in this landscape that have not yet been traced. It will also necessarily throw shadows on areas that cannot be illuminated. The indefinite article "a" in this book's subtitle emphasizes that it is self-consciously provisional, relying on and responding to other narratives of Hindi literary history and always contingent upon what is present (or absent) at this particular moment in the *material* archive of Hindi literature. It also acknowledges that not every area of precolonial Hindi literature is fully addressed here; for example, the tradition of *rīti* or formalist poetry and criticism, which gained prominence at the turn of the seventeenth century, is dealt with only peripherally.

What about the often-contentious word "history"? In the pages that follow, I tell a story—a historical narrative—of how Hindi came to be inscribed, transmitted, and performed in writing, though not in typical storytelling fashion. Each chapter reconstructs a "scene" of vernacular writing in early modern north India, describing and explaining how ideologies of writing, textual genres, practices of inscription and performance, and material text artifacts worked together to form an organic whole. Yet within each individual chapter and throughout the book are signs of *change* over time: for example, clerical communities taking a role in the inscription and transmission of literary works in the sixteenth and seventeenth centuries, paper displacing palm leaf as the primary medium for producing books after the fourteenth century, and communities like the Sikhs self-consciously establishing a *beginning* for their respective scriptural traditions. Marking a beginning or establishing a point of origin is a fundamental part of creating historical consciousness; demonstrating how this is connected to the act of writing and its remembrance is one of my primary concerns. Thus, this book is a "history" of writing in Hindi in that it is an attempt to reconstruct a series of changes through which the vernacular came to be inscribed and transmitted in writing and also to understand how those who wrote in Hindi imagined that history themselves.

"Writing" may be a less contentious concept than "history," but it is no less slippery in terms of its semiotic range. The challenge hinges on the term's own hinge-like character as a word that connects within our imagination the act of textual composition and the act of inscription. In contemporary English, the post-print ideology of universal literacy—part of the "media ideology" of print itself—has led to the encroachment of the concept of "writing" onto most forms of verbal art: in everyday parlance one "writes" music, "writes" poetry, "writes" lyrics, and so forth.[3] In contrast, the lexicon of Hindi, especially that of the precolonial period, encodes more subtle distinctions between types of compositional and inscriptional activity. For example, the act of composing a literary or scholastic work is often articulated using the verb *racā-* (from Sanskrit *rac-*, to fashion, create) or phrases like *granth bāṁdh- / gāṁṭh- / joṛ-* (to tie/join together a work). One may also simply "say" a verse (*pad kah-*, *sher kah-*) and it is understood that the speaker composed it herself or himself. In contrast, the verb *likh-* (Sanskrit *likh-*, to scratch, inscribe, paint) is used specifically to refer to the act of inscription, i.e., writing something down. The composers of early Hindi works and their audiences in the fourteenth through eighteenth centuries were sensitive to this distinction between verbal composition and inscription, or what I call "graphic literacy": the ability to decipher and re-create visual representations of language (graphemes or written "letters"). I have therefore found it occasionally necessary to use phrases like "writing as inscription" and "writing as composition" to make such distinctions clear. More often, I have simply used terms like "compose" and "inscribe," following the usage of corresponding terms in Hindi itself like *racā-* and *likh-*. The main forms or modes of textual composition discussed in this book are literary and scholastic in nature; other forms of writing, such as record keeping and epistolary writing, are discussed primarily in terms of their relationship to literary and scholastic writing.

The final word in the title, "Hindi," carries with it an exceedingly complicated history and often leads to confusion because in the past as well as in the present, it has been used to designate a literary register and tradition (or rather, a complex of literary registers and traditions) as often as to refer to a language.[4] In this book I use "Hindi" not as is commonly done today—to denote the modern, standardized dialect sometimes known by the name *khaṛī bolī* and inscribed in the Devanāgarī script—but as it was used by composers in the early modern period: to refer to a transregional literary language, a loosely standardized register of the vernacular that was used for literary and scholastic compositions in verse and could be understood by audiences in such dispersed locales as Golkonda in the south, Lahore in the north, Murshidabad in the east, and Surat in the West. This was *not* the spoken language of these regions, each of which was home to multiple local languages and dialects, but rather a "link language" or "cosmopolitan vernacular" (to use Pollock's terminology).[5] In addition to the term *hindī* (Persian, literally "of the region of Hind," i.e., east of the Indus River), peoples of the early modern period referred to this literary register using the Persian terms *hindavī* and *hindustānī* ("of [the land] of Hind") as well as the Sanskrit term *bhāṣā* (spoken or vernacular speech, as opposed to Sanskrit) or its *tadbhava* equivalent, *bhākhā*. For the most part, I use *bhāṣā*, the term that precolonial composers themselves used most frequently to characterize the language in which they composed.

Defining "Hindi" in this manner not only follows the usage of the term by composers and audiences in the period under consideration but also acknowledges the fact that "Hindi literature" has always been defined as much in terms of *literary* as linguistic criteria. The language of literary works and written texts more generally in precolonial India was not the language of spoken speech: phenomena such as entextualization and structures such as prosody ensure that the language in written documents and literary works will always be somewhat removed from the context-specific language of social interaction (one of the fundamental conditions of the technology of writing).[6] This written, literary register of Hindi was lexically broad enough and grammatically malleable enough to accommodate works, traditions, and aesthetic sensibilities from all over the northern part of the subcontinent (many of which are now associated with separate linguistic and literary traditions such as Avadhi, Maithili, and Marwari).

Defining "Hindi literature" in this way allows us to substantially expand the archive for Hindi by putting materials from a wider range of linguistic registers, literary genres, and sectarian traditions into conversation with one another. For example, this book considers manuscripts of works and anthologies that would have been considered within the ambit of *bhāṣā* at the time of their composition but are now associated with separate literary traditions like those of Gujarati, Punjabi, and Rajasthani. Studying manuscripts of Hindi works copied in the Gurmukhi script (now associated with the language of Punjabi), the Arabic script (now associated with Urdu), or in the Kaithī, Mahājanī, or other shorthand scripts (now associated with accountancy and recordkeeping) not only brings to notice formerly unknown or unacknowledged copies of works of the Hindi canon but also makes us more aware of exchanges and resonances between different literary and manuscript cultures. Linguistically speaking, the language of, say, early poets associated with the Punjabi tradition like Baba Farid (thirteenth century) and Guru Nanak (fifteenth century) is mutually intelligible with the language of early poets of the Hindi heartland such as Amir Khusrau (twelfth century) and Kabir (fifteenth century). More important, sources dating to the early modern period often consider the compositions of all of these poets to belong to the same language and literary tradition, for which they use the aforementioned terms of *hindavī*, *hindī*, or *bhāṣā/bhākhā*.[7] (Indeed, the song notebooks and scriptural anthologies discussed in chapters 2 and 4 group these very same poets together.) To put it another way, in the terminology used by premodern audiences themselves, poets like Baba Farid, Guru Nanak, Amir Khusrau, and Kabir composed in the same transregional vernacular that I have defined above as the referent of "Hindi."

VERNACULARIZATION IN THEORY AND IN PRACTICE

The question of how and why *deśa-bhāṣā*, or "languages of place," developed into vehicles of literary and intellectual discourse in second-millennium South Asia has recently received renewed attention in academic circles. Scholars in the twentieth century tended to attribute the rise of such vernacular languages and literatures to a popular, broadly subaltern movement against the hegemony of Sanskrit and Brahminical religion. According to this argument, poets and scholars writing in the language of the common people freed literary, philosophical, and religious knowledge systems from the stronghold of Sanskrit, jealously guarded by Brahmin pandits for over one and a half millennia. In the reasoning of many scholars, the vehicle and engine for this vernacular revolution was *bhakti*, the devotional mode of religiosity that spread from the Tamil lands in the south up through north India over the course of the early second millennium.

Literary histories of Hindi, beginning in the 1920s, reflect the influence of this narrative: scholars as diverse as George Abraham Grierson (1851–1941), Ramchandra Shukla (1884–1941), and Hazariprasad Dvivedi (1907–1979) all agreed that although the use of Hindi as a medium of composition may have begun with the epic *rāso* genre and with scattered Nath and Siddha poems in the twelfth through fourteenth centuries, Hindi truly came into its own as a literary language and tradition with the devotional lyrics of the "early medieval period" (*purv-madhyakāl*, c. 1318–1643 CE). Devotional poetry in Hindi was, in Grierson's words, "popular in the best sense of the term—namely, that which is known and loved by all, literate and illiterate alike," and, in Shukla's analysis, the path (*mārg*) that liberated the heart of the Hindu race (*jāti*) from the despair caused by both political defeat at the hands of Muslim sultans and spiritual alienation from the esoteric religious traditions of the time.[8]

At the turn of the current century, Pollock revived the discussion by positing a radically different narrative and logic: charting the literary development of Sanskrit in the first millennium and vernaculars in the second, he argues that it was courtly elites that pioneered literary activity in the vernaculars. In this narrative, Sanskrit (along with Prakrit and Apabhramsha) monopolized the domain of literature (*kāvya*), both because it was *written* (allowing it to transcend time and place and thus become "cosmopolitan") and because it had been fashioned, through grammars, rhetorical treatises, and the construction of analytical metalanguage, into a "workly" language that could serve as a medium for expressive and intellectual works. In contrast, *deśa-bhāṣā* or regional vernaculars, being unwritten and unrefined, could be the medium of song (*gīta*) but never of literary expression, being limited, epistemologically speaking, to particular places and times.[9] According to Pollock, in the second millennium, courtly elites transformed these vernacular languages into mediums for *kāvya* by committing them to writing and refashioning them in terms of the rhetorical, stylistic, and generic conventions of the superposed language of Sanskrit. This movement was part of a shift in the cultural idiom of power in South Asia from the imperial and cosmopolitan to a more regional and localized articulation. The use of the vernacular for religious hymnody and liturgy—both outside the realm of *kāvya*—was a secondary and reactive development.[10]

Pollock's thesis has generated a vibrant and sometimes contentious discussion among scholars. Among the critical responses, Christian Novetzke, writing on Marathi in the Yadava kingdoms of the thirteenth century, has argued that language and literature are indeed political in the manner theorized by Pollock but that the political agents that drove vernacularization as a historical process were, in fact, "nonelites" who wrote outside of the traditional loci of literary composition, i.e., the royal court and the established aesthetic domain of Sanskrit. For Novetzke, vernacularization then was "the strategic use of the topos of everyday life within a social, political, artistic, linguistic, and cultural process in which the quotidian . . . expands at the center of a given region's public culture."[11] Francesca Orsini, writing on north India, has argued that the literary culture of this region was, in a sense, "always already" multilingual. Taking this as our point of departure would mean confronting a much more complex and codependent process of literary development than the bipolar model of cosmopolitan/vernacular and high/low allows us to imagine; Orsini consequently suggests that we may (eventually) discard the term "vernacular" for the term "multilingual."[12]

I am not ready to do so just yet, in part because the poets and audiences of the fourteenth through eighteenth centuries did not imagine *bhāṣā* to be just one language among equals. They did imagine it to occupy a particular place in what Andrew Ollett has called the "language order" of India, a schema in which the characters, expressive potentials, and values of multiple languages are reckoned *in relation* to one another.[13] Yet within this schema, *bhāṣā* was not initially understood to have the same potential for literary (or scholarly or religious) expression as Sanskrit, Prakrit, or Apabhramsha. Poets, scholars, and preachers had to perform intellectual as well as physical labor to establish *bhāṣā* as a medium of literary and intellectual expression. That is why, as I detail in this book, the pioneers of every new genre in Hindi felt compelled to explain why and how they were using the vernacular in their works, and why scribes, calligraphers, artists, and bookmakers spent so much time carefully adapting and reinventing the paratextual, visual, and material conventions of books as they gave material form to these new genres. In order to be taken seriously as literature (or scholarship or scripture), works in Hindi needed to look and feel, as well as read, like serious books.[14]

Yet the sites of that labor were more diverse than Pollock's model might suggest. The quotidian work that produced the north Indian vernacular as a written (literized) and deliberately fashioned (literarized) medium of the verbal arts and sciences was performed by various types of people—including monks, traders, merchants, clerks, gurus, princes, and professional poets—across varied social and institutional contexts that included monasteries, temples, private homes, public squares, markets, and royal ateliers. This reflects the fact that *bhāṣā* was imagined in the language order of the time as linguistically and aesthetically capacious: it could encompass, for example, the *Vīsaladev Rāso* and similar bardic epics composed in the western dialects of Gujarat and Rajasthan from the fifteenth century onward, the allegorical romance of the *Candāyan* composed by the Sufi poet Maulana Daud in eastern "Hinduki" during the fourteenth century, the poet Vishnudas's re-creation of the *Mahābhārata* in a late *madhyadeśī* dialect at the court of Gwalior during the fifteenth century, Surdas's ornate devotional lyrics in the "sweet" tongue of the Braj region during the sixteenth century, and Bhikharidas's literary manual, the *Kāvya Nirṇay*, composed in a highly Sanskritized register during the eighteenth century. Chronicles recited in the pleasure palaces of royal courts, hymns sung at humble gatherings of devotees on the banks of sacred rivers, and dense treatises on metaphysics penned by princes or by celibate renouncers could all be composed and enjoyed in this language. These varied geographical, vocational, social, political, and religious contexts are reflected in the textual content and material form of early books in the vernacular—and this is why it behooves us to begin our study of Hindi literature with the material archive itself.

MATERIALITY MATTERS (BUT SO DOES CULTURE)

The arguments outlined above show that materiality—including the material properties of an object, the technical and artistic practices they make possible, and the agentive "thingness" of textual artifacts—plays a significant role in shaping literary, religious, and intellectual culture. The act or practice of reading also has a material dimension insofar as it is determined by the material properties of the textual artifact (for example, a small book can be held in the hand and read while standing virtually anywhere, but a large volume requires the reader to sit at a table or stand before a lectern), involves embodied actions and practices (deliberate as well as involuntary movement of the eyes, sitting in particular postures, vocalizing while reading aloud), and takes place in specific material circumstances (for example, on the dung-plastered floor of a verandah or on a religious teacher's cushioned throne, using light from a clay oil lamp, or perhaps employing a wooden book stand). Reading is not simply an intellectual or social activity—it is also a physical activity, so the material circumstances of its pursuit will shape its intellectual and social dimensions.

Those same intellectual and social dimensions can shape reading practices as much as the material dimension, so we must avoid falling into material or technological determinism in understanding how reading and writing practices form. Reading culture (the beliefs, assumptions, and normative practices regarding the embodied, social, and intellectual practice of reading) is, after all, part of culture, and cultural practices can prove remarkably resistant to changes in technology and materials, sometimes even driving those changes. For example, scholars frequently point to the introduction of cloth paper to South Asia during the thirteenth century as a major turning point in the artistic and media history of the subcontinent, suggesting that this freed scribes and artists to explore new formats and forms.[15] Yet we currently possess relatively little evidence upon which to base such claims. The first unambiguous reference to the use of paper appears in Jain sources dating to the fifteenth century, even though different types of paper had likely entered India via Tibet, Kashmir, and Malabar trading towns at least as early as the twelfth century; this suggests that the adoption of paper as a writing medium was slow and geographically uneven.[16] Scholars of the intellectual and literary history of India have suggested that paper revolutionized or at least strengthened networks of textual specialists like Brahmin *pandits*; for example, the historian Rosalind O'Hanlon has suggested that the introduction of paper to India during the early sultanate period (roughly 1200 to 1500 CE) made possible the increased circulation of works of the Puranic genre in Sanskrit and their performance in various social contexts, mediated by local vernaculars.[17] Yet the extant manuscript record for this period—which includes many palm leaf manuscripts of Puranic and other Sanskrit works but relatively few paper manuscripts—suggests instead that Brahmin and other ritual and religious specialists resisted or ignored the use of paper for several centuries after its introduction. Furthermore, paper manuscripts of Sanskrit works (as well as works in Prakrit and Apabhramsha) that date to the fourteenth through sixteenth centuries overwhelming follow the material, visual, and structural conventions of their palm leaf archetypes.[18]

The greatest amount of experimentation with the material form and visual layout of books during the early centuries of the second millennium appears to have occurred within the emerging realm of vernacular book culture. The primary reason was that the vernacular of north India was linguistically, lexically, prosodically, and aesthetically hybrid and dynamic. Unlike the literary cultures and linguistic ideologies of Sanskrit and Persian (the two cosmopolitan languages during the thirteenth through eighteenth centuries), the culture of *bhāṣā* did not privilege purity or refinement in matters of lexicon or style or ever develop strict rules or structures of authority for adjudicating such matters. On the contrary, connoisseurs of literature in *bhāṣā* from the fourteenth through the eighteenth centuries often identified rusticity as the language's distinguishing strength and reveled in the poetic effects that could be achieved with such a loosely structured grammar and such a hybrid lexicon (which included words from Arabic, Persian, Turkish, Sanskrit, and Prakrit, in addition to words from local and tribal languages). Furthermore, the literary pioneers of Hindi could not avoid the accusation of novelty—their compositions in *bhāṣā* were manifestly a new phenomenon—and so developed ways to theorize and celebrate that novelty.[19] It therefore makes sense that vernacular literary culture, with its celebration of hybridity and novelty, became the sphere in which scribes, calligraphers, monks, painters, illuminators, paper makers, and bookbinders experimented with new forms and techniques. This demonstrates one of the central claims of this book: that media change—at least in the realm of writing—occurs at the intersections of literary, intellectual, and material cultures.

ON METHODOLOGY: OF READING CLOSE AND DISTANT

Given the multifaceted character of writing as a form of media, any study of precolonial book culture in South Asia must combine approaches and insights from multiple disciplines, including art history, material history, social history, linguistics, philology, and literary studies. I can hardly claim to have expertise in all of these areas but have learned a great deal from these disciplines and their practitioners in the process of writing this book. Methodologically, my analysis of the practices and artifacts of writing has concentrated on three operations.

The first is close reading: analysis of the linguistic, semiotic, and aesthetic functioning of verbal texts to understand how they make meaning and make critical distinctions and associations. This is traditionally the domain of philology and literary studies. Performing a close reading of literary, religious, and scholarly works is essential to grasp how different poets, saints, and scholars thought about writing as a practice, technology, and artifact. It also proves critical in reconstructing how audiences and performers—from singers and preachers to teachers and, in the case of the seventeenth-century merchant Banarsidas, nonprofessional reciters who simply enjoyed entertaining their friends—"used" these texts and made meaning with and through them.

The second operation is close examination of textual artifacts, including codex books, loose-leaf books, and bound notebooks, as well as registers, account books, and even scraps of paper inserted or pasted into books as notes and emendations. This requires examination of materials and reconstruction of the practices that produced them. In the course of this research, I found myself learning about the stitches used in binding signatures (or gatherings) of folios together, the types of cloth and leather used for book covers, the methods of producing ink, and the techniques of ruling a manuscript before inscribing it. In this regard, I have benefited immensely from the studies of Indic and Islamicate books undertaken by art historians and the growing number of book historians working in and on the Central and Southern Asian regions. As evidenced by the size and success of recent book history workshops in India and the publication of a half-dozen monographs and as many edited volumes on pre- and postprint book culture in South Asia over the last ten years, the field of book history in South Asia is coming into its own.[20] It is more of a field than a discipline, drawing upon methods from art history, material history, and literary history in order to see connections between form and content that would otherwise remain opaque or invisible. I hope that the current book contributes to the further development of approaches in this growing field.

The final operation belongs to the method of "distant reading," one of the many text-specific subfields within the emerging discipline of digital humanities. Stated succinctly, distant reading aggregates large corpora of texts or data and subjects them to quantitative analysis in order to draw empirical observations about relationships, trends, processes, and structures. That "data" can be anything: a single "text," a whole canon of literary works, author names, the titles of works, dates of publication. Though I do not discuss the data in detail here, several of my observations about the contours of vernacular book culture are occasioned or supported by evidence gathered through such distant reading. This includes the quantitative analysis of textual data gathered from literary works and data that I myself produced and collected regarding manuscript copies of works. I employed rudimentary forms of computer-assisted quantitative analysis not in order to test hypotheses (since that would risk reproducing certain biases in the way that we currently understand literary genres, linguistic distinctions, religious differences, and the like) but to make large-scale patterns visible.

For example, calculating the frequency of words and strings of words—or even just syllables and strings of syllables—and their positions within prosodic structures helped me to notice recurring terms and phrases in the body of lyric poetry attributed to *nirguṇ bhakti* poets like Kabir, Ravidas, Dadu, Sundardas, and Haridas Niranjani. Having noticed this, I was able to hypothesize how singers, upon hearing a verse, wrote it down or memorized it but then deployed its metrically discrete units in new and improvised ways during recited or sung performance; this in turn accounts for the variation in the order of poetic lines, half-lines, quarter-lines, and other units of text across a large corpus of singers' notebooks. Similarly, over fifteen years spent in libraries, archives, museums, monasteries, temples, and private collections, I recorded and aggregated data about every manuscript I encountered that had been copied by scribes of the Niranjani Sampraday community during the seventeenth through nineteenth centuries, including the scribe's name, the date of copying, and the location at which the book was copied. Analyzing this simple data revealed that the majority of Niranjani scribal activity occurred in several cities but also in certain smaller towns in the regions of Marwar and Mewar. By then associating this geographical data with documentary evidence regarding regional trade and settlements of certain merchant castes, I was able to see (and empirically demonstrate) that Niranjani monks were busiest copying books wherever there were large communities of Bihani merchants—one of the social groups from which the Niranjanis recruited monastic initiates and lay devotees (fig. 0.2). With this correlation in mind, I re-examined the notebooks and found copious evidence of the mercantile and clerical forms of vocational literacy that their users possessed.

The study presented here is based on my direct inspection of a little over five hundred manuscripts as well as data collected from manuscript catalogues regarding approximately two hundred additional manuscripts. This is not, in the terms and scales used by contemporary data science and statistics, a particularly large sample size. Nevertheless, without a sense of the overall magnitude of the Hindi manuscript archive—the ability to make such estimates is still years away—and in the absence of any other data set related to the archive of text artifacts in Hindi, this book at least constitutes a beginning. The reader may simply sit back and enjoy the journey through five hundred years of literary and book history, noting the changes in landscape and individual details as they pass into and out of view. Yet it helps to have a sense of "what's under the hood" of the vehicle that is conveying you through that landscape, and quantitative analysis is part of that metaphorical engine.

THE CAST OF CHARACTERS

Much of the book's argument is illustrated through examples taken from religious traditions in early modern north India. The following map of that religious landscape highlights categories and characterizations used in contemporary scholarship and in doing so outlines some of the conventional wisdom regarding precolonial sects that I seek to modify or refute in my analysis.

The early modern period saw an efflorescence of sectarian religious activity in north India, with various Sufi orders or *silsilahs*, Hindu sects or *sampradāys*, and independent devotional entrepreneurs competing for followers and patronage. The sectarian distinctions most relevant for what follows are among the traditions and communities associated with *bhakti* devotionalism. This mode of religiosity simultaneously emphasized the individual's direct relationship with God and the importance of the religious community (reflected in the concept of *satsaṅg* or "the company of the righteous"). Scholarship on *bhakti* in north India typically divides *bhakti*-oriented traditions into two major groups: those of the *saguṇ* persuasion, which practice devotion to a deity "possessing attributes" (*sa-guṇ*) such as Krishna or Ram, and those of the *nirguṇ* persuasion, which espouse devotion to an ineffable Divinity beyond or "without attributes" (*nir-guṇ*). Each tradition is understood to possess its own canon of saints, writings, and constellation of sectarian communities. *Saguṇ* traditions are represented primarily by Vaishnava communities (who worship one or more avatars of Vishnu) while *nirguṇ* traditions are sometimes grouped together with Sikhism (and even Sufism) as examples of either monism or monotheism. This book addresses the Hindi writings of Sufi authors separately from those of the *bhakti* saints but points out how the former's lexicon of written textuality informed the latter's development of written scriptures.

I give the greatest amount of attention to *nirguṇ bhakti* precisely because this tradition is often assumed—erroneously—to have eschewed writing and writing culture. Two communities, the Dadu Panth and Niranjani Sampraday, coalesced around charismatic saint-poet figures in Rajasthan at the turn of the seventeenth century, maintained monastic orders, and produced scholars that composed in the vernacular. They also produced prodigious amounts of manuscripts. I occasionally refer to other *nirguṇ* religious orders like the Kabir Panth, a monastic order that follows the teachings of the saint Kabir and spread across the Gangetic plain in the seventeenth century, as well as the Ramsnehi Sampraday, a federation of monastic orders that coalesced around local saint figures in southeastern Rajasthan at the turn of the nineteenth century.[21]

The *saguṇ* Vaishnava tradition and its sectarian communities are discussed primarily in the context of scholastic writing and the development of vernacular scriptures. Two sects, the Vallabha Sampraday (also known as the Pushtimarg) and the Gaudiya Sampraday, were founded by charismatic saints at the beginning of the sixteenth century, established a presence in Braj (the region associated with the deity Krishna) by the middle of that century, and produced a significant body of poetry and scholarship in Sanskrit as well as in the vernacular. For lack of space, other communities in Braj that wrote in the vernacular, such as the Radhavallabhis and Haridasis, have not been addressed; however, these traditions also contributed to the development of Hindi as a written medium of literary and intellectual exchange.

Finally, the Sikh tradition receives special attention in the context of hymnody and scriptural writing. Founded by Guru Nanak (1469–1539) toward the end of the fifteenth century, Sikhism understood itself to be a distinct religious tradition from early on in its history. It expressed this through its approach to scripture as well as through the establishment of socially and politically independent communities in Punjab, the region with which it is most closely associated. The Sikhs maintained a presence in Rajasthan as well, where they engaged in robust exchanges with communities like the Dadu Panth and Niranjani Sampraday, a fact revealed by the manuscript record.

Notably absent from the main narrative of the book are the Jains, a community that produced copious amounts of written literature in Hindi (as well as in several other languages). Jainism has long maintained a multilingual literary culture somewhat distinct in linguistic ideology and practice from other communities, which is why it does not figure prominently here.[22] Nevertheless, discussions of Jain practices of writing appear frequently because these practices influenced those of the aforementioned communities in important ways.

FORMAT OF THE BOOK

In each chapter of this book, I describe one "scene" of vernacular writing in precolonial north India. Each includes a set of historical actors (poets, patrons, copyists, performers, preachers), genres (the epic romance, the devotional hymn, the scholastic treatise, the scriptural anthology), practices (writing, reading, singing, teaching), and material artifacts produced by and used in these practices (codices, notebooks, liturgical manuals, and the like). In each scene, I highlight the connections among three elements. First is the ideology of writing. How did historical actors imagine writing (inscription and/or textual composition) as a creative act or, in some cases, as a religious act? How did they use their respective concepts of writing to construct (or deconstruct) a particular epistemology or cultural program? How did this ideology of writing and the particular characteristics of the vernacular language known as Hindi shape each other? The second element is the material text artifacts themselves—the "manuscripts." What were their physical, material, and visual characteristics, from orthography and calligraphy to illustrations, paratexts, and bindings? What can these material and visual elements, in addition to the textual content, tell us about practices of inscription, circulation, and use in performance? The third element is the practices themselves: combining evidence from material text artifacts with documentary and other sources, I attempt to reconstruct the embodied and social practices of writing and reading in the vernacular in second-millennium north India.

Each individual chapter demonstrates how these three aspects were interrelated and together constituted a scene of writing that made sense as a whole, paying particular attention to how they developed as part of the broader process of vernacularization in the late medieval and early modern period. In order to foreground the material and the particular, I begin and end each chapter by focusing on a single artifact, such as an illustrated story, a notebook, or liturgical manual, as an entry point into the intellectual, social, and performative world discussed.

Chapter 1: Storytellers and Storybooks

The first scene of vernacular writing is that of the epic romance or *pem-kathā*, a genre inaugurated at the courts of regional nobles (or warlords) in the sultanate north. The poets patronized by these Persianized elites self-consciously refashioned the local vernacular and folk narratives into a literary idiom while committing both to writing. Beginning with the first poet to compose such a work, Maulana Daud, author of the *Candāyan* (*Tale of Chanda*, 1379 CE), these authors reflected on the significance of writing in the vernacular in the introductory passages of their romances. In doing so, they left substantial evidence with which to reconstruct the relationship among ideologies of writing, linguistic difference, and the social contexts of literary performance in fourteenth- through sixteenth-century sultanate India. Although the pioneers of this genre were practitioners of Sufism—and this had clear consequences for the ways in which they imagined the significance of writing—the *pem-kathā* itself appealed to audiences across various religious, social, and geographical contexts. The manuscript copies of works discussed in this chapter were produced in such distant locales as Jaunpur, Malwa, and Bijapur, and for a clientele that included Mughal generals, wealthy merchants, and even humble accountants and traders.

Through a close reading of the poets' reflections on writing, a close examination of individual copies of works, and a broader survey of the archive of *pem-kathā* copies as a whole, I demonstrate that in the imaginations of these poets and their audiences, what made a "vernacular" literary work (*bhākhā kabi*) was the affective power of the language of *bhāṣā*, its inscription within the technological and stylistic modalities of Persian (and more generally Islamicate) writing, and its transmission through highly scripted and codified practices of performance and reception. In the process, I show how these poets created a vocabulary in the vernacular for speaking (and writing) about written scripture—a vocabulary later appropriated and developed by religious communities associated with *bhakti* during the sixteenth through eighteenth centuries. The commitment of *bhāṣā* to writing in the context of the *pem-kathā* transformed it ontologically and materially, producing a new type of text artifact that could be a canvas for the book arts, an object of connoisseurship, and a form of currency in social and political relations. Copies of the *pem-kathā* circulated within a multilingual book culture but retained a distinct form that allows us to identify an emerging *vernacular* book culture in sultanate India.

Chapter 2: Saints, Singers, and Songbooks

The second scene of writing that I investigate is that of itinerant monks, singers, religious professionals, and devotees of the so-called *nirguṇ bhakti* tradition, who kept personal notebooks of songs and sayings. Founded or inspired by poets like Kabir, Ravidas, Dadu Dayal, and Haridas Niranjani, who preached devotion to a *nirguṇ*, ineffable divinity, these religious communities and traditions coalesced in the late mid-sixteenth through mid-seventeenth centuries. The predominant textual forms in the notebooks of their members are the lyric (*pad*) and the epigrammatic couplet (*sākhī*). The most prominent poets of the tradition pursued an incisive critique of writing as a prosthetic of memory and as a technology of authority and control. Performing close readings of their poetry alongside their hagiographies, I argue that beliefs regarding these saints' putative illiteracy are in fact an integral part of what makes such readings of their poetry possible in the first place.

Despite these saints' apparent distrust of writing, their followers copied their compositions into tens of thousands of manuscripts. These handwritten personal notebooks, most often called *guṭakā* in Hindi, functioned like briefcases in which itinerant sadhus and religious specialists kept notes for singing and sermonizing, religious stories for reciting, astrological charts to consult on behalf of clients, lists, records of transactions, spells, recipes, and any manner of *yād-dāsht* (remembrance) that the user might want to keep for future consultation. This repository of songs, sayings, and stories functioned like a machine that, in the hands of a competent human operator, could generate ever new and fresh performances of texts to delight, instruct, and enlighten. In the details of their script, format, and conventions, these notebooks reflect the application of "vocational" forms of literacy, like accounting and bookkeeping, to the inscription and circulation of vernacular literature, in turn revealing the role played by "middle" castes and classes in the process of vernacularization and the role played by literacy and writing in the spread of so-called "oral" genres like the *bhajan* (hymn).

Chapter 3: Pothīs, *Pandits, and Princes*

The third scene of writing is the world of intellectuals, both religious and literary, and the scholastic "book" (*pothī*). I perform close readings of works by monks of the aforementioned Niranjani Sampraday and Dadu Panth to show how they fashioned themselves as poets (*kavi*) and as intellectuals (*paṇḍit*) while presenting their compositions as works of literature (*kāvya*) and scholarship (*śāstra*). In the process, I demonstrate that the introduction of the vernacular of Hindi into the world of writing and contemporary scholarly discussions destabilized prevailing generic distinctions and conventions, allowing vernacular intellectuals to essentially "rewrite" the norms and conventions of scholastic discourse.

These monk-intellectuals and the scribes who transmitted their works in writing accomplished this restructuring while producing loose-leaf collections of wide paper folios that are most commonly called *pothīs*. Details within these manuscripts reveal the rigorous and tightly controlled structures and processes of copying and editing that ensured textual stability and authority, and gesture toward these books' use as scripts for pedagogical performance. Evidence of such manuscripts' circulation among diverse groups of intellectuals and religious communities gives us a sense of the shape of intellectual networks in this time and place and demonstrates that, far from being anti-intellectual or antischolastic, *nirguṇ bhakti* religious communities played an important role in building those intellectual and scholastic networks.

Chapter 4: The Guru's Voice and the Sacred Book

The fourth chapter investigates the scene of writing within the religious communities of the Niranjani Sampraday, the Dadu Panth, and the Sikh tradition to demonstrate how these groups used the technology of writing and the material object of the bound codex to re-present the songs and sayings of their respective saints in the form of a unified scripture (most often called *granth* or *vāṇī*). Close readings of the hagiographical traditions of these communities reveal that the Sikhs and Dadu Panthis in particular, and the Niranjanis to a lesser extent, self-consciously marked for remembrance the origins and inauguration of their scriptures, an act that sealed the authority of the written text. Such remembrances also reflect a subtle understanding of how the utterances of the saints, though eternal and transcendent, unfold within historical time. The large, bound, beautifully calligraphed and illuminated codices in which these traditions anthologized these words are remarkable objects in terms of their size, organization, decoration, and paratextual detail. These material aspects reflect their use in manifestly *public* liturgical performances with a visual as well as aural dimension. In all three of these traditions, codex scriptures came to be metonymically associated with the guru and, by extension, with God or the Divine itself. These scriptures also helped to anchor evolving notions of the religious community as a polity by standing not only as symbols of the guru's (including the Divine Guru's) authority but also as the material instantiation of His word—in other words, as a written Law.

Conclusion: Building a Library for Hindi

I conclude the book by reconstructing and reflecting upon the processes through which the modern archive of Hindi literature—as a set of material practices and institutions and as an object of knowledge—was produced in the late nineteenth and early twentieth centuries. This story centers on the efforts of two distinct disciplines and their respective institutions: literary history and the library, and art history and the museum. The Nagari Pracharini Sabha and similar literary institutions attempted to "recover" precolonial Hindi literature by undertaking massive surveys of manuscripts, documenting and collecting hundreds of thousands of handwritten books and documents that took various forms and contained a wide variety of genres and linguistic registers. Scholars and archivists associated with these institutions produced survey reports, library catalogues, journal articles, dictionaries, monographs, and critical editions that attempted to tame the wild profusion of manuscript material by offering classifications, taxonomies, and chronologies of literary genres, movements, and styles. Their scholastic imperatives, historiographical modalities, and bibliographical practices drew primarily from the work of European and Indian Indologists working with materials in Sanskrit, Prakrit, and Apabhramsha. Consequently, these scholars tended to miss or ignore the information encoded in the material, visual, and paratextual aspects of the handwritten books with which they otherwise worked so carefully. Ignoring these traces within the material archive allowed the pioneering historians of Hindi to create an entirely new scheme of generic and chronological classification for the language and its literature. In this manner, modern scholars and institutions "produced" Hindi manuscripts (*hastalikhit granth*) as the raw material to be transformed by scholarly analysis into literary knowledge. Similarly, art historians in the early twentieth century transformed copies of Hindi works into the raw material of art history. Copies of illustrated works in Hindi were dispersed, sold, and eventually acquired by museums as art artifacts; the folios were separated so that the illustrations could be reconceived, catalogued, exhibited, analyzed, and valued as individual art objects. Physically severed from the books of which they were once a part, they became separated from the practice of reading and the domain of literature in the imagination of art historians. I close with a reflection on how we might better attune ourselves to the lives of early books in Hindi—and South Asian languages in general—by noticing the clues that have survived despite epistemic and material ruptures.

ON CONVENTIONS, SCHOLARLY AND OTHERWISE

It can be potentially misleading or at least confusing to speak of "manuscripts" in a nonprint society. Wherever possible, I have tried to employ terms like "book," "notebook," "codex," and so forth to describe the text artifacts discussed in this study. Nevertheless, I do sometimes use the term "manuscript" to avoid confusion or excessive repetition. The same is true with "object": although I make the case above that we should conceptualize books as agentive "things," norms of English usage have compelled me to use the term on occasion. I use "Hindi" to denote not only the standardized, modern-day language associated with that term but also a spectrum of literary registers that were employed from the fourteenth century through the early nineteenth century and written using several different scripts. I refer to that same language as *bhāṣā* and sometimes simply as "the vernacular," generally synonymously. The one exception occurs in the concluding chapter, in which I discuss efforts to create a modern "Hindi" free of loanwords from Arabic, Persian, and Turkish, and written exclusively in the Devanāgarī script.

Pronouns present peculiar problems, particularly *à propos* passages penned in vernacular patois or professional parlance. The Hindi verb conveys the gender of a subject, but the pronoun does not; thus the gender of a subject (or object) of a verse can often be ambiguous. Early Hindi poets regularly exploit this ambiguity for poetic, aesthetic, and theological effect. In my translations I have tried to maintain this ambiguity when possible; otherwise I have used the context to make a choice about how to impute gender to subjects (or objects). Obviously, such an approach can never fully do justice to the shifting valence of gender in early Hindi literature.

Academic English also presents difficulties for attuning attention to gender: the usage of male pronouns for the generic human subject often elides the presence and agency of women in the context of both historical narrative and theoretical exposition. Where I have employed male pronouns in general descriptions—for example, "the scribe would write in *his* notebook," "the disciple transcribed the verses as *he* listened to the guru," et cetera—it is consciously to reflect the fact that in early modern north India the sphere of writing and reading was predominantly a male space from which women were often excluded.[23] A substantial body of contemporary documentary evidence and modern scholarly research demonstrates that women were very much part of the literary and religious world of early modern India and actively shaped this world as poets, saints, nuns, devotees, patrons, and connoisseurs. Whenever appropriate I have tried to include feminine as well as masculine pronouns to reflect women's participation in processes of literary production, transmission, performance, and enjoyment. This is an admittedly imperfect solution to a perennial problem of scholastic writing. The history of women's participation in the development of precolonial book culture in South Asia remains to be written.

Most of the documents cited in this book, if they mention a date, use either the lunar Vikrami Samvat calendar or the lunar Hijri calendar. To avoid confusion, I have been careful to note *VS* for dates given according to the Vikrami Samvat calendar, *H* for dates given according to the Hijri calendar, and *CE* for dates according to the Common Era reckoning. Any date unaccompanied by one of these notations is reckoned in terms of the Common Era.

Some readers may find my use of terms for certain writing scripts to be unfamiliar. In particular, I refer to the abjad script used for Arabic, Persian, Turkish, precolonial Hindi (or Urdu), *'ajamī* languages, and various other languages within the Islamicate world as simply "Arabic script." This script, as it was used for precolonial Hindi after 1300 CE in its *naskh* and *nastaʿlīq* calligraphic styles and variants, was heavily modified, having been adapted centuries earlier for use in writing Persian. I nevertheless refer to this as "Arabic script" to avoid the potential clumsiness and confusion generated by terms like "Perso-Arabic script," since the relationship between script and language in the precolonial world is far more complex than can be conveyed through a single term. My usage of this convenient shorthand should in no way suggest a simple or direct relationship between the Arabic language and South Asian works written in this script. Similarly, I refer to the abugida script used for various Indic languages, including Hindi as well as Sanskrit, in late medieval and early modern north India as simply "Nāgarī"—not to ignore but rather to include the many variants in orthography and script seen in precolonial documents that we now speak of as being in "Devanāgarī script." The only distinction that I make in this regard is between Nāgarī and Kaithī (and other shorthand scripts), since it is observed in precolonial sources and relates directly to the different modes and forms of literacy I discuss at length.

Precolonial Hindi presents several challenges related to transcription and transliteration because it was written in multiple scripts and because conventions of poetic recitation occasionally demanded that a reader deviate from or modify sounds as they were written on the page. For the sake of consistency and clarity (and because this is a book about *writing*) I have reproduced quotations exactly as they appear in written documents rather than making changes to reflect the ways performers adjusted their pronunciation to account for poetic meter and so forth. For the sake of consistency, I have followed the ISO 15919:2001 conventions for transliterating Hindi in the Nāgarī script into Roman and applied these rules to my transliterations from Arabic, Kaithī, and Gurmukhi scripts as well.

This made it necessary for me to deviate from the ISO 15919:2001 conventions in the following ways. Since precolonial scribes used a single superscript *bindu* (dot) to denote both 1) a nasalized vowel or 2) a nasalized consonant that precedes another consonant in a cluster, I have distinguished the two in my transliteration by using *ṁ* to denote a nasalized vowel and *ṅ*, *ñ*, *ṇ*, *n*, and *m* to denote nasalized consonants *except* when necessary to maintain poetic meter. In block quotations from verse, I have included the final short vowel *a* at the end of words to give readers a sense of both the metrical rules of the language and the conventions of oral performance; however, when using terms from Hindi in the body of my writing, I have omitted the final *a* vowel to reflect standard prose pronunciation. At some points it has been necessary to distinguish certain graphemes (letters) used in the Arabic script; I have transliterated these using the conventions of the American Library Association and the Library of Congress. For example, I transliterate the unvoiced fricative /ʃ/ (as in "should") as *ś* from documents in the Nāgarī script and as *sh* from documents in the Arabic script.

All titles of works and terms in languages other than English are given according to the foregoing transliteration scheme. The names of authors, historical individuals, and places are given according to accepted English spellings (without diacritics) for easier reference in English language materials. I hope that readers encountering this sometimes cumbersome way of writing Hindi and other South Asian languages will not be discouraged but rather find a new appreciation for just how complex, subtle, and magical the technology (and art) of writing can be.

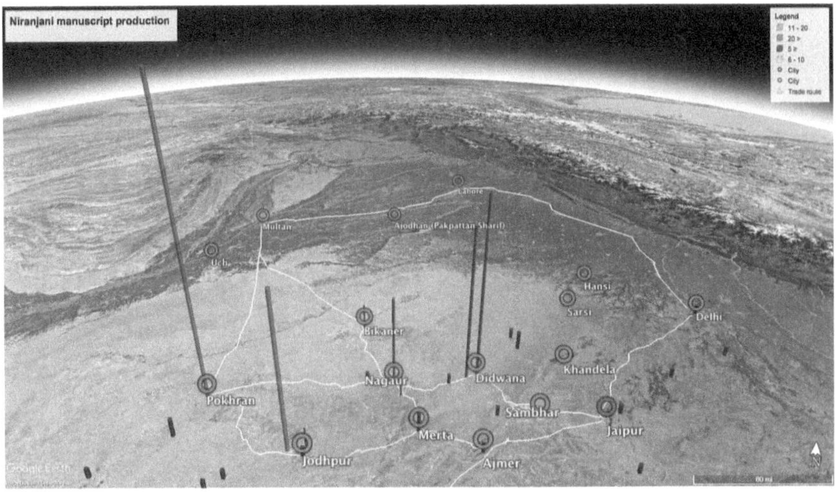

FIGURE 0.2 Map of Niranjani manuscript production c. 1650–1850. Production volumes are represented as vertical bars rising from their respective geographical locations.

Generated using Google Earth™ version 7.3.6.9345

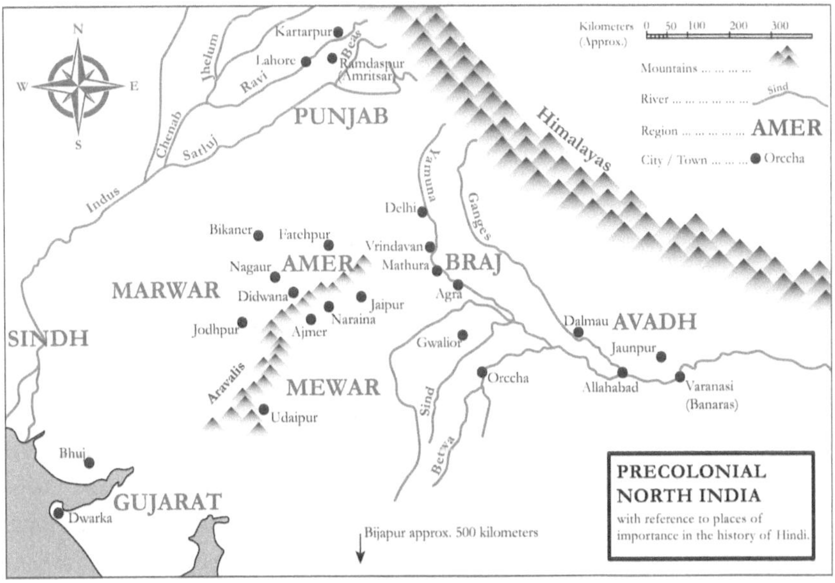

FIGURE 0.3 Map of north India

Image by author

I
Storytellers and Storybooks

sāsatarī ākhara bahu āe | au desī cuni cuni saba lāe
paḍhata sohāvana dījai kānūṃ | ehi ke sunata na bhāvai ānūṃ

Many letters from the śāstras *appear here,*
And I have hand-picked all of the vernacular words.
It is pleasant when recited, so lend me your ears—
Once you've heard this, no other [poem] gives such pleasure!

—Qutban, *Mirgāvatī*, 1503 CE

In the year 1110 Hijri (1698 CE), Dilir Khan, a Pashtun general and noble at the court of the Mughal Emperor Aurangzeb, commissioned the scribe Babullah bin Sayid Muhammad Zahir Husan al-Husayni al-Bukhari al-Najafi to make for him a copy of the poet Surdas's *Nal Daman*, a versified romance in the north Indian vernacular. Although Surdas had composed the *Nal Daman* in 1659 CE, a little less than forty years earlier, the work was a retelling of a much older story: the tale of the star-crossed lovers Nala and Damayanti, who are cursed by a god, separated from each other, and made to overcome enormous obstacles in order to be reunited. The story is at least as old as the Sanskrit *Mahābhārata* (composed from the ninth through fourth centuries BCE), of which it forms a part. By the time Surdas penned his version, the narrative had already been retold numerous times in several South Asian languages, most recently in Persian and to great acclaim by the Mughal poet laureate Shaikh Abu al-Faiz ibn Mubarak "Faizi" (1547–1595 CE).[1] So the seventeenth-century Surdas—not to be confused with the more famous bearer of that name, the sixteenth-century Krishna devotee, Surdas of Braj—was participating in a rich and long-standing tradition of interlingual retellings.

Surdas was a Hindu from the northwestern region of the Punjab, but it was literary conventions, rather than the poet's linguistic or literary background, that determined how he would compose his version of the narrative. Surdas says as much in the introduction, relating how upon "reading" about Nala and Damayanti in the *Mahābhārata*, he became so consumed by the fire of love that it was "as if I were bitten by a snake or lifted up on a wave." Like the pining lovers of the story, he was unable to sleep, eat, or drink, and his "body became kindling for love's fire / gripped again and again by love's flame." In this state of love-induced madness, Surdas resolved to share the story of Nala and Damayanti in another tongue and thus spread the fire from himself to the whole world.[2] The appropriate language for such a tale, according to Surdas, was *pūrab dī bhāṣā*, "the vernacular of the east," a literary register associated with the region now known as Avadh, and with the genre of the "love epic" known in modern scholarship as the *pem-kathā* (love story) or *prem-ākhyān* (love legend). He writes at the end of the *Nal Daman* that although he was well-versed in his native Punjabi ("I know my language as well, down to each and every dot") he composed his "account of love's truth in that language in which there are many poems."[3] His work would find the widest possible audience: "A pleasant garden is one that everyone can share /A pleasant story is one [composed] in a language that everyone understands."[4] Love epics in the eastern vernacular were well-known and well-loved throughout northern India and the Deccan during Surdas's time, so writing in that language promised him a large and knowledgeable readership. There is also an aesthetic rationale behind this choice: in Surdas's time, it was widely understood that the vernacular of north India, and especially "the vernacular of the east," was the ideal medium for expressing "love in separation" (*'ishq-firāq* in Surdas's words, analogous to the concept of *viraha* in Indic literatures). The shared association of certain languages with certain emotions and types of literature was even codified in literary manuals of the time like the *Tuhfat al-Hind* (1676 CE) of Mirza Khan.[5] Thus the language, narrative structure, motifs, and conventions of the *pem-kathā* had already been established through nearly three hundred years of tradition when Surdas sat down to begin his poem.

Similarly, when the scribe Babullah sat down in 1698 to make a copy of the *Nal Daman* for his patron, Dilir Khan, the way he should do so was already a matter of common sense established by at least two centuries of tradition. There existed conventional techniques of transliterating sounds from Indic languages into the Arabic abjad script, rules for ruling a page, protocols for pagination, and ideals to be followed in illustrations. So although a wealthy patron like Dilir Khan could probably have commissioned his copy of the romance in any of the formats and scripts available at the time—including loose-leaf paper and palm-leaf manuscripts, wide-format saddle-stitched codices, and long paper scrolls, to name just a few—it is no surprise that he commissioned the Persian-literate Babullah to make a bound codex in the so-called "portrait" format. It is also no surprise that within this codex, each individual stanza of Surdas's work was neatly copied into a carefully ruled and outlined block of text while each hemistich was carefully copied into a column, with the *dohā* diptych that ends each stanza copied in a differently colored ink (gold) from the rest of the text (black) and receiving its own ornamental box (fig. 1.1).

None of the visual and material elements of Dilir Khan's copy of the *Nal Daman*—now housed in the Chhatrapati Shivaji Maharaj Vastu Sangrahalaya in Mumbai—was arbitrary; they were all the results of a long history of experimentation, innovation, and gradual codification that had played out over the preceding three centuries. These elements also gave the copy an aesthetic, monetary, and social value that, at the time of its copying or at a later point of sale or exchange, could have been reckoned in fairly precise terms: the late seventeenth-century Deccan was a paradise for connoisseurs and practitioners of the book arts, with plenty of calligraphers, illustrators, and bookmakers available to produce deluxe copies, and plenty of political elites and literati ready to commission and purchase them. It does not appear that Surdas or Babullah followed established conventions blindly or mechanically—indeed, the beauty of conventions, whether in literary genres or in book making, is that they set the parameters for innovation. Both Surdas's epic and Babullah's copy bear traces of their creators' particular imaginations and idiosyncrasies even while they conform to broader literary and aesthetic norms.

Literary and book-making traditions do not appear ex nihilo and fully formed; they develop over time and in conversation with one another. When it appeared in the fourteenth century, the *pem-kathā* or Sufi romance represented a new genre in South Asian literature; over time it was gradually given a material form that was unique and recognizable, just like its textual content. And just as the *pem-kathā* combined elements from Arabic, Persian, Sanskrit, and other Indic literary traditions but was more than the sum of its parts, so too the manuscript codices fashioned to contain the *pem-kathā* drew from multiple book-making and aesthetic traditions, combining them to produce a material text artifact with its own distinct character. All of this took place amid broader discussions on literary aesthetics, language, and affect being pursued by poets, scholars, and artists in the fourteenth through sixteenth centuries.

SPEAKING, SINGING, AND WRITING: THE *CANDĀYAN* AND THE BEGINNINGS OF WRITING AND LITERATURE IN THE VERNACULAR

A growing number of historians of Hindi literature believe that the Hindi literary tradition begins with the invention of the Sufi romance and its first known example, the *Candāyan* (1379 CE) of Maulana Daud. There are multiple reasons for giving Daud's work and the genre that it inaugurates this distinction. First, it is the earliest known work in a register of the vernacular that continued to be used for literary composition over the next five hundred years.[6] Second, it employs meters and verse forms like the *caupaī* and *dohā* that would come to be closely associated with *bhāṣā* literature. Third, it is the first work of a genre that would come to occupy a central place in the vernacular literary imagination until well into the nineteenth century. Not all scholars agree; some locate Hindi literature's beginnings in other centuries and in other genres.[7] Yet if we take seriously Sheldon Pollock's contention that writing and the self-conscious identification of poetry or belles lettres as such (whether Indic *kāvya* or Arabic-Persian *adab*) are essential to the constitution of literature proper, then the *Candāyan* stands out sharply as the first work in a north Indian vernacular to have been consciously written as literature.

Practices of inscribing the vernacular had already existed for some time when Maulana Daud picked up the pen toward the end of the fourteenth century. Much of this activity took place in the hundred years preceding the composition of the *Candāyan*, in the context of Persian works containing what Francesca Orsini has characterized as "traces of oral practices in writing."[8] For example, there are scattered inscriptions of vernacular utterance in *malfuẓāt*, dialogic memoirs dedicated to recording the conversations and sermons of Sufi *pīrs*. Two such *malfuẓāt*, the *Nafā'is al-Anfās* ("Delicacies of Speech," 1331–1337 CE) of Rukn al-Din and the *Shamā'il al-Atqiyā* ("Virtues of Devout Men," 1330s CE) of Rukn al-Din Kabir record some of the "Hinduī" verses recited by the Chishti *pīr* Shaikh Fariduddin Ganj-i Shakar (1175–1266 CE) in the context of conversations that ostensibly took place, or were at least transcribed, in Persian. The *Hidāyat al-Qulūb wa 'Ināyat 'Allām al-G͟huyūb* (*Guidance of Hearts and Favor of the Knower of the Hidden*), composed by Mir Hasan in the Deccan from 1344 to 1367 CE, claims to record the discourses of another Chishti saint, Zayn al-Din Shirazi, including several verses in Hindi.[9] Although it is difficult to ascertain whether all of the discourses and deeds recorded are historically accurate, there is no question that the *malfuẕāt* themselves were composed in the four decades immediately preceding the composition of the *Candāyan*. Available copies of these works date only to the sixteenth and seventeenth centuries, but the orthographic and other writing conventions give us a sense of how vernacular utterance may have been recorded in this period.[10] Meanwhile, in the realm of courtly literature, Amir Khusrau (1253–1385 CE), a poet at the courts of three consecutive sultans of Delhi and of several nobles, composed macaronic verses that included snippets of the vernacular and is credited with composing several lyrics in Hindavi that have since become standards of the Sufi musical repertoire.[11] Here again, the lack of early manuscript copies makes it difficult to say how much of what has come down to us is the "original" compositions and what they looked like on paper (i.e., in the orthographic practices of Khusrau's time), yet the significance of Khusrau's *reḵẖtah* (Persian, "mixed") verses in Hindavi and Persian is clear: they had likely been circulating in written form for decades when Maulana Daud began to compose the *Candāyan*.

All of these developments took place in the shadow of the sultanate court of the Tughlaq dynasty of Persianized Afghan lords, and Daud was at the center of their politics beginning in the 1360s.[12] Though the Persian-literate Daud was writing in the town of Dalmau in Avadh, at the provincial court of a warlord (himself a vassal of the sultan), he was connected to both the world of professional poets at court and the world of Sufi *pīrs* (preceptors) at *khānqāhs* (Sufi hospices). It is likely that he was aware of the aforementioned forays into entextualizing the vernacular.[13]

Yet Daud's literary project was of a wholly different nature. As Aditya Behl has argued, the *Candāyan* represents the self-conscious inauguration of a new genre.[14] The source of the narrative, the romance of Prince Laur and Princess Chanda, was an "oral" epic sung by folk performers in the region of Avadh. Daud gave the story an altogether different form, incorporating literary and rhetorical devices from Persian and Indic traditions, such as densely poetic descriptions of cities (Sanskrit *nagara-varṇana*, Persian *shahr-āshob*), characters (Sanskrit *nakha-śikha*, Persian *sarāpā*), and seasons (Sanskrit *ṛtu-varṇana*, Hindi *bārah-māsā*). He introduced Sufi symbolism into the narrative so that his poem could be enjoyed simultaneously as an erotic romance and as an esoteric allegory of Sufi mystical practice. In contrast to earlier written instantiations of *bhāṣā* (like those in the *malfuẕāt*), Daud's version was not simply a transcription of song (*gīt*, *gāthā*) but a written literary work ("*kavi*," in the poet's own words) from the very moment of its conception, and its identity as such demanded a different kind of inscriptional program and material form.[15]

Daud was acutely aware of the significance of bringing *bhāṣā* from the realm of orality into the domain of writing and made vividly present the performative and literate contexts in which he composed. In the opening section of the *Candāyan*, modeled on the panegyric openings of the Persian *masnavī* genre, Daud praises his patron, Juna Shah, an *iqṭāʿ-dār* or noble of the Tughlaq court, comparing him to the legendary polyglot of Sanskrit antiquity, Vararuchi. Daud emphasizes Junah Shah's linguistic and literary proficiency:

khānajahāṁ ghari juga juga khānī / ati nāgara budhivanta binānī
catura sujāna bhākha saba jānā / rūpavanta mantarī sayānā
bahuta binānu daï re gaṛhā / caudaha paḍhatu hiye pai paḍhā
pothi purāna abahirai lagāvai / paṇḍita kai mukha bakata na āvai
* * *
bhayo rāju phuni baruraci jorata aratha agāha
khauṁda khāna jīnā aura gunī kā āha

The Khān-jahān comes from a house of nobles dating back ages,
he is exceedingly cultivated, intellectual, and knowledgeable.
Clever and learned, he knows all languages.
He is handsome and a good minister.
God has fashioned him with great wisdom;
he studied the fourteen [arts] until he could read (or recite) them by heart.
He elucidates books (*pothi*) and *purānas*,
[such that] not a word comes out of the pandits' mouths.
* * *
[Thus] another Vararuchi appeared in the kingdom,
who produces readings of endless depth [from texts.].
There is no other person,
so virtuous as this master.[16]

However hyperbolic this may be—Daud similarly praises the reigning Sultan Firoz Shah Tughlaq as being an all-knowing pandit—the verse reflects the ideal of a highly literate and multilingual ruler that found at least some realization in the multilingual literary culture of sultanate courts.[17]

Daud's language and lexicon reflect the beginnings of a movement that would reinscribe the semiotic world of the vernacular in terms of this culture. The multivalence of the verb *paḍh-* (to read, recite, study) means that we can translate the second half of the third couplet (*caudaha paḍhatu hiye pai paḍhā*) alternatively as "he studied the fourteen arts [until] he recited them by heart" or more literally, "he studied the fourteen arts [until] he read them on his heart." Though the latter rendering may sound awkward in English, it hews closer to the sense of the original: in the Islamicate and specifically Sufi intellectual culture in which Daud composed, the Neoplatonic concept of memory as writing on the tablet of the heart was a well-known convention.[18] Daud's use of the term *pothī* is also remarkable, as it collapses the concepts of a text, a scripture, and a material manuscript into one term that signifies Islamic scriptural and juridical texts as well as Indic scriptures and *śāstras*. In precolonial Hindi, *pothī* most often refers to an unbound group of loose folios made of palm leaf or paper; this was the predominant format for written texts in Indic languages at the dawn of the north Indian sultanates. Daud does not write that his patron performs exegesis of *pothī*s in order to make the sultan's piety or authority intelligible to a non-Muslim audience or for the purpose of proselytization, as some twentieth-century scholars have suggested.[19] Instead, Daud's use of Indic terms like *pothī* pulls notions of written textuality from the Indic context into the realm of Persianate, Islamicate literary culture while simultaneously reimagining that culture in the exotic and dream-like world of the romance narrative itself. For Daud and his audience, not only the tale of Lorik and Chanda but also the language in which Daud recounted it were grounded in the exotic landscape of northern "Hindustan": this was, as Surdas later put it, the "language of the east," in which Daud was living and writing, the language of love (*pem*). Thus Daud re-presented to the Persianized, polyethnic elites the modes, practices, and material objects of their own literacy through the fantastic prism of the Indian vernacular.[20]

This "double move" of bringing the vernacular into the world of Islamicate literacy and literary practices while reimagining those practices in the aesthetic and lexical landscape of north India is most apparent in Daud's praise for his Sufi teacher, Shaikh Zainuddin. Daud describes how he acquired true literacy and composed the *Candāyan*:

shekha jainudīṁ hauṁ pathi lāva / dharamu panthu jihi pāpu gavāṁvā

* * *

ughare naina hiye ujiyāre / pāyo likhi nau akkhara kāre
puni mai akhira kī sudhi pāï / turakī likhi likhi hindukī gāï

Shaikh Zainuddin brought me to the path,
the righteous path on which I renounced my sins.

* * *

My eyes were opened and my heart illuminated,
and I learned to write the nine black letters.
Then I gained an understanding of the letters.
Writing away in Turkish, I sang in Hindukī.[21]

Only after the shaikh brings Daud to the right path and opens his eyes (i.e., the eyes of the heart) is the poet able to both write and comprehend the significance of the "nine black letters," the first half of the *kalimah*, the profession of faith in Islam (*lā ilāha illā–llāh*, "There is no god but Allah"). The emphasis on their visual form ("black") gestures toward the *'ilm-ul ḥurūf* or "science of letters," a form of esoteric letter mysticism practiced among multiple Sufi orders in north India at the time, which ascribes metaphysical powers to the letters of the Arabic alphabet.[22]

Yet the term that Daud uses for "letters" is *akkhara/akhira* (Sanskrit *akṣara*), literally "imperishable," which in fourteenth-century north India could refer to a phoneme of the alphabet, a spoken syllable, or their written representations and figured within a metaphysics of "imperishable sound" (*nāda*) that undergirded contemporary yogic and tantric practices. For actual yogis and other Hindu ascetics of the time, the repetition of specific *akṣara* was part of both transformative verbal formulas used during initiation rites (known as *bīja-mantra* or "source formulas") and other verbal formulas repeated to achieve various physical or metaphysical aims. (Laurik, the hero of the *Candāyan*, himself takes on the appearance and lifestyle of a Hindu ascetic for part of the narrative, establishing a convention that would be observed in all subsequent works of the genre.) The *kalimah* was employed in an analogous fashion by some Sufi orders of the time, repeated as part of *ẕikr* ("remembrance") during initiation rites and other ritual performances to effect a movement to higher states (*maqām*) of spiritual consciousness or gnosis.

Daud thus sets up a series of rough equivalences between the Muslim practice of *ẕikr* and the Hindu practice of *jap-* (repetitive incantation), between the *kalimah* and *mantra*, and between *ḥarf* (Arabic, letter of the alphabet) and *akṣara*. Yet the condensed poetic syntax of the *caupaī* verse makes this homology more than a mere comparison or analogy: the letters (*ḥurūf*) of the *kalimah* formula are not simply *like* the *akṣara* or imperishable syllables of a mantra; they *are* the imperishable *akṣara* of a mantra. The practice of *ẕikr*, the *kalimah*, and the esoteric interpretation of its written graphemes have been made part of the metaphysical and aesthetic landscape of Hindustan. Daud succinctly outlines the relationships among language, literacy, and knowledge: one must have the eyes of their heart opened by a qualified teacher before they can begin to acquire true literacy; further effort is then required to understand the significance of what is written. This particular matrix of pedagogical authority, literacy, and knowledge would appear repeatedly over the following two centuries in the songs of the *nirguṇ* saints (the subject of the next chapter).

Daud then characterizes his literary undertaking: *turakī likhi likhi hindukī gāï*, "Writing away in Turkish, I sang in Hindukī." Here, "Turkish" refers to the Arabic script used by Muslim elites of the Delhi sultanate, collectively referred to as "Turks" in contemporary vernacular and Sanskrit sources. "Hindukī" refers to the language of "Hind," the spoken vernacular of north India. Daud sets forth an image of himself "writing away" in the Arabic script—used by cosmopolitan literati from Pandua in Bengal to Granada in Spain—while singing in the local language of Hindustan. This image would be realized in visual form by later illustrators of the *Candāyan*. Daud's composition acts as a hinge between the domain of literacy and literature—the cosmopolitan realm of *turakī*—and the domain of orality and song—the local yet exotic realm of *hindukī*.

Daud self-consciously and explicitly characterizes his work as literature—not in the lexicon of Persianate letters or *adab* but in the Indic lexicon of *kāvya*. At the end of his preface, he writes, "In the year 781 [Hijri], I recited this succulent poem" (*barasa sāta sai hoï ikyāsī / tihi jāha kavi saraseü bhāsī*). This is literature proper: a "poem" (*kavi*) that is "full of *rasa*" (*saraseü*). Daud addresses the connoisseurs and literati among his audience: "Take to heart and ponder this poem (*kavi*) sung by Daud / Contemplate those utterances that are well-wrought and mend those that are broken" (*dāüda yeha kavi gāī mana mahi lehu bicāri / jurata bolu cita rākhahu ṭūṭata lehu savāṁri*).[23] Through this type of apologetic, a convention of both Persian and Sanskrit literary genres of the period, he indicates that he is presenting this work for the delectation of—but also appraisal and criticism by—"men of letters" (Persian *adībān*, Sanskrit *kovida*), in the social realm of the literate and the literary. In a media landscape without the technology of printing, this was a way of making a work "public," stamping it with a verbal (and written) mark of "publication."

"LEND ME YOUR EARS!" ORALITY AND WRITING IN THE *PEM-KATHĀ* GENRE

Daud's *Candāyan* set the conventions of the *pem-kathā* genre upon which later poets would innovate, articulating their thoughts on the matrix of orality, writing, and (vernacular) literature and enriching the lexicon of written textuality in *bhāṣā*. The first of these later poets, Shaikh Qutban Suhravardi, in 1503 CE completed his *Mirgāvatī*, the story of a prince's adventures in pursuit of a shapeshifting, doe-like (*mirgāvatī*) princess. Qutban dedicated the work to his patron, Hussain Shah, the deposed sultan of Jaunpur. Although the sultan was living in exile at the time, memories of the grandeur of the Jaunpur court—the same that Daud praised one hundred and twenty-four years earlier—were still fresh. Painting a lavish portrait, Qutban praises his patron as the ideal reader: "Wise, intelligent, and knowledgeable, [Shah Hussain] recites from books (*pothī*) and knows all of their meanings" (*paṇḍita au budhivanta sayānāṁ / pothā bāṃca aratha saba jānāṁ*). He is multilingual (*bhākhā sab janai*) and consequently able to produce multiple meanings or implications (*arath*, Sanskrit *artha*) from a given verbal utterance, rhetorical device, or motif. Qutban continues, "He reads the most difficult Puranas, then tells and explains their meaning, [giving] ten meanings for every utterance. Stunned, the pandits are speechless!" (*paḍhahī purāna kaṭhina jo hoī / aratha kahahī samuṁjhāvahī soī / eka eka bola kā dasa dasa bhāvā / paṃditanha acakara bakati na āvā*).[24] Reading is thus an act of performance in which the skilled reader "recites aloud" (*baṁc-*) and produces for his learned listeners (the pandits) multiple interpretations of the text—so many as to amaze or thrill them. Reading, in Qutban's world, is neither an individual pursuit nor an act of mere reception, but rather a social pursuit in which real-time exegesis is as essential to obtaining pleasure or knowledge from a literary work as the content of the work itself.

Like Daud, Qutban paints this picture in the colors of north India, in the process reinscribing terms from the vernacular with meanings that reflect a milieu of written and multilingual textuality. The "books" that the sultan reads are *pothī*, and the works that the sultan explains for his rapt audience are *purāṇa*. Whereas in Sanskrit, *purāṇa* refers specifically to a class of works that combine historical, cosmological, and devotional material, Qutban uses the term in the vernacular as a synecdoche for scriptural and esoteric works in general (and in doing so gestures toward Hussain Shah's multilingual competency).[25] Qutban even reimagines the textual history of the Qur'an in the idiom of north India: while praising the "four companions" (*cār yār*) of the Prophet Muhammad, he writes that "Usman wrote down the divine utterances / As he learned them from the lips of Muhammad" (*usamāna bacana daiīya kai likhe / jo re mohaṁmada adharahu sikhe*).[26] This is the first appearance in the written record of Hindi of the birth of scripture described as the transcription of divine utterance (*bacan*, from Sanskrit *vacana*) from the mouth of a human prophet or guru. It appears again later, not only in other works of the *pem-kathā* genre but also in the hagiographical works of *nirguṇ* devotional communities and the Sikhs—all of which were influenced by Muslim and in particular Sufi beliefs and practices—as these communities record the birth of their own scriptures.

Like Daud, Qutban prefaces his narrative with a reflection on the nature and significance of his project. Yet more than a century later, he was composing in a changed literary landscape: the *Candāyan* had established the vernacular romance as a fixed feature, so much so that the prominent Sufi and scholar 'Abdul Quddus Gangohi attempted to translate it into Persian in the 1470s. During the fifteenth century, Rajput kingdoms to the south in Gwalior had been commissioning versions of the Hindu epics in *bhāṣā*, and Qutban's home region of Avadh had begun to experience an efflorescence of vernacular hymnody in the songs of saints like Kabir and Ravidas. Qutban expands the notion of what constitutes vernacular literary composition to include aspects of prosody, lexicon, and literary topoi. He introduces his story,

gāthā dohā arila ārajā / soraṭha caupāïnha kai sājā
sāsatarī ākhara bahu āe / au desī cuni cuni saba lāe
paḍhata sohāvana dījai kānūṁ / ehi ke sunata na bhāvai ānūṁ

dui re māṁsa dina dasa mahāṁ jorata yaha re orāneūṁ jāi
eka eka bola moṃti jasa provā ikaṭhā cita mana lāi

I have arranged it in *gāthā*, *dohā*, *aril*, *arajā*,
 soraṭhā, and *caupāi* meters.
Many syllables from the *śāstras* appear,
 and I have hand-picked all of the local (*desī*) words.
It is pleasant when recited, so lend me your ears—
 no other [poem] gives such pleasure when heard!

After two months and ten days of composing,
 I completed it.
Assaying every single utterance like a pearl,
 I joined them together with full concentration.[27]

Qutban adapts a motif from Arabic and Persian literary cultures—the poet as jeweler or craftsman—to characterize the vernacular poet in Hindustan: just as a jeweler makes existing gems and pearls more beautiful by arranging them in a novel sequence on the string of a necklace, a poet makes existing themes and rhetorical devices more beautiful by arranging them in an innovative manner on a string of narrative invention. Extending this analogy, Qutban suggests that a vernacular poet takes existing metrical forms, words, and narratives from the language of the region (*deś*) and makes them more beautiful by arranging them (*sājā*) in strikingly new formations on the string of the Persian *maṡnavī* genre. He proudly lists the prosodic forms that he has employed—the *gāthā*, *dohā*, *aril*, *arajā*, *soraṭhā*, and *caupāī*—all of which are distinctively *vernacular* meters, inherited from Apabhramsha via Maru-Gujar ("Old Rajasthani") or Madhyadeshi languages.

The *kaḍavak* or stanza-based structure of the text also appears to be inherited from these earlier literary vernaculars, which had significant consequences for the written and visual presentation of the literary work in book form. Qutban draws attention to the lexical heterogeneity that characterizes vernacular literature: his poem uses "scholarly syllables" (*sāsatarī ākhar*), meaning the phonology, morphology, and lexicon of cosmopolitan literature; he also includes a carefully curated (*cuni cuni*) assortment of local (*desī*) words. At a broader structural level, Qutban has, at the request of his patron, taken a tale from Hindustan with its attendant landscapes, costumes, flora, and fauna, and restrung it into a *maṡnavī*-like romance. If Daud imagined his *Candāyan* as a hinge between the oral world of vernacular song and the written world of Persian literature, then Qutban imagines his *Mirgāvatī* as a hinge between the prosody, lexicon, and topoi of the local and the narrative structure, conventions, and reading protocols of the cosmopolitan.

The next two works of the genre—the *Padmāvat* (1540 CE) of Malik Muhammad Jayasi and the *Madhumālatī* (1545 CE) of Mir Sayid Manjhan Rajgiri—were composed a mere generation later but in a significantly different political and literary context. In the mid-sixteenth century these poets' patrons, the Afghan warlords of the late sultanate dispensation, vied with the Persianized Turkic Mughals for control of north India. Those same patrons were also busy expanding and improving transportation and communication networks that in turn facilitated the development of devotional centers like Braj in which vernacular lyrics were produced and the circulation of those lyrics over great distances. Meanwhile, the exchanges of esoteric knowledge and praxis among Sufis, yogis, and practitioners of Hindu *bhakti* that had transpired over the previous two centuries were beginning to be committed to writing in Persian, in works like the *Rushd-nāma* (c. 1480 CE) of 'Abdul Quddus Gangohi, a *risālah* or treatise on spiritual practice that incorporates yogic techniques (and contains approximately two hundred and fifty verses of vernacular lyric); the *Ḥaqā'iq-i Hindī* (1566 CE) of Mir 'Abdul Wahid Bilgrami, a kind of interpretive lexicon of vernacular lyric replete with examples; translations and adaptations of the Sanskrit *Amṛtakuṇḍa* and other treatises on yoga like the *Baḥr al-Ḥayāt* (c. 1550 CE) of Shaikh Muhammad Ghawth; and, particularly important, another of Jayasi's compositions, the *Kanhāvat* (1540 CE), a vernacular retelling of popular narratives concerning the god Krishna.[28]

This burgeoning literature in Persian as well as in the vernacular reflects the vibrancy of exchanges in two performative domains. The first is the musical performance of lyric poetry in *samā'* gatherings of Sufis, in *satsaṅg* gatherings of Hindu devotees, and in *dhrupad* performances for and among musical connoisseurs. Although their performance protocols and theological underpinnings were distinct, all three practices involved the recitation and singing of vernacular lyrics that drew from a common vocabulary of motifs, symbols, and associations, as well as from the shared aesthetic logic of *rasa*. The second domain is the performance of *pem-kathās* like the *Candāyan*, *Mirgāvatī*, *Padmāvat*, and *Madhumālatī* themselves. As Francesca Orsini has suggested, the social space of the *ahātā* or *caupāl* (covered meeting areas) in which such romances were performed and enjoyed by religiously and socially heterogenous groupings of people across the Gangetic plain made such religious and literary exchanges possible and made the *pem-kathā* a productive and long-lived cultural form.[29]

Jayasi's and Manjhan's works reflect the maturity of the genre: both poets present highly developed descriptions of the matrix of orality, writing, inscription, reading, prosody, and topoi toward which Daud and Qutban had earlier gestured as the defining features of vernacular literature. Jayasi, a Sufi of the Chisti *silsilah* who dedicates his work to the Afghan warlord Sher Shah Suri, characterizes his poem (*kabi*) thus:

ādi anta jasi kaththa ahai / likhi bhākhā caupāī kahai
kabi biāsa rasa kaṃvalā pūrī / dūrihi niara niara bhā dūrī
niarhi dūri phūla saṃga kāṃṭā / dūri jo niaraiṁ jasa guru cāṃṭā
bhaṃvara āi banakhaṃda huti lehiṁ kaṃvala kai bāsa
dādura bāsa na pāvahiṁ bhalehiṁ je āchahiṁ pāsa[30]

I tell the story in *caupaīs*, just as it goes from beginning to end,
having written it in the vernacular.
A poem develops like juice (*rasa*) fills an orange:
those who are far may be close, and those who are close may be far.
Those who are close may be like the thorns on a flower,
and those who are far may be like ants on brown sugar.
The bee comes from the forest to take in the fragrance of the lotus,
but the frog doesn't catch the fragrance, even though he is near to it.

The general ideas and tropes may be inherited from earlier poets but Jayasi has further integrated the genre into the literary imagination of the region. He states that he has not invented the narrative but has taken it from somewhere; this is the literary and cultural landscape of Hindustan itself, the aforementioned milieus of *ahātās* and *caupāls,* sessions of *samā*ʿ and *satsaṅg*, in which such narratives circulated orally. He has "written" (*likhi*) the story in the vernacular (*bhākhā*) but "tells" it (*kahai*) in *caupāī* verses; Jayasi thus maintains the distinction between written text and sung (or recited) lyric that we observed first in Daud's *Candāyan* and later in Qutban's *Mirgāvatī*. Yet the realm of literary inscription is no longer solely the domain of "Turki" (as was the case in Daud's time): now *bhākhā* too can be a "written" language.[31] The reference to *bhākhā* still indicates the distinction between the vernacular and the cosmopolitan languages of Persian, Arabic, and Sanskrit; moreover, the mention of the *caupaī* meter indexes the vernacular to its distinctive prosodic forms. Vernacular literature is still characterized by a particular relationship of orality and writing, prosody and narrative, but its written existence has been naturalized.

Jayasi further develops the epistemology of reading and the notion of the ideal reader outlined by his predecessors. As Behl has suggested, the key to unlocking the hermeneutic and aesthetic workings of the Sufi *pem-kathā* lies in its multisensory characterization of reading (or listening).[32] In Jayasi's *rasa*-laden metaphor, both the symbolic potentials of the text (such as the allegory of the individual soul's yearning for God, symbolized in the hero's desire for the heroine) and the aesthetic triggers of its performance (such as motifs, rhetorical devices, and images intended to stimulate erotic and/or reverential love in the listener's heart) are as subtle and difficult to perceive as a distant fragrance. Like the bee in the forest that smells the lotus from far away, the literary connoisseur or Sufi adept will recognize these meanings and triggers from a distance while the froglike layman or dilettante will miss them completely even though the source of the fragrance (the verbal signifiers) be right "under his nose," so to speak. To properly experience a work of the genre meant not only to cognize its "meaning" but also to effect the appropriate aesthetic and emotional response to it—to taste *rasa* (which was invariably the *rasa* of love, *pem* or *ʿishq*).

Among the *prem-kathā* poets, Jayasi articulates in the most extensive and elegant manner a notion of written scripture (*purān*), including its origins and sacrality. He exhorts his audience to "Become enlightened by recognizing the Creator / As His testimony is written in the scriptures (*purān*)" (*ehi bidhi cīnhahu karahu giānū / jasa purāna mahaṁ likhā bakhānū*). Praising the four companions of the Prophet, he writes that "Usman, that virtuous wise man / Wrote in the scriptures (*purān*) those verses (*āyat*) that he had heard" (*puni usmāna paṃdita baṛa guni / likhā purāna jo āyata sunī*). All four of these great caliphs "recited that very same book (*granth*): the scripture (*purān*) that the Creator had sent / And so those who wander, coming to hear it, then stick to the Path" (*jo purāna bidhi paṭhavā soī paṛhata girantha / aüra jo bhūle āvata te suni lāgata tehi pantha*).[33] Jayasi's confident and repeated use of the term *purān* shows that it has come to designate in the vernacular a class of revealed religious texts that we can roughly translate as "scripture" because they are explicitly "written" (*likhā*), even if their origin is the spoken word of God or His prophets. This sense of written textuality is reinforced by Jayasi's use of the Sanksrit term *granth* for "book." In Sanskrit itself, *granth* (lit. "tying" or "binding") can refer to any extended textual composition, written or unwritten—what is "bound" together here are verses and stanzas, not necessarily leaves of a manuscript. Yet in Jayasi's verse, the *granth* is clearly the written instantiation of God's word: the "book" from which the caliphs read, the *purān* that God "sent," which contains *āyat* (Arabic, lit. "sign," a verse of the revealed Qur'an). Jayasi thus provides a model for scripture within the vernacular imagination: God "sends" (*paṭhavā*) His divine word via human prophets; it is first heard (*sunī*) and then transcribed (*likhā*) by a competent devotee. God is consequently present in scripture and can be perceived (*cīnha-*) by those who *listen*. The divine aura is present in the written scripture but is activated by oral recitation and received through listening, which "brings one to the Path" that leads back to God, its source. Completing the *Padmāvat* in 1540, Jayasi captures this image just before various *nirguṇ*-oriented religious communities in north India, including the Sikhs, Dadu Panth, and Niranjani Sampraday, began to establish their own vernacular scriptures.

Finally, the *Padmāvat* marks an important change in the materials and material practices of writing in northern India that was largely ignored in the cosmopolitan literatures of Persian and Sanskrit. In a verse praising God in the opening, Jayasi uses the metaphor of writing to express God's ineffability:

ati apāra karatā kara karanā / varani na koī paraï baranā
sāta saraga jauṁ kāgara karaī / dharatī sāta samunda masi bharaī
jāvaṃta jaga sākhā bana ḍhāṃkhā / jāvaṃta kesa rovāṁ paṁki pāṁvā
jāvaṃta reha kheha jahaṁ tāīṁ / megha būṃda au gagana tarāīṁ
saba likhanī kaī likha saṁsārū / likhi na jāï gati samuṃda apārū
eta kīnha saba guna paragaṭā / abahūṁ sumuṃda būṃda nahiṁ ghaṭā

Absolutely endless are the deeds of the Creator:
no one can describe them.

Were the seven heavens to be made into paper,
    and the earth and the seven seas filled with ink,
And as many branches, of as many trees,
    as there are in the forests of the world,
And as many hairs, feathers, and fur as exist,
    and as much salty efflorescence (*reh*) there be in the earth as far as it extends,
And as many drops as there may be in the clouds
    and as many stars as there be in the sky—
Were they all to be made into pens and should all of *saṁsāra* write,
    still the endless ocean of His deeds could not be written!
He has accomplished all this and made all His qualities manifest,
    and still that ocean has not decreased by a drop.[34]

As beautiful as this particular rendering may be, the motif itself is hardly Jayasi's invention: it appears, for example, in verses 13:109 and 31:27 of the Qur'an and in the *Śivamahimnaḥ Stotram*, a Shaivite liturgical text composed in Sanskrit during the tenth century.[35] (Jayasi was certainly familiar with the former and there is reason to believe that he was also aware of the latter.) Yet the details of Jayasi's verse reflect a shift in the *techne* of writing in India, as is shown by comparison with the aforementioned verse of the *Śivamahimnaḥ Stotram*:

asita-giri-samaṁ syāt kajjalaṁ sindhu-pātre sura-taruvara-śākhā lekhanī
    patram urvī
likhati yadi gṛhītvā śāradā sarvakālaṁ tadapi tava guṇānām īśa pāraṁ
    na yāti

Were the ink like the Black Mountain
    in an ocean-like pot,
the pen like the branches of the gods' wish-fulfilling tree,
    and the leaf like the expanse of the earth,
even if Śāradā (Sarasvati, the goddess of speech) took up [these
    implements]
    and wrote for eternity,
nevertheless she would not reach
    the end of your qualities.[36]

Where does Jayasi's metaphor depart from its Indian antecedents? The *lekhanī* (reed stylus) is still there, as is the *masi* (ink made from lampblack). The key difference is in the writing surface: *kāgar* (Arabic *kāghaẕ*, "paper") in Jayasi's verse, as opposed to *patram* (Sanskrit "leaf") in the *Śivamahimnaḥ Stotram*. The rest of Jayasi's metaphor is thoroughly Indic, all the way down to the mention of *saṁsāra*, making the presence of paper all the more remarkable.[37] Paper was gradually introduced into north India after the establishment of sultanates at the turn of the thirteenth century, but scribal communities working in Sanskrit, Prakrit, and Apabhramsha appear to have largely ignored the new writing medium for the following two centuries; when they did make use of paper they reproduced the layouts, formats, and aesthetics of palm leaf manuscripts rather than exploring the possibilities of the new material. Even more important, the introduction of paper (and concomitant introduction of new types of pens, brushes, and techniques for writing) went almost totally unremarked in Sanskrit literary and scholastic works during the sultanate period. Similarly, in the domain of Persian and Arabic sources, though documentary and ethnographic works note Indians' use of leaves for writing, this medium never makes it into literary or religious writings in these languages.[38] It is thus the linguistic and literary space of the *vernacular* where the intersection of new and old materials and practices of writing are negotiated. The lexical hybridity of the vernacular allowed it to register the appearance of new materials, new inscriptional practices, and new types of written artifacts (e.g., the use of *purān* to refer to written scripture) in a way not seen in cosmopolitan languages of the period. This in turn made it possible for the *nirguṇ* religious traditions to use writing to think through epistemological questions in new ways.

Just as they were aware of the vernacular's character as a space of mixing and hybridization, poets were sensitive to its particular aesthetic potentials, especially in regard to eros (*śṛṅgāra*, *'ishq*). According to Jayasi's contemporary, Mir Sayid Manjhan Rajgiri, a Sufi of the Shattari order and a poet at the court of the Afghan warlord Islam Shah, it is the language of *bhāṣā* itself that contains *rasa*, as well as the content of a work.[39] Narrating the origin of his composition, he speaks of "the *rasa*-filled vernacular" (*rasa-bhākhā*) and implores his audience to "Listen to what I say as I sing / This ambrosial story of savory *rasa*."[40] *Listening* is the key: Manjhan emphasizes that the correct oral recitation of his work is essential to both an intellectual comprehension of its content and an aesthetic experience of *rasa*. He cautions: "People! Read my letters (or syllables, *ākhar*) having understood them. / Do not repeat a single one [of them] without understanding [it]!"[41] It is an appeal to two distinct but interconnected types of literacy, the graphic and the discursive. To correctly read or recite (*paḍh-*) from the written text of Manjhan's poem required an understanding of vernacular orthography in the Arabic script; scribes of the time had to adapt it to represent the exotic sounds of the north Indian tongue. Each individual syllable needed to be pronounced correctly to reproduce the meter and rhythm of the work as well as rhetorical and sonic effects such as alliteration, and only a correct reading of the text could bring about in listeners an experience of the work's *rasa*. At the same time, to understand the work's allegorical and mystical significations, readers and listeners needed knowledge of both Sufi theology and praxis and Indian literary aesthetics. A work like the *Madhumālatī* required a skilled reader (or reciter) to mediate it for audiences: well-read, knowledgeable, and above all a *rasik* or connoisseur, like the patrons described in the prefaces of *pem-kathā*s.

The composers of the Sufi romances evince an acute awareness of what it meant to not only compose in the vernacular but also *write* in it: *bhāṣā* was a space in which languages, lexicons, and concepts mixed, and in that way it reflected, at least to some degree, the multilingual courtly settings in which these poets composed and performed their works. The Islamicate courts took part in the thriving Persianate book culture of the fourteenth through eighteenth centuries, with sultans, princes, nobles, warlords, and wealthy merchants from Anatolia to Bengal devoting significant time, resources, and attention to the production of ornately embellished and lavishly illustrated codices. It was into this transregional, elite culture of book production, circulation, collection, and enjoyment that the *pem-kathā* in Hindi was born, and it was with this culture in mind that the composers of romances produced their epic works. Yet the textual content did not translate neatly into existing manuscript forms or inscriptional practices; realization in material form required negotiation among different aesthetic conventions—including Persian, Sanskrit, Prakrit, and Apabhramsha—and experimentation with new practices of inscription and impagination. The result was a new type of book that was as rich a mix of materials and forms as the *pem-kathā* genre itself.

SHOWING AND TELLING: COPIES OF THE *CANDĀYAN*

The commitment of Hindi to writing gave the language a material form that could be fashioned into a symbol and currency of wealth and political power in lavishly calligraphed and illustrated books. As written codices, the *Candāyan* and the Sufi romances that followed it helped to constitute the system of patronage and connoisseurship that made these vernacular works possible in the first place.[42] The romance became a material artifact through which ruling elites could demonstrate their wealth, connoisseurship, and participation in the broader norms of transregional Persianate book culture, which at the time stretched from the Ottoman Empire in the west to the sultanate of Bengal in the east, and from Timurid Transoxiana in the north to the Deccan sultanates in the south. Deluxe copies of romances circulated among elites as they were gifted, received, or seized in various political and financial exchanges and transactions. The production of these codices was collaborative and labor-intensive, with *kāghazī* (paper makers) producing and burnishing paper, *khaṭ-kash* (rulers) ruling the areas to be inscribed, a *kātib* (scribe) or *khwush-navīs* (calligrapher) copying the text, one or more artists (*naqqāsh*) creating the illustrations, and a *jild-sāz* (bookbinder) binding the papers between covers of leather, cardboard, or cloth.[43]

The earliest known copies of the *Candāyan* were most likely made during the early to mid-sixteenth century, almost two centuries after the composition of the work.[44] Nevertheless, sixteenth- and seventeenth-century copies as well as copies of later Sufi romances give us insight into the manuscripts that preceded them, displaying similarities with the extant Persian manuscripts of the fourteenth and fifteenth centuries as well as noteworthy differences. Collectively, they suggest a spirit of experimentation and innovation in which patrons, scribes, and artisans drew liberally from the Persianate book arts while incorporating aspects of Indic book culture to produce a new type of book that was distinctly Indian and distinctly vernacular in character. Looking closely at their formats, layouts, calligraphic styles, illustrations, and paratextual elements allows us to reconstruct a synoptic history of how early experimentation gradually led to the development of norms for inscribing Hindi. Here I outline the major features of this development using the earliest copies of the *Candāyan* and, where relevant, copies of other works from the genre.

Little is known about the book ateliers of the north Indian sultanates in the fourteenth through sixteenth centuries, but copies of the *Candāyan* dating to the mid-sixteenth century confirm scholars' general assumptions regarding book production during this period. These copies were made on indigenous cloth paper (as opposed to palm leaf or imported paper) by teams of Persian-literate scribes working with Indian artists. These artists appear to have belonged to the same indigenous (likely Jain) community responsible for illustrated Jain and Hindu manuscripts of the period. The now-known copies of the *Candāyan* are all remarkably similar in their codicological aspects and were clearly deluxe copies made for elite patrons. They are in the Arabic script and bound in codex format with text on the right-hand folios and illustrations on the left-hand folios (fig. 1.2). Like the Arabic and Persian *kitāb*-style codices of the period, these books were read "right to left" with foliation running in the opposite direction to that of books in English and other left-to-right scripts. In these copies of the *Candāyan*, each right-hand folio contains a stanza of the narrative while its facing left-hand folio contains a full-page illustration of the action or dialogue described. A reader or listener would thus have been able to relish the visual presentation of the episode on the left as it was being orally narrated from the text on the right. None of the extant manuscripts has folios measuring larger than approximately thirty by thirty centimeters, suggesting that these editions were to be enjoyed in private by a small number of individuals rather than performed before a large audience.[45] These were books for well-heeled connoisseurs' private delectation.

Although Daud and the poets who followed him in the tradition adopted the narrative structure of a Persian *mas̱navī*, they also employed Indic verse forms and stanzaic structures, compelling the Persian scribes of the time to innovate strategies and techniques for rendering the text on the page. A folio from a roughly contemporaneous copy of a Persian *mas̱navī*, Amir Khusrau's *K̲h̲amsah* (*Quintet*, composed 1298–1302 CE, fig. 1.3), gives a sense of the nature and scope of this innovation. This copy was produced in India around 1450, making it one of the few extant examples from the sultanate period, and follows the general conventions of such illustrated romances in India and throughout the contemporary Persianate world. The text, all couplets (*bait*), is laid out in four vertical columns enclosed by bounding lines (*jadwal*) drawn with red ink. The equal length of the hemistiches (*miṣrāʿ*) in each couplet gives the columns a pleasing symmetry while the employment of a single verse form throughout the composition allows the text to "flow" across the page—and leaves scribes and painters free to incorporate illustrations in any area of the folio. The overall effect is similar to that of modern newspaper printing, in which columns of text are made to "wrap" around illustrations and headlines written in larger font. At the center of the folio, in a "white space" marking a section (*bāb* or *faṣl*) break, is a section heading inscribed in red ink: *guftār andar mawʿiẓa o naṣīḥat wa dāman-i mardān-rā giriftan* ("Discussion on admonition and advice and on asking [accomplished] men for assistance"—literally, "pulling their robes"). The content of such headings varied between copies and was often the prerogative of the scribe.

Early copies of the *Candāyan* and other vernacular romances look quite different. Daud and subsequent poets composed their works in stanzas called *kaḍavak*, a form inherited from traditions in Madhyadeshi and Apabhramsha literatures. Each *kaḍavak* consists of several couplets in the *caupaī* meter (16 + 16 syllables or morae) followed by a couplet in the *dohā* meter (13 + 11 morae). Consequently, a stanza consisted of multiple verse forms of unequal length and the overall length of stanzas could vary considerably across the work. Confronted with the asymmetrical and irregular character of vernacular verse, Persian scribes came up with inventive ways of calligraphing *pem-kathā*s. These included staggering couplets within square boxes made of *jadwal* (fig. 1.4), arranging the longer *dohā* couplets into rhombus shapes at oblique angles and the shorter *caupaī* couplets into vertical columns (figs. 1.5 and 1.6), or placing the *caupaī* into two bound columns and centering the final *dohā* within a separate box (fig. 1.2).[46] Although each arrangement offers its own visual charm and interest, by the seventeenth century, the one in the final example (fig. 1.2), with its economy of space and scribal effort, had become the standard method of calligraphing vernacular romances, even in deluxe copies commissioned by wealthy patrons.

The Sufi poets' arrangement of their narratives into stanzas also led scribes, artists, and binders to reimagine the structure of the codex book as a whole. All early copies of the *Candāyan,* and almost all deluxe copies of the other *pem-kathā*s that date to the precolonial period, present one stanza per folio. Illustrated copies present the calligraphed stanza on the right-hand folio and a visual illustration on the left-hand folio, yet even in more modest, unillustrated codices, it was the norm to inscribe one stanza per folio. This format would have made it easier for scribes to calligraph stanzas of varying length while maintaining a uniform appearance across the book as a whole.

The stanza-wise organization of the codex reproduced and amplified the textual and performative dimensions of the romance: as Daud himself wrote, vernacular verse belonged to the domain of song—"I sang in Hinduki"—and there is sufficient textual and documentary evidence that the *Candāyan* and similar *pem-kathā*s were sung. (Tulsidas's *Rāmacaritamānas* of 1574 CE, composed on the model of the *pem-kathā*, serves as an example of such narrative works in *caupaī-dohā* stanzas still sung today.)[47] The *kaḍavak* or stanza was the textual "unit" of song. Each turn of the page revealed a new moment in the narrative and punctuated the beginning and end of a sung stanza, giving the singer or reciter and their audience a chance to "breathe" in between imbibing the breathtaking verses and visuals and then expiating upon their meaning and significance.

The way scribes and calligraphers copied the *Candāyan* reveals that audiences were familiar with the conventions for inscribing the vernacular, even during the period when those were still being established. The orthographic conventions followed in the various manuscripts vary, meaning that the Persian-literate scribes tasked with copying or transcribing this work in *bhāṣā* were still developing strategies for representing the north Indian vernacular in the Arabic script as late as the early sixteenth century. The language included distinct classes of dental and retroflex consonant stops, aspirated and unaspirated consonants, "tongue-flap" consonants, and other exotic sounds unaccounted for in the Arabic alphabet or its modified form used for Persian. The calligraphers who inscribed the extant copies used different techniques to represent these sounds, including diacritical marks, innovative uses of existing letters in the Arabic alphabet, and new combinations of letters. Some readers, like that of the so-called Lahore-Chandigarh copy of the *Candāyan* (fig. 1.6), annotated their copies with diacritical marks to clarify the pronunciation of certain words. This practice recalls Manjhan's appeal to his readers to "read [his] letters [only] having understood them," since proper re-creation of the aural text was critical to ensuring its correct semiotic and aesthetic reception.[48] Nevertheless, the general *absence* of diacritical marks in early copies of the *Candāyan* and similar works suggests that shared conventions of writing and reading the vernacular in Arabic script existed among audience communities.

The style and quality of calligraphy in these copies of the *Candāyan* raises questions regarding scribal skill, contemporary tastes, and the technical challenges involved in vernacular book culture during the sultanate period. All extant copies are inscribed in variations of the *nas̱ḵẖ* script (written more or less along a straight horizontal line, in contrast to the "hanging" or cascading *nastaʿlīq* script that became popular in South Asia later on). Art historian Qamar Adamjee points out that, while the script and style of calligraphy are broadly similar to those in contemporary Persian manuscripts made in India, they are generally inferior in terms of quality, with different copies exhibiting either overly crowded or overly loose assemblies of letters and words.[49] Adamjee suggests that some of these deficiencies may have been the result of Indian scribes' lack of familiarity or confidence with the Arabic script, but I propose a different explanation: that the scribes commissioned to make these luxury books, expert in the art of composing balanced lines of Persian calligraphy through years of practice, had to retrain their eyes and hands to produce similarly balanced arrangements in the vernacular with its strange combinations of letters and sounds and its uneven lines of verse. The *Candāyan* manuscripts represent an early stage in the development of vernacular calligraphy, characterized by invention and experimentation—though not all of the experiments were successful in terms of visual aesthetics.

In addition to inscribing Daud's text, all but one of these scribes (the calligrapher responsible for the copy held in the Chhatrapati Shivaji Maharaj Vastu Sangrahalaya in Mumbai) appended a Persian heading to each stanza, providing additional insight into the *Candāyan*'s circulation and reception. These copies clearly circulated in multilingual (and expressly Persophone) social contexts, providing material evidence that the picture Daud and his fellow poets painted of a multilingual literary culture in sultanate India was not an idealized fiction but, to at least some extent, a social reality. Many of the headings are plain descriptions of the content of their respective stanzas and thus serve a straightforward navigational function in the long narrative: for example, the Persian heading at the top of the folio in figure 1.2 simply says, "Description of the archers" (*sifat-i tīr-andāzān goyad*).

Yet a few of these hint at the interpretive function that such headings would come to perform later. For example, in the stanza in which King Rupchand, the story's primary antagonist, reacts to a wandering ascetic's description of the story's heroine, Chanda, Daud describes how Rupchand "twisted his limbs and drew [the ascetic] close . . . Like a sleeping man who sits up awakened, his heart leaped in his chest." Rupchand implores the ascetic (named Bajir) to describe Chanda further, awarding him a horse for this service.[50] The scribe responsible for the copy in the John Rylands Library (fig. 1.8) provides the Persian heading, "The king's falling in love upon the [mention of] the name of Chanda and his presentation of a horse to Bajir" (*'āshiq shudan-i rāo bar nām-i cāndā va asp dahānīdan bājīr rā*). The mention of "falling in love" (*'āshiq shudan*) marks a subtle but important exegetical move on the part of the scribe. He has interpreted the textual "signs"—the king's twisting limbs (*aṅgarānā*), his restless heart, his questions to the ascetic—in order to draw a conclusion regarding the character's mental and emotional state. The scribe's paraphrase does conform to the interpretive rules of the genre: restless limbs, a restless heart, and importunate requests for descriptions of an individual are conventional signs of lovesickness (*virah* or *firāq*) in the *pem-kathā*. The scribe has demonstrated the "proper" way of reading the stanza—the kind of sensitive reading that Daud and subsequent poets in their respective prefaces implored their readers to practice. Other headings appear to suture text and illustration together: for example, in the copy held by the John Rylands Library, the heading "Bajir tells Rupchand about the parting of Chanda's hair" (*sifat-i farq-i cāndā guftan-i bājir bar rūpcand*) accompanies a stanza describing Chanda's hair and an illustration of Bajir and Rupchand speaking to each other. By making explicit the relationship between the text on the right-hand folio and the illustration on the left, the book's scribe stitched together the facing folios of the codex verbally much like the binder stitched them together literally.

While scribes performed a certain type of critical reading by inscribing headings, the painters and illustrators performed another type of reading through their illustrations. Their stylistic variations give a sense of how widely the work circulated and further insight into the experimental and emergent character of the early vernacular codex. Just as the textual structure of Daud's *Candāyan* challenged scribes to innovate strategies of layout, calligraphy, and orthography, the work's narrative and literary devices challenged illustrators to devise similarly innovative strategies of visual depiction. How was a painter to represent a stanza that compares the heroine's teeth to red ants and diamonds? What type of illustration should accompany a stanza that describes at least five different actions and moments in time? Adamjee has classified and characterized the various ways of depicting action, dialogue, physical description, and emotional or psychological states, arguing that different artists employed very different approaches to representing time, space, and emotion.[51] Even this brief mention of their diversity is a reminder that these painters, like their scribal counterparts, had to critically *read* the literary work—either on their own or collaboratively with the help of an intermediary who understood literary conventions—in order to produce illustrations that were, in essence, *readings* of the text.

An example is the stanza in which Rupchand falls in love with Chanda, one of several consecutive stanzas in which Rupchand listens to the ascetic, Bajir, describe Chanda's beauty. Different copies of the *Candāyan* reflect different ways illustrators (or teams of illustrators) read the text. The illustrators of the John Rylands copy (fig. 1.8) repeated the same basic composition across six illustrations: each painting in the series depicts Rupchand and Bajir in conversation, accompanied by one to four of Rupchand's courtiers and encompassed by architectural elements suggesting a royal court. Bajir holds small cymbals (*mañjīrā*), an iconic reference to musical performance and his sung description of Chanda, while Rupchand's hand gestures and posture suggest that he is asking questions and listening. Yet in the illustration in which Rupchand "falls in love" (fig. 1.8), the painters have pushed away all architectural detail, placing the characters in a disc of blue encircled by a horizon of gold. Bajir has been relegated to the lower left quadrant, appearing "silent" with his eyes cast down, his cymbals hanging from his hand; the focus is now wholly on Rupchand, who occupies the center of the painting. The knuckle of his index finger on his lips, he gazes downward in contemplation. The illustrators have conveyed the king's heightened emotional state through contrast: while the other illustrations feature iconic representations of speech and action in a lavish and detailed courtly setting, this illustration "zooms in" on the character of Rupchand, pushing out extraneous visual details and foregrounding iconic depictions of mental restlessness (*caṭapaṭī* in Daud's verse).

The illustrators of the Lahore-Chandigarh copy followed a different strategy, representing different dialogic layers of the text spatially. Their illustrations of the conversation between Rupchand and Bajir are divided into five or six separate areas: in the lower register, Rupchand speaks with Bajir while two women speak in the middle right register, courtly furnishings occupy the middle left register, architectural or natural scenes occupy the upper left register, and the author Maulana Daud himself recites his story in the upper right register (fig. 1.9). The illustrators have represented the relationship between narrative frames in spatial terms: at the top of the space—where the reader's eye would move first—the poet speaks. At the bottom of the space, Bajir and Rupchand converse, the latter's questions and the former's answers indicated through iconic hand gestures. In the middle of the space, in a separate register, is the object of which they speak: Chanda, in conversation with a maidservant. Her position between the two male characters speaking of her beauty and the poet Daud and his work is a fortuitous if not intentional and clever move: though her description ostensibly comes from Bajir's mouth, it is Daud's rhetorical and poetic devices that produce the effect and affect of "wonder" (*camatkār*) in the reader or listener. Like the illustrators of the copy in the John Rylands Library, the painters of this copy repeat the composition for each stanza of the episode but change details in each iteration. The human figures' gestures and postures change, giving the impression that they are animated—an effect that would have been heightened as the reader turned each folio. In both copies, the painters (with the possible help of an intermediary) have performed critical readings of Daud's text and re-created those readings in visual form.[52] Sultanate-period audiences would have consisted of connoisseurs who recognized in these illustrations a "text" that must be read in conversation with the stanza on the facing folio. The presence of multivalent, iconic figures throughout these illustrations—such as peacocks, herons, black buck, lions, and other fauna; date palms, lotuses, pipal trees, and other flora; and deities, lamps, and royal regalia, as well as other objects—suggest that audiences needed to be familiar with these figures' literary as well as visual significance to fully appreciate the "meaning" of the paintings and their resonance with the written text.[53]

Daud's vernacular romance challenged Indian scribes and illustrators to innovate new strategies for representing Hindi's sounds, arranging and calligraphing its metrical forms, annotating its narrative content, and representing, interpreting, and amplifying its textual content in visual form. They collectively and collaboratively produced codices that in their visual and material forms reflected and re-produced the relationships of writing and reading, telling and listening, and performing and explaining that undergirded Daud's romantic epic. Each turn of the page punctuated the stanzaic rhythm of the epic, presenting the reader with a new "scene" of written verbal and painted visual text reflecting each other across the crease between the folios, stitched together not only by thread but also through the illustrators' and scribes' performative reading of the narrative. This recursive practice of writing and reading (or telling and understanding) and the relationship between written textuality and oral performance is nowhere better dramatized than in the Lahore-Chandigarh copy. The author of the *Candāyan* himself, Maulana Daud, appears in every illustration, always sitting in the top register, dressed in a white *dhoti* and fine translucent kurta, adorned simply with a turban and prayer beads (*subḥa*) (fig. 1.9). As indicated by his hand gestures and posture, he recites from the written text of the *Candāyan* that sits before him on a folding bookstand (*raḥl*).[54] Daud's figure is animated, changing position and gestures each time the reader turns the page. He even reacts to the events that he himself recounts in the narrative: for example, when a fistfight breaks out between the heroine, Chanda, and her co-wife, Maina, Daud stands up and stares at the women fighting below from the safety of his corner, his book and other appurtenances absent from the frame (possibly because he knocked them over as he leaped up)! Nothing in this copy of the *Candāyan* is static: each element of the two-page spread responds to another element in some way, either as a reading, as a visualization, or as an affective or aesthetic response. Each spread anticipates, organizes, and scripts a series of retellings that come full circle: the cycle begins with the iconic representation of the author Daud's written text in the illustration, proceeds with the figure of Daud reciting from that text, the written transcription of the stanza on the right folio (along with the Persophone scribe's summary reading of the stanza), the reader/reciter's recitation, and the visual reading/text on the left, coming back around to the author's own reaction to the narrative depicted in the illustration.

Each copy of the *Candāyan* thus constitutes a reflection on its own origins, materiality, and performance. Their complexity is enhanced by the fact that all the copies were the products of corporate and collaborative labor, requiring coordination and cooperation among paper rulers, scribes, artists, bookbinders, and patrons. Being the work of so many skilled hands, manuscripts of the *Candāyan* are things of great beauty, and that is the point: in the hands of a skilled poet like Daud, the vernacular song (*gīt*) had been transformed into vernacular *literature* (*kabi, kabit*) and as such could serve as a canvas for the book arts and an object of elite consumption.[55] In the two centuries that followed Daud's composition of the work, illustrated copies of the *Candāyan* and other Sufi *pem-kathā*s became objects of desire for Indian bibliophiles among not only the Persophone elite but also merchant and Rajput communities, causing the genre to quickly evolve its own distinct, and distinctly vernacular, book form.

THE SHAPE OF A GENRE

The many manuscript copies of *pem-kathā* works in archives and libraries across South Asia and in collections in Europe and the Americas include lavishly illustrated volumes commissioned by the wealthy and powerful as well as simple, unillustrated copies made by individuals for their own enjoyment. Some are in the form of discrete codices while others are bound together with multiple other works. They are copied in the Arabic script, the Nāgarī script, the shorthand Kaithī script, the Gurmukhi script (used in the region of the Punjab), and even the Bengali script (which was used for multiple languages in precolonial eastern India). This diversity attests to the popularity of the individual romances and to their collective popularity as a genre; it also reflects the variety of social and performative contexts in which these stories were enjoyed.

Yet what is most striking about these manuscripts is how much they have in common: despite being copied in different social and geographical contexts, in different times, and in different scripts, they almost all follow the same basic format and conventions. First, they are always in codex form: whether in a right-to-left script (such as the Arabic script) or a left-to-right script (such as Nāgarī), *pem-kathā*s were copied into bound collections of folios. In copies made by professional scribes commissioned for the purpose, the scribe copied the text onto loose folios that had been folded and organized into multiple groupings (called signatures or quires by book historians); these signatures were then stitched together individually and finally bound together by a professional binder and placed in a protective cover. Covers were most often made of cardboard covered in worked leather or cloth. For one's own use, an individual could purchase a block of folded signatures and, after copying the text, have them bound; alternatively, an individual could commission a blank, bound codex and fill its pages with texts of his or her choice.

What makes the almost exclusive use of the codex book format for the *pem-kathā* striking is the fact that works of other genres, when copied in the Nāgarī, Kaithī, Bengali, and other scripts, were most often *not* copied into codex books. Religious narratives, songs, and scholastic works were copied into manuscripts in the loose-leaf *pothī* format or the small, bound *guṭakā* format. In other words, there was clearly a convention or consensus among scribes and readers in the fourteenth through eighteenth centuries that a *pem-kathā* belonged in a very particular type of manuscript book—and that convention stretched across communities of political elites, merchants, clerics, clerical professionals, and other groups, as well as across religious, sectarian, and even linguistic boundaries.

The second convention that came to be inextricably associated with the *prem-kathā* is the stanzaic layout of the text. Scribes arranged each *kaḍavak* into two blocks, the first consisting of two columns containing the half-lines of the *caupaī* verses (arranged horizontally) and the second consisting of the two lines of the *dohā* verse (arranged vertically) (fig. 1.2). By the early sixteenth century, this had become the standard format, regardless of writing script. In almost all copies of the *Candāyan*, *Mirgāvatī*, *Padmāvat*, and *Madhumālatī*, and even in copies of lesser-known romances like the *Nal Daman*, the text is always broken into stanzas, with each *caupaī* broken into half-lines and arranged in columns and each *dohā* centered in two lines at the bottom. These elements are all centered along a vertical axis that bisects each folio. More expensive, commissioned copies tend to contain one stanza per folio, but even the most modest copies made by the owners themselves observe the convention of leaving empty "white space" between stanzas and giving each half-line of verse its own line on the page. The fact that scribes followed this convention in every kind of script is remarkable because no other genre looked like this. Across the precolonial archive as a whole, the overwhelming majority of works copied in Nāgarī and Kaithī scripts are in *scriptio continua*: no spaces are left between words or lemma and no line breaks are made for verses or stanzas. (See, for example, figs. 2.1, 2.4–2.7, 3.1, 3.4, 3.5, 4.1–4.4.) To put it another way: other works copied in Nāgarī, Kaithī, and similar scripts usually appeared as one big block of text.

Two examples of *pem-kathā* works copied in the Kaithī script vividly illustrate how the conventions traveled between writing scripts (and their respective reader communities). The first is a late sixteenth-century manuscript of Qutban's *Mirgāvatī* now held by Bharat Kala Bhavan, Banaras Hindu University (fig. 1.10). This illustrated copy was commissioned by a patron who was clearly more comfortable reading in the shorthand Kaithī script (widely used for mercantile and clerical purposes but also, obviously, for literary works) than in the more formal Nāgarī or Arabic scripts. Yet in all other respects, the manuscript follows the visual and material conventions of the genre: the scribe has copied one stanza per folio, separating the hemistiches of the *caupaīs* into columns and centering the *dohā* at the bottom. The unruled lines may cause the calligraphy to appear rough, but like the deluxe copies of the *Candāyan* discussed earlier, this copy of the *Mirgāvatī* featured rich illustrations on each right-hand folio that accompanied the stanzas on each left-hand folio. Even more remarkable is a copy of Jayasi's *Padmāvat*, copied in Kaithī in 1710 CE and also held by Bharat Kala Bhavan, consisting of large folios (measuring approximately 36 x 30 cm) upon each of which is inscribed one to two stanzas of the epic, enclosed in doubled red *jadwal* lines (fig. 1.7). Those lines and the illustrations overlap, with the illustrations stretching and flowing across each folio, filling every bit of available space and uniting each two-page spread into a panoramic whole. (The stanzas inscribed on the folio contain poetic descriptions of the amorous pleasures to be had during the spring and summer months while the trees, flowers, fountain, instruments, peacock feather fans, and singing figures in the illustration call to mind the olfactory, sonic, haptic, and visual sensations extolled in the verses.) This manuscript was clearly commissioned by and for a wealthy and knowledgeable client with specific notions of how the book should "look" and how its verbal and visual texts should be experienced—even though that connoisseur happened to prefer to read in a so-called "shorthand" script.[56]

Finally, paratextual material like headings and marginal notations connected audiences of the *pem-kathā* across social, linguistic, and geographical boundaries. Among the many copies in various scripts, relatively few are free of such scribal interventions. For some readers, the entire manuscript was a canvas for the inscription of interpretive notes and pleasurable associations. An anonymous but avid reader of both the vernacular and Persian who made a copy of the *Padmāvat* for himself in the 1790s so thoroughly covered it with vocalization marks, word glosses, paraphrases, explanations, and literary references in Persian that one often has to struggle in order to locate Jayasi's text on the page (fig. 1.11)! This reader—whose literary and intellectual interests, judging by the other contents of the manuscript, included lexicons of Hindu deities, Persian poetry, and Persian narrative genres like the *maṣnavī*—performed his own reading of the romance in the margins, providing an explanation and exegesis of religious symbols, literary motifs, and knotty or obscure turns of phrase. In this way, even a modest, unillustrated copy of a work shared an important characteristic with more extravagant, illustrated copies: it functioned as an assemblage of readings inscribed or "performed" on the page for the reader/reciter to reproduce through reading, reciting, and explaining. Shantanu Phukan has given an illuminating account of a similarly annotated copy of the *Padmāvat*, by a Sufi named Muhammad Shakir Amrohavi in 1674: the diligent inscription of vocalization marks, glossing of words and phrases, and obviously joyful noting of the Persian literary associations that the *Padmāvat* called forth from Muhammad Shakir's memory collectively provide a trace of the work's "literary *life* in the experience of Mughal readers," in which "a Hindi text turns out to imply Persian as well."[57]

THE BIRTH OF VERNACULAR BOOK CULTURE

Recognizing how many conventions and expectations sultanate- and Mughal-era readers of Hindi shared across social, religious, caste, and geographical boundaries allows us to do away with certain binaries that have prevented a fuller understanding of vernacular literary culture in precolonial India. The first is indeed the binary of "vernacular literary culture" and "cosmopolitan literary culture."

We can distinguish a distinctly vernacular set of literary and manuscript practices, but these drew from and overlapped with practices in the cosmopolitan languages of Sanskrit, Prakrit, Persian, and Arabic. We therefore cannot study the history of literary and book culture in Hindi independently from the other languages. The next and perhaps most pernicious binary is that of Hindi/Urdu, a thoroughly modern distinction that collapses language, lexicon, script, and religious identity into two oppositional terms. The *pem-kathā* developed within a matrix constituted by the language of *bhāṣā*, a lexical register containing both *tadbhava* and *tatsama* terms from Sanskrit and Prakrit as well as words from Persian, Arabic, and Turkish, prosodic forms inherited from Apabhramsha and Madhyadeshi literatures, and a manuscript tradition that utilized multiple scripts and multiple approaches to visual illustration. The *pem-kathā* thus resists any attempt to fit it within a single linguistic or literary tradition. These same elements, along with the aforementioned paratexual and codicological evidence, point to the social and religious diversity of the individuals and groups that enjoyed these romances, making it similarly impossible to characterize the *pem-kathā* as an "Islamic" or "Hindu" literary genre.

Vernacular literary and book culture provided a sphere in which people, things, and practices could "meet" in a manner not possible elsewhere. Francesca Orsini has forcefully argued that the *pem-kathā* as a performative, oral genre cut across social boundaries yet left them intact: thus a Sufi Shaikh, a Hindu *munshī* (scribe or secretary), and a Jain merchant, for example, could all find meaning and pleasure in the performance of a *pem-kathā*, even if the identity and nature of those respective meanings and pleasures were distinct.[58] The *ahātā* in which *pem-kathā*s were recited and enjoyed was the social and physical space where the lives of such different peoples could intersect. While the evidence from written copies of *pem-kathā*s supports Orsini's argument, I suggest that it also reflects a shared, material *book culture* in which people from very different backgrounds developed, nurtured, and exercised notions of taste and discrimination related to the object of the written book. Generals of sultanate and Mughal courts, *munshī*s residing in *qaṣbahs*, merchants moving between trading towns, and initiates of Sufi religious orders shared expectations of what a copy of a *pem-kathā* should look like and how it should read. The fact that certain conventions and practices of layout, inscription, illustration, and binding developed that were specific to the *pem-kathā* and were a mix of elements from other book cultures demonstrates that a distinctly vernacular mode of book production and book culture had evolved.

Manuscripts of the early vernacular romances show that the vernacular—as a language, a literature, and a composite, improvised way of doing things—served as the primary arena for encounters between different literary and artistic traditions. The refined (*saṁskṛta*), classical languages of Sanskrit and Persian, precisely because they possessed robust criteria and institutions for regulating literary language, lexicon, conventions, and the material practices of literary inscription and illustration, stood at a relative disadvantage to register—let alone leverage—changes in the linguistic, literary, and material world of writing that came about in north India following the establishment of sultanate rule. The vernacular, always already hybrid, composite, or corrupted (*apabhraṁśa*), was well suited to serve as a ground for experimentation by authors, scribes, illustrators, and bookmakers willing to mix the lexicons, literary conventions, and material practices of multiple literary and book cultures. Authors writing in Sanskrit and Persian during the sultanate and early Mughal periods did pursue literary experiments that acknowledged the ongoing civilizational encounter, such as Sanskrit *mahākāvyas* written for sultans during the fifteenth and sixteenth centuries and Amir Khusrau's Persian chronicles in the early fourteenth century. Yet none of these experiments generated new genres or new types of book formats like the vernacular *pem-kathā* did.

The conventions for inscribing the *pem-kathā* became so closely associated with the genre that publishers continued to observe them even after the popularization of print technology in colonial South Asia. Scholarly studies of print have tended to emphasize its disruptive energies, in particular its potential to restructure patterns and practices of layout, design, circulation, and reception.[59] Print technology did bring about changes in Hindi, including the ubiquitous use of word breaks and line breaks, new norms of pagination, and new types of paratexts. Yet in the case of the *pem-kathā*, the conventions established by precolonial scribes continued to be followed and are observed to this very day. Jayasi's *Padmāvat* was the first precolonial *pem-kathā* to be printed in 1865; its success spurred the publication of nine more editions over the next thirty-five years.[60] In these early printed editions, the technology of lithography, in which the image to be printed was handwritten onto a stone or metal plate, easily allowed for re-creations of the *pem-kathā*'s calligraphic layout. Yet even publishers that used moveable type, such as the Baptist Mission Press in Calcutta, reproduced the same layout and conventions. For example, in George Grierson's 1896 critical edition and translation of the *Padmāvat*, not only the Nāgarī text but even Griereson's transliterations into the Roman script have been typeset to mimic the stanzaic layout of a calligraphed manuscript[61] (fig. 1.12). Any reader of the genre today, whether in the Arabic or Nāgarī script, will immediately recognize a *pem-kathā* on the page, for its stanzas, individual verses, and paratextual elements are still arranged in the same manner.

MANUSCRIPTS AND MARKETS

Precolonial copies of *pem-kathā* works were rarely objects for "private" enjoyment as we understand books to be today; instead, they circulated within networks of connoisseurs who used books as a currency of social status, political power, and monetary wealth. Markets were never far from the scenes and contexts in which the *pem-kathā* was performed. At religious festivals (*melā* or *utsav*), *kathā*s and commerce went hand in hand: taking place at the shrines of Sufi *pīr*s and Hindu gurus and often lasting for several days, such festivals attracted not only local devotees but also pilgrims and monks from distant cities, providing a large, if short-term, revenue opportunity for merchants selling cloth, jewelry, precious stones, food, talismans, ritual implements, and sundry. Attendees came to satisfy not only their sense of devotion but also a desire for the pleasures to be derived from music, storytelling (including the performance of *pem-kathā*s), food, and purchasing goods. It is difficult to estimate the extent to which books were a regular commodity in the precolonial period, but the ubiquity of printed books for sale at religious festivals during the colonial period suggests that a market existed. There is no doubt that religious professionals used these festivals as an opportunity to trade in books: as indicated by the colophons in manuscripts, it was common for monks and other peripatetic religious professionals to copy manuscripts while attending. The more holy men at a religious festival, the better the chances of finding a desired work from which to make or commission a copy.

The *caupāl* or outdoor space that served as the socially heterogenous arena of *kathā* performance could be a home, a temple, a courtyard, or even a riverbank, but it was often a literal marketplace. The Sufi *pem-kathā*s themselves mention the performance of *kathā*s in the authors' home cities and in the fictional cities of the narratives; that the marketplace could be a theater for storytelling (religious or otherwise) is also suggested by sixteenth- and seventeenth-century hagiographical narratives about Hindu saints.[62] Even when *kathā*s were performed in private, the market was never far away. For example, Banarasidas (1586–1643), a Jain merchant, recorded his life story in the versified *Ardhakathānak* (Half a Tale, 1641 CE). He relates how, even while living penniless and alone in the city of Agra, he managed to procure (most likely on loan) copies of both the *Mirgāvatī* and the *Madhumālatī*. He would recite from these at his home in the evenings to an audience of one or two dozen friends, and always to the acclaim of these literary aficionados.[63] These gatherings combined business and pleasure: Banarasidas's friends were merchants and businessmen themselves, and his *kathā* recitation sessions yielded valuable contacts (one of whom, a sweet seller, eventually helped Banaridas to get back on his feet).

Political ties, articulated through gestures of fealty, largesse, patronage, and alliance, could also involve books. Persianate book culture provided a common "language" of elite connoisseurship and kingship among Islamicate regimes during the late medieval and early modern periods. Beginning in the late sixteenth century, bibliophilia as a mode of elite self-fashioning reached a new level of intensity under the Mughals in northern India and under various sultans in the Deccan region. The ability to commission, procure, enjoy, and assess the quality of deluxe copies of literary works was one of the distinguishing characteristics of a worthy ruler; thus Abul Fazl spends a considerable number of words in his *'Ā'īn-i Akbarī* describing the grand book atelier (*kitāb-k̲h̲ānah*) assembled by his patron, Akbar, and describing the emperor's unparalleled ability to adjudicate the quality of calligraphy and illustration.[64] Participating in Mughal court culture meant emulating such connoisseurship, so ministers, generals, *subahdārs*, and other courtiers commissioned or bought their own copies of the works being enjoyed at court.[65] Books were one of the more important forms of wealth that a ruler seized when he defeated a political rival; the destruction or, more commonly, the disaggregation and distribution of a rival's library were some of the forms of symbolic violence used to establish the end of one political dispensation and consolidate the beginning of another. Yet books also performed an important role in effecting and maintaining peaceful relations, as when the ruler of the sultanate of Bijapur in the Deccan, Ibrahim Adil Shah II, sent approximately two thousand books from his royal library as part of the arrangements for the marriage of Akbar's daughter with Ibrahim Adil's son.[66] Books could thus be a form of *k̲h̲il'at*, ceremonial gifts that contained and/or transmitted some of the aura of the giver.[67]

This system of book valuation did not exist only in a strictly "abstract" or symbolic sense: the value of a book could often be calculated in exact monetary terms. The Mughal imperial library was a highly rationalized and systematic affair, with volumes regularly inspected and appraised; the royal libraries of the Deccani sultanates were arranged and managed along similar lines.[68] Persianized elites within the Mughal empire and Deccani sultanates circulated and studied treatises detailing how to collect and maintain a personal library, including how to employ qualified staff to manage it.[69] Accordingly, when assessing the monetary value of a noble's estate, Mughal officials estimated the value of the noble's library, based in part upon the quality of workmanship and the types of materials used in the volumes. Members of the Persianized elite with sufficient means tried to create book ateliers of their own, often by recruiting calligraphers, illustrators, and bookbinders who had been dismissed from or become disaffected with the royal courts at which they worked. One indicator of the vibrancy of this book culture is that practitioners of the book arts—calligraphers, illustrators, and book binders—were constantly shifting employment between various royal courts and private patrons: far from being treated as mere "artisans," these professionals enjoyed celebrity status and were actively courted by patrons offering "greener pastures."

Rajput rulers of the period were no less invested in bibliophilia than their Mughal and Deccani counterparts, though Rajput patronage of the book arts has been generally less studied in modern scholarship. Rajput kings in Rajasthan, like the Kacchwahas of Amer/Jaipur, built their own book ateliers (*pothī-khānā*) that emulated the Mughal imperial *kitāb-k̲h̲ānah*.[70] The copious production of illustrated, bound codex manuscripts at the courts of Amer/Jaipur, Marwar, and Mewar during the mid-seventeenth through eighteenth centuries suggests that Rajput rulers consciously appropriated and adapted the techniques and practices that they observed among the Mughal elite, producing their own type of illustrated codex.[71] Rajputs apparently also treated books as a form of symbolic capital in a manner akin to their more Persianized counterparts: as evidenced by the provenance of volumes in present-day royal libraries, the acquisition of a rival or subordinate's library through annexation or other means appears to have been part of the practice of kingship. Within these collections are copies of *pem-kathā*s, beautifully calligraphed in Nāgarī and Kaithī scripts and bound in a type of hybrid codex format.[72]

Even the more "humble" literate classes, including merchants like Banarsidas, clerks and professional scribes (*munshī*, *kāyasth*, *khatrī*), moneylenders (*seṭh*, *mahājan*), and a wide range of literate professionals in state employ (such as *paṭavārī*, *qānūngo*, and the like) had access to books through local markets.[73] Booksellers bought and sold copies of works and helped their clients locate and procure specific volumes. Members of these communities also lent and borrowed books within their social and professional circles, and if an individual found a book particularly useful or pleasurable, they would often make a copy for themselves. Books were exchanged as gifts between close friends and colleagues, and teachers gave books to their students both for edification and as a performance of teacherly munificence and nurture.[74]

Books in early modern India present a challenge to understanding for those of us living in the postprint ecumene. In certain contexts, such as the buying and selling of books in the bazaar, they appear to function like commodities divorced from the contexts of their own production and with an exchange value that can be reckoned in monetary terms. Yet in other contexts they appear to be non-fungible and resistant to commodification, as in the case of books given by a

Sufi teacher to his disciples; such books would partake in the teacher's aura and authority (*walāyat*) and thus could not easily be assimilated into a system of either use value or exchange value. To speak of books functioning as a form of "currency" within a "market" is then to speak both literally and metaphorically at the same time: a book could circulate as a nonfungible form of currency within an intellectual, religious, literary, or political network; it also could be assessed in terms of monetary value and circulate as a commodity within those very same networks.

BURNED BY THE FIRE OF LOVE: A ROMANCE FROM INCEPTION TO RECEPTION

From its inception in the heart of its author, Surdas, to its material manifestation as a deluxe copy for a Mughal general, the *Nal Daman* reflects the ideologies and conventions of reading, writing, and performance that undergirded the *pem-kathā* genre. Surdas himself models the ideal reader as he recounts the origin of his work: having read the tale of Nal and Daman, he not only apprehended the story's meaning but also *experienced* love itself, that is, *'ishq*, the *rasa* of the story. Like the characters of the romance, he became "frail" and "senseless," his body "a heap of fire." This act of sensitive reading in turn begot an act of literary creation: the story "awakened a suppressed fire" within Surdas, after which he "breathed out love like breathing out fire." He composed his own version to "manifest the flame that the world knows, the searing of which is pleasurable." Engulfed in the fire of love through the act of reading, Surdas sought to spread that fire to the rest of the world by the very same means.

He did so not through the language in which he first experienced the story (Sanskrit) but rather in the language in which such love stories *should* be told. This was "the eastern vernacular," organically suited to the expression and transsubjective communication of love—the language through which the fire could "jump" from one human subject to another. Surdas therefore emphasizes the relationship between affect and language—"Look at what I have to say: it is the angst of love in separation, in the eastern vernacular" (*yāro peha kachū maiṁ akhiyā / iśqa firāqa pūrabī bhakiyā*)—and de-emphasizes the relationship between language and identity: "the land may be eastern [but] my mind is Punjabi!" (*pūraba desa paṃjābī matihā*). After all, he writes, "Everyone knows *that* language, and whoever reads it understands its meaning. That's the reason this love story comes to you in the vernacular of the east" (*uta bhākhā maharaga saya koī / paḍhai jo matalaba samajhai soī / tisa kārana yaha prema kahānī / pūraba dī bhākhā bica ānī*). That the language of a work should be appropriate to its affective content was common sense, and the appropriate language for love was *bhākhā*. The passage recalls the "language order" (to borrow Andrew Ollett's apt characterization) articulated by the Mughal courtier Mirza Khan in his *Tuḥfat ul-Hind* (The Gift of India, c. 1675 CE). In his threefold classification of languages "in which books and poetry may be composed" (*kitābhā o dīvānhā taṣnīf tavān kard*), Mirza Khan lists Sanskrit, Prakrit, and *bhākhā*, defined as the language of "ornate poetry and the praise of the lover and the beloved. This is the language of the world in which we live." It was the language of the exotic north Indian plains, where love stories seemed to grow out of the landscape itself.

This understanding of language and its relationship to landscape, genre, and affect would have been common sense as well for Dilir Khan, the noble who commissioned a copy of the *Nal Daman* in 1698. Though "Dilir Khan" was a title held by several men at the time, the patron of this manuscript was most likely 'Abdurrauf Miyan, an Afghan noble and soldier at the court of the Mughal Emperor Aurangzeb (r. 1658–1707). Dilir Khan grew up at the sultanate court of Bijapur in the Deccan and when Bijapur fell to the Mughals, joined the Mughal army, fighting in campaigns across the region.[75] He would consequently have been well acquainted with modes of book connoisseurship among the Persianate elite: the Bijapur court was a major center for the book arts in India, beginning with Ali Adil Shah I (r. 1558–1579) and flourishing under his successors. In the seventeenth century, the Bijapuri kings commissioned the production of luxury copies of works in the vernacular of Dakkhani, which was closely related to and mutually intelligible with the literary *bhāṣā* of north India; in fact, Dakkhani composers referred to their language as *bhāṣā*. These works included the *Pem Nem* of Hasan Manju Khalji (H 999, 1590/91 CE) and the *Kitāb-i Nauras* (c. 1599 CE) of the Sultan of Bijapur himself, Adil Ibrahim Shah II (r. 1580–1627), as well as *rāgamālā*s containing Dakkhani poetry. The ornate calligraphy and illumination of such vernacular books was something that even recent immigrants from Iran—at that time a substantial section of the nobility at Deccani courts—could enjoy, even if they did not fully understand the language.[76]

Dilir Khan invested substantial resources in commissioning his copy of Surdas's *Nal Daman*: besides paying for the expert labor of calligraphy, illumination, and binding, he paid for some of the finest materials available, including fine-grained paper and gold and silver inks. Such investment was itself a performance of his connoisseurship: it demonstrated his financial ability to commission luxury goods as well as his political and social "pull," since calligraphers, illustrators, and illuminators were in high demand in the Deccan and could choose from among many potential patrons. And of course, Dilir Khan's possession of a personal copy of a *pem-kathā* signaled his ability to enjoy the allegorical, religious, and aesthetic qualities of the vernacular romance.

The scribe's colophon on the final folio of the codex is correspondingly an encomium to his patron and to the work itself. In an elegantly calligraphed, wedge-shaped colophon (a conventional form in contemporary Islamicate manuscripts), Babullah writes in Persian that the *Nal Daman* is a "perfume that increases love, excites yearning, [a] compendium of mixed delights, [a] mine of lovers' secrets, [a] fountain spring of reality and metaphor," and calls his patron, Dilir Khan, a "noble son, of great power, felicitous, esteemed and of great courage, possessing good manners, arisen from an auspicious sign, the Rustam of the age, the Haitham of the epoch, the grand vizier of the throne, generous and manly . . . liberal and munificent."[77] Babullah makes clear that Surdas's poem is a monument to love but this particular copy is a monument to the greatness of Dilir Khan. This is the paradoxical way a colophon speaks: although it symbolically closes the moment of a book's creation and records the present owner, it also inaugurates an anticipated and ongoing process of transfer in which the book will be passed between numerous hands. Thus the colophon always addresses an imagined future reader. Babullah's colophon establishes the eminence of the work and its patron and thus the value, reckoned in monetary and nonmonetary terms, of the object he and others fashioned. Recording the critical details of its creation ensured that it would be properly valued and appreciated by whosoever might acquire it through purchase, gift, or conquest.

Dilir Khan's copy of the *Nal Daman* encapsulates all that was new, fresh, innovative, and particular to the Hindi romance genre and its material form. The *pem-kathā*, pioneered by Sufi poets at regional courts, marks the transformation of the vernacular into a medium for literary art to be experienced through oral recitation and through specific, affective modes of response and appreciation. These poets transformed the vernacular into the raw material—the linguistic ink and thematic paper, if you will—with which scribes could calligraph the spoken tongue of north India and, along with illustrators, illuminators, and binders, make Hindi and its poetry a canvas for the book arts. When applied to the vernacular romance, these arts became hybrid, innovative, and novel, incorporating conventions, tastes, and techniques from Islamicate as well as Indic manuscript traditions. The *pem-kathā* codex was a distinct object in terms of its orthographic, visual, and textual conventions; now it brought the vernacular into the world of elite consumption in which Hindi books gradually came to be collected, enjoyed, and appraised alongside books in Persian and Arabic. Codices like Dilir Khan's copy of the *Nal Daman*, in terms of their literary content and material form, exuded the taste (*rasa*) of the vernacular but were most often consumed alongside tasty delights in other languages.

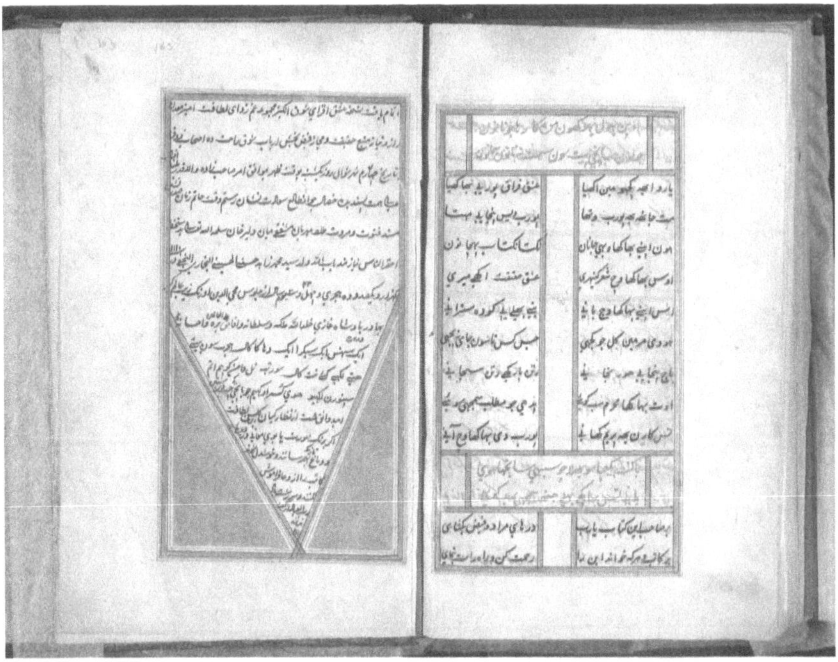

FIGURE 1.1 *Nal Daman* of Surdas, copied in 1698 CE by Babullah for Dilir Khan

Accn. No. 22.3229, Folios 162b and 163a. Chhatrapati Shivaji Maharaj Vastu Sangrahalaya, Mumbai

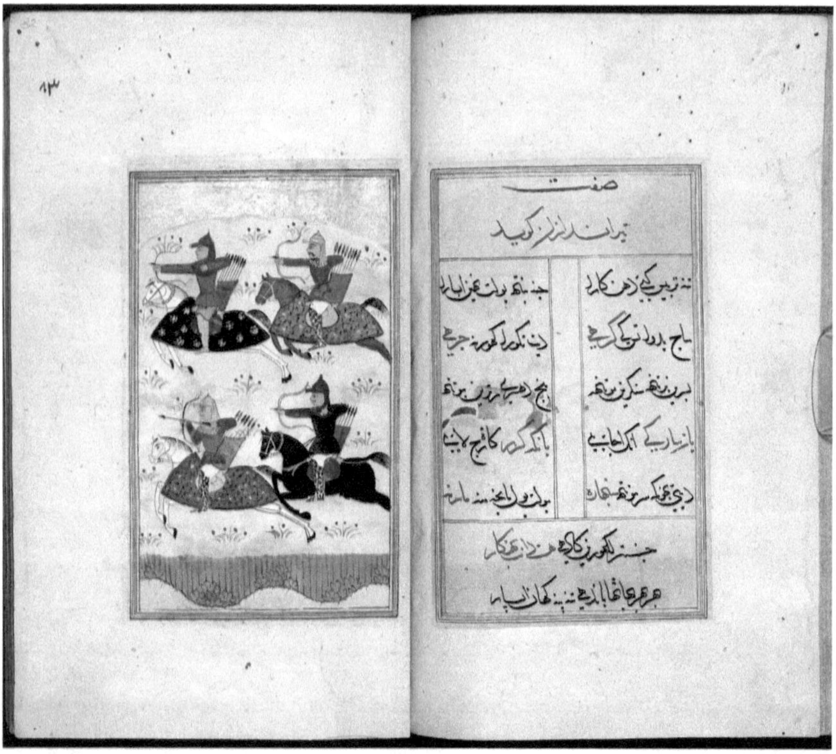

FIGURE 1.2 *Candāyan* of Maulana Daud. Manuscript copied circa 1570

Hindustani Ms. 1, Folios 82v and 83r, John Rylands Library, Manchester

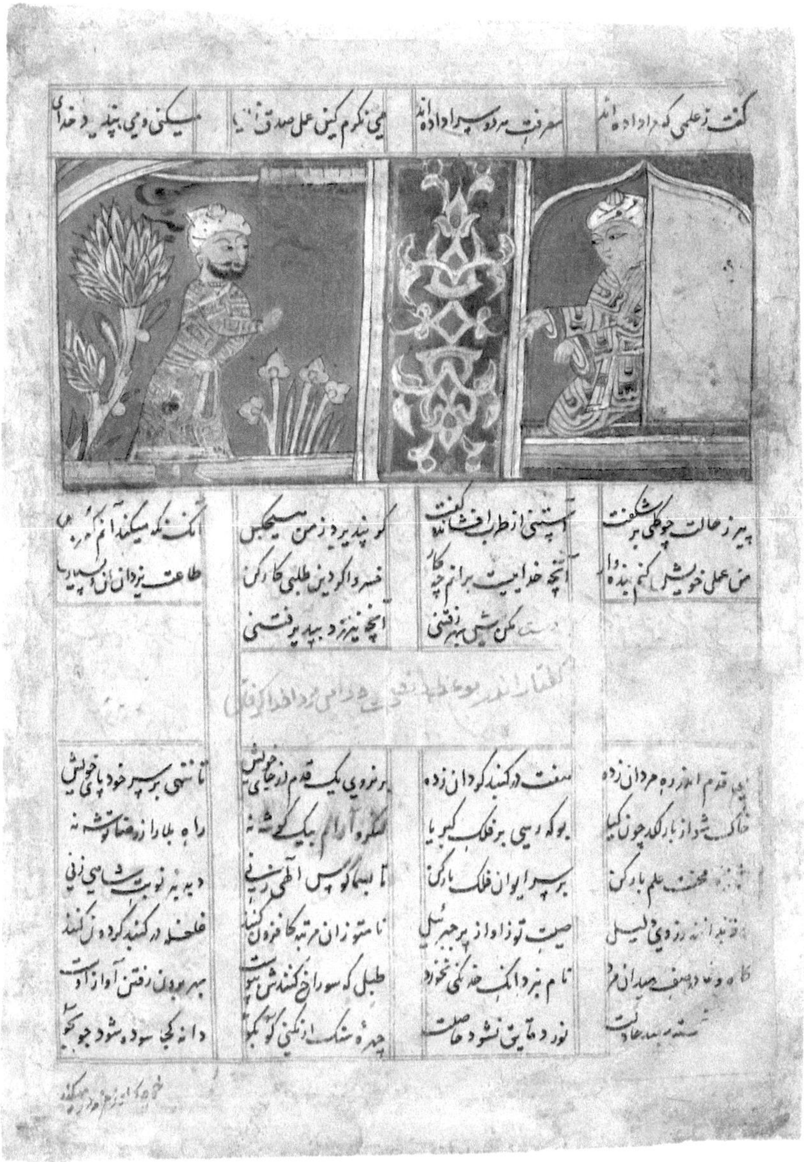

FIGURE 1.3 Folio from the *Khamsah* of Amir Khusrau Dihlavi (India, copied c. 1450)

Accn. No. 1976.283, Metropolitan Museum of Art, New York

FIGURE 1.4 *Candāyan* of Maulana Daud. Copied mid-sixteenth century

Accn. No. 57.1, folios 42v and 43r, Chhatrapati Shivaji Maharaj Vastu Sangrahalaya, Mumbai

FIGURE 1.5 *Candāyan* of Maulana Daud, likely copied in the late fifteenth century. Rice paper has been applied over the text on the right-hand folio. The heroine's friend, Biraspat, describes the arrival of the hero, Laurik, in the city of Govar after his victory in battle.

Accn. Nos. 230v and 231r, Bharat Kala Bhavan, Varanasi

FIGURE 1.6 *Candāyan* of Maulana Daud. The hero, Laurik, enters Chanda's bedchamber.

Accn. Nos. K-730-E 1 and 2, Government Museum and Art Gallery, Chandigarh

FIGURE 1.7 *Padmāvat* of Malik Muhammad Jayasi. A description of the amorous pleasures to be had during the warm months of the year.

Accn. No. 10864-1, Bharat Kala Bhavan, Varanasi

FIGURE 1.8 *Candāyan* of Maulana Daud. Rupchand falls in love with Chanda as he listens to the ascetic Bajir describe her.

Hindustani Ms. 01, folios 41v and 42r, John Rylands Library, Manchester

FIGURE 1.9 The *Candāyan* of Maulana Daud. Rupachand falls in love with Chanda as he listens to the ascetic Bajir describe her.

Accn. No. K-7-30-I, Government Museum and Art Gallery, Chandigarh

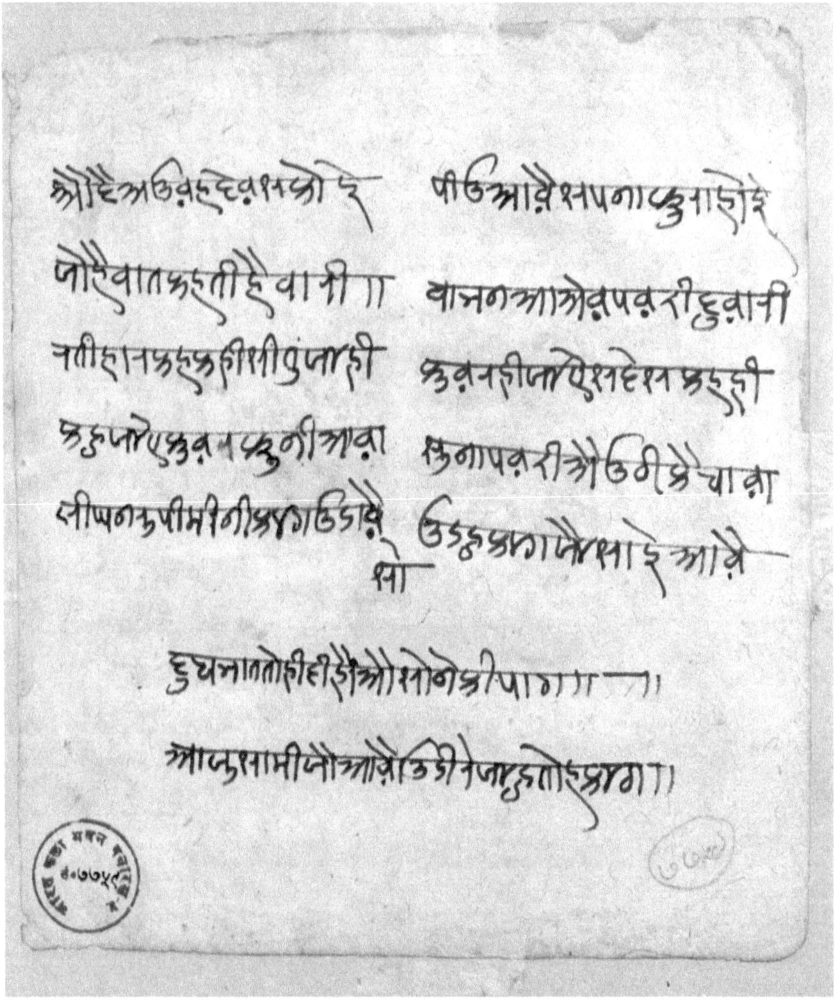

FIGURE 1.10 *Mirgāvatī* of Qutban, copied in the Kaithī script

Accn. No. 7759(r). Bharat Kala Bhavan, Varanasi

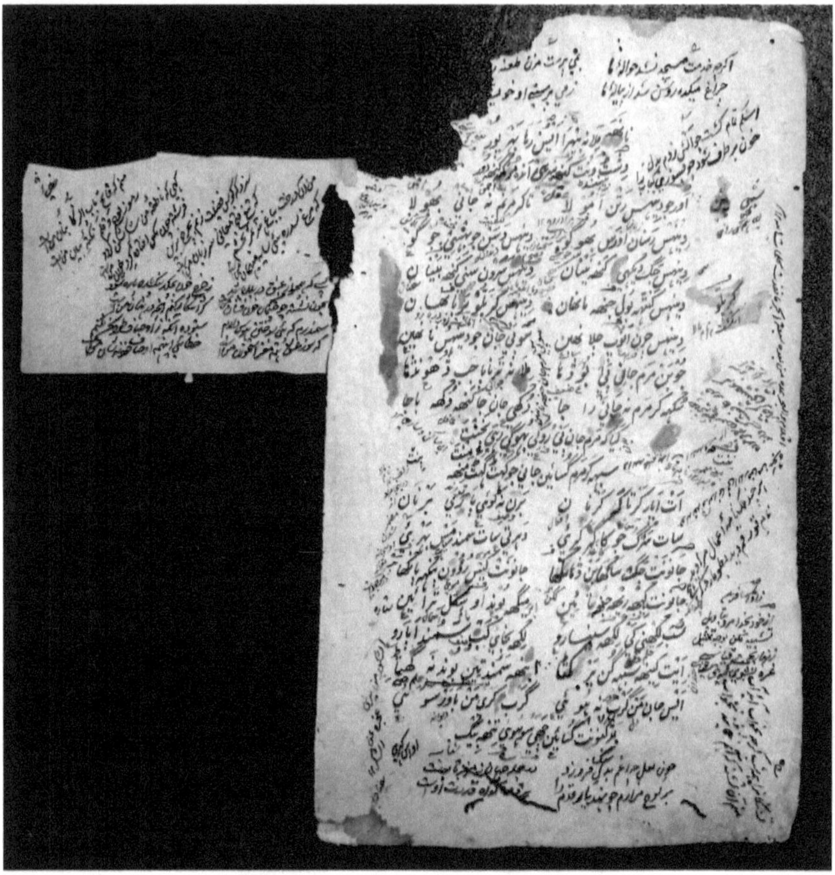

FIGURE 1.11 *Padmāvat* of Malik Muhammad Jayasi. Folio has been removed from the codex for photographing. The owner has attached a slip of paper in order to make additional notes and emendations on this page and the next.

Ms. 477, A.C. Joshi Library, Punjab University, Chandigarh. Photo by author

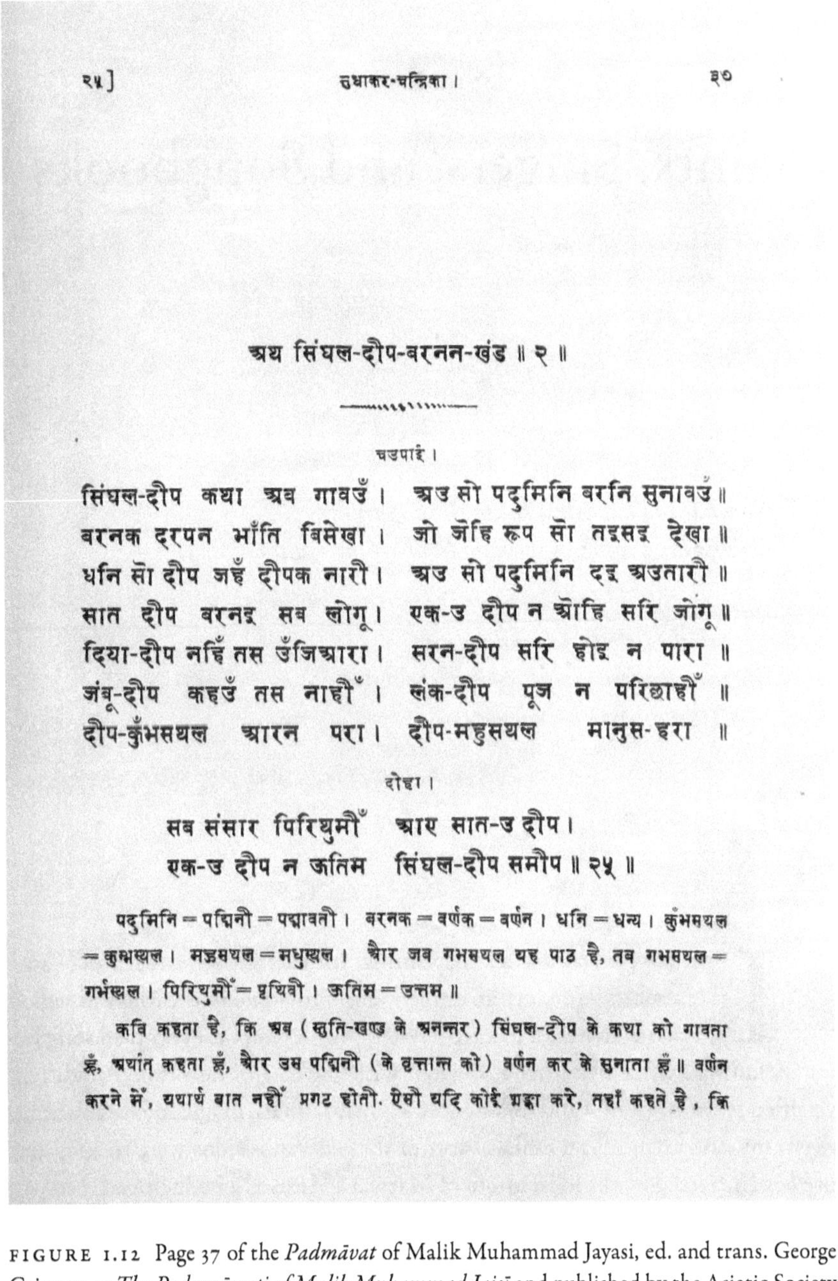

२५] सुधाकर-चन्द्रिका। ३७

अथ सिंघल-दीप-बरनन-खंड ॥ २ ॥

चउपाई।

सिंघल-दीप कथा अब गावउँ। अउ सो पदुमिनि बरनि सुनावउँ॥
बरनक दरपन भाँति बिसेखा। जो जेहि रूप सो तइसइ देखा॥
धनि सो दीप जहँ दीपक नारी। अउ सो पदुमिनि दइ अउतारी॥
सात दीप बरनइ सब लोगू। एक-उ दीप न ओहि सरि जोगू॥
दिया-दीप नहिँ तस उँजिआरा। सरन-दीप सरि होइ न पारा॥
जंबू-दीप कहउँ तस नाहीँ। लंक-दीप पूज न परिछाहीँ॥
दीप-कुँभसथल आरन परा। दीप-महुसथल मानुस-हरा॥

दोहा।

सब संसार पिरिथुमीँ आए सात-उ दीप।
एक-उ दीप न ऊतिम सिंघल-दीप समीप॥ २५॥

पदुमिनि = पद्मिनी = पद्मावती। बरनक = वर्णक = वर्णन। धनि = धन्य। कुँभसथल = कुम्भस्थल। मह्रुसथल = मधुस्थल। और जब गभसथल यह पाठ है, तब गभसथल = गर्भस्थल। पिरिथुमीँ = पृथिवी। ऊतिम = उत्तम॥

कवि कहता है, कि अब (स्तुति-खण्ड के अनन्तर) सिंघल-दीप के कथा को गावता हूँ, अर्थात् कहता हूँ, और उस पद्मिनी (के वृत्तान्त को) वर्णन कर के सुनाता हूँ॥ वर्णन करने में, यथार्थ बात नहीँ प्रगट होती. ऐसी यदि कोई शङ्का करे, तहाँ कहते है, कि

FIGURE 1.12 Page 37 of the *Padmāvat* of Malik Muhammad Jayasi, ed. and trans. George Grierson as *The Padumāwati of Malik Muḥammad Jaisī* and published by the Asiatic Society of Calcutta, 1896

Photo by University of Toronto

2

Saints, Singers, and Songbooks

masi kāgada kai āsirai kyūṁ chūṭai saṁsāra
rāṁma binā sūjhai nahīṁ dādū bharama vikāra

How can one escape saṁsāra
with the help of ink and paper?
Without Ram, no solution comes to mind,
it's just confusion and agitation.

—Dadu Dayal (d. 1603), *sāṁc kau aṅg*, v. 90

In the year 1689 CE, beginning in the lunar month of Pausa (December–January), an anonymous individual in the Marwar region of Rajasthan began to keep a notebook, or *guṭakā*. He copied song lyrics, including hymns by saints associated with the *nirguṇ* devotional tradition, versified stories of saints and folk heroes, mantras, spells, magic squares, yantras, diagrams, and astrological tables. Most of these compositions were in a register of *bhāṣā* inflected by the local idiom of Marwari. He used a wide-tipped reed pen on rectangular folios of cloth-made paper. These folios were stacked, pierced with holes along their left edges, and bound into a cloth and cardboard binding, making them easy to carry and leaf through. Judging from the wear and tear as well as ink smudges, water damage, evidence of rebinding, subsequent inscriptions and corrections, and other bits of textual and material evidence, the notebook's owner used it frequently. Together with the presence of several dated colophons—a relatively rare occurrence in manuscripts of this type—these features show that this *guṭakā* served as a notebook or briefcase of sorts for a religious professional for a period of more than a decade.

The content of the notebook (Ms. 26334, held in the Rajasthan Oriental Research Library in Jodhpur) is copied in a mixture of the shorthand Kaithī script and the more calligraphic Nāgarī script.[1] In Kaithī, the owner drew horizontal lines across the page from which he "hung" individual letters. These lines are uneven, irregularly spaced, and drawn freehand. In contrast, the material inscribed in Nāgarī is usually neater and straighter, each individual character copied separately with its own horizontal line drawn carefully above (fig. 2.1). The notebook's owner mostly used Kaithī for works like hymns and narratives and Nāgarī for texts like mantras, spells, and astrological notes. He often combined the two scripts, apparently letting his hand slip back into the habit of writing certain characters in Kaithī even as he transcribed a text in Nāgarī. It is a visual trace of muscle memory and reminder of the embodied character of writing. This combination of Kaithī and Nāgārī—in a single manuscript, within individual texts, and in the person of the scribe—also draws attention to an important but largely forgotten aspect of early writing in Hindi: that from at least the early seventeenth through the mid-eighteenth century, Kaithī and Nāgarī scripts were hardly as distinct from each other as modern scholars typically assume, and there is little evidence to suggest that Hindi was associated with the Nāgarī script in the manner that early advocates of Hindi as a national language would claim during the nineteenth and early twentieth centuries.[2]

It is clear that the owner of the notebook did not know Sanskrit, even though he occasionally tried to imitate conventions found in Sanskrit manuscripts. For example, before transcribing a lyric (*pad*) dedicated to "Munilal Parshvanath," the notebook's owner adds *atha saṅgīta likṣate*, "Here music is written [*sic*]," in grammatically incorrect Sanskrit. He follows the *pad* with a colophon—*śrī pārśvanātha jī kā saṅgita līkhate mī paisa badī 6 saṁ[vat] 1746*, "The song of Shri Parshvanath Ji is written [here] on the 6th of the dark half of the month of Pausa, Samvat 1746 (1690 CE)"—in a language that could perhaps most accurately be described as a vernacular approximation of Sanskrit.[3] Yet for the most part, such paratextual material is largely absent from the notebook. The owner occasionally assigned verse numbers to lyrics but otherwise provided no rubrics or navigational apparatus: there are no folio numbers or raga notations, and very few subject or section headings. The contents of the notebook often appear to spill over the page: lyrics and mantras fill the extra space between columns of tables; a recipe for cooking eggplant to obtain yogic powers nestles between magic squares; verses and cryptic notes pile upon one another in the empty space left at the bottom of a folio after the end of a story (fig. 2.2).

The ad hoc and idiosyncratic way the material has been copied and the complete lack of navigational paratexts suggest that this was a notebook created by an individual for his own use. Such a *guṭakā* was a portmanteau of sorts in which an owner could carry all manner of *aide-mémoire*, documents, records, and liturgical texts. This individual was apparently a follower of one of the *nirguṇ sant* traditions of Rajasthan, quite possibly the Niranjani Sampraday, and likely worked as a *jyotiṣa* (astrologer) and ritual specialist. Yet his notebook does not conform to any of the canons of Hindi literature or north Indian religion as defined by modern scholars. He appears to have sung the hymns of so-called heterodox *nirguṇ* saints like Kabir (fl. fifteenth century), Haridas Niranjani (d. 1601), and Jangopal (fl. 1600–1620); yet he also cultivated a knowledge of astrology and arcane yogic practices for obtaining extraordinary powers, knowledge systems that these saints fiercely critiqued. He apparently also performed the regional epic of *Ḍholā Māru*—a tradition now thought to be part of the "feudal" culture that *nirguṇ* saints were supposed to have rejected—and evidently attempted to obtain knowledge of talismans from a Muslim religious specialist, copying Islamicate magic squares, esoteric diagrams, and incantations in a shaky mimicry of the Arabic script. All this in addition to copying the aforementioned song dedicated to Parshvanath—a figure revered in Jainism, a tradition contemporary *nirguṇ* poets fiercely critiqued—and a condensed version of a prose *pem-kathā* set in the time of the Delhi Sultan Firoz Shah Tughlaq (r. 1351–1388).[4]

Even among those hymns of the *nirguṇ* saints that the *guṭakā*'s owner chose to copy—and by extension chose to perform, for notebooks such as this were meant to aid in musical performance—it is difficult to discern clear theological criteria for inclusion. Instead, there is a distinct *aesthetic* logic that informs the choice of verses. The notebook's owner copied and sang songs that he enjoyed, that moved him or appealed to him in a particular way. This notebook thus reflects his personal canon as well as his occupational and social world, rather than a sectarian canon or tradition. The *guṭakā* and the hundreds if not thousands of such notebooks like it kept in Indian archives can be approached as the material for literary history as prosopography, with the goal of gradually reconstructing generic, theological, and aesthetic distinctions as they were observed in everyday contexts.

WRITING IN A WORLD OF SPEECH AND SONG

Like Ms. 26334, the *guṭakā*s that fill the cabinets (*alamārī*) of north Indian libraries and archives were primarily instruments used in the creation of oral performance events like singing, sermonizing, teaching, providing astrological or religious consultation, and other rituals that constituted the center of social and religious life in north India during the sixteenth through early nineteenth centuries. Modern scholars have tended to emphasize the oral dimension of this textual world to the near exclusion of the written, particularly in the case of the poetic genres associated with *nirguṇ bhakti*: the tradition of poets and sectarian communities who preached devotion (*bhakti*) to an ineffable, undivided, unqualified (*nirguṇ*) godhead. (The term is most often defined in opposition to *saguṇ bhakti*, the worship of anthropomorphic deities like Ram and Krishna among Vaishnava communities.) Since the pioneering studies of *bhakti* poetry in the first quarter of the twentieth century, there has been a tendency to assume that the lyrics and didactic couplets (*sākhī*) that made up the popular core of devotional poetry and liturgy among *nirguṇ bhakti* traditions were composed, circulated, and performed in a purely oral sphere. Several of the most famous saint-poets of the tradition came from subaltern caste communities and are believed to have lacked formal education and graphic literacy; they are assumed to have composed their poetry "orally." This includes two saints from Banaras—Kabir, who came from the *julāhā* community of weavers, and Ravidas (c. 1450–1550), who came from the *camār* community of leather workers—and two saints from Rajasthan—Dadu Dayal (1544–1603), who came from the *dhuniyā* community of cotton carders, and Haridas Niranjani, who came from the *sāṁkhlā* community of agricultural laborers. Scholars of Hindi generally believe that these saints' hymns and sayings traveled on the tongues of wandering sadhus and pilgrims across the regions of modern-day Rajasthan, Gujarat, Punjab, Uttar Pradesh, Bihar, and Madhya Pradesh, being shared during sessions of communal singing and existing strictly in oral form until, years or sometimes centuries later, they were committed to writing. The scholar Linda Hess puts it succinctly and elegantly: "Religious 'literature' in medieval India was sung. It spread across the country like wildfire on the lips of devotees and wandering ascetics who walked from region to region or met in conventions of holy men on the banks of some sacred river, where a chief activity was *bhajan*, or devotional singing."[5] Devotional poetry spread quickly and among a diverse range of social groups precisely because it was sung, and singing was a central, if not the primary, form of communal worship.

Yet a significant amount of textual, documentary, and material evidence suggests that writing was also an integral part of this tradition from its very beginnings and an inseparable component of textual circulation throughout the tradition's history. The singers, preachers, and anthologizers of the sixteenth, seventeenth, and eighteenth centuries may indeed have been able to memorize hundreds of hymns and aphorisms, made easier by the mnemonic properties of meter and rhyme, yet they just as often worked from written notes, anthologies, and liturgical handbooks.

"IF THE SEVEN SEAS WERE INK": THE THEORY AND PRACTICE OF WRITING IN *NIRGUṆ* POETRY

The tradition of *nirguṇ* poetry in north India is known for criticism of books and book learning, part of its broader critique of privileged forms of religious knowledge and attempt to establish new types of religious and intellectual authority. Beginning with the poetry of Kabir, the putative founder of the tradition (or at least its earliest exponent in north India) and continuing in the compositions of Dharmdas (fl. second half of fifteenth century), Ravidas, Dadu Dayal, Haridas Niranjani, and even the highly scholastic works of Sundardas (1596–1689) of the Dadu Panth, there is skepticism toward reading and learning from written texts. The following *sākhī* of Kabir, which comes to us through the scriptural tradition of the Dadu Panth discussed in chapter 4, is frequently cited as an example of the *nirguṇ* saints' disdain for book learning:

> pothī paḍhi paḍhi jaga muā paṇḍita bhayā na koï
> ekai ākhara prema kā paḍhai so paṃdita hoï
>
> The world could keep reading books (*pothī*) till it up and died,
> and still no one would become learned (*paṇḍit*).
> [But the person] who reads one letter of love—
> *he* will become learned.[6]

This couplet is succinct, linguistically simple, and poetically unadorned, but nevertheless dense with meaning. Kabir speaks specifically of the *pothī*, the unbound collection of wide-format folios made from palm leaf or paper that was the ritual equipment of the Brahmin pandit (fig. 3.1). The seated pedagogue would recite aloud from such books, ceremoniously flipping over each folio as he progressed through the text (figs. 3.2, 3.3). Through the iconic image of the *pothī*-reciting pandit (a frequent target of ridicule in *nirguṇ* poetry and a ubiquitous sight in Kabir's hometown of Banaras), Kabir took aim at contemporary structures of religious and intellectual authority that were monopolized by the Brahmin community.[7]

In this world, authority (*adhikār*) to speak on religious matters was based upon mastery of a corpus of (mostly Sanskrit) texts; the content was determined by sectarian and/or intellectual tradition or lineage. In theory, this standard of authority did not necessarily presume graphic literacy—many texts and parts of texts were transmitted orally and memorized as part of an individual's religious and scholastic training—but available material on religious scholars and specialists in cities like Banaras suggests that written texts were so extensively utilized that literacy was effectively a prerequisite for study.[8] In the first line of the couplet, Kabir mocks the notion that the *external*, bodily activity of reading or reciting (*paḍh-*) from a written text could bring about any kind of *internal* transformation of the individual. He emphasizes reading as an embodied and as a social practice: he criticizes the *social* fact that if you read from a written text, other people will *think* that you are a wise man.

Kabir contrasts the external practice of reading with the internal practice of disciplined affective and gnostic experience (*anubhav*): "he who reads one letter (*ākhar*) of love (*prem*) becomes learned." This is not worldly love but rather love of God, a specific affective state that may be spontaneous (*sahaj*) in nature but can only be accessed through deliberate and mindful practices, the most important of which is remembrance of God (*smaran* or *simran*, from Sanskrit *smaraṇa*). Writing, as a technology for the externalization of memory, is antithetical to the practice of remembrance not only because it eliminates the need to actively remember but also because remembrance, as a fully embodied practice, is a way of re-cognizing (*lakh-* or *pahacān-*) the presence of the divine other (*paramātmā*, the highest self) within the self (*ātmā*). There is an elegant ontological parallelism here: if you remember a text or sign (the names of God, his attributes, his deeds, etc.), then that text or sign resides within you, just as God himself resides within you. Purushottam Agrawal has identified this epistemological privileging of embodied experience over external textual knowledge as part of Kabir's attempt to distinguish poetic (*kāvyokt*) forms of knowledge and devotion from scholastic forms. This is in turn an expression of what Agrawal calls *deśaj ādhunikatā*, an emergent "indigenous modernity."[9] For Kabir and other *nirguṇ* poets, experience (*anubhav*) leads to knowledge (*gyān*, from Sanskrit *jñāna*), not the other way around.

The prosodic form of Kabir's couplet and the very name of the genre to which it belongs tell us something about the alternative epistemology he is proposing.

Composed in the *dohā* meter, this type of didactic epigram was known as a *sākhī*, which can be translated as "witness" (from Sanskrit *sākṣin*, "seeing with the eyes"). This term reinforces the sense of the poem's content as embodied, firsthand knowledge. A *sākhī* bears "witness" in two senses: as a verbalization of what the saint herself or himself has experienced through spiritual endeavor and as a witness to the saint's wisdom—in other words, each time the *sākhī* is recited, it is a testament as much to the saintliness of the saint as to the truth of her or his utterance. The compact structure and rhyme scheme of the *dohā* meter made the *sākhī* perfect for oral transmission, memorization, and recitation in a number of pedagogical performance contexts, including sermons (*pravacan*).[10] The fact that the earliest known manuscripts of *nirguṇ bhakti* communities (which date to the first quarter of the seventeenth century) are anthologies of such *sākhī*s reflects the importance of this form in the transmission of religious knowledge.[11] Hagiographical works of these communities from the late sixteenth and early seventeenth centuries dramatize episodes in which the guru teaches his disciples by reciting *sākhī*s to them: thus the transmission of knowledge from teacher to student is itself a moment of witnessing in which knowledge is transmitted through direct, oral means without the mediating presence of writing.[12]

The polysemy of the terms used in the poem—particularly of the verb *paḍh-* (to read, to study, to recite) and of the substantive *ākhar* (both "syllable" and "letter," from the Sanskrit *akṣara*, literally "imperishable," i.e., "sound") also gestures toward the *nirguṇ* saints' emphasis on direct oral transmission and the soteriological efficacy of sound. Translating *paḍh-* as "to recite" rather than as "to read" and *ākhar* as "syllable" rather than as "letter" creates the following reading:

> The world could keep reciting from books until it up and died,
> and still no one would become learned.
> [But the person] who recites one syllable of love,
> *he* becomes learned.

This rendering brings out more vividly the critique of reading from texts: one may read aloud from manuscripts all they like, but the wisdom or truth contained therein will not become part of the individual; it will always remain external. This is a clever inversion of the way the act of reading is construed in the deep structure of Sanskrit: the reader "makes the text speak" (*vācayati*). In contrast, Kabir and other saints of the *nirguṇ* tradition suggest that the individual who asks the text to speak is not doing the cognitive or mnemonic labor required to recognize God within themselves. Reciting a single syllable of love aloud can bring wisdom because "reciting" in this case involves the vocalization of an internal emotional state, making it externally audible and thus efficacious in the same way that the sounds of God's name and qualities are efficacious.

The idea that vocalizing or simply hearing God's name (most often *rām* in *nirguṇ* traditions) can effect spiritual transformation and bring about salvation is a central tenet of the tradition. Dadu Dayal puts it this way in one of his *sākhīs*: "Oh Dadu, do not let the Name be distant from your inner self for even a moment—keep it in your heart / Thousands of the fallen have been saved simply by saying *rām*" (*dādu nimakha na nyārā kījie antara thaiṁ uri nāma / koṭi patita pāvana bhāye kevala kahatāṁ rāma*).[13] Chanting *rām* was a ubiquitous activity in *nirguṇ* communities like the Dadu Panth, Niranjani Sampraday, and later Kabir Panth; Kabir's use of the term *ākhar* in the earlier couplet alludes to this practice of chanting (*jap-*) auspicious syllables (*mantra*), which was appropriated from earlier ascetic traditions, particularly those associated with the Naths.[14]

If the dubious character of writing as a prosthetic of memory was the primary target of the *nirguṇ* saints' epistemological critique, then the sacred character of its materiality was the primary target of their ontological and broader metaphysical critique, which extended to notions of purity and impurity in general. In early modern India, beliefs in the sacrality and corresponding ritual purity of certain forms of writing were ubiquitous and traversed confessional and sectarian distinctions. Here, the term "sacredness" refers to a metaphysical understanding of the status of a substance. Within Hindu traditions, manuscripts of religious and scholastic works, being physical instantiations of verbal texts with soteriological and other metaphysical efficacies, were often understood to possess certain metaphysical properties themselves, or at least belonged to a class of substances that were ritually "pure" (*pavitra*). In some sectarian traditions and in the case of particular types of works like the *purāṇas*, elaborate rules and rituals were prescribed for copying, storage, opening, recitation, and ritual veneration. Many of these prescriptions are given in the works themselves, usually in the concluding sections or *phalaśruti* (lit. "fruit of hearing," a description of the material and spiritual benefits to be gained by listening to, copying, or commissioning a copy).[15] Such beliefs and practices were particularly prevalent and codified among the Jain community, in which commissioning a copy of a work for use by monks or providing monetary or other support to community libraries (called *granth-bhaṇḍār* or "book warehouses") were common means of obtaining spiritual merit (*puṇya*).[16]

Bhakti religiosity itself, at least in its Vaishnava form, appears to have reinforced and expanded the veneration of religious works by establishing new canons and new structures of patronage. Communities like the Pushtimarg and Gaudiya Sampraday, which developed in the Braj region during the sixteenth century and spread through Rajasthan, Gujarat, and Bengal during the seventeenth and eighteenth centuries, invested the *Bhāgavata Purāṇa*, its vernacular transcreations, and its ancillary texts with new theological and ritual significance while building patronage networks among Hindu political elites (particularly Rajputs), powerful merchants, and their own monastic leadership. Consequently, the commissioning and gifting of lavishly illustrated and calligraphed copies of the *Bhāgavata Purāṇa* and related works became a means through which relationships of patronage and exchange were enacted, while the copies themselves became focal points of religious ritual.[17] Again, the image of the *pothī*-reading pandit in Kabir's couplet is the archetype of this very *public* kind of reading and reinforced notions regarding the respective purity of objects, persons, and forms of labor: an individual from a ritually pure caste community (the Brahmin) recites a religious work (a ritually purifying activity) using a manuscript of that work (a ritually pure object). Members of subaltern castes, such as Ravidas, were excluded from the pedagogical and ritual contexts in which such texts were performed, their physical substance understood to be a threat to the purity of the objects and activities.[18]

The *nirguṇ* saints' critique of writing cut to the heart of contemporary notions of purity and impurity and challenged ideas regarding the transformation of substances through different types of labor. In a *pad* lampooning the logic of purity, Ravidas sings:

> tara tāri apavitra kari mānīe re jaise kāgarā karata bīcāraṁ
> bhagati bhāgaütu likhīai tiha ūpare pūjīai kari namasakāraṁ
>
> Used for toddy, the tree is thought to be impure (*apavitra*),
> but turned into paper, it is used for contemplation!
> And when one writes about devotion and God on it,
> people bow down and worship it![19]

Ravidas satirizes the conventional characterization of some substances as innately pure and others as impure, suggesting that it is human agency that makes them so. The supposedly purifying water of the Ganges can be used to make (polluting) wine, and he himself is a member of a so-called "impure" caste, but through God's intercession has become a saint revered by even Brahmins.[20] The poet throws this contradiction into stark relief as he speaks of writing: when *tāḍī* sap is extracted from the palmyra palm (*Borassus flabelifer*) in order to make liquor (a polluting substance), the tree itself is understood by upper-caste Hindus to be impure.[21] Yet when the leaves are inscribed with one's thoughts, they are considered a totally different substance—paper (*kāgarā*). And when one writes upon them words of devotion, especially a work like the aforementioned *Bhāgavata Purāṇa*, they become an object of extraordinary purity and sanctity and are accordingly worshiped. In all three cases, it is human agency realized as labor that transforms the substance of the tree, which itself has no essential essence that is pure or impure. Ravidas implicitly critiques the differential valuation of labor: the physical labor of making toddy supposedly produces an impure substance, while the intellectual labor (*bicār*) of writing produces a pure substance. If, as Ravidas suggests, distinctions of purity between the two resulting substances are arbitrary, then such distinctions between the two forms of labor must also be arbitrary.

For *nirguṇ* saints, the self is the substance that is to be transformed, the object upon which one must apply labor. The self is the pen that writes and the paper upon which the Word is written. Their nondualist theology rejects the reality of the physical body but at the same time sees it as a tool for attaining gnosis: by using the body to chant, recite, sing, and listen to tales of God, His qualities (*guṇ*), and His deeds (*carit, kīrti*), the devotee activates remembrance, remembrance then engenders love, and love—if cultivated long enough through these techniques—produces the emotional state of *prem rasa*, the "juice," "elixir," or "aesthetic-affective state" of love.[22] The challenge is to avoid becoming a servant of the demands (*kām*, *tṛṣṇa*, etc.) of the body and instead transform it into an instrument that serves the program of liberation. This imperative is captured beautifully in a couplet attributed to Kabir and preserved in the Dadu Panthi manuscript tradition:

> yahu tana jalauṁ masi karauṁ likhauṁ rāma kā nāüṁ
> lekhaṇi karūṁ karaṁka kī likhi likhi rāma paṭhāüṁ
>
> I shall burn this body and turn it to ink,
> and write the Name of Ram.
> I shall turn my bones into a pen,
> and writing away, I shall send [it] to Ram.[23]

The couplet alludes to how ink was produced by burning certain plants to produce soot that was then mixed with oils and/or gums; a bone resembles a reed pen in that its hollow center provides a reservoir for ink.[24] Guru Nanak (1469–1539), the first guru of the Sikh tradition (and a saint-poet included within the canons of *nirguṇ* religious sects) extends this metaphor to the mind:

jāli mohu ghasi masu kari mati kāgadu kari sāru
bhāū kalama kari citu lekhārī gura puchi likhu bīcāru
likhu nāmu sālāha likhu likhu antu na pārāvāru
bābā ehu lekhā likhi jāṇu
jithai lekhā maṁgīai tithai hoï sacā nīsāṇu

Burn your attachment (*mohu*) and grind it into ink,
pulp your intellect (*mati*) and turn it into paper (*kāgadu*).
Fashion a pen from your love, let your consciousness (*citu*) be the scribe (*lekhārī*),
then ask the teacher and write [his] contemplations (*bīcāru*).
Write praises of the Name,
keep writing and writing [though] the end is never reached.
O Baba, know to write such an account (*lekha*),
[so that] when that account is asked for,
it will be a mark of truth (*sacā nīsāṇu*).[25]

The mind in all its different aspects must be transformed and disciplined into an instrument for the remembrance of God through repeated and constant inscription in memory. Consciousness itself becomes a scribe that writes on the mind or heart (*mati*), but it *transcribes* the words and thoughts (*bīcāru*) of the guru, a term that simultaneously references both him and God.

The final verse of the hymn evokes a particular kind of vocational, quotidian literacy: Guru Nanak speaks of *lekhā*, a term used for both the written account of a financial transaction and the account book itself (cf. Persian *daftar*). Nanak came from a Khatri family of merchants and village accountants (*paṭvārī*) and worked as a bookkeeper before taking up his ministry. This experience appears to have shaped his religious imaginary and that of the tradition he founded: the devotee must transform himself into a bookkeeper who dutifully transcribes the words of the guru so that when the account book (his *mati* or heart/mind) is demanded of him for reconciliation, the account (what is written, the *bīcāru* inscribed on his heart) tabulates as "true" (*sacā*). The final line exploits the multiple meanings of both *sacā* (true, authentic, genuine, from Sanskrit *sat*) and *nīsān* (mark, stamp, trace, signature, from Persian *nishān*): the account book of one's heart should be an "accurate mark," i.e., an account of Truth. It also should bear a "genuine signature" or "genuine stamp": in the context of merchant houses and Mughal administration, the *nishān* was the stamp (and sometimes signature) of the supervising officer who validated the account. Here, it is the impress of God on the heart. There is no trace of that mythic sphere of writing, captured in the epics and *purāṇas*, in which the immortal *rishi* dictates to his disciple, Ganesh dictates to Vyas, or Sarasvati dictates to the poet. Instead, the image comes from the mundane, quotidian world of everyday bookkeeping and trade. This parallels a contemporary change in the nature and acquisition of literacy and the emerging use of "vulgar" scripts like Kaithī for literary purposes. It is also reflected in the very notebooks in which this poetry was inscribed.

The level of detail in Guru Nanak's lyric suggests that he was truly using writing to "think through" theological and epistemological questions. And although Nanak might appear to be an outlier in the *nirguṇ* tradition when compared with Kabir, Ravidas, and Dadu, these supposedly "illiterate" saints used similarly detailed analogies and metaphors of writing to articulate their theologies.[26] Yet their critiques, at the levels of both content and form, were deeply embedded in the epistemological imagination of their time, which was very much postliterate in character. In contrast to the agents imagined in Walter Ong's theoretical state of "primary orality," everyone in early modern north India operated in a literary and intellectual environment that had been shaped by literacy and written textuality for centuries.[27] Indeed, the fierceness and consistency with which these saints attack the hegemony enjoyed by literate intellectuals and ritual specialists tells us how pervasive that hegemony was.

At the level of form, these saints composed their hymns and sayings within genres and prosodic structures that had been created and developed in literate contexts. The *dohā* meter of the *sākhī* genre had developed within the Apabhramsha literary tradition. Courtly poets and Jain intellectuals, as well as saint poets like the Buddhist Siddhas, had been composing *dohā* for centuries when the form came into early Hindi via scholastic Jain compositions in the Madhyadeshi literary idiom.[28] The *samān savaiyā* meter used by Ravidas and the *sarasī* meter used by Guru Nanak in the hymns quoted above were being used by literate court poets in Hindi as early as, if not before, the beginning of the *nirguṇ* poetic tradition in the late fifteenth century. This followed the pioneering use of meters like the *dohā* and *caupaī* in *bhāṣā* by the literate, courtly poets composing in and for sultanate courts of the Gangetic Plain and by Vishnudas at the Rajput court of Gwalior in his transcreations of the Hindu epics (*itihās*), the *Pāṇḍav Carit* (Deeds of the Pandavas, 1435) and the *Rāmāyaṇ Kathā* (Tale of the Rāmāyaṇa, 1442).[29] In this postliterate context, the songs and sayings of the *nirguṇ* saints—as well as their Vaishnava cousins farther east in Braj—were composed, circulated, and enjoyed.

In fact, it appears that these compositions were able to travel so far and wide precisely because they were composed in prosodic forms shared with literate, courtly traditions. The most poignant piece of evidence is in the so-called

Fatehpur manuscript, one of the earliest nonsectarian manuscripts of Hindi poetry. Copied by a teacher in 1582 for his pupils, the sons of a Rajput warlord near Fatehpur, Rajasthan, the *pothī*-style manuscript includes *pads* by Kabir and Ravidas alongside those of court poets like Vidyapati (c. 1352–1448) and even princes like Indrajit of Orccha (fl. 1600), and makes no distinction between compositions by "religious" and "literary," "elite" and "subaltern," or "literate" and "illiterate" poets.[30] As this manuscript attests, the technology of writing helped poetic works move back and forth between the popular-religious and elite-courtly spheres.

At the level of thought as well, writing shaped the metaphors and analogies through which these saints articulated their prescriptions for memory. For a poet who is said to have been illiterate, Kabir turns with remarkable frequency to the metaphor of writing to express the practice of remembrance. Among his better-known *sākhīs* is the following verse, preserved in the manuscript tradition of the Dadu Panth:

sāta samaṃdara kī masi karauṁ lekhani saba banarāï
dharatī saba kāgada karauṁ taū hari guṇa likhyā na jāï

If I were to turn the seven seas to ink,
  And make a pen of all the forests,
And if I were to turn the whole earth into paper,
  Still Hari's virtues could not be [fully] written.[31]

Ravidas too uses writing to think through and articulate his relationship with God and the way to accomplish spiritual transformation. In the following hymn, found in both the *Guru Granth Sāhib* and Dadu Panthi sources, he speaks of learning to know God in the manner of learning an (alternative) alphabet:

cali cali mana hari caṭasāla paḍhāṁüṁ
gura kī sāṭa gyāṁna kai akhira visarai tau sahaji samādhi lagāüṁ
prema paṭī śruti lekhani karihūṁ rarau mamauṁ likhi aṃk dikhāṁüṁ
ihi bidhi mukati bhaye sanakādika hridau bidāre prakāsa batāṁüṁ

Let's go, my heart, to study in Hari's school!
If I forget the letters of gnosis (*gyān*) with the guru,
  Then I'll enter intuitive meditation [*sahaj samādhi*].
I'll make love my writing board [*paṭī*] and heard wisdom [*śruti*] my
  stylus,

Writing "*ra*" and "*ma*" I'll show those marks [*aṅk*].
I'll open my heart and tell of how [the saint] Sanaka and others,
Obtained liberation in this way.[32]

The guru (either the human guru or God Himself) is both the teacher and the object of teaching geared toward imparting affect rather than knowledge, emotion rather than cognition. The letters or syllables *ra* and *ma* are the *aṅk* (lit. "mark," "letter," or "digit") that form the Name of God, i.e., *rām*. It is in and on the heart that this writing takes place. Yet despite shifting from the page to the heart, Ravidas is still constrained by the structure of writing: he is left with only the *aṅk*, a mark or impression of God, and an impression is always as much an absence as a presence. Ravidas can push the language of *bhāṣā* only so far: the impression left by literacy on the language cannot be erased completely, like the impressions left on the palimpsest of the writing board (*paṭī*). Like Plato in the *Phaedrus*, the *nirguṇ* saints are unable to escape writing's nature as a kind of displacement: they struggle against language in order to make God present but in the end find only His trace, be it Ravidas's *aṅk* or Nanak's *sacā nīsāṇu*.[33]

The *nirguṇ* saints were certainly not the first Indian poets to struggle with this problem of language, and their tradition was not the first in South Asia to express discomfort with writing and its pedagogical limitations. Some scholars of Indian intellectual and religious history—among them historian of Hindi literature Ramchandra Shukla—have suggested that Kabir, Ravidas, Dadu, and their peers were simply reiterating in a less rigorous fashion philosophical and theological concepts that had already been explored in the Indic (read: Sanskrit) tradition.[34] Many of the rhetorical figures used in poems attributed to these saints have earlier precedent, evincing not simply the saints' reuse of material but also the corporate nature of authorship.[35] For example, Kabir's reflection on the impossibility of enumerating God's virtues borrows a motif that had been in use since at least the tenth century when it appeared in the *Śivamahimnaḥ Stotram*, and appears in Jayasi's *Padmāvat* of 1540.[36] Critiques of book learning can be found in Sanskrit, Arabic, and Persian texts that circulated in India during the late medieval and early modern period, as well as aphorisms privileging memory over writing.[37] The most common anxiety expressed in these works regards the need for a human mediator: without a qualified teacher to make the meaning of a text clear, a student (or any other underqualified reader) is in danger of making grievous errors and producing fallacious meanings.[38] At least at the level of rhetoric, the Sanskrit intellectual and literary tradition in particular continued to privilege orality over literacy, despite the fact that writing had by then been an integral part of literary and intellectual life for almost two millennia.[39]

Yet there *is* something that makes these saints' utterances new and fresh: the entrance of history itself through the historicization of acts of inscription in hagiographical works and the valorization of vulgar, quotidian forms of writing. Whereas authors operating within the literate social contexts of Sanskrit, Arabic, and Persian focus on the need for human mediation of written texts, the *nirguṇ* saints deny any epistemological privilege or pedagogical utility whatsoever to writing. As Ravidas's verse about the *tāḍī* tree demonstrates, these saints attempted to vulgarize the act of writing and divest its artifacts of immanence. And as the hymns and epigrams of Kabir and Dadu make clear, they privileged the *event* of speech—singing, chanting, or recitation—over its written trace. The content of these saints' poetry is only part of what makes this reading of their utterance possible; such readings could not be activated without the operation of a particular authorial persona, which is only partly constructed within the poetry itself.

"MY HAND NEVER TOUCHED A PEN": REMEMBERING THE SAINTS AND THEIR WORLD

Reading *nirguṇ* saints' poetry as a critique of writing requires making frequent reference to the poets' biographies—or perhaps more accurately, to their authorial personas.[40] The *nirguṇ* devotional tradition produced the versified hagiographical narratives that introduced early modern audiences to the lives and personalities of the saints; through the prism of these life stories, the saints' utterances were understood and their latent critiques of writing activated. These hagiographical traditions—which come to us in written form, with early copies dating to the seventeenth century—are almost as old as the poetic tradition, suggesting that the corpus of hymns and sayings and the corpus of hagiographical narratives developed in a dialectical relationship.[41] Internal dating in several of these works tells us that they were composed within a generation of the saints' lifetimes.[42] These include the hagiographies of Anantadas (fl. 1588–1600), the *Bhaktamāl* (Garland of Devotees, c. 1600) of Nabhadas Ramanandi, the *Dādū Janm Līlā* (Divine Play of Dadu's Birth, 1620) of Jangopal Dadupanthi, the *Bhaktamāl* (1660) of Raghavdas Dadupanthi, the *Dayāl Jī Kī Pañc Paracai* (The Five Vignettes of Dayāl Jī, a.k.a. Haridas Niranjani, c. 1738–1779) of Hariramdas Niranjani, and the *Paracaï* (Hagiography, c. 1800) of Raghunathdas Niranjani.[43] Some are sectarian in provenance, but the canon of saints and poetry that they extoll is largely shared among the various communities that collectively make up the *nirguṇ* tradition, including the Kabir Panth, Dadu Panth, Niranjani

Sampraday, and Ramsnehi Sampraday. It is again thanks to the written tradition that we have evidence of how these hagiographies traversed sectarian distinctions: copies were made by monks from each of the aforementioned communities.

The hagiographical tradition produces figures of these saints—their origins, their lives, their personalities—that enable one to read their poetry as a critique of writing. This is not to deny their existence as historical individuals or the veracity of the accounts presented by hagiographers. These works make the saints' often complicated lives legible as examples of righteous conduct and the historical unfolding of God's divine play (*līlā*)—and thus a concrete example of the saints' message or teachings (*upadeśa*, lit. "imperative"). In the case of Kabir, Ravidas, Dadu, and Haridas Niranjani, these works of *paricay* (from the Sanskrit *paricaya*, meaning "introduction to" or "knowledge of") establish the individual's charisma by emphasizing his or her skill in composing and singing verse. Whether it be Anantdas's stories of Kabir singing God's virtues at a gathering of the faithful at his home in Banaras and Ravidas telling stories of God near the local temple, Jangopal's recounting of how Dadu sang with his disciples in the cities and towns of Rajasthan, or Raghunathdas's description of Haridas ministering to the merchants of the city of Didwana, the saints are always depicted in the act of singing and reciting poetry to enthrall devotees and please God. There is no mention of writing or any premeditated composition of verse; *sākhī*s and *pad*s seem to issue from the saints' mouths spontaneously.[44] Hagiographers also spend considerable time dramatizing and remarking upon the subalternity of these figures. Anantdas repeatedly mentions the "low" caste identities of Kabir and Ravidas and sets critical episodes in their life stories around their respective occupations of weaving and leather working. Jangopal tells his audience that Dadu never gave up cotton carding, continuing to work even as he sang and ministered.[45] No reference is ever made to formal education or literacy, and none is needed—the saints' subaltern caste identities and occupations precluded the possibility of access to even vocational forms of literacy.[46]

Hagiographers bring to life the ritual and social contexts in which the saints' lyrics and poetry were orally performed and encourage their audiences to take part. In his chronicle of the life of Ravidas, Anantdas re-creates in vivid detail the sights, sounds, smells, and tastes of a religious festival (*mahochai*, Sanskrit *mahotsava*) at which hymns (*bhajan*) are sung and stories (*kathā*) are performed:

> karai kathā kīrataṁna bārū / āṁna kathā nāhīṁ paisārū
> maṃdira mahala kīyā bahuterā / tahāṁ tahāṁ bhaktana kā ḍerā
> naṁgara ke loga darasa koṁ āvai / tinasoṁ bāṃbhana khare risāvai
> *   *   *

loga mahājaṁna daraṁniṁ jāhīṁ / biprā suṁniṁ mana maiṁ
pachitāṁhī
sakala loka maṁniṁ āṁnaṃda hūvā / bipra dukhī ati jari bari mūvāṁ
sakala soja le rāṁnīṁ āī / pāṁna sugaṁdha gulāla miṭhāī
hari bolo hari bolo hoī / bāga baṁnyo baikūṁṭhā soī
kathā kīratanu bahu vidhi kīno / bāṃṭi prasāda sabaniṁ ko dīno
pīchai ḍerā naṁgari bicāre / mahimāṁ kari bājāra uchāre
āṁni paṭaṃbara māṁga saṁvāre / carana dharata gurudeva padhārai

They sang such excellent songs and told such excellent stories
that no other story even came up.
Encampments of devotees were set up all around,
like so many palaces and temples.
The people of the city came to see,
and the Brahmans were infuriated by all this.
* * *
Merchants and common people came to see,
and hearing about it, the Brahmans silently grieved.
All of the people felt euphoric,
[but] the Brahmins burned with pain.
The queen made all of the arrangements:
betel nut, fragrances, colored powder, and sweets.
"Say Hari! Say Hari!" was [heard],
and so the garden and forest became like Vaikunth (the abode of
Vishnu).
They sang songs and told stories of God in various styles,
and gave all sorts of food offerings (*prasād*) to everyone.
Later they thought to set up camp in the city,
and the market buzzed with [talk of] its greatness.
A great saffron-colored sheet was ordered and stretched out,
on which the feet of the eminent guru (Ravidas) would step.[47]

Performances of the saints' poetry are not only experienced through the ears; they are a multisensory feast so powerful that it can transform an ordinary garden (or square, courtyard, or bazaar) into a heavenly abode. Just as the saints do in their poetry, Anantadas emphasizes the soteriological efficacy of singing, reciting, and hearing God's qualities and deeds, telling his audience that "those who obtain *darśan* of Hari's devotees experience bliss" because "when Hari's devotees sing songs and tell stories, they win everyone's hearts with love!" (*kathā kīratana harijaṁna karaī / pema sahita sabake mana haraī*). Such grand celebrations required significant monetary investment and logistical support, so Anantdas reminds his listeners of the spiritual merit to be gained by patronizing such revivals: "Those whose doorsteps are graced by the feet of Hari's people / have their sins cut away and their souls saved" (*jini kai dvārai jana paga dhārai / kāṭhi pāpa so jīva udhārai*).[48]

Devotees took such reminders seriously. The hagiographical tradition of the Dadu Panth in particular not only prescribes patronage of oral performance but also records historical instances of it. Jangopal (fl. 1600–1630), a merchant of Rajasthan and a direct disciple of Dadu Dayal, composed his *Dādū Janm Līlā* like an account book (*lekhā*), recording the devotees who contributed their wealth and labor to organizing such performances. These devotees, whom Jangopal identifies by personal name, clan name, and village, help broadcast the guru's message and expand the footprint of the emerging *panth* (lit. *path*, i.e., sect) by organizing and financing festivals like those described above. Jangopal's accounts are replete with detail, mentioning even the equipment and supplies necessary for *kirtan* and *kathā*, including *sauri* (thin sheets on which devotees sit), *pālike* (cots for the guru and senior disciples), *pichaurā* (heavy blankets), *bichāṁvane* (stuffed mattresses for sitting), and *jājam* (heavy sheets used as rugs). Individual devotees' charity and labor are rewarded by the guru with miraculous visions, boons, and blessings.[49]

Even after a saint had departed the world, to listen to their life retold in one of these works was to imaginatively witness their poetic performances and speech acts as if they were happening "in real time." Hagiographers embedded and recontextualized the saints' poetry as dialogue in their narratives, creating dramatic scenes of encounter between gurus, holy men, and their rivals. Dadu speaks in *sākhīs* and *caupaīs* as he counsels the Mughal Emperor Akbar in the *Dādū Janm Līlā*, Kabir and Ravidas discuss the nature of reality by reciting *pad* and *kavitt* in the *Kabīr-Ravidās-Saṁvād*, and Haridas Niranjani converts even ghouls to the worship of God with his *caupaīs* in Raghunathdas's *Paracaī*.[50] Lyrics and epigrams are the intellectual currency of the saint: religious knowledge is to be evoked through *rasa*-filled verse, not expounded in dry prose. The "magical" effects of poetic meter on the psyche and the astonishing images and rhetorical effects of poetry (like the *ulaṭabāṁsī* or "upside-down," paradoxical images for which the *nirguṇ* saints were known) accomplish an affective change in the listener.[51] This affective power of versified religious discourse brings about *anabhai viśvās* or *anabhai pad*: a state of having *experienced* truth, i.e., God. Dialogical genres of the seventeenth and eighteenth centuries like the *goṣṭhī* (Sanskrit, "discussion," "assembly") and the Sikh *janmasākhīs*, as well as certain commentarial genres in

Hindi, present their material in the form of a discussion in which the disciple asks questions and the guru responds in *sākhīs*, *caupaī*, *chappay*, and the like. Such genres reflected actual pedagogical practices insofar as reciting and explaining poetic verses was a central part of religious teaching.

The antagonists in these hagiographies are, by and large, the same literate elites that the saints parody in their poetry, and the hagiographers dramatize the ineffectual nature of the elites' brand of literacy to great effect. The antagonists usually appear with their respective props in hand: the Muslim *qāẓī* with his *kitāb* (i.e., the Qur'an), the Brahmin pandit with his *pothī*, and the royal emissary with his *pātī* ("missive," from Sanskrit *patrikā*). Time and again, these representatives of the religious and political establishment prove no match for the quick-witted and eloquent saints: while their authority is dependent upon the documents that they hold, the saints' authority lies in their words, issuing spontaneously as an expression of their holy being. For example, in the *Dādū Janm Līlā*, a *qāẓī* arrives from Ajmer (a center of Muslim religious intellectuals), *kitāb* in hand, to accuse Dadu of blasphemy; he denounces Dadu's mixing of Muslim and Hindu belief, asserting that "A Muslim is one who [recites] the *kalamā*, a *kāfir* (infidel) is one who says *rām*" (*musalamāṁna kalamāṁ thaiṁ hoï / rāmu kahaiṁ kāphara haiṁ soï*).[52] Dadu easily turns the *qāẓī*'s words against him with a *caupaī*:

> kāphira so jo bolai kāpha / dila apaṇī nahīṁ rākhai sāpha
> sāṁī kūṁ pahicāṁnai nāṁhī / kūṁḍa kapaṭa sabaü nahī māṁhī
>
> A *kāfir* is he who tells lies (*kāf*),
> who does not keep his heart clean/pure (*sāf*),
> who does not recognize the Lord,
> and who is just a pot of deceit, without character.[53]

The verse not only includes wordplay (the invented etymology of *kāfir* from *kāf*) and alliteration (*kūṁḍa kapaṭ*) but also, with its use of one- and two-syllable words and internal rhyme, possesses a musical quality. (The hagiographer Jangopal in fact took the verse from one of Dadu's hymns.)[54] The aesthetic contrast between the *qāẓī*'s simple, declarative speech and Dadu's rhetorical flourishes emphasizes the contrast between the figure of the *qāẓī*—oratorically flat-footed and devoid of knowledge because he carries it in his hand rather than in his heart—and the figure of the saint—an embodiment of living knowledge, rhetorically charismatic, who carries his authority and knowledge in his heart and on his tongue.

In the evidentiary paradigm of these hagiographies, the spoken word always trumps the written. Writing is fungible and vulnerable to forgery; speech is not. In the *Dādū Janm Līlā*, local Brahmins and *baniyās* (merchants) conspire against Dadu, convincing the *pañcāyat* (village council) and the local official (*sikadār*) to write a decree: "Whoever consorts with Dadu will have to give five hundred rupees [as fine]" (*jo kauū dādū kai jaihai / saikā pāṃca rupaīyā daihai*). The Brahmins and *baniyās* take the edict to the king for ratification only to find that it has miraculously changed: "The official wrote correctly and gave it to the king but the letters (*akhir*) changed when read aloud: 'Whoever does *not* go to Dadu will have to give five hundred rupees'" (*likhi sikadāra chītī daī sāṃcī / akhira phire bahuri bāṃcī /dādū kai joī nahī jaihai / saikā pāṃca rupaīyā daihai*).[55] The Brahmins and *baniyās* enact their power through the inscription of law; however, the unwritten law of God—which is always on the side of the guru—is supreme. Writing is not a dependable source of truth because it is vulnerable to the mischievousness of men; in contrast, spoken utterance is always made before God, and God can intervene if necessary to set things right. In Anantadas's *Kabīr Paracaï*, the wily Brahmins of Banaras forge a letter (*dal*) in Kabir's name, inviting holy men (*sant*) far and wide to attend a religious festival being organized by Kabir. As the monks and holy men arrive in droves, the Brahmins gleefully note their names in a list (*lekhan lehī*), anticipating the shame that will befall Kabir when he confronts a crowd he is not prepared to host. Yet God himself arrives, appearing in the form of Kabir and organizing a tremendously successful *mahotsav*.[56] The Brahmins' forged letter brings Kabir even greater fame, and the list of festival attendees is now a record of Kabir's many admirers among the holy men of north India.

Conspicuously absent from these hagiographies is any mention of the *guṭakās* or song notebooks, most likely because this mode of writing and type of material text artifact are not targets of the *nirguṇ* tradition's broader critique.[57] In the Brahmins' *pothī*, the *qāẓī*'s *kitāb*, and the village council's decree, writing is meant to transform oral utterance by fixing it and giving it a new kind of authority—here, producing something supplementary to the utterance.[58] Even if the written text is read aloud and used as a foundation for extemporaneous exegesis, the fixed text is still understood to precede and supersede oral recitation. In the case of the song notebook, writing is not intended to fix the text but is truly *notational*: it does not constitute a stable "work" that precedes or supersedes the event of oral performance in terms of chronology or authority. A closer look at the material, visual, and textual aspects of these notebooks reveals traces of this relationship between written note and performance event and elucidates how the notebooks functioned as complex textual machines.

"THUS SONG IS WRITTEN": *GUṬAKĀ* NOTEBOOKS

The song notebooks that constitute a large portion of the manuscript collections of north India are the traces of a process through which songs and sayings moved back and forth between performance and paper. The scribbles in *guṭakā*s are a hinge between past and future: they record, often in an ad hoc fashion, verses and utterances heard during oral performances and are used as notes to inform and inspire new performances. The material form of the *guṭakā* mirrors this character, its folios hinging on a threaded binding made along the vertical axis of the paper folios (figs. 2.4 and 2.7). *Guṭakā*s were like perpetual performance machines in which textual material could be collected, recycled, recombined, and then reproduced in performance. Reconstructing how they worked is difficult, in part, because we cannot access the other member of the dyad to which each belonged: the living individual who used the notebook. The notebook was truly a prosthetic in that it was an extension of the performer, and they worked together to produce oral events. Nevertheless, *guṭakā*s themselves carry many traces of the process with which we can partially reconstruct the world in which they functioned.

In the liturgical context of communal singing, it was the sonic dimension of the text that mattered soteriologically and socially, and this is reflected in the form and conventions of the *guṭakā*. Its layout, manner of inscription, and even bindings are geared toward use in creating a particular sensory and social experience through song. Very little, if any, attention is given to visual appearance; indeed, in most notebooks there is little evidence that the scribe cared enough to make his writing legible to others. It seems clear that those who copied the contents—primarily hymns and epigrams—did not intend to circulate them as written works (in all the senses that the term "work" conveys in poststructuralist criticism, especially as a bounded, stable object that "closes in upon a signified").[59]

The notebook's role in musical performance is discernable at even the level of script and orthography. The orthography of *guṭakā* notebooks is often (though not always) distinct from that of the scholastic *pothī* discussed in chapter 3 and the scriptural codices discussed in chapter 4, despite the fact that the same lyrical compositions are often found in all three types of manuscript. Like *pothī*s and scriptural codices, *guṭakā*s are copied in *scriptio continua*, i.e., without leaving blank spaces in between individual words or lemmata. This reflects a culture of reading aloud, a normative practice depicted in the hagiographical literature of the sixteenth through eighteenth centuries: in the process of orally vocalizing the glyphs that he or she sees on the page, the reciter recognizes individual words, making the visual indication of word breaks redundant.[60] In the case of the *guṭakā*, it might be more appropriate to say that the user "sang aloud" from the notebook. The format of *scriptio continua* would not have posed an obstacle to musical performance since the abugida or syllabic character of Nāgarī-derived scripts, including Kaithī, meshes with the syllabic and moraic prosody of *pad*-style hymns. In musical performance, a singer must match syllables to beats, making the question of where one word ends or another begins largely irrelevant.[61]

The feature of *scriptio continua* may have been shared between the *guṭakā* and other types of manuscripts, but there the similarities end. Vernacular and particularly local phonology and pronunciation are more frequently represented in *guṭakā*s than in other types of manuscripts such as *pothī*s and *vāṇī*s (scriptural anthologies). In notebooks like Ms. 26334, the characteristic sounds and features of local speech and pronunciation are represented on the page, often through innovative and novel uses of the script (in Ms. 26334, certain diphthongs, the replacement of nasal consonants with nasalized vowels, the reduplication of consonants, and other features of Rajasthani dialects). In contrast, vernacular texts copied in *pothī* and *vāṇī* manuscripts tend to reflect *tatsama* pronunciation, i.e., the forms of words that follow the phonological and morphological rules of Sanskrit. Unlike *pothī* and *vāṇī* manuscripts, which were overwhelmingly copied in the Nāgarī script, many *guṭakā*s were copied in the Kaithī script or in a mixture of Kaithī and Nāgarī. And whereas *pothī*s and *vāṇī*s were carefully ruled and then inscribed, with the horizontal *rekhā* or top line individually inscribed over each letter, the owners of many *guṭakā*s simply drew a horizontal line across the page from which they "hung" their letters. The owners appear to have been more concerned with quickly and efficiently capturing the sounds of the sung vernacular than with employing "standard" orthography, making the copy visually attractive, or even bothering to make it legible to others. These are all indications that the writings copied in *guṭakā*s were truly notes for oneself.

These notebooks were literally made to travel: their small dimensions (typically between 12 and 24 centimeters in width and 8 and 14 centimeters in height) and sturdy bindings and covers made them far more portable and resistant to wear than other types of manuscripts. *Guṭakā*s were bound using the simple technique of "stab binding" in which paper folios are stacked one on top of another, their inner edges are pierced, and a string is passed through the holes and then tied in a series of weaves and knots along the newly created spine. The resulting single "signature" (or text block) was then pasted or sewn into a cardboard and cloth cover; this often included a flap that folded over both leaves of the cover, protecting the folios inside. Many existing examples also include strings attached to the outside of the binding for tying the notebook shut. Technically speaking, this was the simplest, easiest, and cheapest manner of binding available. Some *guṭakā*s extant today began as collections of loose folios but were later bound—usually *guṭakās* in which text disappears into the fold, the orientation of the text is different on the recto and verso (because the folio was intended to be vertically flipped while reading), or containing multiple hands or multiple types of paper. In contrast, *pothīs* consisting of loose folios had to be kept in a folded cloth (*basta*) or tied between boards of wood or cardboard to prevent their folios from being scattered. Such manuscripts did not lend themselves to being transported or to quick consultation. A *guṭakā* could easily be carried in the hand or in a bag and quickly opened and consulted. Some individuals, after filling their *guṭakās*, apparently chose to have additional folios added: this involved unbinding the original text block, folding more folios around it, then rebinding the new and enlarged text block. Consequently, some *guṭakās* contain earlier blocks of folios "nested" inside later groups. The practice of folding and saddle stitching the folios caused such notebooks to become increasingly round as more folios were added. This is one possible source of the name *guṭakā*, which comes from the Sanskrit *guṭikā*, meaning "lump" or "ball."[62]

The *guṭakā*'s material form constitutes one link between quotidian, vocational forms of writing and the emergent domain of literary inscription in the vernacular. The *guṭakā* was made in the same manner as the *bahī*, a type of ledger kept by clerks, accountants, secretaries, and bureaucrats working in merchant houses, royal courts, and local administrations since the late sultanate period (fig. 2.3).[63] The way the folios were cut, folded, stitched, and bound was essentially the same, giving these genres an almost identical material form (though *bahīs*, on average, tend to be slightly longer than *guṭakās*). They were also inscribed in a similar manner, using the shorthand Kaithī script (or a mixture of Nāgarī and Kaithī scripts) hung from loosely drawn lines.[64] This formal resemblance in turn reflects a major change in the nature of literacy during the sixteenth and seventeenth centuries. Communities with expertise in "mundane" forms of graphic literacy like record keeping and accounting were now participating in the inscription, circulation, and performance of literary and religious works (or, more precisely, of hymns and epigrams that would eventually be accorded the status of literature and scripture). During the late medieval period in north India, graphic literacy in the Nāgarī script had tended to coincide with discursive literacy in Sanskrit, Prakrit, or Apabhramsha: literary and religious specialists in Hindu and Jain communities acquired graphic literacy in the process of learning these cosmopolitan languages and gaining mastery over their various genres. In contrast, the clerical and mercantile communities that inscribed the *bahīs* and *guṭakās* did not generally acquire graphic literacy as part of a "classical" education; instead, they learned it as a technical or vocational skill to be used in the completion of quotidian transactions and tasks. These were not the Persian-literate *munshīs* of the Mughal administrative and intellectual classes who gained literacy in the context of well-defined curriculums of literature, ethics, statecraft, and epistolary writing, or the Brahmin ritual specialists who acquired literacy as part of their training in Sanskrit grammar, hermeneutics, Puranic history, and the like (and who occasionally worked in the administrations of Mughal, Maratha, and Rajput states as well).[65] These were upstarts, communities positioned within the channels of economic and political power but not near their apexes. In the *guṭakās* of the seventeenth and eighteenth centuries, they leveraged their technical skills to gradually enter the privileged spheres of literature and scholarship. In this way, they resembled their *kāyasth* cousins in the Maratha states of western India and in the Mughal administration of the north.

Guṭakās like Ms. 26334 contain fascinating examples of how these clerical and mercantile communities applied their vocational literacy to the inscription of literary material. The third folio contains two examples of *madhyākṣarī* verse (a type of riddle) on its recto and verso. The notebook's owner inscribed the *madhyākṣarī* in tabular form: rather than copying out the verse in *scriptio continua*, he arranged the two verses into ruled rows and columns, using the leftover space of a third column for miscellaneous verse fragments and mantras. He even drew dotted lines between the riddles and their solutions, making it easier to visually collocate the two. These are all features of *bahīs* and other types of documentary writing from the period, not literary manuscripts. The text even runs parallel to the spine of the notebook, as is the convention in *bahīs*. And just as these scribes repurposed their bookkeeping skills for poetry, they repurposed and reused the *guṭakā* itself, often making cardboard (*gattā*) covers and flyleaves from the folios of discarded *bahīs*. Even the textual contents—*sākhī*, *pad*, *kathā*, and *paricay*—were recorded, in a certain sense, to be recycled according to certain codes of performance.

NOTES, NOT WORKS

The material found in *guṭakās* is, in a general sense, notes for performance. The majority consists of *pads* to be sung in communal worship in the manner of hymns (*bhajan*, *kirtan*). Consequently, *guṭakās* give us enormous insight into the repertoires of individual singers and the communities of which they were a part, and provide clues with which to reconstruct performance practices and modes of transmission. In notebooks that we can confidently attribute to members of *nirguṇ* sectarian traditions such as the Dadu Panth, Niranjani Sampraday, Kabir Panth, and Ramsnehi Sampraday, the majority of hymns are the work of associated saints: Kabir, Ravidas, Namdev, Dadu Dayal, Rajjabdas Dadupanthi, Haridas Niranjani, Sevadas Niranjani.[66] Yet many of these notebooks also contain hymns by poets associated with *saguṇ*, Vaishnava traditions, in particular the Krishna-centered traditions of the Braj region: lyrics by Surdas, Paramanandadas, Haridas Radhavallabhi, and Nandadas, as well as Vaishnava poets of a more westerly persuasion like Mirabai and Narasi Mehta. In this way, many *guṭakā*s appear to reflect personal and local repertoires and canons. These are hymns and saints that formed an organic unit in the mind of a singer or, because singing was often a communal activity, in the collective imagination of a social group.[67]

These repertoires look quite different from the canons drawn up by modern scholars. For example, ever since the publication of Ramchandra Shukla's *Hindī Sāhitya Kā Itihās* in 1929, scholars of Hindi have overwhelmingly grouped the saint poets of the fifteenth through eighteenth centuries into two major "streams" or *dhārā*: the *saguṇ bhakti* stream, which includes the cults of Krishna and Ram, and the *nirguṇ sant* stream, which includes Sufi traditions in addition to the poets and communities discussed here.[68] This distinction may correspond roughly to the contours of sectarian canons as they were written down in anthologies dating to the mid-seventeenth century; however, it is *not* reflected in song notebooks, which allow us to trace the popular canon as it was actually sung and heard in the sixteenth, seventeenth, and eighteenth centuries.[69] Evidently, sadhus belonging to *nirguṇ* monastic orders like the Dadu Panth and Niranjani Sampraday sang compositions by poets from both "streams": householders and other individuals with no particular sectarian affiliation were often even more ecumenical in their choices of saints and songs to sing.[70]

In those notebooks for which any method of selection and organization can be deduced, the primary criterion for including and organizing hymns appears to have been their aesthetic and musical qualities, not the theological commitments of their composers. Hymns with similar themes and motifs are often grouped together: expressive modes, such as *virah* (longing for God as a beloved), *vinay* (petitions to God), *smaran* (rememberance of God), and praise for the palliative and redeeming qualities of God's Name (*nām*) function like unwritten rubrics that can accommodate songs by a wide range of poets. Sometimes this even includes poets associated with the courtly tradition of *rīti* poetry, if it happens to deal with devotional themes.[71] For example, the seventeenth-century owner of a *guṭakā* now in the collection of the Nagari Pracharini Sabha once noted down a hymn by Kabir praising the qualities of the Divine Name (*rām*), and right after it a similar hymn by Tulsidas praising the Name.[72] Modern scholarship places Kabir, an implacable partisan of *nirguṇ* theology, and Tulsidas, a steadfast devotee of the *saguṇ* deity King Ramachandra, at opposite ends of the theological and ideological spectrum. Yet in the imagination of this notebook's owner, they were joined by the thing that they had in common: an insistence on the soteriological efficacy of the vocable *rām*. The "logic" at work is performative rather than theo-logical or ideo-logical.

The logic of performance is writ large across the pages of *guṭakā*s: the paratextual element that most often appears is a notation of the raga in which a hymn is to be sung. Usually it comes immediately before the hymn, sometimes highlighted with vermillion or turmeric powder. In some *guṭakā*s, compositions in the same raga are grouped together, suggesting that raga acted as an organizing principle in the mind of the owner. In other *guṭakā*s, the raga changes with each hymn. It is difficult to reconstruct how these ragas sounded; we simply do not know the melodic structures to which names like *dhanāśrī*, *gaurī*, or *bhairavī* referred in the sixteenth through eighteenth centuries.[73] To make matters more complicated, there is little evidence with which to link the ragas in these *guṭakā*s to the musical systems expounded in Sanskrit treatises of the period, like the *Saṅgīta Śiromani* (1425) and *Saṅgīta Darpaṇa* (1625?), or to vernacular musicological treatises composed in courtly settings, like the *Mānakutūhal* (c. 1488). The fact that the owners tended to use the vernacularized terms for ragas (*dhanāsarī* for Sanskrit *dhanāśrī*, *gauṛī* for Sanskrit *gaurī*, and so forth) further suggests that their musical system was vernacular in character, distinct from musicological knowledge as cultivated in royal courts of the period.[74]

Just as the rubric of a raga did not indicate a strict sequence of musical notes but rather a pattern upon which a singer was expected to improvise, so too the lyrics noted in a *guṭakā* provided a loose pattern for improvisation. These notes appear not to have dictated the structure of a hymn as a whole but instead provided material with which singers improvised by shifting, combining, and repeating verses and phrases to achieve different effects. An individual might distinguish the verses with a *visarga* sign (:), with a single or double *daṇḍa* "stick" (|), or by simply leaving a space between characters. Some individuals numbered the verses but many did not, suggesting that for many singers, the order was either arbitrary or subject to change. The fluid structure of these hymns is demonstrated by variations in their form across various *guṭakā* manuscripts. In the amalgamated corpus of several hundred of these notebooks dating to the seventeenth and eighteenth centuries, there is significant variation in the order of verses within a given composition and even in the word order of individual verses. A single hymn will appear in dozens of *guṭakā*s, but the order of its verses will often vary. Even half lines or phrases may be transposed from one verse to another. The *ṭek* or refrain may appear at the beginning of a *pad*, after the first verse, or at the end of a *pad*. This variation reflects the movement of these lyrics back and forth between performance and writing and speaks to the improvisational and emergent character of the *pad* form in the hands of devotional singers.

Fluidity is built into the structure of the lyric form. The prosodic structure of a *pad*, reckoned in terms of syllabic feet (*varṇa*) or morae (*mātra*), led to certain formulaic phrasings in saint poetry. Terms like *rasa rasaïnā* (alchemy of rasa), collocations of terms like *tana mana dhana* (body, mind, and wealth), and poetic tag lines containing the poet's *chāp* or *nom de plume*, on the basis of their syllabic weight, pleasing alliteration, or internal rhyme, functioned like building blocks.[75] These could easily be inserted into different parts of a *pad* and combined with other formulaic phrases to produce new meanings and aesthetic effects. The frequent appearance of particular terms, phrases, and verbal formulae across hundreds of *pads* by dozens of saint-poets reflects these elements' use in composing and recomposing hymns: they not only shaped the way the "original" poet created a *pad* but also aided the performer in remembering and re-presenting the *pad* in new and fresh ways. *Guṭakās* reflect this process: the considerable differences in the order of phrases and verses as they are found in different notebooks illustrate the varying forms in which singers heard, copied, remembered, or performed a hymn.[76] This offers considerable insight into the way singers modified lyric material per the emergent demands of performance: emotional affect, aesthetic effect, rhythmic and musical requirements, and most important, audience response.[77] The saints themselves emphasized the role of emotional and affective experience—*prem, anubhav, rasa*—in bringing about salvation, so it makes sense that performance was dynamically oriented toward producing emotional effects. Inscriptional practices were in turn oriented toward aiding such performances.

In this sense, the world of vernacular song (*gāthā*) was indeed different from the domain of literature proper (*kāvya*), but not exactly in the manner that Sheldon Pollock has theorized. Pollock posits that in first-millennium South Asia, *kāvya* was understood to exist only in Sanskrit, in part because Sanskrit was a written language and writing allowed the literary object to traverse time and space (thereby entering the domain of the cosmopolitan). In contrast, *gāthā* could accommodate *deśī* or vernacular languages because it was located within the realm of the oral (and thus the local). Vernacular *kāvya* was only possible after the vernacular had been committed to writing, first in political inscription (in stone, on copper plates, and so forth) and only later as literature.[78] Yet here we have an example of vernacular *gāthā* circulating in a form of writing not accounted for in Pollock's model. These compositions are manifestly song, not literature: composers nowhere suggest that they are poets (*kavi*) or their compositions poetry (*kavita*). Singers did not inscribe these songs in a manner that would fix or stabilize the text in the fashion of a literary work; nevertheless, writing was integral to the works' circulation across sizeable geographical and temporal distances. These songs entered the domain of writing in the form of notes in notebooks, not as political inscription. And as we will see in subsequent chapters, it was from these notebooks that literary and religious intellectuals would later cull the same songs in order to re-present them as literature and scripture in other types of manuscripts.

This once again demonstrates the relationship among genre, performance modalities, and different types of writing. The notional and fluid mode of writing found in *guṭakā*s suits the *nirguṇ* lyric and the way that it is sung in communal worship; it does not work with, say, the narrative-focused lyrics of contemporary Vaishnava saints like Surdas, Nandadas, Paramandadas, and Tulsidas. As Kenneth Bryant has argued in the context of Surdas's poetry, such narrative-based lyrics accomplish their dramatic and emotional effects by unfolding sequentially over time.[79] They do not lend themselves to the kind of mix-and-match method of inscription and performance described here. Nor does this mode of writing suit other types of texts found in the *guṭakā*s themselves. For example, many notebooks contain *sākhī*s, which sadhus would deploy as teaching aids during *pravacan*.[80] The *sākhī* itself was the basic textual unit, an independent couplet; there are variations in a given *sākhī* across copies, but they are minimal, usually limited to individual lemmata. Since the *sākhī* is compressed, dense, and often telegraphic in character, it almost always requires exegesis on the part of the performer or teacher, which in turn depends heavily on the identity of the authorial persona. It therefore makes sense that sadhus organized the *sākhī*s in their notebooks according to the saints who composed them, prefacing each collection with a simple rubric such as *Kabīr re dohe* ("Kabir's couplets"). Some took the time to number the *sākhī*s of each saint for ease of reference, but others did not. Many notebooks forego the thematic division of a given saint's *sākhī*s, called *aṅg*, which characterizes *nirguṇ* sectarian anthologies.[81] Some sadhus also copied *kathā*s into their notebooks; being narratives, these *kathā*s are largely stable across copies and usually accompanied by a minimum of paratextual material, including verse numbers for ease of navigation.

The *guṭakā* functioned as a briefcase for the *nirguṇ* monk, who often traveled as part of his work, ministering to branches of the community in different cities and towns, participating in annual religious festivals, and sometimes working as a ritual specialist for householder clients. These monks often traveled for nine months out of the year, returning to monastic centers or staying at the houses of lay devotees during the monsoon season, when travel became difficult, using that time to make copies of works for themselves and others.[82] Many *guṭakās* belonging to sadhus of *nirguṇ* communities like the Dadu Panth and Niranjani Sampraday contain vernacular works of astrology (*jyotiṣa*) and augury (*śakunāvalī*). Little is known about these knowledge systems as they existed in vernacular sources of the period, and the notes in *guṭakās* often are only tables, lists, or calculations.[83] Like the other types of notes, these inscriptions and drawings are tools used to remember, to calculate, and to perform ritual acts, and "mean" little on their own without the mediating labor of a human agent. Knowledge was embodied in the person; the content of his notebook was simply his equipment. The presence of such material in *guṭakās* forces us to reconsider conventional wisdom regarding *nirguṇ*-oriented devotional communities: modern scholars have tended to assume that monks of the Dadu Panth, Niranjani Sampraday, Ramsnehi Sampraday, and similar orders eschewed astrological and tantric knowledge systems, forms of the privileged esoteric and ritual knowledge that *nirguṇ* saints critiqued in their poetry.[84] Monks' notebooks reveal a more complex reality: *nirguṇ* sadhus practiced astrology even as they sang and preached a theology that asserted God to be the exclusive agent (*kartā*) of events, valorized affective devotion toward that God over esoteric knowledge, and dismissed the efficacy of ritual. Did these devotional communities then understand the *nirguṇ* saints' critique of such "superstitions" in a manner different than our own? Did they simply ignore or neglect this part of the saints' thought? More inquiry is needed, but initial observations suggest that monastic and householder members of *nirguṇ* devotional traditions understood astrology to be a descriptive science that functioned independently of belief systems like theology and cosmology.[85] They could therefore appropriate the technology of *jyotiṣa* much like they appropriated the technology of yoga, adapting it to meet the particular demands and assumptions of a *nirguṇ bhakti* ontology.[86]

NOTES AND NOTEBOOKS IN EARLY MODERN NORTH INDIA

The case of the *guṭakās* used in *nirguṇ* devotional traditions draws attention to the wider world of notebooks and note-taking in early modern India. Much of the raw material from which modern literary historians have culled works for their literary canons is not books in the modern sense of edited, authorized, "published" works intended for circulation on paper. Instead, this material is the jottings of aficionados, connoisseurs, and performers, snapshots of dynamic texts moving back and forth between performance and paper. The various literary cultures of north India developed different practices of note-taking and different formats for notebooks; these in turn corresponded to the genres, performance practices, and social worlds of their respective literary cultures.[87]

For example, in the Persianate world of letters, the *safīnah* (lit. "boat") or *bayāẓ* (lit. "white") was an indispensable piece of equipment. The *safīnah* or *bayāẓ* was essentially a bound commonplace book used for poetry: *shāgirds* or aspiring poets would use it to copy exemplars of good verse composed by their *ustād* (teacher) and great poets, to draft and revise their own compositions, and to transcribe verses that they heard in *mushā'iras* (gatherings for the recitation of poetry). *Munshīs* and *adībān* (connoisseurs) would use it to memorize verses by classical and contemporary poets and to record insightful or amusing biographical information about them. This set of practices was common across Persianate societies extending from South Asia to Anatolia during the late medieval and early modern period, so the *safīnah* or *bayāẓ* became a recognizable part of a learned individual's personal effects and a kind of "common currency" among littérateurs from the Deccani sultanates in southern India to the lands of the Ottoman Empire. Its close association with *adab* (the cultivation of tastes and manners) gave the notebook the character of an icon: in Mughal, Safavid, and Ottoman paintings of the sixteenth through eighteenth centuries, idealized depictions of nobles, princes, and kings, as well as portraits of historical individuals like the Mughal Emperor Babur, are reading from a *safīnah* or *bayāẓ*, their eyes squinting in concentration or half closed in meditative bliss.[88] With the rise of vernacular genres based on Persian models in the seventeenth and eighteenth centuries, including the *g̲h̲azal*, *mars̲īya*, *naẓm*, and *qasīdah*, the *safīnah/bayāẓ* came to be part of the literary culture of *bhāṣā* as well. Early composers of works in these genres and their audiences were conversant in Persian as well the vernacular, and many early specimens of *safīnah* and *bayāẓ* that contain vernacular poetry also contain compositions in Persian. For example, Ms. 477 of the A. C. Joshi Library is a codex containing the *Padmāvat* along with Persian poetry, a *mas̲navī* in Hindi, miscellaneous Hindi verses, and copious notes made in Persian in the margins.[89] In this context, the distinction between a personal notebook and a book intended for circulation is often subtle. Some poets deliberately crafted their *safīnah* with the intention that they be copied and used by others as literary primers.[90] Others, rather than copying works into their *safīnah* as they came across them, instead chose a set of poets and/or works in advance and copied them—or had them copied by a professional scribe—all at once; such *safīnah* are more like tailor-made literary anthologies than notebooks per se.[91] Yet all of these codices were called *safīnah/bayāẓ*, reflecting a typology of the written word that corresponded to the material form of the artifact as well as to patterns of textual circulation and the social relationships underlying them. This typology is unmarked by the postprint binary of published/unpublished. Individuals frequently lent, borrowed, gifted, and inherited notebooks; this was one of the ways (along with oral performance) through which this literature circulated.[92] It was also the material and social basis for the process through which anthologies of poetry and anecdotes concerning poets called *taẕkirah* (lit. "memory" or "mnemonic") came to be produced for the vernacular in the eighteenth and nineteenth centuries.[93]

Like *safīnah* or *bayāẓ*, the term *guṭakā* refers to a type of textual artifact defined by its material form and by a set of practices of inscription and circulation. These practices could vary from community to community and from individual to individual. For example, in the Sikh community, the term *guṭakā* refers to manuscripts in the same material form as *nirguṇ* notebooks but containing a set of four to six canonical works of the tradition. Occasionally, a guru of a monastic order would have a disciple copy a set of texts into a *guṭakā*-type manuscript for him. Among Hindu and Jain lay communities, *guṭakā*s kept by householders could include devotional hymns, nondevotional literary texts, records of trade transactions, travelogues, doodles, and any other material that the owner needed to remember. One such *guṭakā*, Ms. 12218 in the Rajasthan Oriental Research Institute Jodhpur, appears to be the notebook of a Jain householder: between 1694 and 1716, the owner copied Hindi works of *stuti* (religious eulogy) dedicated to the Jain *tīrthaṅkars*; the *Kalyāṇamandir Bhāṣā* (*Śivamandir*) of Banarasidas, a Hindi transcreation of the Sanskrit *Kalyāṇamandir* hymn; a set of songs about different watches of the night; a list that collates the days of the week with Jain *tīrthaṅkars*, deities, *muṇis*, and ritual observances; a Hindi transcreation of the Sanskrit *Bhaktāmar Stotra*, a Jain liturgical work; a table of financial transactions; a travelogue recounted by one Thakur Balakidas, a *khatri* of Multan, in 1709 VS (1653 CE), and miscellaneous verses in the vernacular.[94] The notebook provides a sense of its owner as a person: he was an observant Jain, organizing his ritual observances according to a prescribed weekly calendar. He was also a lover of poetry: he copied down nondevotional songs and verses that he enjoyed (and perhaps even performed). Finally, he was a merchant who took an interest in the lives and tales of other merchants like Thakur Balakidas and on at least one occasion found it expedient to use his *guṭakā* for recording business transactions.

Every notebook has a history, and for notebooks that are the works of multiple hands, this history can be quite complex. As mentioned earlier, *guṭakā* manuscripts could be enlarged by having their folios removed from their binding, wrapping a new set of folios around this original text block, and rebinding the resulting set of folios. Notebooks that belonged to monks of *nirguṇ* religious orders appear to have largely passed from one monk to another; even when the resulting *guṭakā* is the work of multiple hands, the contents often constitute a theologically or aesthetically coherent whole. Yet it is also not uncommon to find *guṭakās* that combine "layers" of divergent religious material. For example, occasionally *guṭakās* contain both *nirguṇ* and Jain material copied in different hands and during different stages of compilation—a striking phenomenon, because the Jains were frequently the target of criticism in *nirguṇ* traditions like the Dadu Panth and Niranjani Sampraday.[95]

These types of textual artifacts demonstrate the need for a prosopographical approach to literary history that reconstructs "micro" literary and religious canons and aggregates this information in order to trace the contours of larger audience communities. This is one way to produce what Ulrich T. Kragh calls "localized literary histories"—a detailed sense of what people were reading (or listening to) in a given place and time—and reconstruct how texts actually "moved" from person to person and from social context to social context.[96] Such an approach has the potential to reveal reader communities and relationships between social groups and literary genres that are not visible (or indeed thinkable) in literary histories that take genre or sectarian canon as their organizing principle.

SINGING THE SONGS AND TELLING TALES OF THE SAINTS

The *guṭakā* introduced at the beginning of the chapter, Ms. 26334 in the Rajasthan Oriental Research Institute, demonstrates just how rich such microhistories of literature can be. Bound in a cover of cardboard and cloth, bulging a bit with the girth of its more than two hundred folios, this wide-format notebook was copied in both Kaithī and Nāgarī scripts (and occasionally in a script that mixed Kaithī and Nāgarī). Its owner jotted its contents in a rough hand and a notional mode, providing little paratextual material that would help another person to navigate. This was *his* briefcase, *his* ritual equipment. How might we use it to reconstruct the ideological and performative world of *nirguṇ* religious devotion that this anonymous sadhu inhabited?

Early folios in the *guṭakā* contain hymns, introduced summarily with the cursory note *atha saṅgīta likṣateḥ* ("thus is written [*sic*] song") in pseudo or pidgin Sanskrit. Among the many *pads* included are hymns by the *nirguṇ* saints Haridas Niranjani, Kabir, and Jagjivandas Niranjani, but the owner also copied lyrics by the Jain poet Jinharsh. The first hymn by Haridas gives a sense of the emotive and aesthetic qualities that characterize the majority of these hymns:

jaugīyyā tu āvu rai īṇaṁ desa
nījara paṛai kāṁī nāṁtha mhārau
yyaī karu ādesa (ṭek)

kara jauṛī pāīnaṁ paṁṛu re mīlīyyau jāṁṇaṁ ṇaṁ dyau
tumhārai ghara āvu āī dekhī darasa phala lyau 1
āyyau sāṁvuṇaṁ māṁsa sajanī bharā jala thala tāla
jaugīyyau kīṇaṁ bilamāṁī rākhyau birahani behāṁla 2
bichuṛiyyāṁ ke bhava bhayyā re ai dīnaṃdu bhara jāī
aika berī kauü daunaṁ pherī naṁgara hamārai āī
jaugīyyā tu āvu rai īṇaṁ desa 3
vā muratī maṁnaṁ mau basī re cīta tai dura naṁ jātha
kevula kai naṁhī aura kauī darasaṇaṁ dehau nātha
jaugīyyā tu āvu rai īnaṁ desa
nījara paṛai kāī nāṁtha mhārau huyyaī karu ādesa 4

Yogi, come to this land.
Won't you be near me, my lord?
This is my request. (refrain)

Joining my hands, I fall at your feet.
    Having found you, I won't let you go.
I will come to your house,
    and having seen you, will get the fruits of *darśan*. v 1

Oh girlfriend, the rainy month of *sāvan* has come,
    the lakes and ponds are all full.
Yogi, why do you tarry?
    This *virahinī* is beside herself. v 2

The feeling of separation has arisen.
    Oh sun, please rise!
And circling one time in [your] loop,
    come to my town.
Yogi, come to this land. v 3

That figure has settled in my mind,
    and never leaves my consciousness.
There is no other, only [you].
    Give [me] *darśan*, oh lord.

Yogi, come to this land.
Won't you stay near me, my lord?
This is my only request. V 4

The hymn is metaphorical, drawing on the rich motif of the *virahiṇī*, a woman suffering the pangs of separation from her beloved. Here, the *virahinī* or individual soul longs to be reunited with the yogi, i.e., God. There is little that is explicitly "devotional"; the term *nāth* ("lord") can just as easily refer to a husband or lover as to God, and *darśan* can refer to the sight of any person or thing, not only God. The "point" of the *pad* is not to express a theological, cosmological, or didactic *meaning*, but rather to elicit a devotional *feeling*: the singer (who, in the antiphonal singing practices of religious gatherings, would have been the sadhu as well as his audience) sings in the voice of the *virahiṇī*, simultaneously witnessing and vicariously experiencing her restlessness and suffering. As she sings about longing for her lover, the performer inhabits her persona, separated from and restless for union with God. This is precisely the affective "experience"—the *anubhav* discussed at the beginning of the chapter—that the *nirguṇ* saints valorize over the mechanical practice of book learning.

The performative logic of singing, reciting, and hearing about God in order to access this experience and be saved from the cycle of birth and death is at work in all the hymns in the manuscript, including verses in praise of the Name, declarations of love for Hari (God), warnings against falling into the trap of *māyā* (illusion), and references to the subtle body that is manipulated through yogic practice. Among these is a *pad* attributed to Kabir that states this logic explicitly:

kabīra karamaṁ kiyā parabata jītā līyyā aikahī nāṁvaṁ
rāī māṁnaṁ baisanarā jālata ketā gāṁvaṁ (1)
kabīra pada gāṁyyā maṁnaṁ haraṣīyyāṁ sākhī kahāṁ āṁṇaṃda
auta naṁ nāṁva naṁ jāṁṇīyyāṁ taba laga gala mai phaṁda (2)

Kabir accomplished a mountain of works
and was victorious through the One Name.
How many villages burned down,
as if by one little flame! V 1

Kabir sang a *pad* and his heart became glad,
reciting a *sākhī*, he became blissful.
If you don't know the avatar or the Name,
that's when the noose goes around [your] neck. V 2

For Kabir, it is not reading the *śāstras*, the *sūtras*, the *purāṇas*, or any other religious work that brings salvation but rather speaking a single word: the Name of God. That little, two-syllable vocable (*rā-ma*), that tiny flame, burns all karmic bonds. One attains salvation in the active process of singing, not in the passive process of reading: one sings a hymn (*pad gāṁyyā*) and recites an epigram (*sākhī kahāṁ*) and thus attains happiness and bliss (*haraṣīyyāṁ, āṁṇaṃda*). Conversely, not knowing God's Name or His deeds is essentially a death sentence.

Kabir and his fellow *nirguṇ* saints, being model devotees of God, not only preach this mode of worship but also demonstrate it, both in their poetry and as idealized figures in hagiographical works. The hymn quoted above manages to work in both modes simultaneously: Kabir's voice exhorts the listener to do as he does, recite God's name and sing his praises; at the same time, the use of the third person allows the verses to be read as a story *about* Kabir and his path to salvation.[97] To sing these verses was to "make present" the saint through his voice and to recount the truth of his life and spiritual achievements—in other words, to "witness" Kabir, his speech, and his deeds. Each time the owner of this notebook and his audience sang these verses, they bore witness to this truth made manifest (once again) through their own speech.

The point of this and other hymns was to make manifest the saints and their truth, and to effect an affective change in the participants in *satsaṅg* (to generate within them the feeling of love for God) through the dynamic and emergent practice of sung performance. The owner of the notebook inscribed these lyrics to achieve that end. This means that he had little need for the conventions that characterized fixed literary texts, such as verse numbers, section headings, and rubrics. In the sections of the manuscript that contain hymns, he used these elements sparingly and inconsistently (if at all). He transcribed the hymns in an idiosyncratic manner that reflected the way they were sung. The language, even in the compositions by Kabir, a saint from Banaras in the east, is marked by the phonology and morphology of Marwari, the spoken vernacular of central Rajasthan.[98] The scribe appears to have been unconcerned with preserving the prosody of the hymns "on the page," insofar as he transcribed words phonetically and interpolated sounds and syllables that "broke" the poetic meter.[99] Instead, it seems that he transcribed these pieces *as they sounded* to him and as they would be sung by him and by others, using local pronunciation and diction. Even the overall structure as transcribed reflects musical performance: for example, in the hymn by Haridas Niranjani, the scribe has included part of the refrain in his transcription of the third and fourth verses. This reflects how *pads* were likely sung but is distinct from the conventional practice in contemporary *pothī* manuscripts of literary and religious works, in which the refrain is transcribed just once at the beginning of each *pad*.[100] Even the punctuation is idiosyncratic: in some places he marks each half-line of verse and in other places only whole verses, using circles, a *visarga* mark, or sometimes just an empty space. Sometimes he marks refrains by writing *ṭek* ("refrain") and sometimes he does not. No pattern or system is apparent to a reader, because the manuscript was never intended to be "read" in the first place, at least not in the modern sense and not by anyone other than the scribe himself. It was intended to help the scribe create moments of rapture, affection, and transcendence in his listeners and fellow singers during the oral performance events that the saints argued were so critical for the transmission of knowledge, the attainment of spiritual goals, and the formation of a community of the righteous—the *sādhu jan* or "righteous people."

In the *satsaṅg* gatherings that created and cemented bonds among members of this community, singing was perhaps the central but certainly not the only such oral performance event. Storytelling and preaching were also important activities at *mahotsav*s, and the owner of Ms. 26334 apparently led devotees in these as well. His *guṭakā* contains the *Śrī Dhruv Carit*, a vernacular retelling of the story of Vishnu's exemplary devotee, Dhruv, composed by Jangopal, the author of the *Dādū Janm Līlā*. The *kathā*, when recited, would have delighted listeners with miraculous tales of how God protects his devotees. There is also a section of folios simply titled *duhā vupadeś aṅg kā*, "couplets on didactic [*sic*] themes," containing *sākhī*s covering a wide range of topics related to knowing, loving, and serving God. These verses are numbered—perhaps to aid the owner in locating a particular verse—but do not follow any conventional organizational scheme. They instead appear to have been chosen and arranged by the scribe himself as he compiled his teaching materials. Like Kabir, Dadu, Haridas, and the great saints and gurus who had come before him, he would have taught his listeners by reciting the couplets and then expounding upon their meaning and significance. In this way, he and his audiences reenacted the scenes of saints and disciples depicted in the hagiographical literature recited.

Yet this sadhu also engaged in ritual and vocational activities that are not typically associated with *nirguṇ* beliefs and practices. His *guṭakā* contains astrological notes as well as spells, magic recipes, and diagrams (*yantra*) used in yogic and tantric practices. Some of the more remarkable instances include Islamicate magic squares containing Arabic numerals, an anthropomorphic diagram inscribed with letters of the Arabic alphabet, an inscription of the *basmalah*, and a spell in the Arabic script (fig. 2.8). The shaky, tentative hand suggests that the scribe imitated a written model without necessarily being able to read the Arabic script.[101] Nevertheless, these scribbles are traces of exchanges among *nirguṇ* monks, tantric practitioners, and Muslim esoteric specialists during the seventeenth century. Besides religious, ritual, and esoteric material, the owner copied folk narratives, oral epics, and riddles into his notebook: a version of the Rajasthani romance *Ḍholā Mārū*, a regional *pem-kathā* called the *Kutub Śatak*, a *bārah-māsā* ("twelve month") poem describing a *virahiṇī*'s longing for her lover during the various seasons, and *madhyākṣarī* riddles in verse. The sadhu who copied the notebook does not appear to conform to our image of the typical *nirguṇ* devotee, skeptical of ritual, critical of existing social structures (such as those glorified in the *Ḍholā Mārū* narrative), dismissive of "decadent" erotic poetry (like that found in the *bārah-māsā*), and openly hostile toward arcane esoteric knowledge systems like those associated with tantra, *'ilm-i g̱haibī* (occult sciences), or *jādū-ṭonā* (magic). Was he a professional bard in addition to being a religious teacher? Did he make money by performing astrological calculations and protective spells for clients? Did he simply copy works that he enjoyed? One thing is clear: this sadhu and his notebook, and the hundreds or possibly thousands of similar notebooks that lie unexamined in archives across north India, compel us to reexamine our assumptions regarding the relationship between theological commitment and everyday praxis among *bhakti* communities in early modern India.

These *guṭakā*s also encourage us to rethink histories of precolonial Hindi literature that conflate generic and social distinctions. The conventional taxonomy since the publication of Shukla's *Hindī Sāhitya Kā Itihās* in 1929 posits a separate audience for each major literary tradition, associating subaltern devotees and monks with *nirguṇ bhakti* poetry, followers of popular Vaishnavism with *saguṇ bhakti* poetry, Sufis with *prem-kathā*s, and feudal elites with heroic epics and *rīti* poetry. *Guṭakā*s and similar notebooks reveal much more complex relationships between genres, religious traditions, and social groups. This complexity increases over time: this particular *guṭakā*, once it left the hands of its first owner, apparently passed through the hands of other individuals, accumulating even more diverse content along the way. The folios appended later contain couplets by Biharilal (1595–1663), court poet to Raja Jaisingh of Amber; the narrative of Chandan Maliyagiri (a folk hero of Rajasthan), a short liturgical text dedicated to the Jain *tīrthaṅkar* Parshvanath; and even a sketch of a Jain *tīrthaṅkar* cut out from another manuscript and pasted onto one of the *guṭakā*'s folios. What modes and patterns of circulation produced such a composite collection, and what kinds of individuals found it worthwhile to collect (if not also perform) such a wide variety of works? Such questions demand a mode of literary historiography that takes as its starting point neither genre nor literary tradition but rather the written artifact itself, the most intimate trace of the lived literary world.

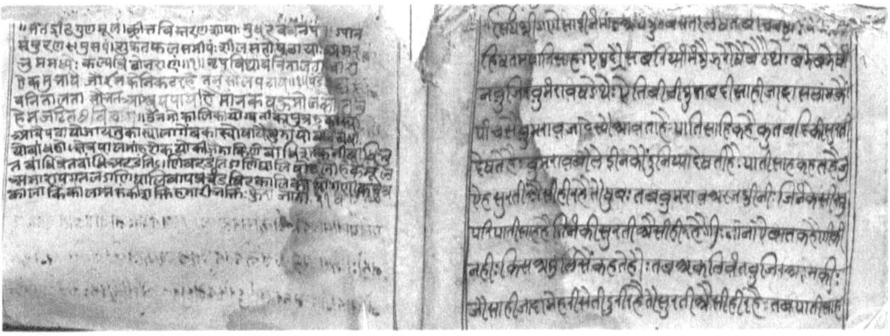

FIGURE 2.1 A late seventeenth-century *guṭakā* containing multiple hymns, miscellaneous verses, narratives, mantras, spells, and other material. On the left-hand folio are a fragment of a *kathā* narrative work and an invocation to a deity of the *śākta* pantheon in the Nāgarī script; on the right-hand folio is a copy of the *Kutub Śatak* narrative in a mixture of the Nāgarī and Kaithī scripts.

Ms. 26334, Rajasthan Oriental Research Institute, Jodhpur. Folios unnumbered

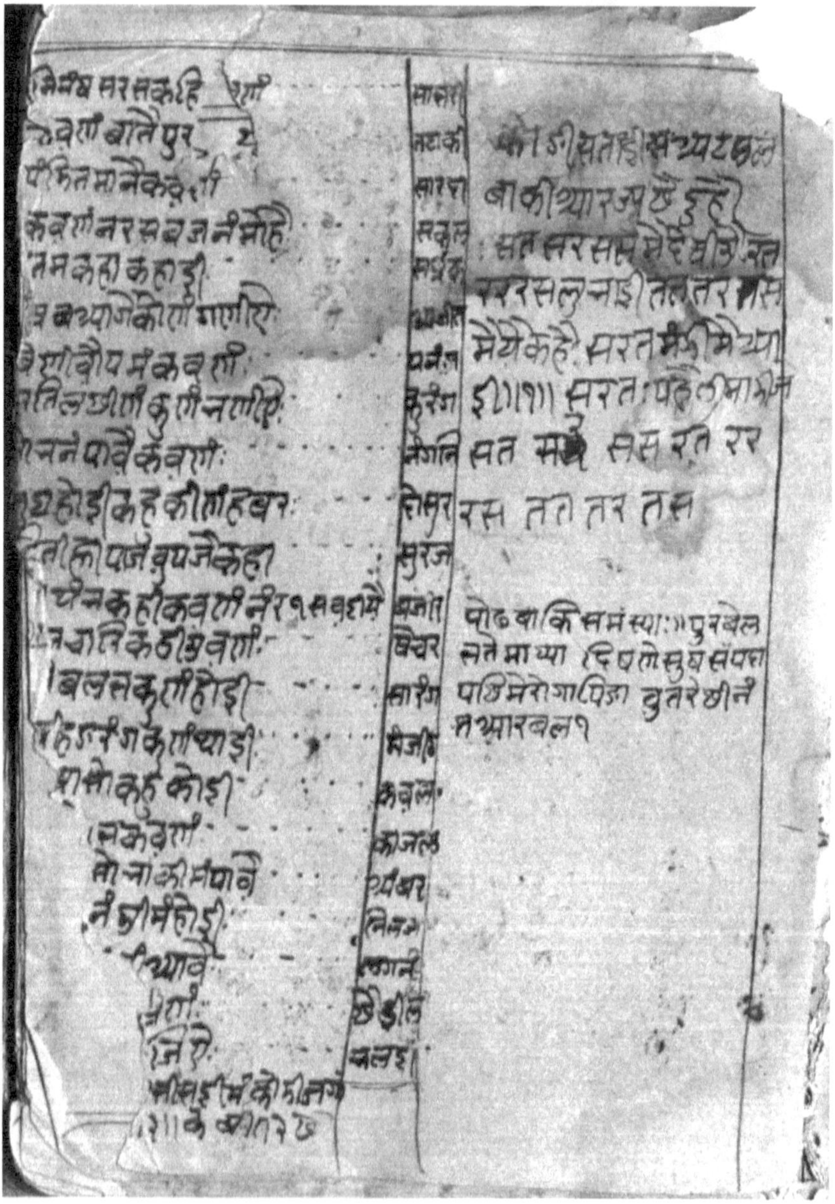

FIGURE 2.2 A table containing a *madhyākṣarī* riddle verse in the left-hand column and a verse fragment and mantra in the right-hand column

Ms. 26334, Rajasthan Oriental Research Institute, Jodhpur. Folio unnumbered

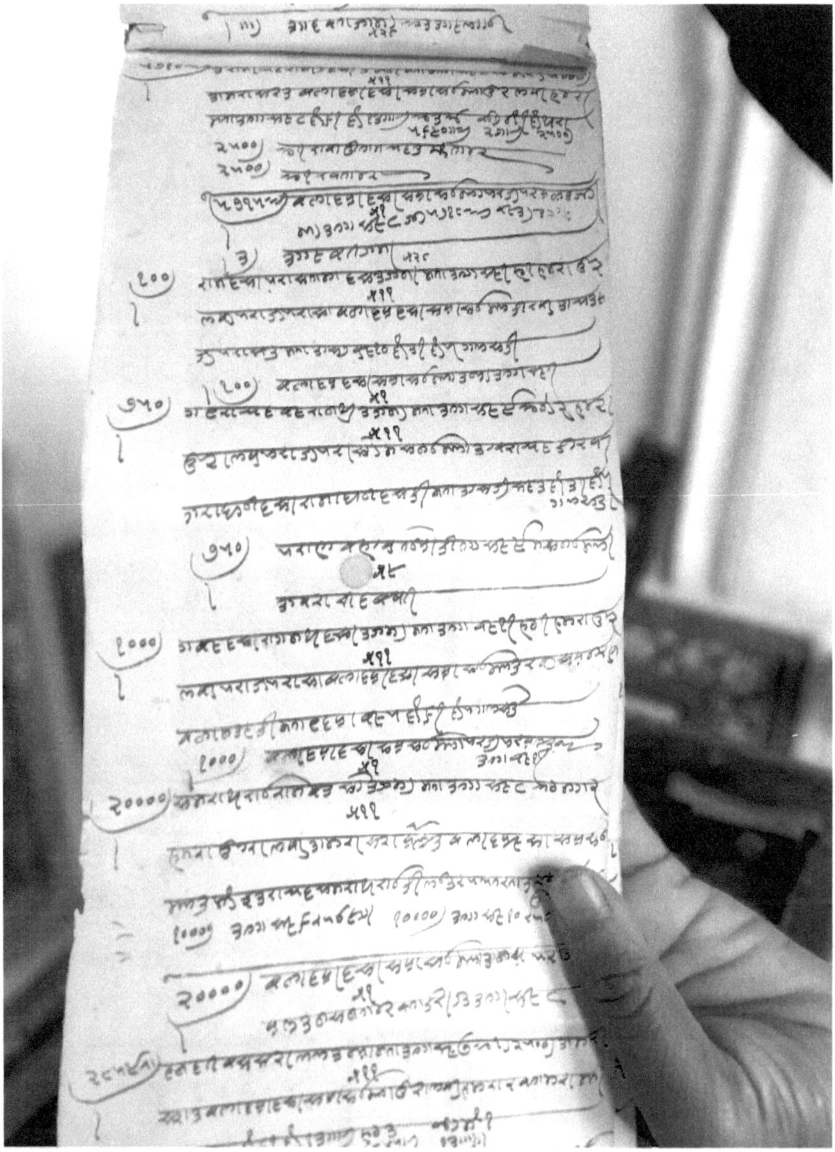

FIGURE 2.3 A *bahī* record book, Morarkaji Haveli, Navalgarh, Rajasthan

Photograph courtesy of Manpreet Kaur

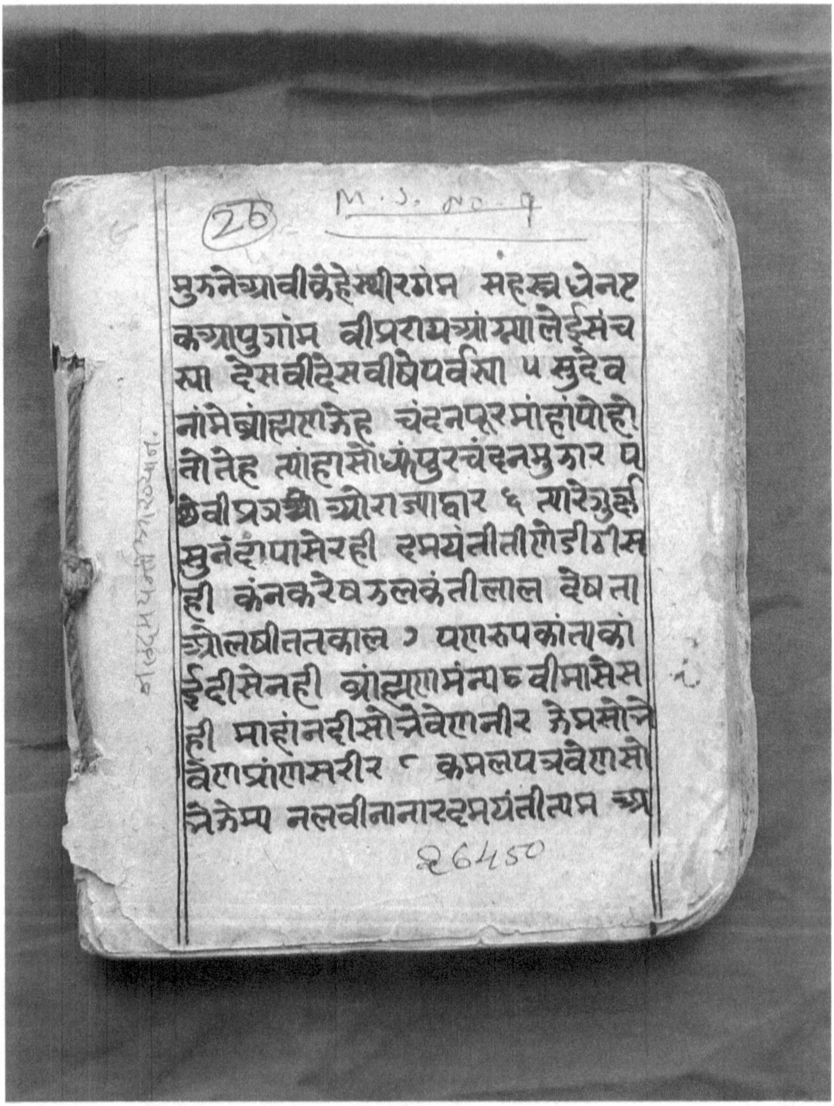

FIGURE 2.4 Ms. 26450, Oriental Institute, Maharaja Sayajirao University, Baroda. Binding of a *guṭakā* notebook (copied 1665–1670 CE). Note the simple saddle-stitch binding with thick thread through a single signature of folios.

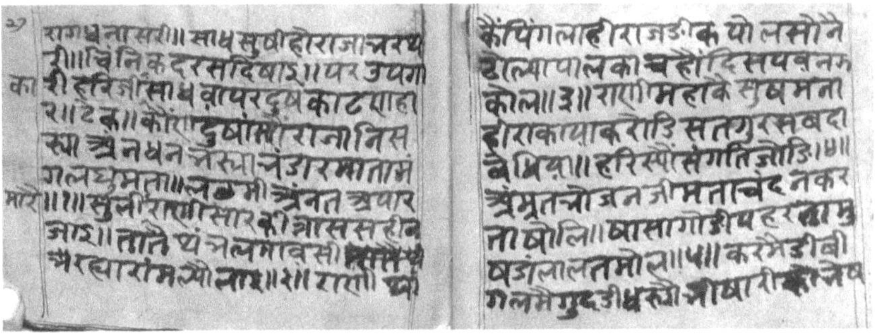

FIGURE 2.5 *Guṭakā* folios containing hymns by Dadu Dayal. The raga, *dhanāsarī* (Sanskrit *dhanaśrī*), is noted in the top left-hand corner of the left-hand folio and is highlighted with red powder. The end of each verse within a hymn is marked by the presence of two *virām cinhā* or *daṇḍa* (vertical lines) and is numbered. Corrections are noted in the left margin of the left-hand folio.

Ms. 14362, Rajasthan Oriental Research Institute, Jodhpur, Folios 27b and 28a

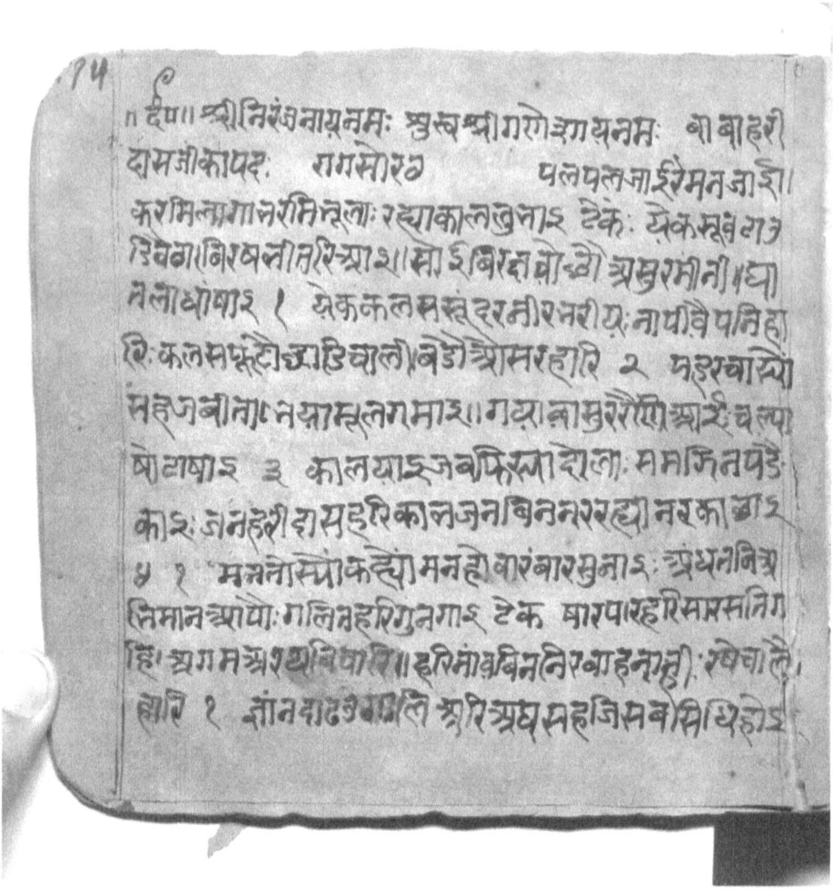

FIGURE 2.6 Ms. 11583 (1672 CE?), Rajasthan Oriental Research Institute, Folio 20b. The folio begins with the auspicious *bhālā* symbol, an invocation to God (Niranjan) and Ganesha, and the heading "*Pads* of Baba Haridas," followed by a notation of the raga: *soraṭha*. The owner of the *guṭakā* has marked individual verses and half lines by leaving a space and/or inscribing a *visarga* (:) at the end of a poetic line; however, he has not been consistent in this practice (or in numbering the verses) across the manuscript.

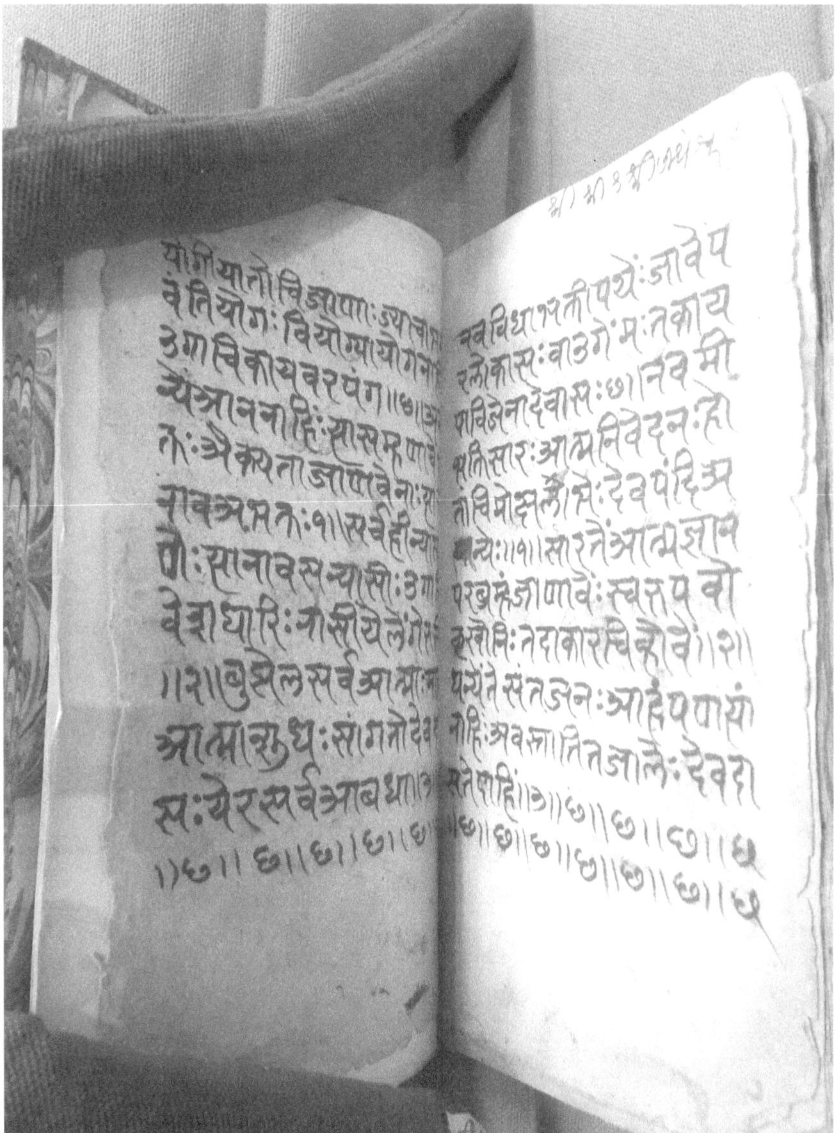

FIGURE 2.7 Ms. Indien 698, Bibliothèque nationale de France. The notebook's owner has inscribed *śrī* (signifying radiance, glory, and/or Lakṣmī) multiple times along the upper margin of the right-hand folio and has filled the leftover space in the final lines of each folio with the auspicious syllable *cha*.

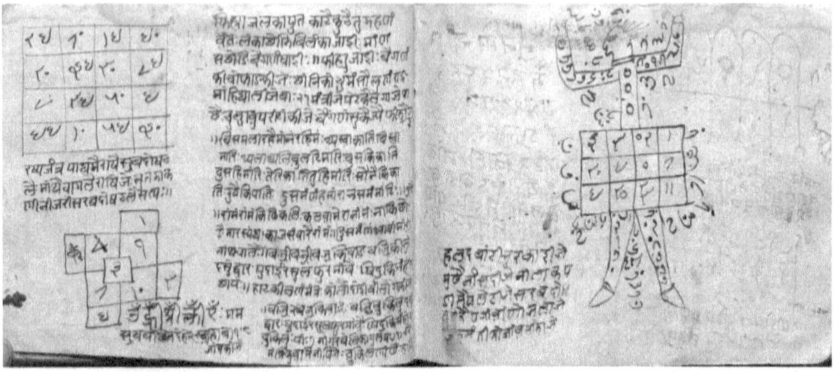

FIGURE 2.8 Two folios from Ms. 26334, Rajasthan Oriental Research Institute, Jodhpur. The left-hand folio contains two magic squares, part of a recipe to attain yogic powers, and a versified spell preceded by the *basmalah* in Nāgarī script. The right-hand folio contains an anthropomorphic diagram with letters of the Arabic alphabet inscribed around the figure and a magic square in the center of the figure's body.

3

Pothīs, Pandits, and Princes

paṇḍita so ju paḍhai yaha pothī
jā maiṁ brahma bicāra nirantara aura bāt jānauṁ saba thothī

A pandit is he that studies this *book:*
in whom there is constant thought of Brahma,
and who knows all other matters to be trivial.

—Sundardas (1596–1689), *Pad* 31, *Sundar Granthāvalī*, ed. Pandit Harinarayan Sharma

In late May 1830 CE, the monk Rupdas Niranjani was apparently tired. He had just finished copying a *pothī* of ninety-one folios (one hundred and eighty-two pages). The manuscript contained seven different works of religious scholarship in Sanskrit and in Hindi. In the early folios, Rupdas's letters are elegantly inscribed with tight strokes and arranged in unerringly straight lines of equal length; however, by the last several folios, his pen strokes have become looser, and occasionally a line of text sags slightly in the middle like a clothesline. Despite his fatigue, Rupdas closed the manuscript with all the conventions appropriate to a proper "book" containing scholastic or religious material. On the final folios, he penned a colophon in alternating lines of red and black ink. He noted the date, the day of the week, and even the location of Venus within Taurus, then his location: the hermitage (*dhām*, lit. "abode") of Haridas Niranjani, in the town of Didwana. He gave the name of the individual for whom he copied the *pothī* (one Baldev) and his own name, but only after first giving the name of his guru, Harkishandas, with requisite laudations (*śrī śrī* 108 *śrī*). Rupdas identified himself as Harkishandas's disciple (Hindi *siṣa*, from Sanskrit *śiṣya*), servant (*khānajād*, Persian *k̲h̲ānazād*), and slave (*gulām*, Persian *g̲h̲ulām*), and recorded the name of the particular Niranjani saint from which his own guru-disciple lineage sprang, Khemdas. He closed the manuscript with an invocation to Ram and a request that Ram bless him with auspiciousness. Rupdas inscribed all of this in a language that was neither Sanskrit nor Hindi nor the local language of Marwari, but rather a macaronic combination of all three.[1]

On every folio of the manuscript, Rupdas followed the textual and visual conventions of the *pothī*, a format that had already been in use for several centuries, across several regions, and in multiple languages including Sanskrit, Prakrit, and Apabhramsha. Over the previous three centuries, these conventions had been gradually adopted in copies of works in Hindi, Punjabi, Gujarati, and Bengali as well. The conventions included the wide, "landscape" proportions of the unbound folios, the practice of inscribing the text on each side of a folio in opposite orientations (so that the folio could be flipped along the long upper edge), the folio numbers and abbreviated section headings inscribed in the upper left margins, and the use of red ink for paratextual material. Even the double rule lines Rupdas inscribed in the margins followed a model that had been used in paper copies of Sanskrit, Prakrit, and Apabhramsha works since the fourteenth century (and in the palm leaf manuscripts that preceded them).[2] Yet there are also elements that mark this particular *pothī* as part of "vernacular" manuscript culture. The first is the language used for the paratextual material, which mostly follows the grammar and morphology of Hindi but evokes the "feel" of Sanskrit through long compounds and a few formulaic phrases (for example, *gaṇeśāya namaḥ* "obeisance to Ganesha," *arjuna uvāca* "Arjuna spoke"). The linguistic purity of the paratextual material appears to have been less important to Rupdas and his readers than the simple fact that it was different from the language of the works themselves, standing out just as the red ink of these rubrics stood out from the blocks of body text inscribed in black ink.

Rupdas's adherence to these conventions tells us something important about him and the social and intellectual context in which he worked. While Rupdas's Sanskrit was not perfect, he was competent enough to correct minor errors as he copied works in the language; his various patrons were clearly confident in his abilities. Rupdas's use of pidgin Sanskrit-Hindi in the paratextual material therefore suggests not a lack of linguistic knowledge but a diligent adherence to norms of inscription. He knew these conventions from more than forty years of experience copying manuscripts for gurus and devotees in cities and towns across the region: manuscripts dating back to at least VS 1845 (1788/1789 CE) and containing his "signature" (his name together with his guru-disciple lineage), are scattered in government and sectarian libraries across Rajasthan. Rupdas performed this scribal labor as part of his monastic duties: it was one way he rendered *sevā* (service) to the senior Niranjani monks he studied under and served. This labor was also part of his professional activity and identity: copying, editing, and presenting copies of scholastic and religious works in exchange for pedagogical guidance, political patronage, or simply money, Rupdas and monks like him built and maintained the networks of vernacular intellectuals that arose in the late sixteenth century and continued to thrive through the late nineteenth century, until printing in Hindi eventually reshaped the landscape of written discourse.

A LITERARY AND INTELLECTUAL COMMUNITY ON PAPER

In a limited sense, the *pothī* was similar to the "book" as we think of it in today's postprint world: a copy of a self-contained, unified work intended to circulate *in writing* among an imagined community of readers. Part of what constitutes that community are shared expectations of how a book should look, feel, and be used. Yet in important respects, the *pothī* differed markedly from our contemporary notion of the book: for example, its folios were never bound, so the manner in which it was physically held, recited from, stored, and organized in libraries was quite different from that of the codex. Furthermore, the ways the *pothī* was used in pedagogical, musical, and literary performance bear a greater resemblance to the vocalized reading practices (i.e., reading aloud) of medieval and early modern Europe and the Islamicate Middle East and Central Asia than to the silent reading that is the norm today.[3] Vernacular epics like the *Rāmacaritamānas* (Lake of the Deeds of Rama, 1574) of Tulsidas, courtly poetry like the *Satasaī* (Seven Hundred Verses, c. 1662) of Biharilal, works of literary theory and criticism like the *Rasikapriyā* (Beloved of Connoisseurs, 1591) of Keshavdas, and commentaries and translations of Sanskrit works like the *Bhagavadgītā*, *Bhāgavata Purāṇa*, and the *Śatakatraya* of Bhartrihari were transmitted on paper across vast distances and over centuries, but ultimately they were experienced as orally recited verse or as music in royal courts, *pāṭhaśālā* (schools), *maṭh* (monasteries), and gatherings of religious devotees or literary aficionados. At the same time, the material artifact of the *pothī* itself served as a token or type of currency in intellectual and social exchanges between intellectuals, pedagogues, students, and representatives of political authority.

This scene of writing closely corresponds to the model of vernacularization proposed by Pollock, in which the reinvention of everyday language as a medium for literary and intellectual exchange is made possible by the double developments of literization and literarization.[4] The commitment of literary and scholastic works to writing (literization) allowed them to circulate as stable texts across time and space and to be incorporated into practices of bibliophilia and connoisseurship among elite audiences. Inscribing a Hindi work onto paper made it something that could travel and could be illustrated, annotated, commissioned, collected, valued, and exchanged. The fact that these texts were modeled to a significant extent on genres in the privileged language of Sanskrit (literarization) made it possible for readers to use them in the aesthetic and affective regimes of pleasure connected with those genres. Elite audiences were primed to develop an appreciation for *itihās* (epic), *nīti* (ethics or statecraft), *kāvya śāstra* (literary theory), and similar genres in Hindi because they already knew how to appreciate those genres in Sanskrit. Once again, we can extend Pollock's theory into the domain of material texts—but not without significant modification. Just as vernacular intellectuals emulated the conventions of genres found in Sanskrit, Prakrit, and Apabhramsha, scribes emulated the material and visual conventions of the manuscripts in which works of those genres were found. Nevertheless, there is evidence of the experimentation, mixing, and hybridity that characterize vernacular manuscript culture in everything from the orientation of folios to the language of rubrics.

As a trace of intellectual life in the vernacular from the seventeenth through early nineteenth centuries, *pothī*s and the works contained within them contradict conventional wisdom regarding the historical development of Hindi and the process of vernacularization more generally. The following analysis centers primarily on the Dadu Panth, Niranjani Panth, and similar communities within the *nirguṇ* devotional tradition because even though they are generally understood by modern scholars to have eschewed scholasticism, the manuscript record reveals that their monks (and sometimes their lay devotees) were sedulously engaged in composing, circulating, and teaching works of scholarship in a refined register of Hindi. The extent of vernacular education during the early modern period as reflected in the manuscript archive forces us to reconsider historiography that locates the origins of vernacular education in the colonial period, with the founding of Fort William College in Calcutta in 1800 and subsequent efforts by colonial administrators to construct curricula and materials for the teaching of Hindi.[5] The manuscript record also contradicts conventional distinctions between popular, religious writings and courtly literature by revealing that the monks of these religious sects were reading the literary and philosophical works of court pandits, while their own original works ended up in the libraries of pandits, princes, and kings.

BHĀṢĀ, KĀVYA, ŚĀSTRA: LITERATURE AND SCHOLARSHIP IN THE VERNACULAR

The construction of new literary and scholastic genres in Hindi during the sixteenth and seventeenth centuries involved fusing, shifting, and innovating upon generic distinctions and conventions; this also led to the creation of new types of intellectuals and intellectual networks. These were vernacular intellectuals in that they composed in Hindi, even if they were also conversant in Sanskrit. Some hailed from the communities of pandits and *ustād*s that had previously monopolized the spheres of scholarship and religious authority at royal courts and at more provincial sites of political and religious power like the *koṭ* (fort of a local lord), *qaṣbah* (provincial town), *maṭh*, or local temple.[6] Others among these new intellectuals represented an insurgent intellectual and social force encroaching on the domain of Brahmin and *'ulamah* authority; these included the merchant and clerical castes and communities that were gradually applying their vocational forms of literacy to the composition, inscription, and circulation of literature and often participated in *nirguṇ* religious communities. While the former, more elite type of vernacular intellectual has recently received scholarly attention, the latter, more provincial "upstarts" have remained largely neglected.[7] Consulting the manuscript archive sheds considerable light on this latter group, revealing that provincial religious intellectuals shared many of the same concerns and strategies as their more elite counterparts and directly engaged with them, in the process building a vast and complex intellectual network.

Allison Busch elegantly diagnosed the new intellectuals' condition as "the anxiety of innovation."[8] Poets and pedagogues composing at Mughal and Rajput courts were acutely aware of the novelty of using the vernacular for literary and intellectual thought, so even while emphasizing the "freshness" of their compositions, these poets insisted on those compositions' grounding in the Sanskritic tradition. How to resolve this apparent contradiction? Busch identifies a solution in the verbal formula *apanī mati anusār*, "according to my understanding." This phrase shows up in the writings of the pioneers of literary theory and rhetoric in Hindi, including Keshavadas (1555–1617), Cintamani Tripathi (fl. 1670), and Matiram (fl. 1620–1675). It most often appears at critical moments in which composers of *rīti granth*s (treatises on literary style) depart from or modify a concept as it has been inherited from the Sanskrit tradition, submitting that they have simply re-presented the knowledge of Sanskrit works "according to [their] understanding."[9] This verbal formula articulates a particular kind of relationship between the speaker and the Sanskrit tradition: the poet humbly but firmly attests that he is not only familiar with but also participates in that tradition, having reflected upon and digested its material using the faculty of his intellect (*mati*). The formula posits an agentive and mediating role for the vernacular scholar: he presents the ideas of the Sanskrit tradition according to (*anusār*) his *own* (*apnī*) understanding. The new intellectuals in Hindi thus positioned themselves as mediums who gave early modern audiences (who venerated Sanskrit intellectual traditions but were more comfortable in the vernacular) access to the knowledge systems contained in Sanskrit.

One consequence of this fusing of Sanskrit material with vernacular sensibilities was the creation of new kinds of texts and modes of scholastic inquiry. Until recently, the originality of Hindi scholastic works in the precolonial period has been largely ignored by modern scholars, who have tended to dismiss these texts on theology, philosophy, and most important, literary theory—the aforementioned *rīti granth* genre—as poor regurgitations of Sanskrit works and theories. On the contrary, even though vernacular intellectuals modeled aspects of their writing on Sanskrit archetypes, they altered and expanded the scope of existing genres and conventions. They mixed elements adopted from Sanskrit literary and scholastic writing with rhetorical strategies and aesthetic techniques taken from the vernacular genres that had emerged over the past few centuries, including those found in the *pad* and *sākhī* genres. Some of these writers innovated their own original modes of analysis and exposition along the way. The *rīti granth* itself is an example of the tendency in the vernacular to mix and adapt elements from multiple sources and traditions. It takes its manner of exposition largely from Sanskrit *alaṁkāra-śāstra* (the science of rhetorical and poetic devices), giving a technical definition (*lakṣaṇa*) for each literary trope or rhetorical device followed by an example (*udāharaṇa*) used in an original verse of poetry. Authors of *rīti granth*s sometimes even adopted the taxonomy of such tropes and devices wholesale from well-known Sanskrit works.[10] Yet this is where the similarities with Sanskrit *alaṁkāra-śāstra* end. Hindi composers like Keshavdas, Cintamani, and Jasvant Singh composed their *rīti granth*s—definitions, examples, and all—completely in verse, whereas Sanskrit composers of *alaṁkāra-śāstra* frequently used prose to present their ideas. These Hindi poeticians addressed topics like *chanda-śāstra* (the science of prosody) and *alaṁkāra-śāstra* in the same work, something rarely done by their Sanskrit counterparts. They also expanded existing literary typologies far beyond their treatment in Sanskrit: one was the classification of literary heroines (*nāyikā-bheda*), which Hindi poets developed into an independent literary genre in its own right.[11] Most strikingly, the authors of *rīti granth*s composed large amounts of original poetry to illustrate the poetic tropes and figures that they defined—far more than the authors of Sanskrit works of literary theory typically did. Thus the *rīti granth*—the most technically sophisticated expression of belles lettres in precolonial Hindi (and therefore the most disparaged by many modern Hindi critics)—was a hybrid cultural production in terms of its conceptual material, form, and style.

VERNACULAR INTELLECTUALS BEYOND THE ROYAL COURT

This negotiation among tradition, innovation, and invention extended beyond the genre of the *rīti granth* to other forms of literary and scholastic writing in the vernacular. It also extended beyond the social sphere of courtly literati and political elites (a more heterogenous and dispersed group than the English term "courtly" might suggest) to include scholars, intellectuals, and littérateurs from monastic orders, merchant clans, and clerical communities located in small cities, *qaṣbah*s, and villages across north India. Beginning at the turn of the seventeenth century, composers working within the devotional and social milieu of *bhakti* religious communities expanded the scope of what could be called *kāvya* by redefining it in terms of its affective power: specifically, its capacity to elicit the emotion of religious love and devotion, *bhakti*. These upstart poets and poeticians rearticulated literary theory in terms of devotion while rearticulating devotion in terms of literary theory. Earlier poets in Hindi, including the Vaishnava poet Nandadas in his *Rāsapañcādhyāyī* (Five Chapters on the *Rās* Dance of Krishna, mid-sixteenth century CE) and the court poet Keshavdas in his *Rasikapriyā* (1591) and *Kavipriyā* (c. 1601), had gestured toward the roots of poetic art in devotion, but this formulation found its full expression beginning only in the early seventeenth century with the works of Dadu Panthi and Niranjani monks.[12] These monastic scholars, now joined by their counterparts employed at Rajput and Mughal courts, also expanded the scope of *śāstra* or the scientific treatise by introducing innovations into its structure, form, and analytical methods. This shared project of constructing a corpus of literary and scholastic works in the vernacular gradually joined the courtly-political and popular-devotional domains into an expansive intellectual network.

In contrast to the saints they revered, the monks of *nirguṇ*-oriented religious orders like the Dadu Panth and Niranjani Sampraday were both literate and educated—which is to say that they had generally received at least some formal training in works and disciplines like Vedānta, the *purāṇas*, and literary theory. Whereas saints like Kabir, Ravidas, and Dadu demurred from calling themselves poets or their works poetry, these *nirguṇ* monks evince little hesitation in asserting their literary and scholastic credentials or referring to their compositions as works (*granth*) of literature and scholarship. If the earlier saints' illiteracy was part of what produced their aura as iconoclastic visionaries, then literacy and erudition were part of what established these later monks' authority. Many of them came from clerical and merchant communities and so already possessed vocational literacy: the ability to read and write in different scripts, draft documents and records, and perform simple mathematical operations. Some initiates, like Sundardas of the Dadu Panth and Tursidas of the Niranjani Sampraday, were sent to Banaras be trained in Sanskrit and disciplines like Advaita Vedānta, Mīmāṁsa, and Puranic exegesis. This combination of graphic and discursive literacy enabled the monk-scholars to not only provide solid ideological foundations for their respective communities but also vastly expand the geographical and social reach of their traditions through the production of written works on theology, metaphysics, ritual praxis, and literary theory.

Monk-scholars of the Dadu Panth and Niranjani Sampraday redefined *kāvya* by positing emotion, particularly the emotion of *bhakti*, as poetry's central cause and concern. Contemporary court poets like Keshavdas and Cintamani, following the pronouncements of earlier theoreticians writing in Sanskrit, defined *kāvya* in terms of the presence of *rasa* (the aesthetic sentiment conveyed or produced by a work of art) and the employment of poetic and rhetorical devices (*alaṁkāra*).[13] The subject (*vastu*) of poetry was confined to a clearly delimited domain of tropes and motifs that in the hands of *rīti* poets came to be increasingly dominated by the erotic mood (*śṛṅgāra rasa*).[14] The monk-scholars of *nirguṇ* religious orders challenged this definition of poetry obliquely, allowing the edifice of literary form to stand but gutting its inner, affective content and establishing *bhakti* as the highest form of literary sentiment. Their critique is captured most succinctly and elegantly by the Dadu Panthi monk Sundardas (1596–1689):

dohā
racanā karī aneka bidhi bhalau banāyau dhāma
Sundara mūrati bāharī devala kaune kāma

Composing works in many different ways,
grand abodes have been built.
[Yet] what use is a temple,
if the beautiful image (*mūrti*) is outside?[15]

The *sākhī* can be read in two complementary ways: first, even a poem that is beautiful in terms of form has little value if it lacks the presence of God (the *mūrti*) within it. Second, the image of God is beautiful in itself and therefore does not require a grand or sophisticated poetic edifice in order for its beauty to be perceived. In both cases, it is the beauty of God that is the soul of poetry, whether or not the poet builds an elaborate verse superstructure around it. This definition still allows plenty of room for the theorization and valorization of poetic craft: echoing Sanskrit poeticians like Anandavardhana and Mammata, Sundardas establishes a three-tier scheme of "high," "medium," and "low" poetry and devotes an entire *aṅg* (anthological section) of his *sākhīs* to prescriptions on rhetorical style (*vacan-vivek*).[16] As Dalpat Rajpurohit has demonstrated, Sundardas—hailing from a Jain family of merchants and educated in Sanskrit at Banaras—was not only replying to his courtly counterparts (such as Keshavdas) but also using their own terms and conceptual structures against them in order to establish devotional sentiment as the highest quality of poetry.[17] Later Dadu Panthi and Niranjani monks further developed this devotional theory of *kāvya*. For example, Hariramdas Niranjani, writing in the early eighteenth century, begins his treatise on prosody, the *Chandaratnāvalī* (Necklace of the Jewels of Prosody, 1738), by explaining that knowledge of poetic meter is necessary for a poet to properly produce devotional sentiment in his audience, and treats major aspects of Sanskrit and *rīti* poetics such as *alaṁkāra* in a somewhat cursory fashion, remarking only on their role in producing that sentiment.[18] It is clear that the question of how poetry produces meaning was not as important for these monks as how it produces affect, particularly the affect of devotion.

Nirguṇ poets also redefined the scope and aims of *kāvya* by appropriating and redeploying its conventions in new ways. The most important convention was the poet's presentation of his work for consideration by connoisseurs. For example, when the Niranjani monk Bhagvandas composed his *Vairāgya Vṛnd* (Collection on Renunciation, 1673), a vernacular commentary on the Sanskrit poems of Bhartrihari, he prefaced it with the following apologetic:

piṁgula amara lakhyau nahī nahi kavita kī rīti
grantha artha parakāśa kūṁ antari upajī prīti

chanda bhaṁga akṣara kaṭita aratha vipara jai hoi
dūkhana taiṁ bhuṣana karaiṁ kauvida kahiye soi

I have not seen the [works of] Pingala or Amara,
nor the rules of poetic composition.

[Yet] a passion (*priti*) arose within [me]
to illuminate the meaning of the *granth* [i.e., the *Vairāgya Śataka*].

If the meter be broken or syllables omitted,
or a contradictory meaning is produced,
those who change these flaws into adornments
are called the learned (*kovid*).[19]

Such an apologetic, a convention appropriated from Sanskrit *kāvya*, is meant to be read against the grain: Bhagvandas's references to Sanskrit works on prosody like the *Chandasūtra* of Pingala and works of lexicography like the *Amarakośa* establish his familiarity with the literary tradition, and his appeal to the "learned" (*kovid*) is an invitation for connoisseurs and critics to consider his composition a serious work of belletristic and scholastic writing (despite its being composed in the vernacular). At the same time, Bhagvandas ties his literary work back to the definition of *kāvya* articulated earlier by Sundardas: love (*prīti*), the affective expression of *bhakti*, occasions and animates his poetry.[20]

This redefinition of *kāvya* was concomitant with a redefining of the *kavi* (poet) and his work. Monks of the Dadu Panth and Niranjani Sampraday fused the figure of the *kavi* as literary poet with the figure of the *kavi* as "sage" or "seer," a usage of the term dating to the Vedic period. Manohardas, a monk of the Niranjani Sampraday, introduces his *Vedānta Mahāvākya Bhāṣā* (Commentary on the Great Sayings of Vedānta, 1660 CE) by explaining the purpose of the text and the nature of his work:

ātma lābha teṁ aura na koī, yaha bhākhata haiṁ muni saba soi
lābha artha kavi karaiṁ vakhāṇa, ātma koṁ īsvara kari jāṁṇa

There is nothing [greater] than self-knowledge,
so all the sages (*muni*) say.
For the purpose of such knowledge the poet (*kavi*) describes
[how] to know the God within.[21]

Having thus reformulated what it meant to "do" *kāvya*, these monks could recharacterize the whole tradition of *nirguṇ bhakti* poetry in *bhāṣā* as a continuation of *chand-baddh* (versified) revelation stretching back to the Vedic seers. The Niranjani monk Bhagvandas does precisely this in the introduction to his *Jaiminī Aśvamedhaparva* (Jaimini's Book of the Horse Sacrifice, 1698): in the opening, the Vedic *kavi* and *kovid* of yore gather together, along with the goddess of speech herself, Sarasvati, to request Bhagvandas to recite the narrative of the sacrifice in *bhāṣā*.[22]

Just as they expanded the scope of *kāvya*, Dadu Panthi and Niranjani monks expanded the scope of *śāstra* to encompass the various types of scholastic writings that they produced. Shastric writing in Sanskrit was capacious to begin with, the term *śāstra* signifying a system of ideas or rules that could be simultaneously descriptive and prescriptive and encompassing topics as varied as astrology, sexual intercourse, agriculture, horses, gemology, and, of course, *kāvya* and *dharma*.[23] Nevertheless, the range of possible objects was explicitly delimited, *śāstra*'s methods and conventions were well defined, and most important here, *śāstra* was primarily composed in Sanskrit (and Prakrit), a language that could claim the universality necessary to carry the normative, hegemonic weight of such pronouncements, at least in northern India.[24] Consequently, the idea that *śāstra* could be composed in *bhāṣā* was itself a revolutionary assertion. In a manner not unlike the *rīti* poets who claimed to re-present the Sanskrit tradition "according to [their] understanding," monks of the Dadu Panth and Niranjani Sampraday presented themselves as humble mediums bringing knowledge from the world of Sanskrit into the vernacular. Yet their modest claims belied drastic innovations. For example, the Niranjani monk Dhyandas opens his *Ekādaśī Māhātmya* (Panegyric of the Eleventh Day of the Lunar Fortnight, c. 1660) with the following appeal to the goddess Sarasvati:

> pūjūhauṁ surasati sura raī, śubha ākṣari dai mo samujhaī
> sahaṃsakṛta bhākhā kari, gāūṁ kathā sāstra ukti banāūṁ
> haṃsavāhinī prabla hūjai, vimala vāṁnī mokuṃ dījai
>
> I worship Sarasvati, the Queen of Speech,
>   may she give me understanding and auspicious letters (speech).
> Having made Sanskrit into the vernacular (*bhākhā*),
>   I sing stories (*kathā*) and craft statements (*ukti*) of *śāstra*.
> May she whose mount is the swan be powerful!
>   May I be given immaculate speech (*vāṇī*).[25]

Such a verse would have struck contemporary readers of *śāstra* in Sanskrit as odd. Invocations to Sarasvati were not unheard of in the genre but were a convention more associated with literary compositions (*kāvya*).[26] Similarly, Dhyandas's appeal to the community of literary connoisseurs at the end would have been more at home in a work of *kāvya* than a work of *śāstra*. Nevertheless, Dhyandas clearly states that this is the latter. Again, this characterization would have appeared strange to any reader of Sanskrit *śāstra*: Dhyandas declares that he "sings stories" and "voices statements of *śāstra*" (*gāūṁ kathā sāstra ukti banāūṁ*), thus combining three genres and modes of discourse (*gāthā*, *kathā*, and *śāstra*) that would have had no place together in the world of Sanskrit. Yet they make perfect sense in the context of the performance practices of *nirguṇ* religious communities: at *mahotsav*s and smaller gatherings, gurus, monks, and lay devotees would gather to sing hymns, listen to stories of God and the saints, and receive religious instruction in the form of sermons. In the ritual and social world of *nirguṇ* religious orders, *gāthā*, *kathā*, and *śāstra* belonged together.

Writing was a constitutive element of this new, vernacular form of *kāvya* and *śāstra*, and authors "perform" the act in their compositions as they describe the process. This begins with the conception of the literary or scholastic work *qua* work (*granth*): often, an author will simply assert that he experienced a "passion," "feeling," or "desire" to compose the work, recalling the aforementioned definition of *kāvya* as occasioned by and eliciting religious passion or devotion. Sometimes the author describes how the work was commissioned, as when the Dadu Panthi monk Caturdas tells his audience that in May 1635 CE, his guru Santdas ordered him to compose a commentary on the eleventh book of the *Bhāgavata Purāṇa*.[27] Authors of scholastic works often emphasize the amount of study that went into a given composition, including the consultation of written sources. Hariramdas Niranjani, in his *Chandaratnāvalī*, assures his audience that "Having looked at all ideas concerning meter, and having examined all the works (*granth*) on meter by poets (*kaviyan*), Hariram has expounded and discussed his ideas."[28] Even authors' colophons can gesture toward the intellectual, institutional, or sectarian (and implicitly literate) contexts of composition that imbue their works with authority. In the final lines of his *Nāmaprakāś* (Illumination of the Names, 1768 CE), Hariramdas mentions not only where he completed the work (Dhanop) but also the name of his guru (Balakdas), "under whose tutelage he composed the work" (*ācaraja guru saranabala granth kāryau harirāṁma*) and the location of his "home" monastery, Didwana.[29] The gesture toward his prestigious monastic lineage—Didwana was the monastery associated with Haridas, the putative founder of the Niranjani Sampraday—and his explicit reference to his guru's supervision of the project provides Hariramdas's work with a sectarian imprimatur of quality and accuracy. Anantadas (a.k.a. Anathdas), composer of the *Vicāramāl* (Garland of Cogitation, 1670 CE), gestures not only to his work's written origins but also to its written future. He closes with the following *phalaśruti*: "Whoever copies (*likhai*) and reads from (*paḍhai*) [this work] with great love and then reflects [upon it], will have the light of wisdom shine upon them each moment like the sun."[30] The suggestion that not only studying the text but also simply *inscribing* it with the appropriate affect (*ati prīti*, "extreme love") points to the possibility that some Hindu *bhakti* traditions, like their counterparts in the Jain community, understood the commissioning and inscription of religious works to generate spiritual merit (*puṇya*) for those involved.

Even as they rehearse the acts of writing and reading in their works, these authors also gesture toward the oral modes through which those works were transmitted, performed, and explicated. A particularly clever example is found in the *Jñānasamudra* ("Ocean of Knowledge," 1653) of Sundardas, a dialogue between guru and disciple that outlines three major methods of obtaining metaphysical knowledge. Sundardas ends the work with the following *phalaśruti*:

> dohā
> yahaī jñāna samudra hai yaha guru śiṣa saṁvāda
> sundara yāhi kahai sunai tākai miṭahiṁ bisāda
>
> *This* is the Ocean of Knowledge:
>   this dialogue between guru and disciple.
> Sundar says that the one who recites or listens to it
>   will have their sufferings dispelled.

Sundardas emphasizes that the dialogue (*saṁvād*) is the "ocean of knowledge" contained within his work and suggests that its soteriological and palliative potential is unlocked through re-creating that dialogue orally. It is the mode of question and answer, of thesis, antithesis, and synthesis, that generates knowledge (*jñān*) in the first place; the text must therefore be performed in a dialogical manner, through "reciting and listening" (*kahai sunai*). Simply "reading" the text (silent or private reading) fails to activate the epistemological machinery. The *Jñānasamudra* is a script for pedagogical performance, in which the reciter (the guru) brings to life the idealized characters of the guru and disciple for his students. It is a re-enactment of the face-to-face, oral modes of knowledge transmission idealized in the songs and sayings of the *nirguṇ* saints. This recitation in turn provided a foundation—or better yet, a stage—upon which the guru could then engage in further, extemporaneous exegesis. This again highlighted the character of knowledge as being embodied in the guru and the character of the text artifact as occupying a nodal, but not determinative, place in a broader set of hermeneutical practices and their accompanying modes of oral address.[31]

Such practices bring us back to the metaphysical understandings of sound that undergirded *nirguṇ* traditions' theology and praxis. An echo of this metaphysics is discernible in monk-scholars' concern with modes of auspicious utterance. For example, Sundardas begins his *Jñānasamudra* with a *maṅgalācaraṇ* ("auspicious undertaking," an appeal to God that precedes the literary work proper and is intended to ensure its successful completion) in the *chappay* meter. Although such *maṅgalācaraṇ* verses were themselves de rigueur in literary and scholastic works, Sundardas actually incorporates an autocommentary into the last two lines, explaining to his audience why auspicious utterance is necessary to avoid obstacles in the first place.[32] Hariramdas begins his treatise on prosody by identifying the inauspicious syllables and *gaṇa* (metrical feet) that should be avoided at the beginning of a composition lest they bring about ill effects.[33] *Nirguṇ* monks inherited these beliefs regarding *maṅgalācaraṇ* verses and certain combinations of syllables from Sanskrit *kāvya* but joined them to a specifically *nirguṇ* metaphysics of sound. For example, Sundardas addresses his *maṅgalācaraṇ* not to Ganesh (who is typically invoked at the start of any work) but rather to the guru and the saints, the vocalized remembrance of which effects physical and spiritual salvation. Hariramdas cautions against the use of inauspicious syllables and poetic feet or the erroneous application of meter in religious poetry precisely because it was the aural experience of that poetry that was understood to produce *bhakti* in the listener. Such beliefs about the power of poetic utterance were taken seriously and constituted some of the rules governing poetic competitions and demonstrations of literary competency in pedagogical contexts.[34]

The corpus of literary and scholastic writings composed by monks of *nirguṇ* religious orders reveals the extent to which these monks engaged with the literary and religious ideas of their day and participated in a broader network of vernacular intellectuals that included scholars at royal courts, pandits at schools (*pāṭhaśālā*), and even kings, princes, and local lords (*rāo*, *sāmant*). This overturns the conventional wisdom among historians of Hindi who, since the 1920s, have generally denied the existence of scholasticism or even intellectual consistency in the compositions of *nirguṇ* authors, instead characterizing *nirguṇ bhakti* as an amalgamation of Islamic monotheism, folk wisdom, and yogic practices.[35] Such a conclusion is perhaps understandable if one reduces the *nirguṇ* textual tradition to the genres of the epigram (*sākhī*) and lyric (*pad*), with which the *nirguṇ* tradition came to be identified in the early twentieth century as writers like Kshitimohan Sen, Rabindranath Tagore, and Evelyn Underhill compiled and translated lyrics attributed to saints like Kabir and Dadu.[36]

The many works of *śāstra* and *kāvya* composed by *nirguṇ* monks and preserved in the written archive tell a different story. Monks of the Dadu Panth, Niranjani Sampraday, and similar *nirguṇ* religious orders like the Ramsnehi Sampraday and Carandasi Sampraday participated in the rapidly expanding field of vernacular scholarship during the seventeenth and eighteenth centuries. They engaged with the writings and ideas of Vaishnava *bhakti* communities like the Pushtimarg, Vallabha Sampraday, and Ramanandi Sampraday; of Advaita Vedāntins in urban centers like Banaras; of Sikh communities in the Punjab and northern Rajasthan, and of courtly intellectuals among the Rajput and Mughal nobility. Monks of the Niranjani Sampraday and Dadu Panth were particularly successful in expanding their respective sects' reach and influence in discussions of Advaita Vedānta. In addition to Sundardas's *Jñānasamudra*, Manohardas Niranjani's *Vedānta Mahāvākya Bhāṣā* (Commentary on the Great Sayings of the Vedānta, c. 1660), *Ṣaṭa Praśnottarī Bhāṣā* (Commentary on the Six Questions and Answers, n.d.), and *Jñānamañjarī* (Bouquet of Knowledge, 1659) and Bhagvandas Niranjani's *Amṛtadhāra* ("Stream of Nectar," 1671) helped to constitute what Michael Allen has recently called the "Greater Advaita Vedānta tradition," a largely unexamined corpus of early modern texts that, being written in the vernacular or in genres not typically associated with Advaita Vedānta, fall outside the assumed canon of Sanskrit works.[37] Although such vernacular texts may have been peripheral to the debates being pursued by Sanskrit pandits of the period, they were the medium through which many inhabitants of seventeenth- and eighteenth-century north India, including monks, teachers, merchants, courtiers, and even kings, learned about and debated this system of thought.[38]

Vaishnava theology and literary theory were two additional domains in which *nirguṇ* monks pursued exchanges with other religious groups and courtly interlocuters. Beginning in the mid-sixteenth century, Vaishnava devotion to Ramachandra and Krishna had spread rapidly across northern India, driven in part by the growth of Vaishnava sects like the Ramanandi Sampraday, Gaudiya Sampraday, Pushtimarg, and Radhavallabhi Sampraday. In the regions of modern-day Rajasthan and Madhya Pradesh, Krishna worship also became a central part of the royal cults at Rajput courts. Consequently, at the beginning of the seventeenth century, there was a need to establish theological foundations for the beliefs, ritual praxis, and literary aesthetics of Vaishnava devotion.[39] This need was answered by monks of not only the Vaishnava orders themselves but also of the Dadu Panth and Niranjani Sampraday, who composed treatises, commentaries, and vernacular versions of important Vaishnava works in Sanskrit. Works like Dhyandas's aforementioned *Ekādaśī Māhātmya Bhāṣā* (which provides narrative explanations for the importance of rituals performed on the eleventh day of the lunar fortnight), Bhagvandas's 1703 CE *bhāṣā* commentary on the tenth book of the *Bhāgavata Purāṇa* (which details Krishna's exploits in Braj), and Caturdas's *bhāṣā* commentary on the eleventh book (which addresses the superiority of *bhakti* over knowledge and renunciation) were used in a collective attempt to ground contemporary Vaishnava rituals and beliefs in canonical Sanskrit works like the *purāṇas*, the epics, and even the Upanishadic corpus. As evidenced in scribal colophons and their presence in various collections, these works met a demand among not only monks but also householder devotees (especially merchants and clerical communities), kings, and Rajput nobility. These same groups were also the audience for works of vernacular poetry and literary theory. Bhagvandas's *Vairāgya Vṛnd*, though presented as a work on renunciation, was in fact a highly literary exegesis on the courtly *kāvya* creations of Bhartrihari; Sundardas's *savaiya* poems were so high in literary quality that they were made part of literary curricula at *pāṭhaśālās*, while his *vacan-vivek* verses became a guide for aspiring religious poets; Hariramdas's *Chandaratnāvalī* was used by poets across Rajasthan and Punjab as a textbook on poetic meter. In these works, the monk-scholars addressed ideas and topics—sometimes explicitly, often implicitly—put forward by courtly poets like Keshavdas and Cintamani Tripati, and even by Rajput kings such as Jasvant Singh of Marwar (who composed the *Bhāṣābhūṣan*, "Ornament of Language," in 1660) and Savant Singh "Nagaridas" of Kishangarh (who composed the *Bihāracandrikā,* "Moonlight Dalliance," in 1731 and the *Brajasār*, "Essence of Braj," in 1742).[40]

In addition to textual evidence in the form of references, allusions, concepts, and lexicon shared between these monks and their interlocutors, the manuscript archive provides "hard" evidence that *nirguṇ* monks composing in far-flung locales like Didwana, Dhanop, Fatehpur, and the Narmada Valley were self-consciously in conversation with the works of courtiers and kings at the courts of Jodhpur, Jaipur, Gwalior, and Delhi, and with monks at the Ramanandi complex at Galta and the Pushtimargi temples of Vrindavan and Nathdwara. The libraries of *nirguṇ* monasteries contain *pothīs* of works by Vaishnava scholars, courtly poets, and kings, while *pothīs* of treatises by *nirguṇ* monks are found in the royal collections of Rajput courts and in the collections of Vaishnava monasteries in and beyond the region of Rajasthan, and even among Sikh communities of the Punjab.

BOOKS FOR SCHOLARS: THE *POTHĪ*

Just as the monks of *nirguṇ bhakti* communities, in order to participate in the scholarly discussions of their day, crafted works according to the textual conventions of *śāstra* and *kāvya* (even as they reshaped those conventions), the scribes who copied the works did so according to the textual, visual, and material conventions associated with manuscripts of those genres (while also subtly reshaping those conventions). These monks composed works that *sounded* like scholarly treatises and poetry when read aloud; then scribes copied them so that they *looked* like books of scholarship and poetry. The material form of scholastic and literary texts was determined by processes of production and performance modalities rooted in a shared intellectual culture that spanned northern India. Consequently, works of scholarship and literature (as well as other genres like *purāṇa* and *itihāsa*) were most often inscribed in the type of manuscript that contemporary vernacular sources call the *pothī*.[41]

In contrast to the idiosyncratic personal notebooks discussed in the previous chapter, the *pothī* reflected a set of shared conventions observed by scribes working across several languages and regions, and across the late medieval and early modern periods. Paper *pothī*s were used from Gujarat to Bengal and from Kashmir to the Deccan, and for texts in Sanskrit, Prakrit, Apabhramsha, Maru-Gurjar, Punjabi, Hindi, and Bengali. Scribes (both professional and private) working in Hindi produced *pothī*s that observed the textual and visual conventions of this transregional book format even as they innovated certain elements that came to distinguish the *pothī*s of works in Hindi from examples in these other languages. Whether aware of it or not, these scribes copied works for an imagined, idealized reader, an individual with expectations of what they would see on the page and how they would navigate and use the text, and who possessed certain qualifications. Consequently, the *pothī* reflects the performative, intellectual, social, and political world in which it functioned.

The paper *pothī* is a collection of loose folios, usually short in height and broad in width, based on the model of the palm leaf *pothī* or *pustakam*, the most common form of "book" in the subcontinent before the popularization of paper beginning in the fourteenth century (fig. 3.1). The expansion of the paper-making industry during the late sultanate and early Mughal periods accelerated paper's displacement of palm leaf as the most common material for manuscripts in the north—though certainly not everywhere, and not all at once.[42] Nor did its introduction in the twelfth century bring about an immediate change in the format or conventions of the *pothī*; paper specimens maintained the proportions, textual orientation, layout, and illumination programs of their palm leaf archetypes for centuries afterward. Paper did eventually bring about a few significant changes, most notably in dimensions: in contrast to palm leaf, paper could easily be produced in large sheets and cut to various sizes, and artisans exploited this quality by creating *pothī*s in many different sizes both large and small. The plasticity of dimensions and the ability of paper to accept different types of ink and paint in turn led to new approaches to illustration and illumination, beginning in the Jain manuscript tradition. Nevertheless, the vast majority of *pothī*s reflect a general conservatism in style, with most scribes following earlier conventions and using only two colors of ink, black and red.

In contrast to the bound *guṭakā*, the unbound *pothī* is not well suited for travel and not as convenient to consult: its loose folios cannot easily be "leafed through" and must be carefully handled to avoid accidents, such as placing them in the wrong order or letting them be blown away by the wind. Unlike the palm leaves that they emulate, the paper folios of a *pothī* cannot be pierced and bound with string (even though many include vestigial decorations where holes would have been made in a palm leaf manuscript; see fig. 3.1). Even the technique of binding the folios by placing them between two boards and wrapping a string around the resulting stack (another vestige of the earlier palm leaf manuscripts) risks damaging the folios, because string can abrade the soft edges of the paper.

The most common mode of binding a paper *pothī* was (and still is) the *basta*: a rectangular piece of cloth that derives its name from the Persian verb *bastan*, "to bind" or "to close."[43] One "binds" the stack of folios in the *basta* simply by wrapping them in the cloth and tying the corners or edges of the cloth into a knot (a literal "*granth*").[44] *Basta*s are most often red-dyed cotton but can be made of any material and dyed any color; the *basta*s used in Jain and Sikh communities—traditions that ascribe particular importance to books—are often ornate and beautiful, providing a canvas for embroidery and other forms of embellishment commensurate with the status of the work contained. Multiple *pothī*s were sometimes "bound" together in a single piece of cloth, leading to libraries using the *basta* as an organizational unit: even today, some manuscript libraries and catalogues continue to organize *pothī*s according to the *basta* in which they are kept.[45] The logics behind such collections—for example, the rationale for binding a given group of *pothī*s together in a single *basta*—have been largely forgotten. Nevertheless, the historical practice of using the *basta* to bind and organize works and the storage of those *basta*s in trunks called *sandūk* (Arabic *ṣandūq*) exemplifies how the physical, material form of the book shapes practices of knowledge organization and the institutional structures responsible for them.

The material form of the *pothī* corresponds to a particular practice of embodied reading in which the reader or reciter sits cross-legged in front of the text, which is laid on a cloth or cushion to show respect and to protect it from dirt. Occasionally the *pothī* is placed on a small wooden stand akin to the *raḥl* used for codices. The *pothī* and this manner of reciting from it are iconic in that an actual *pothī*, a painting of a *pothī*, a sculpture of a *pothī*, or the mention of a *pothī* in a text such as a hymn or a hagiography all produce a common set of significations, meanings, and associations.[46] Kabir satirizes the figure of the pandit reciting from a *pothī* in his hymns. More laudatory examples include the Pushtimargi hagiography, *Caurāsī Vaiṣṇavan Kī Vārtā* (Tales of the Eight-Four Vaishnavas, mid-seventeenth century), in which the composers Gokulnath and Hariray affectionally describe Vallabhacharya, the founder of the sect, giving wisdom to his disciples as he recites from *pothīs*.[47] Eighteenth-century painters of the Nathdwara school, a Pushtimargi center in Rajasthan, often depicted Vitthalnath, son and successor to Vallabhacharya, as well as other scholars of the sect, sitting cross-legged before *pothīs* as they teach their disciples (fig. 3.2). The *pothī* thus works as a metonym for a particular kind of authority grounded in the ability to mediate written texts. Its function as an icon of intellectual, religious, and literary culture entered the colonial imagination through images like James Prinsep's 1831 lithograph of a Brahmin reciting from a Puranic text in Banaras (fig. 3.3) and persists in modern paintings of saints like Tulsidas and Sundardas seated before stacks of *pothī*-style folios, absorbed in the work of writing. The *pothī* was, of course, an icon long before the emergence of vernacular literature in north India: visual and sculptural depictions of Sarasvati, the goddess of speech and of poetry, holding a *pothī* of the palm leaf variety date to as early as the second century CE.[48] In this sense the *pothī* is quite literally an icon, or at least part of one—the icon of Speech Herself, from whom the poet and scholar request the gift of eloquence. Sarasvati is also she whom the student propitiates once a year during Sarasvati *puja* when the material implements of writing such as notebooks, pens, and schoolbooks are worshiped and blessed.[49]

The textual content of *pothīs* is presented according to shared, transregional conventions rather than scribal preference or local usage. The texts are linguistically and orthographically more standardized and Sanskritized than those found in *guṭakā* notebooks. The composers tended to employ a transregional register of *bhāṣā* that was largely free of localized vocabulary and expressions. In the particular generic, performative, and social context of vernacular *śāstra* or scientific writing, authors tended to use a Sanskritized register of language, favoring *tatsama* words over their *ardhatatsama* and *tadbhava* counterparts, and long *samāsa* or compounds, a distinctive feature of Sanskrit.[50] The scribes who copied these works also followed standardized practices of orthography adopted from Sanskrit, maintained the phonology associated with the transregional register of *bhāṣā* (as opposed to the phonology of local languages and dialects like Marwari), and preferred to use *tatsama* terms rather than their more vernacular equivalents. These tendencies cannot be sufficiently explained as faithful reproduction of the works as the scribes "received" them. (Indeed, the general absence of autographed copies of works from this period means that the available material is the creation of scribes, not of the authors themselves.) That the standardized and Sanskritized modes of representing language in *pothīs* are an aspect of scribal practice, not simply a facet of the original texts, is revealed through comparison: those who copied scholastic or literary works into *pothī*s and lyric or epigrammatic poetry into *guṭakā*s followed different practices for each genre and type of manuscript. Scribes tended to follow transregional and Sanskritized phonology and orthography when copying works of *kāvya* and *śāstra* into *pothī*s and local phonology and modes of orthography when copying hymns and sayings into notebooks. They also often made editorial emendations when inscribing a *pothī*. By comparing the versions of lyrics and epigrams in *guṭakā* and *pothī* manuscripts, we find that the scribes often "muted" or minimized localized features of the text, replacing *tadbhava* words with their *tatsama* equivalents and changing case markers and verb endings to conform to the usage found in the more transregional register of *bhāṣā*.

The scribes who copied *pothī*s were not mere copyists but copyeditors in their own right, applying norms of orthography, punctuation, spelling, morphology, and phonology to produce a book that would meet the expectations of the idealized reader, a member of the class of vernacular intellectuals and literati. They copied works in the Nāgarī script, carefully inscribing each letter and its accompanying *śirorekhā* (superscript line) individually, unlike the rough shorthand found in many *guṭakā*s. The quality of hands found in *pothī* manuscripts is generally high—nothing like the scribbles seen in many *guṭakā*-type notebooks—and although the text layout (horizontal lines of text of equal height with narrow gaps in between) leaves relatively little room for calligraphic embellishment, many scribes took pains to make their inscriptions beautiful as well as legible (see fig. 3.3). *Pothī*s are copied in *scriptio continua*, in consonance with the vocalized reading practices that were part of pedagogical and literary performance. Nevertheless, word breaks did begin to appear in the paratexts of eighteenth-century Hindi manuscripts, especially in colophons. A scribe would sometimes "justify" a line of text (i.e., position the individual words at regular intervals so as to fill the width of the text block) if the line came at the end of a folio or needed to be broken in order to accommodate illumination. This reveals that scribes not only recognized individual lemmata (words) as they copied but also could, when aesthetic concerns demanded it, visually represent those words as distinct. This careful arrangement of individual words, along with the creative and often geometrical arrangement of syllables, punctuation marks, and even diacritical marks like the *anusvāra* (superscript dot indicating a nasal consonant) and *candra-bindu* (superscript dot and crescent indicating a nasalized vowel) on the page suggest a general concern with the visual aesthetic of the book: a copy of a serious work of literature or scholarship needed to look the part.

The existence of shared protocols among vernacular readers in sixteenth- through nineteenth- century north India is nowhere more vividly reflected than in the rich paratextual material found in *pothīs*. Nestled between segments of the "body text" (the literary or scholastic work proper) are ancillary inscriptions—opening formulae, section headings, verse numbers, colophons, and the like—that direct the reader in how to use or perform the text, as well as provide a wealth of contextual and historical information. In many *pothīs*, these paratexts are highlighted by the use of red ink or *hiṅgul* powder ("cinnabar" or mercury sulfide), making them "rubrics" (from Latin *rubrica*, red ochre) in multiple senses of the term: they are both "written in red" and "directions" or "rules" for performing the work (see figs. 3.1 and 3.4).[51] These include navigational apparatuses such as section headings and verse numbers to aid the reader in locating specific passages. Section headings can be simple ("Devotion's form") or elaborate ("Thus concludes 'Stealing the Horse,' the Fourth Section of the Commentary of Jaimini on the Horse Sacrifice Chapter of the *Mahābhārata*").[52] Verse numbering schemes can be quite sophisticated, with separate numbering sequences for different types of verse (*kavitt*, *dohā*, *caupāī*, *arill*) used within a single work. In manuscripts that contain both a "root text" (*mūl pāṭh*) and a commentary (*ṭīkā*), scribes often used separate numbering sequences (or in some cases employed complex numbering schemes that collated the root and commentary verses).[53] Verse numbers also played a role in editing and quality control. Many *pothīs* conclude with a tally of verses copied, and while some simply give the total number, many give separate tallies for each type of verse. In theory, this acted as a safeguard against the omission or repetition of verses while copying, since the tally of the copy could be checked against that of the original.[54] Professional scribes used such tallies to calculate their fees, as was often the practice with Sanskrit manuscripts.[55] In addition to verse numbers, folio numbers (usually marked in the margin on the verso side of a folio) were indispensable, as the loose, unbound folios of a *pothī* were always in danger of falling out of order.

Other paratexts mark narratological and dialogical shifts in the text, which in turn provide cues to the reciter regarding how to perform it. One of the most common is the marking of direct speech, usually with the Sanskrit finite verb *uvāca* ("said"): for example, *arjuna uvāca* ("Arjun said"). Rubrics such as "Arjuna asks a question," "Here, Bhartrihari laments the pursuit of worldly pleasures," and "The poet now explains the difference between types of renunciation" mark important heteroglossic shifts and thus guide the reader in mediating the text for an audience. A brief example is in the opening of Manohardas's *Vedānta Mahāvākya Bhāṣā*, a vernacular commentary on the metaphysical propositions of the Upaniṣads, presented in the form of a dialogue between guru and disciple. In November 1737, a scribe by the name of Jairamdas made a copy of the *Vedānta Mahāvākya Bhāṣā* that includes numerous paratextual cues for how to make sense of the manuscript's content and present it in a pedagogical setting. (It is likely that at least some of these paratexts were added by Jairam or an earlier scribe.) The manuscript begins as follows, translated and transcribed here as it appears in the original, with paratextual material (highlighted using red *hiṅgul* powder in the manuscript) given in bold.

> [In Sanskrit:] **Obeisance to the One Consisting of Truth, Consciousness, and Bliss** || **Obeisance to the Guru** || [In Hindi:] **The composer asks for the joy of freedom from obstacles when composing the work** || **Dohā** || Oh Ganesh, grant me auspiciousness | Oh Sarasvati, grant me auspiciousness || Oh Mahesh, grant me auspiciousness || Oh Parvati, grant me auspiciousness || **1** || **The purpose and subject matter of the work is stated** || **Caupāī** || There is nothing [greater] than self-knowledge | So all wise men say | For the purpose of such knowledge | the poet describes how to know the God within || **2** || **Those qualified to [study or teach] this work are stated by way of a question** || **Question** || A doubt came to the disciple's mind | The soul is separate from God | The individual soul is unknowing and God is all-knowing | How can one that is unknowing and one that knows be one? || **3** | . . .

The rubrics succinctly explain what the text is "doing": posing a question, providing an answer, or presenting an opening invocation to prevent the appearance of any obstacles to the composition or performance of the work. In this regard they function like commentaries. They also indicate how to perform the work: every verse is preceded by an indication of the meter in which it should be recited. More important, these paratexts correlate the discursive world of the text—the dialogue between an idealized guru and disciple—with the performative world of the text, i.e., that of the actual guru reciting the *Vedānta Mahāvākya Bhāṣā* for his disciples. The *Vedānta Mahāvākya Bhāṣā* is a treatise explaining certain metaphysical propositions, and such notes guide the reciter in presenting its theses (*pakṣa*), antitheses (*vipakṣa*), questions (*praśna*), answers (*uttara*), doubts or objections (*āsaṅkā*), and solutions (*samādhāna*). As a script for pedagogical performance, it enables the reciter to re-create the type of face-to-face, oral, dialogical exchange between teacher and student that is idealized within the text itself.[56] This is the same recursive and repetitive character of vernacular *śāstra* to which Sundardas gestures at the end of the *Jñānasamudra*: it is always both a representation of an archetypical teaching "event" and a script for re-producing such events in one's own time and place.[57]

The *pothī* thus functioned as the lynchpin in ritualized pedagogical performances practiced in *pāṭhaśālā*s (schools) and sectarian *maṭh*s. As a visual and material icon, it formed part of the tableau of teaching in which the guru sat, *pothī* laid out before him, in front of his disciples; as a script, it provided not only the scholastic work but also cues for actualizing the work as a dialectic disquisition. Despite the significant epistemological and institutional shifts in the late eighteenth through early twentieth centuries with the arrival of colonialism and indigenous intellectual responses to it, the material book has continued to play this role in many traditions of religious teaching, including in *nirguṇ* communities like the Dadu Panth and Niranjani Sampraday.[58]

As the introductory and concluding verses of Manohardas's *Vedānta Mahāvākya Bhāṣā* and Sundardas's *Jñānasamudra* indicate, an individual needed to possess certain qualifications in order to claim the right or authority (*adhikār*) to mediate or teach a work of *śāstra*.[59] Within sectarian religious contexts, similar qualifications and authority were also required to simply transmit such works in writing. The copying of *pothī*s in monastic settings was a tightly controlled process, documented in colophons.[60] In *pothī*s copied by monks of religious orders like the Niranjani Sampraday and Dadu Panth, the scribe typically indicates whether he has copied the work for his guru or for himself using the Sanskrit compound *paṭhanārta*, "for the purpose of reading/study"; e.g., *svāmī Rāmadāsa paṭhanārtha* ("for the purpose of study by Svami Ramdas").[61] The scribe then gives his own name, preceded by his guru-disciple lineage, often going all the way back to the founder of the religious order. This is a form of *praśasti* or praise for one's guru and a declaration of one's own intellectual pedigree—an important assurance addressed to an anonymous reader and not just to the immediate individual for whom the text was copied. *Pothī*s often changed hands within monastic orders, moving from guru to disciple (recall the Mughal *farmān* notarizing the transfer of the Gosvamis' libraries to their nephew, Jiva) and from one monk to another, both within and between different religious orders. Manuscripts copied by monks also sometimes made their way to householder devotees and kings. In this context, the scribe's rehearsal of his guru-disciple lineage addresses an imagined future reader by giving a guarantee of accurate textual transmission: it asserts that the copyist has received spiritual as well as intellectual training sufficient to the task of transmitting the text.

This confirms that reading, writing, and even copying texts were considered intellectual rather than merely mechanical processes. An individual needed to possess the requisite *adhikār* to properly mediate and transmit a work, either through speech or through writing. Other details mentioned in colophons also function as part of the imprimatur: a scribe's mention of the town, temple, or monastery at which he completed the manuscript and the number of days that it took him to do so provide the reader with information about the sectarian or institutional context and the amount of care and time invested in inscription. This contrasts markedly with the practice of some professional scribes of the period, who copied works for money and whose work did not presuppose an understanding of the content of a text.

In a world without print or mass-produced copies of works, the colophon thus functioned in a manner somewhat analogous to the copyright page found in modern books: it provided the reader with the information necessary to ascertain the accuracy, quality, and provenance of a copy of a work. This information was as indispensable to the vernacular scholars of early modern north India as it is to scholars today, since each group is bound together professionally by shared norms of citation and shared criteria for sources and editions. In fact, the entire mode of book production in early modern north India made this information even more valuable, because a scholar who desired a copy of a work would have to either commission a copy or make one himself—and this always required an existing manuscript. A manuscript carrying a sectarian authorization or an authentication of its quality theoretically possessed fewer errors and therefore would require less editorial labor during the copying process. Ultimately, the colophons found in *pothī*s gesture toward an imagined *community* of readers, the same *kavi-kul* or society of the learned whom Bhagvandas addresses in the opening and closing sections of his *Vairāgya Vṛnd*. Copyists used the colophon to locate themselves not only temporally and geographically but also within an imagined political, social, and institutional dispensation. This is why *pothī*s copied by Hindus and Jains in north India, in addition to providing the date according to the *saṁvat vikramī* calendar, sometimes mention the name and regnal year of the Mughal emperor. This is the case with the famous "Fatehpur manuscript," a collection of exemplary *pad*s collated by a teacher for his students, the sons of a Rajput warlord near Fatehpur. The *pothī* contains lyrics enjoyed by the Rajput and Mughal nobility of the time, and the scribe, Ramdas Ratan, closes the manuscript by locating Fatehpur within "the dominion of *śrī* Akbar." Shared connoisseurship of such poetry in *bhāṣā* is part of what constituted the combined Rajput-Mughal nobility, and that community of connoisseurs was the "dominion" in which Ramdas's *pothī* participated, even if it was produced in a provincial city like Fatehpur.

PRODUCING A *POTHĪ*

Producing a *pothī* required the work of multiple hands and a combination of technologies. The folios were first cut to size from large sheets of paper, then ruled using a *misṭara*, a tool introduced into South Asia, together with paper itself, by central Asian immigrants during the early sultanate period. There were two types of *misṭara*: a wooden board with raised ridges onto which the paper was pressed, leaving embossed lines; and a board across which strings were strung at regular intervals, which the scribe used as guides as he inscribed the lines of text. (Later *pothīs*, especially from the late nineteenth and early twentieth century, reveal the use of pencil to rule folios.) So even though the *pothī* retained a size and format that bespoke its connection to the earlier tradition of palm leaf books, it was produced using materials, technologies, and techniques adopted from the manuscript culture of the Islamicate world.[62]

Once the folios of the manuscript were ruled, the copyist went to work—though not always by himself. Most colophons mention only one scribe, yet some mention a second individual: the reciter.[63] This individual would read aloud from an existing copy while the copyist listened and transcribed the recited text; in the colophons of *pothīs* thus produced, the scribe sometimes assures the reader that they have "copied [the text] as heard" (*bāṁcai sūnai tīsu*). In this way, orality remained a part of textual transmission even when that transmission occurred "in writing."[64] Even if the colophon does not mention a reciter in addition to the scribe, the presence of such a textual mediator and the role of orality in written transmission are sometimes revealed through errors. An excellent example is in an 1863 copy of Anandaram's *Paramānand Prabodh* ("Apprehension of the Ultimate Bliss," 1762 CE), a commentary in *bhāṣā* on the *Bhagavadgītā*. The text of the Hindi commentary has been transcribed with relatively few errors, but the Sanskrit verses of the *Bhagavadgītā* itself are riddled with phonological, orthographical, and even morphological errors. The unevenness of the copy suggests a scribe who was familiar with the vernacular but not with Sanskrit, and who consequently misheard sounds, misrecognized words, and substituted *tadbhava* words for their Sanskrit equivalents.[65] (These mistakes did not prevent the anonymous scribe from complaining in the colophon that he "copied [the book] with great labor," enduring pain in his "hands, buttocks, neck, eyes, and face.")[66]

For many monastic scribes, copying manuscripts was a form of seasonal labor. During the monsoon season in north India, when rains made travel difficult, monks of the region's various sects would remain at monasteries and the houses of beneficent lay devotees, spending part of that time copying works for themselves, their gurus, and lay devotees.[67] For others, the work was occasional: colophons reveal that some monks copied works at different points throughout the year, though most often while residing at a temple or monastery. Yet others appear to have occasionally employed their skills for monetary renumeration, copying religious and scholastic works for householder patrons. This further complicates our understanding of literacy during this period. Many monks of the Dadu Panth, Niranjani Sampraday, and similar monastic orders hailed from merchant and clerical backgrounds and thus possessed certain forms of "vocational" literacy, like record-keeping and accountancy. As they copied *pothīs* for their gurus, fellow monks, and themselves, they parlayed this vocational literacy into participation in the privileged discursive domains of literature and scholarship. At the same time, their literacy remained vocational insofar as it was part of their role as a monk, but also because they could practice it commercially, as a form of skilled labor.

PARATEXTS, PARA-SANSKRIT, AND MULTILINGUAL PREACHING AND PEDAGOGY

The multilingual character of many *pothīs* draws attention to the multilingual character of the intellectual, literary, and religious culture of early modern north India. Works composed in one language were often mediated through one or more other languages. Even in manuscripts that appear to be "monolingual" in that they contain a work composed in a single language, traces of the manuscripts' multilingual performance contexts can be found. Marginal notes, headings, and other paratextual material reveal the ways even the classics of Sanskrit literature were mediated through the vernacular. For example, each folio of the early seventeenth-century *pothī* of the *Bhāgavata Purāṇa* held in the Brooklyn Museum includes, in the upper and lower margins, "captions" inscribed in *bhāṣā*. Highlighted with red ink, these vernacular notes summarize the action that is described in the Sanskrit text and represented in the accompanying illustration.[68] The exquisitely illustrated seventeenth-century copy of the *Rāmāyaṇa* in the Chattrapati Shivaji Maharaj Vastu Sangrahalaya reflects a similar relationship between languages, texts, and images: the recto of each folio contains a full-page illustration while the verso contains the corresponding Sanskrit verse and a summary or "heading" for the episode in *bhāṣā*.[69]

The multilingual nature of literary and pedagogical performance is writ large upon *pothīs* that contain vernacular commentaries or adaptations of Sanskrit works. In copies of works like Manohardas's *Vedānta Mahāvākya Bhāṣā*, Bhagvandas's *Vairāgya Vṛnd*, Anandram's *Paramānand Prabodh*, and Prince Indrajit of Orchha's *Vivekadīpikā* ("Lamp of Discrimination," c. 1600, a prose commentary on the poems of Bhartrihari), the Sanskrit "root text" (*mūl pāṭh*) is followed by explanation and exegesis in *bhāṣā*. These were scripts for pedagogical performance, supplying the guru with the original text in Sanskrit and the vernacular "tools" necessary to mediate and explain it to his students.

Even copies of works composed exclusively in the vernacular contain traces of multilingualism in their paratextual material. These paratexts are almost always in Sanskrit or what could be called "para-Sanskrit," a language "distinct from" yet "analogous to" Sanskrit in its form and function. This macaronic language tends to use Sanskrit nouns (declined and undeclined) and verbal roots (sometimes conjugated according to the rules of Sanskrit grammar, at other times suffixed with vernacular verb endings) together with postpositions, conjunctions, and syntactic markers from Hindi.[70] This language could in some places be described as *bhāṣā* made to "sound like" Sanskrit, with case endings and verb suffixes from Sanskrit appended to vernacular roots. The attempt to make the vernacular "sound like" something else draws attention to these paratexts' formal and aesthetic function. Openings, headings, notes, and colophons not only conveyed information to the manuscript's user about the content and how to use it. They also helped to fashion the text contained in the manuscript as a literary or scholastic work. Just as contemporary readers of printed literary and academic works have certain formal expectations that are so conventional as to be banal—for example, that a book should have a title, contain chapter and section headings, include page numbers, footnotes, abbreviations of Latin phrases, and so forth—audiences in early modern India had their own sets of expectations. *Pothīs* possess those elements that made a text look *and* sound like a work of literature or scholarship: openings, colophons, headings, and notations that, when recited, re-created the sound and aura of Sanskrit.

EXCHANGES INTELLECTUAL AND OTHERWISE

Pothīs served as a currency of exchange in early modern north India, and that exchange could be intellectual, social, political, and/or monetary in nature. Mentions of scribes, gurus, patrons, and rulers in colophons make each *pothī* the receipt of a transaction. Among monastic orders like those of the Dadu Panth and Niranjani Sampraday, the most common transaction occurred between disciple and guru and involved the exchange of service (*sevā*) and blessing (*prasād*). When a disciple copied a *pothī* "for reading by" (*paṭhanārth*) his guru, he would often record this act of service in the colophon, stating that "such-and-such disciple inscribed the work for reading by such-and-such guru." The student offered his service in the form of the physical and intellectual labor required to copy the book; in return, the guru—who, in *nirguṇ* traditions, stood as a proxy for God Himself—offered blessings in the form of spiritual instruction and advancement within the monastic structure. Occasionally a guru might lend or procure a copy of a work for one of his disciples to copy for his own use; such largesse was part of the role of mentor and surrogate parent. Such acts could bind gurus and disciples across generations. For example, in the Niranjani Sampraday one Bhudhardas reports in the colophon of his copy of the *Rāmājña Rām Kathā* that his guru, Raghavdas, had arranged "through his grace" (*prasādena*) to get a copy of the work in the summer of 1703 CE so that Bhudhardas could copy it "for his own study" (*ātmapaṭhanārtha*). By 1705 CE, Bhudardas was already having his own disciples copy works for him, as evidenced in the colophon of a 1705 copy of Tulsidas's *Rāmacaritamānas*, made for Bhudhardas by the junior monk Gangaram.[71] A disciple's continuing reverence and devotion (*niṣṭhatā*) to his guru was rewarded with the guru's continuing grace (*prasād*), a mutually perpetuating exchange recorded and performed in the colophons of these and similar *pothī*s.

Copies of works produced by one religious community and found in the collections of another point to a type of exchange that was as much social and institutional as theological and literary. The Niranjanis and Dadu Panthis provide a perfect example: by far, the greatest number of manuscripts of Niranjani works outside of the community's own collections are in the monastic libraries of the Dadu Panth, and vice versa.[72] This constant cross-fertilization reflects the fact that the two communities were closely intertwined, if not indistinguishable, in the seventeenth century: they claimed several of the same saints and scholars as their own and courted patronage and devotees from the same merchants of the region, establishing *maṭh*s in the same cities and towns.[73] Farther north in the Punjab, Niranjani and Dadu Panthi works on theology and poetics made their way into the collections of the Sikh community. Copies of Sundardas's *Jñānasamudra* and *Savaiya Granth*, Hariramdas's *Chandaratnāvalī*, and Niranjani and Dadu Panthi vernacular adaptations of Sanskrit works nestled between Sikh religious texts in anthologies that the Sikh tradition calls *guṭakā*: bundles of *pothī*s inscribed in the Gurmukhi script and bound together.[74] Similarly, copies of scholastic works by monks of the Sikh Sevapanth—including the *Pāras Bhāg* (Fortune of the Philosopher's Stone), an eighteenth-century *bhāṣā* adaptation of the Persian *Kīmiyā-yi Saʿādat* (The Alchemy of Happiness, 1058/59) of Abu Hamid Al-Ghazali—were kept in the monastic libraries of the Dadu Panth. Collectively, these manuscripts are the material trace of vibrant discussions on matters of theology, metaphysics, and literary theory pursued by members of the Sikh, Dadu Panth, and Niranjani communities from the early seventeenth through the nineteenth century—a shared history that has been largely forgotten by modern scholars and even by the communities themselves.[75]

*Pothī*s inscribed by monks for lay devotees and other householders mark the exchange of scribal labor and religious knowledge for patronage that sometimes came in the form of monetary renumeration. There was an apparent demand for copies of works on theology and literary theory among members of the same merchant and clerical communities that supplied initiates and material patronage to the monastic orders of the Dadu Panth and Niranjani Sampraday. This makes sense given that these communities' scribal skills enabled the sects to broadcast their works in writing; much of this literature also spoke directly to householder concerns regarding how to live ethically and achieve salvation despite being implicated in the social and material webs of *saṁsāra*.[76] The monastic scribes who copied the works of Sundardas, Hariramdas, Bhagvandas, and the like for householder devotees sometimes acknowledge their shared confessional identity by using shared appellations in their colophons.[77] Niranjani and Dadu Panthi monks also copied works for other householder patrons, including texts from their own traditions and various others in Sanskrit and in *bhāṣā*; such copying, in contrast to the careful editorial practices followed within monastic structures, could be mechanical in nature, insofar as it did not presuppose an understanding of a manuscript's content or even the language in which it was composed.[78]

Copies made by monks for ruling elites, including local lords (*sāmant, rāṇā*), Rajput kings and princes, and members of the Mughal nobility, throw light on exchanges between spiritual and temporal authority in the seventeenth and eighteenth centuries. Both Rajput and Mughal ideologies of rule emphasized the importance of moral, ethical, literary, artistic, and religious education to the constitution of political authority. In the medieval period, various Sanskrit genres like *subhāṣita* and the Persian genres of *akhlāq* and *adab* had served the purpose of providing such an education to courtly elites; however, by the late sixteenth century, there was an increasing demand for pedagogical materials in the vernacular.[79] This demand was particularly strong among ascendant Rajput clans eager to fashion new idioms of Hindu kingship, including the Tomar Rajputs of Gwalior at the turn of the sixteenth century and the Kachwaha, Rathore, Sisodia, and Chauhan courts in Rajasthan during the late sixteenth and seventeenth centuries.

To meet this need, intellectuals employed at Rajput and Mughal courts such as Keshavdas, Kavindracharya Sarasvati, Cintamani Tripathi, Vrind, and Sundar Kavi composed works of *nīti* (ethics), *kāvya-śāstra*, and *kathā* (in this context, didactic narratives) that quickly came to form a curriculum for princes and sons of the nobility.[80] Monastic orders like the Dadu Panth and Niranjani Sampraday also responded by presenting copies of their works to local rulers. For example, Niranjani monks presented copies of Manohardas's *Vedānta Mahāvākya Bhāṣā* in 1722, Bhagvandas's *Vairāgya Vṛnd* in 1737, and Manohardas's *Jñānamañjarī* in 1748 to the Kachwaha court at Jaipur.[81] While Manohardas's works explained concepts of Advaita Vedānta, Bhagvandas's *Vairāgya Vṛnd* contained a vernacular translation of and commentary on Bhartrihari's famous *śataka*—itself a classic of the *subhāṣita* genre, which provided a literary and ethical education to courtly elites. All three works would have spoken to the interests of Jai Singh II and his son, who were heavily invested in reviving scientific knowledge in Sanskrit as well as Vedic ritual practices.[82] A generation later and three hundred kilometers west at the Rathore court of Marwar, the Niranjani monk Mangaldas copied a collection of vernacular works on Advaita Vedānta in 1778 for the princes Sher Singh and Guman Singh. The Rathore royal family had maintained an interest in Advaita Vedānta since the time of the princes' great-great-grandfather, Raja Jasvant Singh (d. 1678), who himself composed four works on the subject; these same works were studied in the Niranjani Sampraday. The princes' grandfather, Raja Bakht Singh, had also received a copy of Niranjani and Dadu Panthi works in 1739/40 CE while staying at his palace in Nagaur. Within the Ahhichatragarh fort there, Bakht Singh regularly hosted sadhus like those of the Niranjani Sampraday and Dadu Panth in a special *nivās* (residential quarters).[83]

As the foregoing examples illustrate, the exchange of *pothīs* among these monastic orders and royal courts punctuated a relationship that involved intellectual exchange as well as exchanges between religious and political authority. Rajput kings studied the compositions of Dadu Panthi and Niranjani monks, and the monks studied the compositions of Rajput kings.[84] This intellectual interaction could extend over generations, so when Mangaldas Niranjani, in the colophon of the primer that he prepared for Sher Singh and Guman Singh, rehearsed the princes' royal lineage and his own guru-disciple lineage, noting the date and location at which he presented the manuscript, he was marking a transaction that renewed the ties between those two intertwined lineages. These ties produced not only prestige but also material advantages for the religious communities, in the form of tax-free land grants, financial support for architectural projects, and sometimes monetary gifts.[85]

THE WORLD OF VERNACULAR INTELLECTUALS IN EARLY MODERN NORTH INDIA

The "grunt work" of the process we now call vernacularization was performed by individuals like Rupdas, the monk described at the beginning of the chapter. Like his fellow monks, he moved back and forth between the cities and towns of the region, copying the works of his monastic tradition as well as the classics of the Sanskrit canon and of the emerging vernacular canon for his teachers, senior monks, and householder devotees. In this way, sadhus established *bhāṣā* as a medium of scholarly and literary discourse, not only in cities but also in *qaṣbah*s and villages from Gujarat to Bengal. This was also how they established and maintained the intellectual networks of the time, in which texts and ideas circulated through human encounters and through the (sometimes painful) physical labor of copying works by hand. Rupdas's labor was both physical and intellectual: the loose and sometimes sagging lines of his manuscript speak to physical fatigue, but the editorial marks—insertions and corrections inscribed in the margins, on the rare occasion that he omitted part of a verse while copying—and his diligence in noting the date of completion of each section speak to the mental sharpness with which he continued to work. His declaration of his monastic lineage at the close of the *pothī* affirms his intellectual and spiritual credentials and his authority to transmit the works contained therein.

The *pothī*'s use by Baldev (the recipient of the manuscript) would have been an embodied as well as intellectual affair involving vocalized reading, likely in a ritualized manner in which the position and posture of the reader and the arrangement and handling of the manuscript followed certain norms, like those depicted in contemporary paintings. Its performance would have been an act of alchemy in which the written words were transformed into spoken discourse once again in an encounter between teacher and student. As Hindi sources of the period put it, he would have "made the text speak" (*granth bāṁc-*).[86]

The *pothī*s in present-day archives paint a different picture of early modern intellectual culture and scholastic networks than that found in much of the literary and religious historiography on the period. Studies of *nirguṇ* religiosity that take their material exclusively from the lyric and epigrammatic poetry of *nirguṇ* saints tend to conclude—quite reasonably—that the tradition's critique of Brahminical ritual and pedagogical practice put *nirguṇ* religious sects in a distant and antagonistic relationship to not only Sanskrit pandits but also courtly elites (the political counterparts of the Brahmin ritual complex). The manuscript record tells a more complicated story: poets of the Dadu Panth and Niranjani

Sampraday certainly pursued such critiques, but they and their monastic brethren also pursued discussions with Rajput kings and Brahmin pandits on matters of metaphysics, theology, and literary theory. They studied works outside of their own sectarian canon, including those of authors and traditions with which they disagreed; thus copies of works like Tulsidas's *Rāmacaritamānas* and Keshavdas's *Rasikapriyā*—a work that criticizes *nirguṇ* religiosity and a work criticized by *nirguṇ* poets, respectively—were copied and read by Niranjani monks at Didwana in the seventeenth and eighteenth centuries. Debate, after all, requires familiarity, acquired through the close study of competing traditions' literature.

This was all made possible by individuals and communities that had traditionally practiced mundane forms of literacy but were now using those skills to broadcast *kāvya* and *śāstra* in the vernacular. These monks of merchant and clerical backgrounds leveraged their literacy to drastically expand their communities' sphere of influence: although the numerical strength of the Dadu Panth's and Niranjani Sampraday's monastic orders does not appear to have been particularly great in comparison to those of other communities, they wielded an intellectual influence disproportional to their size precisely because they were quick to embrace literacy and manuscript culture. The diligence with which they copied and circulated their works helped establish them as the preeminent authorities on Advaita Vedānta, yoga, devotional literary aesthetics, and astrology in the vernacular, not only in their home region of Rajasthan but also in parts of the Punjab.[87] The *pothī* was the primary—but not the only—conduit of their influence. They also constituted and expressed religious authority through another form of written media: the holy book.

FIGURE 3.1 *Vairāgya Śataka* of Bhartrihari with the *Vivekadīpikā* commentary of Indrajit, copied VS 1764 (1707/1708 CE). Rubrics, margins, and the diagram in the center of the folio are inscribed in red ink.

Bhandarkar Oriental Research Institute Ms. 387-1892-95, Folio 1b

FIGURE 3.2 Vallabhacharya and Vitthalnath of the Vallabha Sampraday and disciples. Vitthalnath teaches from a *pothī* while the disciple sitting before him inscribes another *pothī*. Two more *pothī*-type manuscripts on bookstands are in the lower third of the painting. A disciple appears to be performing obeisance to the *pothī* on the right. Nathdwara, Rajasthan, mid-eighteenth century

Collection of Anuj Ambalal; photograph courtesy of the Art Institute of Chicago

FIGURE 3.3 “A Preacher Expounding the Poorans. In the Temple of Unn Poorna, Benaras.” In James Prinsep, *Benaras Illustrated, in a Series of Drawings,* plate 5.

British Library, Item No. 75115

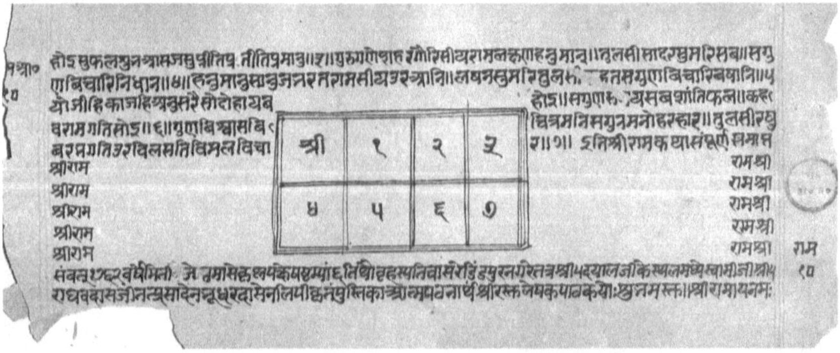

FIGURE 3.4 *Rāmājña Rām Kathā*, copied 1703

Rajasthan Oriental Research Institute, MS 27519, Folio 10b

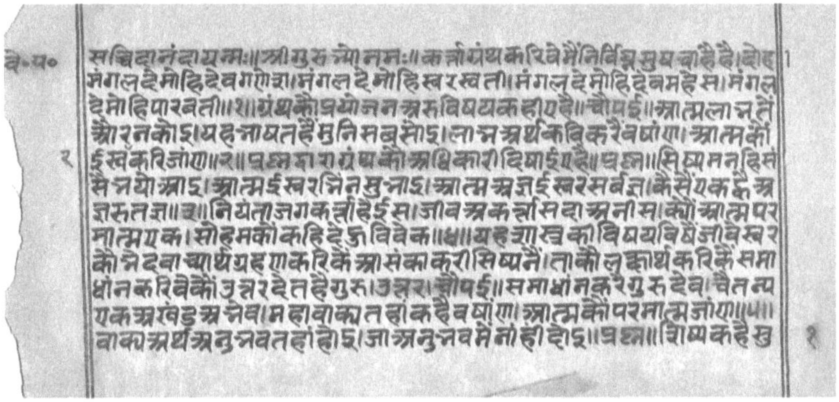

FIGURE 3.5 The *Vedānta Mahāvākya Bhāṣā* of Manohardas Niranjani. Manuscript copied in 1797 CE by the monk Jairamdas. Rubrics are highlighted with red *hiṅgul* powder.

Rajasthan Oriental Research Institute, Jodhpur, MS 26579, folio 1B

4
The Guru's Voice and the Sacred Book

suṇi pāḍe kiā likhahu jañjālā
likhu rāma nāma guramukhi gopālā

Listen pandit!
Why do you write entanglement?
Remain obedient to Gopal,
and write the Name of Ram.

—Guru Nanak (1469–1539), Rāmakali M. 1 Dakhaṇī Oaṁkāru

In a small *galī* or lane near the Niranjani Sampraday monastery in the town of Didwana is an unassuming gate that opens into a small courtyard. In the middle of the courtyard stands the *samādhi* or funerary monument of Amardas (d. 1785), a guru and saint-poet of the Niranjani Sampraday. The brothers Damodarlal and Radheshyam Parik and their family have maintained the *samādhi* for generations, and on certain days of the year (or when a visitor requests), they open the door of the shrine so that one may pay homage to the saint. Amardas's personal effects are arranged reverently in the center of the monument's sanctum: his *gudaṛī* (patchwork shawl), sandals, and *vāṇī*. In the Niranjani tradition, a *vāṇī* (lit. "utterance" or "voice") is a collection of the songs and sayings of a saint arranged in a particular order and copied into a distinctive and very large codex book. From the mid-seventeenth century, Niranjani gurus like Amardas carried such *vāṇīs* containing the words of Kabir, Namdev,

Haridas Niranjani, and other poets of the Niranjani tradition (as well as poets of the closely related Dadu Panth). These anthologies provided a textual script and visual focal point for gatherings of devotees during which the guru would preach and teach. Today, Amardas's *vāṇī* is not read but instead performs another kind of work: set on a *raḥl* bookstand in the sanctum, it stands in for the guru himself, an object of reverence suffused with his aura and constituting the material instantiation of his "voice."

This particular *vāṇī* began as the voice of the guru Amardas in a very different sense. According to the manuscript's colophon, in May 1783 CE, after a month and a half of "back-breaking" scribal labor, five monks of the Niranjani Sampraday, all Amardas's disciples, completed this anthology of 714 folios (equaling 1,428 pages). Lakshman, Lakshmidas, Bhudhar, Ramdas, and Jairam put considerable time and energy into producing a volume that was clearly legible, easily navigated, and visually impressive. To this end, they inscribed a comprehensive table of contents at the beginning of the manuscript and added extensive rubrics in red ink. Though they did not add the type of decorative embellishments and illumination found in some other *vāṇī* manuscripts, they did inscribe double lines in red ink along both the margins and the edges of the folios, giving the pages a visually pleasing symmetry (figs. 4.1 and 4.2). The five scribes collectively copied 16,364 verses by at least 46 different saint-poets, spanning a range of genres that included the *sākhī*, *pad*, *paricay* (hagiography), *stuti* (eulogy), and *kathā*. They organized this mass of material according to author, raga, and theme; this structure, in combination with the table of contents, folio and verse numbers, and other navigational apparatuses, would have allowed their guru, Amardas, to quickly and easily recall and "make speak" (*bāṁc-*) the words of the saints. This was an all-in-one, comprehensive collection of material for preaching, teaching, and leading congregational singing, made portable and durable by its sturdy binding, cardboard and cloth cover with protective fore-edge flaps, and outer binding thread. The changing career of Amardas's *vāṇī* as a textual tool, ritual focal point, and object of veneration reflects a significance and power that is not limited to the book's utility as a mnemonic prosthesis or repository of textual information.

The Niranjani *vāṇī* is one of several types of written vernacular scripture that emerged among religious communities during the late sixteenth and early seventeenth centuries. Using the term "scripture" to describe such an artifact is not without problems: English "scripture" is derived from Latin *scrīptūra* ("writing," "inscribing"), and cognates in Romance languages are similarly derived.[1] Though historically, all three of the major Semitic religions—Judaism, Christianity, and Islam—have their roots in oral tradition, each has come to embrace an idea of its own scripture as essentially *written*.[2] The situation in premodern South Asia was significantly different: orality was integral to the structure of the earliest known stratum of sacred texts, the Vedas (first and second millennia BCE), as well as to the rules of their transmission: inscribing them was largely prohibited, at least until the early modern period.[3] Orality continued to be valorized over writing in later religious texts such as the *śāstras*, *sūtras*, *purāṇas*, and epics (despite the fact that writing was clearly part of their composition and circulation).[4] In contrast, Buddhist and Jain communities in South Asia developed "cults of the book" by the early centuries of the first millennium, in which physical copies of canonical works were understood to possess both power and agency. As Jinnah Kim has demonstrated in the case of Mahayana Buddhism, practices of imagining and fashioning manuscripts as stupas and mandalas, and beliefs about the ability of sacred books to effect changes in the material world, reached their height in the early centuries of the second millennium.[5] In the case of Jainism, a robust and codified system of commissioning, producing, giving, and receiving copies of certain Jain religious works (most often for use by Jain monks but occasionally for rulers or householders) developed in which each of these practices or acts was understood to produce spiritual merit (*puṇya*). Such practices continued into the early modern period and the present.[6]

Similar beliefs and practices within the complex of sectarian traditions now recognized as Hinduism have gone relatively unremarked by modern scholars, especially the late medieval and early modern traditions associated with *bhakti*.[7] Nevertheless, there was a clear trend toward the establishment of canonized sacred texts in the form of physical books among *bhakti*-oriented religious communities during the sixteenth and seventeenth centuries, particularly in traditions of the *nirguṇ* persuasion. This important shift has yet to receive sustained research, and its causes remain largely unexplained.[8] Evidence suggests that the increased importance of writing to the canonization and authorization of religious scripture during that time was the result of multiple converging trends. The first was the increasing experimentation with genre made possible by the process of vernacularization. The innovation of new genres in *bhāṣā* made possible the conceptualization of the *granth* or *vāṇī* as an anthology of canonized saints. Religious communities committed their devotional texts to writing while creating organizational and exegetical techniques that would help to establish these works as religious scripture. The second contributing factor was the exchange between Islamicate and Indic forms of religiosity and material culture that began during the sultanate period and continued through the Mughal period. This eventually led to innovations in the material form of the manuscripts in which devotional texts were inscribed: the scriptural volumes produced in the late sixteenth through eighteenth centuries reflect a mix of elements appropriated from the Islamicate *kitāb* and the Indic *pothī*. Finally, the emphasis on the written aspect of scripture was driven in part by what William Pinch and Patton Burchett have identified as an emergent notion of "religion" and religious publics during the late sixteenth and early seventeenth century in northern India. This new mode of religiosity—which was closely tied to *bhakti* devotionalism—located power in the figure of God (as opposed to human bodies) and accorded with the political dispensation of Mughal and Rajput states.[9] The holy book, as a material symbol of universal authority and of the textual community that it helped to bring into being, became a focal point for the rituals through which religious communities imagined and enacted their own polities. Studying this process in the context of three such communities—the Sikhs, the Dadu Panth, and the Niranjani Sampraday—reveals that these traditions developed their respective notions of scripture and polity in conversation with one another.

SCRIPT AND SCRIPTURE

The definition of scripture, much like the definition of literature, is bound up in history and woven together with the concept of writing. Various peoples of South Asia, as elsewhere, have established, challenged, and revised notions of what constitutes sacred utterance over time and in the context of specific and historically contingent constellations of discourses, institutions, and power relations.[10] The factor that has remained consistent is the mutually constitutive relationship between medium and message: whether the sacred text has been transmitted exclusively through oral channels or established through commitment to writing, religious communities have defined and distinguished their scriptures, at least in part, through the material and embodied processes through which they are transmitted and reproduced. The establishment of written scriptures in Hindi that began in the late sixteenth century is remarkable because the concurrent production of scriptural anthologies across multiple religious communities reflects an emergent identification of scripture with written textuality and the elevation of the vernacular as a language of revelation.

No exact equivalent to the English term "scripture" exists in South Asian languages because the notion of an inherent relationship between sacred utterance and writing was not widespread until the early modern period. Nevertheless, communities from the Vedic period onward clearly distinguished certain forms of speech from others as "sacred" in the sense that these modes of speech, or speech acts, were consecrated or "set apart for" the deity or for a ritually significant purpose.[11] This phenomenon can be observed across different categories and genres of text (e.g., *saṁhitā, stotra, śāstra, purāṇa, itihāsa*) and across multiple religious traditions. For our purposes here, "scripture" can be heuristically defined as a text that has attained a special status, understood to be not just descriptive or evocative of something else sacred but a sacred thing itself.[12] As Catherine Bell suggests, it is "held sacred in comparison to other objects or other texts... It is the written word elevated into a service that eliminates the lines between medium and message, only to reimpose these lines in less sacred contexts."[13]

This fusion of medium (writing) with message (the revelations and dictums of the saints) shows how a historical change in media intersects with ideological, social, and political changes in early modern India. The inscription of sacred texts and their veneration has a long history in South Asia; yet the collection, collation, inscription, and ritual veneration of discrete and unified anthologies of saintly utterance—and in a quotidian tongue accessible to all—at the turn of the seventeenth century represents something truly new. The three foremost communities in this movement—the Sikhs, Dadu Panth, and Niranjani Sampraday—were clearly aware of this novelty because rather than attempting to obscure it, they emphasized it in their hagiographical writings and the paratextual material of the anthologies themselves. Even if these traditions understood the saints' words to be timeless, they also understood those words to be uttered and inscribed in historical time, a fact to be celebrated.

The written vernacular scriptures of early modern communities were produced through the intertwined processes of literization and anthologization. Literization, the commitment of language to writing, played a critical role in the establishment of *bhāṣā* as a language of revelation and scripture: the inscription of the saints' songs and sayings made it possible to imagine them *as texts* (as opposed to oral events) and to impose upon them hierarchical and taxonomic structures of organization—and thereby establish precedence. Writing them down allowed one to order the saints and their utterances according to a theological rubric (which I call anthologization) and to fix the form of those sayings in order to stabilize their transmission and establish a shared and authoritative recension. This was one of the ways fledgling religious communities attempted to control the potential mushrooming and competition of guru-disciple lineages. Communities like the Sikhs, Dadu Panth, and Niranjani Sampraday, centered around the guru-disciple relationship, were structurally inclined to develop multiple branches over time. Establishing a discrete and fixed scriptural corpus and setting rules for its transmission meant that all of those branches would ultimately lead back to the same root.

The material instantiation of saints' utterances also gave the vernacular and texts composed in it a new ontological character: the saints' words could now be "seen," making it possible for devotees to obtain *darśan* (reciprocal visual apprehension) of them. The words, transformed into a material substance, could be literally bound into the discrete object of a codex and thus imagined as a unitary body (corpus). This was equally true for an anthology of utterances by an individual saint like the *Dādū Vāṇī* and for an anthology that contained an entire canon of saints, such as the *Guru Granth Sāhib*. To borrow a metaphor from the seventeenth-century Dadupanthi hagiographer Madhavdas, the "sea of God's saints and their virtues" may be infinite, but the discrete and delimited material object of the bound holy book made it possible to imagine and map the contours of its shores. In the Sikh tradition, the inscription of the saints' utterances into a material volume also made it possible to "close the book" of revelation, as Guru Gobind Singh did explicitly in 1708, announcing that the line of human gurus was ended and henceforth the written scripture would act as the Guru of the community.

Finally, the materialization of saintly utterances in the form of a book made possible new ways of imagining communities, expressed and reproduced through a set of rituals that had the sacred book as their center. Possession of a written scripture marked a "people of the book" (*ahl al-kitāb* in Arabic, *ahl-i kitāb* in Persian), a status with distinct social and political significance in Mughal-ruled north India. For communities like the Niranjani Sampraday, scriptural anthologies figured in acts of ritual veneration (like those performed at the *samādhi* of Amardas) that affirmed membership in a decentralized but egalitarian system of monastic governance. For communities like the Sikhs, the elevation of the scriptural anthology to the status of the Guru led to the development of both a religious polity that recognized the holy book as its sovereign and a correspondingly "courtly" ritual idiom. In the Dadu Panth, the complex development of multiple scriptural anthologies was part of an equally complex tension between competing drives to centralize and decentralize authority.

The terms that these traditions use to designate their scriptural anthologies reflect the complex interplay of orality and writing that characterize the scriptures as discursive text and material book. The *tatsama* Sanskrit term *vāṇī* (and its *tadbhava* equivalent, *bāṇī*) mean "speech," "language," or "words." The compositions of an individual saint are thus collectively referred to as the saint's *vāṇī*. Given its derivation and literal meaning, the term always suggests a sonic or oral "event" that presupposes a speaker, either human or divine. A *vaṇī* is the "voice" of the guru that is "made to speak"'(*bāñc-*) by a reciter. The other term most often used for these scriptural anthologies is *granth*, from the Sanskrit nominative *grantha* ("tying, binding, stringing together," and thus "a knot").[14] In Sanskrit, Prakrit, and Apabhramsha, it most often refers to a literary "work," a set of verses or utterances that have been "tied together" into a unified textual object. The emphasis is on the discursive "text," yet it is hard to ignore the material resonance of the metaphor: it calls to mind the palm leaf *pothī* archetype with a string running through or around its individual leaves to "bind" them together, and even later, paper *pothīs*, often "tied" together in a *bastā*. This literal sense comes across in the way that sixteenth- and seventeenth-century Hindi authors use the term in religious contexts: *granth* refers to a bound codex copy of a scriptural anthology. Such anthologies consisted of multiple compositions that were metaphorically tied together and inscribed on paper folios that were literally stitched together.

Given the *nirguṇ* saints' epistemological and social critique of writing, the inscription and veneration of those same saints' utterances in the Dadu Panth, Niranjani Sampraday, and Sikh tradition can initially be perplexing. Indeed, the enthusiasm with which these traditions transcribed, collated, copied, circulated, and revered the saints' words has puzzled many historians of Hindi literature, some of whom have dismissed these communities as "hypocrites" that strayed from the path prescribed by their gurus.[15] Yet a close look at the religious and political contexts of the late sixteenth through early eighteenth centuries together with the hagiographical traditions of the communities themselves reveals that things are more complicated.

THE SCRIPTURAL TURN OF THE LONG SEVENTEENTH CENTURY

The trend among some *bhakti* communities toward establishing written scriptures appears to have developed in response to the political exigencies of Mughal rule, intersectarian competition, new theological ideas, and changing notions of what constituted "religion" and "religiosity" in general. At the turn of the seventeenth century, *bhakti* communities in northern India began refining and consolidating their textual canons; they continued to do so for roughly the next one hundred years. One reason appears to have been heightened competition for monastic initiates, lay devotees, and royal patronage.[16] In the context of sectarian competition for a limited pool of devotees and resources, it became imperative to differentiate one's theological, ideological, and aesthetic traditions from those of other groups. Communities drew this distinction and consolidated their identity by embracing some poets and works as their own while ejecting others from their canons.[17] A survey of approximately three hundred anthological manuscripts produced within several different religious orders from the late sixteenth through early nineteenth centuries reveals that most manuscripts copied from 1582 to 1635 CE, regardless of their sectarian provenance, include an ecumenical assortment of saint poets and poems; this suggests that songs by *nirguṇ* saints like Kabir, Ravidas, and Dadu, and songs by *saguṇ* Vaishnav devotees like Tulsidas, Surdas, and Mirabai were often performed together, or at least by the same performer.[18] By the middle of the seventeenth century, things had begun to change: manuscript anthologies reflect clear ideological and sectarian boundaries, with groupings of particular saint-poets taking shape. For example, over the course of the seventeenth century, manuscripts from the Pushtimarg, a Krishna-worshiping Vaishnava community centered in the region of Braj, increasingly featured only members of the *aṣṭachāp* or "eight seals" group of poets associated with the community through hagiographical writings like the *Caurāsī Vaiṣṇavan Kī Vartā* (Tales of the Eighty-Four Devotees of Vishnu, late seventeenth century CE).[19]

In several cases, the refinement of a sect's religious canon and the establishment of its saints' lyric poetry as scripture (as distinct from mere "song") proceeded in a dialectical relationship with the production of its hagiographical tradition. That tradition emphasized the centrality of the scriptures while establishing the spiritual credentials of the saints whose compositions were anthologized therein. As Vasudha Dalmia has noted in the case of the Pushtimarg, the imperative of asserting sectarian difference led to an emphasis on scripture in its *vārtā* (hagiographical) literature, which was "the *Bhāgavata Purāṇa* and the canon that the *sampradāya* itself [was] creating, much of it in Brajbhāṣā and some of it orally transmitted."[20] The production of *vartā* hagiographical works aided in the scripturalization of saint-poets' lyrics: Gokulnath, the author, and Hariray, the compiler of and commentator on the *vārtās*, incorporated the lyrics into dialogues and narratives depicting interactions between the saints and the Pushtimarg's founder, Vallabhacharya, thus recasting them as utterances of revelation during the *līlā* or "divine play" of the sect's founder and his disciples. The narratives themselves circulated orally until Hariray transcribed and collated them in the mid-seventeenth century.[21]

The Gaudiya Sampraday, another Vaishnava sect with roots in Braj, provides a different example of how hagiographies could help to establish scriptures. Over the course of the sixteenth century, a group of Gaudiya monks in Vrindavan, known as the Gosvamis, produced a rich theological literature in Sanskrit that would eventually become the scriptural core of the Gaudiya Sampraday (and was recorded in the Mughal *farmān* discussed in the preface of this book). These works and their delivery from Braj to devotees in Bengal around the turn of the seventeenth century were the subject of a vernacular hagiography, the *Prem Vilās* (The Revelry of Love) of Nityanand.[22] The narrative follows three Gaudiya monks as they struggle to transport the works of the Goswamis to Bengal, lose the books to bandits, and later recover them from the bandits' patron, a king named Vir Hamvir whom they successfully convert. The books (referred to as *granth* in the narrative) play a pivotal role in reforming the corrupt king and rescuing the mission: the disciples convert the king by reciting from their scriptures and initiate him into the Sampraday by touching him with one of the books.[23] Among those is the *Caitanya Caritāmṛta* of Krishnadas Kaviraj, a hagiography in Bengali that entextualizes the utterances of the sect's founder, Caitanya, within a narrative of his life. It all forms a striking *mise en abîme*: the vernacular hagiography of the *Prem Vilās* demonstrates the sacredness of the Gaudiya scriptures by narrating their loss and miraculous recovery, and among these scriptures is another vernacular hagiography, the *Caitanya Caritāmṛta*, that demonstrates the sacredness of the Gaudiya scriptures by narrating their enunciation on the lips of the sect's founder and his companions. Those same books may have later become objects of worship in a more monumental sense. According to a Gaudiya tradition recounted by Måns Broo, before the books were recovered, a second set of copies was made and sent from Vrindavan to Bengal. When the books were eventually located and found to be redundant, they were sent to the most senior scholar in Vrindavan, Jiva Gosvami. Finding them damaged and without the means to properly maintain these revered objects, Jiva had the *granth*s interred in the manner of ascetics: the body of a holy person, being already purified through *sādhanā* (spiritual practice), does not need to be purified through the fire of cremation and is therefore buried directly in the ground. Just steps from Jiva's own *samādhi* in Vrindvan lies a small octagonal dome known as the *granth samādhi* that is believed to contain the remains of these books.[24]

As the Gaudiya Sampraday, Pushtimarg, and other competing Vaishnava communities in Braj were establishing their various scriptural works in the late sixteenth and early seventeenth centuries, one of their shared textual foundations—the Sanskrit *Bhāgavata Purāṇa*—was taking on a new kind of material importance. A compendium of narratives concerning the deity Vishnu, including his avatar as Krishna, it provided a source of narrative, theological, and aesthetic material from which both the Sanskrit and vernacular lyrical and scholastic traditions of these Vaishnava communities drew heavily.[25] As Mackenzie Brown suggests, there is also something particular about the late medieval Puranic genre, especially the *Bhāgavata Purāṇa*, that lends importance to written copies. In the

Bhāgavata Purāṇa, the *Bhāgavata Māhātmya* (Eulogy to the Bhagavata) emphasizes the identification of the text with Krishna himself, in a manner similar to hypostasis, suggesting one possible reason for the importance of material copies. Brown ties this emphasis to the egalitarian ethos of *bhakti*: although recitation of the *purāṇas* remained firmly within the occupational domain of Brahmins, members of almost any caste or community, including women, could commission, donate, and listen to a copy of a *purāṇa* being recited (at least in theory). The manuscript record would appear to support Brown's argument: the sixteenth and seventeenth centuries witnessed the production of beautifully calligraphed and lavishly illustrated copies of the *purāṇas*, especially the *Bhāgavata Purāṇa*, commissioned by kings, princes, wealthy merchants, and other Vaishnava devotees.[26] Hagiographical sources like the *Caurāsī Vaiṣṇavan Kī Vartā* and the *Caitanya Caritāmṛta* also suggest that copies of the *Bhāgavata Purāṇa* played an important role in ritual gatherings of devotees.

Branches of these sects grew outward from Vrindavan and across the Mughal lands, thanks in large part to Mughal and Rajput patronage.[27] This combined support of the Braj region and its Vaishnava sects constituted a cooperative, elite cultural project that involved literature, visual art, and architecture. The type of religiosity theorized, patronized, and—in the case of Hindu members of the nobility, practiced—by these kings, princes, and nobles was, to quote William Pinch, "a religion of temples, monasteries, and physical symbols,"[28] among them the book (*kitāb*, *granth*). Just as the increasingly paper-based nature of intellectual exchange between elites encouraged devotional groups like the Dadu Panth and Niranjani Sampraday to commit their poetry to writing and re-present it as *kāvya* and *śāstra*, so too the bibliocentric literary and religious culture of the Mughal and Rajput nobility encouraged religious sects to entextualize and write down their traditions. Possession of written scriptures (or at least written texts) made a community legible as a religious tradition within the imperial gaze.

During the reign of Akbar (r. 1556–1605), the Mughal court began a vast information-gathering project about Indian lands, customs, and knowledge systems, including religion, that lasted decades and centered largely (though not exclusively) on the translation, study, and production of written texts.[29] The breadth of the Mughals' interests and the significance of books in the Mughal episteme can be discerned from Abul Fazl's description of the imperial library in his *Āʿīn-i Akbarī* (Institutions of Akbar, 1589–1598), an encyclopedic record of Akbar's empire:

> His Majesty's library is divided into several parts: some of the books are kept within, and some of them without the harem. Each part of the library is

> subdivided according to the value of the books and the estimation in which the sciences are held of which the books treat . . . Prose and poetry, Hindi [i.e., Sanskrit], Persian, Greek, Kashmiri are all kept separately. In this order they are also inspected. Experienced people bring them daily and read them before His Majesty, who hears every book from the beginning to the end . . . Among books of renown, there are few that are not read in His Majesty's assembly hall . . . Scholars of language (*zabān-dānān*) are constantly engaged in translating Hindi, Greek, Arabic, and Persian books (*kitāb*) into other languages.[30]

Abul Fazl's awe-inspiring description establishes the epistemic basis for the emperor's just and enlightened rule: the library is encyclopedic and panoptic, containing the totality of the world's knowledge, all of which the emperor absorbs with interest. Beginning with Akbar, Mughal kings and princes commissioned Persian translations of Indic texts on everything from poetry to mathematics, yoga, history, flora, and fauna, or sometimes commissioned digests of Indic works and knowledge systems in Persian or *bhāṣā*.[31] Some of the early classics of Hindi writing on religion and philosophy, including the *Yogavāsiṣṭhasār* ("Digest of the *Yoga Vāsiṣṭha*") of Kavindracharya Sarasvati and the *Vijñānagīta* (Song of Knowledge) of Keshavdas were composed in this context.[32] The consumption of such works was not limited to the imperial court; the imperial library and atelier served as "tastemakers" for the broader Persianized nobility, who commissioned their own copies.

The Mughals' bibliocentric knowledge practices shaped their understanding of South Asian religions more generally: in the *Āʿīn-i Akbarī*, Abul Fazl refers to the *Mahābhārat*, *Rāmāyaṇa*, Vedas, and *Harivaṁśa* as *kitāb*, "books." He also introduces the "nine schools" of Indian thought (Nyāya, Vaishesikā, Mīmānsa, Vedānta, Sānkhya, Patānjala, Jaina, Bauddha, and Nāstika, in his reckoning) by describing their proponents' shared method of writing on *pothīs*: "In this country there are eight sects who professedly teach the doctrines of the beginning of the world and of the next world . . . Formerly they wrote with an iron stylus on the leaves of the palm and the *tūz* tree, but now on paper, and from left to right. The leaves are kept separate and it is not the practice to stitch them together. Their mystic idealism enlightens the understanding and invigorates the soul."[33] For Abul Fazl, the identification of a religious or philosophical tradition as such begins with the identification of a written text, reflecting the influence of Islam, in which the archetypal book, the Qur'an, played a critical role in defining the tradition and its community.[34] We can also see a reflection of the belief among some Muslim elites in Mughal north India that an Indian religious tradition that possessed a scripture could potentially be considered *ahl-i kitāb*, a "people of the book," and therefore be entitled to certain rights and protections within an Islamic polity. Communities that prospered under the patronage of the Mughal court were largely those with both the cultural capital of written scriptures and the technical and discursive literacy to explicate them, in particular Jains and Brahmins.[35]

At Rajput courts within the Mughal Empire, there was an even greater demand for religious specialists, especially those who could explicate Sanskrit scriptures in the vernacular. The re-presentation of philosophical and religious systems in *bhāṣā* (and often in the idiom of *bhakti*) was integral to the way rulers like those of Amer, Jodhpur, Bikaner, Bundi, and Kota articulated new notions and modes of Hindu kingship from the late sixteenth through early eighteenth centuries.[36] For many, this meant patronizing one of the various Vaishnava sects of Braj, most often the Pushtimarg or Gaudiya Sampraday. For some, like the court of Jaipur in the early eighteenth century, this meant patronizing multiple *bhakti* sects as well as *smarta* Brahmins and Vedic ritual specialists. In all cases, possession of a written scripture or scriptures was critical to participation in court religion. It was the criterion by which a religious sect could be identified as distinct and legitimate in the eyes of the crown and thus a prerequisite for participation in religious and philosophical discussions at court. It was also a mode of giving and receiving patronage: commissioning deluxe copies of scriptural works became an important expression of royal piety as well as connoisseurship (most especially in the case of the *Bhāgavata Purāṇa*).[37]

The hagiographical literature of the Sikhs, Dadu Panth, and Niranjani Sampraday shows a keen awareness of these developments at Mughal and Rajput courts. For example, Jangopal's *Dādū Janm Līlā* locates Dadu and his community in both the Mughal and Rajput dispensations, recounting his visits to Mughal and Rajput courts and discussions with Akbar, the Kacchwaha Rajput King Bhagvandas, and their respective ministers. These rulers summon Dadu in order to determine the theological and doctrinal positions of the saint and his flock. Regardless of the extent to which we can ascertain the historical veracity of such accounts, these narratives reflect concern with being *legible* as a religious community in the gaze of the Mughal and Rajput states.

For Mughal and Rajput elites desiring to know and govern their subjects, a written scripture served a metonymic function, standing in for the community of people that recognized its authority and abided by its precepts. For the communities themselves, a written scripture provided a medium through which transactions of religious and temporal power could be pursued. Sometimes, as in the case of the Pushtimarg and Gaudiya Sampraday at the Jaipur court, the relationship thus constituted was one of patronage. In contrast, for the Sikhs, Dadu Panth, and Niranjani Sampraday, the establishment of a written scripture could be as much an expression of spiritual and political sovereignty as an attempt to liaise with political elites.

THE *GURU GRANTH SĀHIB* AND THE SIKH COMMUNITY

Nowhere is this phenomenon more clearly exemplified than in the case of the Sikh community, a tradition that from early in its history understood itself to be a distinct *dīn* (Arabic, "religion," "faith").[38] The effort to define and establish an authoritative anthology of saintly utterances and the importance of material copies are in consonance with that understanding and with ideas and practices of literacy among the Sikh Gurus and their followers. Sikhism, founded by Guru Nanak (1469–1539) toward the end of the fifteenth century, has much in common with both *nirguṇ sant* and Vaishnava *bhakti*, and even includes saints from both of these traditions within its scriptural canon. In the *Guru Granth Sāhib*, the lyrics and sayings of saints like Kabir, Ravidas, Namdev, and Surdas, as well as Sufi saints like Baba Farid and Bhikan, constitute what is called the *bhagat bāṇī* ("words of the devotees"). Yet the compositions by the Sikh gurus, which form the textual core of the Sikh canon and carry the greatest theological authority, articulate a mode of religiosity that is distinct from its *nirguṇ* and *saguṇ* cousins, in part because of its emphasis on certain forms of writing. The Sikh Gurus preached a type of religiosity that was explicitly universalist and addressed to all castes and both genders—and that consequently possessed the potential to become *law*. Perhaps for this very reason, from the late sixteenth through early eighteenth centuries, the community struggled to maintain unity and continuity in the chain of human and scriptural authority represented by the Guru and the *Granth*.[39] At certain historical junctures, possession of an authoritative copy of the scripture conferred religious authority upon its human custodian. The combination of universalist ideology, emphasis on internal continuity, and a *bhakti*-style theology that—to borrow William Pinch's words from a different context—posits "a distant yet ever-present Lord, God as a thing apart, God with an upper-case 'G,'" favors an understanding of the Sikh traditions as a *dīn* or *maẕhab* (Arabic, "way," "law," "creed") rather than a mere "sect" (*sampradāy*, *panth*).

Literacy and writing appear to have been integral to the Sikhs' theological thought, literary idiom, and communal identity from early on in the community's history. Guru Nanak, born in a town near Lahore during the period of the Lodi sultanate, hailed from a *khatrī* clan of merchants and clerks. He trained in vocational forms of literacy like bookkeeping and received education in Persian—making him less like his *nirguṇ sant* contemporaries Kabir and Ravidas and more like the merchant and clerical communities that would come to populate the Sikh and *nirguṇ bhakti* traditions beginning in the late sixteenth century.[40] The Sikh hagiographical tradition emphasizes Guru Nanak's mercantile literacy to great effect in stories that present him as a "bad" merchant but an extraordinary saint, giving away food and goods rather than selling them for profit.

Sikh hagiographies also attest that Guru Nanak's words, in the form of hymns called *śabad* (Sanskrit *śabd*, "sound") and short verses called *salok* (Sanskrit *śloka*) were written down during his lifetime, either by merchant disciples or by Nanak himself.[41] Bhai Gurdas (d. 1637), companion of the fifth Sikh Guru, theologian, and one of the collators and scribes of the *Ādi Granth* (the anthology that would later be expanded and dubbed the *Guru Granth Sāhib*), writes of Guru Nanak's "*kitāb*"—the book in which Nanak recorded his hymns and poems. Significantly, Bhai Gurdas mentions the *kitāb* for the first time while describing Nanak's visit to Mecca, the center of the Islamic world and the *ahl-i kitāb* or "people of the book." The authorities there—*qāẓī*s (judges) and *mullah*s (clerics)—challenge Guru Nanak to open his book and ascertain from it whether Hindus or Muslims are better. Nanak bests the lot by replying that neither can attain heaven without performing good deeds.[42] Sikh tradition asserts that Guru Nanak gave this manuscript to his successor, Guru Angad, as a symbol of the transfer of spiritual authority, and that later gurus added their own compositions to the manuscript, passing it on to their respective successors in a ritual of ceremonial investiture.[43]

The transfer of this anthological manuscript and its accompanying authority became the focal point for struggles over succession and leadership during the sixteenth century. This led to the appearance of multiple factions or lineages within the Sikh community, each possessing its own copy of the anthology. Each faction also produced hagiographical literature that attempted to authenticate the provenance of its respective copy and thus bolster its claims to authority. In 1581, when Guru Ramdas (1534–1581) passed leadership of the community to his younger son, Arjan (1563–1606), his elder son, Prithi Chand (1558–1618), contested the succession, using his possession of the aforementioned *kitāb* to stake a claim as the rightful Guru. The manuscript, known today as the Guru Harsahai *pothī*, remained in the possession of Prithi Chand and his descendants Miharavan and Hariji as they established a competing lineage of gurus. Within this lineage, known by the patronymic "Sodhi," the *Gosaṭi Guru Miharivānu* (Guru Mihirvan's Discussion, late seventeenth century) was composed; the hagiographical work asserts the Guru Harsahai *pothī* to be the spiritual patrimony received from Guru Nanak and his successors.[44] The second such manuscript, or rather set of four bound codices, called the Goindval *pothīs*, contains compositions by Guru Nanak that were likely copied from the Guru Harsahai *pothī* as well as compositions by Guru Amardas and the aforementioned *bhagats* (Kabir, Ravidas, Surdas, Sheikh Farid, etc.) that appear to have been added to the second section of the Guru Harsahai *pothī* later. The Goindval *pothīs* can safely be dated to the period of Guru Amardas (d. 1574), most likely to 1570–1572.[45] The Guru's son, Baba Mohan, retained possession of the *pothīs* even when Guru Amardas transferred leadership of the community to his son-in-law, Bhai Jetha (Guru Ramdas), in 1574; his descendants, known as the Bhalla family, continued to hold on to the *pothīs* in order to retain authority and prestige while challenging Guru Ramdas's legitimacy.[46] One of the family members, Sarupdas Bhalla, composed the hagiographical *Mahimā Prakāś* ("Light of Glory") in 1576, asserting that the *pothīs* were originally copied for Guru Amardas by his grandson, Sahnasram, supporting the Bhalla family's claim to legitimate possession of the book.[47] When the Bhallas eventually made peace with Guru Arjan (son and successor to Guru Ramdas), they effected the compromise by lending the *pothīs* to the Guru so that he could compile an authoritative recension of the scripture; in return, the Bhallas were allowed to retain their copies and attendant prestige.[48]

Within the context of this struggle for spiritual authority among the Sodhis, Bhallas, and the appointed Gurus, Guru Arjan took the decisive action of collating, structuring, inscribing, and establishing an authoritative recension of Sikh scripture in 1604.[49] This lengthy and meticulous process involved the work of several editors and scribes, including the aforementioned scholar and chronicler Bhai Gurdas. Guru Arjan and his team made important contributions to the anthology's structure, revising the raga-based organization of hymns introduced in the Goindval *pothīs* and adding the new rubric of *ghar* (lit. "house"), a classification of musical and metrical rhythm. Guru Arjan also authorized significant additions, including the *rāgamālā* or "garland" of musical modes that closes the scripture and a hagiographical work describing a meeting between Guru Nanak and the king of Sri Lanka. Finally, Guru Arjan introduced two textual (or perhaps paratextual) elements of great importance: the *mūl mantar* ("root mantra"), which he inscribed himself at the beginning of the *pothī*, and a comprehensive table of contents.[50] Guru Arjan ritually "established" (*sthāp-*) this copy of the *gurabāṇī* or "saints' words"—known today as the Kartarpur *pothī* or *Ādi Granth* ("Original Book")—at Ramdaspur, the site of his *gaddī* or throne. Sikh tradition remembers and celebrates this momentous occasion annually in the Prakāś Utsav or Festival of Manifestation.

Guru Arjan's establishment of an authoritative written scripture was not simply an inward-looking response to tensions within the Sikh community; it was also an outward-looking announcement addressed to the social and political milieu of the Mughal-Rajput dispensation. At the same moment, Guru Arjan and his advisors were initiating changes in the way the Sikh *saṅgat* (lit. "assembly," i.e., the religious community) was imagined and administrated. These included a vast expansion of the institution of *masand*, a system of revenue collection in which members of the community were deputized to collect one-tenth of the earnings of each devotee household, as well as to adjudicate disputes in their respective jurisdictions. They also included an ambitious architectural program at Ramdaspur that saw the construction of the Darbār Sāhib ("Venerable Court"), a large shrine in which the *Ādi Granth* was eventually enthroned.[51] The office of the Guru was being gradually reimagined as that of a sovereign, the religious leadership as the nobility of a royal court, and the community of believers as a polity. Guru Arjan's compilation and ritual establishment of a scriptural text at his "capital" of Ramdaspur in 1604 made the burgeoning Sikh community legible as an independent religion, marked by specific textual, canonical, and theological boundaries, in the eyes of Rajput and Mughal political elites.[52]

Guru Arjan's compilation of the *Ādi Granth* at Ramdaspur marks the beginning of the formation of the *Guru Granth Sāhib* as a discrete and definitive scriptural text—but not its end. Later Gurus expanded it over the course of the seventeenth century until the tenth Guru, Guru Gobind Singh (1666–1708), ended the line of human Gurus and invested the written text of the *Guru Granth Sāhib* with supreme authority over the community in 1708. Throughout this history, Sikh hagiographical tradition emphasized the importance of written copies of the Gurus' and saints' utterances and adjudicated claims to authority in terms of the *written* transmission of those utterances. This draws attention to the theological and historical significance of writing in the Sikh religious imagination.

Hagiographical writings within the Sikh community, such as the *Janam Sākhīs*, the *Gosaṭi Guru Mihariwānu*, and the *vārs* (lit. "occasion," a type of ode) of Bhai Gurdas emphasize the unbroken written (and therefore authoritative) transmission of Sikh scripture even as they acknowledge and celebrate the historical origin of the revelation contained therein. Hagiographers like Bhai Gurdas assert that the truths articulated by Guru Nanak and his successors are the same as propounded "in the Vedas and Puranas" and by "all the saints"; yet the narratives presented in Bhai Gurdas's *vārs* have the texture of historical, not mythical, time. His descriptions of the early community read like inventories of the individual members, families, locations, administrative functions, and events, replete with detail. These hagiographical traditions, together with the Gurus' hymns and verses in the *Guru Granth Sāhib* itself, frame literacy and writing in a particular relationship to revelation and theology. Guru Nanak was not like his contemporaries Kabir and Ravidas, whose presumed illiteracy made it possible to read their poetry as a critique of writing as a mnemonic technology and an icon of religious authority. In contrast, hagiographies of Guru Nanak emphasize both his vocational literacy and his knowledge of "Turki"—a synecdoche for the Persian language and also the Persian literary and intellectual tradition.

Nanak speaks frequently of writing as an act of faith, in which he "will ask my Guru and write His words of love."[53] Later Gurus extend and amplify this idea of writing as an act of devotion: Amardas urges the faithful to "write with pen, paper, and ink pot / The Name of Ram and Hari's nectar-like words (*aṁmrita-bāṇī*)."[54] The term "guru" signifies both God and the human guru, so such directives can be read both metaphorically, as exhortations to act according to God's decrees, and literally, as instructions to inscribe the words of the Sikh Gurus. To act is to write, and to write is to act. The meaningful choice is not between writing and not writing but rather between writing worldly knowledge (mundane writing) or knowledge of God (elevated writing). As Guru Amardas says, "[Those who forget the Guru's word] write falsehood and practice falsehood . . . Those turned toward the Guru write meditations upon the truth."[55]

The Gurus' writings outline a theology in which all acts, including acts of writing, can be traced back to the original act of writing performed by God Himself. Yet only those acts (of writing) marked with His seal are authorized. In the *Japu Jī*, the verses that open the *Guru Granth Sāhib,* Guru Nanak states in a manner reminiscent of Islamic Hadith writings that "The names of all species and manner of beings / Were written by [His] moving pen."[56] All speaking and all writing has its roots in that original, creative act by a God that is Himself *akhar*—literally "imperishable," but also "syllables" or "letters": "Through *akhar,* words are written and spoken / Through *akhar,* destiny is declared on the forehead / He that wrote this, has not writing upon *His* head."[57] God brings entities, events, and conditions into being through writing: "He writes a command (*hukum*) and one obtains happiness or pain, by [His] command one is high or low." Indeed, the participle *likhiā* ("written") functions as a synecdoche for destiny in the hymns of the Sikh Gurus contained in the *Guru Granth Sāhib.*

God writes, and so it is; thus the supreme Guru's command is written into, and as, law: Guru Nanak says in the opening verses of the *Guru Granth Sāhib,* "Nanak, proceed according to what is written in the sovereign's command."[58] This way of imagining the Guru's word and written scripture as law gradually allowed the Sikh community to imagine and build itself as a polity with its own governmental structures and political authority and to create an elaborate, courtly ritual practice around the material object of the written scripture. In the Gurus' theological imagination, the sovereign's command (*hukum*) is "writ" in multiple senses of the word: it is "written," a "command," "scripture," and "authority" itself. The sovereign's word carries his authority because it bears his "seal" or "mark": "Writ cannot be erased [that carries] the seal of the word (*sabadu nisāṇā*)."[59] This is the same mark that Nanak invokes as the "true" seal or mark (of God) upon one's deeds.

The material logic of the metaphor is important. A seal is an impression, an absence that paradoxically evokes a presence; a sovereign's seal upon a written document proves that it has been in his presence and thus authorizes that which is written. In the thought of the Sikh Gurus, God's seal upon both utterance and deed evokes His presence and gives authorization. Similarly, Guru Nanak's seal authenticates and authorizes his command as the Guru in Sikh scripture: each of his successors "seals" their hymns by writing in the concluding verse not their own name but rather the *chāp* ("seal," "impression") of "Nanak." Sikh readers of the *Guru Granth Sāhib* know that a given hymn may have been "written" by Guru Amardas, Guru Ramdas, or Guru Arjan because the notation *mahalā* indicates the identity of each hymn's composer. Yet it is Nanak's *chāp* within these same hymns that "marks" them as authentic, as scriptural utterances authorized by *the* Guru. For as Sikh hagiography affirms, Guru Nanak was *present* in each of his successors: his soul or "light" (*jotī*) was absorbed into their respective souls.[60]

It is therefore no surprise that early authorized copies of the Sikh scriptural anthology often carry the literal signatures of the Gurus. Guru Ramdas authenticated the Goindval *pothīs* with his signature; Guru Arjan "sealed" the Kartarpur *pothī*, the archetype of the *Guru Granth Sāhib* that he had commissioned and ritually installed at Ramdaspur in 1604, by inscribing the *mūl mantar* himself. He later repeated this practice to authorize copies made from the Kartarpur *pothī* (or from other authorized copies).[61] Other, later Gurus also signed their names to *bīrs* (copies of the *Granth*) to sanction them, and these signed copies, by virtue of carrying the mark of the Guru's presence, subsequently became objects of veneration in their own right.[62]

THE *DĀDŪ VĀṆĪ*, *PAÑC VĀṆĪ*, AND *SARVĀṄGĪ*S OF THE DADU PANTH

While Guru Arjan was compiling a definitive recension of Sikh scripture, the monks of the Dadu Panth were compiling the words of their sect's founder, Dadu

Dayal, and the many saints that the Panth recognized into its own authoritative scripture. Like the Sikhs, the Dadu Panth commemorated and celebrated the compilation and inscription of these scriptures in hagiographical writings and ritually installed one scripture, the *Dādū Vāṇī* or "Words of Dadu," in the manner of a sovereign at the monastic center in Naraina. This is probably not a coincidence.

The Sikhs and Dadu Panth were engaged in a robust exchange of texts and ideas at the turn of the seventeenth century: several compositions attributed to Guru Nanak and Guru Angad were added to Dadu Panthi anthologies dating to the first quarter of the sixteenth century, including the *Sarvāṅgī* and *Pañc Vāṇī* anthologies.[63] Both communities included compositions by some of the same saints in their respective canons, including hymns by Kabir, Ravidas, Surdas, Namdev, Pipa, and Trilochan. In 1660, when the Dadu Panthi hagiographer Raghavdas penned his encyclopedic eulogy of the saints, the *Bhaktamāl* or "Garland of Devotees," he praised Guru Nanak, along with Dadu, Kabir, and the Niranjani saint Jaggan, as the four *mahants* (superiors) of the four *nirguṇ sampradāys*: Sikhism, the Dadu Panth, the Kabir Panth, and the Niranjani Sampraday, respectively.[64] In Raghavdas's words, the Sikhs and the Dadu Panthis stemmed from a common root, the worship of "the one, unqualified, unformed, undying" Divinity. They furthermore complemented each other, Nanak being "in the form of the Sun, giving light to the whole world," and Dadu being "in the form of the Moon, nourishing all with the nectar [of his moonlight]."[65] As the manuscript record reveals, intellectual exchanges would continue throughout the eighteenth and into the early nineteenth century, with compositions by poets of the Dadu Panth making their way into Sikh *guṭakās* and Sikh theological works like the *Pāras-Bhāg* (Fortune of the Philosopher's Stone, early eighteenth century) being studied by Dadu Panthi monks.[66] It would seem that much of this dialogue took place between Dadu Panthi monks and members of the Udasi and Sevapanthi communities, monastic sects within the broader Sikh fold that were active in the region of Fatehpur, an important center for the Dadu Panth. Sikh tradition also reports that the tenth and final Sikh Guru, Guru Gobind Singh, visited the Dadu Panthi monastery at Naraina in the early eighteenth century and met the *mahant* of the Dadu Panth, Jaitram.

Given these connections between the Dadu Panth and the Sikhs, it is striking that both compiled their respective scriptural anthologies at almost exactly the same time. While Sikhs commemorate Guru Arjan's installation of the *Ādi Granth* at Ramdaspur as occurring on August 29, 1604, the Dadu Panth claims that the *Dādū Vāṇī* or "Words of Dadu," a comprehensive anthology of Dadu's hymns and sayings, was compiled and installed at its monastery in Naraina on

June 24th, 1604—roughly a month after Dadu's death and a mere two months before the inauguration of the Ādi Granth.[67] The fact that parts of the Dadu Panthi source that gives this date, Madhavdas's *Sant Guṇ Sāgar*, date to later in the seventeenth century and are thus imagined "reconstructions" of events, only strengthens the impression that the Dadu Panth found it important to establish their scripture as being at least as old as the *Ādi Granth* of the Sikhs, if not its very twin.[68]

As in the case of the Sikh tradition, the Dadu Panth's hagiographical works emphasize the fidelity with which the guru's words were transmitted in writing as well as the meticulous editorial work that went into producing the authorized scriptural anthology. Jangopal makes sure to mention in his *Dādū Janm Līlā* that Dadu was accompanied at all times by his faithful devotee and scribe, Mohandas Daftari. Mohandas's very surname, *daftarī* (Persian, "office keeper"), suggests that he hailed from a clerical background. Jangopal relates that he "recited Hari's (God's) virtues as he collected them from the guru and wrote them down."[69] This emphasis on first-person witness echoes the same emphasis in the *sākhī* genre of epigrams; the verse also suggests a deliberate effort to "collect" (*sāṁc-*) the guru's utterances during his lifetime. Mohandas "witnessed" the guru's speech with his own ears, and this speech, once written down, would be presented in scriptural anthologies as the spiritual "witness" of and by the guru in the form of *sākhīs*.[70]

Just as Sikh tradition records the editorial rigor with which the *Ādi Granth* was compiled, the Dadu Panthi tradition records how Garibdas, the son and spiritual successor of Dadu, supervised his best monks as they collated and edited his father's words into an authoritative recension, carrying out an order that had come from the mouth of Dadu himself. Madhavdas narrates the compilation of the *Dādū Vāṇī* thus:

> dādu guru nija āyasu pāvata, rajjaba mohana śrī jagannātha
> sākhi hu śodha anukrama rākhata, tāla ru rāga garībahiṁ sātha
> aṃga saiṃtīsa sākhi likhī saba, rāga satāisa śabdahiṁ gāthā
> yoṁ kari saṃta likhī guru vāṇi ju, sthāna ru sthāna bhaī vikhyātā

> Receiving orders from the guru Dadu himself,
> Rajjab, Mohan, and the great Jagannath
> revised and ordered the *sākhīs*
> and [did the same] for the *tālas* and ragas, together with Garibdas.
> All the *sākhīs* were written down in thirty-seven chapters (*aṅg*),
> and the devotional songs in twenty-seven ragas.

In this way the true ones (*sant*) inscribed the words of the guru
  (*guruvāṇī*)
  and it became famous everywhere.[71]

Madhavdas leaves no room for doubt that the guru himself willed his words to take the form of a written *granth* and hand-picked individual disciples to complete the task. Among them was Mohandas, the same monk who had transcribed Dadu's every word; Rajjab, an accomplished poet himself and the compiler of another scriptural anthology; and Garibdas, the living recipient of the guru's authority. The chain of textual transmission and leadership could not be clearer. Madhavdas also describes the structure of the scripture in considerable detail, mentioning the thematic or *aṅg*-based organization of epigrams and the rhythmic (*tāl*) and melodic (*rāg*) organization of hymns. By introducing these innovations into the organization of material, the Dadu Panth produced a distinctive type of scriptural anthology and pioneered an editorial practice that helped guarantee stable textual transmission. Over the seventeenth and eighteenth centuries, this practice would be emulated by other *nirguṇ* monastic orders like the Kabir Panth, Ramsnehi Sampraday, and Niranjani Sampraday.

Madhavdas's evocative description of the life of the Dadu Panth after its founder's passing makes clear that the creation of the *Dādū Vāṇī* (or, in Madhavdas's words, the *guru vāṇī*, a name that again suggests comparison with the *Guru Granth Sāhib* of the Sikhs) inaugurated a new epoch in the way that the guru's message of liberation reached the faithful. Just as the guru himself had once plied the roads and trails of the region, delivering his revelations and insights to devotees in far-flung towns and villages, his monks would now follow those same roads, quite literally carrying his words, in written form, to devotees:

jo apano guru-paṃtha upāsaka, pāsa rakhe guruvāṇī pujāī
dāsa garība daī saba ko sudha, saṃta sudhānahiṁ vāṇī dharāī
deśa diśā nija sādhuna ko paṭi, mādhava vāṇi ju kīrati gāī

Those practitioners who adopted the guru's path
  kept a *Guru Vāṇī* and worshiped it.
Garibdas reminded and instructed everyone
  that a *sant* should keep [a copy of] the *vāṇī*.
In every land and direction where he sent his sadhus,
  The glory of the *vāṇī* was sung, says Madhav.[72]

The guru—or rather his physical manifestation in human form, which hagiographers like Madhavdas and Jangopal are careful to point out is merely an illusion adopted for the sake of convenience—may be gone, but his essence, his word (*vāṇī*), is still very much present. It is the duty of his disciples to "keep" the guru's *vāṇī*, and here the word "keep" (*dhar-*) is polysemic, meaning both keep a copy of the book in hand and keep the words of the guru in their heart. This *vāṇī*, in its material as well as spoken form, is to be "venerated" or "worshiped" (*pujā-*) just as the guru himself was worshiped when he was physically present. For the *vāṇī* both confers and receives glory, as reflected in the polysemy of the final line: "the glory of the *vāṇī* was sung" (*vāṇi ju kīrati gāī*). The guru's hymns extoll the glories of God, and devotees' performance of those hymns celebrate the glory of the guru's word. This is the birth of scripture: when the medium itself becomes the message and the means to access the sacred becomes something sacred in its own right.

The *Dādū Vāṇī* was the first but not the only scriptural anthology produced within the Dadu Panth. The industry and diligence with which the monks of the Panth transcribed, collated, and copied the words of numerous saints suggests an effort to produce a comprehensive written treasury of *nirguṇ* devotional utterances and to locate Dadu, his disciples, and their words within the broader universe of *nirguṇ* devotion. The first collection, the *Pañc Vāṇī* or "Five Voices," is more a type of scriptural anthology than a fixed scriptural text. As its title suggests, so-called *Pañc Vāṇī* manuscripts contain the songs and sayings of five prominent saints, usually Dadu, Namdev, Kabir, Ravidas, and Hardas, each of whom is given a separate section. Although early *Pañc Vāṇī* manuscripts (which date to the first half of the seventeenth century) consistently include compositions by these same five saints, the particular selection by any one saint can vary from one manuscript to another. Later *Pañc Vāṇī* manuscripts also vary in the selection of saints: Dadu, Kabir, and Ravidas are always included, but the others may change. Occasionally, short selections from other saints are also appended, making the actual number of saints greater than five.[73] The colophons at the end of these voluminous bound manuscripts identify the scribes, but only as copyists—the compiler(s) responsible for selecting and collating the contents of a *Pañc Vāṇī* are never identified. Manuscript evidence suggests that the practice of copying *Pañc Vāṇī* manuscripts began at roughly the same time that the *Dādū Vāṇī* was compiled, meaning that as soon as an authoritative recension of their guru's utterances had been established, monks of the Dadu Panth began copying and performing them alongside those of other prominent members of the *nirguṇ* "family" of saints.[74] The *Pañc Vāṇī* manuscript tradition consequently reflected a particular constellation of saints but did not delineate which of their utterances were "canon": the saintly figures were important, rather than specific texts.

The *Pañc Vāṇī* manuscript tradition reflects an effort to establish a corpus of preeminent *nirguṇ* saints with Dadu as its head, and the *Sarvāṅgī* tradition reflects an effort to place Dadu and his disciples within a comprehensive mapping of the *nirguṇ* devotional universe. Two monks of the Dadu Panth separately undertook the colossal task of compiling such an anthology, which, as the title "*Sarvāṅgī*" suggests, is "complete" (literally, "possessing all parts"). The first was the aforementioned Rajjab, a Muslim disciple and able poet who had helped to compile Dadu's compositions in 1604. Rajjab completed his *Sarvāṅgī* sometime in the 1620s, after collecting and collating the songs and sayings of eighty saint-poets.[75] He opens the collection by explaining the purpose and benefit of such an anthology:

tatabetā taravara bhale mata madhu ānyā chāna
sarabaṃgī mānau sahata prāṇa puṣṭi rasa pāna

The philosophers are a great tree,
  the nectar of which I have sifted and brought.
The *Sarvāṅgī* is like honey:
  having tasted it, one's soul is nourished.[76]

Rajjab continues by saying that the utterances of the saints contained in his anthology are "a grand feast" and "a fragrant perfume" for the faithful supplied directly "through God's grace."[77] Echoing the sonically centered theology of the *nirguṇ* saint-poets, he assures the listener that the utterances themselves are a nectar that bestows well-being and liberation: like a beekeeper or a perfumer, he has merely "sifted" the great mass to bring to the listener the most potent and flavorful extract or essence.

The second monk to attempt a comprehensive anthology of saintly utterances was Gopaldas, a second-generation disciple of Dadu who completed his *Sarvāṅgī* in 1628. Gopaldas situates his work scripturally and historically in the colophon:

> Thus Gopaldas, disciple of Santdas and grand-disciple of Swami Dadu Dayal, completes this jewel of thought, this volume (*pothī*) named the *Śrī Sarbamgī*. May it be completed on the day of the new moon in the bright half of the month of Phalgun in the year *saṁvat* sixteen hundred and eighty-four, in the settlement and auspicious place that is Sambhar, in the kingdom of Mirza Zulqarnain . . . Reciting from this book (*pustak*), the ignorant become wise, both error and

karma are destroyed, and tangled souls become freed. I have brought together the wisdom of all the sadhus in one place [so that] a disciple may meditate upon and comprehend the words of the True People (*sati pūrikh*).[78]

Some of those 138 True People whose words are contained in the *Sarvāṅgī* belong to antiquity or occupy a mythological or semidivine status within the Indian tradition, reinforcing the impression that the *Sarvāṅgī* is a comprehensive compendium of *timeless* sacred utterances. Yet the historical unfolding is understood to continue right up to the present moment, including in the words of Dadu Dayal, from whom Gopaldas was removed by only one generation. Gopaldas marks his own temporal and geographical location, emphasizing the historicity of the *Sarvāṅgī*'s origin rather than placing it in mythical time or casting it as a miraculous event. He simultaneously locates himself within his sect's sacred geography, at the merchant town of Sambhar where Dadu lived for many years, and within the Mughal political dispensation, in the *subah* or district of the Mughal Governor Mirza Zulqarnain.

The sheer size of these anthologies as well as the rich variety of their poetic content suggests that Rajjab and Gopaldas were attempting to create truly exhaustive compendiums that could address "every part" (*sarv-aṅg*) of *nirguṇ* religiosity. Both give pride of place to compositions by Dadu and his disciples and include *pad*s and *sākhī*s by all of the major figures of the *nirguṇ* canon. Yet they also include verses by dozens of saint-poets that fall outside what is today considered the realm of *nirguṇ* devotion, including poems attributed to Sufis like Baba Zindapir, Baba Farid, and Qazi Muhammad; Nath yogis like Gorakhnath and Matsyendranath; devotees of Krishna such as Surdas, Paramanandas, and Vidyapathi; and devotees of Ramachandra such as Agradas. These collections also contain several compositions attributed to Guru Nanak, revealing another link between the Dadu Panth and the Sikh community. Rajjab and Gopaldas pull a dizzyingly wide array of saintly stars from across the religious cosmos of the time, arranging them into distinctly *nirguṇ* constellations. They accomplish this in part by organizing their copious material into thematic sections based on the aforementioned concept of *aṅg*, literally "part" or "limb," but here denoting an "aspect" of religiosity. The methodical arrangement along with the linguistic diversity of the material itself—including Punjabi, Rajasthani, eastern dialects of Hindi, and bits of Persian and Sanskrit, a variety not found in the *guṭakā* notebook of any individual sadhu—suggests that Rajjab and Gopaldas compiled their anthologies using written sources and not from memory.[79] At the same time, mnemonic, musical, and associative technologies associated with orality appear to have had a role: the repetition of key words and phrases in successive verses and the importance of raga as an organizational rubric suggest the workings of human memory in structuring the material.

The Dadu Panth and Sikh community inaugurated authoritative, written recensions of their respective gurus' utterances not only at the same time but also in a similar manner. Both produced anthologies that delineated the boundaries of their respective theological galaxies by incorporating the hymns and sayings of saints associated with previous and even competing religious traditions (e.g., the *bhagats* of the *Guru Granth Sāhib*, such as Kabir and Farid, and the Vaishnava poets included in the *Sarvāṅgīs*, such as Surdas and Paramanandadas). At the same time, both positioned the works of their own gurus at the center. Both traditions presented the inscription of these scriptures as *historical* moments in the ongoing and timeless revelation of Truth by the saints—figures who themselves transcend spatial and temporal boundaries. They did so primarily through hagiographies that located the activities of listening to, transcribing, collating, and copying the gurus' speech in specific geographical and chronological circumstances, but also through paratextual material in the manuscripts themselves, such as the Sikh gurus' inscriptions in *bīrs* and Rajjab and Gopaldas's colophons at the end of their respective anthologies.

THE *VĀṆĪ* OF THE NIRANJANI SAMPRADAY

In contrast, the Niranjani Sampraday lacks any hagiographical remembrance of the circumstances in which its scriptural canon was determined and set to paper; indeed, it lacks the very concept of a single scriptural anthology with supreme authority. Yet the manner in which the Niranjani monks of the seventeenth and eighteenth centuries organized, copied, and used scriptural anthologies reveals just how closely they were involved in exchanges with the Dadu Panth and the Sikhs. This is one of several ways that the manuscript record shows connections between the Niranjani Sampraday and these other communities: Guru Nanak's compositions are found in Niranjani anthologies, large numbers of Niranjani works are found in Dadu Panthi monastic libraries, and copies of Niranjani works are found in Sikh manuscript anthologies.[80]

The development of a written scripture within the Niranjani Sampraday was influenced by the Sikh and Dadu Panthi models that preceded it, yet written scripture as such never attained a comparable importance in the development of Niranjani communal identity. *Vāṇī* is the term used within the Niranjani Sampraday to designate a bound volume of sayings, songs, hagiographical poems, stories, and treatises by Niranjani and some non-Niranjani saints. So far, I have not found any copies that date prior to the 1690s, though it is almost certain that the tradition began earlier.[81] Identifying a beginning for the *Vāṇī* is made more difficult by the fact that no hagiographical work makes reference to it, providing another point of contrast with the Sikh and Dadu Panthi cases: whereas the latter groups used hagiography to establish the authority of their scriptures, no such effort by the Niranjani Sampraday is apparent.[82]

Nevertheless, the Niranjani *Vāṇī* resembles the Sikh and Dadu Panthi scriptures in aspects of its organization, material form, and ritual use, suggesting that it played the role of a sacred scripture.[83] Like the *Pañc Vāṇī* of the Dadu Panth, the Niranjani *Vāṇī* is a scriptural tradition defined by a canon of saints rather than by a canon of texts. The core of a *Vāṇī* manuscript consists of lyrics and epigrams by Kabir, Gorakhnath, Haridas, Dadu, Sevadas Niranjani, Tursidas Niranjani, and Namdev; these poets are found in almost every Niranjani *Vāṇī*, and the selection of their compositions is largely (but not absolutely) consistent. Copies of the *Vāṇī* can also contain material from other Niranjani poets, including Dhyandas, Santdas, Khemdas, Manohardas, Bhagvandas, Jagjivandas, and Pipadas, and even works by poets of other traditions, including the poetry of Sundardas, the hagiographies of Anantadas, and poems attributed to Vaishnava figures like Swami Ramanand and Nath figures like Bhartrihari. In this respect, the *Vāṇī*s resemble the Dadu Panth's *Sarvāṅgī*s in the breadth of saints and traditions that they incorporate (although the *Sarvāṅgī*s include a greater number of individual poets).[84] Copies of the *Vāṇī* also bear a striking resemblance to another type of manuscript found in the Dadu Panth, a bound codex produced at least as early as the 1630s, which Horstmann describes as "the whole or parts of the Dādū Vāṇī or the whole or parts of the *pañcvāṇī* plus additional material from the regionally and religiously related traditions."[85] Several poets and texts are included in both the Niranjani *Vāṇī* and these Dadu Panthi codices, including Haridas, Khemdas, the hagiographies of Anantadas, and religious parables like the story of Mohmard Raja. Perhaps most strikingly, the Niranjani *Vāṇī* shares a distinct physical form with Dadu Panthi anthologies: it is a codex bound along the vertical edge, approximately 25 cm in height by 15 cm in width, holding between five hundred and six hundred folios (figs. 4.1, 4.3).

Within the Niranjani community, these anthological codices were understood to be unified *granth*s and treated as sacred objects. Copies of the *Vāṇī* are kept in Niranjani *samādhi*s as well as in temples, installed as objects of veneration along with the personal effects of the saint or, in the case of the temples, along with Shiva lingams and images of Lord Ramachandra.[86] They are an important part of the "wealth" connected to a given *samādhi* or temple and are sometimes worshiped, along with other articles and images, during the performance of *āratī* (evening prayer), much like an image of the deity is worshiped in Vaishnava traditions. Their colophons reveal that they were most often copied by Niranjani monks for their gurus and were used in congregational worship. In this regard, the *Vāṇī* parallels the model of the *Ādi Granth*, which is both the word of the guru when recited and the person of the guru when its material form is worshiped.

The Niranjani *Vāṇī* provides another example of the importance of the materiality of scripture that contrasts with the scriptures of the Sikhs and the Dadu Panth. In the Niranjani *Vāṇī*, the material assemblage of folios into a bound codex helped to constitute a canonical assemblage of authorial figures and texts. Each copy had at its core a fixed canon of saints but could also hold any number of texts and authors from a broad (yet still delimited) canon. Including such works within *Vāṇī* manuscripts appears to have helped establish their scriptural authority within the Niranjani Sampraday insofar as it made them part of a venerated textual artifact that was "more sacred" than other inscribed objects. Lyric poems and hagiographical narratives were not considered "scripture" when scribbled in a *guṭakā* notebook, but they became canon when inscribed in a guru's *vāṇī*.[87] Such *vāṇīs* were essential to the Niranjani practices of sermonizing (*pravacan*) and communal singing (*samāj-gāyan*) and became associated with the figure of the guru—but not, it appears, with the identity of the community as a whole, as was the case in the Sikh tradition and Dadu Panth.

METHODS OF ANTHOLOGIZATION OR *GRANTHĪKARAṆ* IN THE MAKING OF SCRIPTURES

Simply inscribing a text did not establish its character as sacred scripture. Particular methods of organizing, presenting, and framing the content had to be applied to elevate the utterances contained therein and to emphasize the theological and doctrinal unity of the anthology thus produced. The textual and material object was imagined as a unitary entity whose whole was more than simply the sum of its parts.

Most compilers frame their respective anthologies as a unified *granth* through introductory and/or concluding verses. These include invocations (*vandan*), benedictions (*maṅgalācāraṇ*), and statements of the benefits to be gained by reciting and listening to the contents of the anthology (*phalaśruti*). For example, the *Ādi Granth* begins with the *mūl mantar* (root mantra), "The One Oṁkār, named

Truth, the Creator, without fear or hatred, of timeless form, unborn and self-existent, known through the Guru's grace" (*ika oṁkāra sati nāmu kartā purakhu nirbha-u niravairu akāla mūrati ajūnī saimaṁ gura prasādi*).[88] Attributed to Guru Nanak, this formula functions as an article of faith in a manner similar to the *kalimah tayyibah* ("There is no god but Allah, Mohammad is the messenger of Allah") in Islam. Each individual section of the *Ādi Granth* begins with the mantra *ika oṁkāra satgura prasādi*, "One Oṁkār, by the grace of the Guru." Gurinder Singh Mann has compared the usage of this second, shorter mantra in the *Ādi Granth* to the *basmallah* ("In the name of God, the Merciful, the Compassionate") that begins each chapter (*surah*) of the Qur'an.[89] Mann also suggests that the appearance of this formula at the beginning of each section gestures back to the act of writing: "a claim is made that the inscription begins by his grace, as mediated to the scribe through the human guru. At every juncture of his labor, thus, the scribe remembers God and seeks his help through the guru."[90]

The compilers of the *Ādi Granth* frame the scripture as a whole by placing at its beginning the two daily prayers, the *japujī* (chant) and *so daru rahirās* (supplication at the [Divine's] gate), and at its end the *rāgamālā* (garland of ragas). Like two bookends, these works bracket the main content of the *Granth*, the hymns and sayings of the Gurus and *bhagat*s. The *japujī* and *so daru rahirās* are recited by devotees at the beginning of the morning and the end of the evening, respectively, constituting sacred ritual performances that frame (or bookend) the activities of each day, and are appropriately placed at the beginning of the volume. The *rāgamālā* is placed at the end, almost in the manner of an appendix: it is a technical and esoteric text that outlines the derivations of the various ragas and *rāginī*s (musical modes and their subdivisions), including those used in the *Granth* itself.[91] Its inclusion reflects the importance of singing and musical performance to how the *Granth* is "made to speak." Yet it appears after Guru Arjan's "seal" that closes the collection.[92] Put another way, the most-recited portions of the *Ādi Granth* are appropriately placed at the opening of the work while the technical apparatus—which would have been intelligible only to trained *rāgī*s or hymnodists—was placed at the end, with the hymns that were sung throughout the day forming the main "body" of the scripture.

The hymns themselves are organized by raga into thirty-one sections that are further subdivided according to author, with the hymns of the Sikh Gurus coming first and those of Guru Nanak appearing at the very beginning. The assignment and ordering of the ragas occurred over years, with substantial revisions being made between the Guru Harsahai, Goindval, and Kartarpur *pothī*s. The exact logic behind the final ordering, which dates to the time of the Kartarpur *pothī* (1604), has not yet been deciphered, but as Mann has pointed out, the arrangement of ragas in the *pothī*s that preceded it involved a complex balancing of considerations of raga and *rāginī*, the season of the year, and the time of day when it was most appropriate to perform a given raga.[93] These organizational rubrics were likely preserved in the Kartarpur *pothī* and subsequent expansions of the *Granth*. Within each raga section, the hymns of the Gurus are carefully organized by meter and genre (with shorter compositions toward the beginning and longer ones toward the end), while the compositions of the non-Sikh *bhagat*s are put together at the end of the raga section without any distinction of meter or genre, in a section simply titled *bāṇī bhagatan kī*, "words of the devotees."[94] The use of a special coding system for the compositions of the Gurus in which each is designated by the term *mahal* (Arabic, "palace") and a number (Guru Nanak is *Mahal* 1, Guru Angad is *Mahal* 2, and so forth) further distinguishes the *Ādi Granth* as a uniquely Sikh scripture and establishes a hierarchy of scriptural authority among the saints it anthologizes.

The structure and organization of the *Ādi Granth* also reflect its use as a living text in Sikh devotional life since the early seventeenth century: the *var*s of Bhai Gurdas, as well as internal evidence in the Gurus' hymns, suggest that communal singing was the primary congregational ritual.[95] Such singing also took place in the court of the Guru, so the extant early manuscripts of the *Ādi Granth* were probably used in singing, just as printed copies are used today in singing at gurdwaras. At the same time, the inclusion of the *japujī* and *so daru rahirās* made the *Ādi Granth* a scripture that belonged in households, where it was used in families' performance of daily prayers.

In the Dadu Panth, three of its four types of scriptural anthologies—the *Dādū Vāṇī* and the two *Sarvāṅgī*s—show marked similarities, especially in their opening formulae. The figure of the guru (both human and Divine) is central to the theology and praxis of the Dadu Panth; accordingly, all Dadu Panthi scriptural anthologies begin with the *guru kau aṅg* or "chapter on the guru." This opening section contains *sākhī*s extolling the guru and stressing his importance in the disciple's search for liberation. For example, the *Dādū Vāṇī* opens with the following two verses, composed in a type of hybrid or para-Sanskrit:

> *sākhī*
> dādū namo namo niraṃjanaṁ namaskāra gurudevataḥ
> vandanaṁ sarva sādhavā praṇāmaṁ paraṃgataḥ (1)
>
> parabrahma parāparaṁ so mama deva niraṃjanam
> nirākāraṁ nirmalaṁ tasya dādū vandanam (2)

sākhī

I bow to Dadu, I bow to Niranjan,
  I salute the Divine Guru.
I praise all of the holy ones (*sādhavā*)
  [and] pay obeisance to those have crossed over (*pāraṃgataḥ*) (1)

The ultimate and highest Brahma—
  he is my Lord, Niranjan,
without form and totally pure.
  I praise Him [and] Dadu. (2)[96]

In a certain sense, the scriptural character of the *Dādū Vāṇī* or "Dadu's words" is captured in the polysemy of the final line, *tasya dādū vandanam*, which could mean both "Dadu praises Him (the Guru)" and "I praise Him and Dadu." The dense syntax and formulaic use of action words in the verses themselves, along with how the verses were performed, suggests that both meanings were understood simultaneously. In reciting this phrase, the devotee took on the voice of Dadu himself as Dadu praised God; at the same time, to recite Dadu's verse was to pay tribute to Dadu, the saint and guru. The sacrality of the object (God) is shared with the medium used to access the object (Dadu's words, his *vāṇī*). Once again, the medium is the message.

This and other Sanskritized opening invocations to the guru in the Dadu Panth's anthologies accomplish three things: first, they announce the book as a unified scripture consisting of the saints' revelations and teachings. Second, they establish the primacy of the guru and the character of the scriptural book itself *as the guru*. This is accomplished through a series of equivalences: the guru's *vāṇī* or word *is* the guru, and the book is the *vāṇī*, therefore the book is the guru. Third, they re-create the aura of ritual recitation by mimicking the phonology and morphology of Sanskrit, presenting verbal formulas that "sound like" Sanskrit. The paratextual material is replete with such vernacularized, hybrid Sanskrit, particularly in the opening and closing invocations that mark different sections of the anthologies, including the *Sarvāṅgīs* of Gopaldas and Rajjab as well as some of the *Pañc Vāṇī* collections.[97] The aural effect in liturgical performance would have been powerful, with the guru reciting from the *granth*, intoning words and sounds that would have been familiar to the audience from Sanskrit, each time he opened and closed his liturgy.

In general, *Pañc Vāṇī* anthologies of the Dadu Panth and *Vāṇī* anthologies of the Niranjani Sampraday lack the elaborate opening formulae and *phalaśrutī* found in the aforementioned collections, yet their identities as unified, scriptural books are established through other means. In an exhaustive table of contents at the beginning of the manuscript, each section (corresponding to an individual saint, a type of composition, a theme, and/or the title of an individual work) is given with its corresponding folio number and the total number of verses recorded within the section (fig. 4.1). The significance of this innovation should not be underestimated: available evidence within the north Indian manuscript archive as a whole suggests that the Sikhs and Dadu Panth introduced this practice into vernacular book culture; no other Hindi manuscripts from the late sixteenth or early seventeenth century include one. Such tables reinforced the impression of the book as a deliberately formed, structured, and unified whole, and together with the verse tallies given at the end of each section, established the fidelity and quality of the book's transmission and editing. Dadu Panthi and Niranjani scribes consistently tallied the total number of verses when they completed copying a section; this tally could be compared against the written archetype and checked against the table of contents. The colophon of the anthology usually included a final tally of all verses, along with a full exposition of the scribe's (or scribes') guru-disciple lineage, traced back to the first generation of the founding saint's disciples. These measures and attestations assured the anthology's user that the copy met the monastic order's scribal standards and carried the sect's imprimatur.

The importance of the guru-disciple relationship is reflected in Niranjani *vāṇīs*: scribes tend to give pride of place to the compositions of saints of their own lineage, inscribing those works at the beginning of the manuscript and placing the works of other saints in later sections. For example, Amardas Niranjani had his disciples inscribe the *pads* and *sākhis* of his own guru, Sevadas, at the beginning of his *vāṇī*, and the scribes of a late eighteenth-century Niranjani *vāṇī*, Ms. 2165 in the Rajasthan Oriental Research Institute, Jaipur, similarly placed the compositions of Sevadas (their guru's guru) at the beginning of the manuscript, embellishing them with decorative applications of red and black ink (figs. 4.4, 4.5, 4.6).

Dadu Panthi and Niranjani scribes "sealed" their anthologies by inscribing powerful verbal formulas. At the end of each major section, the scribe would write a short invocation to God and/or the guru, followed by the formula *śubham astu* ("may it be auspicious," adopted from Sanskrit manuscripts) and often ending with a graphic representation of an auspicious phoneme, such as "*ra-ra-ra-ra-ra-ra-ra-ra-ra-ra-ra-ra-ra-ra*" or "*raṁ-raṁ-raṁ-raṁ-raṁ-raṁ-raṁ-raṁ-raṁ*" (figs. 4.2, 4.5).[98] These visually striking representations of a mantra give cause for reflection: certainly they were unnecessary as a mnemonic device, since writing the syllable *ra* or *raṁ* once would have sufficed to indicate whatever the reader was supposed to recite. These inscriptions therefore suggest that the graphic representations of powerful sounds, their material manifestation through ink and on paper (as well, perhaps, as the *act* of inscribing them), were understood to be powerful and efficacious in their own right.

FASHIONING THE GURU FROM PAPER AND INK: SCRIPTURE IN MANUSCRIPT

The creation of these impressively large, beautiful, and always bound codices helped to establish their contents as a unified, recognizable whole: just as the compilers bound the hymns and sayings of the saints together through their editorial practices, the papermakers, binders, and scribes responsible for the material copies literally bound these works together into codices (*granth* or *kitāb*). The Sikh community made the boldest material and aesthetic gestures, again reflecting its early understanding of itself as a religious tradition. The distinctiveness of Sikh religious scripture begins with script itself: by the time the Guru Harsahai *pothī* was copied in the 1530s, the Sikh leadership had already begun to develop a new script they evocatively named Gurmukhī (lit. "from the mouth of the guru").[99] Gurmukhi was adapted from the Laṇḍā and Ṭākarī scripts used by merchant and scribal communities like the *mahājans*, *kāyasths*, and the *khattris*, from which Guru Nanak and his family members hailed.[100] The development of a visually distinct script and rules of orthography was a statement of not only religious difference but also political autonomy.[101] The Nāgarī and Arabic scripts were used for religious texts but also for the everyday purposes of administration in Mughal and Rajput states and the literary practices that undergirded the culture-power matrix of Mughal and Rajput courts. When Guru Arjan established the *Ādi Granth* as the Sikh community's primary scripture in 1604, and with it Gurmukhi as the script of Sikh scripture, he did so in the context of increasing Sikh assertions of political autonomy. Gurmukhi came to be used not only for scripture but also for the documentation and management of the Sikh proto-state. Early copies of the *Ādi Granth* display clean handwriting and standardized orthography.[102] Such uniformity and care are precisely the elements that distinguish a copy of scripture from, say, a *guṭakā*, or even a *pothī* of a nonscriptural work.

In fact, calligraphy provided the primary means through which Sikh scribes visually embellished copies of the Gurus' words. This practice began as early as the Goindval *pothīs* (1570s), which consist of large, landscape-oriented folios covered in a fluid and even Gurmukhi script. The style recalls Persian calligraphy in the *nasta'līq* hand that was so valued at Mughal and provincial courts (fig. 4.7).[103] This calligraphy is surrounded by *beyne's-sütur*, a cloud-like embellishment made with ink that fills the horizontal space between lines of text, another feature adapted from deluxe copies of Persian and Arabic works.

The sacrality of Sikh scripture was expressed visually in a largely Islamicate idiom. Copies of the Granth from the seventeenth and eighteenth centuries often include an ornamented frontispiece (*'unvān*) containing a dome-like form or "crown" (*tāj*) and one or more cartouches (fig. 4.8). Blocks of text are often enclosed in *jadwal* drawn in multiple colors of ink. Along with palmettes, *sāz* (floral or vegetal designs), and radiant lines along the margins, these embellishments and illuminations give a strong sense of the book's identity as an exceptional, special, or sacred object. These elements also give weight to Mann's suggestion that the Qur'an, as a focal point of communal ritual in Islam, provided an archetype for the Sikh *Ādī Granth*.[104] This is not to suggest that the visual elements of *bīrs* were intended to imitate copies of the Qur'an (since these same elements could be found in other types of books) but rather that it was the character of the Qur'an as a *public* book—visually and aurally accessible to all, even if it could not be *read* by all—that informed Sikh material practices related to scripture. Copies of the Sikh Granth, with their large size and high quality of calligraphy and embellishment, were clearly intended to be viewed by large numbers of people and to inspire awe and reverence.

The production of such copies would have been no small affair, requiring multiple types of specialized professionals including papermakers, margin rulers, scribes, artists, and binders. Furthermore, commissioning a copy of the sacred anthology required obtaining an archetype from which to copy, and during the tenures of Guru Arjan and Guru Hargobind, this meant obtaining permission from the Guru himself: such authorized copies received the Guru's signature and blessing.[105] In this sense, the Granth, functioning as a concrete metonym for the Guru, carried the literal *nisān* (stamp or signature) of the Guru himself—recalling again the idea of God's mark or the "seal of truth" (*sacā nīsāṇu*) that Guru Nanak implored his followers to see inscribed upon all their deeds.

Anthological manuscripts of the Dadu Panth and Niranjani Sampraday conform to a single archetype, once again reflecting the symbiotic exchange that characterized the sects' early development. This archetype is visually distinct: a codex in portrait orientation, of unusual height (approximately 25 centimeters) and consistent width (approximately 15 centimeters). Yet these codices were fashioned not in the manner of their Islamicate *kitāb* counterparts but instead like *guṭakās*: folios were laid in a pile and then folded and stitched into a single quire or signature before being sewn and pasted into a cloth cover. This method of assembly gave the anthologies the striking, rounded appearance seen in figure 4.3. This format is surprisingly robust and therefore appropriate to an all-in-one liturgical omnibus that the guru could carry with him as he ministered to communities of devotees in far-flung towns and cities.

The scribes of the Dadu Panth and Niranjani Sampraday evidently invested great time and labor in making these codices impressive in appearance. This effort constituted an act of *sevā* or service to one's guru, and the resulting book was evidently intended to reflect his exalted status. Although the Nāgarī script does not lend itself to the type of fluid calligraphy possible with the Arabic script or the Gurmukhi script, Dadu Panthi and Niranjani monks found inventive ways to turn writing into a form of visual embellishment. They often used alternating colors of ink to create geometric designs in the center of folios (reminiscent of the vestigial thread-hole ornaments in *pothī*-type manuscripts), inscribed alternating lines of red and black text, or even created checkered designs (figs. 4.5, 4.6). In contrast to Sikh anthological manuscripts with their Islamicate influences, the folios of Dadu Panthi and Niranjani *vāṇīs* follow the visual and compositional conventions of Indic *pothīs*: they are ruled by vertical margin lines in red ink, and illumination is primarily in the form of medallions in the center of folios or floral decorations accompanying colophons. The purpose behind such embellishments and the large size of these codices appears to be the same: to constitute a focal point for communal worship and to inspire awe and reverence. One can imagine a Niranjani guru like Amardas, sitting with his *vāṇī* opened before him on a *gaddī*, reciting *sākhīs* and expounding their meaning for an assembly of devotees, and leading them in singing the hymns of the saints as he consulted this encyclopedic repository of their songs.

THE DIVINE COURT AND RELIGIOUS POLITIES

These holy books both constitute and reflect a new kind of textual community that emerged in early modern north India, which we might term, following Brian Hatcher, a "religious polity." A textual community does not require a physical book in order to coalesce; the Sikhs, Dadu Panth, and Niranjani Sampraday began with members united through the oral performance of a shared repertoire of hymns and sayings.[106] But the collation of saints' poetry into a single collection and the transformation of that collection into a material book—the saints' words made manifest—had a discernible effect on how these communities imagined themselves. The ceremonial investiture of the scriptural book as the figural sovereign of the community inaugurated a new dispensation and established the book as the supreme authority or supreme law. This single gesture thus encompasses what Hatcher has identified as the distinguishing features of the polity as a religious and social formation in early modern South Asia: the religious polity was brought about through self-conscious moments of "creation" or "breaks" with the past, centered around the figure of a sovereign, and involved a "choice to follow a certain rule and live in relation to a disciplinary habitus."[107] The concrete materiality of the holy book and the courtly idiom it anchored—expressed through ritual but also through architecture and the shaping of public spaces—also corresponded to the reification of the religious community's spiritual "sovereignty" into concrete modes and institutions of self-governance. Indrani Chatterjee has termed this "monastic governmentality," a precolonial mode in which the household—either that of the spiritual leader's family joined through marriage and blood or that constituted by guru and disciple relationships—structured administrative formations and politics.[108] For communities like the Sikhs and Dadu Panth especially, the holy book stood at the center of increasingly elaborate administrative structures that governed the lives of their devotees and that sometimes conflicted with the agents of Rajput and Mughal power.

These communities inaugurated their scriptures and polities at a historical moment when *bhakti* religiosity more generally was beginning to take on a distinctively "public" character. Christian Novetzke has suggested that *bhakti* itself is essentially a technology of building publics that are unified but open-ended, social units "created through shared cultural phenomena and reinforced by *demonstrations in public* of these shared cultural phenomena" (emphasis mine).[109] What makes these communities "public" is the demonstration or enactment of community in modes, spaces, or contexts that look *outward* toward the larger social sphere. The holy books of the Sikhs, Dadu Panth, and Niranjani Sampraday, as well as their other symbols of sovereignty or authority, spoke directly to the broader social imaginary and in this sense were public demonstrations.

The social imaginary to which they spoke, or at least the domain within the social imaginary that we might call the "*bhakti* public," had been explicitly articulated only a few years earlier by the Ramanandi poet Nabhadas in his hagiographical compendium, the *Bhaktamāl* (c. 1600).[110] Writing at the monastery of Galta, not far from modern-day Jaipur and close to the Dadu Panth's area of activity, Nabhadas formulated the transregional and transtemporal community of *bhakti* thus:

bhakta bhakti bhagavanta guru catura nāma vapu eka
inake pada baṃdana karata nāsai vighana aneka

The devotee and devotion, God and guru—
four names for but one body.
Worshiping their feet
destroys many an obstacle.[111]

Nabhadas's encyclopedic eulogy of saints both human and divine outlines the broad contours of the public "body" (*vapu*), while his emphasis on the *catuḥ sampradāy* or four Vaishnav sects inaugurated by Ramanuja, Madhava, Nimbarka, and Vishnuswami suggests a center (or perhaps head) for that body.[112] The *Bhaktamāl* inspired several similar works, the earliest of which were produced by the same communities that Nabhadas conspicuously ignored in his compendium: the Dadu Panth and the Niranjani Sampraday.[113] These begin with Raghavdas's *Bhaktamāl* (1660), which posits a *catuḥ sampradāy* of *nirguṇ* sects—consisting of the Sikhs, Kabir Panthis, Dadu Panthis, and Niranjanis—to complement the four Vaishnava sects.[114] The Niranjani monk Pyareram, assimilating material from both of the aforementioned works and Anantadas's *paracaīs*, produced his own *Bhaktamāl* in 1827.[115] In consonance with its identification as a distinct religion, the Sikh community's hagiographical literature, including the *janm sākhīs* and *vars*, imagines a different constellation of saints and traditions, putting Guru Nanak into literal conversation with such figures as the Sufi saint Baba Farid (d. 1266) and the ascetic Gorakhnath (fl. fourteenth century).

Within the context of these sometimes complementary, sometimes competing imaginings of the *bhakti* public, the Sikhs, Dadu Panth, and Niranjani Sampraday staked their claims to sovereignty and articulated their respective polities. They appropriated and adapted motifs and idioms from earlier works and traditions, such as the notion of the Divine Court (*darbār*) in which God is ruler and of the city of Begumpur ("City Without Sorrow"), a utopia in which distinctions of caste and creed do not exist.[116] Yet they translated these literary tropes into concrete ritual and social practices, as well as architectural idioms and programs of spatial organization.[117]

The idea of the Divine Court in the Sikh tradition begins with Guru Nanak himself, who refers to the *dargāh* (court) of the Lord in his hymns.[118] Guru Nanak even established the first Sikh settlement, founding the town of Kartarpur at the turn of the sixteenth century. Then Guru Arjan, at the turn of the seventeenth century, reimagined the Sikh community as a sovereign polity, reorganizing and expanding the *masand* system while establishing his capital at

Ramdaspur. There he built the Harmandir Sahib (popularly known as the "Golden Temple") in 1595, constructing it in the manner of a *dīvān* or hall of royal audience. In this hall he installed the Kartarpur *pothī* (the first copy of what would eventually become known as the *Guru Granth Sāhib*) as a sacred scripture in 1604. Those involved in its compilation and editing made clear in their writings that the book was the Guru and sovereign authority of the community. Bhai Gurdas praises not only the Guru's spiritual authority but also his temporal authority, and identifies "the Word of the Satguru," i.e., the scripture, with the living Guru.[119] Bura Sandhu, another scribe, writes that the Kartarpur *pothī* manifests the very body of Guru Nanak, and to appear before it is to have an audience with the Guru.[120] In 1708, faced with the potential destruction of the entire Sikh leadership by the Mughal military, the tenth and last Guru, Guru Gobind Singh, formally invested the *Granth* as the perpetual Guru of the community. After his death later that year, the *Granth* indeed became the supreme textual authority through which the Sikh community would reconstitute and govern itself going forward: for all practical purposes, it stood as a constitution or law.

Since the turn of the eighteenth century, ritual performance involving the Granth has followed an elaborate courtly idiom: the *Granth* is first awoken from sleep (*sukh-āsan*) in its sleeping chamber, then brought in a ceremonial procession to the center of the gurdwara, the symbolic *dīvān*. It is placed on a *takhat* (Persian *tak̲h̲t*, throne), underneath a regal canopy where the reciter, or *granthī*, waves a flywhisk above the *Granth* as he recites from it, recalling the treatment given to royal personages. Members of the community not only listen to the text being recited but also physically enact reverence or obeisance to the *bīr* by bowing their heads, joining their hands, and prostrating themselves before it. *Darśan*, or visual communion with the granth/guru/sovereign, is experienced through the eyes and through physical proximity to the *bīr*.

In the Dadu Panth, the *Dādū Vāṇī* became the symbolic sovereign of a monastic administration articulated in a courtly idiom. Madhavdas recounts in his *Sant Guṇ Sāgar* how Dadu's son and successor, Garibdas, invested the *Dādū Vāṇī* as the supreme authority of the community in regal fashion in 1604, installing the book in a temple appropriately called its "palanquin." He writes that "the *guru vāṇī* (word of the guru) was residing in splendor (*virajit*) in the temple," and along with Dadu's shawl, sandals, and cap, was "placed on a throne, and above this a heavy curtain was hung." Sitting like a monarch on a throne, below a canopy, the scripture presided over the proceedings as its subjects—the devotees—celebrated its coronation with sermons, singing, and feasting. From that day forward, "those who followed the guru's path (*panth*) kept a *guru vāṇī*, which they worshiped."[121]

Even today, a copy of the *Dādū Vāṇī* sits in state on a throne and under a canopy in the main temple at the Dadu Panth's central monastery in Naraina (fig. 4.9). The monastic complex, established in the late sixteenth century and enlarged during the seventeenth and eighteenth centuries, shares elements with palace architecture in the region, and the main temple with its elevated, stage-like sanctum resembles the halls of audience common in the fort-palaces of regional lords and nobles (fig. 4.10).[122] Devotees and visitors often join their hands, bow, or prostrate themselves in front of the enshrined copy of the *Dādū Vāṇī* before participating in other worship activities in the temple.

The Dadu Panth's structure of spiritual authority rested on guru-disciple lineages that naturally began to segment in the early seventeenth century. Influential monks like Sundardas established their own monasteries and lineages, posing a potential challenge to the authority of the guru at Naraina. Garibdas's establishment of an authorized, standardized recension of the founder's compositions as the supreme authority of the community impeded such segmentation by tying the various lineages back to the singular icon of the *Dādū Vāṇī*. Madhavdas emphasizes the scripture's importance as a criterion for participation in the monastic community, reporting that during its inauguration at Naraina, "Garibdas reminded everyone that holy men (*sant*) must remember to keep the *vāṇī*."[123] However far the Panth's sadhus might wander, the *vāṇī* would always tie them back to a single figure of authority (and to Naraina). To be a loyal subject of the sovereign, of the scripture, was to keep a copy and revere it.

Those subjects lived under the authority and protection of the guru. Hagiographical traditions tell of Mughal emperors and their governors (*subahdār*) challenging the will or prestige of the guru at Naraina, only to find their authority ineffective against his divinely sanctioned power. The annual *melā* commemorating Dadu's passing became an occasion for the Dadu Panth to renew and publicly demonstrate its identity as a polity, as monks and lay devotees from around the region gathered at Naraina. Today, during the *melā* (which occurs during the month of *phālagun* and lasts one week), the monastic complex at Naraina becomes a city unto itself, its lanes (*gali*), squares (*cauk*), and ceremonial gates (*pol*) filled with monks and lay devotees. The various monastic lineages and militarized *nāgā* contingents assert their prestige in regal processions that culminate with the arrival of the living guru and the scripture.[124] The religious polity of the Dadu Panth thus finds its full expression once a year, even if only temporarily, in the form of a city-state.

The Niranjani Sampraday appears to have been even more decentralized in character than the Dadu Panth during the seventeenth and eighteenth centuries: several of Haridas's disciples went on to establish their own monasteries and lineages in the early seventeenth century, and by the eighteenth century there were independent Niranjani *maṭhs* at Didwana, Shekhawati, Merta, Bikaner, Nagaur, Jaipur, and Jodhpur. All of these monasteries and lineages appear to have been accorded equal prestige within the Sampraday: Raghavdas gives the names of thirteen Niranjani *mahants* in his *Bhaktamāl* but makes no distinctions between them. The Niranjani poet Hariramdas, writing his *Paramārthasatasaī* in the early years of the eighteenth century, lists twelve Niranjani *mahants* and concludes by stating that "There is no trickery or obstruction among these abbots (*adhikārī*), each with his own monastery (*nijadhām*) / The twelve Niranjani *mahants* will always dwell in Hariram's heart."[125] A decentralized structure appears to have increased the symbolic importance of the written *vāṇī*. As each *mahant* was an authority unto himself, the *vāṇī* that he carried wherever he traveled, made especially for him by his disciples and containing a written record of his monastic lineage, became part of his charismatic figure, like his *gudaḍī* (patchwork blanket), sandals, and other personal effects. It was so strongly understood to be an extension of the guru himself that it followed him into the next world, never "speaking" again but instead standing as a silent object of worship for the devotees who came to pay their respects to the saint at his *samādhi* (fig. 4.11).

Nevertheless, the Niranjani settlement at Gadha Dham gradually became a de facto center for the broader Niranjani community in Didwana. Originally a settlement of Maheshwari merchants; the community is said to have converted en masse at the turn of the seventeenth century, becoming devotees of Haridas Nirajani and his monks. The settlement includes a monastic complex and temples but also residential areas in which monastic living quarters (*nivās*, *āśram*) and lay devotees' houses were built side by side. Until the mid-twentieth century, the main monastic complex that contains Haridas's *samādhi* was a gathering place for the community each evening, the blowing of horns calling the residents to gather for hymns and religious stories.[126] At the annual *melā* commemorating Haridas's passing during the month of *phālagun*, members of the Niranjani Sampraday gather there; like Naraina during the Dadu *melā*, Gadha Dham becomes a city unto itself, its lanes and courtyards populated by lay devotees and monks, including sadhus of other religious orders. Leaders of the community—senior monks and prominent lay devotees—meet to make decisions and plans for the coming year. Though now a shadow of the large festival it once was, the Niranjani *melā* is the ritual occasion and space in which the Niranjanis reconstitute administrative, social, and spiritual ties.[127] During this temporary gathering of the community into a miniature city-state, the doors of Niranjani saints' *samādhis* are opened so that the faithful can pay their respects before the relics, including the *vāṇīs*.

THE SOUND OF THE GURU'S VOICE, THE SIGHT OF THE GURU'S BODY

In 1605, the Sikh scribe Bura Sandhu wrote that the Kartarpur *pothī* that he and his colleagues had prepared manifested the very body (*deh*) of Guru Nanak, so to stand before it was to have an audience with the Guru.[128] In the Sikh community, as well as in the Dadu Panth and Niranjani Sampraday, the physical scripture of the holy book both concretized textual canons and provided a lynchpin for intersecting threads of textual, divine, and human authority. Written scriptures like the Sikh *Granth*, the *Dādū Vāṇī*, the *Sarvāṅgīs*, and the Niranjani *vāṇī* metonymically fuse the saints of the past, their words, and the present-day performers or mediators of those words into a single whole. In the Hindi idiom, the guru, monk, or devotee "makes the book speak" (*granth bāñc-*) and in doing so makes the saints speak.

In the case of a prominent teacher like Amardas Niranjani, the human guru and his book existed in parallel chains of transmission: Amardas traced his spiritual lineage back to Haridas, who according to Niranjani tradition received initiation from Gorakhnath himself. The *vāṇī* that Amardas carried contained the teachings of those saints and many others that had been transmitted to him through his human guru, Sevadas. Those teachings also had been transmitted in writing, from one generation of disciples to the next, through the sect's meticulous scribal practices. The guru-disciple lineage recorded in the colophon of his *vāṇī* thus records and authenticates both the chain of human spiritual authority and the chain of textual authority. In a certain sense, they were one and the same: the saints spoke *through* Amardas each time he recited from the *vāṇī*. So when Amardas became forever silent in 1785, entering a state of permanent *samādhi* and leaving his physical body, his copy of the *vāṇī* became silent as well. The present-day custodians of his *samādhi*, the brothers Damodarlal and Radheshyam Parik, do not read from the manuscript but rather preserve it with great care and with the same reverence and affection that they show to Amardas's other relics. This shows just how rich the so-called "afterlife" of a book can be.

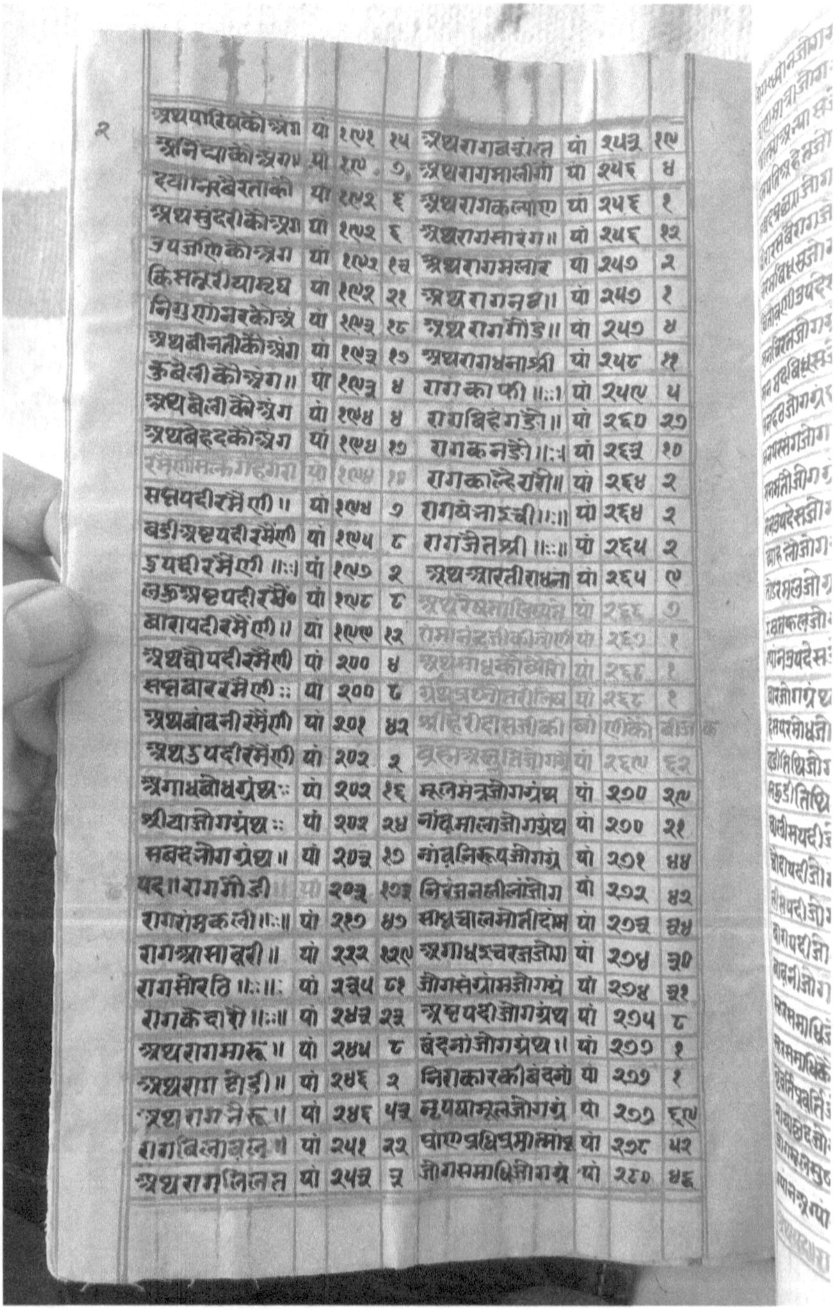

FIGURE 4.1 Table of contents in the *vāṇī* of Amardas Niranjani, copied 1783 CE

Photo by author

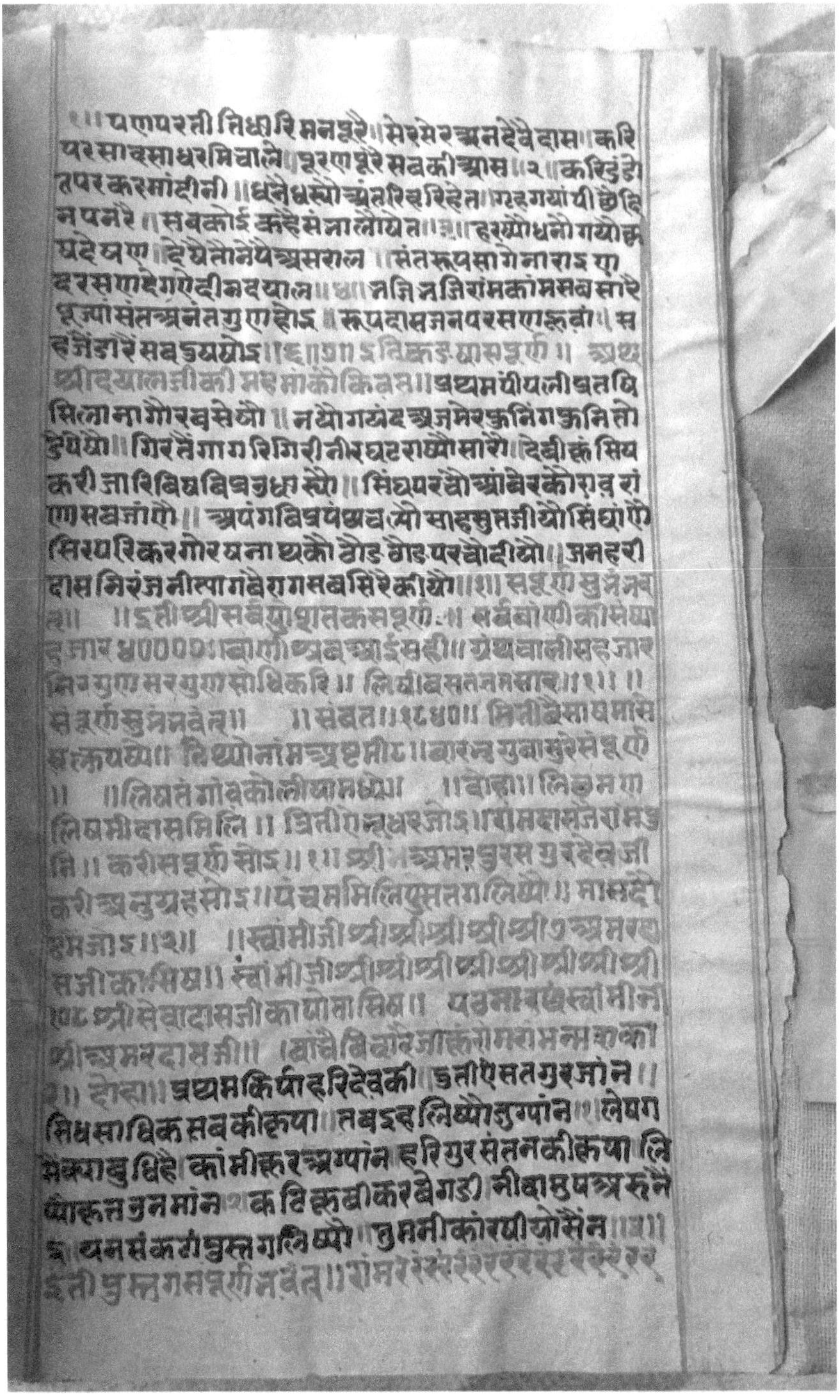

FIGURE 4.2 Final folio and colophon of the *vāṇī* of Amardas Niranjani, copied 1783 CE

Photo by author

FIGURE 4.3 The author scans the *vāṇī* of Amardas Niranjani at his *samādhi* in Gadha Dham, Didwana, in February 2012

Photo by Balakdas Niranjani

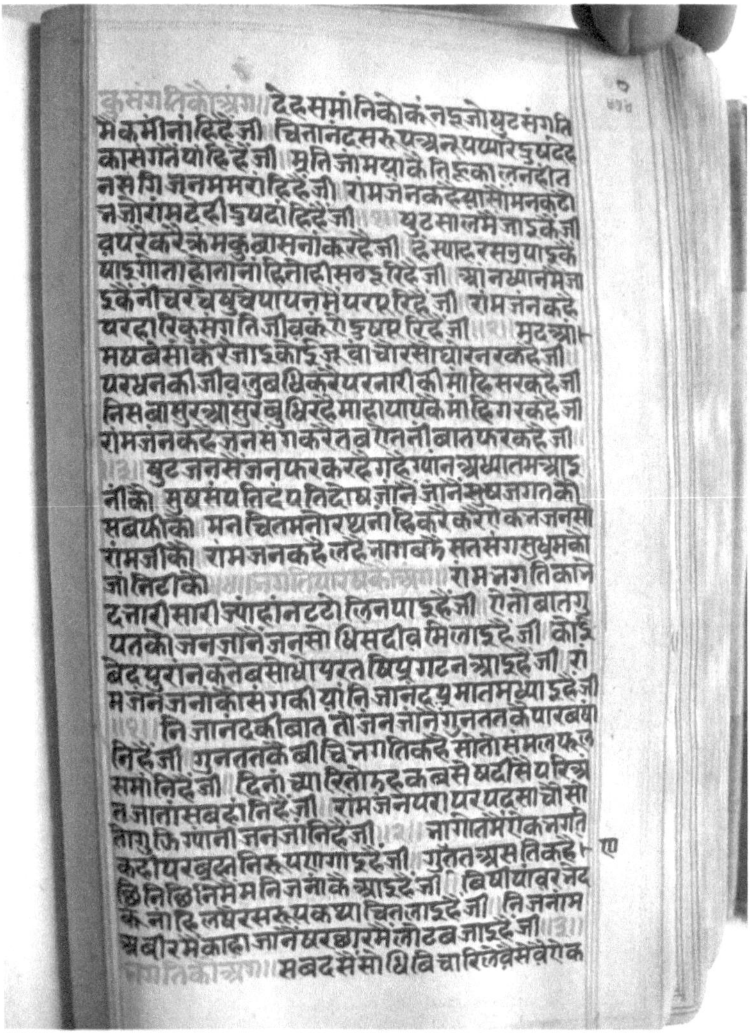

FIGURE 4.4 A *vāṇī* manuscript of the Niranjani Sampraday. Copied prior to 1850 CE

Ms. 2165, Rajasthan Oriental Research Institute, Jaipur. Photo by author

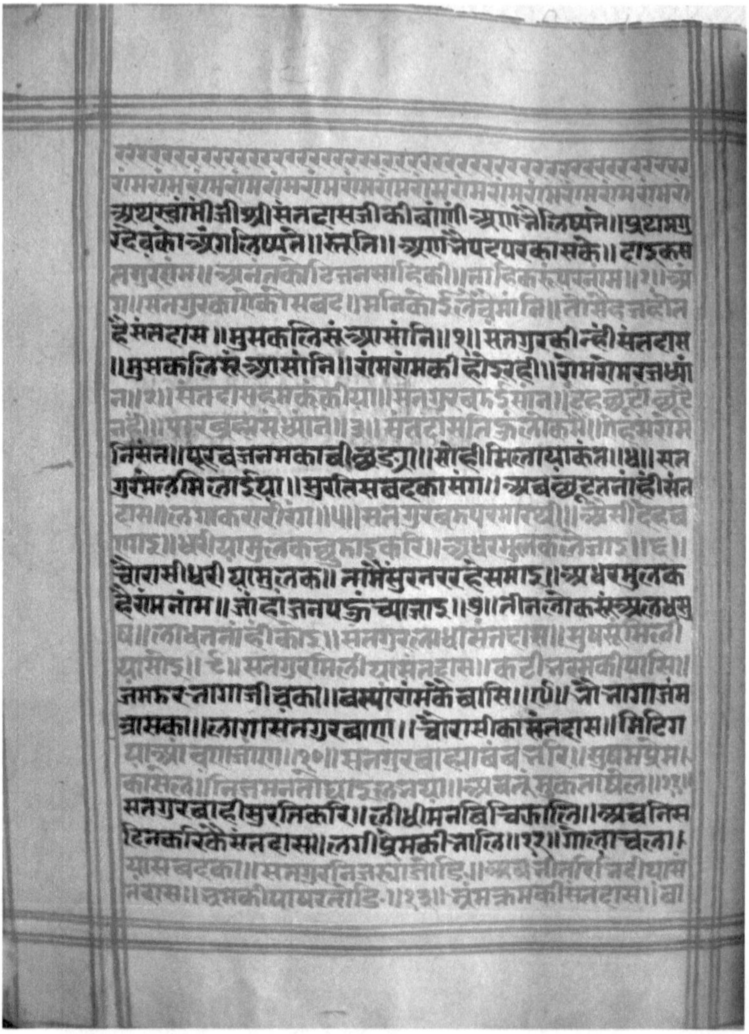

FIGURE 4.5 The first folio of a *vāṇī* manuscript of the Niranjani Sampraday. The lines are inscribed in alternating bands of red and black ink. The first line contains the syllable *ra* while the second line contains sixteen instances of the divine Name or mantra *rām*.

Ms. 2165, Rajasthan Oriental Research Institute, Jaipur. Photo by author

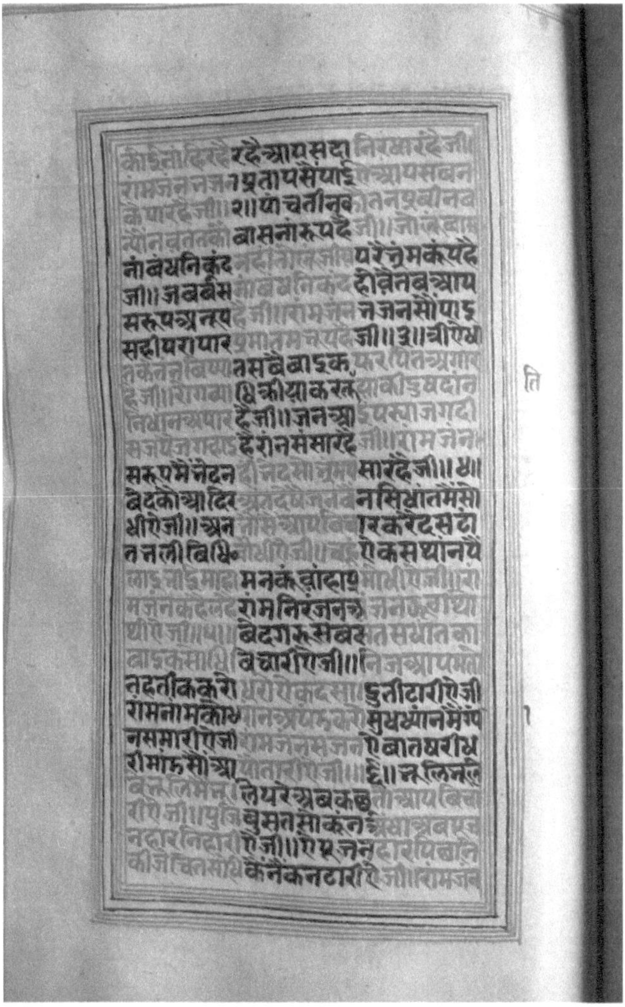

FIGURE 4.6 Folio from a Niranjani *vāṇī*. The text is inscribed in alternating blocks of red and black ink and framed with margin lines in red, black, and yellow ink.

Ms. 2165, Rajasthan Oriental Research Institute, Jaipur. Photo by author

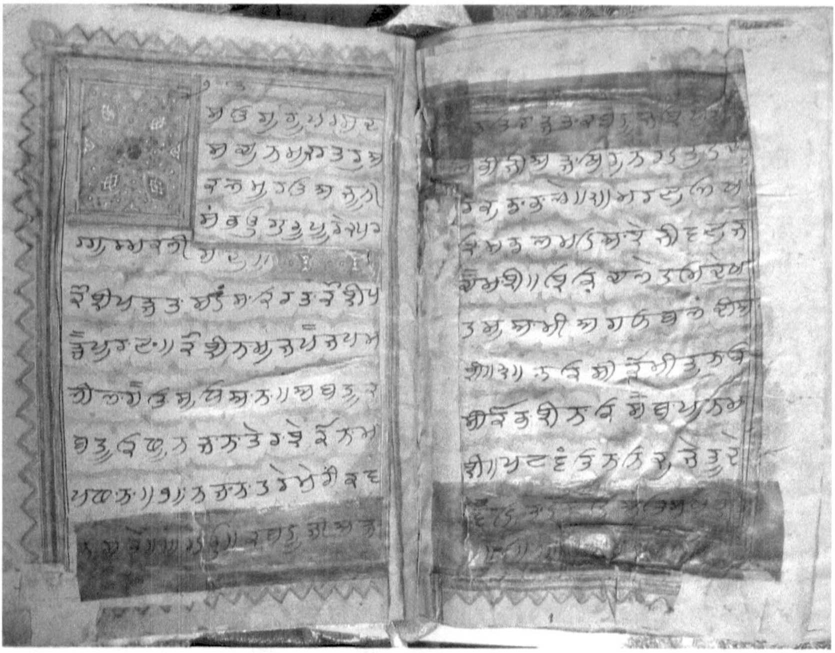

FIGURE 4.7 The opening folios of the Goindval *pothīs*, copied 1570s CE

Photograph courtesy of Gurinder Singh Mann

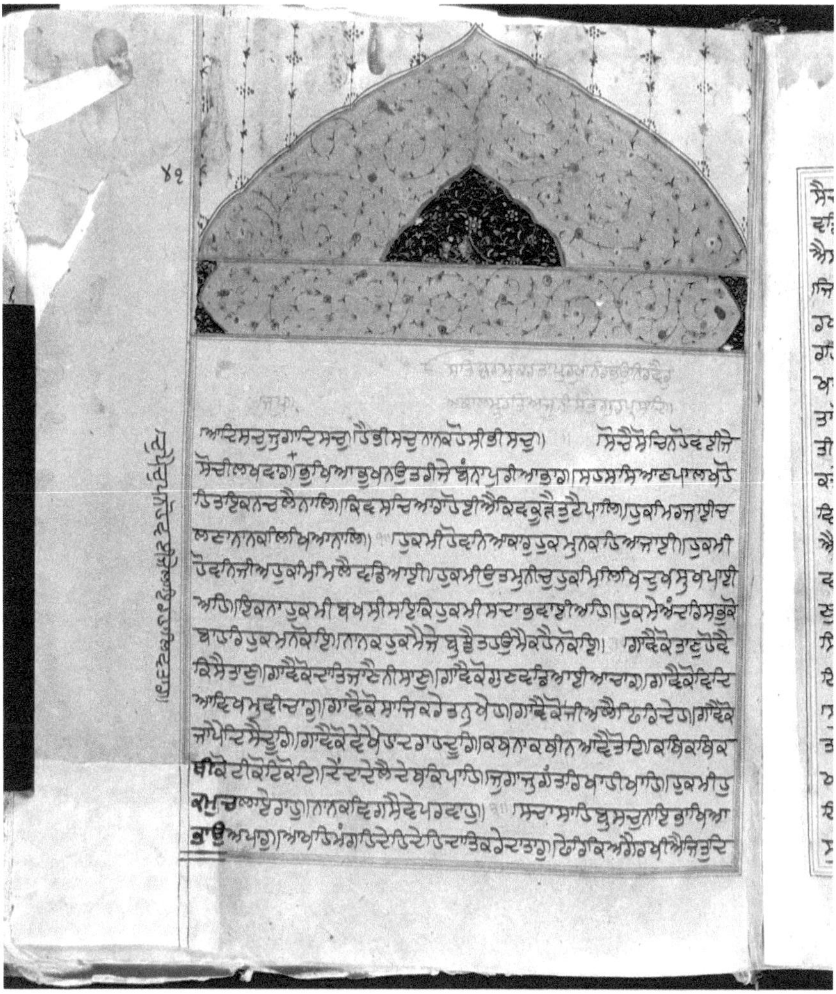

FIGURE 4.8 Copy of the *Ādi Granth* (*Guru Granth Sāhib*), copied c. 1660–1675 CE

Ms. Or. 2748, British Library, London

FIGURE 4.9 The *Dādū Vāṇī* enshrined on the *takẖt* or throne in the Dadu Mandir, Naraina. The manuscript is kept under the parasol toward the rear; the printed copy in the foreground is used in liturgy and communal singing. When it is not in use, a one-rupee coin is placed on top.

Photo by author

FIGURE 4.10 Interior of Dadu Mandir, Naraina

Photo by author

FIGURE 4.11 Amardas's *gudaḍī* (quilt) and other personal belongings in his *samādhi*, Gadha Dham, Didwana

Photo by author

Conclusion

Building an Archive for Hindi

jalād rakṣet tailād rakṣed rakṣec chithilabandhanāt
mūrkhahaste na māṁ dadyād iti vadati pustakam

The book says, "Protect me from water, oil, and loose binding,
And do not place me into the hands of fools!"

—verse traditionally appended to colophons in Sanskrit, Prakrit, and vernacular manuscripts

To conclude this tour through the history of the handwritten book in Hindi, let us return to the Nagari Pracharini Sabha or Committee for the Promulgation of Nagari in Banaras and its manuscript collection. The handwritten books that fill the Sabha's almirahs arrived there because they no longer served the purposes for which they were created—they had become "useless" as books because print technology and printed books had displaced them in their performative, pedagogical, social, and ritual contexts. Furthermore, those contexts had been radically altered or had ceased to exist as colonial modes of government, trade, education, and entertainment reshaped the cultural landscape of northern India and Indian religious reformers restructured the ritual and textual practices of their communities. These inscribed artifacts now served a new purpose, and their very identities as "things" consequently changed: they were no longer "books" but rather "manuscripts," referred to as *hastalikhit granth* ("handwritten book") and *pāṇḍulipi* (lit. "yellowish writing") in Hindi. For modern historians, manuscripts containing martial poetry in Hindi (the *rāso* and *virudāvalī* genres) or paeans (*praśasti*) became "historical documents" (*aitihāsik dastāvez*); for art historians, illustrated manuscripts became objets d'art to be appreciated in museums and private collections; for literary scholars, *guṭakās*, *pothīs*, and *vāṇīs* containing religious and courtly poetry became the raw material from which the literary history of Hindi was to be reconstructed.

The collecting and cataloguing practices of libraries and other literary and cultural institutions transformed the heterogenous collections of paper, palm leaf, birch bark, and cloth that had once tied together the north Indian literary and social landscape into modern "archives" structured according to clearly defined genres, document types, religious traditions, and linguistic divisions. These distinctions dovetailed with the emerging contours of modern historical, literary, and religious scholarship, producing such taxonomies as much as they were produced by them. In the process of organizing these artifacts, surveyors, collectors, archivists, and scholars erased traditional distinctions, characteristics, and taxonomies of the documents. Understandings of the relationships among written text, oral performance, genre, patronage, and religious tradition were forgotten as modern institutions worked to create the archive of Hindi "literature" (*sāhitya*).

Handwritten books became the abstract archive of Hindi literary history, the textual raw material from which a new type of scholar produced interpretive and authoritative historical knowledge about the Hindi language, its literature, and the nation (*rāṣṭra*) of Hindi speakers. They also became a material archive as the myriad handwritten documents once held by thousands of individuals and institutions, including religious *maṭhs*, *pāṭhaśālās*, madrasahs, and community libraries, were gradually aggregated and organized in brick-and-mortar libraries, archives, and institutions for the promulgation and celebration of the Hindi language and its literature. The Nagari Pracharini Sabha was the first institution to undertake a systematic survey and collection of Hindi manuscripts, and the scholars involved established many of the foundational tenets and practices of modern literary historiography and criticism in Hindi. The Sabha consequently receives the greatest amount of attention in the analysis that follows. A set of comparisons with other institutions, such as the Rajasthan Oriental Research Institute in Jodhpur and the Chhatrapati Shivaji Maharaj Vastu Sangrahlaya (formerly the Prince of Wales Museum) in Bombay highlights how different scholarly modalities and archival practices—as well as the language politics of the early twentieth century—effectively made parts of the material archive of Hindi literature either disappear or become impossible to imagine.

THE NAGARI PRACHARINI SABHA AND THE RECOVERY OF HINDI LITERATURE

In March 1893, a small group of students at Queen's College in Banaras resolved to form the Nagari Pracharini Sabha, an organization whose express purpose was the promotion of the Hindi language in the Nāgarī script. For two decades a fierce debate had been underway in British India—and most fiercely in the North-Western Provinces and Oudh (NWPO)—over the language and script in which governmental business, especially the courts, should be administered. (The British colonial government, following its Mughal predecessor, had till then conducted its business in Persian but was gradually replacing Persian with the vernacular.) The Nagari Pracharini Sabha was one of several organizations devoted to promoting "Hindi," which, as they understood it, consisted of a Sanskrit-derived lexicon largely devoid of Persian, Arabic, or Turkish words and was written in the Nāgarī script. As the Sabha declared in its first formal statement in July 1893, "The chief goal of this Sabha will be to bring about the progress of the Nagari language."[1] For them, the vernacular of north India and the Nāgarī script were inseparable.

The Sabha quickly grew to include dozens of members, including high-profile figures from the Brahmin and *kāyasth* communities. Their mission to promulgate Hindi received a major fillip in 1900, when the lieutenant governor of the province and their ally, Sir Antony MacDonnell, declared that Hindi in Nāgarī would be made a language of the courts. This victory bolstered Hindi activists' ambitions to establish Hindi as the national language (*rāṣṭra-bhāṣā*) of British India; yet just like a nation, a national language must have a history. If the Sabha's leaders and sympathizers were to persuade colonial authorities and the Indian public that Hindi written in the Nāgarī script was indeed the "language of the people" (*jan-bhāṣā*) of north India, then they would have to establish that it had historically been the medium through which the "public" (*jantā*) had voiced its aspirations and transmitted knowledge in the form of literature.

Unfortunately, Hindi's published history was remarkably scant at the time. The nineteenth century had seen three compendiums published on the subject: Shivsingh Sengar's *Śivasiṁh-Saroj* (The Lotus of Shivsingh, 1883), Garcin de Tassy's *Historie de la littérature Hindoui et Hindoustani* (History of Hindi Literature, 1839), and George Grierson's *The Modern Vernacular Literature of Hindustan* (1889). The first two authors wrote their books in a manner reminiscent of the *tazkirah* or biographical compendiums of poets, introducing poets in alphabetical order and adding short excerpts from their oeuvres when possible.[2]

Neither provided a chronology or periodization of Hindi literature, offered an interpretation of its historical development, or suggested a criterion for assessing literary value. Grierson proposed a rough periodization of Hindi literature that would inform the work of later historiographers but lacked the scope and depth of a proper historical *narrative*; scarcity of information about authors' dates also frustrated his efforts to arrange works and authors into a chronological framework.[3]

Hindi activists apprehended a need for a "modern" and "scientific" history of Hindi literature along the lines of European literary histories.[4] It was a project that would require massive financial investment, labor, and methods and practices borrowed from several disciplines, including philology, linguistics, paleography, and historiography. When the officers of the Sabha began to look for models, they cast their gaze toward Bengal and Europe, and toward the classical languages of Sanskrit and Prakrit. Bengali littérateurs and intellectuals had begun the process of constructing a literary history for the language decades earlier, with a robust discussion underway by the mid-nineteenth century.[5] These intellectuals had also demonstrated, through their reconstruction of a literary history for Bengali, the modes through which a "modern" vernacular literature could be distinguished—another aspiration that the leaders of the Nagari Pracharini Sabha and its allies harbored for Hindi.

It is no coincidence that Bengal was also the site of early paleographic and philological research: in 1784, Sir William Jones had founded the Asiatic Society in Calcutta, which soon began the systematic collection, cataloguing, and study of manuscripts in Sanskrit and other ancient Indian languages. As the society's agents began to catalogue the manuscripts they had collected from the region, they realized that a significant portion of the material was actually in the vernacular of Bengali. Thus the philological and antiquarian effort to collect manuscripts of works in Sanskrit—imagined as a project of "recovering" a lost past and lost knowledge—had the unintended consequence of producing the first modern collection of Bengali literature—"modern" in terms of its organizational logic, institutional character, and way of imagining its object.[6] These intertwined developments provided the proponents of Hindi with a model for producing both a literary past and a contemporary practice of literary science.

After opening its library of printed Hindi books to the public in 1896, the Nagari Pracharini Sabha began to formulate a plan for building an archive of Hindi manuscripts. The Sabha's officers, especially Shyamsundar Das—one of the original founders, the general secretary, and the initiator of the manuscript survey—envisioned an institution built according to the collecting and bibliographic practices established by Orientalist scholars of Sanskrit in Europe and in India. These practices had been recorded since the mid-nineteenth century in library catalogues and antiquarian journals, as well as in detailed reports of "manuscript tours" undertaken by such leading Indologists as Georg Bühler, Peter Peterson, and Ramkrishna Gopal Bhandarakar.[7] European Orientalists and administrators in the eighteenth and nineteenth centuries were generally impressed by the size and quality of Indian libraries but completely dismayed by their physical appearance. They found nothing comparable to the Baroque wall libraries that were popularized across Europe during the Enlightenment, with volumes arranged, spines out, on fine wood shelves and rooms filled with luxurious furniture designed to facilitate private reading and contemplation. Instead, they encountered dark and often subterranean storerooms that were opened only to retrieve or return books. Instead of shelves upon which bound volumes could be arranged, displayed, and browsed—an activity integral to the literary and intellectual culture of eighteenth- and nineteenth-century European salons, libraries, and bookstores—Indian libraries were filled with wooden trunks (*ṣandūq*), boxes, and bags (*basta*) that concealed the identity of the books that they contained. Indian libraries consequently employed specialized personnel who, through memory or the use of well-guarded handwritten catalogues, located, retrieved, stored, and organized the collection.[8] Even in small personal libraries—say, the collection of a village pandit or the library of a *qāẓī* living in a *qaṣbah*—books were usually wrapped in cloth and stored in trunks to protect them from the ravages of moisture, heat, and insects.[9]

Orientalist scholars' imperative to rescue the written record of Indian literature from supposed indigenous neglect—actualized through the surveying, collection, and centralized storage of manuscripts in modern, scientifically organized libraries built on the European model—was characterized by the same anxieties that animated colonial collecting and scholastic practices in general. Indigenous bibliographical and library practices were thought to be aesthetically unpleasing and irrational, and made European scholars and administrators dependent upon native expertise for access to Indian textual knowledge.[10] The contrast between Indian and European libraries provides an apt metaphor for the way this bibliographic project was imagined: European Indologists and their Indian colleagues would exhume India's written heritage from its hidden entombment in trunks and boxes scattered across the region and make it visible, searchable, and browsable in a direct and unmediated fashion familiar to the modern reader. No longer bound by the chains (*silsilah*) of Islamic pedagogical lineages or the sacred threads (*janeū*) of Brahmin scholastic initiation, readers would be able to peruse volumes on myriad subjects without having to rely upon the largesse of traditional custodians and mediators.

A similar attitude was reflected in the way that the Sabha's leadership characterized its mission to create an archive of Hindi literature. As Shyamsundar Das wrote in his autobiography,

> The Sabha believed very strongly that much literary and historical information dealing with India, especially with North India, lay hidden in Hindi manuscripts wrapped in cloth and shut up in dark buildings. If anyone knew something [of such manuscripts] or if a collection of such manuscripts was to be found in someone's house [and he did nothing], then whether through illusion or ignorance or greed, he was preventing the preservation and enrichment of his own native language by [not] presenting these hidden treasures to the public.[11]

In order to make knowledge of Hindi's literary history available to the public, the raw material of that history (manuscripts) would have to be rescued from the public itself. As the Sabha and similar organizations gradually extracted the Hindi manuscript archive from the traditional sites of its production and circulation, they unwittingly destroyed existing knowledge systems and practices related to the storage, classification, organization, documentation, valuation, conservation, exegesis, and performance of written materials.

The Sabha's plan to create an archive for Hindi literature had two major elements: an ambitious survey of Hindi manuscripts across northern India and the construction of a modern library facility to house those manuscripts. The Sabha began its first survey of Hindi manuscripts in 1899, after obtaining a pledge of 400 rupees annually for the project from the Government of the North-Western Provinces and Oudh. The first year's survey was an extremely modest undertaking, with Shyamsundar Das and the Sabha's president, Radha Krishna Das, approaching pandits, aristocratic families, and individual households in the Banaras region and documenting the titles, authors, and bibliographic information for any Hindi manuscripts that they found. Nevertheless, buoyed by the discovery of several unknown works, they repeated the annual survey for five more years, visiting different districts within the province, as well as Jaipur, Jodhpur, and Rewah. From 1906 to 1950, the Sabha continued the survey, published a report once every three years, and gained increasing financial support from the government of the NWPO as well as from the government of Punjab and a few princely states. Despite persistent problems with training and retaining survey staff and with finding resources for the publication of the reports, by 1950 the Sabha had managed to collect manuscripts of more than 14,673 works by an estimated 6,095 authors.[12] Meanwhile, the Sabha began plans in 1898 to build a headquarters, launching a major fundraising campaign for the purpose in 1901 and completing construction of the building in February 1904. The grand edifice was a three-story red brick mixture of Georgian and Indo-Saracenic architecture that rivaled Banaras's Town Hall in size. In addition to administrative and publication offices, the building housed a spacious storeroom for manuscripts and a grand, two-storied, arcaded reading room in which scholars could consult both manuscripts and printed books in the collection[13] (figs. 0.1, 5.1).

The Nagari Pracharini Sabha quite literally *produced* the modern archive of Hindi language and literature by surveying, collecting, and cataloguing this vast body of manuscripts. Yet three factors gave that archive a very particular shape. The first was the Sabha's express mission of popularizing "Hindi in the Nāgarī script"—as opposed to the Arabic script, which by that time had come to be associated with the literary traditions of Urdu. Nāgarī was also preferred over Kaithī and other shorthand scripts (despite the participation of prominent *kāyasth*s in the Sabha). Consequently, the group showed little interest in collecting manuscripts copied in the Arabic script, even though some of the oldest works in Hindi, the *pem-kathā*s, were most often in this script. (Many early copies of other major works in Hindi, including the *Rāmacaritamānas* of Tulsidas and the *Sūrasāgar* of Surdas, were also in the Arabic script.) Although the Sabha proudly noted the acquisition of manuscripts in Kaithī and Gurmukhi scripts in its survey reports, these constituted a minuscule percentage of the volumes collected. A huge part of the written literature of north India was left out simply on the basis of the script in which it was copied. Meanwhile, manuscripts of the vernacular in the Arabic script were gradually being acquired by libraries specializing in Urdu and by "Islamic" libraries such as the Khuda Bakhsh Library in Patna, the would-be "Muslim" counterparts of the "Hindu" Nagari Pracharini Sabha.[14]

The second factor that shaped this archive of Hindi was geography. The Sabha was headquartered in Banaras, within the British administrative unit of the North-Western Provinces and Oudh (redesignated the United Provinces of Agra and Oudh in 1902). Although this region was rich in Hindi manuscripts, the Sabha frequently expressed ambitions of expanding into Bengal, Punjab, the Central Provinces, and the northern princely states to amass a comprehensive archive of Hindi literature. These ambitions were repeatedly frustrated by the financial and administrative limitations imposed by the Sabha's location: it successfully lobbied its own provincial government to fund its survey activities and related publications for several years but was less successful in acquiring financial assistance from other provinces and princely states, in part because they had chosen to pursue their own manuscript surveys. While the Sabha officers' connections among the literati and erstwhile ruling families of the United Provinces yielded access to these communities' private manuscript collections, the Rajput princes, *mahants*, and pandits of other regions were more hesitant to grant access to their libraries.

The third factor becomes perceptible only by viewing the Nagari Pracharini Sabha's manuscript collection in its totality. It then shows what appears to be an implicit set of religious distinctions, actualized through choices regarding which textual genres should be collected. Although some Islamic and Jain texts were added to the Sabha's collection, it appears that the surveyors were uninterested in collecting works that they understood to be Islamic or Jain "religious" literature. Thus there are no copies of Jain *phāgu* songs or Shia *marṣiyah* elegies, even though such works were composed in the same language (and, in some cases, in the same style) as works that the Sabha did collect. (In comparison, the Rajasthan Oriental Research Institute collected many Jain works—unsurprising given the large number of Jain *granth bhaṇḍār*s in the region and the presence of Jain intellectuals among the institute's early officers—but few works related to Islam.) As a result of these three factors, the archive of Hindi literature that the Nagari Pracharini Sabha produced was distinctly "eastern" (in terms of the broader "Hindi belt"), was distinctly Hindu, and excluded a wide variety of works and genres that were either written in a script other than Nāgarī or were assumed to belong to a religious tradition other than Hinduism.

Nevertheless, the officers and scholars of the Nagari Pracharini Sabha used this archive to construct an authoritative framework for understanding Hindi literary history that persists, at least in part, today. Soon after the manuscript survey was initiated in 1901, scholars working with the Sabha began using the manuscripts they had surveyed and collected to reconstruct Hindi literary history, publishing articles and essays on the "recovered" Hindi works. Many of these scholars had assisted in the surveys and would later become prominent scholars at Allahabad University and Banaras Hindu University; they published their research in the Sabha's *Khoj Reports* (Search Reports) and in the *Nāgarī Pracāriṇī Patrikā*, the journal of Hindi language and literature that the Sabha had launched in 1896. Its manuscript collection played a central role in some of the earliest monographs addressing the history of Hindi literature; for example, the Mishra brothers (Ganeshbihari, Shyambihari, and Shukdevbihari) published their encyclopedic compendium of Hindi authors in 1913 at the bequest of, and with archival support from, the Sabha.[15] Pitambardatt Barthwal, who had assisted in the manuscript surveys and in 1933 became the first individual to complete a doctoral degree in Hindi literature, made extensive use of the Sabha's archives to write his dissertation, which he later published as the influential *Traditions of Indian Mysticism Based Upon the Nirguna School of Hindi Poetry* in 1936.[16]

Yet the decisive moment for the formation of Hindi literary history came in 1929, in the form of a synoptic history that Ramchandra Shukla composed as the introduction to Shyamsundar Das's colossal dictionary, the *Hindī Śabd Sāgar* (Ocean of Hindi Words). Both Shukla and Das had played central roles in developing the institution of the Sabha and in cataloguing and documenting the massive amount of material collected through the manuscript surveys. On the basis of the works contained in the Sabha's collection, Shukla first proposed, in the introduction to the *Hindī Śabd Sāgar*, what would become the canonical periodization and taxonomy of Hindi literature. According to Shukla, Hindi literature, being a reflection of "the public's mentality" (*jantā kī cittavr̥tti*), could be broadly divided into four epochs (*kāl*), each with its own distinct ethos and corresponding mode of literary production. The first he dubbed the "early period" or "period of the heroic ballad" (*vīragāthākāl*), reckoned to extend from 994 to 1319 CE; the second was the "early medieval" or "period of the devotional" (*bhaktikāl*), 1319–1643 CE; the third was the "late medieval" or "period of formalism" (*rītikāl*), 1644–1844 CE; finally, the "modern period" or "period of prose" (*gadyakāl*) was reckoned to extend from 1845 onward.[17] This periodization continues to frame much scholarly discussion of Hindi literary history to this day.

Despite having worked with manuscripts in the Sabha's collection for several years, Shukla ignored their material and formal aspects entirely, abstracting from their content a genre-centered taxonomy of literary forms that told the history of Hindi in terms of great authors and their works. The significance of this approach is reflected in Shukla's periodization, which assigns literary genres a chronology based solely upon the times at which seminal works were composed, rather than the periods in which they were copied and circulated. In Shukla's narrative, literary genres appear to rise and fall in popularity in tandem with the political and social circumstances of their composition. For example, the great popularity of the *pem-kathā* during the "late medieval period" (approximately 1644–1844 CE), which is reflected in the manuscript record, is simply not *thinkable* within Shukla's generic and chronological framework, which locates the *pem-kathā* firmly within the "early medieval period" (1319–1643). Like the implicit logic of the Sabha's manuscript collection, Shukla's generic classifications assume certain correspondences between generic distinctions and religious distinctions; literary forms and motifs in his analysis become elements of sectarian identity rather than expressive modes that can be shared across multiple traditions and communities. For example, Shukla presents the *pem-kathā* (or, in his terminology, the *prem-gāthā* or "love ballad") as a literary form particular to Sufism and characterizes it as a sub-branch (*śākhā*) of *nirguṇ* literature; he in turn characterizes *nirguṇ* literature as a branch of resurgent Hindu devotional religion (*bhakti*), the zeitgeist of the early medieval period.[18] The diversity of social contexts, not to mention the great temporal span, reflected in manuscripts of *pem-kathā* works has disappeared and the genre has been fixed within a very specific, and very narrow, social and temporal domain. How could such a taxonomy possibly account for a poet like Surdas, the Punjabi Hindu who composed the *pem-kathā* of *Nal Daman* in 1659?

BIBLIOGRAPHIC TECHNOLOGIES AND THE DISAPPEARANCE OF WORKS, GENRES, AND PEOPLE

Shukla's reimagining of Hindi's literary record was to a significant extent made possible by the collecting and cataloguing practices of the Nagari Pracharini Sabha itself. The seemingly banal procedures and documents through which cataloguers like Shukla, Das, and Barthwal described and entered manuscripts into the Sabha's ever-growing register tell us a great deal about how these men and their peers in similar institutions produced an interpretive history of Hindi literature from a great mass of handwritten books. By 1903, having learned from the difficulties and challenges during the first three years of the manuscript survey, Das implemented a system that largely emulated the bibliographic and codicological practices of contemporary Sanskrit scholars.[19] Each of his subsequent survey reports gave a serially numbered list of manuscripts that included the title of the work; the name of the author; whether the work was in verse or prose; the writing material (paper, palm leaf, etc.); the number of folios and the number of lines of text per folio; the appearance of the manuscript (its physical condition); whether it was complete or incomplete; whether the work as recorded in the manuscript was "correct" or "corrupted"; the script in which it was copied; the "place of deposit" (the location where it was acquired or found); a brief description of what the work "is" (e.g. a "translation" of another work, an example of a particular genre, etc.); and two excerpts, one from the beginning of the manuscript and one from the end.

Nevertheless, in the Sabha's survey reports, most of the entries are not for manuscripts per se, but rather for literary *works*: each entry is for a discrete work by a known, individual author—despite the fact that many manuscripts contained multiple works by multiple authors. This cataloguing structure reflects the dominant mode of literary historiography globally at the turn of the twentieth century. Literary history, itself a "hybrid genre" that "conjoined literary criticism, biography, and intellectual/social background within a narrative of development" had, over the past half-century, taken a decidedly nationalist turn.[20] The history of a literature was understood to be the story of great writers and works that collectively gave expression to the evolving "mind" of the nation.[21] The Sabha's survey reports, intended to make the recovery and writing of Hindi literary history possible, provided data about "great works" and "great authors" so that their collective story as the expression of the nation's ethos could be written.[22]

Such a privileging of works and authors inevitably caused certain other kinds of data and information to be pushed into the background or ignored. The Sabha's survey reports include no typology of manuscript forms and few details regarding a manuscript's physical and material form (whether or not it was bound, the materials used in its production, the arrangement of text, etc.). The philological imperative to find the oldest recensions of works and to reconstruct the ur-texts of supposedly corrupted works encouraged cataloguers to privilege older manuscripts and neglect or ignore later and undated copies. They paid little attention to documenting provenance, meaning that critical information about where and how manuscripts were acquired, the individual and institutional hands through which they passed, and any earlier contexts of their performance were lost.

The structural logic of the survey report is, to a significant extent, a product of its own particular character as *medium*: a printed paper book in which data is presented in sequential lists and in tabular form. The materials and processes of print media imposed limitations upon the kinds of relationships that could be documented or modeled. To create a printed catalogue that recorded and represented the relationships between different aspects of various manuscripts (such as date of composition, date of copying, dimensions, script, extent of completion, etc.) in a manner akin to present-day relational databases would have required labor and printing costs far exceeding the Sabha's resources and the ability of most individuals and institutions to purchase a copy. The most the Sabha could do was to provide indices of authors and works at the end of reports and catalogues.

In the early twentieth-century world of print media, creating a catalogue of manuscripts organized according to author and work was perhaps the most efficient and effective method of making data available to researchers; however, this approach provided no practical way to identify or cross-list manuscripts with multiple works or authors. Manuscripts for which a discrete work or individual author could not be identified were generally relegated to tables at the end of the survey report and excluded from the all-important indices of authors and works.

The fate of tens of thousands of such manuscripts in India is illustrated by the case of the ubiquitous *pad-saṁgraha* ("collection of lyrics") and *sphuṭakar pad* ("miscellaneous lyrics"). These terms have been used by cataloguers from the time of the Sabha's early surveys as a designation or "title" for a manuscript containing works by multiple authors. They are most often applied to poetic miscellanies for which an institution lacks the necessary time, staff, expertise, resources, or patience to investigate the contents. Such anthological manuscripts, being "illegible" in the language and logic of the catalogue and archive, simply disappear from view. This is the fate of the vast majority of *guṭakā*-type manuscripts.

Dozens of archives and libraries of Hindi literature sprung up in the wake of the Nagari Pracharini Sabha's success. The Sabha itself had a hand in launching several, such as the prestigious Hindi Sahitya Sammelan of Allahabad (founded in 1910).[23] Others, like the Bihar Rashtrabhasha Parishad (est. 1950), Rajasthan Oriental Research Institute (est. 1954), Rajasthani Shodh Sansthan (est. 1955), and Vrindavan Research Institute (est. 1968), represented efforts by state governments and private organizations to preserve, document, and promote regional or local literary traditions in Hindi (or in idioms and registers that were increasingly considered "dialects" of Hindi by literary historians). At the same time, the royal houses of princely states like Jaipur, Jodhpur, and Udaipur began to invest resources in the study and conservation of their histories, which included the establishment of modern library facilities and the reorganization of royal collections along the lines of European bibliographic practices. All the while, older Indological libraries like the Asiatic Society branches in Calcutta and Bombay continued to collect vernacular manuscripts along with manuscripts of Sanskrit and Prakrit works, eventually cataloguing them and making them available to researchers.

The catalogues of these archives collectively reflect the divergent ways institutions, cataloguers, and librarians have imagined the linguistic and literary landscape of north India. As a researcher's point of entry into the archive, the library catalogue presents itself as a map of the linguistic and literary terrain of the archive. Yet it does not simply represent a pre-existing landscape; it *creates* that landscape through acts of classification and taxonomical structures. Catalogues often make distinctions between genres and traditions that would have been unintelligible or meaningless to audiences in precolonial north India. Schemes of classification even cause certain works to "fall through the cracks" created by modern generic and linguistic distinctions. For example, the Rajasthan Oriental Research Institute in Jodhpur divides the collection into two parts: the first set of catalogues documents the Sanskrit manuscripts in the collection while the second set documents the Hindi and Rajasthani manuscripts. (The reasoning behind cataloguing Hindi and Rajasthani manuscripts together—and whether and when "Hindi" and "Rajasthani" designate distinct languages and literatures—is itself a complex linguistic, literary, and historical question.) Catalogues of the Hindi and Rajasthani manuscripts are organized according to "subject" (*viṣay*); among the twenty-three enumerated are philosophy (*darśan*); Brahminical rules of conduct (*dharmaśāstra*); Puranas; literature (*kāvya*), which is subdivided into "poetry," "historical poetry," and "miscellaneous poetry"; ethics; drama; "devotional literature" (*bhakti sāhitya*); astrology; music; "Jain literature"; and so forth.

Where, in such a taxonomy, would one place a work such as the *Vairāgya Vṛnd* of Bhagvandas, a vernacular commentary (*ṭīkā*) on an anthology of courtly Sanskrit poetry written by a monk who refers to himself as a literary poet while expiating on spiritual detachment and the need for devotion (*bhakti*)? Bhagvandas's work is found among the entries for *bhakti sāhitya* in the library's catalogue, even though other commentaries on Sanskrit poetry are among the entries for *kāvya*. The *Vairāgya Vṛnd* is also absent from the catalogues of Sanskrit manuscripts, even though its manuscripts contain Sanskrit poetry. In the logic of the catalogue, works like the *Vairāgya Vṛnd* (a literary commentary cum religious treatise), the *Vedānta Mahāvākya Bhāṣā* of Manohardas (a commentarial work of Advaita Vedānta), and the *Chandaratnāvalī* of Hariramdas (a work on prosody with examples from religious poetry) must be made to fit into a single entry and thus into a single generic or formal category—in the case of these three works, the category of *bhakti*.

Some archives organize their manuscripts in such a way that it provokes, like Borges's description of a fictional Chinese encyclopedia, "the laughter that [shatters] . . . all the familiar landmarks of . . . our thought that bears the stamp of our age and our geography—breaking up all the ordered surfaces and all the planes with which we are accustomed to tame the wild profusion of existing things."[24] For example, the manuscript catalogue of the University of Lucknow's library divides its contents as follows: Arabic, Urdu, Turkish, Persian, Sanskrit, Palm-leaf, Kaithi, Hindi. Aside from its bifurcation of the vernacular into "Hindi" and "Urdu," the classification scheme alternates between language (Arabic, Turkish, Sanskrit, etc.), script (Kaithi, Urdu, Hindi,) and writing material (palm leaf)![25] If this scheme provokes laughter, it should also shatter the "familiar landmarks" of the literary archive that we find natural or logical and thus take for granted.

Modern archival practices caused not just works but also people to disappear. The organizing rubrics of twentieth-century archives and libraries often break up collections (and even individual manuscripts) inherited from the polyglot and polymathic individuals and institutions of the precolonial period. For Manuscript 26334 in the Rajasthan Oriental Research Institute, the notebook of hymns, epigrams, stories, hagiographies, mantras, spells, magic squares, yantras, diagrams, and astrological tables that belonged to the peripatetic religious specialist discussed in chapter 2, the cataloguer, compelled to find a title for this "work," named it *Kutub Śat Ādi Guṭakā* ("*guṭakā* of the *Hundred Verses about Kutub*, etc."), after a condensed prose version of a *pem-kathā* found in the *guṭakā*.[26] This already obscures the diverse contents of the *guṭakā*, and the cataloguer gives the manuscript's "subject" (*viṣay*) as *itihās* ("epic" or "history")! When the existence of such a multilingual and multireligious collection (containing Islamic and Jain material in addition to works of Hindu *bhakti*) becomes obscured, so too does the figure of the historical subject who copied, performed, and explained these texts to his audience. This was not an "exceptional" individual, a participant in elite literary circles, or a member of courtly society, but a sadhu practicing the polyglot literary and religious culture of his day. Yet there is no space to imagine him in an archive that literally and figuratively separates manuscripts of Jain works from manuscripts of Hindu and Islamic works and manuscripts of Sanskrit works from manuscripts of Hindi and Rajasthani works. Nor is there space for the owner of Manuscript 477 in the AC Joshi Library (discussed in chapter 1), who read the *Padmāvat* of Jayasi, Persian and vernacular stories of Islamic and Hindu kings, lexicons of Hindu deities, and poetry in Persian and Hindi, in an archive and literary history that see only works and authors divided by language, genre, or subject.

FROM MANUSCRIPTS TO PRINTED BOOKS

Another major initiative undertaken by the Nagari Pracharini Sabha and similar institutions was the publication of critical editions of "classical" works of Hindi literature like the *Padmāvat*, *Rāmacaritamānas*, and *Pr̥thvīrāj Rāso*, and collections of the hymns and epigrams of saint-poets like Kabir. Diligent and industrious scholars like Das, Shukla, Mata Prasad Gupta, Agarchand Nahata, and others collated dozens of the oldest manuscripts available for a given work, compared and recorded variants, reconstructed passages, and created stemmata of manuscript recensions and traditions.[27] They thus produced authoritative or "authentic" (*prāmāṇik*) versions, often printed with critical apparatuses, notes, and introductions that explained the literary and historical significance of the given work. These printed books—a new type of codex for a new type of reader, mass-produced and identical in their form and content—played a large role in the formation of a modern Hindi "public," in great measure because they quickly became part of college and university syllabi across the Hindi belt of north India.[28] In contrast to manuscript copies, which had transmitted texts in a serial fashion, with one copy producing another through discrete social and intellectual networks, these printed copies were produced en masse and broadcast across wide geographical and diverse social spaces as they were sold in shops, universities, book fairs, and religious fairs, and by mail order.

Paradoxically absent from these printed editions of the "classics" was an indication of the large bodies of manuscripts from which they had been produced, despite the inclusion of critical apparatuses and descriptions of editorial practices. The imperative to reconstruct an original or ur-text from which recensions branched reduced manuscript copies to "pure" or "corrupted" instantiations of a single work. The "text" was assumed to be one and unitary; its material, written form had little to no significance in and of itself, being a mere trace of a particular recension. Consequently, editors paid little attention to the social, religious, or material contexts in which manuscripts were produced and their possible significance for particular readings of the text. Furthermore, the value of those different readings could only be reckoned in binary terms: either "authentic" (*prāmāṇik*) or "corrupted" (*vikār*) in relation to a putative "original" (*mūl*) work.[29] This approach was fraught with contradiction in regard to the *pad*s and *sākhī*s composed by (putatively illiterate) saint-poets: editors of anthologies frequently assumed that no "original" manuscript tradition existed and therefore readings had to be adjudicated according to beliefs regarding the biography of the poet.[30] The drive to recover discrete works by discrete individuals reduced the abundance of manuscript versions to raw material for the production of a *single* work, a process aptly described by Jaroslav Strnad as an obsession with "finding the source" rather than "mapping the stream."[31]

FROM BOOKS TO ART: THE FATE OF THE ILLUSTRATED *PEM-KATHĀ*S

While the surveyors, cataloguers, and scholars dedicated to the promotion of Hindi literature transformed handwritten books into the raw material of Hindi literary history, art historians, collectors, and museum curators transformed illustrated copies of Hindi works into the raw material of Indian art history. These specialists collectively converted the illustrations that accompanied stories into objects of expert knowledge in the domains of painting and calligraphy; in doing so, they often removed the images from their literary or narrative contexts, although they acknowledged the sources of the images. These illustrations, divorced from their performative contexts, were no longer imagined as part of a practice of reading and storytelling but rather as aesthetic objects to be contemplated in isolation and on their own terms. This process through which illustrated manuscripts were reimagined had a material as well as an intellectual dimension: the images within manuscripts could be reconstituted as examples of visual art in large part because they were quite literally ripped from books, then sorted, organized, stored, and displayed according to emerging protocols of museology and conservation.

Like literary history, the discipline of art history in India had its roots in the antiquarian and Orientalist scholarship of colonial officials and scholars, particularly in the writings of archaeologists and historians. South Asian scholars like Ananda Coomaraswamy (1877–1947) and Calambur Sivaramamurti (1909–1983) took up the emerging discipline of art history and guided it in new directions that included, in some cases, distinctly nationalist interpretive frameworks, another parallel with the practice of literary history at the time. This involved a shift in ways of seeing, initiated through government art schools and gallery and museum practices. According to Christopher Pinney, these practices encouraged a move away from "theatrical," interactive engagements with images, in which the beholder remained aware of his or her own presence vis-à-vis the object (as in the practice of *darśan*) and toward a disembodied relationship in which the viewer imagines himself or herself to be an "absent beholder."[32] It also involved the development of a concept of "Indian art" for which a history of evolution and change could be written. By 1874, drawing upon the writings of European archaeologists, historians, ethnographers, and travelers, Henry H. Cole could write confidently of a tradition of "Indian art" that stretched from the Vedic period to the present, and that "by studying the art and production of India—inseparable from the history of nations—we learn not a little of its people themselves."[33] From this point forward, individual artifacts from South Asia in European and Indian collections were imagined as instantiations of an Indian art tradition that changed over time and included multiple branches (imagined in communal terms as "Hindu," "Jain," "Islamic," etc.) but that was ultimately unitary in character, being the expression of the "mind" of the Indian nation.

These shifts occurred in tandem with the emergence of two institutions: the university (including art schools) and the museum. The former trained European and Indian specialists in authoritative frameworks and methods of art history and criticism.[34] The latter, built by civic groups and provincial governments in India, provided a space in which artifacts could be experienced as art objects, socializing visitors into particular practices of viewing and discussion. In Carol Duncan's words, in terms of both architecture and function, museums represented a new type of "temple" in which the "ritual" of detached aesthetic consumption was performed by and for the public.[35] For example, the Prince of Wales Museum in Bombay, financed by government and private donors and formally opened in 1922, was intended to further public understanding and appreciation of the sciences and arts. As Lady Lloyd, wife of the governor of Bombay, put it at the inauguration ceremony, "the stranger who visits it will have the history of its community unrolled before his eyes, he will be presented with a fascinating picture of the natural surroundings in which the community lives . . . and of its achievements in every sphere of art and science."[36]

In 1955, the museum acquired sixty-eight folios of an illustrated manuscript that had previously belonged to a family in Bhopal and that the superintendent of Persian and Arabic epigraphy in the Archeological Survey of India, Ziauddin Abdul Hayy Desai, had identified as belonging to the *Candāyan* of Maulana Daud.[37] Each folio was richly illustrated on one side and calligraphed on the other (fig. 1.4). In the late 1950s, two prominent art historians and collectors, Karl Khandalavala and Moti Chandra, confirmed that the folios belonged to the *Candāyan*, of which fragmentary copies had recently been identified in the collections of the Bharat Kala Bhavan in Banaras, the Raza Rampur Library in Uttar Pradesh, a Sufi *k̲h̲ānqāh* at Maner Sharif in Bihar, the Lahore Museum, the Staatsbibliothek in Berlin, and the John Rylands Library of the University of Manchester.[38] Over the next three decades, these dispersed copies would collectively lead a double life: for scholars of Hindi like Parmeshwari Lal Gupta, Mataprasad Gupta, and Vishvanath Prasad, they were the source of a literary text that they arduously reconstructed according to the editorial procedures described earlier. The material and visual aspects of the manuscripts held little interest for them and played no role in their editorial decisions.[39] In contrast, for art historians like Khandalavala and Chandra, the visuality and materiality of the folios were everything: analyzing them meant identifying distinct stylistic, iconographic, and material elements in the illustrations in order to locate the copies within specific geographical, temporal, and social contexts. They and later scholars like Basil Gray, Anand Krishna, Regine Pachner, and Rai Krishnadasa compared the folios to the dispersed folios of other illustrated manuscripts in order to hypothesize the dates of their creation, the religious or ethnic identity of the artisans who painted them, and the identity of the patrons who commissioned them. With the exception of Parmeshwari Lal Gupta, the literary scholars and art historians moved, worked, and published in separate circles; discussions of the manuscripts' visual programs and calligraphic layout seldom appear in the writings of the literary scholars, while the narrative of the *Candāyan* and its literary qualities receive only passing mention in the writings of the art historians.[40]

The scholastic concerns and practices of art historians dovetailed with contemporary museological practices of collecting, cataloguing, storing, and exhibiting manuscripts. No single institution possessed a complete copy of the *Candāyan* (indeed, the work has never been reconstructed in its entirety), and all of the institutions holding fragments, with the exception of the John Rylands Library, received their respective groups of folios unbound. (The copy acquired by the John Rylands Library had been previously rebound in a modern leather binding and was missing several folios.) Twelve folios from the same copy that was the source of the folios in the Prince of Wales Museum were eventually sold to the Philadelphia Museum of Art, Asian Art Museum of San Francisco, San Diego Museum of Art, Metropolitan Museum of Fine Arts, Virginia Museum of Fine Arts, Brooklyn Museum, and Cleveland Museum of Art, while fifteen folios were acquired by private collectors. This dispersal underscores how the folios were understood and valued as individual paintings within the global art market.[41]

In this condition—unbound, dispersed, and isolated—each folio, or rather the illustration on the verso of each folio, could be reconceptualized as an independent art object. Several came to be permanently exhibited in the Miniature Painting Gallery of the Prince of Wales Museum (now the Chhatrapati Shivaji Maharaj Vastu Sangrahalaya) as examples of the evolving synthesis of "Indic" and "Islamic" styles of painting—one of the primary themes of the master narrative of Indian art in the second millennium.[42] Each folio is framed and exhibited so that only the side containing visual illustration can be viewed. Each is accompanied by a separate label explaining the illustration's significance in the history of Indian painting (but without any mention of the text inscribed on the back). Even though the accompanying signage mentions that these are illustrations of the story of Laurik and Chanda, there is no acknowledgment or visual suggestion in the spatial arrangement of the folios that these "paintings" were once bound together *as a book* or constituted a *single* object. Instead, they collectively represent a moment in the historical development of Indian "miniature" painting.

This material disaggregation also allowed those folios' individual meanings to be reinscribed. The museum's internal cataloguing process, carried out by hand sometime after 1961, created a separate catalogue item for each folio rather than treating them as parts of a single object. The register of artifacts lists each folio separately under the title of its respective "subject," i.e., the subject of the visual illustration on the folio's verso. Yet the cataloguer has often inferred the "subject" from the Persian heading on the other (recto) side. In such deluxe copies of the *Candāyan*, each stanza along with its Persian heading was inscribed on the right-hand folio of the manuscript while the visual illustration was painted on the facing left-hand folio. The cataloguer has entered not the subject of the painting on the catalogued folio but rather the subject of whichever folio would have followed it in the manuscript. This catalogue in turn became a source of information for museum signage, publications, scholarly studies, and social media posts by art historians and aficionados.[43] Folios from other copies of the *Candāyan* have met similar or worse fates: some of the illustrated folios held by Bharat Kala Bhavan have been mounted on cardboard with chemical adhesive, making it impossible to examine the text inscribed on the other side.

Perhaps the most poignant case is that of the *Candāyan* copy originally acquired by the Central Museum of Lahore around 1922. The copy included twenty-four detached folios (figs. 2.6, 2.10). With the Partition of India and Pakistan in 1947, it was decided to similarly partition the collections of the Central Museum, with roughly 60 percent of artifacts remaining in Pakistan and 40 percent being sent to India. The museum's copy of the *Candāyan* was accordingly partitioned, with fourteen folios remaining in Lahore and ten being sent to India, where they eventually came to their present home in the Government Museum and Art Gallery in Chandigarh. The fate of this exquisite manuscript gestures to the fate of the *pem-kathā* genre specifically and to the archive of illustrated vernacular works generally. In the communalized historical imagination of the early twentieth century, Hindus and Muslims were understood to ultimately embody two distinct "nations" (*rāṣṭra*, *qaum*), each with its own language and literature: Hindi for the Hindus, Urdu for the Muslims.[44] As both Hindi and Urdu, Hindus and Muslims, could stake a plausible claim to the linguistic and literary inheritance of the *Candāyan*, it was perhaps inevitable that the Lahore-Chandigarh copy, as it is now called, would be divided up along with the physical geography and social fabric through which it had once circulated.[45]

Dilir Khan's 1698 copy of the *Nal Daman* of Surdas too entered the collection of the Prince of Wales Museum in the 1940s, but not before it was transformed into an art object through rather radical means. When Dilir Khan had it made, the copy was beautified with fine calligraphy and illumination but lacked any illustrations. Yet when the museum purchased the manuscript, it was replete with painted illustrations of kings, nobles, musicians, and ascetics. These were added later, possibly by a precolonial connoisseur; the practice of reusing paintings in manuscripts was not uncommon in Mughal India. Yet the way they have been incorporated suggests a modern owner or art dealer: pasted right over the text, they obscure large portions of the work (at least sixty-four stanzas). In any case, the paintings bear no relation to Surdas's literary work, but this fact went unnoticed because the twentieth-century individuals who sold, acquired, and catalogued the book understood its value to be determined by its visual and material aspects, not by its textual content. The disciplinary divide between art history and literary history ensured that literary scholars have remained almost completely unaware of the work's existence, and the few art historians who have examined the book erroneously describe its paintings as "illustrations" of Surdas's *Nal Daman*.[46]

THE LIVES OF BOOKS

In the spring of 2020, while leafing through a *guṭakā* of religious and philosophical works in the royal library of the City Palace in Jaipur, I came across several blossoms of the *kaner* (desert rose) pressed between two folios. It was likely they had been placed there a century or two earlier. Who had done so, and why? For a medical purpose, or simply a desire to preserve an otherwise ephemeral object of beauty? Later, I discovered between the folios of a codex containing Keshavdas's *Rasikapriyā* and a Hindi rendition of the *dān-līlā* (story of Krishna's "toll play") a tiny elephant and his driver. An artist of the royal book atelier had sketched them on thin paper and cut them out to use as a stencil when composing paintings. How did the elephant and driver make their way into the middle of a story about Krishna and the milkmaids of Braj? By accident? As a bookmark? Or perhaps as the plaything of a child who had acquired them as a toy?

Every handwritten book is unique and bears traces of the life that it has lived. That life begins with its construction, preparation, and inscription, and continues as the book is acquired, read, and performed by multiple individuals over time in different geographical, social, literary, and religious contexts. To study a book in all of its textual, visual, and material dimensions is therefore to reconstruct the social, literary, and religious lives of the people through whose hands it passed as well.

What can a method of writing literary history that begins with the material archive teach us that other approaches cannot? The first thing it reveals is the relationship between textual genre and material form. Narrative structures, prosodic forms, and performance modalities shape the physical construction and appearance of a book. In the case of the *pem-kathā*, the stanzaic structure of the narrative and the use of multiple prosodic forms led to the development of a distinctive style of codex with recognizable conventions for arranging text and illustrations. In the case of the *pad* and *sākhī*, hymnodic and pedagogical modes of performance, as well as the occupational exigencies of a traveling monk, favored a notational mode of inscription that was made in robust, bound *guṭakā*s, the form of which had been adapted from notebooks used for recordkeeping and accounting. In the case of scholastic writing, the imperative to recast the vernacular of *bhāṣā* in the model of *kāvya* and *śāstra* drove the development of new paratextual practices as well as the adoption of the *pothī*, with its literary and scholastic associations, as the primary written vehicle for these new vernacular genres. The role that the *pothī* played in constituting scholastic and literary networks also attracted early purveyors of vernacular *kāvya* and *śāstra*. Finally, in the case of scriptural anthologies known as *granth* and *vāṇī*, the creation of a specific bound codex provided a material dimension to the binding of various saints' words into a distinctive canon, which in turn bound various individuals into a distinct religious community. Calligraphy and illumination marked these books as elevated and sacred.

Paying attention to the relationship between different types of texts and their material forms in turn reveals the development of a vernacular book culture reflected in visual, material, and performance practices that drew from existing writing cultures while mixing and adapting their various elements. Books in the vernacular look different than their counterparts in the classical languages of Sanskrit, Persian, and Arabic. The differences may be readily apparent, as in the textual layout of the *pem-kathā*, or more subtle, as in the para-Sanskrit of paratexts in *pothī*s. Yet they are always there, reminders that the vernacular is a space of mixing and hybridity that, in its complexity and occasional messiness, mirrors the quotidian in a precolonial South Asia characterized by different languages, literary cultures, and religions.

That quotidian world of everyday scribes, sadhus, merchants, devotees, and provincial poets drove the process of vernacularization in north India as much as the literary projects of political elites and courtly communities. Grand, self-conscious, and deliberate gestures, such as Daud's inauguration of writing "Hinduki" in "Turki," announced the commitment of *bhāṣā* to writing and its arrival in the domain of literature; however, the quiet labor of small-town literary aficionados and devotees also literized and literarized the vernacular over time, as these people jotted down poetry and songs, composed and copied works of scholarship, and attempted to give their religious scriptures a physical shape that befitted their sacred character. Precolonial Hindi literature and its material forms were the products of many hands.

A method of literary historiography that begins with the material archive is therefore a type of prosopography that seeks to recover not only works and genres but also people. Each material text artifact, whether a codex *kitāb*, a *guṭakā*, a *pothī*, or a *granth*, can potentially provide information about local, micro-level literary and religious canons, generic distinctions, performance practices, pedagogical structures, and everyday linguistic and literary exchanges. This is especially the case with manuscripts that contain more than a single work. Yet even the single, brief marginal note of an anonymous reader can reveal the existence of historical individuals with complex tastes, beliefs, and social lives.

Aggregating the linguistic, literary, religious, and social data made available helps to break down distinctions between audience communities introduced by earlier modes of writing literary history. Earlier literary histories of Hindi that took genre or theological orientation as their unit of analysis understandably tended to divide audience communities along generic or religious lines. Yet the manuscript record reflects a radically different literary and religious terrain of precolonial north India. This included individuals who preached *nirguṇ* devotion but practiced tantra and magic; or enjoyed Persian stories, vernacular Sufi romances, and Hindu religious works with equal enthusiasm; or studied works on renunciation while amassing wealth through trade networks.

Redrawing the lines between audiences also reveals forgotten connections between various traditions and communities. Beginning with the material archive draws attention to the communities that circulated religious and scholastic works in addition to the communities that composed them. Members of the Sikh, Dadu Panth, and Niranjani communities copied, read, studied, and perhaps even performed each other's compositions on subjects ranging from philosophy to prosody. The material archive also makes visible the robust exchange of ideas between these religious communities and courtly intellectuals such as poets, pandits, and kings. To retrace the circuits of religious and intellectual networks in precolonial India, a good place to start is with the books that the literati and intelligentsia read.

Finally, a method of writing literary history that begins with the material archive forces us to reimagine our relationship with it rather than taking its shape for granted, reminding us that the institutional, material, textual, literary, and religious terms and distinctions through which we encounter the archive are as much (if not more) a product of modern practices of collection, organization, and interpretation as a reflection of the precolonial past. In the case of Hindi, such an approach may actually provide both the energies and methods needed to preserve the archive by re-establishing its value for scholars of literature, religion, and history: not as a site of extraction of texts, data, and information from written documents but as a site of encounter and study in which to grapple with the materiality of earlier forms of writing. In attempting to identify and understand the ways earlier peoples produced, used, and interacted with written media, we stand to gain perspective on our own relationship with writing. Thus, the archive's value can be assessed not only in terms of its connection to the past but also in terms of its relevance to the present. Such insights can only be gained through an engagement with these artifacts in their full materiality—not through images or reproductions in printed or digital form.

The value of Hindi's archive is determined by how we engage with it. Realizing that value requires getting our hands dirty with the dust and ink of the books that the composers, copyists, performers, and audiences of Hindi literature have left. Doing so will reveal countless enchanting surprises: an unknown work, an unforeseen connection between genres, a clue to a reader's identity. Or perhaps a flower, or an elephant.

FIGURE 5.1 Reading hall of the Nagari Pracharini Sabha, Banaras

Photo by author

Notes

PROLOGUE

1. Perhaps the most deleterious development for the Sabha has been a legal conflict among members of its administration over control of the institution; this made it impossible to undertake any restorative or other initiatives for several years. Ashutosh Bhardwaj, "With Nagari Pracharini Sabha's ruin, Hindi is losing a major centre and its best think-tank," *The Print*, December 12, 2020, https://theprint.in/opinion/with-nagari-pracharini-sabhas-ruin-hindi-losing-major-centre-best-think-tank/564809/. The legal dispute was resolved in February 2024.
2. Asked about the state of Osmania University's manuscript collection in 2017, librarian assistant Fazaluddin Ahmed replied, "Since these manuscripts won't create doctors, engineers or IT professionals, they lie here in the darkness of locked almirahs, neglected. *Bahut kam log aate hai padne ke liye. Aur padne layak scholars bhi hain kahan*? (Very few people come to read them. And anyway, where are the scholars competent to read them?)." Papri Pal, "1000-year-old manuscripts cry for attention in Osmania University Library," *The Times of India*, April 18, 2017, http://toi.in/9JQ4_Y/a24gk.
3. Established by the Government of India in 2003, the National Mission for Manuscripts has pursued an ambitious program of first cataloguing, then digitizing, the totality of India's manuscript collections in partnership with the various institutions that hold them. It has partnered with more than forty institutions on digitization initiatives and possesses an extensive database of manuscript holdings across the country, but access varies significantly, and the mission's online database of manuscripts, Kriti Sampada, faces significant challenges in usability and data quality. https://www.namami.gov.in/our-programmes (accessed September 12, 2022). The sometimes lofty and utopian rhetoric of large-scale digitization initiatives (LSDIs) like the Google Books Library Project and the Open Content Alliance often ignore major questions regarding the objects of digitization, their putative audiences, and factors affecting accessibility. See Elisabeth Jones, "The Public Library Movement, the Digital Library Movement, and the Large-Scale Digitization Initiative: Assumptions, Intentions, and the Role of the Public," *Information & Culture* 52, no. 2 (2017): 229–63.
4. On the size and extent of the manuscript wealth of India, see Sheldon Pollock, "Literary Culture and Manuscript Culture in Precolonial India," *Literary Cultures and the Material Book*, ed. Simon

Eliot (London: British Library, 2007), 77. On the size and scope of the National Mission for Manuscripts' cataloguing project, see http://namami.gov.in/content/manuscript-database (accessed September 13, 2022).

5. In addition to the efforts of the National Mission for Manuscripts, dozens of important archives and libraries like the Oriental Institute of the Maharaja Sayajirao University of Baroda, the Rajasthan Oriental Research Institute, Mansingh Pustak Prakash, Rajasthani Shodh Sansthan, Maharaja Sawai Mansingh II Museum, Raza Rampur Library, Khuda Bakhsh Library, and Osmania University have pursued initiatives to educate scholars, researchers, and administrators on the value of manuscripts and how to work with them.
6. Bruno Latour, *Reassembling the Social* (New York: Oxford University Press, 2005).
7. "Heritage" itself is a fraught term in popular discussions of Indian history and a fetishized commodity in political and commercial constructions of "Indian" and "regional" products and services. See David Geary, *The Rebirth of Bodh Gaya: Buddhism and the Making of a World Heritage Site* (Seattle: University of Washington Press, 2017) and Helle Jørgensen, *Tranquebar-Whose History? Transnational Heritage in a Former Danish Trading Colony in South India* (New Delhi: Orient BlackSwan, 2014).
8. On commonplace books, see Peter Stallybrass, Roger Chartier, John Franklin Mowery, and Heather Wolfe, "Hamlet's Tables and the Technologies of Writing in Renaissance England," *Shakespeare Quarterly* 55, no. 4 (2004): 379–419.
9. Quoted by Irfan Habib in "A Documentary History of the Gosā'ins (Gosvāmīs) of the Caitanya Sect of Vṛndāvana," in *Govindadeva: A Dialogue in Stone*, ed. Margaret H. Case (New Delhi: Indira Gandhi National Centre for Arts, 1996), 144. On the library of the Gosvamis, see also Pragati Sharma, *Braj Kī Akabarakālīn Pustak Ṭhaur Aur Usakā Sūcī Patra* (Vrindavan: Vrindavan Shodh Sansthan, 2016).
10. Latour, *Reassembling the Social*, 70–82.
11. Bill Brown, "Thing Theory," *Critical Inquiry* 28, no. 1 (autumn 2001): 4.
12. Marshal McLuhan, *Understanding Media: The Extensions of Man* (New York: McGraw-Hill, 1964), 12.
13. Ronald Deibert, *Parchment, Printing, and Hypermedia: Communication in World Order Transformation* (New York: Columbia University Press, 1997).
14. Plato, *Phaedrus*, 276a. Matthew Cobb, "Why your brain is not a computer," *The Guardian*, February 27, 2020, https://www.theguardian.com/science/2020/feb/27/why-your-brain-is-not-a-computer-neuroscience-neural-networks-consciousness.
15. Deibert, *Parchment, Printing, and Hypermedia*, 34–35.

INTRODUCTION

1. Despite the Niranjani Sampraday's significant influence on the religious and literary culture of Rajasthan and north India more generally during the seventeenth through eighteenth centuries, it is largely neglected in modern scholarship. Only one monograph has been published in Hindi, Ratanlal Mishra's *Nirañjanī Sampradāy: Sādhanā Evaṁ Sāhitya* (Navalgarh: Mahamaya Mandir, 1998), which presents several new pieces of information but contains numerous errors. In Marwari, Bhamvar Kasana has published a short booklet, *Nirañjanī Panth* (Didwana: College Book House, 2006), containing a description of important oral traditions. Until recently, the only published source of Niranjani literary and hagiographical works was Swami Mangaldas's *Mahārāj Śrī Haridās Jī Kī Vaṇī* (Jaipur: Nikhil Bharatiya Niranjani Mahasabha, 1962), which includes short works and excerpts from several Niranjani poets in addition to a substantial introduction on the

history of the Sampraday. Although several monographs on individual Niranjani authors appeared in the second half of the twentieth century, all drew the majority of their material from Mangaldas's collection and from Parasuram Chaturvedi's chapter on the Niranjanis in *Uttarī Bhārat Kī Sant-Paramparā* (Allahabad: Bharati Bhandar, 1951). Hindi scholar Neha Baid has recently published two critical editions of works by the Niranjani poet Hariramdas, the *Chandaratnāvalī* (Jodhpur: Rajasthani Granthagar, 2010) and *Nām-Prakāś* (Jodhpur: Rajasthani Granthagar, 2013).

2. Sheldon Pollock, *The Language of the Gods in the World of Men: Sanskrit, Culture, and Power in Premodern India* (Berkeley: University of California Press, 2006), 75–89, 283–89.
3. On the concept of "media ideology," see Ilana Gershon, "Media Ideologies: An Introduction," *Journal of Linguistic Anthropology* 20, no. 2 (2010): 283–93.
4. On the difficulties of defining Hindi for analytical purposes see Michael Shapiro, "Hindi," in *The Indo-Aryan Languages*, ed. Dhanesh Jain and George Cardona (London: Routledge, 2003), 276–82. Joshua Pien has recently put forward a provocative thesis that a distinct form of precolonial Hindi used as a lingua franca can be traced back to two major migrations in the early modern history of north India. See "Tracing Dehlavi: The Origins of the Hindi-Urdu Lingua Franca" (Ph.D. diss., University of Pennsylvania, 2022).
5. On the concept of a "cosmopolitan vernacular," see Pollock, *Language of the Gods*, 283–329.
6. On the entextualization of language and/or speech, see Richard Bauman and Charles L. Briggs, "Poetics and Performance as Critical Perspectives on Language and Social Life," *Annual Review of Anthropology* 19 (1990): 59–88; Karin Barber, "Text and Performance in Africa," *Bulletin of the School of Oriental and African Studies* 66, no. 3 (2003): 324–33; Laurie Honko, "Text as Process and Practice: The Textualization of Oral Epics," in *Textualization of Oral Epics* (Berlin: de Gruyter, 2000), 6–16; see also the essays in Michael Silverstein and Greg Urban, eds., *Natural Histories of Discourse* (Chicago: University of Chicago Press, 1996), especially Urban's essay, "Entextualization, Replication, and Power," 21–44.
7. On the language of the early Sikh scriptures, see Christopher Shackle, *An Introduction to the Sacred Language of the Sikhs* (London: School of Oriental and African Studies, 1983).
8. George Abraham Grierson, "The Popular Literature of Northern India," *Bulletin of the School of Oriental Studies* 1, no. 3 (1920): 88; Ramchandra Shukla, *Hindī Sāhitya Kā Itihās* (Kashi: Nagari Pracharini Sabha, 1929), 63–64.
9. Pollock, *Language of the Gods*, 3–5.
10. Pollock acknowledges that processes played out somewhat differently in north India due to the establishment of Persianate literary culture under the Islamicate sultanates after 1200 CE but maintains that religious compositions in the north Indian vernacular were understood to be manifestly nonliterary "song." Pollock, *Language of the Gods*, 392–94.
11. Christian Lee Novetzke, *The Quotidian Revolution: Vernacularization, Religion, and the Premodern Public Sphere in India* (New York: Columbia University Press, 2016), 10.
12. Francesca Orsini, "How to Do Multilingual Literary History? Lessons from Fifteenth- and Sixteenth-Century North India," *The Indian Economic and Social History Review* 49, no. 2 (2012): 225–46; Francesca Orsini, "Vernacular: Flawed but Necessary?" *South Asian Review* 41, no. 2 (2020): 1–3.
13. Andrew Ollett, *Language of the Snakes: Prakrit, Sanskrit, and the Language Order of Premodern India* (Oakland: University of California Press, 2017), 3–5.
14. The precolonial hagiographical and biographical traditions regarding Hindi poets often recount their struggles for recognition and acceptance among societies of the learned and sometimes describe the respective fates of their writings. Nandadas, the sixteenth-century poet and devotee of Krishna, is said to have dismissed his own vernacular poems and consigned them to a river. A copy of Tulsidas's epic *Rāmacaritamānas* (1574 CE) was allegedly subjected by Brahmin pandits

to a trial in which it was placed under a stack of Sanskrit works and locked in a temple; the next day, upon opening the temple, the pandits found that Tulsidas's composition had miraculously risen to the top of the pile.

15. See for example Karl Khandalawala, *The Development of Style in Indian Painting* (Madras: MacMillan, 1974), 57.
16. See Masatoshi A. Konishi, *Hāth-Kāghaz: History of Handmade Paper in South Asia* (Shimla: Indian Institute of Advanced Study, 2013), 21–44. Palm leaf continued to be widely used as a writing material well into the early modern period, not only in the south but also in Bengal and Orissa.
17. Rosalind O'Hanlon, "Performances in a World of Paper: Puranic Histories and Social Communication in Early Modern India," *Past and Present* 219 (May 2013): 87–126. O'Hanlon provides an insightful analysis of how manuscripts functioned within the oral performance tradition of Puranic works "as linked discursive fields within which many different social, political or religious concerns could find expression" (97). Yet the suggestion that "the coming of paper amplified this role" is not substantiated by manuscript or documentary evidence.
18. On the few examples of paper manuscripts dating to this period, see Konishi, *Hāth-Kāghaz*, 33–43. A few scholars have noted the slowness with which scribes, artists, and patrons in South Asia adopted new materials and formats. Milo Beach remarks, "While paper was plentiful in India after about 1400, so entrenched were traditional attitudes that Hindu artists and craftsmen only slowly took advantage of the freedom that the new materials allowed, to vary the size and shape from the severely restricted palm-leaf format. And even then the folios were seldom bound." *Mughal and Rajput Painting* (Cambridge: Cambridge University Press, 1992), 1. I thank Patton Burchett for bringing this passage to my attention.
19. On the challenge of newness and beginnings in Hindi literature, see Allison Busch, "The Anxiety of Innovation: The Practice of Literary Science in the Hindi *Rīti* Tradition," *Comparative Studies of South Asia, Africa and the Middle East* 24, no. 2 (2004): 45–59; Allison Busch, "Hindi Literary Beginnings," in *South Asian Texts in History: Critical Engagements with Sheldon Pollock*, ed. Yigal Bronner, Whitney M. Cox, and Lawrence J. McCrea (Ann Arbor: Association for Asian Studies, 2011), 203–55.
20. These works include (but are not limited to): Bidur Bhattarai, *Dividing Texts: Conventions of Visual Text-Organization in Nepalese and North Indian Manuscripts* (Berlin: De Gruyter, 2020); Swapan Chakravorty and Abhijit Gupta, eds., *Print Areas: Book History in India* (Delhi: Permanent Black, 2004); Swapan Chakravorty and Abhijit Gupta, eds., *Moveable Type: Book History in India* (Ranikhet: Permanent Black, 2008); Swapan Chakravorty and Abhijit Gupta, eds., *Founts of Knowledge: Book History in India* (New Delhi: Orient Blackswan, 2016); Florinda De Simini, *Of Gods and Books: Ritual and Knowledge Transmission in the Manuscript Cultures of Premodern India* (Berlin: De Gruyter, 2016); Jinah Kim, *Receptacle of the Sacred: Illustrated Manuscripts and the Buddhist Book Cult in South Asia* (Berkeley: University of California Press, 2013); Bhavani Raman, *Document Raj: Writing and Scribes in Early Colonial South India* (Chicago: University of Chicago Press, 2012); Saraju Rath, *Aspects of Manuscript Culture in South India* (Leiden: Brill, 2012); A. I. Venkatacalapati, *The Province of the Book: Scholars, Scribes, and Scribblers in Colonial Tamilnadu* (Ranikhet: Permanent Black, 2012); Vincenzo Vergiani, Daniele Cuneo, and Camillo Alessio Formigatti, eds., *Indic Manuscript Cultures through the Ages: Material, Textual, and Historical Investigations* (Berlin: De Gruyter, 2017); Eva Wilden, *Manuscript, Print and Memory: Relics of the Caṅkam in Tamilnadu* (Berlin: De Gruyter, 2014).
21. A brief introduction to the Kabir Panth may be found in David N. Lorenzen, "Traditions of Non-Caste Hinduism: The Kabir Panth," *Contributions to Indian Sociology* 21, no. 1 (1987): 263–83; For an introduction to the Ramsnehi Sampraday, see Gopikishan Citara, *Rāmasnehī Santakavi Dāyaladās Aur Unakā Kāvya* (Jalore: Shrimati Naju Devi Solanki, 2006).

22. For an introduction to the multilingual manuscript culture of the Jains, see Nalini Balbir, "Functions of Multiple-Text Manuscripts in India: The Jain Case," in *The Emergence of Multiple-Text Manuscripts*, ed. Alessandro Bausi, Michael Friedrich, and Marilena Maniachi (Berlin: De Gruyter, 2019), 33–35.
23. There are important exceptions to this exclusion, particularly among women of politically elite households, that deserve close study. For example, women of the Mughal harem were literate in Persian as well as the vernacular and composed poetry themselves. Contemporary chronicles and records also reveal that these women played a large role in shaping and administering the Mughal imperial library. For a brief survey, see Angbin Yasmin, "Literacy and Literature: Study of Attainments of Women in Mughal India," *Proceedings of the Indian History Congress* 73 (2012): 391–99. In Rajasthan, female members of Rajput courts are reported to have commissioned important literary and scholastic works in addition to composing poetry themselves.

1. STORYTELLERS AND STORYBOOKS

1. On the tale of Nala and Damayanti in Sanskrit, see Deven Patel, *Text to Tradition: The Naiṣadhīyacarita and Literary Community in South Asia* (New York: Columbia University Press, 2014). Surdas's vernacular retelling has more in common with later literary renderings of the narrative like the Sanskrit *Naiṣadhīyacarita* and Persian *Nal Daman* of Faizi than the earlier version recorded in the *Mahābhārata*. On written and oral retellings of the story in various languages, see the essays in Susan Wadley, ed., *Damayanti and Nala: The Many Lives of a Story* (New Delhi: Chronicle Books, 2011). Faizi's work has been printed as *Maṣnavī Nal Daman-i Fayẕī*, ed. Muhammad Tayyib Siddiqi (Patna: Book Emporium, 1987). For a discussion of the work in English, see "Faizi's *Nal-Daman* and Its Long Afterlife" in Muzaffar Alam and Sanjay Subrahmanyam, *Writing the Mughal World: Studies on Culture and Politics* (New York: Columbia University Press, 2012), 204–48.
2. Surdas, *Nal Daman*, Ms. 22.3229, Chhatrapati Shivaji Maharaj Vastu Sangrahalaya.
3. Surdas, *Nal Daman*. The reference to "dots" (Arabic *nuqṯa*) suggests that Surdas wrote (or was at least literate) in the Arabic script.
4. Surdas, *Nal Daman*.
5. Mirza Khan, being concerned more with the genre of love lyrics than that of epic romances, writes that the vernacular of the Braj region, between the Yamuna and Ganges rivers, is best for "the praise of the lover and the beloved." *Tuhfat al-Hind*, ed. Muhammad Ziya al-Din as *A Grammar of the Braj Bhakha. The Persian Text Critically Edited from Original MSS., with an Introduction, Translation and Notes* (Calcutta: Visva-Bharati Book-Shop, 1935), 34–35.
6. The identification of linguistic attributes that link the language of the *Candāyan* to the register of *bhāṣā*, as well as what distinguishes this language from those of earlier works, is addressed in Imre Bangha, "The Emergence of Hindi Literature: From Transregional Maru-Gurjar to Madhyadeśī Narratives," in *Text and Tradition in Early Modern India*, ed. Tyler Williams, Anshu Malhotra, and John S. Hawley (New Delhi: Oxford University Press, 2018), 15, 19–25.
7. Ramchandra Shukla, for example, locates the beginnings of Hindi literature in the *rāso* heroic ballads of the tenth through fourteenth centuries, and in the poetry of Amir Khusrau (d. 1253–1325) and Vidyapati (fl. c. 1400). *Hindī Sāhitya Kā Itihās*, rev. ed. (Kashi: Nagari Prachrini Sabha, 1950) 29–59. Hazariprasad Dvivedi considers Hindi to have developed out of Apabhramsha, including Buddhist and Nath poetry; nevertheless, he considers the *nirguṇ bhakti* poetry of the "eastern Aryan" region to be the first expression of a distinctive Hindi literature. *Hindī Sāhitya Kī Bhūmikā* (Bombay: Hindi Granth Ratnakar, 1940), 33–36.

8. Francesca Orsini, "Traces of a Multilingual World: Hindavi in Persian Texts," in *After Timur Left: Culture and Circulation in Fifteenth-Century North India*, ed. Francesca Orsini and Samira Sheikh (New Delhi: Oxford University Press, 2014), 411–444.
9. See Carl W. Ernst, "The Interpretation of the Sufi Tradition in India: The *Shama' 'il al-Atqiya* of Rukn al-Dīn Kāshānī." *Sufi* 22 (1994): 5–10.
10. *Nafā'is al-Anfās*, scan of microfilm of original manuscript courtesy of Carl Ernst, folios 190–91. Ernst reckons this to be a seventeenth-century manuscript. Neither the author nor the scribe "marks" or distinguishes utterances in the vernacular from the Persian text—it is simply transcribed as part of the reported speech of the dialogue.
11. Paul E. Losensky and Sunil Sharma, *In the Bazaar of Love: The Selected Poetry of Amīr Khusrau* (New Delhi: Penguin Books India, 2011), xxvii–xxxiv, 105–16. On the available textual evidence for Amir Khusrau's vernacular compositions, see, in Urdu, Gopi Chand Narang, *Amīr Khusrau Kā Hindavī Kalām: Ma'nuskhah-yi Barlin, Zakhīrah-yi Ishpringar* (Chicago: Amir Khusrau Society of America, 1987). The same text was printed in Hindi as *Amīr Khusaro Kā Hindavī Kāvya: Śpriṅgar Saṅgrah Kī Barlin Prati Sahit* (New Delhi: Simant Prakashan, 1990). On Amir Khusrau's works in contemporary Sufi performance, see Regula Qureshi, *Sufi Music of India and Pakistan: Sound, Context, and Meaning in Qawwali* (Cambridge: Cambridge University Press, 1986).
12. Aditya Behl, *Love's Subtle Magic: An Indian Islamic Literary Tradition, 1379–1545* (New York: Oxford University Press, 2012), 53–54. The Tughlaq state likely employed the vernacular in written documentation at local levels of its fiscal administration; the use of Persian at all levels was introduced only later by the Mughals during the reign of Akbar. See Najaf Haider, "Language, Caste and the Secretarial Class in Mughal India," in *The Development of a Nation: Essays in Memory of R.S. Sharma*, ed. D. N. Jha (New Delhi: Manohar, 2014), 251.
13. Sultanate bureaucracy, including tax collection and accounting, was carried out in the vernacular, as we know from the eighteenth-century Mughal historian Ghulam Husain Taba'taba'i: "Earlier in India the government accounts were written in Hindavi according to the Hindu rule. Raja Todar Mal acquired new regulations (*zawābit*) from the scribes (*nawīsindagān*) of Iran, and the government offices then were reorganized as they were there in *wilāyat* (Iran)." *Siyar al-Muta'akhkhirīn*, vol. 1 (Lucknow: 1876), p. 200, quoted in Alam and Subrahmanyam, "The Making of a Munshi," in *Writing the Mughal World*, 314.
14. Behl, *Love's Subtle Magic*, 61–108.
15. Daud identifies his work *as poetry*: "In the year 781 [Hijri], I brought this *rasa*-laden poem (*kavi*) to light. *barasa sāta sai hoye ikhyāsī / tihi yāha kavi saraseu bhāsī*." *Candāyan*, ed. Shyam Manohar Pandey (Allahabad: Sahitya Bhavan Private Limited, 2018), *kaḍavak* 17. No complete copy of the *Candāyan* exists; Pandey's critical edition is the most comprehensive. Other editions based on manuscript copies include Parmeshwarilal Gupta, ed., *Maulānā Dāūd Ḍalamaī Kṛt Candāyan: Mūl Pāṭh, Pāṭhāntar, Ṭippaṇī, Evaṁ Khojapūrṇ Sāmagrī Sahit* (Bombay: Hindi Granth Ratnakar, 1964); Vishvanath Prasad and Mataprasad Gupta, eds., *Candāyan* (Agra: Agra Vishvavidyalaya, 1962). For critical studies, see Naseem Akhtar Hines, *Maulana Daud's Cāndāyan: A Critical Study* (New Delhi: Manohar Publishers & Distributors, 2009), and Shiv Kumar Shandilya, *Maulānā Dāūd Kṛta Cāndāyan Kā Bhāṣā Svarūp Evaṁ Bimbātmak Saṁcetanā* (New Delhi: Bhasha Prakashan, 1978). On the literary tradition of the Sufi romance, including a discussion of the *Candāyan* as the inaugural work of the genre, see Behl, *Love's Subtle Magic*. On the folk antecedents of the *Candāyan*'s narrative, see Shyam Manohar Pandey, *Lok Mahākāvya Lorikī: Lorik Aur Candā Kī Lok-Gāthā: Mūlapāṭh, Bhāvārth, Śabdārth, Tathā Ṭippaṇiyāṁ* (Allahabad: Sahitya Bhavan, 1979).
16. *Candāyan*, *kaḍavak* 10. Readings and verse numbers follow Pandey 2018, with minor emendations after comparison with manuscripts and published editions to reconstruct the phonology of the original where, in my opinion, Pandey has made unnecessary changes in the interest of

standardization. All translations are my own unless otherwise noted. The name Vararuchi can refer to one of several composers in Sanskrit; this figure is most likely a composite and thus stands as an exemplar of the polyglot.

17. Behl, *Love's Subtle Magic*, 2, 55, 292.
18. For examples from a range of Islamicate sources, see Annemarie Schimmel, "The Book of Life Metaphors Connected with the Book in Islamic Literatures," in *The Book in the Islamic World: The Written Word and Communication in the Middle East*, ed. George N. Atiyeh (Albany: State University of New York Press, 1995), 71–81.
19. For example, Naseem Hines characterizes Daud as an "evangelist" who "had to introduce the idea of Sufism to his audiences who came from all walks of life." "In Quest for the Correct Combination: The Home-coming Episode in Maulana Daud's Indo-Sufi Masnavi *Candayan*," in *The Banyan Tree: Essays on Early Literature in New Indo-Aryan Languages*, ed. Mariola Offredi (Manohar: New Delhi, 2000), 15–25. For critiques of this position, see Behl, *Love's Subtle Magic*, 3; also Tony K. Stewart, "In Search of Equivalence: Conceiving Muslim-Hindu Encounter through Translation Theory," *History of Religions* 40, no. 3 (2001): 260–87.
20. Aditya Behl has characterized this reimagining in the Sufi romance tradition as a "masquerade." *The Magic Doe: Qutban Suhravardī's* Mirigāvatī, ed. Wendy Doniger (New York: Oxford University Press, 2012), 23.
21. *Candāyan, kaḍavak* 9.
22. C.f. Abul Fazl's Illuminationist-influenced description of writing in the *Ā'īn-i Akbarī*, which asserts that the blackness of Arabic letters conceals "the thousand rays" of God's knowledge that they contain. Abu al-Fazl ibn Mubarak, *The A'īn-i Akbarī*, ed. and trans. Heinrich Blochmann (Calcutta: Asiatic Society of Bengal, 1927), 97.
23. *Candāyan, kaḍavak* 17. Daud is possibly making a pun on *kavi saraseü bhāsī*, since the phrase could also be read as "Saraswati [the goddess of poetry] illuminated this poem." He calls his composition a poem (*kavitu*) once more at the beginning of *kaḍavak* 18, "I shall recite this poem (*kavitu*) with knowledge in my heart / It's delightful when recited, [so] lend an ear and listen," and invites his audience to "listen" to his "*kabitā*" once more in an aside made in *kaḍavak* 331.
24. Qutban, *Mirgāvatī, kaḍavak* 10. Readings are taken from two critical editions: Dick Frederik Plukker, "The *Miragāvatī* of Kutubana: Avadhī Text with Critical Notes" (PhD diss., Universiteit van Amsterdam, Faculteit der Wiskunde en Natuurwetenschappen, 1981); and Parameshwarilal Gupta, *Maulānā Dāūd Kṛt Candāyan: Mūl Pāṭh, Pāṭhāntar, Ṭippaṇī, Evaṁ Khojapūrṇ Samagrī Sahit* (Delhi: Hindi Granth Ratnakar, 1964).
25. The term *purāṇa* is used in a similar fashion by the devotional poets discussed in the next chapter.
26. Qutban, *Mirgāvatī, kaḍavak* 5.
27. Qutban, *Mirgāvatī, kaḍavak* 11.
28. See Simon Digby, "'Abd Al-Quddus Gangohi (1456–1537 AD): The Personality and Attitudes of a Medieval Indian Sufi," in *Medieval India: A Miscellany* 3 (Aligarh: Aligarh Muslim University, 1975), 1–66; Francesca Orsini, "'Krishna Is the Truth of Man': Mir 'Abdul Wahid Bilgrami's Haqā'iq-i Hindī (Indian Truths) and the Circulation of Dhrupad and Bishnupad," in *Culture and Circulation*, ed. Allison Busch and Thomas de Bruijn (Leiden: Brill, 2014), 222–47; Francesca Orsini, "Inflected Kathas: Sufi and Krishna Bhaktas in Avadh," in *Religious Interactions in Mughal India*, ed. Vasudha Dalmia and Munis Daniyal Faruqui (New Delhi: Oxford University Press, 2014), 195–232. Heidi Pauwels, "When a Sufi Tells about Krishna's Doom: The Case of Kanhāvat (1540?)," *Journal of Hindu Studies* 6 (2013): 21–36. Carl Ernst, "Sufism and Yoga According to Muhammad Ghawth," *Sufi* 29 (1996): 9–13; Carl Ernst, "The Islamization of Yoga in the 'Amrtakunda' Translations," *Journal of the Royal Asiatic Society*, Third Series, 13, no. 2 (July 1, 2003): 199–226. On the phenomenon of translation and equivalence across Indic and Islamic systems of thought in precolonial India, see Stewart, "In Search of Equivalence."

29. Francesca Orsini, "Inflected Kathas: Sufis and Krishna Bhaktas in Awadh," in *Religious Interactions in Mughal India*, ed. Vasudha Dalmia and Munis Daniyal Faruqui (New Delhi: Oxford University Press, 2014), 195–96.
30. Malik Muhammad Jayasi, *Padmāvat*, ed. Mataprasad Gupta (Allahabad: Sahitya Bhavan, 2006; originally 1963), v. 24. Subsequent citations are to this edition.
31. Jayasi reflected on the alphabet and the significance of writing in another composition, the *Ākharāvaṭ*. See Mujib Rizvi, *Sab Likhanī Kai Likhu Saṁsārā: Padmāvat Aur Jayasī Kī Duniyā* (New Delhi: Rajkamal, 2019), 51–52.
32. Behl, *Love's Subtle Magic*, 286–324.
33. Jayasi, *Padmāvat*, vv. 8.1, 12.4, 12.8.
34. Jayasi, *Padmāvat*, v. 10.
35. On the date of the *Śivamahimnaḥ Stotra*, see Elaine Fisher, *Hindu Pluralism: Religion and the Public Sphere in Early Modern South India* (Oakland: University of California Press, 2017), 206, n. 2.
36. Puṣpadanta, *The Mahimnastava or, Praise of Shiva's Greatness*, ed. W. Norman Brown (Poona: American Institute of Indian Studies, 1965), 8.
37. Jayasi may be the first vernacular poet in north India to mention paper. A similar verse attributed to the fifteenth-century poet Kabir also mentions paper (see chapter 2), but neither the verse nor the lifetime of Kabir himself can be dated with any certainty.
38. For example, Ibn Battuta notes in his memoir of his travels through South Asia in the 1330s that the Maldivian chancellery used paper for copies of the Qur'an and for theological works and palm leaf for official missives and orders. Ibn Batuta, *Rihla*, ed. H. A. R. Gibb and C. F. Beckingham as *The Travels of Ibn Battuta, A.D. 1325–1354*, vol. 4 (London: Hakluyt Society, 1958), 832.
39. On Manjhan and his milieu, see the introduction in Manjhan, *Madhumālatī: An Indian Sufi Romance*, ed. and trans. Aditya Behl and Simon Weightman (Oxford: Oxford University Press, 2000).
40. Mir Sayid Manjhan Rajgiri, *Madhumālatī*, ed. Mataprasad Gupta (Allahabad: Mitra Prakashan, 1961) *kaḍavak* 39 (*kaḍavak* 37 in Shivgopal Mishra edition.)
41. Manjhan, *Madhumālatī*, *kaḍavak* 42.
42. As Behl writes, "The panegyric was an ideal form that set the style and laid out the content of political authority but also created the material circumstances for its own production. The praise of kings and noblemen, and particularly of the military nobility of the period, gave poets access to the resources and sponsorship they needed to compose poetry within a courtly culture that patronized skilled literary figures, calligraphers, scholars, and artists. In return, the poet composed poetry that gave the patron pleasure and allowed him to establish his political authority through the symbolic forms and the cultural style of the period." *Love's Subtle Magic*, 48.
43. Although we possess little documentation of book production during the early sultanate period, we do have some knowledge of the sixteenth century, in which most of the copies of the *Candāyan* considered in this chapter were produced. See Éloïse Brac de la Perrière, *L'art du livre dans l'Inde des sultanats* (Paris: PUPS, 2008); Éloïse Brac de la Perrière, "The Art of the Book in India under the Sultanates," in *After Timur Left: Culture and Circulation in Fifteenth-Century North India*, ed. Francesca Orsini and Samira Sheikh (New Delhi: Oxford University Press, 2014), 302–38; John W. Seyller, *Workshop and Patron in Mughal India: The Freer Rāmāyaṇa and Other Illustrated Manuscripts of ʿAbd al-Raḥīm* (Zürich: Artibus Asiae), 1999.
44. On the dating of early copies of the *Candāyan*, see Qamar Adamjee, "Strategies for Visual Narration in the Illustrated 'Chandayan' Manuscripts" (Ph.D. diss., New York University, 2011), 94–113, 122–27.
45. As, for example, in the case of the epic of *Amir Hamza* first commissioned by the Mughal Emperor Akbar in the late 1550s. The gigantic manuscript consisted of large, unbound folios with

illustrations on one side and the corresponding text on the other, so that they could be held up before an audience while being read. John W. Seyller and Wheeler. M. Thackston, *The Adventures of Hamza: Painting and Storytelling in Mughal India* (Washington, D.C.: Freer Gallery of Art, 2002). As Adamjee notes, some of the extant folios of *Candāyan* copies have been cut down from their original size. *Strategies for Visual Narration*, 122.

46. Although various geometric arrangements of verse can be found in late medieval and early modern albums of Persian calligraphy (*safīnah* and *muraqq'a*) from central and western Asia, such arrangements were clearly *not* standard conventions for the inscription of *maṣnavīs*.

47. Philip Lutgendorf, *The Life of a Text: Performing the Ramcaritmanas of Tulsidas* (Berkeley: University of California Press, 1991), 97–112.

48. In contrast, later copies of works composed in *bhāṣā* and copied in the Arabic script are replete with vocalization marks. This suggests that the inclusion of such marks had more to do with the particular social and patronage contexts in which an individual manuscript was copied than with any kind of general level or extent of vernacular literacy in a given period or place.

49. Adamjee, "Strategies for Visual Narration," 94–145. Adamjee also speculates on the system behind the idiosyncratic use of colored ink for certain words and phrases in the *Candāyan* manuscript held by the John Rylands Library but is unable to identify a clear logic (141–45). I have so far also been unable to identify the reason for the calligrapher's use of red and blue in addition to black ink.

50. *suni ke cānda rāū aṅgarānā / bājira ahuṭi niyara dhari ānā / jasa ko sūta baiṭhi uṭhi jāgai / rājā hiye caṭapaṭī lāgai. Candāyan, kaḍavak* 63. JRL Hindustani Ms. 01, f.96.b.

51. Adamjee, "Strategies of Visual Narration," 175–222.

52. I see a slight contrast with Molly Aitken's characterization of the relationship between text and image in Rajput paintings such as those that accompany another work of Hindi literature, Keshavdas's *Rasikapriyā* (Beloved of Connoisseurs, 1591 CE): "Paintings narrated, but on their own terms, using a canon of forms and a pictorial iconography that evolved in relationships among paintings and that signified alongside texts, not dependently on them." *The Intelligence of Tradition in Rajput Court Painting* (New Haven, Conn.: Yale University Press, 2010), 4. While the forms and iconography of *Candāyan* illustrations are indeed distinct from that of the verbal text, they are nevertheless *readings* of that text and in that sense depend upon it.

53. Adamjee has also noted the presence of figures like the peacock that, while not mentioned in Daud's text itself, appear to add to the affective power of the paintings. "Strategies of Visual Narration," 182–83, 197.

54. The illustrator(s) of this copy appear to have been unfamiliar with the Arabic script; although the word "Allah" appears multiple times, the rest of the scribbles meant to indicate writing in the illustrations of Daud's book are gibberish composed of roughly drawn letters. The sixteenth-century copy of Qutban's *Mirgāvatī* held by the Bharat Kala Bhavan and discussed below also features a painting of a professional writer or scribe, possibly the author himself, inscribing a loose folio with a reed pen while sitting before a table upon which sit an inkpot and a codex balanced on a *raḥl*.

55. The extensive use of gold and silver paint in the John Rylands copy, for example, evinces the amount of money and resources that patrons invested. The monetary and social valuation of such deluxe copies is discussed in detail below.

56. That patron may have been one Muhammad Sultan Khan, who is mentioned in a colophon in Arabic script. See T. K. Biswas, "An Illustrated Padmāvat in the Bharat Kala Bhavan," in *Indian Art & Connoisseurship: Essays in Honour of Douglas Barrett*, ed. John Guy (New Delhi: Indira Gandhi National Centre for the Arts, 1995), 230–39.

57. Shantanu Phukan, "'Through throats where many rivers meet': The Ecology of Hindi in the World of Persian," *Indian Economic and Social History Review* 38, no. 33 (2001): 36.

58. Francesca Orsini, "The Social History of a Genre: Kathas across Languages in Early Modern North India," *Medieval History Journal* 20, no. 1 (2017): 1–31.
59. Dramatic characterizations of printing's impact on written discourses begin with Marshall McLuhan's *The Gutenberg Galaxy: The Making of Typographic Man* (Toronto: University of Toronto Press, 1962) and include such seminal works as Elizabeth Eisenstein's *The Printing Press as an Agent of Change: Communications and Cultural Transformations in Early-Modern Europe* (New York: Cambridge University Press, 1985).
60. The publication of Jayasi's *Padmāvat* was preceded by the publication of another, modern version composed by Ziyauddin Ibrat and Ghulam Ali Ishrat, in Khari-Boli Urdu, in 1858 and by Mir Bahadur Ali's prose retelling of Mir Hasan Dihlavi's *Sihr al-Bayān* (1785), a *pem-kathā* composed during the colonial period, in 1803. I thank Ihsan Ul-Ihthisam Chappangan for the latter reference. For a list of printed editions (as well as manuscripts) of the *Padmāvat*, see Sreenivasan, *The Many Lives of a Rajput Queen: Heroic Pasts in India c. 1500–1900* (Seattle: University of Washington Press, 2007), 227–231, and Thomas de Bruijn, *Ruby in the Dust: Poetry and History in Padmāvat by the South Asian Sufi Poet Muḥammad Jāyasī* (Leiden: Leiden University Press, 2012), 277–84.
61. Malik Muhammad Jayasi, *The Padumāwati of Malik Muḥammad Jaisī*, ed. and trans. George Abraham Grierson (Calcutta: Asiatic Society, 1896). The first book printed using Nāgarī type within India itself was the *Grammar of the Hindustanee Language* by John Gilchrist, in 1796. It is noteworthy that the first use of Nāgarī type in India was for a vernacular language (rather than Sanskrit). This follows the pragmatic aims of language pedagogy in Company-ruled Calcutta, where the development of Nāgarī and Bengali typefaces addressed the immediate needs of training Company administrators and agents (as well as missionaries and Orientalist scholars). See Bapurao S. Naik, *Typology of Devanagari Vol. 1* (Bombay: Directorate of Languages, 1971). See also Ulrike Stark, *An Empire of Books: The Naval Kishore Press and the Diffusion of the Printed Word in Colonial India* (Ranikhet: Permanent Black, 2007).
62. For example, the sixteenth-century hagiographer Anantadas locates much of the action in his stories about the saints in the markets of Banaras and other cities and towns. *The Hagiographies of Anantadās: The Bhakti Poets of North India*, ed. and trans. Winand Callewaert (Richmond: Curzon, 2000).
63. Banarsidas, *Ardhakathānak*, ed. and trans. Mukund Lath as *Half a Tale: A Study in the Interrelationship between Autobiography and History* (Jaipur: Rajasthan Prakrit Bharati Sansthan), 1981, vv. 334–35. Banarsidas's penury makes it exceedingly likely that he borrowed the copies of the *Mirgāvatī* and *Madhumālatī*; there is also reason to suspect that the reading of *udār* ("great," v. 335) in Lath's text should be corrected to *udhār*; thus we have *madhumālati mirgāvati pauthī doï udhāra*, "The *Madhumālatī* and *Mirgāvatī*, both on loan . . ."
64. Abu al-Fazl, *Ā'īn-i Akbarī*, 96–109.
65. See Seyller, *Workshop and Patron in Mughal India*, 11, 22–24.
66. Recounted by Rafi Uddin Shirazi in his *Taẕkirah al-Mulk* (History of Kings, 1611), quoted in Richard Skelton, "Documents for the Study of Painting at Bijapur in the Late Sixteenth and Early Seventeenth Centuries," *Arts Asiatiques* 5, no. 2 (1958): 97–125.
67. On instances of *khil'at* both beneficent and malignant, see Michelle Maskiell and Adrienne Mayor, "Killer Khilats, Part 1: Legends of Poisoned 'Robes of Honour' in India," *Folklore* 112, no. 1 (2001): 23–45.
68. John W. Seyller, "The Inspection and Valuation of Manuscripts in the Imperial Mughal Library," *Artibus Asiae* 57, no. 3/4 (1997): 243–349; Keelan Overton, "Book Culture, Royal Libraries, and Persianate Painting in Bijapur, circa 1580–1630," *Muqarnas* 33 (2016): 91–154.
69. For example, an anonymously authored seventeenth-century work in the East India Office collection (simply called the *Bayāẓ-i khushbū'ī* by catalogers), instructs the reader in the furnishing and

management of a proper personal library, while the writings of *munshīs* like Chandrabhan "Brahman" (d. c. 1670) prescribe syllabi for those training to enter imperial service. D. N. Marshall and V. D. B. *Mughal Bibliography: Select Persian Sources for the Study of Mughals in India* (Bombay: New Book Company, 1962), 506. The prestigious post of Imperial Librarian was given to prominent individuals like the *subahdār* (provincial governor) of Kashmir, Mohammad Tahir Ashna (1628–71), and the celebrated calligraphist and poet Mir Muhammad Salih Kashafi (d. 1651).

70. See Gopalnarayan Bahura, *Literary Heritage of the Rulers of Amber and Jaipur, with an Index to the Register of Manuscripts in the Pothikhana of Jaipur (Khasmohor Collection)* (Jaipur: Maharaja Sawai Man Singh II Museum, 1976), 12–15.

71. The production of codex books at Rajput courts is thus similar to the practice of painting: as Molly Aitken has demonstrated, painters at Rajput courts responded to Mughal techniques and subjects while maintaining their own "habit," which Aitken defines as an embodied, psychomotor reality. Aitken, *Intelligence of Tradition*, 83–87. Book artisans at Rajput courts (including painters) similarly created books that formally mimicked Mughal codices but remained within a habit or habitus defined by *pothī*-centered book culture.

72. See, for example, a copy of Sadhan's *Mainasat* (composed c. 1567) copied in Nāgarī with some Kaithī features, and formatted per the conventions described above, in the Kacchwaha Royal Pothikhana in Jaipur (Ms. 1877, Maharaja Sawai Man Singh II Museum, Jaipur. Undated). Rajput patrons also commissioned romances in the *pothī* format; see, for example, a copy of Manjhan's *Madhumālatī* made in 1741 CE and now held by the University of Pennsylvania (Ms. Indic 28, item 3024): copied in a Kaithī-influenced Nāgarī script, its wide, loose folios and red and black margin lines follow the conventions of the *pothī*-type manuscripts described in chapter 3.

73. On urban book markets, see Alam and Subrahmanyam, "The Making of a Munshi," 317.

74. For example, the prominent seventeenth-century *munshī* Chadrabhan recounted in a letter to his son how he passed on his copies of Persian classics to his disciples after having finished with them. Quoted in Alam and Subrahmanyam, "The Making of a Munshi," 317. On Chandrabhan and his pedagogical pursuits, see Rajeev Kinra, *Writing Self, Writing Empire: Chandar Bhan Brahman and the Cultural World of the Indo-Persian State Secretary* (Oakland: University of California Press, 2015).

75. Dilir Khan 'Abdurrauf Miyana came from a family of Afghan tribal chiefs that had served first at the Mughal courts of Jahangir and Shah Jahan and later defected to the court of Bijapur. It has been suggested that the patron mentioned in the colophon of the *Nal Daman* may be Dilir Khan Daudzai (birthname Jalal Khan Rohilla), a prominent Afghan at Shah Jahan's and, later Aurangzeb's court; however, Daudzai died in 1683, fifteen years before the inscription of the colophon. See the *Maāṯẖir-ul-Ulmarā* of Nawwab Samsadudaula Shah Nawaz Khan and 'Abdul Hayy, trans. Henry Beveridge, revised and annotated by Baini Prashad (Kolkata: Asiatic Society, 2003; originally 1941), 499–505; also the *Maāsir-i-Ālamgriri* of Saqi Must'ad Khan, trans. Jadunath Sarkar (Kolkata: Asiatic Society, 2008; originally 1947), 145, 147.

76. In his Persian *dībācah* or introduction to the *Kitāb-i Nauras* of Adil Ibrahim Shah II, Nur al-din Zahuri Torshizi showcases the Indian arts for recent West Asian immigrants, emphasizing the genres they could appreciate, such as painting and calligraphy. Mulla Nuruddin Zahuri, *Dībācah-yi Kitāb-i Nauras*, ed. Sayyid Muhammad Yunus Ja'farī, *Qand-i Pārsī* 63–64 (2014): 199–256. See especially 218–21. I thank Zoë High and Thibaut d'Hubert for including me in their reading sessions of Zahuri's *dībācah*.

77. On the shape and illumination of colophons in Islamicate manuscripts see François Déroche, *Islamic Codicology: An Introduction to the Study of Manuscripts in Arabic Script* (London: Al-Furqān Islamic Heritage Foundation, 2006), 180, 233–34.

2. SAINTS, SINGERS, AND SONGBOOKS

1. It would be more accurate to describe this as a Kaithī-like script used in the region of Rajasthan and Gujarat. See George A. Grierson, *Linguistic Survey of India Vol. IX, Indo-Aryan Family, Central Group Part II* (Calcutta: Office of the Superintendent Government Printing, 1908), 4, 19, 63.
2. Some of these advocates were the same philologists and literary historians involved in early attempts to collect and study manuscripts in Hindi, like Shyamsundar Das and Ramchandra Shukla, discussed in the concluding chapter of this book. On the movement to make Nāgarī the official script of Hindi, see Christopher R. King, *One Language, Two Scripts: The Hindi Movement in Nineteenth-Century North India* (New Delhi: Oxford University Press, 1999).
3. The owner of the notebook has garbled the Sanskrit passive *likhyate*, misspelled *saṅgīta*, and used the Hindi possessive postposition *kā*.
4. The latter work is the anonymously authored narrative known as the *Kutub-śatak* (Hundred Verses About Kutub, undated). For details, see the conclusion.
5. *The Bijak of Kabir*, trans. Linda Hess and Shukdeo Singh (New York: Oxford University Press, 2002; originally published by Northpoint Press, 1983), 6.
6. Kabir, *sākhī* 33.3. In *Nirguṇ Bhakti Sāgar / Devotional Hindi Literature: A Critical Edition of the Panc-Vani or Five Works of Dadu, Kabir, Namdev, Raidas, Hardas with the Hindi Songs of Gorakhnath and Sundardas, and a Complete Word-Index*, ed. Winand Callewaert and Bart Op de Beeck (New Delhi: Manohar, 1991), 302.
7. For examples of Kabir's criticism of Brahmin pandits, see the *Guru Granth Sāhib, aṅg* 343–45, 654. Verses attributed to Kabir in the Sikh *Ādi Granth* (early *Guru Granth Sāhib*) single out the Brahmins of Banaras for special scorn; see his compositions in *aṅg* 857. The satirical image of a Brahmin pandit reading from a *pothī* is found frequently in the anthological manuscripts of *nirguṇ* devotional communities; see for example *sākhī* 46.23 in the *Sarvāṅgī* of Gopaldas, attributed to Gorakhnath.
8. See, for example, Rosalind O'Hanlon, "Speaking from Siva's Temple: Banaras Scholar Households and the Brahman 'Ecumene' of Mughal India," *South Asian History and Culture* 2, no. 2 (2011): 253–77; Rosalind O'Hanlon, "Performance in a World of Paper: Puranic Histories and Social Communication in Early Modern India," *Past and Present* 219, no. 1 (May 2013): 87–126; Anand Venkatkrishnan, "Ritual, Reflection, and Religion: The Devas of Banaras," *South Asian History and Culture* 6, no. 1 (2015): 147–71. The same was true for Jain monks of the time, who were trained using texts in Prakrit and Apabhramsha as well as Sanskrit. See John E. Cort, "The Intellectual Formation of a Jain Monk: A Śvetāmbara Monastic Curriculum," *Journal of Indian Philosophy* 29 (2001): 327–49.
9. Purushottam Agarwal, *Akath Kahānī Prem Kī: Kabīr Kī Kavitā Aur Unakā Samay* (New Delhi: Rajkamal Prakashan, 2009), especially 53–53, 86–94.
10. On the formal qualities of the *sākhī* as liturgical device, see Karine Schomer, "The *Dohā* as a Vehicle of Sant Teachings," in *The Sants: Studies in a Devotional Tradition of India*, ed. Karine Schomer and W. H. McCleod (Delhi: Motilal Banarsidass, 1987), 61–90; also Monika Horstmann, "The Example in Dadupanthi Homiletics," in *Tellings and Texts: Music, Literature, and Performance in North India*, ed. Francesca Orsini and Katherine Butler Schofield (Cambridge, UK: Open Book Publishers, 2015), 31–60.
11. These are the *pañc-vāṇī* and *sarvāṅgī* anthologies of the Dadu Panth of Rajasthan, compiled in the first two decades of the seventeenth century. In addition to the *Nirguṇ Bhakti Sāgar* cited above, see *The Sarvangi of the Dadupanthi Rajab*, ed. Winand Callewaert (Leuven: Departement Orieàntalistiek, 1978); *The Sarvāṅgī of Gopaldas, a 17th Century Anthology of Bhakti Literature*, ed. Winand Callewaert (New Delhi: Manohar, 1993); *Rajjabadās Kī Sarbaṅgī, The Sarbangi of Rajjabdas: a Dadupanthi Source of the 17th Century*, ed. Shahabuddin Iraqi (Aligarh: Granthayan, 1985).

12. Perhaps the greatest testament to the oral character of this genre and the mode of knowledge transmission privileged by the *nirguṇ* saints is that variations of this verse by Kabir and the motif it presents are found throughout the body of *nirguṇ sant* poetry. For example, two quite similar *sākhīs* are attributed to Dadu Dayal (who identifies Kabir as his spiritual guru): the first reads, *ekai akhira pīva kā soī sati kari jāṁṇi / rāma nāma sata gara kahyā so dādū paravāṁṇi*, "Understand that even just one letter of the beloved is Truth / If one says 'Ram's Name is Truth,' then *that*, oh Dadu, is epistemological proof (*pramāṇa*)" (Ds. 2.2, *Dādū 443 pads*, critical edition by Monika Horstmann, based on the Caturvedi edition and the oldest manuscripts in the Callewaert Microfilm Collection, reprinted in Callewaert and Op de Beeck, *Nirguṇ Bhakti Sāgar*). The second reads, *dādū akṣara prema kā koī paḍhegā eka / dādū pustaka prema bina kete paḍhaiṁ aneka*, "Oh Dadu, [better] that one read one letter of love / Than read any number of books without love" (*sākhī* 118, *Śrī Dādū Vāṇī*, ed. Ramprasaddas Swami, Jaipur: Shri Dadu Dayalu Mahasabha, 2007). For an anonymously authored *sākhī* that uses this motif in the Dadu Panthi manuscript sources, see the *Sarvāṅgī* of Gopaldas, v46.16.
13. *Sākhī* 2.23, in Horstmann, ed., *Dādū 443 pads*. The Name of God, i.e., Rām, could even flip the balance of power and religious authority between a subaltern hymnodist like Kabir or Ravidas and the very Brahmin pandits they criticized: as Ravidas says, "My caste and clan has always tanned animal [hides] around Banaras / Now the Brahmins stretch themselves across the ground paying it respect since your servant Ravidas found refuge in your Name." (*merī jāti kuṭabāṃḍalā ḍora ḍovaṃtā nitahi bānārasī āsa pāsa / aba bipra paradhāna tihi karahi ḍaṃḍaüti teri nāma saraṇāï ravidāsu dāsā.*) *The Life and Works of Raidas*, ed. Winand M. Callewaert (New Delhi: Manohar, 1992), v. 39/98 (*Guru Granth Sāhib* 1293, *mahal* 7).
14. On practices of chanting and repetition of words and vocables in *nirguṇ* saint traditions, see Pitambardatt Barthwal, *Traditions of Indian Mysticism Based Upon Nirguna School of Hindi Poetry* (New Delhi: Heritage Publishers, 1978; originally 1930), and Parsuram Chaturvedi, *Uttarī Bhārat Kī Sant-Paramparā* (Allahabad: Bharati Bhandar, 1951). The importance of vocalizing the Name of God in the tradition can be gleaned from Ravidas's hymn, "Oh Murari, your Name is my *ārati* (worship) and my ablutions (*majanu*)," preserved in the Sikh *Ādi Granth*, AR 694, 3.1.1. On the *bhakti* saints' appropriation of certain forms of tantric practices (and the rejection of others), see Patton Burchett, *A Genealogy of Devotion: Bhakti, Tantra, Yoga, and Sufism in North India* (New York: Columbia University Press, 2019), 239–75.
15. Mackenzie Brown, "Purāṇa as Scripture: From Sound to Image of the Holy Word in the Hindu Tradition," *History of Religions* 26, no. 1 (August 1, 1986): 68–86; Florinda De Simini, *Of Gods and Books: Ritual and Knowledge Transmission in the Manuscript Cultures of Premodern India* (Berlin: De Gruyter, 2016); Kali Kumar Dutta, "The Ritual of Manuscripts," *Our Heritage: Bulletin of the Department of Post-Graduate Training and Research, Sanskrit College, Calcutta* 19, no. 1 (1971): 15–43. See also Jinah Kim, *Receptacle of the Sacred: Illustrated Manuscripts and the Buddhist Book Cult in South Asia* (Berkeley: University of California Press, 2013).
16. John E. Cort, "The Jain Knowledge Warehouses: Traditional Libraries in India," *Journal of the American Oriental Society* 115, no. 1 (Jan–Mar 1995): 77–87; see also Nalini Balbir, "The Cambridge Jain Manuscripts: Provenances, Highlights, Colophons," in *Indic Manuscript Cultures through the Ages: Material, Textual, and Historical Investigations*, ed. Vincenzo Vergiani, Daniele Cuneo, and Camillo Alessio Formigatti (Berlin: De Gruyter, 2017), 47–76; Nalini Balbir, "Is a Manuscript an Object or a Living Being?: Jain Views On the Life and Use of Sacred Texts," in *The Death of Sacred Texts: Ritual Disposal and Renovation of Texts in World Religions*, ed. Kristina Myrvold (Surrey: Ashgate, 2010), 107–24.
17. On the manuscript culture of Vaishnava *bhakti*, see Brown, "Purāṇa as Scripture," 71, 81; also Måns Broo, "Rites of Burial and Immersion: Hindu Ritual Practices on Disposing of Sacred Texts in Vrindavan," in Myrvold, ed., *The Death of Sacred Texts*, 91–106. For examples of the *Bhāgavata Purāṇa*

as an object of royal and ritual patronage, see Tadashi Shimizu, *The Bhāgavata-Purāṇa Miniature Paintings: From the Bhandarkar Oriental Research Institute Manuscript Dated 1648* (Tokyo: The Centre for East Asian Cultural Studies, 1993); B. N. Goswamy and Eberhard Fischer, *Pahari Masters: Court Painters of Northern India* (Zürich: Artibus Asiae, 1992).

18. Gurinder Singh Man suggests that the idea of equal access to the physical copy of the Qur'an may have inspired the early Sikh community's development of a ritual culture around the *Guru Granth Sāhib*. See chapter 5.

19. Anthologized in the Sikh *Ādi Granth* as 38 *malār* 1. Reading taken from *The Life and Works of Raidas*, ed. Winand Callewaert and Peter Friedlander (New Delhi: Manohar, 1992), v. AG 47 (page 203). Manuscripts of the *Sarvāṅgī* of Gopaldas curiously give *tatakāra* ("immediately") for *tara tari*.

20. Callewaert and Friedlander, eds., *Life and Works of Raidas*, vv. AG 47.1, 3.

21. See Robert L. Hardgrave, Jr., "Political Participation and Primordial Solidarity: The Nadars of Tamilnad," in *Caste in Indian Politics*, ed. Rajni Kothari (Hyderabad: Orient Longman 2004, originally 1970), 99.

22. This idea of *prem rasa* has resonances with the concept of the same name discussed by Sufi poets in the *pem-kathā* genre, but the two concepts are distinct in theology, epistemology, and manner of realization.

23. *Sākhī* 2.21, in *Kabīr Granthāvalī*, ed. Parasanath Tivari (1961), reprinted in Callewaert and Op de Beeck, *Devotional Hindī Literature*, 281–302.

24. On the preparation of ink see Shivaganesha Murthy, *Introduction to Manuscriptology* (Delhi: Sharada Publishing House, 1996), 54; Sanjay Lal Sah, "Prācīn kāl meṁ lekhan kā ādhār: syāhī," *Kriti Rakshana* 9, no. 6 (2014): 3–8.

25. *Sirī rāg, Mahalu* 1. *Guru Granth Sāhib*, 16. I thank Manpreet Kaur for introducing me to this verse and for her guidance in translating and understanding it.

26. The motif of the *lekhā* (account book), for example, appears in a *pad* by Shaikh Bahaudi preserved in manuscripts of Gopaldas's *Sarvāṅgī*; see v. 126.42.

27. Walter J. Ong, *Orality and Literacy: The Technologizing of the Word* (New York: Routledge, 1988; originally 1982), especially 31–77; Walter J. Ong, *The Presence of the Word: Some Prolegomena for Cultural and Religious History* (New Haven, Conn.: Yale University Press, 1967), 22–35. The earliest instances of inscription in South Asia date to the third century BCE and are political inscriptions related to the Mauryan Empire. See Richard Salomon, *Indian Epigraphy: A Guide to the Study of Inscriptions in Sanskrit, Prakrit, and the Other Indo-Aryan Languages* (New York: Oxford, 1998), 133–42.

28. Imre Bangha, "The Emergence of Hindi Literature: From Transregional Maru-Gurjar to Madhyadeśī Narratives," in *Text and Tradition in Early Modern India*, ed. Tyler Williams, Anshu Malhotra, and John S. Hawley (New Delhi: Oxford University Press, 2018), 10–13.

29. The lack of reliable dates for poets like Kabir and Ravidas makes it difficult to determine whether they were contemporaries of poets like Vishnudas and Qutban or came after them, but there is little doubt that Daud preceded the earliest of the *nirguṇ bhakti* poets by at least half a century, and that he in turn drew inspiration from earlier texts in the literary dialect of Madhyadeshi. On the language and compositions of Vishnudas of Gwalior, see Vishṇudās, *Mahābhārata: Pāṇḍav-Carit* (Vidya Mandir Prakashan, 1973).

30. The Fatehpur manuscript has been published in facsimile; see *Pad Sūradāsajī Kā: The Padas of Surdas*, ed. Gopalnarayan Bahura and Kenneth E. Bryant (Jaipur: Maharaja Sawai Man Singh II Museum, 1984).

31. The *Sarvāṅgī* of Gopaldas, v. 62.2 (*sākhi* 8.2 in Callewaert and Op de Beeck). This is a common trope found in the premodern poetry of several South Asian languages; see discussion below. For other references to reading, writing, and the material equipment of literacy in Kabir's poetry in

early written sources, see *Guru Granth Sāhib* 871.5.4, 1371.137, and 1373; *Sarvāṅgī*, vv. 19.164, 19.166. These are, of course, *written* sources compiled long after the historical Kabir's lifetime; here, I use "Kabir" to refer to the authorial persona, not to any historical individual.

32. *Pad* 76, in Callewaert and Friedlander, eds., *Life and Works of Raidāsa*, 216. The trope of the writing board (*paṭī/pāṭī*) upon which one learns to write and read continues to appear into the seventeenth century, in the writings of the Sikh gurus and Dadu Panthi saints like Sundardas.

33. For more instances of the motifs of writing and reading in the poetry of Ravidas, Dadu, and other *nirguṇ* saints from early written sources, see Gopaldas, *Sarvāṅgī*, vv. 23,1.2; 46,2.2; 25,71; 62,37; 62,39; 112,20.18; 125,7.

34. A representative example of this line of thinking is found in Ramchandra Shukla, *Hindī Sāhitya Kā Itihās* (Kashi: Nagari Pracharini Sabha, 1940) (revised edition of introduction to Das, *Hindī Śabd Sāgar*, 1920), 69–70.

35. On the notion of corporate authorship in South Asian religious poetry, see Christian Novetzke, "Divining an Author: The Idea of Authorship in an Indian Religious Tradition," *History of Religions* 42, no. 3 (2003): 213–42.

36. On this motif in the *Śivamahimnaḥ Stotra* and *Padmāvat*, see chapter 1. Given the difficulty of dating Kabir's lifetime and compositions, there is a possibility that Jayasi's use of the motif predates its use in the verse attributed to Kabir.

37. Take, for example, the oft-quoted Sanskrit aphorism, "[Concerning] the knowledge contained in a book and the wealth possessed by another / At the time of need, neither that knowledge nor that wealth is of any use" (*pustakasthā tu yā vidyā parahastagataṁ dhanam / karyakāle samutpanne na sā vidyā na tad dhanam*). On anxieties about book learning among Muslim intellectuals in early modern India, see Nile Green, "The Uses of Books in a Late Mughal Takiyya: Persianate Knowledge Between Person and Paper," *Modern Asian Studies* 44, no. 2 (March 1, 2010): 241–65.

38. An entertaining example is found in the *Fawā'id al-Fu'ād*, a transcription of conversations with the Sufi *pīr* Nizamuddin Auliya made by his disciple, Amir Hasan Sijzi. Nizamuddin recalls how his own teacher, Shaikh Fariduddin, became angry when a disciple offered to bring a better manuscript of a particular work than the copy from which the shaikh was reading. What angered Fariduddin was the disciple's suggestion that he did not know the text well enough to be able to correct from memory all of the errors in the copy. *Nizam ad-din Awliya, Morals for the Heart: Conversations of Shaykh Nizam ad-din Awliya recorded by Amir Hasan Sijzi*, ed. and trans. Bruce Lawrence (New York: Paulist Press, 1992), 109.

39. Sheldon Pollock, *The Language of the Gods in the World of Men: Sanskrit, Culture, and Power in Premodern India* (Berkeley: University of California Press, 2006), 82–89.

40. On the construction of authorial personas in *bhakti* poetry, see John Stratton Hawley, "Author and Authority," in *Three Bhakti Voices: Mirabai, Surdas, and Kabir in Their Time and Ours* (New Delhi: Oxford University Press, 2005), 21–47.

41. This is not to suggest that unwritten hagiographical traditions did not play an important role in remembering and broadcasting the saints' life narratives; such traditions are still very much alive and have informed the written tradition (and vice versa). See, for example, Swami Narayandas, *Śrī Dādū Panth Paricay: Dādū Panth Kā Itihās* (Jaipur: Sri Dadu Dayalu Mahasabha, VS 2035 / 1979 CE), and Mangaldas, *Śrī Mahārāj Haridās Jī Kī Vāṇī* (Jaipur: Nikhil Bharatiya Niranjani Mahasabha, 1962). On patterns and themes in the hagiographical literature of this period, see Winand M. Callewaert and Rupert Snell, eds., *According to Tradition: Hagiographical Writing in India* (Wiesbaden: Harrassowitz, 1994).

42. For example, the *Dādū Janm Līlā* was composed by Jangopal, a first-generation disciple of Dadu Dayal who had known the guru personally; the work also includes descriptions of Dadu's sons and several of his disciples living at the time who would later be canonized themselves. The *Bhaktamāl*

of Raghavdas of the Dadu Panth similarly includes descriptions of saint-poets in the Panth and in the Niranjani Sampraday who, if not living at the time of the work's composition, were quite likely known personally by the author.

43. Anantdas, *The Hagiographies of Anantadās: The Bhakti Poets of North India*, ed. and trans. Winand Callewaert (Richmond: Curzon, 2000); Nabhadas, *Bhaktamal, with Commentary of Priyadas*, ed. Rupkala (Lucknow: Tejkumar Press, 1914); Jangopal, *Dādu Janm Līlā*, ed. and trans. Winand Callewaert as *The Hindi Biography of Dadu Dayal* (Delhi: Motilal Banarsidass, 1988); Raghavdas, *Bhaktamāl*, ed. Agarchand Nahata (Jodhpur: Rajasthan Oriental Research Institute), 1965; Hariramdas, *Dayāl Jī Kī Pañc Paracai*, Ms. 24778, 1817 CE, Rajasthan Oriental Research Institute, Jodhpur; Ragunathdas, *Paracaï*, in Mangaldas, *Śrī Mahārāj Haridās Jī Kī Vāṇī*, 218–42. I have included the *Bhaktamāl* of Nabhadas, a poet of the ostensibly *saguṇ*-oriented Ramanandi Sampraday, because copies circulated within the sectarian communities of the *nirguṇ* tradition, reflecting the fact that Nabhadas praises many of the same figures revered by the *nirguṇ* sects, including Kabir, Namdev, and Ravidas. That the hagiographies of Anantdas (associated with the Ramanandi Sampraday) were circulated among *nirguṇ* sects like the Niranjanis has already been noted by David Lorenzen in *Kabir Legends and Ananta-Das's* Kabir Parachai (Albany: State University of New York Press, 1991).

44. See Anantdas, *Kabīr Paracaī*, vv. 1.6(1), 4.8, *Raidās Paracaī*, vv. 2.9, 4.11, 11.3, 11.8.2.

45. Anantdas, *Kabīr Paracaī*, vv. 1.1–4, 2.2–4, 4.13, 5.9, 7.1, 10.1, 11.3; *Raidās Paracaī*, vv. 1.2–13, 2.5, 4.12–6.20, Jangopal, *Dādū Janm Līlā*, vv. 4.3–6.

46. That the saints' putative illiteracy (*nirakṣaratā*, "being without letters") is established by hagiographical works is underlined by the fact that it is never mentioned or even alluded to in their poetry. Even the famous *sākhī* attributed to Kabir, "I've never touched paper, my hand has never grasped a pen / The saints of the four ages made their thoughts known with their mouths" (*masi kāgad chauṁ nahīṁ kalama gahauṁ nahi hātha / cāroṁ juga kai mahātama kabirā mukhahiṁ janāī bāta*), is not found in any early manuscript, suggesting that it too is part of a collective effort by multiple authors writing in his name and over time to construct an image of the saint that is consistent with his perceived message.

47. Anantdas, *Raidās Paracai*, vv. 4.10–11, 11.8.0–6.

48. Anantdas, *Raidās Paracai*, vv. 11.3–4.

49. Jangopal, *Dādū Janm Līlā*, vv. 12.21–26.

50. Jangopal, *Dādū Janm Līlā*, vv. 5.26–28; *Kabīr-Ravidās-Saṁvād*, Ms. 12422, Rajasthan Oriental Research Institute Jodhpur, ff. 29b–32a; Raghunathdas, *Paricaï*, v.6.17–18.

51. On the psychic and affective dimensions of poetic meter and rhythm, see Alexander Freer, "Rhythm as Coping," *New Literary History* 46, no. 3 (2015): 549–68. On the "upside down" language and "rough rhetoric" of Kabir and similar saints, see Hess and Singh, *The Bijak of Kabir*, 7–14.

52. Jangopal, *Dādū Janm Līlā*, v. 2.11.

53. Jangopal, *Dādū Janm Līlā*, v. 2.11.

54. Dadu, *Dādū Vāṇī*, ed. Caturvedi, v. 13.19.

55. Jangopal, *Dādū Janm Līlā*, v. 2.8–10.

56. Anantadas, *Kabīr Paracaï*, ed. Lorenzen, vv. 10.1–12.

57. The Sikh tradition constitutes an important exception in the broader galaxy of *nirguṇ*-oriented religious traditions: Guru Nanak is frequently depicted in the *janamasākhī* literature carrying a *pothī* of his poetry. This *pothī* is accorded importance as the earliest form of what would eventually become the *Guru Granth Sāhib*, the sacred scripture of the Sikhs. Yet because the Sikh tradition understands Guru Nanak's *pothī* to be more than simply a song notebook, it really belongs in a different class of material text; I discuss it in the context of sacred scriptures in chapter 4.

58. On writing as supplement, see Jacques Derrida's reading of Jean Jacques Rousseau in *Of Grammatology* (Baltimore, Md.: Johns Hopkins University Press, 1997, originally 1974), 141–64.

59. Roland Barthes, "From Work to Text," trans. Richard Howard, in *The Rustle of Language* (New York: Hill and Wang, 1986, originally 1971), 56–64.
60. This harkens back to the original meaning of *lēmma* in Greek: "something assumed." Individual "words," or units of meaning, or signifiers, are entities "assumed" to exist among the jumble of sounds that one hears when they read aloud, and thus can be picked out. On *scriptio continua* and the history of reading aloud, see William A. Johnson, "Toward a Sociology of Reading in Classical Antiquity," *The American Journal of Philology* 121, no. 4 (December 1, 2000): 593–627; Frank D. Gilliard, "More Silent Reading in Antiquity: Non Omne Verbum Sonabat," *Journal of Biblical Literature* 112, no. 4 (1993): 689–94. To state that reading aloud was a normative practice is not to suggest that silent reading did not occur but rather that it was an exception. Print culture did not bring an end to reading aloud in either northern India or any other region of the subcontinent. See Francesca Orsini, *Print and Pleasure: Popular Literature and Entertaining Fictions in Colonial North India* (Ranikhet: Permanent Black, 2009).
61. A succinct introduction in English to prosody and musical performance in the Hindi tradition may be found in Rupert Snell, *The Hindi Classical Tradition: A Braj Bhāṣā Reader* (London: School of Oriental and African Studies, 1991), 24–25.
62. Monier Monier-Williams, *A Sanskrit-English Dictionary* (Oxford: Clarendon Press, 1872), s.v. "guṭikā."
63. On the *bahī* and recordkeeping in sultanate and Mughal India, see Najaf Haider, "Language, Caste and the Secretarial Class in Mughal India," in *The Development of a Nation: Essays in Memory of R.S. Sharma*, ed. D.N. Jha (Delhi: Manohar, 2014), 251.
64. On the script used in *bahīs*, see Grierson, *Linguistic Survey of India Vol. IX Part II*, 4, 9, 63. *Bahīs* continued to be used into the early twentieth century; see for example photographs of a "street banker" in Udaipur writing in a *bahī* and merchants holding *bahīs* in Chitorgarh, in Martin Hürlimann, *India: The Landscape, the Monuments, and the People* (Bombay: D. B. Taraporevala Sons, 1932), 239, 246. Earlier depictions of *bahī*-wielding individuals engaged in clerical or mercantile activity include ethnographic drawings and prints in the so-called "Company style"; see Item 2007681228, "The Scribe" (1825 CE), in the Library of Congress, https://www.loc.gov/item/2007681228/. Farther south in the Marathi-speaking region of western India, singers' notebooks were called *vahī*—a modified pronunciation of *bahī*. On Marathi *kirtankars'* notebooks, see Christian Novetzke, "Note to Self: What Marathi *Kirtankars*' Notebooks Suggest about Literacy, Performance, and the Travelling Performer in Pre-Colonial Maharashtra," in Orsini and Schofield, eds., *Tellings and Texts*, 169–84.
65. On clerical communities in the Mughal world, see Muzaffar Alam and Sanjay Subrahmanyam, "The Making of a Munshi," *Comparative Studies of South Asia, Africa and the Middle East* 24, no. 2 (2004): 61–72; Rosalind O'Hanlon and Christopher Minkowski, "What Makes People Who They Are? Pandit Networks and the Problem of Livelihoods in Early Modern India," *Indian Economic and Social History Review* 45, no. 381 (2008): 381–416; Rosalind O'Hanlon, "The Social Worth of Scribes: Brahmins, Kayasthas and the Social Order in Early Modern India," *Indian Economic and Social History Review* 45 (2010): 563–95.
66. The reception and canonization of Namdev's poetry proceeded in the north in a manner distinct from that of his home region of western India: there he is understood to belong to the family of Varkari saints who worship a quite anthropomorphic form of Krishna called Vithoba, while in northern India he and his compositions came to be associated firmly with *nirguṇ* traditions like that of the Dadu Panth, Niranjani Sampraday, and the Sikh community.
67. Such groups are today called *bhajan maṇḍalī* or "hymn circles." Contemporary sources from the seventeenth and eighteenth centuries do not use any particular term for these loosely organized groups but mention informal *satsaṅg* gatherings in a manner suggesting that meeting to sing hymns outside of any sectarian institutional context was a common occurrence.

68. Shukla, *Hindī Sāhitya Kā Itihās*, 60–231. In Shukla's terminology, these traditions are, respectively: 1) *saguṇ kṛṣṇa-bhakti śākhā*, 2) *saguṇ rām-bhakti śākhā*, 3) *nirguṇ jñānaśrayī śākhā*, and 4) *prem-mārgī śākhā*.

69. Even the sectarian canons reflected in the written anthologies of communities like the Dadu Panth, Niranjani Sampraday, and Kabir Panth were the products of long processes of refinement and reorganization. Sectarian anthologies from the early seventeenth century tend to be broadly ecumenical in their inclusion of material from a wide range of saint-poets; anthologies dating to the second half of the seventeenth century and later tend to contain the works of smaller and more theologically homogenous groups. I have explored this process in "Bhakti kāvya maiṁ nirguṇ-saguṇ vibhājan kā aitihāsik adhyayan (A Historical Study of the Nirgun-Sagun Distinction in Bhakti Poetry)," MPhil thesis, Jawaharlal Nehru University, 2007, and "Madhyakālīn bhakti-sampradāyoṁ ke ṭakarāvōṁ kā bhautik ādhār (The Material Foundations of Conflict between Medieval Bhakti Communities)," *Bahuvacan* 24 (2010): 53–76.

70. The conclusions presented here support several observations by Jack Hawley about the theological heterogeneity of material in early manuscript anthologies of *bhakti* poetry. See John S. Hawley, "The Nirguṇ/Saguṇ Distinction," in *Three Bhakti Voices*, 70–86.

71. The Fatehpur manuscript of 1582 CE has already been mentioned in this regard; similar examples can be found in *guṭakā*s that include poems by courtly poets like Keshavdas and Tansen alongside compositions by Surdas, Kabir, and other saints.

72. Ms. 426, Nagari Pracharini Sabha (folios unnumbered, with several missing).

73. This is partly due to the dynamic nature of the raga itself, since the structure could change over time, and to the dynamic nature of a teaching tradition in which different guru-disciple lineages brought about innovations. It is also due to the general absence of a *written* notation system that recognizes fixed pitch values. Like saint poetry, musicological knowledge in precolonial north India existed in a space of overlap between the written and the aural, in the interface between inscribed texts and embodied practices. See Richard Widdess, "The Oral in Writing: Early Indian Musical Notations," *Early Music* 24, no. 3 (August 1, 1996): 391–405; Richard Widdess, *The Rāgas of Early Indian Music: Modes, Melodies and Musical Notations from the Gupta Period to c. 1250* (Oxford: Clarendon Press, 1995).

74. Allyn Miner suggests that individuals familiar with courtly musicological systems may have originally created the raga system used in *bhakti* devotional music of north India, but that this system at some point became independent of the courtly tradition and the two diverged over time ("Ragas in the Early Sixteenth Century," in Orsini and Schofield, *Tellings and Texts*, 397). Miner speaks primarily about the Krishna-centered traditions of the Braj region; I would argue that traditions of raga in the *nirguṇ*-oriented traditions farther west in Rajasthan were probably even further removed from courtly practice even though musicological writing experienced an efflorescence in the late seventeenth and eighteenth centuries.

75. See Heidi Pauwels, "New Indo-Aryan Poetry in Performance: Metre and Oral Formulae as Exemplified in the Poetry of Harirām Vyās," in *Studies in Early Modern Indo-Aryan Languages, Literature, and Culture: Research Papers, 1992–1994, Presented at the Sixth Conference on Devotional Literature in New Indo-Aryan Languages, Held at Seattle, University of Washington, 7–9 July 1994*, ed. Alan W. Entwistle (New Delhi: Manohar, 1999), 311–38.

76. This process of composition and re-composition has historically vexed textual critics concerned with reconstructing an original or *ur*-text. Jaroslav Strnad has suggested a novel and productive alternative that instead maps variations in a corpus of versions of a poem. See "Searching for the Source or Mapping the Stream? Some Text-Critical Issues in the Study of Medieval Bhakti," in Williams, Malhotra, and Hawley, *Text and Tradition in Early Modern North India*, 143–58.

77. On the use of notebooks in contemporary bhakti musical performance, see Linda Hess, *Bodies of Song: Kabir Oral Traditions and Performative Worlds in North India* (New Delhi: Oxford University Press, 2015), 77–90.
78. Pollock, *The Language of the Gods in the World of Men*, 83.
79. Kenneth E. Bryant, *Poems to the Child-God: Structures and Strategies in the Poetry of Sūrdās* (Berkeley: University of California Press, 1978), 40–42.
80. See Monika Horstmann, "Texts and What to Do with Them: Dādūpanthī Compilations," in *Écrire et transmettre en Inde classique*, ed. Gérard Colas and Gerdi Gerschheimer (Paris: École française d'Extrême-Orient, 2009), 27–42; Horstmann, "The Example in Dadupanthi Homiletics"; Schomer, "The *Dohā* as a Vehicle of Sant Teachings."
81. When such *aṅg*-based thematic organization does appear, it usually indicates that the verses have been copied from such a sectarian anthology. See chapter 4.
82. Monika Horstmann, "Dādūpanthi Anthologies of the Eighteenth and Nineteenth Centuries," in *Bhakti in Current Research: Proceedings of the Ninth International Conference on Early Devotional Literature in New Indo-Aryan Languages, Heidelberg, 23–26 July 2003*, ed. Monika Horstmann (New Delhi: Manohar, 2006), 163.
83. I am aware of only one historical study of astrological works in precolonial Hindi: Kshama Joshi, *Hindī Sāhitya Meṁ Jyotiṣaśāstra Kī Paramparā* (Delhi: Deshabharati Prakashan, 2010). This is despite the fact that one of the most famous precolonial Hindi poets and a prominent scholar at the court of the Mughal emperor Shah Jahan, Kavindracharya Sarasvati (fl. 1650), is known to have composed a work on astrology called the *Samarasār*, and other well-known Hindi composers like Banarasidas (1586–1643) are known to have been trained in astrology. On Kavindracarya, see Allison Busch, "Hidden in Plain View: Brajbhasa Poets at the Mughal Court," *Modern Asian Studies* 44, no. 2 (2010): 289; on Banarasidas, see John Cort, "Making It Vernacular in Agra: The Practice of Translation by Seventeenth-Century Jains," in Orsini and Schofield, *Tellings and Texts*, 75. Commentaries in Hindi on astrological works composed in Sanskrit were being written at least as early as the second decade of the seventeenth century; a manuscript containing a prose Hindi commentary on the Sanskrit *Bhuvan Dīpikā* has been found containing a colophon dated 1614 CE; see Thomas Grahame Bailey, "Hindi Prose before the Nineteenth Century," *Bulletin of the School of Oriental Studies* 3, no. 3 (1924): 525.
84. On the critique of tantric, Nath, and Brahminical ritual knowledge in *bhakti* poetry, see Burchett, *A Genealogy of Devotion*, 239–304; Heidi Pauwels, "Who Are the Enemies of the Bhaktas? Testimony about 'Śāktas' and 'Others' from Kabīr, the Rāmānandīs, Tulsīdās, and Harirām Vyās," *Journal of the American Oriental Society* 130, no. 4 (October 1, 2010): 509–39. Partisans of *bhakti* did indeed position their belief systems in opposition to ritual knowledge systems even as they appropriated some of the technologies of those traditions. The manuscript record reveals that astrology was one such technology, even though it receives no mention in scholarly histories of *nirguṇ* devotion.
85. On the shifting relationship between astrology and cosmology in early modern India, see Christopher Z. Minkowski, "Competing Cosmologies in Early Modern Indian Astronomy," in *Studies in the History of the Exact Sciences in Honour of David Pingree*, ed. David Pingree, David Edwin, and Charles Burnett (Leiden: Brill, 2004), 349–84. The presence of astronomical and alchemical notes in *guṭakā*s would appear to complicate Abdur Rahman's suggestion that the rise of *bhakti* and Sufi modes of religiosity in India coincided with (or possibly even effected) stagnation in scientific development. "Science and Social Movements: Bhakti and Sufi Movements," in *History of Indian Science, Technology, and Culture AD 1000–1800*, ed. Abdur Rahman (New Delhi: Oxford University Press, 1998), 415–35.
86. Patton Burchett has described the process through which *bhakti* saints simultaneously criticized Tantrikas, Shaktas, and Nath yogis while appropriating and redeploying their metaphysical terminologies and regimes of bodily practice. See *A Genealogy of Devotion*, 177–94.

87. For an example of early modern notebooks and their relationship to oral performance in southern India, see Novetzke, "Note to Self."
88. For a Safavid example, see British Museum No. 1920,0917,0.298.3, a painting of a youth reading from a *safīnah* by Riza-yi 'Abbasi (based on an earlier model by "Muhammadi of Herat"), c. 1625–26, made for the Safavid emperor Shah Abbas, as well as Walters Art Museum No. 653.17A, a painting of a young man reading, found in a *muraqqa'* compiled in 1693. The Mughal portrait of Babur reading from a *safīnah* was produced at the Mughal court circa 1605 to 1615; see British Museum No. 1921,1011,0.3.
89. Ms. 477, A. C. Joshi Library, Panjab University, Chandigarh. The final work copied into the codex includes a colophon of 2nd Safar, 1212 Hijri (July 27, 1797). See the discussion of this manuscript in chapter 1.
90. This is the case with the *safīnah* of Brindabandas "Khwushgu," who compiled this anthology of Persian poets circa 1730 CE with the express intention of making it a literary primer (Prashant Keshavmurthy, *Persian Authorship and Canonicity in Late Mughal Delhi: Building an Ark* [New York: Routledge, 2016], 170, n. 26). On the position of this work in the Persian literary canon, see Alam, "The Culture and Politics of Persian in Precolonial Hindustan," in *Literary Cultures in History: Reconstructions from South Asia*, ed. Sheldon Pollock (Berkeley: University of California Press, 2003), 176, and Rajeev Kinra, *Writing Self, Writing Empire: Chandar Bhan Brahman and the Cultural World of the Indo-Persian State Secretary* (Oakland: University of California Press, 2015), 12.
91. See for example Accn. 63.32, Chhatrapati Shivaji Maharaj Vastu Sangrahalaya; Accn. 1–85-154.77, Library of Congress, Washington, D.C.
92. Acts of exchange involving *safīnah/bayāẓ* such as lending and gifting, or even simply inscribing verses in another person's *safīnah*, both constituted and performed different types of social relationships. Prashant Keshavmurthy points out the recurrent narrative trope of an established poet inscribing his verses in the *bayāẓ* of a lesser-known, local poet, thus conferring honor upon the latter. Keshavmurthy, *Persian Authorship and Canonicity*, 170 fn. 30.
93. Littérateurs like Mir Taqi Mir (1723–1810), having accumulated in their *safīnah*s a great number of verses and a great number of anecdotes about authors, edited this material and supplemented it with introductory and evaluative commentary in Persian, producing the first *taẕkirah*s of vernacular Indian literature. These became the basis for the first "modern" literary histories of the north Indian vernacular. On *bayāẓ* and the compilation of *taẕkirah*s, see Frances Pritchett, *Nets of Awareness: Urdu Poetry and Its Critics* (Berkeley: University of California Press, 1994), 64–65.
94. On the *Śivamandir* of Banarasidas and vernacular versions of the *Bhaktāmar Stotra*, see Cort, "Making It Vernacular in Agra," 78–79, 88. The colophon accompanying the travelogue suggests that the owner of the manuscript himself may have transcribed the tale as Thakur Balakidas recounted it: "Thus is written the account of faraway lands just as it was told by Thakur Balakidas, resident of Multan, who saw it himself . . ." Yet there is a problem: the scribe gives the date of inscription as the 13th of the bright half of the month of Magha, VS 1609, "in the reign of Śrī Shahjahan Jī." If we take the numeral 6 to be an error and replace it with 7, then the date equates to February 2, 1653, comfortably within the reign of the Mughal emperor Shah Jahan (r. 1628–1658).
95. On Dadupanthi critiques of Jainism, see Monika Horstmann, "Nāth and Dādūpanthī Critique of Jains," *International Journal of Jaina Studies* 13, no. 1 (2017): 1–72.
96. Ulrich Timme Kragh, "Localized Literary History: Sub-Text and Cultural Heritage in the Āmer Śāstrabhaṇḍār, a Digambara Manuscript Repository in Jaipur," *International Journal of Jain Studies* 9, no. 3 (2003): 1–53.
97. It is possible that this *pad* was composed by someone other than the historical individual we recognize as Kabir: composing a *pad* in the style of—and in the voice of—an established saint-poet was a common practice in early modern India and was apparently not understood to violate any

relationship between authorship and authenticity. This type of anamnetic authorship, to use the term Novetzke employs in the context of Namdev's poetry, led to the rapid growth of Kabir's poetic corpus (and those of many of his *bhakti* brethren, especially Surdas). See Novetzke, *Religion and Public Memory: A Cultural History of Saint Namdev in India* (New York: Columbia University Press, 2008), 135–61. On a similar phenomenon in the Surdas corpus, see John Stratton Hawley, "The Early Sūr Sāgar and the Growth of the Sūr Tradition," *Journal of the American Oriental Society* 99, no. 1 (1979): 64–72. The fact that this *pad* is not found in early manuscripts makes it more likely that it is a later composition that evokes Kabir's affect through mimicking his voice.

98. For example, the scribe's transcription of the hymns is marked by the reduplication of semivowels, the substitution of retroflex *ṇ* for dental *n*, and the frequent nasalization of vowels, especially before a nasal or labial consonant or semivowel. Marwari pronouns like *mhāro* and *īṇaṁ* are also used in the *pads*, although in the case of Haridas, a native of central Rajasthan, these could be a feature of the original composition.

99. The original prosody of the two *pads* quoted here is not overly difficult to reconstruct: Haridas's *pad* is most likely in the *sār* or *sarasī* meter and Kabir's *pad* is in the *śaṅkar* meter.

100. The final iteration of the refrain as transcribed in the *guṭakā* even contains a slight variation: emphatic *huyyaī* for *yyaī*. In the musical performance of *pads*, the overlaying of the prosody onto the *tīnatāl* rhythm often resulted in the beginning of the refrain being "appended" to the end of each verse; on this phenomenon see Snell, *The Hindi Classical Tradition*, 24–25; Kenneth Bryant and John S. Hawley, *Sur's Ocean: Songs from the Early Tradition* (Cambridge: Harvard University Press, 2015), xxxi–xxxviii.

101. Little has been written on the occult beliefs and practices behind these writings and diagrams; see Ja'far Sharīf and Gerhard Andreas Herklots, *Qanoon-e-Islam, or, The Customs of the Mussalmans of India* (Lahore: Al-Irshad, 1973, originally 1832).

3. *POTHĪS*, PANDITS, AND PRINCES

1. Ms. 24445, Rajasthan Oriental Research Institute. The *pothī* was given a simple binding at a later date.

2. The earliest known paper manuscripts in these languages date to the fourteenth century. Although Macdonell mentions the existence of an early thirteenth-century manuscript in an Indic language, I have not been able to locate any. *India's Past: A Survey of Her Literatures, Religions, Languages, and Antiquities* (Oxford: Oxford University Press, 1927), 53.

3. See Mark Amsler, *Affective Literacies: Writing and Multilingualism in the Late Middle Ages* (Turnhout: Brepols, 2012); Brian V. Street, *Literacy in Theory and Practice* (New York: Cambridge University Press, 1984); Seyyed Hossein Nasir, "Oral Transmission and the Book in Islamic Education: The Spoken and the Written Word," in George N. Atiyeh, ed., *The Book in the Islamic World: Written Word and Communication in the Middle East* (Albany: State University of New York Press, 1995), 57–70.

4. Sheldon Pollock, *The Language of the Gods in the World of Men: Sanskrit, Culture, and Power in Premodern India* (Berkeley: University of California Press, 2006), 82–83, 283–98.

5. On colonial efforts to establish institutions and practices of vernacular education, see Christopher R. King, *One Language, Two Scripts: The Hindi Movement in Nineteenth Century North India* (New Delhi: Oxford University Press, 1999), 88–116. The project of reconstructing education in *bhāṣā* during the precolonial period has been initiated by Françoise Mallison and Dalpat Singh Rajpurohit; see Françoise Mallison, "The Teaching of Braj, Gujarati, and Bardic Poetry at the Court of Kutch: The Bhuj Brajbhāṣā Pāṭhśālā (1749–1948)," in *Forms of Knowledge in Early Modern*

Asia Explorations in the Intellectual History of India and Tibet, 1500–1800, ed. Sheldon Pollock (Durham, N.C.: Duke University Press, 2011), 171–82; Dalpat Singh Rajpurohit, "Bhakti versus Rīti? The Sants' Perspective," *Bulletin of the School of Oriental and African Studies* 84, no. 1 (2021): 95–113; Dalpat Singh Rajpurohit, *Sundar Ke Svapn: Ārambhik Ādhunikatā, Dādūpanth, Aur Sundaradās Kī Kavitā* (New Delhi: Rajkamal, 2022), 168–84.

6. On the rise of vernacular intellectuals in second millennium South Asia, see Sheldon Pollock, "India in the Vernacular Millennium: Literary Culture and Polity, 1000–1500," *Daedalus* 127, no. 3 (July 1, 1998): 41–74, and chapter 10 of *The Language of the Gods*, especially 494–95.
7. On vernacular intellectuals from among the north Indian nobility, see Allison Busch, *Poetry of Kings: The Classical Hindi Literature of Mughal India* (New York: Oxford University Press, 2011); "The Anxiety of Innovation: The Practice of Literary Science in the Hindi Riti Tradition," *Comparative Studies of South Asia, Africa and the Middle East* 24, no. 2 (2004): 45–59; and "Hidden in Plain View: Brajbhasa Poets at the Mughal Court," *Modern Asian Studies* 44, no. 2 (2010): 267–309.
8. Busch, "The Anxiety of Innovation."
9. For example, Keshavdas uses the phrase to qualify his original typology of lovers' trysts in the *Rasikapriyā* (Delight of Connoisseurs, 1591), v. 5.41. In *Keśav Granthāvalī*, ed. Vishvanath Tripathi (Allahabad: Hindustani Academy, 1987).
10. Busch, "The Anxiety of Innovation," 49. Yet as Busch demonstrates, this theoretical borrowing from Sanskrit should be understood as a deliberate adoption of a classicist idiom, and/or a framework in which vernacular poets demonstrated their virtuosity (and innovation) by composing illustrative verses. See also *Poetry of Kings*, 5–6.
11. In 1737, the poet Ray Shivdas celebrated the novel contributions of Hindi poeticians in the introduction to the *Sarasār*: "Clever poets had heard many individual poems and *dhrupads* / that engaged new categories of *nāyakas* and *nāyikās*. / They looked to the discussions of them in available books / And became aware of new categories that had never before been treated." Quoted and translated in Busch, "The Anxiety of Innovation," 279.
12. Here again we see a contrast: although both vernacular and Sanskrit composers of the sixteenth and seventeenth centuries attempted to reconceptualize classical literary and aesthetic theory through religious categories and vice versa, they did not produce the same results. Vernacular works like the *Rāsapañcādhyayī* of Nandadas, the *Rasikapriyā* of Keshavadas, the *Rasamañjarī* of Agradas, and the *Jñān Samudra* and *Savaiyā Granth* of Sundardas enjoyed great popularity and produced a demonstrable impact on the trajectory of literature and literary theory in the vernacular. In contrast, as Pollock argues, Sanskrit works like the *Bhaktirasāmṛtasindhu* of Rupa Gosvami, the *Bhagavatamuktāphala* of Vopadeva, and the *Alaṁkārakaustubha* of Kavikarnapura may have introduced significant theoretical innovations, but these appear to have carved out a new domain for religious aesthetics rather than influenced the more general discourse of *literary* aesthetics (*A Rasa Reader: Classical Indian Aesthetics* [New York: Columbia University Press, 2016], 23–24). The idea that *bhāv* (emotion) is the soul of poetry rather than its particular mode of semiosis or any of its technical elements is also articulated by Tulsidas in the *Rāmacaritamānas* (1574 CE), but a systematic exploration of that idea in a shastric mode would have to wait for Dadu Panthi and Niranjani writings in the mid-seventeenth century.
13. Although Keshavdas makes the important move of locating the origin of *rasa* within Krishna and his *līlā* (divine play), it is still *rasa* that is the soul of poetry, not devotional sentiment or any other criterion. See *Rasikapriyā* 1.13–16. On the devotional significance of Keshavdas's treatment of *rasa* and poetry more generally, see Busch, *Poetry of Kings*, 44–45, 87–88, 111.
14. These were not the only tropes deemed literary or taken up by vernacular poets at royal courts. *Bhāṣā* poets, including the composers of *rīti granths*, composed works about *vīr* (heroism), war, historical events, *nīti* (ethics/statecraft), philosophy, and various other subjects. Yet what

constituted *kāvya* or literature proper according to the pronouncements and predilections of the *rīti granth* genre and its audience was clearly limited to romance and a few other themes. Material from religious traditions was not excluded from the realm of properly literary themes, but devotional sentiment was not part of the aesthetic program of Sanskrit and *rīti* poets. On the relationship of devotional and literary verse making in early Hindi see Rupert Snell, "Bhakti Versus Riti? The Satsai of Biharilal," *Journal of Vaishnava Studies* 3, no. 1 (1994): 153–61; Allison Busch, "Questioning the Tropes of 'Bhakti' and 'Riti' in Hindi Literary Historiography," in *Bhakti in Current Research: Proceedings of the Ninth International Conference on Early Devotional Literature in New Indo-Aryan Languages, Heidelberg, 23–26 July 2003*, ed. Monika Horstmann (New Delhi: Manohar, 2006), 33–48; Rajpurohit, "Bhakti versus Rīti? The Sants' Perspective."

15. *Sākhī* 17.25, p. 238 in Shastri edition. I am grateful to Dalpat Rajpurohit for bringing this verse to my attention. One may also compare and contrast this with Rajpurohit's translation and exegesis of the verse (and others by Sundardas on the topic of poetry) in "Bhakti Versus Rīti? The Sants' Perspective."
16. *Savaiyā* 14.4 In *Sundaradās Granthāvalī*, ed. Swami Narayandas (Jaipur: Shri Dadu Dayalu Mahasabha, 1989), 173.
17. Rajpurohit illustrates how Sundardas, through the use of *śleṣa* (pun/double meaning) and oblique references, singles out Keshavdas for particular ridicule, criticizing the courtly poet's occupation with sensual themes even as he reuses some of the latter's ideas. "Bhakti Versus Rīti? The Sants' Perspective," 103–104.
18. "That which gives rise to meaning in poetry and wonder in the heart / Has the name of *alaṁkār*, oh poets, take this to heart" (*jihi artha kari kavita ko camatakāra mana hoī / alaṁkāra tihi nāma ko kavi dhāro mana joī*). Hariramdas, *Chandaratnāvalī*, ed. Neha Baid as *Harirāmadās Kṛt Chandaratnāvalī* (Jodhpur: Rajasthani Granthagar, 2010), v. 108.
19. Bhagvandas, *Vairāgya Vṛnd*, 1st *prakāś*, v. 4–5.
20. Tulsidas offers a similar apologetic and a similar appeal to love as the source of poetry in the *Rāmacaritamānas*, v. 1.9.6. Tulsidas, *Śrī Rāmacaritamānas* (Gorakhpur: Gita Press, 2006). Sundardas is even more assertive when addressing his audience, daring them to dive into his "Ocean of Knowledge" (*jñān-samudra*), which is full of oysters of every poetic meter and unfathomable pearls of meaning. *Jñān Samudra*, v. 7. In *Sundaradās Granthāvalī*, ed. Swami Narayandas (Jaipur: Shri Dadu Dayalu Mahasabha, 1989), 1.
21. Manohardas, *Vedānta Mahāvākya Bhāṣā*, v. 2. Ms. 26579, Folio 1B. Rajasthan Oriental Research Institute, Jodhpur.
22. The figure of the *kavi* as a seer who reveals or praises God in Hindi is perhaps first attested in Nandadas's *Rupamañjarī*.
23. On the domain of *śāstra*, see Sheldon Pollock, "The Theory of Practice and the Practice of Theory in Indian Intellectual History," *Journal of the American Oriental Society* 105, no. 3 (1985): 499–519.
24. I say *primarily* in Sanskrit and in northern India because, by the turn of the sixteenth century, *śāstra* was already being composed in the vernaculars of Tamil, Kannada, and Telegu in the south and in Prakrit in the north. I thank Andrew Ollett for pointing out this important chronological and geographical distinction.
25. Ms. 12476, VS 1819 / 1762 CE, Rajasthan Oriental Research Institute, Jodhpur, Folio 1A.
26. An invocation to Sarasvati is found, for example, in the opening of Jayanta Bhatta's *Nyāyamañjarī* (v. 1.5), in which the term refers simply to "speech."
27. Caturdas, *Bhāgavata Purāṇa Bhāṣā*, Ms. 164060, Rajasthan Oriental Research Institute, vv. 60–61. On Caturdas's vernacular version of the eleventh chapter of the *Bhāgavata Purāṇa*, see Monika Horstmann, "Caturdās's Bhāsā Version of the Eleventh Book of the Bhāgavatapurāṇa," in *Transforming Tradition: Cultural Essays in Honour of Mukund Lath*, ed. Monika Horstmann (New Delhi: Aditya Prakashan, 2013), 47–62.

28. *piṃgala mata sakala dekhi avara chanda grantha pekhi kaviyan harirām mala caracarī bakhānī. Chandaratnāvalī*, v. 1.87.
29. Hariramdas Niranjani, *Nāmaprakāś*, ed. Neha Baid as *Nāmaprakāś: Sampādan Evaṁ Samīkṣā* (Jodhpur: Royal Publication, 2015), v. 256.
30. *likhai paṛhai ati prīti juta aru puni karai bicāra / chin chin jñāṁna prakāsa tihi sneï suravi parakāra. Vicāramāl*, v. 43. Ms. 37973, Rajasthan Oriental Research Institute, Jodhpur, f. 25b (numbered as f.9b).
31. Women sometimes became influential gurus in the *nirguṇ* devotional communities of Rajasthan, Punjab, and Haryana. Prominent among them is Sahajobai (fl. c. 1743), who became the leader of the Carandasi community after the passing of her guru, Carandas, and composed the corpus of *pads* known as the *Sahajaprakāś* (Light of Spontaneous Epiphany, n.d.). See Sahajo Bai, *Sahajo Bāī Kī Bānī: Sahaj Prakāś, Jīvan Caritra Sahit* (Allahabad: Belvedere Printing Works, 1962). See also a recent translation of some of Sahajobai's compositions into English: *Sahaj Prakash: The Brightness of Simplicity*, ed. and trans. Harry Aveling and Sudha Joshi (Delhi: Motilal Banarasidass, 2001). In the Niranjani Sampraday, Panna Devi (fl. mid-eighteenth century) is remembered as a powerful *sādhavī* (female ascetic) around whom a community of followers developed in the wealthy trading center of Nawalgarh (Ratanlal Mishra, *Nirañjanī Sampradāy: Sādhanā Evaṁ Sāhitya* [Nawalgarh: Mahamaya Mandir, 1998], 99). There is no question that women made up a significant part of the audience of lay devotees at public preachings, as evidenced in hagiographical works like the *Dādū Janm Līlā* and the *Caurāsī Vaiṣṇavan Kī Vārta*, and in visual representations like James Prinsep's lithographs of Banaras (see fig. 3.3).
32. Sundardas, *Jñān Samudra*, v. 1.1. The language of auspiciousness and inauspiciousness shows up frequently in Sundardas's thought on poetic composition; for example, he criticizes poetry concerned with *śṛṅgār* (erotic sentiment) as being *viparīt* (unfavorable/inauspicious). Sundardas, *Savaiyā Granth*, v. 5, in *Sundar Granthāvalī*, 172.
33. Hariramdas, *Chandaratnāvalī*, vv. 13–17.
34. The written and oral hagiographic record of Sundardas's life is particularly rich with references to poetic "examinations" and competitions held in Banaras and Rajasthan and performances of literary virtuosity in epistolary writing. Swami Narayandas, *Śrī Dādū Panth Paricay: Dādū Panth Kā Itihās* (Jaipur: Shri Dadu Mahavidyalaya, 1978), 555–56, 571–77; see also Rajpurohit, *Sundar ke svapn*, 168–77. Sundardas's compositions would eventually become part of the curriculum for later poets, whose skills were tested in similar fashion. See Mallison, "The Teaching of Braj, Gujarati, and Bardic Poetry at the Court of Kutch," and Rajpurohit, *Sundar Ke Svapn*, 177–87.
35. Ramchandra Shukla's characterization of the *nirguṇ* textual archive is representative: "The compositions of this branch [of *bhakti* poetry] are not literary—they are in the form of miscellaneous epigrams and lyrics of which the language and style are mostly irregular and incoherent . . . The poetic savor (*sarasatā*) that causes one to become immersed in the *rasa* of *bhakti* is also very scarce . . . That development of refined (*saṁskṛt*) intellect, refined heart, and refined speech that attracts educated society is not found in this branch." *Hindī Sāhitya Kā Itihās* (Kashi: Nagari Pracharini Sabha, 1940 [rev. ed. of introduction to Das, *Hindī Śabd Sāgar*, 1920]), 73. Even Pitambardatt Barthwal, a champion of *nirguṇ bhakti*'s intellectual value, could find only an "unconscious philosophy" running through the compositions of *nirguṇ* saints: "It is not, however, contended that these saints consciously undertook to formulate a system or systems of philosophy, for they were not philosophers but mystics, whose unconscious philosophy supplied simply the background of their religion." *Traditions of Indian Mysticism Based Upon Nirguna School of Hindi Poetry* (New Delhi: Heritage, 1978, originally 1936), xi.
36. Rabindranath Tagore and Evelyn Underhill, *Songs of Kabir* (New York: MacMillan, 1915); Kshitimohan Sen, *Dādū* (Calcutta: Vishvabharati Karyalay, 1935); Kshitimohan Sen, *Medieval Mysticism of India* trans. Manmohan Ghosh (London: Luzac, 1936). For an insightful study of how

Tagore's, Sen's, and others' compilations and translations shaped modern understandings of Kabir, see Peter Friedlander, *Kabir Poems in Transformation: A Fountain of Creativity* (Delhi: Primus Books, 2022).

37. Michael Allen, "Greater Advaita Vedānta: The Case of Niścaldās," *International Journal of Hindu Studies* 21 (2017): 275–97.

38. For example, the Rajput king Jaswant Singh of Marwar (r. 1638–1678) composed four works on Advaita Vedānta, while Keshavdas addressed elements of Advaita Vedānta in his *Vijñānagīta* (1610).

39. On the establishment and growth of Krishna worship, see Alan W. Entwistle, *Braj, Centre of Krishna Pilgrimage* (Groningen: E. Forsten, 1987); Jan K. Brzezinski, "Prabodhānanda Sarasvatī: From Benares to Braj," *Bulletin of the School of Oriental and African Studies* 55, no. 1 (1992): 52–75; and the chapters by John S. Hawley, Swapna Sharma, and Srivatsa Goswami in Tyler Williams, Anshu Malhotra, and John Stratton Hawley, eds., *Text and Tradition in Early Modern North India* (New Delhi: Oxford University Press, 2018). On the spread of Ram worship in Mughal India, see Patton Burchett, *A Genealogy of Devotion: Bhakti, Tantra, Yoga, and Sufism in North India* (New York: Columbia University Press, 2019), 129–236. On the spread of Vaishnavism among the Rajput-Mughal nobility, see John Stratton Hawley, *A Storm of Songs: India and the Idea of the Bhakti Movement* (Cambridge, Mass.: Harvard University Press, 2015), 190–229; Norbert Peabody, *Hindu Kingship and Polity in Precolonial India* (Cambridge: Cambridge University Press, 2003). For an example of the importance of written texts in determining a sect's legitimacy, particularly at a royal court, see Monika Horstmann, *Visions of Kingship in the Twilight of Mughal Rule* (Amsterdam: Royal Netherlands Academy of Arts and Sciences, 2006), 18–22.

40. Not all modern scholars consider these two compositions by Nagaridas to be *rīti granths*. I follow the opinion of Heidi Pauwels that these two works are structured like and can be read as poetic handbooks. See Heidi Pauwels, "Romancing Radha: Nāgarīdās's Royal Appropriation of Bhakti Themes," *South Asia Research* 25, no. 1 (2005): 55–78.

41. *Pothī* is the term most commonly used for this type of textual artifact; contemporary sources sometimes refer to such manuscripts as *pustak*, *granth*, and on rare occasions, *guṭakā*, usage that can usually be explained in terms of the particular narrative or rhetorical context.

42. Masatoshi A. Konishi, *Hāth-Kāghaz: History of Handmade Paper in South Asia* (Shimla: Indian Institute of Advanced Study and Aryan Books, 2013), 33–83.

43. John T. Platts, *A Dictionary of Urdu, Classical Hindi, and English* (Delhi: Munshiram Manoharlal, 2004; originally 1884), s.v. "basta." See also Francis Joseph Steingass, *A Comprehensive Persian-English Dictionary* (London: Allen, 1892), s.v. "basta."

44. Modern variations include string or cords sewn onto the outer side of the *basta* and tied around it after the folios have been wrapped in the cloth.

45. The early literary historian of Hindi, Shiv Singh Sengar, is said to have purchased *pothīs* "by the *basta*" from individuals liquidating their collections. Kishorilal Gupta, *Saroj-Sarvekṣaṇ; Hindī Sāhitya Ke Itihās Ke Pramukhatam Sūtra Śivasiṁh "Saroj" Ke Kaviyoṁ Viṣayak Tathyoṁ Evaṁ Tithiyoṁ Kā Vivecanātmak Aur Gaveṣaṇātmak Parīkṣaṇ* (Allahabad: Hindustani Academy, 1967), 23.

46. Here I use the concept of the icon as developed by Erwin Panofsky and William J. T. Mitchell; see Erwin Panofsky, *Studies in Iconology: Humanistic Themes in the Art of the Renaissance* (New York: Harper & Row, 1962), and William J. T. Mitchell, *Iconology: Image, Text, Ideology* (Chicago: University of Chicago Press, 1986).

47. On the dating of the *Caurāsī Vaiṣṇavan Kī Vārtā*, see John S. Hawley, *Surdas: Poet, Singer, Saint*, rev. ed. (New Delhi: Primus Books, 2018), 4–8.

48. Catherine Ludvik, *Sarasvatī: Riverine Goddess of Knowledge: From the Manuscript-Carrying Vīṇā-Player to the Weapon-Wielding Defender of the Dharma* (Leiden: Brill, 2007), 229, 231–32.

49. David R. Kinsley, "Sarasvatī," in *Visions of the Divine Feminine in the Hindu Religious Tradition* (Berkeley: University of California Press, 1986), 63–64. In Jain communities, *pothīs* and other

manuscripts become the object of worship once a year during *Jñān Pañcamī*. John E. Cort, "The Jain Knowledge Warehouses: Traditional Libraries in India," *Journal of the American Oriental Society* 115, no. 1 (January–March 1995): 87.

50. As Allison Busch has argued, the significant lexical variation across sixteenth- through eighteenth-century *bhāṣā* literature can be correlated with differences in generic and performative contexts. Allison Busch, "Riti and Register," in *Before the Divide: Hindi and Urdu Literary Culture*, ed. Francesca Orsini (New Delhi: Orient Black Swan, 2010), 84–120. The preference for Sanskrit-derived or Sanskritized vocabulary in vernacular works of *śāstra* did not necessarily preclude the use of terms from Persian and Arabic, especially in technical, specialized, or esoteric contexts. This suggests a sense of technical register that was not defined in terms of a single "language" or family of languages.

51. *Oxford English Dictionary*, 3rd ed. (2018), s.v. "rubric."

52. Ms. 14460 f.1b and Ms. 16595 f.7b, respectively; Rajasthan Oriental Research Institute, Jodhpur.

53. The scribe who copied Bhartrihari's Sanskrit *Nīti-Śataka* along with Indrajit's *bhāṣā* commentary, the *Vivekadīpikā*, in 1735, discharged his dharma as an editor by assigning special numbers to those Sanskrit verses that he identified as interpolations. British Library (formerly India Office Library) Ms. 3318, noted in Ronald Stuart McGregor, "Some Bhartṛhari Commentaries in Early Braj Bhāṣā Prose," *Bulletin of the School of Oriental and African Studies, University of London* 26, no. 2 (January 1, 1963): 319.

54. I use the qualifier "in theory" because, as is evident from a not insignificant number of *pothīs*, some scribes simply copied verse numbers from the original manuscript mechanically as they went along, reproducing earlier numbering errors.

55. On scribal copying rates for Sanskrit manuscripts, see Jürgen Hanneder, "Pre-modern Sanskrit Authors, Editors and Readers," in *Indic Manuscript Cultures through the Ages: Material, Textual, and Historical Investigations*, ed. Vincenzo Vergiani, Daniele Cuneo, and Camillo Formigatti (Berlin: De Gruyter, 2017), 224.

56. It is of course possible that these rubrics aided private study as well as teaching, but the qualifications (*adhikār*) demanded of a reader as well as educational norms generally precluded the possibility of a novice or student reading such works without the guidance of a qualified teacher.

57. As Whitney Cox elegantly and succinctly puts it, works of *śāstra* were models for and of social practices, including pedagogical practices (Opening remarks, "Regimes of Knowledge in the Early Indic World," University of Chicago, February 7, 2020).

58. See Monika Horstmann, "The Example in Dadupanthi Homiletics," in Francesca Orsini and Katherine Butler Schofield, eds., *Tellings and Texts: Music, Literature and Performance in North India* (Cambridge: Open Book Publishers, 2015), 31; Philip Lutgendorf, *The Life of a Text: Performing the Rāmcaritmānas of Tulsidas* (Berkeley: University of California Press, 1991), 113–33; McComas Taylor, *Seven Days of Nectar: Contemporary Oral Performance of the Bhāgavatapurāṇa* (New York: Oxford University Press, 2016).

59. Sundardas, *Jñānasamudra*, vv. 8–9. Manohardas Niranjani, *Vedānta Mahāvākya Bhāṣā*, v. 77–79 (RORI JOD Ms. 26579 f. 21).

60. The section of text found at the end of a manuscript that gives details of the manuscript's copying is given no particular name in contemporary sources. To my knowledge, the term used in modern sources for this element, Sanskrit *puṣpikā*, is not attested earlier than Otto Böhtlingk's *Sanskrit-Wörterbuch*, first published in 1855, which defines it as *die Unterschrift eines Abschnittes in einem Buche*, the "signature of a section of a book" (Otto von Böhtlingk, *Sanskrit-Wörterbuch Herausgegeben von Der Kaiserlichen Akademie Der Wissenschaften*, vol. 5 [St. Petersburg: Buchdr. der K. Akademie der wissenschaften, 1855], 105). The etymology of *puṣpikā* is somewhat mysterious; the literal meaning is mucus of the mouth or penis, which suggests it is a corruption of *puṣpaka* (flower), since drawings of flowers sometimes appear at the end of manuscripts. The English term

"colophon" appears to be of similarly recent vintage, appearing only in the eighteenth century as a term for the title and publication information in a book. *Oxford English Dictionary*, 3rd ed., s.v. "colophon."

61. While some contemporary and earlier Sanskrit and Prakrit manuscripts appear to distinguish between *paṭhanārtha* (for private study) and *vācanārtha* ("to be recited," i.e., to be read aloud for others) no such distinction seems to have been made in the *bhāṣā* manuscripts of this period. The term *vācanārtha* itself does not appear, only *paṭhanārtha*; any distinction must be made on the basis of other types of evidence.
62. On the Islamicate *misṭara*, see François Déroche, *Islamic Codicology: An Introduction to the Study of Manuscripts in Arabic Script* (London: Al-Furqān Islamic Heritage Foundation, 2006), 165–66, and Adam Gacek, *Arabic Manuscripts: A Vademecum for Readers* (Leiden: Brill, 2009), 231–32.
63. See, for example, Ms. 725-1895-1902, the *Gītā Māhātmya* of Anandram, Bhandarkar Oriental Research Institute, f. 146.b.
64. Kali Kumar Dutta points out that several Sanskrit liturgical texts, including the *Parāśara*, *Devīpurāṇa*, *Vahnipurāṇa*, *Cāṇakyasaṁgraha*, and *Nandipurāṇa*, give specific prescriptions for their copying, including the appointment of two qualified scribes: one tasked with reciting the work, the other with transcribing the spoken text. "The Ritual of Manuscripts," *Our Heritage, Bulletin of the Department of Post-Graduate Training and Research, Sanskrit College, Calcutta* XIX, no. 1 (1971): 28–34. The prevalence of this practice among scribes copying vernacular works in unclear.
65. The anthropologist Franz Boaz noted this phenomenon of assimilating unfamiliar sounds into familiar sounds and patterns. "On Alternating Sounds," *American Anthropologist* 2, no. 1 (1889): 47–54.
66. Folio 231.a, Ms. 166699, Rajasthan Oriental Research Institute, Jodhpur. The full colophon is given as the epigraph to the introduction of this book.
67. The dates recorded in the colophons of many manuscripts corroborate this calendar; see also Monika Horstmann, "Dādūpanthī Anthologies of the Eighteenth and Nineteenth Centuries," in *Bhakti in Current Research: Proceedings of the Ninth International Conference on Early Devotional Literature in New Indo-Aryan Languages, Heidelberg, 23–26 July 2003* (New Delhi: Manohar, 2006), 163.
68. Accn. Nos. 83.164.1 and 83.164.2, Brooklyn Museum. Though the hands are similar, subtle differences suggest that the notes in Hindi and the Sanskrit text were inscribed by different individuals.
69. Accn. Nos. 56.27 and 56.28, Chhatrapati Shivaji Maharaj Vastu Sangrahalaya. This manuscript is particularly striking because the illustrations were clearly produced by artists associated with the Mughal imperial atelier, but all inscriptions are in the Nāgarī script—a relatively rare combination suggesting that the patron was a Hindu of considerable rank in the Mughal aristocracy.
70. It might be more accurate to say that this language mixes phrases (in the technical sense used by linguists) from Sanskrit and *bhāṣā*.
71. MS. 27518, Rajasthan Oriental Research Institute, *Rāmacaritamānas* of Tulsidas, copied 1705 CE. MS. 27519, Rajasthan Oriental Research Institute, *Rāmājña Kathā*, copied 1703 CE.
72. The Niranjani and Dadu Panthi monastic orders possess so many of each other's literature that Swami Mangaldas, a Dadu Panthi monk and the author of the *Śrī Haridās Mahārāj Jī Kī Vāṇī*, found it possible to research the history and literature of the Niranjani Sampraday primarily using the collections of the Dadu Panth.
73. Tyler Williams, "Notes of Exchange: Scribal Practices and Vernacular Religious Scholarship in Early Modern North India," *Manuscript Studies* 2, no. 3 (2019): 5–45; Tyler Williams, "The Ties That Bind: Individual, Family and Community in Northwestern Bhakti," in *Bhakti and Power: Debating India's Religion of the Heart*, ed. John Stratton Hawley, Christian Lee Novetzke, and Swapna Sharma (Seattle: University of Washington Press, 2019), 192–202.

74. AC Joshi Library Mss. 97, 105, 1428, Punjabi University Library Mss. 0152:g, 330, 115369. In the Sikh context the term *guṭakā* most often refers to a bound anthology of religious texts that includes the *nitanem* prayers for daily recitation. Unlike the *guṭakā* notebooks described in the previous chapter, these Sikh anthologies were collated and inscribed in a careful and deliberate manner. Even though they are bound they follow the *pothī* format, from the proportions of their folios to the use of para-Sanskrit paratexts in red ink.
75. On the connection between the Sikh Seva Panth and the Dadu Panth with particular reference to the *Pāras Bhāg*, see Monika Horstmann, "*Pāras-bhāg*: Bhāī Aḍḍan's Translation of Al-Ghazālī's *Kīmiyā-yi Sa'ādat*," in *Patronage and Popularisation, Pilgrimage and Procession: Channels of Transcultural Translation and Transmission in Early Modern South Asia, Papers in Honour of Monika Horstmann*, ed. Heidi R.M. Pauwels (Wiesbaden: Harrassowitz Verlag, 2009), 9–21. Anne Murphy has recently proposed a new model for writing the history of Punjabi literature that takes into account the multilingual nature of literary production in the region of Punjab and thereby gives a place for works in Hindi (Brajbhasha and other literary registers) in the history of Punjabi. "Punjabi in the (Late) Vernacular Millennium," in *Early Modern India: Literatures and Images, Texts and Languages*, ed. Maya Burger and Nadia Cattoni (Heidelberg: CrossAsia), 305–28.
76. Williams, "The Ties That Bind," 193–96.
77. For example, the Niranjani monk Dularam ends his 1863 copy of Hariramdas's *Viṣṇusahasranām* (Thousand Names of Vishnu) by writing "copied . . . by the devotee of Vishnu, Dularam, for study by the devotee of Vishnu, Manganiram." Rajasthan Oriental Research Institute, Jodhpur, Ms. 26094, folio 41.b.
78. See for example the copy of Hariramdas's *Chandaratnāvalī* held in the Shri Saraswati Pustakalaya library in Fatehpur, Rajasthan, which was made in November 1794 "for study by the Brahmin Rambaksh."
79. On *subhāṣita* literature, see Ludwik Sternbach, *Subhāṣita, Gnomic and Didactic Literature* (Wiesbaden: Harrassowitz, 1974); on the education of medieval Hindu elites see Daud Ali, *Courtly Culture and Political Life in Early Medieval India* (New York: Cambridge University Press, 2004), 69–96, 170–82. On Persian didactic literature see Muzaffar Alam, *The Languages of Political Islam: India 1200–1800* (Chicago: University of Chicago Press, 2004), in particular part II, "Shari'a, Akhlaq and Governance"; see also Muzaffar Alam and Sanjay Subrahmanyam, "The Making of a Munshi," in *Writing the Mughal World: Studies on Culture and Politics* (New York: Columbia University Press, 2012), 311-338.
80. Busch, *Poetry of Kings*, 146–56.
81. Mss. 2440.28, 3809, and 5983, Maharaja Sawai Man Singh II Museum.
82. On Sanskritic and Vedic revivalism at the Jaipur court, see Horstmann, *Visions of Kingship*.
83. Man Singh Pustak Prakash, Ms. 1215, "Kavit vedānt sambandhī" copied VS 1834 (1778 CE), and Ms. 1359, "Pad saṁgrah," copied VS 1796 (1739/40 CE). The Advaita-related works of Jasvant Singh, including the *Ānandavilās* (1667), *Anubhavaprakāś* (n.d.), *Siddhāntabodh* (n.d.), and *Siddhāntasār* (n.d.), may be found in Vishwanathprasad Mishra, ed., *Jasavantasiṁh Granthāvalī* (Varanasi: Nagari Pracarini Sabha, 1972).
84. For an example of one such conversation between kings and monks, see Rajpurohit's discussion of Advaita Vedānta in the works of Maharaja Jasvant Singh and Sundardas. *Sundar Ke Svapn*, 86–88.
85. The Niranjani monastery at Didwana and Dadu Panthi monastery at Naraina were built on such land grants at the beginning of the seventeenth century. As late as the turn of the nineteenth century, the Rathore queen Pratap Kumari would give custody of the newly constructed Ram temple in the center of Jodhpur to Niranjani monks. *INTACH Newsletter Jodhpur* (2011), 6. On the connection between the Dadu Panth and the Marwar court, see Rajpurohit, *Sundar Ke Svapn*, 83–86.

86. *Bāṁc-* is etymologically related to the Sanskrit *vācayati* "to make speak," a term that was similarly used in the sense "to read." *Hindī Śabdasāgar*, ed. Shyamsundar Das (Kashi: Nagari Pracharini Sabha, 1929), s.v. "bāṁcanā."
87. Individual Niranjani sadhus also achieved prestige at outposts in the Madyadesh region and the Deccan, but the sects' primary area of influence remained confined to Rajasthan.

4. THE GURU'S VOICE AND THE SACRED BOOK

1. *Oxford English Dictionary*, 3rd ed. (2018), s.v. "scripture."
2. The relationship between orality and writing in the way that scripture is imagined and the way it is practiced in these traditions is admittedly complex. Yet all three acknowledge writing as being integral to the character and transmission of their respective scriptures. In Islam, this is reflected in the collective memory of Caliph Abu Bakr, and in Christianity and Judaism in the figure of Moses and the Tablets of the Covenant. See William Graham, *Beyond the Written Word: Oral Aspects of Scripture in the History of Religion* (Cambridge: Cambridge University Press, 1987), 13–14, 53–55.
3. Frits Staal, *The Fidelity of Oral Tradition and the Origins of Science* (New York: North-Holland Publishing Company, 1986); Frits Staal, C. V. Somayajipad, Adelaide De Menil, and M. Itti Ravi Nambudiri, *Agni, the Vedic Ritual of the Fire Altar* (Berkeley: Asian Humanities Press, 1983).
4. Sheldon Pollock, *The Language of the Gods in the World of Men: Sanskrit, Culture, and Power in Premodern India* (Berkeley: University of California Press, 2006), 83.
5. Jinnah Kim, *Receptacle of the Sacred: Illustrated Manuscripts and the Buddhist Book Cult in South Asia* (Berkeley: University of California Press, 2013), 1, 5–9. See also Gregory Schopen, "The Phrase 'sa pṛthivīpradeśaś caityabhūto bhavet' in the Vajracchedika: Notes on the Cult of the Book in Mahāyāna," *Indo-Iranian Journal* 17, no. 3–4 (November 1, 1975): 147–81. Some important questions about this theory have been raised by David Drewes in "Revisiting the Phrase 'sa pṛthivīpradeśaś caityabhūto bhavet' and the Mahāyāna Cult of the Book," *Indo-Iranian Journal* 50, no. 2 (June 1, 2007): 101–43.
6. See John E. Cort, "The Jain Knowledge Warehouses: Traditional Libraries in India." *Journal of the American Oriental Society* 115, no. 1 (January–March 1995): 77–87; Nalini Balbir, "Is a Manuscript an Object of a Living Being? Jain Views on the Life and Use of Sacred Texts," in *The Death of Sacred Texts: Ritual Disposal and Renovation of Texts in World Religions*, ed. Kristina Myrvold (Surrey: Ashgate, 2010), 107–24.
7. A crucial exception is Florinda De Simini's groundbreaking study of the ritual uses of Sanskrit manuscripts from the sixth through seventeenth centuries, *Of Gods and Books: Ritual and Knowledge Transmission in the Manuscript Cultures of Premodern India* (Berlin: De Gruyter, 2016). See also B. N. Goswamy and Dhritabrata Bhattacharjya, eds., *The Word Is Sacred, Sacred Is the Word: The Indian Manuscript Tradition* (New Delhi: Niyogi Books, 2006); Måns Broo, "Rites of Burial and Immersion: Hindu Ritual Practices on Disposing of Sacred Texts in Vrindavan," in *The Death of Sacred Texts: Ritual Disposal and Renovation of Texts in World Religions*, ed. Kristina Myrvold (Surrey: Ashgate, 2010), 91–106; Kali Kumar Dutta, "The Ritual of Manuscripts," *Our Heritage, Bulletin of the Department of Post-Graduate Training and Research, Sanskrit College, Calcutta* 19, no. 1 (1971): 15–44; Frits Staal, "The Concept of Scripture in the Indian Tradition," in *Sikh Studies: Comparative Perspectives on a Changing Tradition*, ed. Mark Juergensmeyer and N. Gerald Barrier (Berkeley: Graduate Theological Union, 1979), 121–24.
8. Although the importance of the material book in *nirguṇ bhakti* and north Indian *bhakti* traditions more generally has been largely neglected, there are a couple of important exceptions

within the realm of Vaishnava studies and, in particular, studies of the Gaudiya Sampraday: Mackenzie Brown, "Purāṇa as Scripture: From Sound to Image of the Holy Word in the Hindu Tradition," *History of Religions* 26, no. 1 (August 1986): 68–86, and Broo, "Rites of Burial and Immersion."

9. William Pinch, *Warrior Ascetics and Indian Empires* (Cambridge: Cambridge University Press, 2006), 17–20, 211–25; Patton Burchett, *A Genealogy of Devotion: Bhakti, Tantra, Yoga, and Sufism in North India* (New York: Columbia University Press, 2019), 107–23.
10. As Wilfred Cantwell Smith writes, "To observe [a text's role as scripture in human life] at all accurately is to recognize its fundamental historical character: its quality of changing over time—and place; of being ever enmeshed in the particular contexts of those in whose lives and societies the role has been played." *What Is Scripture? A Comparative Approach* (Minneapolis: Fortress Press, 1993), 4.
11. In this sense there is a comparative case to be made between the sacred (săcer > sacre) status of liturgical utterance in classical and medieval South Asia and in Byzantine and medieval Europe. The Latin term *scriptūrā* appears to have been used for sacred writings in the Christian tradition from at least the time of Tertullian (second century CE). On scripture as a general category, see Smith, *What Is Scripture?* A comparative approach has been outlined and demonstrated in two influential collections of essays: Graham's *Beyond the Written Word* and Miriam Levering, ed., *Rethinking Scripture: Essays from a Comparative Perspective* (Albany: State University Press of New York, 1989). For a discussion of "scripture" in the South Asian context, see Thomas Coburn's essay, "'Scripture' in India," in the latter volume. For a synoptic account of Buddhist "scripture" and its relationship with writing in South Asia and beyond, see Donald Lopez, *Buddhist Scriptures* (London: Penguin, 2004), xi–xxii. Select studies of the concept of scripture in the context of late medieval and early modern India include Gurinder Singh Mann, "Scriptures and the Nature of Authority: The Case of the Guru Granth in Sikh tradition," in *Theorizing Scriptures: New Critical Orientations to a Cultural Phenomenon*, ed. Vincent Wimbush (New Brunswick: Rutgers University Press, 2008), 41–54. Gurinder Singh Mann, *The Making of Sikh Scripture* (Oxford: Oxford University Press, 2001); Tony Stewart, *The Final Word: The Caitanya Caritāmṛta and the Grammar of Religious Tradition* (New York: Oxford University Press, 2010).
12. Scripture is a "thing" in Latour's sense, i.e. a nonhuman actor that has a life of its own and is understood to *make* meaning as well as to accrue it. Bruno Latour, *Reassembling the Social* (New York: Oxford University Press, 2005), 70–82.
13. Catherine Bell, "Scriptures: Text and Then Some," in Wimbush, ed., *Theorizing Scriptures*, 24.
14. Monier Monier-Williams, *A Sanskrit-English Dictionary* (1890; Oxford: Oxford University Press, 1979), s.v. "grantha."
15. For example, Parashuram Chaturvedi suggests that the creation of sacralized collections of saintly utterance during the seventeenth century transformed that utterance into something esoteric, mysterious, and alienated from the common people, while the new *nirguṇ* writings of the period, oriented toward expanding sectarian influence, lacked the very qualities that distinguished *nirguṇ sant* religion. *Uttarī Bhārat Kī Sant-Paramparā* (Allahabad: Bharati Bhandar, 1951), 520–21.
16. Richard Burghart suggests that the saturation of north India, and particularly the Gangetic Basin, with various monastic orders led to fierce competition for the limited resources of "devotees and disciples, pilgrimage routes and pilgrimage centers, and political patronage." "The Founding of the Ramanandi Sect," in *Religious Movements in South Asia, 600–1800*, ed. David Lorenzen (New York: Oxford University Press, 2004), 233.
17. For a sophisticated analysis of the relationship between canon formation and community consolidation, see Heidi Pauwels, "Hagiography and Community Formation: The Case of a Lost

Community of Sixteenth-Century Vrindāvan," *The Journal of Hindu Studies* 3, no. 1 (2010): 1–38; Vasudha Dalmia, "Hagiography and the 'Other' in the Vallabha Sampradaya," in *Bhakti in Currrent Reserarch, 2001–2003: Proceedings of the Ninth International Conference on Early Devotional Literature in New Indo-Aryan Languages, Heidelberg, 23–26 July 2003*, ed. Monika Horstmann (New Delhi: Manohar, 2006), 115–38.

18. Williams, "Bhakti Kāvya Meṁ Nirguṇ-Saguṇ Vibhājan Kā Aitihāsik Adhyayan (An Historical Study of the Nirgun-Sagun Distinction in Bhakti Poetry)" (MPhil thesis, Jawaharlal Nehru University, 2007), 53–61. The sample size of manuscripts dating to the period 1582–1635 CE is admittedly small (12) and could consequently reflect survival bias, with manuscripts of the Dadu Panth being overrepresented.
19. Williams, "Bhakti Kāvya Meṁ Nirguṇ-Saguṇ Vibhājan," 53–61. On the development of the Pushtimarg's hagiographical tradition in the *Caurāsī Vaiṣṇavan Kī Vārtā* and *Do Sau Bhāvan Vaiṣṇavan Kī Vārtā*, see Richard Barz, "The *Caurāsī Vaiṣṇavan Kī Vārtā and the Hagiography of the Puṣṭimārgā*," in *According to Tradition: Hagiographical Writing in India*, ed. Winand Callewaert and Rupert Snell (Wiesbaden: Harrassowitz, 1994), 43–64; Richard Barz, *The Bhakti Sect of Vallabhācārya* (New Delhi: Munshiram Manoharlal, 1992); Hariharnath Tandan, *Vārtā Sāhitya* (Aligarh: Bharat Prakashan, 1960). For an example of how the Pushtimarg's *vārtā*s appropriated the figures of prominent saints like those of the *aṣṭhachāp* group, see John S. Hawley, "The Sectarian Logic of the *Sūrdas Kī Vārtā*," in *Bhakti in Current Research, 1979–1982*, ed. Monika Horstmann (Berlin: Dietrich Reimer Verlag, 1983), 191–211.
20. Vasudha Dalmia, "The 'Other' in the World of the Faithful," 137–38.
21. On the composition and transcription of the *Caurāsī Vaiṣṇavan Kī Vārtā*, see the introduction to *Caurāsī Vaiṣṇavan Kī Vārtā (Tīna Janm Kī Līlā Bhāvanā Vālī)*, ed. Dwarkadas Parikh (Mathura: Dwarkadas Parikh, 1960); Tandan, *Vārtā Sāhitya*; and Barz, "The *Caurāsī Vaiṣṇavan Kī Vārtā*," 4–8. John Stratton Hawley compares these studies with available manuscript evidence in *Surdas: Poet, Singer, Saint*, rev. ed. (Delhi: Primus Books, 2018), 4–8. On the earliest known manuscript of the *Caurāsī Vaiṣṇavan Kī Vārtā*, see Emilia Bachrach, *In the Service of Krishna: Illustrating the Lives of Eighty-Four Vaishnavas from a 1702 Manuscript* (Ahmedabad: Mapin, 2020).
22. On the history of the Gaudiya Sampraday in Braj, see Alan W. Entwistle, *Braj: Centre of Krishna Pilgrimage* (Groningen: E. Forsten, 1987), 136–50; on the Goswamis see Entwistle, *Braj*, and Stewart, *The Final Word*, 22–23. On the dating of the *Premavilās* and the events described therein, see Stewart, *The Final Word*, 9, 310–11.
23. *Premavilās* canto 13, quoted and translated in Stewart, *The Final Word*, 40–41.
24. Broo, "Rites of Burial and Immersion," 98–100.
25. The *Bhāgavata Purāṇa* in its current form was compiled over the sixth through tenth centuries. For an overview of challenges regarding its dating (from both text-critical and theological points of view) see Mackenzie Brown, "The Origin and Transmission of the Two *Bhāgavata Purāṇas*: A Canonical and Theological Dilemma," *Journal of the American Academy of Religion* 51, no. 4 (1983): 551–67. On the importance of the *Bhāgavata Purāṇa* to *bhakti* traditions in Braj, see John S. Hawley, "Did Surdas Perform the *Bhāgavata-purāṇa*?" in *Tellings and Texts: Music, Literature and Performance in North India*, ed. Francesca Orsini and and Katherine Butler Schofield (Cambridge: Open Book Publishers, 2015), 209–30; John Stratton Hawley, *A Storm of Songs: India and the Idea of the Bhakti Movement* (Cambridge, Mass.: Harvard University Press, 2015), 70–74.
26. Some of these copies may even have been produced by the same artists, or communities of artists, that produced some of the deluxe copies of the *pem kathās* discussed in chapter 1. See Qamar Adamjee, "Strategies for Visual Narration in the Illustrated 'Chandayan' Manuscripts" (PhD diss., New York University, 2011), 226–27.
27. Hawley, *A Storm of Songs*, 150–57; Burchett, *A Genealogy of Devotion*, 99–126.

28. Pinch, *Warrior Ascetics*, 20.
29. Akbar is of course famous for having enjoyed oral religious disputation between experts from different religious traditions. See Darryl Maclean, "Real Men and False Men at the Court of Akbar," in *Beyond Turk and Hindu: Rethinking Religious Identities in Islamicate South Asia*, ed. David Gilmartin and Bruce Lawrence (Gainesville: University Press of Florida, 2000).
30. Abu al-Fazl ibn Mubarak, *Ā'īn-i Akbarī*, ed. Sayed Ahmad Khan (Aligarh: Sir Syed Academy, 2005), 96.
31. For a discussion of the Mughal translation project, see Audrey Truschke, *Culture of Encounters: Sanskrit at the Mughal Court* (New York: Columbia University Press, 2016); see also John William Seyller, *Workshop and Patron in Mughal India: The Freer Rāmāyaṇa and Other Illustrated Manuscripts of 'Abd Al-Raḥīm* (Washington, D.C.: Artibus Asiae, 1999). As Truschke points out, the process of translation itself was not exclusively written nor exclusively in Sanskrit and Persian: the teams of translators, consisting of scholars in both the source and target languages, often communicated with one another in the vernacular, and "translations" often included material taken from sources other than the putative "source text."
32. See Allison Busch, *Poetry of Kings: The Classical Hindi Literature of Mughal India* (New York: Oxford University Press, 2011), 130–65; Allison Busch, "Hidden in Plain View: Brajbhasa Poets at the Mughal Court," *Modern Asian Studies* 44, no. 2 (2010): 279–92.
33. Abu al-Fazl ibn Mubarak, *Ā'īn-i Akbarī*, Book 4, 68. I have taken assistance from H. S. Jarrett's translation (1894) but made revisions to better reflect the technical terminology used by Abul Fazl.
34. On the Qur'an as the archetypical *kitāb* in Islamicate cultures, see George Atiyeh, "Introduction," in *The Book in the Islamic World: The Written Word and Communication in the Middle East* (Albany: State University of New York Press, 1995), 13–18.
35. On Jains and Brahmins at the Mughal court, see Truschke, *Culture of Encounters*. See also Shalin Jain, "Interaction of the 'Lords': The Jain Community and the Mughal Royalty under Akbar," *Social Scientist* 40, no. 3/4 (April 2012): 33–57.
36. On royal patronage of vernacular literature at Amer/Jaipur, see Gopalnarayan Bahura, *Literary Heritage of the Rulers of Amber and Jaipur, with an Index to the Register of Manuscripts in the Pothikhana of Jaipur (Khasmohor Collection)* (Jaipur: Maharaja Sawai Man Singh II Museum, 1976), 24–47. For the continuing importance of such vernacular intellectuals in the eighteenth century, see Monika Horstmann, *Visions of Kingship in the Twilight of Mughal Rule* (Amsterdam: Royal Netherlands Academy of Arts and Sciences, 2006).
37. On Gaudiyas at court, see Horstmann, *Visions of Kingship*, 20–22. On the Pushtimarg and Rajput courts in Rajasthan, see Norbert Peabody, *Hindu Kingship and Polity in Precolonial India* (Cambridge: Cambridge University Press, 2003). On canon and identity in the Ramanandi Sampraday and its relations with the Kacchwaha court, see Burchett, *A Genealogy of Devotion*, 131–34; William Pinch, "Reinventing Ramanand: Caste and History in Gangetic India," *Modern Asian Studies* 30, no. 3 (July 1, 1996): 549–71; William Pinch, "History, Devotion, and the Search for Nabhadas of Galta," in *Invoking the Past: The Uses of History in South Asia*, ed. Daud Ali (Oxford: Oxford University Press, 1999), 367–99.
38. Within the *Guru Granth Sāhib*, the term *dīn* in the sense of religion or faith occurs nine times. Winand Callewaert, ed., *Śrī Guru Granth Sāhib: With Complete Index* (Delhi: Motilal Banarsidass, 1996). Significantly, the term appears in a *sākhī* attributed to Kabir, *sūra soī pahacānie laḍai dīna kai heta*, "he who fights in the name of religion (*dīna*) is recognized to be a warrior," for which other (non-Sikh) sources give a reading of *dhanīṁ* (bride, wife) instead of *dīn*. On the self-recognition of the Sikh tradition as a distinct religion, see Gurinder Singh Mann, *The Making of Sikh Scripture* (New York: Oxford University Press, 2001), 6–10.
39. See Jeevan Singh Deol, "Text and Lineage in Early Sikh History: Issues in the Study of the Ādi Granth," *Bulletin of the School of Oriental and African Studies, University of London* 64, no. 1

(January 1, 2001): 34–58, and Harjot Oberoi, *The Construction of Religious Boundaries: Culture, Identity and Diversity in the Sikh Tradition* (Delhi: Oxford University Press, 1994).

40. The primary sources for Guru Nanak's early life are the collection of hagiographical narratives known as the *janam-sākhīs* ("life testimonies") that date to at least as early as the first half of the seventeenth century. On the *janam-sākhī* tradition, see W. H. McLeod, *Early Sikh Tradition: A Study of the Janam-Sākhīs* (Oxford: Clarendon Press, 1980); for an example of how Guru Nanak's education is remembered in this literature, see *The B40 Janam-Sakhi*, ed. W. H. McLeod (Amritsar: Guru Nanak Dev University, 1980), 5–10. It is significant that the most popular account of Guru Nanak's childhood and education is supposed to have been told by an author of merchant background, Bhai Bala, another *khatri* and companion (along with the Muslim musician Mardana) of Guru Nanak during the latter's travels. See McLeod, *Early Sikh Tradition*, 15–22.

41. For an example in which a merchant transcribes Guru Nanak's compositions, see McLeod, ed., *The B-40 Janam Sakhi*, 157.

42. Bhai Gurdas, *Vārāṁ Bhāī Guradās: Text, Transliteration, and Translation*, ed. and trans. Jodha Singh (Patiala: Vision and Venture, 1998), *vār* 1 *paüṛī* 33.

43. Mann, *The Making of Sikh Scripture*, 12, 35.

44. Hariji Sodhi, *Gosaṭi Guru Miharivānu*, ed. Govindnath Rajguru (Chandigarh: Punjab University, 1974), 175–78. The work ties inheritance of the *pothī* directly to Miharvan (the son and successor of Prithi Chand in the Sodhi lineage) but contains few details about the *pothī* itself. Gurinder Singh Mann has argued on the basis of orthographical, codicological, and textual evidence that, whether or not the *pothī* formerly in the possession of the Sodhis was *the* autographed copy given by the first Guru to the second, its early sections almost certainly date to the 1530s—the lifetime of Guru Nanak—and that the *pothī* has a textual relationship to the so-called Goindval *pothīs*—the other copy of the Guru's compositions that predates the collation of the *Guru Granth Sāhib* in 1604. Mann, *The Making of Sikh Scripture*, 33–39. On the Guru Harsahai *pothī*, see also Pashaura Singh, *The Guru Granth Sahib: Canon, Meaning and Authority* (New Delhi: Oxford University Press, 2000), 32.

45. On the transmission and dating of the Goindval Pothis, see Gurinder Singh Mann, *The Goindval Pothis: The Earliest Extant Source of the Sikh Canon* (Cambridge, MA: Department of Sanskrit and Indian Studies, Harvard University, 1996), 2–23.

46. This is asserted by a representative of the opposing side in the dispute, the aforementioned Bhai Gurdas, companion of Guru Arjan and one of the compilers of the *Guru Granth Sāhib*.

47. Sarupdas Bhalla, *Mahimā Prakāś*, ed. Shamsher Singh Ashoka and Gobind Singh Lamba (Patiala: Bhasha Vibhag, 1970), *sākhī* 11, vv. 3–9.

48. Mann, *The Making of Sikh Scripture*, 47–49.

49. Bhai Gurdas, one of the compilers of the Kartarpur *pothī* (the archetype of the *Guru Granth Sāhib* commissioned by Guru Arjan), makes note of these tensions in his hagiography of the Sikh Gurus. He criticizes the Sodhis by name but does not mention the Bhallas, providing further evidence that the Bhallas had reconciled with Guru Arjan by the time of writing. Bhai Gurdas, *Vārāṁ Bhāī Guradās*, *vār* 1 *paüṛī* 46–47.

50. The *mul mantar* reads, *ikku ōaṁkāru sati nāmu karatā purakhu nirabhāü niravairu akāla mūrati ajūnī saibhaṁ gura prasādi* ("The One Oṁkār, named Truth, the Creator, without fear or hatred, of timeless form, unborn and self-existent, known through the Guru's grace"). Although tradition attributes the formulation of the *mul mantar* to Guru Nanak, its first written appearance is in the Kartarpur *pothī*, as part of Guru Arjan's "signature" or seal.

51. On the construction of the temple complex at Ramdaspur/Amritsar, see Pardeep Singh Arshi, *The Golden Temple: History, Art, and Architecture* (New Delhi: Harman Publishing House, 1989), 8–15.

52. The Sikhs' religious and political aspirations were understood by the Mughal court, which moved quickly to curb Sikh autonomy. Tensions came to a head in 1606 CE when the Mughal emperor

Jahangir had Guru Arjan arrested and executed at Lahore, setting off a century of warfare between the Sikhs and Mughals.

53. *gura puchi likhaũgī jīu sabadi sanehā. Guru Granth Sāhib, rāgu gaüṛī, pūrabī chanta mahala* 1 (p. 242). See also *salok mahala* 3 (p. 84).
54. *Guru Granth Sāhib, gaüṛī guārerī mahalā* 5.
55. *kūṛu likhihi tai kūṛu kamāvahi . . . guramukhi saco sacu likhahi vīcāru. Guru Granth Sāhib, mājh mahalā* 3, 8.21.22.6–7 (p. 123).
56. *jīa jāti raṅgā ke nāva / sabhanā likhiā vuṛī kalam. Guru Granth Sāhib, japujī* 16 (p. 3).
57. *akharī likhaṇu bolaṇu bāṇi / akharā siri saṅjogu vakāṇi / jini ehi likhe tisu siri nāhi. Guru Granth Sāhib, japuji* 19 (p. 4)
58. *hukumi rajāī calaṇā nanaka likhiā nāli. Guru Granth Sāhib, japujī* 1.7 (p. 1).
59. *likhatu miṭai nahī sabadu nīsānā. Guru Granth Sāhib, rāgu gaüṛī asaṭapadīā, mahala 1*, 221.9 (p. 221).
60. This theological idea is articulated and inscribed in early copies of the Sikh anthology themselves, which often contain a list of the Gurus and the dates on which they died titled *calitra jotī joti samāvaṇe kā* ("account of the merging of light into light"). See for example Government Museum and Art Gallery, Chandigarh, Mss. 2002.1.8 (copied 1698), 2002.1.9 (early nineteenth century), and 2002.1.14 (1798). Details are available in Madanjit Kaur and Man Singh Nirankari, *Descriptive Catalogue of Manuscript Section (Gurmukhi), Government Museum and Art Gallery, Chandigarh*, ed. Kirpal Singh (Chandigarh: Government Museum and Art Gallery, 2005).
61. Gurinder Singh Mann speculates that in the seventeenth century, there may have been a practice of commissioning a copy from the Kartarpur *pothī* or other authorized archetype and then having the copy authenticated by the Guru, who would inscribe the *mul mantar* in his own hand. Mann, *The Making of Sikh Scripture*, 82.
62. See for example the 1676 CE copy of the *Ādi Granth* bearing the *nisān* of Guru Tegh Bahadur; Ms. 2002.1.12, Government Museum and Art Gallery, Chandigarh.
63. Gopaldas's *Sarvāṅgī* contains 101 verses attributed to Guru Nanak and seven verses attributed to Guru Angad. Rajjab's *Sarvāṅgī* contains four verses attributed to Guru Nanak and three attributed to Guru Angad. *Rajjabadās Kī Sarbaṅgī, The Sarvāngī of Rajjabdas: A Dadupanthi Source of the 17th Century*, ed. Shahabuddin Iraqi (Aligarh: Granthayan, 1985), 259, 279, 411, 596. *The Sarvāṅgī of Gopāldās, a 17th Century Anthology of Bhakti Literature*, ed. Winand Callewaert (New Delhi: Manohar, 1993). In manuscripts of the *Pañc Vāṇī* type, their compositions occasionally appear in appended sections containing the works of miscellaneous saints.
64. This fourfold formulation of the *nirguṇ* sectarian world elegantly mirrored the idea of the *catuḥ-sampradāy* or the four major Vaishnava *sampradāya*s recognized in Mughal north India at the time. On this and similar foursomes, see Hawley, *A Storm of Songs*, 128–38.
65. Raghavadas, *Bhaktamāl, Caturadās Kṛt Ṭīkā Sahit*, ed. Agarchand Nahata (Jodhpur: Rajasthan Oriental Research Institute, 1965), vv. 341–342.
66. See for example Punjabi University Library, Ms. 115369, a *guṭakā* copied in 1751 CE that contains, in addition to Sikh works, a section of *chappays* by Rajjabdas. On the *Pāras Bhāg* of Bhai Addan and its importance in the Dadu Panth, see Monika Horstmann, "Pāras-Bhāg: Bhāī Aḍḍan's Translation of Al-Ghazālī's Kīmiyā-Yi Sa'ādat," in *Patronage and Popularisation, Pilgrimage and Procession: Channels of Transcultural Translation and Transmission in Early Modern South Asia, Papers in Honour of Monika Horstmann*, ed. Heidi Pauwels (Wiesbaden: Harrassowitz Verlag, 2009), 9–23.
67. Jangopal gives the date of Dadu's passing as the 8th of the month of Jyaiṣṭh, *saṁvat* 1660 (≈ June 1603), but does not indicate whether it was during the "brighter" or "darker" lunar fortnight of the month.

68. As Monika Horstmann has stated, although extant recensions of the work give its date of completion as 1604, portions of the work were almost certainly composed later—perhaps quite late in the seventeenth century. Monika Horstmann, "Dādūpanthi Anthologies of the Eighteenth and Nineteenth Centuries," in *Bhakti in Current Research: Proceedings of the Ninth International Conference on Early Devotional Literature in New Indo-Aryan Languages, Heidelberg, 23–26 July 2003* (New Delhi: Manohar, 2006), 167.
69. *sikha mohana daphtarī bāṁcau hari guna likhe gura su sāṁcau.* Jangopal, *Dādū Janm Līlā*, ed. and trans. Winand Callewaert as *The Hindī Biography of Dādū Dayāl* (Delhi: Motilal Banarsidass, 1988), v. 13.25.
70. Note the division of intellectual and scribal labor in these narratives: it is the saint who speaks and the disciple who writes. The saint speaks spontaneously (*sahaj*), and thus his utterance has an immediacy and primacy. In contrast, the disciple is always listening, and the act of his writing is secondary in terms of both temporality and importance. Christian Novetzke has noted similar pairings of saints with scribes in the Marathi *bhakti* canon; see the verses from Mahipati's *Bhaktivijay* translated in Novetzke, *Religion and Public Memory: A Cultural History of Saint Namdev in India* (New York: Columbia University Press, 2008), 78.
71. Madhavdas, *Sant Guṇ Sāgar*, ed. Bakshiram Shastri (Bhairan: Mahant Ramvallabhdas Swami, 2000), v 25.6. Quoted in Horstmann, "Dādūpanthī Anthologies," 167–68. The translation given here is my own.
72. Madhavdas, *Sant Guṇ Sāgar*, v. 25.5.
73. Winand Callewaert and Bart Op de Beeck, eds., *Nirguṇ Bhakti Sāgar. Devotional Hindī Literature: A Critical Edition of the Pañc-Vāṇī or Five Works of Dādū, Kābir, Nāmdev, Raidās, Hardās with the Hindī Songs of Gorakhnāth and Sundardās, and a Complete Word-Index* (New Delhi: Manohar Publications, 1991), 11.
74. Horstmann and Callewaert both estimate the compilation of the *Pañc Vāṇī* to have occurred around 1600; see Horstmann, "Dādūpanthī Anthologies," 166–67; Callewaert, *Nirguṇ Bhakti Sāgar*, 9–11.
75. On the date of Rajjab's *Sarvāṅgī*, see Winand Callewaert, *The Sarvāṃgī of the Dādūpanthī Rajab* (Leuven: Departement Orientalistiek, 1978), 73–75.
76. Rajjabdas, *Sarbaṅgī*, ed. Brajendra Kumar Sinhal (Raigarh: Brajmohan Samvariya, 2010), v. 1.7.
77. Rajjabdas, *Sarbaṅgī*, v. 1.9.
78. Gopaldas, *Sarvāṅgī*, 520.
79. As Horstmann points out, the ubiquity of writing in the Dadu Panth from its earliest days further supports the hypothesis that these monks collected and edited their material in writing. Horstmann, "Dādūpanthī Anthologies," 176–77.
80. The *Chandaratnāvalī* or *Necklace of the Jewels of Poetic Meter* (1739) of Hariramdas Niranjani appears to have been particularly popular in the Sikh community: see for example Punjabi University Accn. No. O152:g (Hand number 115403).
81. The Rajasthan Oriental Research Institute holds a few copies of the *Vāṇī*: Jodhpur Ms. 22452, 12561; Jaipur Ms. 2165; the majority of copies I have seen are in the possession of the Niranjani community, particularly families that are custodians of Niranjani *samādhi*s and temples. The relative prominence of these families and the connection of copies of the *Vāṇī* to the *samādhi* or temple in which they are found (they are part of the inherited wealth of the superintending families) suggests an important role for the *Vāṇī* in the community's social structure.
82. The first written hagiography of which we have any knowledge (Hariramdas's *Dayāl Jī Kī Pañc Paracāi*, probably not earlier than 1730 CE) not only trails the compilation of the *Vāṇī* by at least forty years but says nothing about Haridas's compositions, let alone their recording. The second major hagiography, Raghunathdas's *Paracāi* (late eighteenth century), similarly makes no mention

of writing or scripture, even though it describes many other aspects of Haridas's life and the early Niranjani community in detail. The other major source of information on Niranjani poets, the *Bhaktamāl* of Raghavdas of the Dadu Panth, makes no mention of writing either in regard to Niranjani saints. Hariramdas, *Dayāl Jī Kī Pañc Paracāi*, Rajasthan Oriental Research Institute Jodhpur Ms. 24778; Raghunathdas, *Paracaī*, in Swami Mangaldas, *Śrī Mahārāj Haridās Jī Kī Vāṇī* (Jaipur: Nikhil Bharatiya Niranjani Mahasabha, 1962), 217–42; Raghavdas, *Bhaktamāl*, vv. 429–44.

83. The *Vāṇī* has ceased to be used in congregational worship but has remained an object of worship during the performance of *āratī* (see below). Members of the community now use printed editions of hymns during *samāj-gāyan*.

84. The *Sarvāṅgī* of Gopaldas also includes poems by Swamidas, a lesser-known saint poet of the Niranjani Sampraday (v. 37.12). Its inclusion is curious, since the only other Niranjani poet included by Gopaldas in his collection is Tursidas, who was quite well known in the region and whose poetry was read in the Dadu Panth.

85. Horstmann, "Dādūpanthī Anthologies," 169.

86. The term "temple" here requires clarification: there are several temple-like structures at Ghadha Dham where communal singing and sermons took place; their courtyards sometime contain Shiva *lingams*, recalling the Niranjanis' links to the Shaivite Nath Sampraday, as well as images of the *saguṇ* Lord Ramachandra of the *Rāmāyaṇa* narrative, reflecting their engagement with Vaishnavism. It is difficult to date the installation of these *lingams* and images; however, their marginal, rather than central, placement within the temples suggest that they were not part of the original structures.

87. This case of "scripture by association" invites comparison with the apocrypha or deuterocanon in post-Reformation Christianity. See Geza Xeravits and Jozsef Zsengeller, eds., *Deuterocanonical Additions of the Old Testament Books: Selected Studies* (Berlin: De Gruyter, 2010).

88. On the origins and development of the *mūl mantar*, see Pashaura Singh, *The Guru Granth Sahib: Canon, Meaning and Authority* (New Delhi: Oxford University Press, 2000), 84–90.

89. Mann, *The Making of Sikh Scripture*, 101.

90. Mann, *The Making of Sikh Scripture*, 101.

91. See Surinder Singh Kohli, *A Critical Study of Ādi Granth, Being a Comprehensive and Scientific Study of Guru Granth Sahib, the Scripture of the Sikhs* (Delhi: Motilal Banarsidass, 1976); Singh, *Guru Granth Sahib*, 125–50. Winand Callewaert and Mukund Lath suggest that the *rāgamālā* portion of the *Ādi Granth* "has no relevance in the *Granth*, except as a kind of tribute to the importance of music for it." *The Hindi Padāvalī of Nāmdev: A Critical Edition of Nāmdev's Hindi Songs with Translation and Annotation* (Delhi: Motilal Banarasidass Publishers, 1989), 97. Although the *rāgamālā* is no doubt a tribute to the importance of music in the tradition, it seems unlikely that Guru Arjan would have included such a technical text in the compilation of the Kartarpur *pothī* without a more specific and sophisticated ideological and aesthetic program.

92. Separating the central body of hymns and the *rāgamālā* is the "seal" (*mundāvanī*) of Guru Arjan, a hymn generally understood to "close" the main section of the *Granth* by declaring *thāla vica tinna vastū païo sata santokha vīcāro*, "Upon this plate, three things have been placed—truth, contentment and contemplation," with the "plate" taken to mean the *Granth* (*Ādi Granth*, 31.M5). The *mundāvanī* appears at the end of the section of hymns in the Kartarpur *pothī*, but other early manuscripts do not consistently place it there. See Singh, *Guru Granth Sahib*, 53–80. Singh also points out that early scribes and likely the gurus themselves marked the folios that they had proofread with the word *śudh*, meaning "pure" or "without corruptions." Singh, *Guru Granth Sahib*, 53–54.

93. Mann, *The Making of Sikh Scripture*, 87–94.

94. This format and subheading are found as early as the Kartarpur *pothī*. Mann, *The Making of Sikh Scripture*, 94–95.

95. Bhai Gurdas, *Varnan Bhāī Guradās*. In *Bhai Gurdas: The Great Sikh Theologion: His Life and Work*, ed. Gurnek Singh (Patiala: Publication Bureau, Punjabi University, 2007).
96. Dadu Dayal, *Śrī Dādū Vāṇī*, ed. Ramprasaddas Swami (Jaipur: Shri Dadu Dayalu Mahasabha, 2007). After comparison with the same verses in the *Sarvāṅgī* of Gopaldas (see below), it appears that the modern editor may have hypercorrected parts of the text in order to render them more like Sanskrit, for example changing *anusvaras* at the end of a line to *m* and changing final *ha* to *ḥ* (*visarga*). Consultation of the early manuscripts of the *Dādū Vāṇī* will be necessary to determine whether the published text or the reading in Gopaldas is original.
97. Gopaldas, *Sarvāṅgī*, vv. 1–4. Rajjab, *Sarvāṅgī*, v. 1. Such language mixing was not peculiar to the Dadu Panth; examples of similar language can be found in the rubrics of the Niranjani *Vāṇīs* described below. Nor was the use of this type of para-Sanskrit limited to devotional communities: there are examples of similar mixing in court poetry as well, as in the opening *virudāvalī* (string of titles) of the *Mānacarit* (Tale of Mānsingh, 1585). *Mānacaritāvalī: Āmber Ke Suprasiddh Rājā Mānasiṃh Ke Carit Se Sambandhit Pāñc Rājasthānī Racanāoṁ Kā Saṅkalan* (Jaipur: Maharaja Savai Mansingh II Museum, 1990), 2.
98. Some copies also include such a representation at the beginning of the manuscript. See Ms. 2165, Rajasthan Oriental Research Institute, Jaipur. This is also found at the end of the Dadu Panthi manuscript from which Winand Callewaert has produced his edition of the *Sarvāṅgī of Gopaldas*, 520.
99. Mann, *The Making of Sikh Scripture*, 39. Pashaura Singh dates the development of the Gurmukhi script to the lifetime of Guru Nanak on the basis of a marginal inscription in the Goindval *pothīs* crediting Guru Angad with developing it under Guru Nanak's supervision. Singh, *Guru Granth Sahib*, 17.
100. Singh, *Guru Granth Sahib*, 16–17. See also Christopher Shackle, *An Introduction to the Sacred Language of the Sikhs* (London: School of Oriental and African Studies, University of London, 1983). On Laṇḍe and Ṭakarī, see Deambi Kaul, *Śāradā and Ṭakarī Alphabets: Origin and Development* (New Delhi: Indira Gandhi National Centre for the Arts, 2008).
101. Mann (*The Making of Sikh Scripture*, 5) and Singh (*Guru Granth Sahib*, 17) both interpret the development of Gurmukhi as an attempt to create a unique Sikh script that would parallel the use of the Nāgarī script by Hindus for their holy texts and the use of Arabic script by Muslims. They do not, however, ascribe to it a political aspect. There are potential problems with ascribing a one-to-one relationship between script and religious community in this period (see Francesca Orsini, "How to Do Multilingual Literary History? Lessons from Fifteenth- and Sixteenth-Century North India," *The Indian Economic and Social History Review* 49, no. 2 [2012]: 225–46), which is why I suggest here that the development of Gurmukhi be looked at as a political as well as religious gesture.
102. Mann, *The Making of Sikh Scripture*, 45. Singh, *Guru Granth Sahib*, 236 (Plate 1), 262 (Plate 2).
103. On the importance of calligraphy at the Mughal court, see Abul Fazl, *Ā'īn-i Akbarī*, 92–98. On calligraphy at regional courts, see Seyller, *Workshop and Patron in Mughal India*.
104. Mann, *The Making of Sikh Scripture*, 11–12.
105. On scribal practices related to the *Ādi Granth* in the early Sikh community, see Singh, *Guru Granth Sahib*, 60–61, 204.
106. This type of textual community was constituted through the types of texts and performances described in chapter 2. On textual communities and literacy, see Brian Stock, *The Implications of Literacy: Written Language and Models of Interpretation in the Eleventh and Twelfth Centuries* (Princeton, NJ: Princeton University Press, 1983), especially part II, "Textual Communities," 88–240. For a selection of essays on such textual communities in India, see Vasudha Dalmia, Angelika Malinar, and Martin Christof, eds., *Charisma and Canon: Essays on the Religious History of the Indian Subcontinent* (New York: Oxford University Press, 2001).

107. Brian Hatcher, *Hinduism Before Reform* (Cambridge, MA: Harvard University Press, 2020), 74–100.
108. Indrani Chatterjee, "Monastic 'Governmentality': Revisiting 'Community' and 'Communalism' in South Asia," *History Compass* 13, no. 10 (2015): 497–511.
109. Christian Novetzke, "Bhakti and Its Public," *International Journal of Hindu Studies* 11, no. 3 (December 2007): 259.
110. For a comprehensive introduction to the *Bhaktamāl*, see James Hare, "Garland of Devotees: Nabhadas' 'Bhaktamal' and Modern Hinduism" (PhD diss., Columbia University, 2011). For an analysis of the role of Nabhadas and the *Bhaktamāl* in the history of the Ramanandi Sampraday and the formation of a *bhakti* public, see Pinch, "History, Devotion, and the Search for Nabhadas of Galta."
111. Nabhadas, *Bhaktamāl*, in Narendra Jha, ed., *Bhaktamāl: Pāṭhānuśīlan Evaṁ Vivecan* (Patna: Anupam Prakashan, 1978), v. 1.
112. On the idea of the *catuḥ sampradāya* in the *Bhaktamāl* and elsewhere, see John S. Hawley, "The Four *Sampradāy*—and Other Foursomes," in *Bhakti Beyond the Forest*, ed. Imre Bangha (New Delhi: Munshiram Manoharlal, 2013), and *Storm of Songs*, 99–147.
113. Nabhadas was almost certainly aware of the Sikhs and the Dadu Panth, and possibly aware of the Niranjani Sampraday, but mentions none of them in the *Bhaktamāl*. See Hare, "Garland of Devotees," 250, and Patton Burchett, *A Genealogy of Devotion*, 228–35.
114. Raghavdas, *Bhaktamāl*, vv. 341–44.
115. Mangaldas, *Śrī Haridas Jī Mahārāj Kī Vāṇī*, 243.
116. They are found, for example, in a *pad* of Ravidas included in the *Ādi Granth*, *rāg gauḍī* 2. 354. Cf. Dadu's description of the divine court in *pad* 369, in Winand Callewaert and Op de Beeck, *Nirguṇ Bhakti Sāgar*, 258.
117. The reification of courtly motifs into political and social practice within the Sikh tradition has received some serious scholarly attention; see Louis E. Fenech, *The Darbar of the Sikh Gurus: The Court of God in the World of Men* (New Delhi: Oxford University Press, 2008); Sukhvindar Bath, *Pañjāb Kā Darabārī Hindī Kāvya* (Delhi: Sanjay Prakashan, 2006); Jagjiwan Mohan Walia, *Parties and Politics at the Sikh Court, 1799–1849* (New Delhi: Master Publishers, 1982). The courtly idiom within the Dadu Panth and Niranjani Sampraday has yet to receive scholarly attention.
118. E.g., *nānaka dara pardhāna so dargahi paidhā jāe*, "O Nanak, they are respected at the Lord's Gate; they are robed in honor in the Court of the Lord." Ādi Granth 4.14.
119. Bhai Gurdas, *Vārāṁ Bhāī Guradās*, vv. 4.31, 5.21, 39.3, 39.12, 40.6.
120. Mann, *The Making of Sikh Scripture*, 131.
121. Madhavdas, *Sant Guṇ Sāgar*, vv. 25.1–6, quoted in Horstmann, "Dādūpanthī Anthologies," 167–68.
122. On the history of various buildings in the complex, see Narayandas, *Śrī Dādū Panth Paricay: Dādū Panth Kā Itihās* (Jaipur: Shri Dadu Dayalu Mahasabha, 1979). The complex features ceremonial gates, a hall of audience, and a *naubat khānā* (drum house), all hallmarks of royal architecture. The temple in which the enshrined copy of the *Dādū Vāṇī* now sits was constructed in the late 1820s and completed in 1833.
123. Madhavdas, *Sant Guṇ Sāgar*, v. 25.5, quoted in Horstmann, "Dādūpanthī Anthologies," 167–68.
124. For the early history of the Dadu Panth, see Narayandas, *Śrī Dādū Panth Paricay*; on militarized sections of the Panth, see James Hastings, "Poets, Sants, and Warriors: The Dadu Panth, Religious Change and Identity Formation in Jaipur State circa 1562–1860 CE" (PhD diss., University of Wisconsin, 2002). A description of the monastery in the nineteenth century can be found in *The Rajputana Gazetteer*, vol. 2 (Calcutta: Office of the Superintendent of Government Printing, 1879), 161. The author observed the processions and *melā* at Naraina in February 2019, during which a copy of the *Dādū Vāṇī* was carried on an elaborate, covered palanquin pulled by a tractor.

125. Quoted in Mangaldas, *Śrī Mahārāj Haridās Jī Kī Vāṇī*, Part II, 179.
126. Author interview with Parik and Shastri families, Didwana, March 2012.
127. A description of the *melā* at the turn of the twentieth century can be found in K. D. Erskine, *The Western Rajputana States Residency and the Bikaner Agency, Rajputana Gazetteers*, vol. 3B (Allahabad: The Pioneer Press, 1908), 184.
128. Mann, *The Making of Sikh Scripture*, 131.

CONCLUSION

1. Quoted in Christopher R. King, "The Nagari Pracharini Sabha (Society for the Promotion of the Nagari Script and Language) of Benares 1893–1914: A Study in the Social and Political History of the Hindi Language" (PhD diss., Columbia University, 1974), 282.
2. These works were followed by publication of the four-volume *Miśrabandhu Vinod* (Delights of the Mishra Brothers) in 1913–1934, which similarly presented an alphabetical compendium of Hindi authors with excerpts. They were preceded by William Price's *Hindee and Hindoostanee Selections*, published in 1827 as a chrestomathy; however, other than a comment on the age of the *rāso* genre, the collection lacked any interpretive or explanatory content.
3. Nevertheless, Grierson's suggestion that Hindi literature reached its apex with the Vaishnava devotional poetry of the sixteenth and seventeenth centuries and began to decline in the eighteenth had a tremendous influence on later historians. *The Modern Vernacular Literature of Hindustan* (Calcutta: Asiatic Society, 1889), xvi–xxiii.
4. The Nagari Pracharini Sabha had already noted the need "to increase the storehouse of the Hindi language through books of the highest quality . . . and articles . . . on the history of newspapers, etc., history, novels, drama, poetry, prose, philosophy, and other such important subjects after critically studying the lives and best works of ancient Hindi poets to make clear their good qualities." Statement dated July 16, 1893, quoted in King, "The Nagari Pracharini Sabha," 283.
5. We can locate the beginnings of modern literary historiography in Bengali in Kashiprasad Ghosh's essay, "On Bengali Writers," published in 1830. I thank Eduardo Acosta for introducing me to this text and for familiarizing me with the outlines of nineteenth-century literary historiography in Bengali.
6. The Nagari Pracharini Sabha approached the Asiatic Society in 1893 for a descriptive list of any vernacular manuscripts in its possession that might relate to Hindi literature and was encouraged when it received the list a year later. King, "The Nagari Pracharini Sabha," 328–29.
7. Georg Bühler, *Detailed Report of a Tour in Search of Sanskrit Mss. Made in Kaśmír, Rajputana, and Central India* (Bombay: Bombay Branch of the Asiatic Society, 1877); Peter Peterson, *A Third Report of Operations in Search of Sanskrit Manuscripts in the Bombay Circle, April 1884–March 1886* (Bombay: Bombay Branch of the Asiatic Society, 1887); Ramkrishna Gopal Bhandarkar, *Lists of Sanskrit Manuscripts in Private Libraries in the Bombay Presidency* (Bombay: Government Central Press, 1893).
8. On library practices during the late medieval and early modern periods, see Pragati Sharma, *Braj Kī Akabarakālīn Pustak Ṭhaur Aur Usakā Sūcī Patra* (Vrindavan: Vrindavan Shodh Sansthan, 2016); Shaikh Allauddin and R. K. Rout, *Libraries and Librarianship during Muslim Rule in India* (New Delhi: Reliance Publishing House, 1996); Dipak Kumar Barua, "Libraries in Medieval India," *The Modern Review* 14, no. 679 (July 1963): 53–58; Bimal Kumar Datta, *Libraries and Librarianship of Ancient and Medieval India* (Delhi: Atma Ram, 1970).
9. For representative European reactions to Indian manuscript libraries, see John E. Cort, "The Jain Knowledge Warehouses: Traditional Libraries in India," *Journal of the American Oriental Society*

115, no. 1 (January–March 1995): 77–87; Bühler, *Detailed Report of a Tour in Search of Sanskrit Mss.*; Peterson, *A Third Report of Operations in Search of Sanskrit Manuscripts.*

10. European attitudes to Indian bibliographical practices can be gleaned from the following note by Whitley Stokes, Secretary to the Council of the Governor-General of Making Laws and Regulations in British India, in 1868: "Now, I venture to assert that no one who has ever seen a Native list of MSS. would think of entrusting a Native with the preparation of such a catalogue [of Sanskrit manuscripts in Indian and European libraries]. The titles of Sanskrit works (which are all that Native lists present) are often fanciful and insufficient . . . The lists, too, are often untrustworthy." In *Papers Relating to the Collection and Preservation of the Records of Ancient Sanskrit Literature in India*, ed. Archibald Edward Gough (Calcutta: Office of Superintendent of Government Printing, 1878), 2.
11. Shyamsundar Das, *Merī Ātmakathā*, 80, quoted in King, "The Nagari Pracharini Sabha," 329–30.
12. *Hastalikhit Hindī Granthoṁ Kī Khoja Kā Pichale 50 Varshoṁ Kā Paricayātmak Vivaraṇ: Vi. 1957–2007; Ī. 1900–50* (Kashi: Nagari Pracharini Sabha, VS 2006 / 1950 CE), 16. This is not the total number of *manuscripts*, since the Sabha possesses multiple copies of many works as well as many manuscripts of works for which no title or author is currently known.
13. For a fascinating account of the aesthetic imagination of antiquarian libraries in colonial India, see David Boyk's history of the Khuda Bakhsh Library in "Provincial Urbanity: Intellectuals and Public Life in Patna, 1880–1930" (PhD diss., University of California, Berkeley, 2015), 178–231.
14. On the communal character of the Nagari Pracharini Sabha and the prominent role played by Brahmin intellectuals in its development and politics, see Christopher Rolland King, *One Language, Two Scripts: The Hindi Movement in Nineteenth Century North India* (Oxford: Oxford University Press, 1994); and "The Nagari Pracharini Sabha," 255–59. On the Khuda Bakhsh library and its collections, see Boyk, "Provincial Urbanity."
15. Ganeshbihari Mishra, Shyambihari Mishra, and Shukdevbihari Mishra, *Miśrabandhu Vinod: Athavā Hindī Sāhitya Kā Itithās Tathā Kavi Kīrtan* (Prayag: Hindi Granth Prasarak Mandali, 1913).
16. Pitambardatt Barthwal, *Traditions of Indian Mysticism Based Upon Nirguna School of Hindi Poetry* (New Delhi: Heritage Publishers, 1978; originally 1936). Much of the conventional scholarly wisdom regarding *nirguṇ* religiosity challenged in this book has its roots in Barthwal's study.
17. Ramachandra Shukla, *Hindī Sāhityā Kā Itihās* (Kashi: Nagari Pracharini Sabha, 1942) (revised edition of introduction to Das, *Hindī Śabd Sāgar*, 1929), 1–2.
18. Shukla, *Hindī Sāhityā Kā Itihās*, 46, 62–76.
19. When Das began the survey in 1899, James Fuller Blumhardt's *Catalogue of the Hindi, Panjabi and Hindustani Manuscripts in the Library of the British Museum* (London: British Museum Press, 1899), which followed methods used for Sanskrit and Prakrit manuscripts, was just being printed. It is likely that Das had seen a copy by 1903.
20. Lawrence Buell, "Literary History as a Hybrid Genre," in *New Historical Literary Study: Essays on Reproducing Texts, Representing History*, ed. Jeffrey N. Cox and Larry J. Reynolds (Princeton, N.J.: Princeton University Press, 1993), 216.
21. In John Wilson's words, the "living and creative spirit of literature is its nationality." "On the Revival of a Taste for Our Ancient Literature," (*Blackwoods*, 1818, p. 266), quoted in April London, *Literary History Writing 1770–1820* (London: Palgrave Macmillan, 2010), 114.
22. When Das summarized the results of the survey of 1904 in his report, he wrote not of manuscripts and their dates but of works and their dates of composition, articulating in a single paragraph the basic scheme of Hindi's chronological development that Shukla would develop into a full-fledged history of Hindi literature twenty-four years later. *Annual Report of the Search for Hindi Manuscripts for the Year 1904* (Allahabad: United Provinces Government Press, 1907), 2.

23. On the Hindi Sahitya Sammelan and its archive, see Aakriti Mandhwani, "The Hindi Library and the Making of an Archive: The Hindi Sahitya Sammelan from 1911 to 1973," *South Asia: Journal of South Asian Studies* 43, no. 3 (May 3, 2020): 522–36.
24. Michel Foucault, *The Order of Things* (New York: Pantheon, 1970), xv.
25. Kali Prasad, *Catalogue of Oriental Manuscripts in the Lucknow University Library* (Lucknow: Lucknow University, 1951).
26. The work found on folios 6 through 20 of the manuscript is a version of the *Kutub Śatak*, an anonymously authored *pem-kathā* composed in prose and in a language thought to be an early form of Khariboli Hindi, a dialect particular to the Delhi region. Mataprasad Gupta speculates its date of composition to be circa 1500 CE. Mataprasad Gupta, *Kutab Śatak Aur Usakī Hindī* (Varanasi: Bharatiya Jnanpith Prakashan, 1967), 5. Gupta appears to have been unaware of this early copy of the work despite using another copy in the institute's collection to produce his edition.
27. On the history of critical editing of Hindi works, see Kanhaiya Singh, *Hindī Pāṭhānusandhān* (Allahabad: Lokbharati Prakashan, 1990).
28. On the formation of a "Hindi public sphere" and the role of textbooks in its creation, see Francesca Orsini, *The Hindi Public Sphere 1920–1940: Language and Literature in the Age of Nationalism* (New Delhi: Oxford University Press, 2002), especially chapter 3, "The Uses of History."
29. S. M. Katre's characterization of manuscript witnesses used for critical editions neatly captures the sensibility of the twentieth-century editor: "Just as the general character of a witness has a bearing on the credibility of any deposition which he makes, so also the general character of a [manuscript] will aid us in determining the value of its testimony with regard to a particular reading." *Introduction to Indian Textual Criticism* (Poona: Deccan College Post-graduate and Research Institute, 1954), 35–36.
30. For example, Shyamsundar Das, at pains to explain the presence of Punjabi features in the language of the primary manuscript source for his *Kabīr Granthāvalī* (Kabir Omnibus) of 1928, speculates that the features must be the result of Kabir's interaction with sadhus coming to Banaras from the Punjab. *Kabīr Granthāvalī* (Kashi: Nagari Pracharini Sabha, 1928), 5–6.
31. Jaroslav Strnad, "Searching for the Source or Mapping the Stream? Some Text-Critical Issues in the Study of Medieval Bhakti," in *Text and Tradition in Early Modern North India*, ed. Tyler Williams, Anshu Malhotra, and John Stratton Hawley (New Delhi: Oxford University Press, 2018), 143–58. For a thoughtful discussion of critical editing practices of South Asian texts, see Jürgen Hanneder, *To Edit or Not to Edit: On Textual Criticism of Sanskrit Works* (New Delhi: Aditya Prakashan, 2017).
32. Christopher Pinney, "Piercing the Skin of the Idol," in *Beyond Aesthetics: Art and the Technologies of Enchantment*, ed. Christopher Pinney and Nicholas Thomas (Oxford: Berg, 2001), 157–79.
33. Henry Hardy Cole, *Catalogue of the Objects of Indian Art Exhibited in the South Kensington Museum, Illustrated by Woodcuts, and by a Map of India Showing the Localities of Various Art Industries* (London: G. E. Eyre and W. Spottiswoode, 1874), 2.
34. For an overview of English government policies and initiatives regarding Indian art, see Pushpa Sundar, *Patrons and Philistines: Arts and the State in British India, 1773–1947* (Delhi: Oxford University Press, 1995).
35. Carol Duncan, *Civilizing Rituals: Inside Public Art Museums* (London: Routledge, 1995), 7–20.
36. Quoted in "CSMVS Centenary 2022–2023," accessed July 1, 2023, https://csmvs.in/csmvs100/.
37. Khandalavala and Chandra announced the discovery in 1961 in "New Documents of Indian Painting," *Lalit Kalā* 4, no. 3: 51–54.
38. A synoptic account of the discovery of copies of the *Candāyan* can be found in Qamar Adamjee, "Strategies for Visual Narration in the Illustrated *Chandayan* Manuscripts" (PhD diss., New York University, 2011), 9–10.

39. A brief critical overview of editions of the *Candāyan* can be found in Shyam Manohar Pandey, "Maulānā Dāūd and His Candāyan," 129–130.
40. The first three decades of art historical writing on the *Candāyan* is summarized in Basil Gray, "The Lahore Laur-Chandā Pages Thirty Years After" (*Chhavi-2: Felicitation Volume*, 1981, 5–9.)
41. A comprehensive list of known folios from this copy of the *Candāyan* and their respective locations and citations can be found in Adamjee, "Strategies for Visual Narration in the Illustrated *Chandayan* Manuscripts," 285.
42. A recent survey of South Asian art, Vincent Arthur Smith's *Art of India*, is representative of the persistence of this scheme: the book divides Indian art into three periods—the "early" (first millennium), "Islamic" (second millennium), and "twentieth century." *Art of India* (New York: Parkstone International, 2012).
43. An important exception is Kalpana Desai and B. V. Shetti's description clarifying the relationship between stanzas and their respective illustrations in *Jewels on the Crescent: Masterpieces of the Chhatrapati Shivaji Maharaj Vastu Sangrahalaya Formerly Prince of Wales Museum of Western India* (Mumbai: Chhatrapati Shivaji Maharaj Vastu Sangrahalaya, 2002), 264. The current signage accompanying folios on display in the museum appears to be accurate.
44. For a synoptic history of the Hindi-Urdu divide and its communal dimensions, see Alok Rai, *Hindi Nationalism* (Hyderabad: Orient Longman, 2001).
45. There are countless examples of libraries and collections being split—often in ways detrimental to the materials and to their study—between India and Pakistan during the ongoing process of Partition (which, with the passing of generations and knowledge, continues to the present). For example, see Andrew Amstutz, "A Partitioned Library: Changing Collecting Priorities and Imagined Futures in a Divided Urdu Library, 1947–49," *South Asia: Journal of South Asian Studies* 43 no. 3 (2020): 505–21.
46. Desai and Shetti, *Jewels on the Crescent*, 142–43; George Michell and Mark Zebrowski, *Architecture and Art of the Deccan Sultanates* (Cambridge: Cambridge University Press, 1999), 213. Michell and Zebrowski, apparently unaware of the contents of the manuscript's colophon and on the basis of the paintings' style and content, suggest that the manuscript was made for a Rajput patron. The only scholar to have examined the text, as far as I am aware, is Dr. Motichand, in "Sūradās Kṛt 'Nal-Daman' Kāvya," *Nāgarī Pracāriṇī Patrikā* 19, no. 2 (1938): 121–38. I thank Thibaut d'Hubert for sharing a copy of the essay.

Select Bibliography

PRIMARY SOURCES (EDITED)

Abu al-Fazl ibn Mubarak. *Ā'īn-i Akbarī*. Ed. Sayed Ahmad Khan. Aligarh: Sir Sayed Academy, 2005.

——. *The Áín i Akbarí of Abul Fazl*. Vols. 1 and 2. Trans. H. Blochmann. Calcutta: Asiatic Society of Bengal, 1872.

——. *The Áín i Akbarí of Abul Fazl*. Vol. 3. Trans. H. S. Jarrett. Calcutta: Asiatic Society of Bengal, 1894.

Anantadas. *The Hagiographies of Anantadās: The Bhakti Poets of North India*. Ed. and trans. Winand Callewaert. Richmond, Surrey: Curzon, 2000.

Banarsidas. *Ardhakathānak*. Ed. and trans. Mukund Lath as *Half a Tale: A Study in the Interrelationship between Autobiography and History. The Ardhakathanaka*. Jaipur: Rajasthan Prakrit Bharati Sansthan, 1981.

Bhalla, Sarupdas. *Mahimā Prakāś*. Ed. Shamsher Singh Ashoka and Gobind Singh Lamba. Patiala: Bhasha Vibhag, 1970.

Callewaert, Winand, ed. *Śrī Guru Granth Sāhib: With Complete Index*. Delhi: Motilal Banarsidass, 1996.

Callewaert, Winand, and Bart Op de Beeck, eds. *Nirguṇ Bhakti Sāgar. Devotional Hindī Literature: A Critical Edition of the Pañc-Vāṇī or Five Works of Dādū, Kābīr, Nāmdev, Raidās, Hardās with the Hindī Songs of Gorakhnāth and Sundardās, and a Complete Word-Index*. New Delhi: Manohar Publications, 1991.

Daud, Maulana. *Candāyan*. Ed. Vishvanath Prasad and Mataprasad Gupta. Agra: K. M. Institute of Hindi and Linguistics, 1962.

——. *Candāyan*. Ed. Parmeshwari Lal Gupta as *Candāyan: Mūla Pāṭh, Pāṭhāntar, Ṭippaṇī, Evaṁ Khojapūrṇ Sāmagrī Sahit*. Bombay: Hindi Granth Ratnakar, 1964.

——. *Candāyan*. Ed. Mataprasad Gupta as *Candayan: Dāūd Viracit Pratham Hindī Sūfī Prem-Kāvya*. Agra: Pramanik Prakashan, 1967.

——. *Candāyan*. Ed. Muhammad Ansarullah. Patna: Idarah-yi Tahqiqat-i Urdu, 1996.

——. *Candāyan*. Ed. Shyam Manohar Pandey. Allahabad: Sahitya Bhavan, 2018.

Dadu. *Dādū Vāṇī*. Ed. Swami Narayandas as *Śrī Dādū Vāṇī: Śrī Dādū Girārtha Prakāśikā Ṭīkā Sahit*. Jaipur: Dadu Mahavidyalaya, 1969.

Ghazzali, *Kīmiyā-yi Sa'adat*. Ed. and trans. Khadiv Husain. Tehran: Shirkat-i Sihami-i Kitabha-yi Jibi, H. 1354.

Gokulanath. *Caurāsī Vaiṣṇavan Kī Vārtā*. Ed. Dwarkadas Parikh as *Caurāsī Vaiṣṇavan Kī Vārtā: Tīn Janm Kī Līlā Bhāvanāvālī. Saṁ. 1752 Kī Prati*. Mathura: Dwarkadas Parikh, 1959.

——. *Caurāsī Vaiṣṇavan Kī Vārtā*. Ed. Kamala Shankar. Lucknow: Uttar Pradesh Hindi Sansthan, 2008.

Gopaldas. *Sarvāṅgī*. Ed. Winand Callewaert as *The Sarvāṅgī of Gopāldās, a 17th Century Anthology of Bhakti Literature*. New Delhi: Manohar, 1993.

Gurdas, Bhai. *Vārāṁ*. Ed. and trans. Jodh Singh as *Vārāṁ Bhāī Guradās: Text, Transliteration, and Translation*. Patiala: Vision & Venture, 1998.

Hariramdas. *Chandaratnāvalī*. Ed. Neha Baid. Jodhpur: Rajasthani Granthagar, 2010.

Ibn Batuta. *The Travels of Ibn Battuta, A.D. 1325–1354*. Ed. and trans. H. A. R. Gibb, B. R. Sanguinetti, C. Defrémery, and C. F. Beckingham. London: Hakluyt Society, 1958.

Jangopal. *Dādū Janm Līlā*. Ed. and trans. Winand Callewaert as *The Hindī Biography of Dādū Dayāl*. Delhi: Motilal Banarsidass, 1988.

Jasvantsingh, Maharaja. *Jasavantasiṁh Granthāvalī*. Varanasi: Nagari Pracharini Sabha, VS 2029.

Jayasi, Malik Muhammad. *Jāyasī Granthāvalī: Padmāvat, Akharāvaṭ, Ākhirī Kalām, Aur Mahrī Baīsī*. Ed. Mataprasad Gupta. Allahabad: Hindustani Academy, 2011 (originally 1951).

——. *Padmāvat*. Ed. Mataprasad Gupta. Allahabad: Bharati Bhandar, 1963.

——. *Padmāvat*. Ed. and trans. George Abraham Grierson as *The Padumāwati of Malik Muḥammad Jaisī*. Calcutta: Asiatic Society, 1896.

Kabir. *The Bijak of Kabir*. Ed. and trans. Linda Hess and Shukdeo Singh. New York: Oxford University Press, 2002 (originally 1983).

——. *Kabīr Granthāvalī*. Ed. Shyamsundar Das. Varanasi: Nagari Pracharini Sabha, 1920.

——. *Songs of Kabir*. Trans. Rabindranath Tagore. New York: Macmillan, 1916.

Kavindracharya Saraswati. *Kavīndrakalpalatā*. Jaipur: Rajasthan Puratattvanveshan Mandir, 1958.

Keshavdas. *Keśav Granthāvalī*. Ed. Vishvanath Tripathi. Allahabad: Hindustani Academy, 1987.

Kutban (Qutban) Suhravardi. *Mirgāvatī*. Ed. Shivgopal Mishra as *Kutuban Kṛt Mṛgāvatī*. Prayag: Hindi Sahitya Sammelan, 1963.

——. *Mirgāvatī*. Ed. Mataprasad Gupta as *Mṛgāvatī: Kutaban Kṛta Sūfī Prem-Kāvya*. Agra: Pramanik Prakashan, 1968.

——. *Mirgāvatī*. Trans. Aditya Behl as *The Magic Doe: Qutban Suhravardi's Mirigavati*. Ed. Wendy Doniger. Oxford: Oxford University Press, 2011.

Manjhan, Mir Sayyid. *Madhumālatī*. Ed. Mataprasad Gupta as *Mañjhan Kṛta Madhumālatī: Bhūmikā, Sampādit Pāṭh, Pāthāntar, Arth Aur Śabdānukramaṇī*. Allahabad: Mitra Prakashan, 1961.

——. *Madhumālatī*. Ed. and trans. Aditya Behl and Simon Weightman as *Madhumalati: An Indian Sufi Romance*. Oxford: Oxford University Press, 2000.

——. *Madhumālatī*. Ed. Vaqarula Hasan Siddiqi. Rampur: Rampur Raza Library, 2005.

Mann, Gurinder Singh. *The Goindval Pothis: The Earliest Extant Source of the Sikh Canon*. Cambridge, Mass.: Harvard University Press, 1996.

Nabhadas. *Bhaktamāl*. Ed. Rupkala as *Bhaktamal, with Commentary of Priyadas*. Lucknow: Tejkumar Press, 1914.

——. *Bhaktamāl*. Ed. Narendar Jha as *Bhaktamāl, Pāṭhānuśīlan Evaṁ Vivecan*. Patna: Anupam Prakashan, 1978.

Namdev. *The Hindi Padāvalī of Nāmdev: A Critical Edition of Nāmdev's Hindi Songs with Translation and Annotation*. Ed. and trans. Winand M. Callewaert and Mukunda Lath. Delhi: Motilal Banarasidass, 1989.

Nandadas. *Nandadās Granthāvalī*. Ed. Brajratan Das. Kashi: Nagari Pracharini Sabha, VS 2014.

Nizamuddin Auliya. *Fawa'id al-Fu'ad*. Compiled by Amir Hasan Sijzi. Ed. and trans. Bruce Lawrence as *Morals for the Heart: Conversations of Shaykh Nizam Ad-Din Awliya Recorded by Amir Hasan Sijzi*. New York: Paulist Press, 1992.

Raghavadas. *Bhaktamāl*. Ed. Agarchand Nahata. Jodhpur: Rajasthan Oriental Research Institute, 1965.

——. *Bhaktamāl*. Ed. Swami Narayandas. Jaipur: Sri Dadu Dayalu Mahasabha, VS 2026.
Rajjabdas. *Sarvāṅgī*. Ed. Winand Callewaert as *The Sarvāṅgī of the Dādūpanthī Rajab*. Leuven: Departement Oriëntalistiek, Katholieke Universiteit, 1978.
——. *Sarvāṅgī*. Ed. Shahabuddin Iraqi as *Rajjabadās Kī Sarbaṅgī, The Sarbangi of Rajjabdas: A Dadupanthi Source of the 17th Century*. Aligarh: Granthayan, 1985.
——. *Sarvāṅgī*. Ed. Brajendrakumar Sinhal as *Rajjab Kī Sarabaṅgī*. Raigarh: Brajmohan Samvariya, 2010.
Ravidas. *The Life and Works of Raidās*. Ed. Winand Callewaert and Peter Friedlander. New Delhi: Manohar Publishers & Distributors, 1992.
Sodhi, Hariji. *Gosaṭī Guru Miharivānu*. Ed. Govindnath Rajguru. Chandigarh: Punjab University, 1974.
Sundardas. *Sundaradās Granthāvalī*. Ed. Harinarayan Sharma. 2 vols. Calcutta: Rajasthan Research Society, 1937.
——. *Sundaradās Granthāvalī*. Ed. Swami Narayandas. Jaipur: Shri Dadu Dayalu Mahasabha, 1989.
Tulsidas. *Rāmacaritamānas*. Ed. Shyamsundar Das. Prayag: Nagari Pracharini Sabha, 1903.
——. *Rāmacaritamānas*. Gorakhpur: Gita Press, 2003.
Vishnudas. *Mahābhārata: Pāṇḍav-Carit*. Gwalior: Vidya Mandir Prakashan, 1973.
Zuhuri, Nur al-din Muhammad. "*Sih Nasr-i Ẓuhūrī*." Ed. Sayyid Muhammad Yunus Jaʿfari. *Qand-i Pārsī* 63–64 (2014): 199–256.

SECONDARY SOURCES

Agarwal, Purushottam. *Akath Kahānī Prem Kī: Kabīr Kī Kavitā Aur Unakā Samay*. New Delhi: Rajkamal, 2009.
Aitken, Molly Emma. *The Intelligence of Tradition in Rajput Court Painting*. New Haven, Conn.: Yale University Press, 2010.
——. "Parataxis and the Practice of Reuse, from Mughal Margins to Mīr Kalān Khān." *Archives of Asian Art* 59 (2009): 81–103.
Alam, Muzaffar. *The Languages of Political Islam: India, 1200–1800*. London: Hurst, 2004.
—— and Sanjay Subrahmanyam. *Writing the Mughal World: Studies on Culture and Politics*. New York: Columbia University Press, 2012.
Allauddin, Shaikh, and R. K. Rout. *Libraries and Librarianship during Muslim Rule in India*. New Delhi: Reliance Publishing House, 1996.
Allen, Michael. "Greater Advaita Vedānta: The Case of Niścaldās." *International Journal of Hindu Studies* 21 (2017): 275–97.
——. "Greater Advaita Vedānta: The Case of Sundardās." *Journal of Indian Philosophy* 48 (2020): 49–78.
——. *The Ocean of Inquiry: Niscaldas and the Premodern Origins of Modern Hinduism*. New York: Oxford University Press, 2022.
Amsler, Mark. *Affective Literacies: Writing and Multilingualism in the Late Middle Ages*. Turnhout: Brepols, 2012.
Arberry, A. J. *Specimens of Arabic and Persian Palæography*. London: India Office, 1939.
Arshi, Pardeep Singh. *The Golden Temple: History, Art, and Architecture*. New Delhi: Harman, 1989.
Atiyeh, George N., ed. *The Book in the Islamic World: Written Word and Communication in the Middle East*. Albany: State University of New York Press, 1995.
Babb, Lawrence A., Varsha Joshi, and Michael W. Meister, eds. *Multiple Histories: Culture and Society in the Study of Rajasthan*. Jaipur: Rawat Publications, 2002.
Bachrach, Emilia. *In the Service of Krishna: Illustrating the Lives of Eighty-Four Vaishnavas from a 1702 Manuscript*. Ahmedabad: Mapin, 2020.

Bailey, Thomas Grahame. "Hindi Prose before the Nineteenth Century." *Bulletin of the School of Oriental Studies* 3, no. 3 (1924): 523–26.

Bangha, Imre. *The First Published Anthology of Hindi Poets: Thomas Duer Broughton's Selections from the Popular Poetry of the Hindoos, 1814*. Delhi: Rainbow Publishers, 2000.

——, ed. *Bhakti Beyond the Forest: Current Research on Early Modern Literatures in North India, 2003–2009*. New Delhi: Manohar Publishers & Distributors, 2013.

Barber, Karin. *The Anthropology of Texts, Persons and Publics: Oral and Written Culture in Africa and Beyond*. Cambridge: Cambridge University Press, 2007.

——. "Text and Performance in Africa." *Bulletin of the School of Oriental and African Studies* 66, no. 3 (2003): 324–25.

Barthes, Roland. *The Rustle of Language*. Trans. Richard Howard. New York: Hill and Wang, 1986 (originally 1971).

Barthwal, Pitambardatt. *Traditions of Indian Mysticism Based upon the Nirguṇa School of Hindi Poetry*. New Delhi: Heritage, 1978 (originally 1933).

——. *Pītambardatt Baṛthvāl Ke Śreṣṭh Nibandh*. Ed. Govind Catak. New Delhi: Takshila Prakashan, 1978.

Barua, Dipak Kumar. "Libraries in Medieval India." *The Modern Review* 14, no. 679 (July 1963): 53–58.

Barz, Richard. *The Bhakti Sect of Vallabhācārya*. New Delhi: Munshiram Manoharlal, 1992.

Basu, Ratna, and Karunasindhu Das. *Aspects of Manuscriptology: Puṁthibidyāra Digdarśana*. Kolkata: The Asiatic Society, 2005.

Bausi, Alessandro, Michael Friedrich, and Marilena Maniachi, eds. *The Emergence of Multiple-Text Manuscripts*. Berlin: De Gruyter, 2019.

Beach, Milo Cleveland. *Mughal and Rajput Painting*. New Cambridge History of India. New York: Cambridge University Press, 1992.

Beck, Guy L. *Sonic Liturgy: Ritual and Music in Hindu Tradition*. Columbia: University of South Carolina Press, 2012.

——. *Sonic Theology*. Columbia: University of South Carolina Press, 1993.

Bedekar, V. H. *Chandigarh Museum Laur-Chanda: A Study in Styles*. Chandigarh: Government Museum and Art Gallery, 2006.

Behl, Aditya. *Love's Subtle Magic: An Indian Islamic Literary Tradition, 1379–1545*. New York: Oxford University Press, 2012.

Bhati, Hukamsingh. *Rājasthān Meṁ Granthoṁ Kī Khoj*. Jodhpur: Rajasthani Shodh Sansthan and Rajasthani Granthagar, 2004.

Bhattarai, Bidur. *Dividing Texts: Conventions of Visual Text-Organization in Nepalese and North Indian Manuscripts*. Berlin: De Gruyter, 2020.

Bloom, Jonathan. *Paper before Print: The History and Impact of Paper in the Islamic World*. New Haven, Conn.: Yale University Press, 2001.

Brac de la Perrière, Éloïse. *L'art du livre dans l'Inde des sultanats*. Paris: Pressed de l'Université Paris-Sorbonne, 2008.

Brend, Barbara. *Perspectives on Persian Painting: Illustrations to Amīr Khusrau's Khamsah*. London: Routledge-Curzon, 2003.

Bronner, Yigal, Whitney M. Cox, and Lawrence J. McCrea, eds. *South Asian Texts in History: Critical Engagements with Sheldon Pollock*. Ann Arbor, Mich.: Association for Asian Studies, 2011.

Brown, Bill. "Thing Theory." *Critical Inquiry* 28, no. 1 (October 1, 2001): 1–22.

Brown, Mackenzie. "Purāṇa as Scripture: From Sound to Image of the Holy Word in the Hindu Tradition." *History of Religions* 26, no. 1 (August 1986): 68–87.

Bryant, Kenneth E. *Poems to the Child-God: Structures and Strategies in the Poetry of Sūrdās*. Berkeley: University of California Press, 1978.

Buell, Lawrence. "Literary History as a Hybrid Genre." In *New Historical Literary Study: Essays on Reproducing Texts, Representing History*, ed. Jeffrey N. Cox and Larry J. Reynolds, 216–29. Princeton, N.J.: Princeton University Press, 1993.

Burchett, Patton. "Bitten by the Snake: Early Modern Devotional Critiques of Tantra-Mantra." *The Journal of Hindu Studies* 6, no. 1 (May 1, 2013): 1–20.

——. *A Genealogy of Devotion: Bhakti, Tantra, Yoga, and Sufism in North India*. New York: Columbia University Press, 2019.

Busch, Allison. "The Anxiety of Innovation: The Practice of Literary Science in the Hindi Riti Tradition." *Comparative Studies of South Asia, Africa and the Middle East* 24, no. 2 (2004): 45–59.

——. *Braj Beyond Braj: Classical Hindi in the Mughal World*. New Delhi: India International Centre, 2009.

——. "Hidden in Plain View: Brajbhasa Poets at the Mughal Court." *Modern Asian Studies* 44, no. 2 (2010): 267–309.

——. *Poetry of Kings: The Classical Hindi Literature of Mughal India*. New York: Oxford University Press, 2011.

——. "Portrait of a Raja in a Badshah's World: Amrit Rai's Biography of Man Singh (1585)." *Journal of the Economic and Social History of the Orient* 55, no. 2/3 (January 1, 2012): 287–328.

—— and Thomas de Bruijn, eds. *Culture and Circulation: Literature in Motion in Early Modern India*. Leiden: Brill, 2014.

Callewaert, Winand, and Rupert Snell, eds. *According to Tradition: Hagiographical Writing in India*. Wiesbaden: Harrassowitz, 1994.

Callewaert, Winand, and Dieter Taillieu, eds. *International Conference on Early Literature in New Indo-Aryan Languages. Devotional Literature in South Asia: Current Research, 1997–2000: Proceedings of the Eighth International Conference on Early Literature in New Indo-Aryan Languages, Leuven, 23–26 August 2000*. New Delhi: Manohar Publishers & Distributors, 2002.

Case, Margaret, ed. *Govindadeva: A Dialogue in Stone*. New Delhi: Indira Gandhi National Centre for Arts, 1996.

Caube, Vrajabihari. *Lectures on Manuscriptology*. Hoshiarpur: Katyayana Vaidik Sahitya Prakashan, 2004.

Chagtai, Muhammad Abdulla. *Painting during the Sultanate Period (C.E. 712–1575)*. Lahore: Kitab Khana-i-Navras, 1963.

Chakravorty, Swapan, and Abhijit Gupta, eds. *Founts of Knowledge: Book History in India*. New Delhi: Orient Blackswan, 2016.

——, eds. *Moveable Type: Book History in India*. Ranikhet: Permanent Black, 2008.

——, eds. *Print Areas: Book History in India*. Delhi: Permanent Black, 2004.

Chandra, Satish. *Essays on Medieval Indian History*. New Delhi: Oxford University Press, 2003.

Chang, Ku-ming (Kevin), Anthony Grafton, and Glenn W. Most, eds. *Impagination—Layout and Materiality of Writing and Publication: Interdisciplinary Approaches from East and West*. Berlin: De Gruyter, 2020.

Chatterjee, Indrani. "Monastic 'Governmentality': Revisiting 'Community' and 'Communalism' in South Asia." *History Compass* 13, no. 10 (2015): 497–511.

Chatterjee, Kumkum. "Scribal Elites in Sultanate and Mughal Bengal." *Indian Economic & Social History Review* 47, no. 4 (October 1, 2010): 445–72.

Chaturvedi, Parashuram. *Uttarī Bhārat Kī Sant-Paramparā*. Allahabad: Bharati Bhandar, 1951.

Chitara, Gopikishan. *Rāmasanehī Santakavi Dāyaladās Aur Unakā Kāvya*. Jalore: Shrimati Naju Devi Solanki, 2006.

Cohn, Bernard S. *Colonialism and Its Forms of Knowledge: The British in India*. Princeton, N.J.: Princeton University Press, 1996.

Coomaraswamy, Ananda Kentish. *The Essential Ananda K. Coomaraswamy*. Ed. Rama P. Coomaraswamy. Bloomington: World Wisdom, 2004.

Cort, John E. "The Intellectual Formation of a Jain Monk: A Śvetāmbara Monastic Curriculum." *Journal of Indian Philosophy* 29 (2001): 22.

——. "The Jain Knowledge Warehouses: Traditional Libraries in India." *Journal of the American Oriental Society* 115, no. 1 (January–March 1995): 77–87.

——. "The Svetambar Murtipujak Jain Mendicant." *Man*, New Series, 26, no. 4 (December 1, 1991): 651–71.

Crook, Nigel. *The Transmission of Knowledge in South Asia: Essays on Education, Religion, History, and Politics*. New York: Oxford University Press, 1996.

d'Hubert, Thibaut. "La Diffusion et l'usage Des Manuscrits Bengalis Dans l'est Du Bengale, XVIIe-XXe Siècles." In *Eurasian Studies Special Issue: Lecteurs et Copistes Dans Les Traditions Manuscrites Iraniennes, Indiennes et Centrasiatiques (Scribes and Readers in Iranian, Indian And Central Asian Manuscript Traditions), Eurasian Studies* XII, no. 1–2 (2014): 325–60.

——. *In the Shade of the Golden Palace: Alaol and Middle Bengali Poetics in Arakan*. New York: Oxford University Press, 2018.

Dalmia, Vasudha. "Hagiography and the 'Other' in the Vallabha Sampradaya," in *Bhakti in Currrent Reserarch, 2001–2003: Proceedings of the Ninth International Conference on Early Devotional Literature in New Indo-Aryan Languages, Heidelberg, 23–26 July 2003*, ed. Monika Horstmann, 115–38. Delhi: Manohar, 2006.

Dalmia, Vasudha, and Munis Daniyal Faruqui, eds. *Religious Interactions in Mughal India*. New Delhi: Oxford University Press, 2014.

Dalmia, Vasudha, Angelika Malinar, and Martin Christof, eds. *Charisma and Canon: Essays on the Religious History of the Indian Subcontinent*. New York: Oxford University Press, 2001.

Darnton, Robert. *The Case for Books: Past, Present, and Future*. New York: Public Affairs, 2009.

Das, Shyamsundar. *Sāhityālocan Arthāt Sāhitya Ke Aṅgoṁ Aur Upāṅgoṁ Kā Vivecan Aur Nirūpaṇ*. Prayag: Indian Press, 1959.

Datta, Bimal Kumar. *Libraries and Librarianship of Ancient and Medieval India*. Delhi: Atma Ram, 1970.

de Bruijn, Thomas. *Ruby in the Dust: Poetry and History in Padmāvat by the South Asian Sufi Poet Muḥammad Jāyasī*. Leiden: Leiden University Press, 2012.

De Simini, Florinda. *Of Gods and Books: Ritual and Knowledge Transmission in the Manuscript Cultures of Premodern India*. Berlin: De Gruyter, 2016.

Deibert, Ronald. *Parchment, Printing, and Hypermedia: Communication in World Order Transformation*. New York: Columbia University Press, 1997.

Deol, Jeevan Singh. "Text and Lineage in Early Sikh History: Issues in the Study of the Adi Granth." *Bulletin of the School of Oriental and African Studies, University of London* 64, no. 1 (January 1, 2001): 34–58.

Derrida, Jacques. *Of Grammatology*. Baltimore, Md.: Johns Hopkins University Press, 1998.

Déroche, François. *Islamic Codicology: An Introduction to the Study of Manuscripts in Arabic Script*. London: Al-Furqān Islamic Heritage Foundation, 2006.

Desai, Ziyaud-Din A., and A. K. Sharma. *Purā-Prakāśa: Recent Researches in Epigraphy, Numismatics, Manuscriptology, Persian Literature, Art, Architecture, Archaeology, History and Conservation: Dr. Z.A. Desai Commemoration Volume*. Delhi: Bharatiya Kala Prakashan, 2003.

Digby, Simon. "'Abd Al-Quddus Gangohi (1456–1537 AD): The Personality and Attitudes of a Medieval Indian Sufi." In *Medieval India: A Miscellany*, 3:1–66. Aligarh: Aligarh Muslim University, 1975.

——. "Before Timur Came: Provincialization of the Delhi Sultanate through the Fourteenth Century." *Journal of the Economic and Social History of the Orient* 47, no. 3 (2004): 298–356.

Dirks, Nicholas B. *Autobiography of an Archive: A Scholar's Passage to India*. Ranikhet: Permanent Black, 2015.

Dube, Uday Shankar. *Hastalikhit Hindī Granthoṁ Kī Khoj Kā Itihās*. Allahabad: Hindustani Academy, 2009.

Dutta, Kali Kumar. "The Ritual of Manuscripts." *Our Heritage, Bulletin of the Department of Post-Graduate Training and Research, Sanskrit College, Calcutta* XIX, no. 1 (1971): 17–44.

Dvivedi, Hajariprasad. *Hindī Sāhitya Kī Bhūmikā*. Bombay: Hindi Granth Ratnakar, 1963.

——. *Kabīr: Kabīr Ke Vyaktitva, Sāhitya Aur Dārśanik Vicāroṁ Kī Ālocanā*. 3rd ed. Bombay: Hindi Granth Ratnakar, 1950.

Eck, Diana L. *Darśan: Seeing the Divine Image in India*. New York: Columbia University Press, 1996.

Elliot, Simon, Andrew Nash, and Ian Willison, eds. *Literary Cultures and the Material Book*. London: The British Library, 2007.

Eisenstein, Elizabeth L. *The Printing Press as an Agent of Change: Communications and Cultural Transformations in Early-Modern Europe*. New York: Cambridge University Press, 1985.

Entwistle, Alan W. *Braj, Centre of Krishna Pilgrimage*. Groningen: E. Forsten, 1987.

——, ed. *Studies in Early Modern Indo-Aryan Languages, Literature, and Culture: Research Papers, 1992–1994, Presented at the Sixth Conference on Devotional Literature in New Indo-Aryan Languages, Held at Seattle, University of Washington, 7–9 July 1994*. New Delhi: Manohar, 1999.

Ernst, Carl W. *Eternal Garden: Mysticism, History, and Politics at a South Asian Sufi Center*. Albany: State University of New York Press, 1992.

——. "The Interpretation of the Sufi Tradition in India: The Shama 'il al-Atqiya of Rukn al-Dīn Kāshānī." *Sufi* 22 (1994): 5–10.

——. "The Islamization of Yoga in the 'Amrtakunda' Translations." *Journal of the Royal Asiatic Society*, Third Series, 13, no. 2 (July 1, 2003): 199–226.

Falk, Toby, Ellen S. Smart, and Robert Skelton. *Indian Painting: Mughal and Rajput and a Sultanate Manuscript*. London: P. & D. Colnaghi, 1978.

Farquhar, J. N. *An Outline of the Religious Literature of India*. Delhi: Motilal Banarsidass, 1967 (originally 1920).

Faruqi, Shamsurrahman. *Early Urdu Literary Culture and History*. New York: Oxford University Press, 2001.

Fenech, Louis E. *The Darbar of the Sikh Gurus: The Court of God in the World of Men*. New Delhi: Oxford University Press, 2008.

Finkelstein, David. *An Introduction to Book History*. New York: Routledge, 2005.

——and Alistair McCleery, eds. *The Book History Reader*. New York: Routledge, 2002.

Fisher, Elaine M. *Hindu Pluralism: Religion and the Public Sphere in Early Modern South India*. Oakland: University of California Press, 2017.

Flood, Finbarr Barry. "Islamic Identities and Islamic Art: Inscribing the Qur'an in Twelfth-Century Afghanistan." In *Dialogues in Art History, from Mesopotamian to Modern: Readings for a New Century*, ed. Elizabeth Cropper, 91–118. Washington, D.C.: National Gallery of Art, 2009.

——. *Objects of Translation: Material Culture and Medieval Hindu-Muslim Encounter*. Princeton, N.J.: Princeton University Press, 2009.

Freer, Alexander. "Rhythm as Coping." *New Literary History* 46, no. 3 (2015): 549–68.

Freitag, Sandria B., ed. *Culture and Power in Banaras: Community, Performance, and Environment, 1800–1980*. Berkeley: University of California Press, 1989.

Friedlander, Peter. *Kabir Poems in Transformation: A Fountain of Creativity*. Delhi: Primus Books, 2022.

Fuller, C. J. "Orality, Literacy and Memorization: Priestly Education in Contemporary South India." *Modern Asian Studies* 35, no. 1 (2001): 1–31.

Gacek, Adam. *Arabic Manuscripts: A Vademecum for Readers*. Leiden: Brill, 2009.

Garcin de Tassy, Joseph Héliodore Sagesse Vertu. *Histoire de la littérature hindoui et hindoustani*. Paris: Oriental Translation Committee of Great Britain and Ireland, 1839.

Genette, Gérard. *Paratexts: Thresholds of Interpretation*. New York: Cambridge University Press, 1997.

Ghori, S. A. K., and A. Rahman. "Paper Technology in Medieval India." *Indian Journal of History of Science* 1, no. 2 (1966): 133–49.

Ghose, Madhuvanti, ed. *Gates of the Lord: The Tradition of Krishna Paintings*. Chicago: Art Institute of Chicago, 2015.

Goody, Jack. *The Logic of Writing and the Organization of Society*. New York: Cambridge University Press, 1986.

Gordon, Stewart, ed. *Robes of Honour: Khil'at in Pre-Colonial and Colonial India*. New Delhi: Oxford University Press, 2003.

Goswamy, B. N. *A Jainesque Sultanate Shahnama and the Context of Pre-Mughal Painting in India*. Zürich: Museum Rietberg, 1988.

——and Dhritabrata Bhattacharjya, eds. *The Word Is Sacred, Sacred Is the Word: The Indian Manuscript Tradition*. New Delhi: Niyogi Books, 2006.

Gough, Archibald Edward. *Papers Relating to the Collection and Preservation of the Records of Ancient Sanskrit Literature in India*. Calcutta: Office of Superintendent of Government Printing, 1878.

Grafton, Anthony. *Codex in Crisis*. New York: Crumpled Press, 2008.

Grafton, Anthony, and Glenn W. Most, eds. *Canonical Texts and Scholarly Practices: A Global Comparative Approach*. Cambridge: Cambridge University Press, 2016.

Graham, William A. *Beyond the Written Word: Oral Aspects of Scripture in the History of Religion*. Cambridge: Cambridge University Press, 1987.

Gray, Basil. "The Lahore Laur-Chandā Pages Thirty Years After." *Chhavi-2: Felicitation Volume*. 5–9. Banaras: Bharat Kala Bhavan, 1981.

Green, Nile. "The Uses of Books in a Late Mughal Takiyya: Persianate Knowledge Between Person and Paper." *Modern Asian Studies* 44, no. 2 (March 1, 2010): 241–65.

Grewal, J. S. *Sikh Ideology, Polity, and Social Order: From Guru Nanak to Maharaja Ranjit Singh*. New Delhi: Manohar, 2007.

Grierson, George Abraham. *A Handbook to the Kaithi Character*. Calcutta: Thacker, 1899.

——. *The Languages of India: Being a Reprint of the Chapter on Languages, Contributed by George Abraham Grierson to the Report on the Census of India, 1901, together with the Census Statistics of Language*. Calcutta: Office of the Superintendent of Government Printing, 1903.

——. *Linguistic Survey of India Vol. IX, Indo-Aryan Family, Central Group, Part II*. Calcutta: Office of the Superintendent Government Printing, 1908.

——. *The Modern Vernacular Literature of Hindustan*. Calcutta: Asiatic Society, 1889.

Gupta, Kishorilal. *Saroj-Sarvekṣaṇ: Hindī Sāhitya Ke Itihās Ke Pramukhatam Sūtra Śivasiṁh "Saroj" Ke Kaviyoṁ Viṣayak Tathyoṁ Evaṁ Tithiyoṁ Ka Vivecanātmak Aur Gaveṣaṇātmak Parīkṣan*. Allahabad: Hindustani Academy, 1967.

Gupta, Mataprasad. *Kutab Śatak Aur Usakī Hindī*. Varanasi: Bharatiya Jnanpith Prakashan, 1967.

Habib, Irfan. *An Atlas of the Mughal Empire: Political and Economic Maps with Detailed Notes, Bibliography and Index*. New York: Oxford University Press, 1986.

——. "Writing and the Use of Books in the Age of Persian Manuscripts." *Tattvabodh* 1 (2006): 22.

Haider, Najaf. "Language, Caste and the Secretarial Class in Mughal India." In *The Development of a Nation: Essays in Memory of R. S. Sharma*, ed. D. N. Jha, 249–62. Delhi: Manohar, 2014.

Haidar, Navina Najat, and Marika Sardar. *Sultans of the South: Arts of India's Deccan Courts, 1323–1687*. New York: Metropolitan Museum of Art, 2011.

Hanneder, Jürgen. *To Edit or Not to Edit: On Textual Criticism of Sanskrit Works: A Series of Lectures Delivered at the École Pratique Des Hautes Études Paris, March 2015 and the Department of Pali, Savitribai Phule Pune University Pune, October and November 2015*. New Delhi: Aditya Prakashan, 2017.

Havelock, Eric Alfred. *The Muse Learns to Write: Reflections on Orality and Literacy from Antiquity to the Present*. New Haven, Conn.: Yale University Press, 1986.

Hawley, John Stratton. *A Storm of Songs: India and the Idea of the Bhakti Movement*. Cambridge, Mass.: Harvard University Press, 2015.

——. "The Early Sūr Sāgar and the Growth of the Sūr Tradition." *Journal of the American Oriental Society* 99, no. 1 (1979): 64–72.

——. *Sūrdās: Poet, Singer, Saint.* Rev. ed. Delhi: Primus Books, 2018.

——. *Three Bhakti Voices: Mirabai, Surdas, and Kabir in Their Times and Ours.* New Delhi: Oxford University Press, 2005.

Herman, Bernard. "On Southern Things." *Southern Cultures* 23, no. 3 (2017): 7–13.

Hess, Linda. *Bodies of Song: Kabir Oral Traditions and Performative Worlds in North India.* New Delhi: Oxford University Press, 2015.

Hines, Naseem Akhtar. *Maulana Daud's Cāndāyan: A Critical Study.* New Delhi: Manohar, 2009.

Honko, Laurie, ed. *Textualization of Oral Epics.* Berlin: De Gruyter, 2000.

Horstmann, Monika, ed. *Bhakti in Current Research, 1979–1982: Proceedings of the Second International Conference on Early Devotional Literature in New Indo-Aryan Languages, St. Augustin, 19–21 March 1982.* Berlin: Verlag, 1983.

——, ed. *Bhakti in Current Research: Proceedings of the Ninth International Conference on Early Devotional Literature in New Indo-Aryan Languages, Heidelberg, 23–26 July 2003*, New Delhi: Manohar, 2006.

——. *Crossing the Ocean of Existence: Braj Bhāsā Religious Poetry from Rajasthan: A Reader.* Wiesbaden: Harrassowitz, 1983.

——. "Nāth and Dādūpanthī Critique of Jains." *International Journal of Jaina Studies* 13, no. 1 (2017): 1–72.

——. "Pāras-Bhāg: Bhāī Aḍḍan's Translation of Al-Ghazālī's Kīmiyā-Yi Sa'ādat." In *Patronage and Popularisation, Pilgrimage and Procession: Channels of Transcultural Translation and Transmission in Early Modern South Asia, Papers in Honour of Monika Horstmann*, ed. Heidi Pauwels, 9–23. Wiesbaden: Harrassowitz Verlag, 2009.

——. "Texts and What to Do with Them: Dādūpanthī Compilations." In *Écrire et Transmettre En Inde Classique*, ed. Gérard Colas and Gerdi Gerschheimer, 27–42. Paris: École française d'Extrême-Orient, 2009.

——. "Three Brajbhāṣā Versions of the 'Bhāgavata Purāṇa.'" *International Journal of Hindu Studies* 22, no. 1 (2018): 123–74.

——. *Visions of Kingship in the Twilight of Mughal Rule.* Amsterdam: Royal Netherlands Academy of Arts and Sciences, 2006.

——and Bill Heike, eds. *In Favour of Govinddevjī: Historical Documents Relating to a Deity of Vrindaban and Eastern Rajasthan.* New Delhi: Indira Gandhi National Centre for the Arts and Manohar Publishers & Distributors, 1999.

Ishaq, Shaik. *Dakkhinī Hindī Ke Premākhyānak Kāvya, Eka Samīkṣātmak Adhyayan.* Chennai: Publication Division, University of Madras, 2007.

Jackson, Heather J. *Marginalia: Readers Writing in Books.* New Haven, Conn.: Yale University Press, 2001.

Jain, Dhanesh, and George Cardona. *The Indo-Aryan Languages.* London: Routledge, 2003.

Jha, Pankaj. *A Political History of Literature: Vidyapati and the Fifteenth Century.* Oxford: Oxford University Press, 2019.

Jha, Shalin. "Interaction of the 'Lords': The Jain Community and the Mughal Royalty under Akbar." *Social Scientist* 40, no. 3/4 (April 2012): 33–57.

Johnson, William A. "Toward a Sociology of Reading in Classical Antiquity." *The American Journal of Philology* 121, no. 4 (December 1, 2000): 593–627.

Jones, Elisabeth. "The Public Library Movement, the Digital Library Movement, and the Large-Scale Digitization Initiative: Assumptions, Intentions, and the Role of the Public." *Information & Culture* 52, no. 2 (2017): 229–63.

Jørgensen, Helle. *Tranquebar-Whose History? Transnational Heritage in a Former Danish Trading Colony in South India.* New Delhi: Orient BlackSwan, 2014.

Joshi, Priya. "Quantitative Method, Literary History." *Book History* 5, no. 1 (2002): 263–74.

Juergensmeyer, Mark, and N. Gerald Barrier, eds. *Sikh Studies: Comparative Perspectives on a Changing Tradition: Working Papers from the Berkeley Conference on Sikh Studies*. Berkeley: Graduate Theological Union, 1979.

Kasana, Bhamvar. *Nirañjanī Panth*. Didwana: College Book House, 2006.

Katre, S. M., and P. K. Gode. *Introduction to Indian Textual Criticism*. Poona: Deccan College Post-graduate and Research Institute, 1954.

Kaul, Deambi, B. K. *Śāradā and Ṭakarī Alphabets: Origin and Development*. New Delhi: Indira Gandhi National Centre for the Arts and D.K. Printworld, 2008.

Kaur, Madanjit. *The Golden Temple: Past and Present*. Amritsar: Guru Nanak Dev University Press, 1983.

Kellogg, S. H. *A Grammar of the Hindi Language in Which Are Treated the High Hindī, Braj, and the Eastern Hindī of the Rāmāyan of Tulsī Dās*. New Delhi: Munshriram Manoharlal, 1972 (original 1875).

Khandalavala, Karl. *The Development of Style in Indian Painting*. Madras: MacMillan, 1974.

——. "The Mṛigāvat of Bharat Kala Bhavan: As a Social Document and Its Date and Provenance." In *Chhavi: Golden Jubilee Volume*, ed. Anand Krishna, 19–36. Banaras: Bharat Kala Bhavan, 1971.

Kim, Jinah. *Receptacle of the Sacred: Illustrated Manuscripts and the Buddhist Book Cult in South Asia*. Berkeley: University of California Press, 2013.

King, Christopher Rolland. *One Language, Two Scripts: The Hindi Movement in Nineteenth Century North India*. Oxford: Oxford University Press, 1994.

Kinra, Rajeev. "Master and Munshī: A Brahman Secretary's Guide to Mughal Governance." *Indian Economic & Social History Review* 47, no. 4 (October 1, 2010): 527–61.

——. *Writing Self, Writing Empire: Chandar Bhan Brahman and the Cultural World of the Indo-Persian State Secretary*. Oakland: University of California Press, 2015.

Kohli, Surindar Singh. *A Critical Study of Ādi Granth, Being a Comprehensive and Scientific Study of Guru Granth Sahib, the Scripture of the Sikhs*. Delhi: Motilal Banarsidass, 1976.

Konishi, Masatoshi A. *Hāth-Kāghaz: History of Handmade Paper in South Asia*. Shimla: Indian Institute of Advanced Study and Aryan Books, 2013.

Kragh, Ulrich Timme. "Localized Literary History: Sub-Text and Cultural Heritage in the Āmer Śāstrabhaṇḍār, a Digambara Manuscript Repository in Jaipur." *International Journal of Jain Studies* 9, no. 3 (2003): 1–53.

Kshirsagar, Dattatreya Balakrishna. *Nāgaur Kilā Rī Vigat*. Jodhpur: Maharaja Mansingh Pustak Prakash Shodh Kendra, 1991.

Lath, Mukund, and Monika Horstmann, eds. *Transforming Tradition: Cultural Essays in Honour of Mukund Lath*. Jaipur: Prakrit Bharati Academy and Aditya Prakashan, New Delhi, 2013.

Latour, Bruno. *Reassembling the Social*. New York: Oxford University Press, 2005.

Levering, Miriam, ed. *Rethinking Scripture: Essays from a Comparative Perspective*. Albany: State University of New York Press, 1989.

Lord, Albert Bates, Stephen A. Mitchell, and Gregory Nagy. *The Singer of Tales*. 2nd ed. Cambridge, Mass.: Harvard University Press, 2000.

Lorenzen, David N., ed. *Religious Movements in South Asia, 600–1800*. New York: Oxford University Press, 2004.

Losensky, Paul E., and Sunil Sharma. *In the Bazaar of Love: The Selected Poetry of Amīr Khusrau*. New Delhi: Penguin Books India, 2011.

Losty, Jeremiah P. *The Art of the Book in India*. London: British Library, 1982.

Ludvik, Catherine. *Sarasvatī: Riverine Goddess of Knowledge: From the Manuscript-Carrying Vīṇā-Player to the Weapon-Wielding Defender of the Dharma*. Leiden: Brill, 2007.

Lutgendorf, Philip. *The Life of a Text: Performing the Rāmcaritmānas of Tulsidas*. Berkeley: University of California Press, 1991.

Mandhwani, Aakriti. "The Hindi Library and the Making of an Archive: The Hindi Sahitya Sammelan from 1911 to 1973." *South Asia: Journal of South Asian Studies* 43, no. 3 (May 3, 2020): 522–36.

Mangaldas, Swami, ed. *Śrī Mahārāj Haridās Jī Kī Vāṇī*. Jaipur: Nikhil Bharatiya Niranjani Mahasabha, 1962.

Mann, Gurinder Singh. *The Making of Sikh Scripture*. New Delhi: Oxford University Press, 2001.

McGregor, Ronald Stuart, ed. *Devotional Literature in South Asia: Papers of the Fourth Conference on Devotional Literature in New Indo-Aryan Languages, Held at Wolfson College, Cambridge, 1–4 September 1988*. New York: Cambridge University Press, 1992.

——. *Hindi Literature from Its Beginnings to the Nineteenth Century*. Wiesbaden: Harrassowitz, 1984.

——. *The Language of Indrajit of Orchā: A Study of Early Braj Bhāṣā Prose*. London: Cambridge University Press, 1968.

McLeod, W. H. *Early Sikh Tradition: A Study of the Janam-Sākhīs*. Oxford: Clarendon Press, 1980.

——and Daya Ram Abrol. *The B40 Janam-Sakhi*. Guru Nanak Dev University, 1980.

McLuhan, Marshall. *Understanding Media: The Extensions of Man*. New York: McGraw-Hill, 1964.

McWilliams, Mary, and David J. Roxburgh. *Traces of the Calligrapher: Islamic Calligraphy in Practice, c. 1600–1900*. Houston: The Museum of Fine Arts, 2007.

Menariya, Motilal. *Rājasthāna Meṁ Hindī Ke Hastalikhit Granthoṁ Kī Khoj*. Vol. 1. Udaipur: Hindi Vidyapith, 1942.

Michell, George, and Mark Zebrowski. *Architecture and Art of the Deccan Sultanates*. Cambridge: Cambridge University Press, 1999.

Mishra, Bhagirath. *Nirañjanī Sampradāy Aur Sant Turasīdās Nirañjanī*. Lucknow: Lucknow University, 1963.

Mishra, Ganeshbihari, Shyambihari Mishra, and Shudevbihari Mishra. *Miśrabandhu Vinod: Athavā Hindī Sāhitya Kā Itithās Tathā Kavi-Kīrtan*. Vol. 1. Prayag: Hindi Granth Prasarak Mandali, 1913.

Misra, Jogesh. *History of Libraries and Librarianship in Modern India since 1850*. Delhi: Atma Ram, 1979.

Mishra, Ratanalal. *Nirañjanī Sampradāy: Sādhanā Evaṁ Sāhitya*. Navalgarh: Mahamaya Mandir, 1998.

Moretti, Franco. *Graphs, Maps, Trees: Abstract Models for a Literary History*. London: Verso, 2005.

Murphy, Anne. *The Materiality of the Past: History and Representation in Sikh Tradition*. New York: Oxford University Press, 2012.

Myrvold, Kristina. *Inside the Guru's Gate: Ritual Uses of Texts among the Sikhs in Varanasi*. Lund: Lund University, 2007.

——, ed. *The Death of Sacred Texts: Ritual Disposal and Renovation of Texts in World Religions*. Farnham: Ashgate, 2010.

Nahta, Agarchand. *Rājasthān Meṁ Hindī Ke Hast Likhit Granthoṁ Kī Khoj*. Vol. 1. Udaipur: Rajasthan Vishva Vidyapith, 1954.

——. *Rājasthān Meṁ Hindī Ke Hast Likhit Granthoṁ Kī Khoj*. Vol. 2. Udaipur: Udaipur Vidyapith, 1947.

Narayandas, Swami. *Śrī Dādū Panth Paricay: Dādū Pantha Kā Itihās*. Jaipur: Shri Dadu Mahavidyalaya, 1978.

Novetzke, Christian. "Bhakti and Its Public." *International Journal of Hindu Studies* 11, no. 3 (2007): 255–72.

——. *The Quotidian Revolution: Vernacularization, Religion, and the Premodern Public Sphere in India*. New York: Columbia University Press, 2016.

——. *Religion and Public Memory: A Cultural History of Saint Namdev in India*. New York: Columbia University Press, 2008.

O'Hanlon, Rosalind. "Performances in a World of Paper: Puranic Histories and Social Communication in Early Modern India." *Past and Present*, no. 219 (May 2013): 219–58.

——. "The Social Worth of Scribes: Brahmins, Kayasthas and the Social Order in Early Modern India." *Indian Economic and Social History Review* 45 (2010): 563–95.

——and David Washbrook, eds. *Religious Cultures in Early Modern India: New Perspectives*. New Delhi: Routledge, 2011.

Oberoi, Harjot. *The Construction of Religious Boundaries: Culture, Identity and Diversity in the Sikh Tradition*. Delhi: Oxford University Press, 1994.

Offredi, Mariola. *The Banyan Tree: Essays on Early Literature in New Indo-Aryan Languages: Proceedings of the Seventh International Conference on Early Literature in New Indo-Aryan Languages, Venice, 1997*. New Delhi: Manohar, 2000.

Ogborn, Miles. *Indian Ink: Script and Print in the Making of the English East India Company*. Chicago: University of Chicago Press, 2007.

Ojha, Gaurishankar Hirachand. *The Palaeography of India*. Oodeypore (Udaipur): Sujjan Press, 1894.

Ollett, Andrew. *Language of the Snakes: Prakrit, Sanskrit, and the Language Order of Premodern India*. Oakland: University of California Press, 2017.

Ong, Walter J. *Orality and Literacy: The Technologizing of the Word*. New York: Methuen, 1982.

——. *The Presence of the Word: Some Prolegomena for Cultural and Religious History*. New Haven, Conn.: Yale University Press, 1967.

Orsini, Francesca. *The Hindi Public Sphere 1920–1940: Language and Literature in the Age of Nationalism*. New York: Oxford University Press, 2002.

——, ed. *The History of the Book in South Asia*. Farnham: Ashgate, 2013.

——. "How to Do Multilingual Literary History? Lessons from Fifteenth- and Sixteenth-Century North India." *The Indian Economic and Social History Review* 49, no. 2 (2012): 225–46.

——. *Print and Pleasure: Popular Literature and Entertaining Fictions in Colonial North India*. Ranikhet: Permanent Black, 2009.

——. "The Social History of a Genre: Kathas across Languages in Early Modern North India." *Medieval History Journal* 20, no. 1 (2017): 1-31.

——. "Vernacular: Flawed but Necessary?" *South Asian Review* 41, no. 2 (2020): 1–3.

——and Katherine Butler Schofield, eds. *Tellings and Texts: Music, Literature and Performance in North India*. Cambridge: Open Book Publishers, 2015.

——and Samira Sheikh, eds. *After Timur Left: Culture and Circulation in Fifteenth-Century North India*. New Delhi: Oxford University Press, 2014.

Overton, Keelan. "Book Culture, Royal Libraries, and Persianate Painting in Bijapur, circa 1580–1630." *Muqarnas* 33 (2016): 91–154.

——, ed. *Iran and the Deccan: Persianate Art, Culture, and Talent in Circulation, 1400–1700*. Bloomington: Indiana University Press, 2020.

Ouseley, William. *Persian Miscellanies: An Essay to Facilitate the Reading of Persian Manuscripts; with Engraved Specimens, Philological Observations, and Notes Critical and Historical*. London: Richard White, 1795.

Pandey, Manager. *Bhakti Āndolan Aur Sūradās Kā Kāvya*. New Delhi: Vani Prakashan, 2003.

Pandey, Rajbali, ed. *Hindī Sāhitya Kā Bṛhat Itihās*. Kashi: Nagari Pracharini Sabha, VS 2014.

Pandey, Shyam Manohar. *Lok Mahākāvya Lorikī: Lorik Aur Candā Kī Lok-Gāthā: Mūlapāṭh, Bhāvārth, Śabdārth, Tathā Ṭippaṇiyāṁ*. Allahabad: Sahitya Bhavan, 1979.

Panofsky, Erwin. *Studies in Iconology: Humanistic Themes in the Art of the Renaissance*. New York: Harper & Row, 1962.

Patel, Deven M. *Text to Tradition: The Naiṣadhīyacarita and Literary Community in South Asia*. New York: Columbia University Press, 2014.

Patel, Jashu, and Krishan Kumar. *Libraries and Librarianship in India*. Westport: Greenwood Press, 2001.

Pauwels, Heidi R. M. "Hagiography and Community Formation: The Case of a Lost Community of Sixteenth-Century Vrindāvan." *The Journal of Hindu Studies* 3, no. 1 (2010): 53–90.

——. "Imagining Religious Communities in the Sixteenth Century: Harirām Vyās and the Haritrayī." *International Journal of Hindu Studies* 13, no. 2 (2009): 143–61.

——, ed. *Patronage and Popularisation, Pilgrimage and Procession: Channels of Transcultural Translation and Transmission in Early Modern South Asia, Papers in Honour of Monika Horstmann.* Wiesbaden: Harrassowitz Verlag, 2009.

——. "A Tale of Two Temples: Mathurā's Keśavadeva and Orcchā's Caturbhujadeva." *South Asian History and Culture* 2, no. 2 (2011): 278–99.

——. "When a Sufi Tells about Krishna's Doom: The Case of Kanhāvat (1540?)." *Journal of Hindu Studies* 6 (2013): 21–36.

——. "Who Are the Enemies of the Bhaktas? Testimony about 'Śāktas' and 'Others' from Kabīr, the Rāmānandīs, Tulsīdās, and Harirām Vyās." *Journal of the American Oriental Society* 130, no. 4 (2010): 509–39.

Peabody, Norbert. *Hindu Kingship and Polity in Precolonial India.* Cambridge: Cambridge University Press, 2003.

Phukan, Shantanu. " 'Through Throats Where Many Rivers Meet': The Ecology of Hindi in the World of Persian." *Indian Economic and Social History Review* 38, no. 33 (2001): 33–58.

Pinch, William R. "History, Devotion, and the Search for Nabhadas of Galta." In *Invoking the Past: The Uses of History in South Asia*, ed. Daud Ali. Oxford: Oxford University Press, 1999.

——. *Warrior Ascetics and Indian Empires.* Cambridge: Cambridge University Press, 2006.

Pinney, Christopher. "Piercing the Skin of the Idol." In *Beyond Aesthetics: Art and the Technologies of Enchantment*, ed. Christopher Pinney and Nicholas Thomas, 157–79. Oxford: Berg, 2001.

Pollock, Sheldon. "The Cosmopolitan Vernacular." *The Journal of Asian Studies* 57, no. 1 (1998): 6–37.

——, ed. *Forms of Knowledge in Early Modern Asia: Explorations in the Intellectual History of India and Tibet, 1500–1800.* Durham, N.C.: Duke University Press, 2011.

——. "India in the Vernacular Millennium: Literary Culture and Polity, 1000–1500." *Daedalus* 127, no. 3 (1998): 41–74.

——. *The Language of the Gods in the World of Men: Sanskrit, Culture, and Power in Premodern India.* Berkeley: University of California Press, 2006.

——, ed. *Literary Cultures in History: Reconstructions from South Asia.* New Delhi: Oxford University Press, 2003.

——. *A Rasa Reader: Classical Indian Aesthetics.* New York: Columbia University Press, 2016.

——. "The Theory of Practice and the Practice of Theory in Indian Intellectual History." *Journal of the American Oriental Society* 105, no. 3 (1985): 499–519.

Prajapati, Sweta. *A Bibliography of Palaeography and Manuscriptology.* Delhi: Bharatiya Kala Prakashan, 2004.

Price, William, and Tarini Charana Mitra. *Hindee and Hindoostanee Selections.* 2nd ed. Calcutta: Asiatic Lithograph Company's Press, 1830.

Prinsep, James. *Benares Illustrated, in a Series of Drawings.* Calcutta: Baptist Mission Press, 1831.

Pritchett, Frances W. *Nets of Awareness: Urdu Poetry and Its Critics.* Berkeley: University of California Press, 1994.

Rai, Alok. *Hindi Nationalism.* Hyderbad: Orient Longman, 2000.

Rajpurohit, Dalpat Singh. "Bhakti versus Rīti? The Sants' Perspective." *Bulletin of the School of Oriental and African Studies* 84, no. 1 (2021): 95–113.

——. *Sundar Ke Svapn: Ārambhik Ādhunikatā, Dādūpanth, Aur Sundaradās Kī Kavitā.* New Delhi: Rajkamal, 2022.

Raman, Bhavani. *Document Raj: Writing and Scribes in Early Colonial South India.* Chicago: University of Chicago Press, 2012.

Randhawa, Mohinder Singh. *Kangra Rāgamālā Paintings.* New Delhi: National Museum, 1971.

Ranković, Slavica, Leidulf Melve, and Else Mundal, eds. *Along the Oral-Written Continuum: Types of Texts, Relations, and Their Implications.* Abingdon: Marston, 2010.

Rath, Saraju, ed. *Aspects of Manuscript Culture in South India*. Leiden: Brill, 2012.

Rizvi, Mujib. *Sab Likhanī Kai Likhu Saṁsārā: Padmāvat Aur Jayasī Kī Duniyā*. New Delhi: Rajkamal, 2019.

Rowell, Lewis Eugene. *Music and Musical Thought in Early India*. Chicago Studies in Ethnomusicology. Chicago: University of Chicago Press, 1992.

Sah, Anumpam, ed. *Indigenous Methods and Manuscript Preservation*. New Delhi: National Mission for Manuscripts and D.K. Printworld, 2006.

Saha, Shandip. "The Movement of Bhakti along a North-West Axis: Tracing the History of the Puṣṭimārg between the Sixteenth and Nineteenth Centuries." *International Journal of Hindu Studies* 11, no. 3 (December 1, 2007): 299–318.

Salomon, Richard. *Indian Epigraphy: A Guide to the Study of Inscriptions in Sanskrit, Prakrit, and the Other Indo-Aryan Languages*. New York: Oxford, 1998.

Sam, N. "Some Important Aspects of Manuscriptology." *Journal of Manuscript Studies* XXXVI (2003–2004): 121–30.

Sarma, K. V., and Dash Siniruddha. *New Lights on Manuscriptology: A Collection of Articles of Prof. K.V. Sharma*. Chennai: Sree Sarada Education Society Research Centre, 2007.

Sastri, Hiranand. *Ancient Vijñaptipatras*. Baroda: Baroda State Press, 1942.

Schimmel, Annemarie. *Calligraphy and Islamic Culture*. New York: New York University Press, 1984.

——. *Islamic Calligraphy*. Leiden: Brill, 1970.

Schomer, Karine, ed. *The Sants: Studies in a Devotional Tradition of India*. Delhi: Motilal Banarsidass, 1987.

Schopen, Gregory. "The Phrase 'Sa Pṛthivīpradeśaś Caityabhūto Bhavet' in the Vajracchedikā: Notes on the Cult of the Book in Mahāyāna." *Indo-Iranian Journal* 17, no. 3–4 (1975): 147–81.

Schwartzberg, Joseph E. *A Historical Atlas of South Asia*. Chicago: University of Chicago Press, 1978.

Seghal, K. K. *Rajasthan District Gazetteer: Nagaur*. Jaipur: Government Central Press, 1975.

Sen, Kshitimohan. *Medieval Mysticism of India*. Trans. Manomohan Ghosh. London: Luzac & Company, 1936.

Sengar, Shiv Singh. *Śivasiṁh Saroj*. Ed. Trilok Narayan Diksit. Lucknow: Tejkumar Book Depot, 1966 (originally 1878).

Sewell, Robert, Shankara Balakrishna Dikshita, and Robert Schram. *The Indian Calendar, with Tables for the Conversion of Hindu and Muhammadan into A.D. Dates, and Vice Versa*. Delhi: Motilal Banarsidass, 1995.

Seyller, John William. "The Inspection and Valuation of Manuscripts in the Imperial Mughal Library." *Artibus Asiae* 57, no. 3/4 (1997): 243–349.

——. *Workshop and Patron in Mughal India: The Freer Rāmāyaṇa and Other Illustrated Manuscripts of 'Abd Al-Raḥīm*. Washington, D.C.: Artibus Asiae, 1999.

Shackle, C. *An Introduction to the Sacred Language of the Sikhs*. London: School of Oriental and African Studies, 1983.

Shaji, P. L. "Cataloguing of Manuscripts." *Journal of Manuscript Studies* XXXVII (2005): 49–56.

Shandilya, Shiv Kumar. *Maulānā Dāūd Kṛt Cāndāyan Kā Bhāshā Svarūp Evaṁ Bimbātmak Saṁcetanā*. New Delhi: Bhasha Prakashan, 1978.

Sharif, Ja'far, and Gerhard Andreas Herklots. *Qanoon-e-Islam, or the Customs of the Mussalmans of India*. Lahore: Al-Irshad, 1973 (originally 1863).

Sharma, Krishna. *Bhakti and the Bhakti Movement, A New Perspective: A Study in the History of Ideas*. New Delhi: Munshiram Manoharlal Publishers, 1987.

Sharma, Pragati. *Braj Kī Akabarakālīn Pustak Ṭhaur Aur Usakā Sūcī Patra*. Vrindavan: Vrindavan Shodh Sansthan, 2016.

Shastri, Satyanarayan. *Santakavi Turasīdās Nirañjanī: Sāhitya Aur Siddhānt*. Kanpur: Sahitya Niketan, 1974.

Shivganeshmurty, R. S. *Introduction to Manuscriptology*. Delhi: Sharada Pub. House, 1996.

Shukla, Ramchandra. *Hindī Sāhitya Kā Itihās*. Kashi: Nagari Pracharini Sabha, 1942 (originally 1929).

Shukla, Savitri. *Nirañjanī Sampradāy Ke Hindī Kavi*. Bhopal: Madhyapradesh Sasan Sahitya Parishad, 1974.

Silverstein, Michael, and Greg Urban. *Natural Histories of Discourse*. Chicago: University of Chicago Press, 1996.

Singh, Kanhaiya. *Hindī Pāṭhānusandhān*. Allahabad: Lokbharati Prakashan, 1990.

Singh, Kavita, ed. *Scent upon a Southern Breeze: The Synaesthetic Arts of the Deccan*. Mumbai: Marg Foundation, 2018.

Singh, Pashaura. *The Guru Granth Sahib: Canon, Meaning and Authority*. New Delhi: Oxford University Press, 2000.

Skelton, Robert. "Documents for the Study of Painting at Bijapur in the Late Sixteenth and Early Seventeenth Centuries." *Arts Asiatiques* 5, no. 2 (1958): 97–125.

Slaje, Walter, ed. *Śāstrārambha: Inquiries in the Preamble in Sanskrit*. Wiesbaden: Harrassowitz Verlag, 2008.

Smith, Vincent Arthur. *Art of India*. New York: Parkstone International, 2012.

Smith, Wilfred Cantwell. *What Is Scripture? A Comparative Approach*. Minneapolis: Fortress Press, 1993.

Snell, Rupert. *The Hindi Classical Tradition: A Braj Bhasa Reader*. London: School of Oriental and African Studies, 1991.

Snodgrass, Jeffrey G. *Casting Kings*. New York: Oxford University Press, 2006.

Sreenivasan, Ramya. *The Many Lives of a Rajput Queen: Heroic Pasts in India c. 1500–1900*. Seattle: University of Washington Press, 2007.

Stallybrass, Peter, Roger Chartier, John Franklin Mowery, and Heather Wolfe. "Hamlet's Tables and the Technologies of Writing in Renaissance England." *Shakespeare Quarterly* 55, no. 4 (2004): 379–419.

Stark, Ulrike. *An Empire of Books: The Naval Kishore Press and the Diffusion of the Printed Word in Colonial India*. Ranikhet: Permanent Black, 2007.

Sternbach, Ludwik. *Subhasita, Gnomic and Didactic Literature*. Wiesbaden: O. Harrassowitz, 1974.

Stewart, Tony K. *The Final Word: The Caitanya Caritamrta and the Grammar of Religious Tradition*. New York: Oxford University Press, 2010.

——. "In Search of Equivalence: Conceiving Muslim-Hindu Encounter through Translation Theory." *History of Religions* 40, no. 3 (February 1, 2001): 260–87.

Storey, C. A. *Persian Literature: A Bio-Bibliographical Survey*. London: Luzac & Co., 1927.

Street, Brian V. *Literacy in Theory and Practice*. New York: Cambridge University Press, 1984.

Sundar, Pushpa. *Patrons and Philistines: Arts and the State in British India, 1773–1947*. Delhi: Oxford University Press, 1995.

Taher, Mohamed. *Librarianship and Library Science in India: An Outline of Historical Perspectives*. New Delhi: Concept, 1994.

Tandan, Hariharnath. *Vārtā Sāhitya*. Aligarh: Bharat Prakashan, 1960.

Taylor, McComas. *Seven Days of Nectar: Contemporary Oral Performance of the Bhāgavatapurāṇa*. New York: Oxford University Press, 2016.

Tessitori, L. P. *Notes on the Grammar of the Old Western Rajasthani with Special Reference to Apabhramsa and to Gujarati and Marwari*. Mazgaon: British India Press, 1916.

Thackston, Wheeler McIntosh. *Album Prefaces and Other Documents on the History of Calligraphers and Painters*. Boston: Brill, 2001.

Thaker, Jayant P. *Manuscriptology and Text Criticism*. Vadodara: Oriental Institute, 2002.

Tod, James. *Annals and Antiquities of Rajasthan, or The Central and Western Rajput States of India*. London: H. Milford, Oxford University Press, 1920 (originally 1829–1832).

Topsfield, Andrew. "The Royal Paintings Inventory at Udaipur." In *Indian Art & Connoisseurship: Essays in Honour of Douglas Barrett*, ed. John Guy, 189–99. Ahmedabad: Indira Gandhi National Centre for Arts, 1995.

Truschke, Audrey. *Culture of Encounters: Sanskrit at the Mughal Court.* New York: Columbia University Press, 2016.

Utas, Bo, Carina Jahani, and Dariyush Kargar. *Manuscript, Text and Literature: Collected Essays on Middle and New Persian Texts.* Wiesbaden: Reichert, 2008.

Venkat Rao, D. *Cultures of Memory in South Asia: Orality, Literacy and the Problem of Inheritance.* New Delhi: Springer, 2014.

Venkatacalapati, A. Ira. *The Province of the Book: Scholars, Scribes, and Scribblers in Colonial Tamilnadu.* Ranikhet: Permanent Black, 2012.

Venkatkrishnan, Anand. "Ritual, Reflection, and Religion: The Devas of Banaras." *South Asian History and Culture* 6, no. 1 (2015): 147–71.

Vergiani, Vincenzo, Daniele Cuneo, and Camillo Alessio Formigatti, eds. *Indic Manuscript Cultures through the Ages: Material, Textual, and Historical Investigations.* Berlin: De Gruyter, 2017.

Visalakshy, P. *Some Aspects on Manuscriptology.* Thiruvananthapuram: Oriental Research Institute & Manuscripts Library, University of Kerala, 2008.

Wadley, Susan Snow, ed. *Damayanti and Nala: The Many Lives of a Story.* New Delhi: Chronicle Books, 2011.

Widdess, Richard. "The Oral in Writing: Early Indian Musical Notations." *Early Music* 24, no. 3 (1996): 391–405.

——. *The Rāgas of Early Indian Music: Modes, Melodies and Musical Notations from the Gupta Period to c. 1250.* Oxford: Clarendon Press, 1995.

Wilden, Eva. *Manuscript, Print and Memory: Relics of the Caṅkam in Tamilnadu.* Berlin: De Gruyter, 2014.

Wilson, Horace Hayman. *Hindu Religions or, an Account of the Various Religious Sects of India.* Calcutta: Published by the Society for the Resuscitation of Indian Literature, 1899.

Williams, Tyler. "'If the Whole World Were Paper . . .' A History of Writing in the North Indian Vernacular." *History and Theory* 56 (2018): 81–101.

——. "Madhyakālīn Bhakti Sampradāyoṁ Ke Ṭakarāvōṁ Kā Bhautik Ādhār." *Bahuvacan* 24 (2010): 53–76.

——. "Notes of Exchange: Scribal Practices and Vernacular Religious Scholarship in Early Modern North India." *Manuscript Studies* 2, no. 3 (2019): 5–45.

——. "'Publishing' and Publics in a World Without Print: Vernacular Manuscripts in Early Modern India." *Manuscript Studies* 4, no. 1 (2019): 146–68.

——. "The Ties That Bind: Individual, Family and Community in Northwestern Bhakti." In *Bhakti and Power: Debating India's Religion of the Heart*, ed. John Stratton Hawley, Christian Lee Novetzke, and Swapna Sharma, 192–202. Seattle: University of Washington Press, 2018.

——, Anshu Malhotra, and John Stratton Hawley, eds. *Text and Tradition in Early Modern North India.* New Delhi: Oxford University Press, 2018.

Willison, I. R., and Wallace Kirsop, eds. *The Commonwealth of Books: Essays and Studies in Honour of Ian Willison.* Melbourne: Monash University, 2007.

Wimbush, Vincent L., ed. *Theorizing Scriptures: New Critical Orientations to a Cultural Phenomenon.* New Brunswick: Rutgers University Press, 2008.

Wright, Elaine Julia. *Muraqqa' Imperial Mughal Albums from the Chester Beatty Library, Dublin.* Alexandria: Art Services International: 2008.

Wujastyk, Dominic. "Indian Manuscripts." In *Manuscript Cultures: Mapping the Field*, ed. Jörg Quenzer and Jan-Ulrich Sobisch, 159–82. Berlin: De Gruyter, 2014.

Yasmin, Angbin. "Literacy and Literature: Study of Attainments of Women in Mughal India." *Proceedings of the Indian History Congress* 73 (2012): 391–99.

DISSERTATIONS AND THESES

Adamjee, Qamar. "Strategies for Visual Narration in the Illustrated 'Chandayan' Manuscripts." PhD diss., New York University, 2011.

Boyk, David. "Provincial Urbanity: Intellectuals and Public Life in Patna, 1880–1930." PhD diss., University of California, Berkeley, 2015.

Hare, James P. "Garland of Devotees: Nabhadas' 'Bhaktamal' and Modern Hinduism." PhD diss., Columbia University, 2011.

Hastings, James Michael. "Poets, Sants, and Warriors: The Dadu Panth, Religious Change and Identity Formation in Jaipur State circa 1562–1860 CE." PhD diss., The University of Wisconsin-Madison, 2002.

King, Christopher Rolland. "The Nagari Pracharini Sabha (Society for the Promotion of the Nagari Script and Language) of Benares, 1893–1914: A Study in the Social and Political History of the Hindi Language." PhD diss., University of Chicago, 1974.

Plukker, Dick Frederik. *The Miragāvatī of Kutubana: Avadhī Text with Critical Notes.* PhD diss., Universiteit van Amsterdam, 1981.

Rajpurohit, Dalpat Singh. "Bhakti Aur Rīti Kāvya Dhāraoṁ Kā Saṁvād Aur Dādūpanthī Sundaradās Kī Kavitā (A Dialogue of Bhakti and Riti Sensibilities and the Poetry of Dadupanthi Sundardas)." PhD diss., Presidency University (Kolkata), 2018.

Scheper, Catharina Helena. "The Islamic Bookbinding Tradition: A Book Archaeological Study." PhD diss., Leiden University, 2014.

Williams, Tyler. "Bhakti Kāvya Meṁ Nirguṇ-Saguṇ Vibhājan Kā Aitihāsik Adhyayan (An Historical Study of the Nirgun-Sagun Distinction in Bhakti Poetry)." MPhil thesis, Jawaharlal Nehru University, 2007.

——. "Sacred Sounds and Sacred Books: A History of Writing in Hindi." PhD diss., Columbia University, 2014.

MANUSCRIPT REPORTS AND LIBRARY, MUSEUM, AND DEALER CATALOGUES

Aufrecht, Theodor. *Catalogus Catalogorum: An Alphabetical Register of Sanskrit Works and Authors.* Leipzig: Brockhaus, 1891.

Bahura, Gopalnarayan. *Catalogue of Manuscripts in the Maharaja of Jaipur Museum.* Jaipur: Maharaja of Jaipur Museum, 1971.

——. *Catalogue of Manuscripts in the Maharaja Sawai Man Singh II Museum (Pothikhana Collection: Dharmaśāstra).* Jaipur: Maharaja Sawai Man Singh II Museum, 1984.

——. *Literary Heritage of the Rulers of Amber and Jaipur, with an Index to the Register of Manuscripts in the Pothikhana of Jaipur (Khasmohor Collection).* Jaipur: Maharaja Sawai Man Singh II Museum, 1976.

Barnett, Lionel D. *Panjabi Printed Books in the British Museum: A Supplementary Catalogue.* London: Trustees of the British Museum, 1961.

Biswas, Subhas C., and Manibhai Prajapati. *Bibliographic Survey of Indian Manuscript Catalogues: Being a Union List of Manuscript Catalogues.* Delhi: Eastern Book Linkers, 1998.

Blumhardt, James Fuller. *Catalogue of the Hindi, Panjabi and Hindustani Manuscripts in the Library of the British Museum.* London: British Museum Press, 1899.

——. *A Supplementary Catalogue of Hindi Books in the Library of the British Museum Acquired during the Years 1893–1912.* London: British Museum, 1913.

Brown, W. Norman. *A Descriptive and Illustrated Catalogue of Miniature Paintings of the Jaina Kalpasūtra as Executed in the Early Western Indian Style (with 45 Plates).* Washington, D.C.: The Lord Baltimore Press, 1934.

Bühler, Georg. *Detailed Report of a Tour in Search of Sanskrit Mss. Made in Kaśmír, Rajputana, and Central India.* Bombay: Bombay Branch of the Asiatic Society, 1877.

Cole, Henry Hardy. *Catalogue of the Objects of Indian Art Exhibited in the South Kensington Museum, Illustrated by Woodcuts, and by a Map of India Showing the Localities of Various Art Industries.* London: G. E. Eyre and W. Spottiswoode, 1874.

Das, Syam Sundar Rai Bahadur. *An Abstract Account of the Search for Hindi Manuscripts for the Years 1900, 1901 and 1902.* Bombay: Bombay Education Society's Press, 1904.

Desai, Kalpana S., and B. V. Shetti. *Jewels on the Crescent: Masterpieces of the Chhatrapati Shivaji Maharaj Vastu Sangrahalaya Formerly Prince of Wales Museum of Western India.* Mumbai: Chhatrapati Shivaji Maharaj Vastu Sangrahalaya, 2002.

Ehnbom, Daniel J. *Indian Miniatures: The Ehrenfeld Collection.* New York: Hudson Hills Press and American Federation of Arts, 1985.

Ettinghausen, Richard. *Paintings of the Sultans and Emperors of India in American Collections.* New Delhi: Lalit Kala Akademi, 1961.

Fendall, Ramsey. *Islamic Calligraphy (Catalogue of Traces of the Calligrapher: Islamic Calligraphy in Practice, C. 1600–1900 and Writing the Word of God: Calligraphy and the Qur'an, Asia Society, New York October 7th–February 8th).* London: Sam Fogg, 2003.

Gupta, R. D., and M. L. Gupta, eds. *A Catalogue of Hindi Manuscripts in the Vrindaban Research Institute.* Vrindaban: Vridaban Research Institute, 1979.

Haidar, Navina Najat, and Marika Sardar. *Sultans of the South: Arts of India's Deccan Courts, 1323–1687.* New York: Metropolitan Museum of Art, 2011.

Jain, Prem Chand. *Jain Granth Bhandars in Jaipur and Nagaur.* Jaipur: Centre for Jain Studies, University of Rajasthan, 1978.

——. *A Descriptive Catalogue of Manuscripts in the Bhattarkiya Granth Bhandar, Nagaur.* Jaipur: Centre for Jain Studies, University of Rajasthan, 1981.

Kasliwal, Kastoor Chand. *Rājasthān Ke Jain Śāstra Bhaṇḍāroṁ Kī Granth-Sūcī.* Jaipur: Shri Digambar Jain Atishay Kshetra Shrimahaviraji, 1954.

Khuda Bakhsh Oriental Public Library. *Catalogue of the Arabic and Persian Manuscripts in the Khuda Bakhsh Oriental Public Library.* 2nd ed. Patna: Khuda Bakhsh Oriental Public Library, 1970.

——. *Fihrist-i Makẖṭūṭāt-i Urdū: Kẖudā Bakẖsh Oriyanṭal Pablik Lā'ibrerī.* Patna: Khuda Bakhsh Oriental Public Library, 1962.

——. *Kẖudā Bakẖsh Lā'ibrerī Ke Urdū Makẖṭūṭāt Kī Fihrist.* Patna: Khuda Bakhsh Oriental Public Library, 1995.

Lorenzen, David N. *Catalog of Manuscripts in the Kabīr Chaurā Monastery.* México, D.F.: El Colegio de México, 1994.

Marshall, D. N., and Vicaji Dinshah B. Taraporevala. *Mughal Bibliography: Select Persian Sources for the Study of Mughals in India.* Bombay: New Book Company, 1962.

McInerney, Terence, Steven M. Kossack, and Navina Najat Haidar. *Divine Pleasures: Painting from India's Rajput Courts, The Kronos Collections.* New York: The Metropolitan Museum of Art, 2016.

Miller, Bob. *Manuscripts from the Himalayas and the Indian Subcontinent.* Vol. 17. London: Sam Fogg Rare Books and Manuscripts, 1996.

Mishra, Sashibhusan. *Acarya Sri Surendrasuriswarji Jaina Tatvajnanasala's Catalogue of Palm-Leaf Manuscripts with Basic Manuscriptology: Muni Sri Ramasuriswarji (Dahelawala) Maharaja's Collection.* Ahmedabad: Acharya Shri Surendrasuriswarji Jain Tatvajnanashala, 2014.

Nagari Pracharini Sabha. *Khoja Meṁ Upalabdh Hastalikhit Hindī Granthoṁ Kā Traivārṣik Vivaraṇ.* Vols. 1–20. Kashi: Nagari Pracharini Sabha, 1935–1949.

Pandey, Sudhakar, ed. *Hastalikhit Hindī-Grantha-Sūcī.* Varanasi: Nagari Pracharini Sabha, VS 1989.
Pandey, Sudhakar, Karunapati Tripathi, and Mohanlal Tivari, eds. *Hastalikhita Saṁskṛta-Grantha-Sūcī.* Varanasi: Nagari Pracharini Sabha, Vs. 2031.
Prasad, Kali. *Catalogue of Oriental Manuscripts in the Lucknow University Library.* Lucknow: Lucknow University, 1951.
Raghavan, V., K. Kunjunni Raja, N. Veezhinathan, E. R. Ramabai, Siniruddha Dash, and Theodor Aufrecht. *New Catalogus Catalogorum: An Alphabetical Register of Sanskrit and Allied Works and Authors.* Vols. 18, 26, 28–35, 37–65. Madras: University of Madras, 1949.
Raja, Chittenjoor Kunhan, and K. Madhava Krishna Sarma, eds. *Catalogue of the Anup Sanskrit Library.* 2nd ed. Bikaner: Maharaja Ganga Singh Ji Trust, 1993.
Rajasthan Oriental Research Institute. *Rājasthānī-Hindī Hastalikhit Granth-Sūcī.* Vols. 44, 58, 142–44, 153, 158–59, 163, 180, 190, 198–99, 202–204, 207–209, 214, 216. Jodhpur: Rajasthan Oriental Research Institute, 1960.
——. *A Catalogue of Sanskrit and Prakrit Manuscripts in the Rajasthan Oriental Research Institute.* Vols. 71, 77, 81–82, 85, 91, 125–27, 130–32, 136–40, 145–52, 167–69, 186, 212. Jodhpur: Rajasthan Oriental Research Institute, 1963.
Sharma, Ram Kripalu, ed. *Grantha Pārijāta: Hindī Bhāshā Ke Hastalikhit Granthoṁ Kī Vargīkṛt Sūcī.* Jaipur: Shri Sanjay Sharma Sangrahlaya and Shodh Sansthan, 2001.
Varma, Ramkumar, and Rosanalal Alma, eds. *Hastalikhit Hindī Granthoṃ Kī Vivaraṇātmaka Sūcī.* Allahabad: Hindi Sahitya Sammelan, 1971.
Vyas, Kaluram, ed. *Mahārājā Mānasiṁh Pustak Prakāś Ke Granthoṁ Kī Sūcī.* Jodhpur: Maharaja Mansingh Pustak Prakash, 1981.

DICTIONARIES

Böhtlingk, Otto von. *Sanskrit-Wörterbuch in Kürzerer Fassung.* St. Petersburg: Akademie der wissenchaften, 1879.
Callewaert, Winand. *Dictionary of Bhakti: North-Indian Bhakti Texts into Khaṛī Bolī, Hindī and English.* New Delhi: D.K. Printworld, 2009.
Das, Shyamsundar. *Hindī Śabd Sāgar.* Kashi: Nagari Pracharini Sabha, 1969.
Lalas, Sitaram. *Rājasthānī Sabad Kos: Rājasthānī Hindī Bṛhat Koś.* Rajasthani Shodh Sansthan, 1962.
McGregor, Ronald Stuart. *The Oxford Hindi-English Dictionary.* New Delhi: Oxford University Press, 1994.
Monier-Williams, Monier. *A Sanskrit-English Dictionary.* Oxford: Oxford University Press, 1979 (1872).
Platts, John T. *A Dictionary of Urdu, Classical Hindi, and English.* London: W. H. Allen & Co., 1884.
Singh, Bhai Kanha "Nabha." ed. *Guru Śabad Ratnākar Mahān Koś.* Northridge: Bhai Baljinder Singh, 2010.
Steingass, Francis Joseph. *A Comprehensive Persian-English Dictionary, including the Arabic Words and Phrases To Be Met with in Persian Literature.* London: Routledge & K. Paul, 1892.

Index

abjad script, 22–23, 28. *See also* Arabic script
Abul Fazl (Abu al-Fazl ibn Mubarak), 58, 163–64, 235n22, 265n103
account books, 13. *See also* bahī
adhikār, 79, 141–42, 254n56
Ādi Granth, 167–69, 201, 241n14, 266n118; *Dādū Vāṇī* and, 172–73; early copies of, 182, 185, 262n62; editing of, 168, 173; enthroned or established, 168–69, 172, 185; *mūl mantar* in, 180–81; Niranjani *Vāṇī* and, 180; Kabir verses in, 240n7; organization of, 180–82, 264n92; orthography or script of, 185; Qur'an and, 186; *rāgamālā* of, 181, 264nn91–92; scribes for, 167, 185. *See also* Guru Granth Sāhib; Kartarpur *pothī*
Advaita Vedānta, 126, 133, 148, 150, 217, 253n38, 256n83
Afghans, 30, 37–38, 42, 61, 239n75
Agra, 57
ahl-i kitāb/ahl al-kitāb, 159, 164–65, 167
Ā'īn-i Akbarī. *See* Abul Fazl
Aitken, Molly, 237n52, 239n71
Akbar, Emperor, 58, 91, 163–64
ākhara, 37, 42, 79–81. *See also* letter or letters
akhira, 32–33, 86, 93, 241n12. *See also* letter or letters
akṣara, 33, 80, 127, 241n12. *See also* letter or letters
alaṁkāra, 124, 126, 127, 251n18
al-Din, Rukn, 29
Allen, Michael, 133
Amardas, 154–55, 159, 168, 170–71, 184, 187, 193, 204
Amritsar, 261. *See also* Ramdaspur
Amṛtakuṇḍa, 37
Anandram, 1, 143, 145
Anantdas, 88–91, 93, 130, 179, 189, 238n62, 244n43
Apabhramsha: conventions of, 43, 122; as cosmopolitan language, 3, 96; Hindi's relation to, 233n7; Jain monks study, 240n8; literacy in, 96; as literary language, 8, 9; manuscripts in, 11; meters or prosodic forms in, 37, 55, 85; *pothī*s in, 120, 135; scribes writing in, 42; term *grantha* in, 160
Arabic, 23, 28, 40; alphabet or letters of, 33, 46–47, 109, 235n22; books or manuscripts in, 44, 62, 164, 217, 225; as cosmopolitan language, 39, 55; literary motifs in, 36, 87, 88; loanwords from, xviii, 12, 22, 55, 207, 254n50; in magic squares, 109, 118; numerals, 109; scriptures in, 159; translations from, 164
Arabic script, 22–24, 42–43, 76, 233n3, 237n54, 237n56; administrative use of, 185; *bhāṣā* or Hindi works in, 7, 46, 211, 237n48; calligraphy in, 23, 47, 186–87; *Candāyan* copies in, 44, 46–47; cataloguing practices for, 217; Daud's use of, 34; Muslim use of, 185, 265n101; *pem-kathā* copies in, 27–28, 52; right-to-left order of, 44, 52; transliteration into, 28, 46; Urdu and, 211; vocalization marks of, 237n48,
arajā, 36–37

archives, 230n5, 269n23; conditions of, xvi–xvii; construction of, xvi, 20, 205–18; historiography and, xvii–xviii, 2–3, 20–21, 122–23, 149; material, xv, 3, 5, 206, 224–27; organization of, 217–18; redundant (or not), xv–xvi; "thing-ness" of literary, xix
aril, 36–37
Arjan, Guru, 189–90, 262n52; *Ādi Granth* and, 168–69, 172, 181, 185–86; Kartarpur *pothī* and (*see* Kartarpur *pothī*); *mūl mantar* and, 168, 171, 261n50; *rāgamālā* and, 181, 264nn91–92; signature of, 186, 261n50; succession of, 167
artifacts, material textual, 2, 5, 13, 17, 131; in archives, xvii, 205–6; authority of, 93; data from, 13–14; elites' use of, 43, 121; historical consciousness and, 3, 10, 110, 226; illustrations in or from, 21; manuscripts as, xviii, 17, 205; material properties of, 10, 17; in museums, 222–23; in pedagogical performances, 141; practices producing, 13, 17; as "things," 10, 205; types of, xix, xx–xxi, 3, 13, 18, 104–5; venerated, 180; vernacular, 42
astrology, xvii, 76, 102, 129, 150, 217, 247nn83–85. *See also* notebooks: astrological materials in
audiences: affect produced for, 127; *bhāṣā* or Hindi as seen by, 6, 7, 9; elite, 122; expectations of, 145; for Hindi or vernacular works, 6, 134; illustrations as seen by, 50, 237n45; paratextual materials for, 54, 139, 183; participation or responses by, 89, 100, 108; for *pem-kathā*, 17–18, 27, 32, 34–35, 54; recitation or singing to, 42–43, 46, 57, 108–9, 183, 235n23; separate (or not), 110, 216, 226; sultans explain to, 32, 35; terms used by, xix, 6, 7; women in, 252n31
Aurangzeb, Emperor, 26, 61, 239n75
authority: of Brahmins, 79, 123, 241n13; colophons and, 130, 141, 193; of gurus, 20, 166, 174, 190–92; of *hukum*, 171; of intellectuals or pandits, 78–79, 85, 123, 241n13; literacy and, 79, 126; of monks, 126, 141, 149; oral performance and, 92–93; pedagogical, 34, 60; of physical book, 20, 93, 137, 157, 166–68, 188, 190–93; political, 32, 121, 147–48, 170, 236n42; religious, 78–79, 92, 123, 141, 148, 150, 159, 165–70, 178, 191, 193, 241n13; of scribes or copyists, 141, 149; scriptural, 166, 178–80, 182, 188; struggles over, 167–68; of writing, 18, 167, 169–70
Avadh, 27, 30, 36

Baba Farid, *See* Fariduddin, Shaikh "Ganj-i Shakar"
Babullah bin Sayid Muhammad, 26–28, 62, 63
Babur, Emperor, 103, 248n88
bahīs, 96–97, 113
Baḥr al-Ḥayāt, 38
Banaras, xiii, 133, 252n34; Bharat Kala Bhavan in, 221; Brahmins in, 93, 137, 152, 240n7, 252n31; education or scholars in, 79, 126–27; Kabir in or from, 77, 79, 89, 93, 108, 269n30; as literary setting, 137, 238n62; Nagari Pracharini Sabha in, xiii, 205, 207, 210–11; Ravidas in or from, 77, 241n13
Banaras Hindu University, 53, 212
Banarsidas, 12, 59, 238n63
basta, 96, 136, 253nn44–45
bayāẓ, xxi, 103–4, 248nn92–93
Behl, Aditya, 30, 39, 234n15, 235nn19–20, 236n42
Bengal, 82, 135, 149, 208, 211, 232n16, 238n61
Bengali, 120, 135, 162, 208, 238n61, 267n5
Bengali script, 52
bhagats, 166, 168, 178, 181–82
Bhagavadgītā, 1, 143
Bhāgavata Purāṇa, 82–83, 121, 161–63, 165, 241–42n17; commentaries on, 130, 133; dating of, 259n25; in *pothī* format, 144
Bhagvandas Niranjani, 147, 179; *Amṛtadhāra* by, 133; *Bhāgavata Purāṇa* commentary by, 133; *Jaiminī Aśvamedhaparva* by, 128–29; *Vairāgya Vṛnd* by, 127–28, 134, 142, 145, 148, 217
Bhai Gurdas, 167–69, 190, 261n46, 261n49; *vārs* by, 169–70, 182
bhajan. *See* hymns
bhākhā. *See* bhāṣā
Bhaktamāl of Nabhadas Ramanandi, 88, 188–89, 244n43, 266n110
Bhaktamāl of Pyareram, 189
Bhaktamāl of Raghavdas Dadupanthi, 88, 172, 189, 192, 243–44n42, 264n82
bhakti, 37, 133, 165, 166, 241n14, 247nn84–86, 252n35; characteristics of, 15; as emotion, 125–26, 128, 132, 217; as literary period, 213; *nirguṇ/saguṇ* distinction in, 15, 98, 110; "public" communities of, 188–89; raga system and, 246n74; scholarship on, 15, 77, 188;

Sikhism and, 166–67; singing or orality and, 77, 132, 246n74; in subject catalogues, 217–18; vernaculars and, 8–9; writing and, 15, 18, 131, 156–57, 160, 163, 188, 257–58n8, 263n70. *See also* nirguṇ bhakti communities; nirguṇ bhakti literature; nirguṇ bhakti saints; saguṇ bhakti poets

bhakti poetry. *See* devotional poetry

Bhallas, 168, 261n49

Bharat Kala Bhavan, 53, 221, 223, 237n54

bhāṣā (*bhākhā*), 38, 55, 128, 233n6, 255n61, 255n70; in Arabic script, 46–47, 237n48; commentaries in, 133, 139, 143, 254n53; connoisseurs of poetry in, 12, 142; culture of, 11–12; Dakkhani and, 61; defined, 6, 7, 21; *deśa* or *deśī* (*see* deśa bhāṣā); "eastern," 27; emotions expressed in, 27; genres in, 156, 225; Hindu epics in, 36; languages included in, 7; lexicon of, 12, 35, 254n50; literary culture of, 12, 103; as literary language, 9, 12, 18, 250–51n14; in Marwar, 74; meters of, 29, 36, 85; in monastic libraries, 147; novelty of, 12; paratexts in, 144–45; as pedagogical language, 145, 165, 249n5; in *pothīs*, 137, 142, 225; *pūrab dī* or eastern, 27, 32; *rasa*-filled, 42; relation to other languages of, 7, 9–10, 61; Sanskritized, 145; as scholarly language, 129, 133, 149, 164–65, 225; as scriptural language, 158; synonyms for, 7; transregional register of, 137–38; as written language, 18, 30–31, 43, 87, 225; poetry in, 128. *See also* Hindi

Bhikharidas, 10

Bijapur, 18, 58, 61, 239n75

Bilgrami, Mir 'Abdul Wahid, 37

binding, 17, 222; of *guṭakās*, 52, 74, 94–96, 104, 114; loose, 205; of multiple works together, 52; of palm leaf manuscripts, 160; of *pem-kathā*, 52, 55, 61; of *pothīs*, 160 (*see also pothīs*: unbound); of scriptural anthologies, 20, 146, 159–60, 180, 185–87, 225; stitch types for, 13; terms for, 40, 136, 160; of *vāṇī*, 155, 178–80, 225. *See also* book binders

bodies, xix, 1, 83, 118, 162, 190, 193. *See also* embodied practices

book ateliers, 10, 44, 164, 224, 255n69; *kitāb-khānah*, 58–59; *pothī-khānā*, 59

book binders, 12, 44, 46, 51, 52, 58–59, 62, 185, 186

book covers, 13, 44, 52, 95, 97, 155, 187

book cultures, xxi, 1, 12, 18, 22, 55–56; Persianate, 43–44, 58–59, 225; *pothī*-centered, 239n71; South Asian or Indic, xxi, 12, 13, 44; sultanate-period, xxi, 18, 47; vernacular, xxi, 11, 13, 18, 47, 55, 184, 225; women's participation in, 22

book history field, 13

books: as agents, 56, 156; as art, 219–24; authority and, 157, 188; borrowed, 59, 104, 238n63, 248n92; care for, xix, 2, 209; commodified (or not), 57, 59–60; as currency, 18, 43, 57, 60, 103, 121, 145; dispersed folios of, 21, 220–24; expectations for "look" of, 9, 54–55, 121, 135, 138, 145, 239n71; formats of (*see* formats); as gifts, 44, 58–59, 82, 248n92; as gurus, 183, 190; handwritten (*see under* handwritten materials); as icons, 103, 136–37, 141, 170, 190; layout of (*see* layout); liturgical use of, xxi; lost or stolen, xiv, 58, 162; manuscripts versus or as, xvii–xviii, 21, 205, 218–19; materials used for, 5, 13; nonprint, 1–2; notebooks versus or as, xx, 103; pedagogical practices and, xxi, 19; performances with, xxi, 19; size of, 10, 45, 143; terms for, xvii, xix, xxi, 159–60; as "things," xix–xx, 21. *See also* granth; guṭakā; kitāb; pothī; pustakam

bookstands, 11, 51, 136, 151, 155. *See also* raḥl

Brahmins, 90, 207, 209, 217; authority of, 79, 123, 241n13; lithograph of, 137, 152, 252n31; *pandits* (*see* pandits: Brahmin); paper (not) used by, 11; patronage for, 165; *pothīs* used by, 78–79, 82, 92, 93, 137, 240n7; *purāṇas* recited by, 163

Braj, 37, 133, 224; religious communities in, 15–16; "sweet" tongue of, 10; Vaishnavas in, 81, 85, 98, 161–63, 165; vernacular of, 233n5

Brajbhāṣā, 161, 256n75. *See also* Hindi

Brown, Bill, xix

Brown, Mackenzie, 163–64

Buddhists, 233n7

Busch, Allison, xi, 123, 250n10, 254n50

Caitanya Caritāmṛta, 162–63

calligraphers, 9, 12, 17, 236n42–37, 239n69; in Deccan, 28, 61; Persian-literate scribes, 44, 45–47; recruitment of, 58–59

calligraphy: in colophons, 62; embellished, 138, 186, 187; by monks, 187; in Mughal atelier, 58; Persian, 237n46; print editions and, 56, 222; of *purāṇas*, 163; Sikh, 185–86; unruled lines in, 53; vernacular, 47, 50, 61–62

Candāyan, 10, 17, 39, 64, 66, 67, 69, 70; calligraphy of, 45–48, 50, 237n49; circulation and reception of, 47; date of, 29; Daud's self-reflections in, 32, 34; dispersed folios of, 221–23, 234n15, 237n45, 270n41; earliest known copies of, 44–49; genre of, 30; hero of, 30, 33; illustrators or illustrations of, 34, 44–45, 48–51, 221–23, 237nn52–54; importance of, 29, 31, 34, 36, 43; John Rylands copy of, 48, 49, 50, 64, 69, 221, 222, 237n49, 237n55; Lahore-Chandigarh copy of, 47, 49–51, 223; language of, 31–33; as literature, 29–30, 34, 51; material form for, 31, 44–46; meters of, 29; opening section of, 31; orthographic conventions for, 46–48; performances of, 38, 50; as poem, 34, 234n15, 235n23; poetic and literary devices in, 30; Qutban and, 36–37; scribal headings for, 47–48; stanzas of, 45–46, 53, 223; story of, 30; Sufi symbolism in, 30; term *pothī* in, 32. *See also* Daud, Maulana

castes, xix, 54; any or all, 163, 166, 189; merchant, 14, 123; "middle," 19; subaltern, 77, 82, 89, 241n13

caupaī, 29, 33, 36, 45, 85, 91–92, 139, 140; Dadu's use of, 91–92; layout of verses in, 46, 52–53; as vernacular meter, 29, 37–39

Chandaratnāvalī, 127, 130, 134, 146, 217, 231n1, 251n18, 256n78, 263n80

chāp, 100, 171

Chhatrapati Shivaji Maharaj Vastu Sangrahalaya, 28, 47, 222, 255n69, 270n43

chronicles, 10, 56, 89, 233n23

Cintamani Tripathi, 123, 124, 126, 134, 148

circulation: of *Candāyan*, 47–48, 223; evidence for, 17; of Khusrau's *rekhtah*, 30; of material text artifacts, 3, 60, 104, 121–22, 226; monks' role in, 149–50; of notebooks or *guṭakās*, 19, 94, 96, 101–4, 110; oral, 39, 77, 161; paper's impact on, 11; of *pothīs*, 19, 121–22; of *pem-kathā*, 18, 57; print technology and, 56; provincial, 123; removal of works from, xvii, 205; of romances, 44; temporal, 3; transregional, elite, 43–44, 58; of vernacular lyrics, 37; wide or broad, 19, 37, 48, 244n43; writing allows for, 122

codices: anthological, 20, 160, 179–80, 186, 226; blank, 52; bound, 20, 28, 59, 168, 179–80, 185; of *Candāyan*, 44–46, 48; collaborative production of, 44, 50; colophons in, 62; in courtly book culture, 59, 239n71; Dadu Panthi, 20, 179–80, 186–87; genres not using, 52; hybrid, 59; illustrated, 3, 43, 48, 59; illustrations depicting, 237n54; Mughal, 239n71; Niranjani, 20, 154–55, 179–80, 186–87; as notebooks, 52, 103; patronage systems for, 43; *pem-kathā*, 28, 52–53, 62, 224; portrait-orientation, 28, 186–87; *pothī* and, 121; reading practices for, 44–45, 136; romance, 44, 46; *scriptio continua* in, 94; scriptural, 20, 94, 154, 185–87, 225; stanza-wise organization of, 28, 46, 52–53, 224; terms for, 103, 185; text direction in, 44, 52; unillustrated, 46, 52; venerated, 155–56; visual embellishment of, 187; wide-format, 28. *See also* bayāẓ; granth; safīnah; vāṇī

collecting, xviii, 20, 206, 208–9, 211–12, 214, 222

colophons: addressed to future readers, 1–2, 62, 141; authors', 130; book speaks in, 205; complaints in, 1, 143, 155; dates in, 75, 119, 142, 148, 155, 176, 247n83, 248n89, 248n94; details in, 142–45, 184; embellished, 187; by Gopaldas, 176–77, 178; gurus in, 141, 146, 148, 176, 184, 193; in Islamicate manuscripts, 62, 239n77; locations in, 57, 119, 130, 142, 144, 148, 176; in Niranjani *Vāṇī*, 180, 193; reciters in, 143, 248n94; in *Pañc Vāṇī* manuscripts, 175; patrons in, 62, 145, 237n56, 239n75; in *pothīs*, 139, 141–46, 176–77; by Rupdas, 119–20; scribal, 1–2, 62, 134, 141, 143, 147; terms for, xviii, 254–55n60; verse tallies in, 139, 184; word breaks in, 138

commentary (genre), 91, 127–28, 130, 133, 217; manuscripts with root text and, 139, 143, 144–45, 247n83, 254n53

commonplace books, xviii, 103

conservation, xvii, 210, 216, 220

copyeditors. *See* editors or editing

copying, xviii–xix, 46, 178, 254–55n60; binding and, 52; of diagrams, 76; errors in, 243n38; mechanical, 147; by monks, 14, 19, 121, 141, 143–44, 146–47, 149, 175; in notebooks, 103; of *pothīs*, 138–39, 141–44, 149; rates for, 139, 254n55; rules for, 81, 255n64; by Rupdas, 119–21, 149; as seasonal labor, 143–44; as transcription, 143, 255n64; spiritual benefits of, 81

cosmopolitan languages, 3, 9, 11, 39, 42, 55, 96, 100

cosmopolitan literature, 37, 40, 54
courts, judicial, 207
courts, royal: Afghan, 42; calligraphers et al. at, 58–59, 236n42, 265n103; Deccani, 61; Delhi, 134; in illustrations, 49; intellectual exchanges with, 125, 127, 132–34, 148; Islamicate, 43; Jodhpur, 134; literary practices of, 185; literature composed in, 9; multilingual, 43; performances in, 10, 121; popular-religious sphere and, 85–86, 122; provincial or regional, 17, 30, 62, 186; Rathore, 147, 148; religion at, 133, 165; ritual idioms of, 159, 171, 188, 190; Sanskrit at, 3, 217; scholars at, 123, 132; sultanate, 30, 31, 55, 61, 85; treatises composed in, 99, 125; Tughlaq, 31. *See also* Bijapur; Gwalior; Jaipur; Jaunpur; elites: courtly; Mughals; patrons: court; poets: court; Rajputs
Cox, Whitney, 254n57
critical editions, xiv, xviii, 21, 218, 269n29

Dadu Dayal: antagonists of, 92–93; anthologies including, 161, 172–73, 175–77, 178–79, 183; *caupāī* by, 91, 92; community of, 18; date and background of, 77; as guru, 182–83; hagiographies of, 88–89, 91–92, 165, 173, 243n42, 252n31, 262n67; hymns by, 98; influences on, 87; Kabir and, 241n12; on Name, 81, 241n12; *pad* by, 266n116; "poet" label rejected by, 126; recurring terms or phrases of, 13; *sākhī*s by, 81, 91; speech privileged by, 88, 93, 109; transcriptions of, 173–74; translations of, 132; writing for or literacy of, 74, 77–78, 85, 89, 93, 241n12
Dādū Janm Līlā. *See* Jangopal Dadupanthi
Dadu Panth: canon of, 88; chanting in, 81; as community, 163, 165, 187–89, 191; courtly idiom in, 190, 266n117; founding of, 15; guru in, 182, 191; Kabir and (*see* Kabir: in Dadu Panth); libraries of, 146–47, 178, 255n72; literary theory in, 125–28, 147, 150, 250n12; manuscripts of, 15; material book or codex in, 141, 163, 179, 186–88, 193; *melā* of, 191–92, 266n124; monks of, 19, 98, 102, 122, 125–30, 132–33, 141, 144, 145, 147–50, 172, 175–76, 187, 255n72, 256n85; notebooks of, 98, 102, 105; orality stressed by, 91; scholars or scholarship in, 15, 125–30, 133, 150; scribes in, 184, 187; scriptures of, 20, 40, 78, 83, 157–59, 172–75, 178–80, 182, 187–88, 246n69 (*see also* Dādū Vāṇī; Pañc Vāṇī; Sarvāṅgīs); Sikhs and, 16, 146, 172, 177–78, 189, 226; writing in, 20, 160, 163, 243n32, 263n79
Dādū Vāṇī, 172–75, 179, 193, 241n12, 265n96; as anthology, 159; date of, 172–73; editing of, 173; opening verses of, 182–83; structure of, 174; venerated, 172, 190–91, 202, 266n122, 266n124
Daftari, Mohandas, 173, 174
Dakkhani, 61
Dalmau, 30
Damayanti. *See* Nal Daman
Das, Shyamsundar, xiv, 208, 210, 213, 240n2, 269n30
Daud, Maulana, 10, 17, 29, 39, 242n29; "double move" of, 32; illustrations of, 34, 49–51; intellectual culture of, 32; literacy of, 33–34; patron of, 31–32, 35; performative context of, 31, 38; political context of, 30; Qutban and, 36–38; "sang in Hinduki," 46, 225; as Sufi, 32–33, 235n19. *See also* Candāyan
Deccan, 27–28, 30, 44, 58, 59, 61, 103, 135, 257n87
Deibert, Ronald, xx–xxi
Delhi, 30, 134, 269n26
Delhi sultanate, 30, 34, 76
deśa bhāṣā, xxi, 7–8
deśī or *desī* languages, xxi, 26, 36–37, 100
Devanāgarī, 6, 22–23. *See also* Nāgarī
devotional poetry: anthologies of, 246n70; aural experience of, 38, 77, 89–90, 97–100, 108, 132, 246n73; authorial personas of, 88, 243n35, 243n40, 249n97; debates on definition of, 126–28; depiction of esoteric or ritual knowledge in, 102, 247n84; depiction of reading or writing in, 78, 88–89, 92, 170, 242n31, 243n33, 244n46; in hagiographies, 89, 91, 108; meters for, 132; *nirguṇ*, 13, 77–79, 88, 91, 101–2, 108, 126, 128, 149, 233n7, 241n12, 252n35; as poetry (or not), 126; soteriological power of, 90, 108; Vaishnava, 16, 98, 101, 267n3
dhrupad, 38, 250n11
didactic couplet/epigram. *See* sākhīs
Didwana, 89, 119, 130, 134, 150, 154, 192, 204, 256n85
dohā, 28–29, 36–37, 45–46, 52–53, 80, 85, 126, 131, 139
doodles, xvii, 104
Dvivedi, Hazariprasad, 4, 8, 233n7
Dwivedi, Mahavirprasad, xiv

editors or editing, 19, 138, 142, 149, 168, 173, 174, 185, 254n53; of print editions, xx, 219, 221, 265n96, 269n29
education, 89, 96, 125, 127, 147–48, 167, 261n40; vernacular, 122
elites: connoisseurship of, 58–59, 61–62, 122; courtly, 3, 8, 86, 125, 147–48; deluxe copies for, 43–44, 51, 52; feudal, 110; Hindu, 82, 163; Mughal, 59, 164, 165, 169; Muslim, 34, 164; parodies of, 92; Persianate or Persianized, 17, 32, 58–59, 61, 164; political or ruling, 28, 43–44, 52, 59, 82, 125, 147–49, 163, 165–66, 169, 225, 233n23; Rajput, 165, 169; vernacular intellectuals, 123; women, 233n23
embodied practices, 2, 10–11, 17, 75, 79, 136, 149, 157, 239n71, 246n73
epic romance, 16, 17, 233n5. *See also* pem-kathā
epics, xiv, 122, 236n45; bardic, 10; in *bhāṣā*, 36, 121; heroic, 110; Hindu, 85, 156; love (*see* pem-kathā); in notebooks, 110, 218; oral, 30, 110; regional, 76; Sanskrit, 134
epigrammatic couplet. *See* sākhīs
epistemology, xx–xxi, 16, 81, 85, 141, 160, 241n12

"Faizi," Shaikh Abu al-Faiz ibn Mubarak, 26–27, 233n1
Fariduddin, Shaikh "Ganj-i Shakar," 7, 29, 166, 177, 178, 189, 243n38
Fatehpur, 86, 134, 142, 172, 256n78
Fatehpur manuscript, 86, 142, 242n30, 246n71
festivals, 57, 89, 91, 93, 101, 192
formats, xvii, 44, 52, 187, 232n18; changed (or not), xxi, 11, 42, 56, 135, 143; choices between, 28; Dadu Panth preferences in, 186–87; for notebooks, 103; Niranjani preferences in, 186–87; for *pem-kathās*, 28, 46, 52, 56; in sultanate era, 32

Gangohi, 'Abdul Quddus, 36, 37
Garibdas, 173–74, 190–91
gāthā (meter), 36–37
gāthā (song), 30, 100, 130, 173. *See also* songs
Gaudiya Sampraday, 15, 81, 133, 161–62, 165, 258n8
Ghawth, Shaikh Muhammad, 38
Gobind Singh, Guru, 159, 169, 172, 190
Goindval *pothīs*, 168, 171, 181, 185–86, 200, 261n44, 265n99
Golden Temple, 190
Gopaldas, 176–78, 183, 240n7, 240n11, 241n12, 242n19, 265n96; ecumenism of, 177, 262n63, 264n84; paratextual material of, 183 (*see also* colophons: by Gopaldas); tropes used by, 242n26, 243n33. *See also* Sarvāṅgīs
Gorakhnath, 177, 179, 189, 193, 240n7
Gosaṭi Guru Miharivānu, 167, 169, 261n44
Gosvamis, xix, 141, 161–62, 250n12
granth, xxi, 5, 81, 128, 163, 253n41; *bhaṇḍārs*, 81, 212; etymology and meaning of term, 159–60; handwritten (*hastalikhit*), xvii, xviii, 21, 205; Jayasi's use of term, 40; literary or scholastic works as, 130; made to speak (*granth bāṁc-*), 149, 193; *nirguṇ* monks' use of term, 126; *samādhi*, 162; scripture, as, 20, 156, 159, 179, 183, 185, 225; unified, 179, 180
Grierson, George, 8, 56, 207–8, 267n3
Gujarat, 10, 77, 82, 135, 149, 240n1
Gujarati, 7, 120
Gurmukhi, 7, 23, 52, 146, 211; calligraphy in, 186–87; development of, 185–86, 265n99, 265n101
guru-disciple lineages: included in books, 120–21, 141, 148, 176, 184, 193; segmentation of, 158, 191–92, 246n73
Guru Granth Sāhib, 159, 166–71, 240n7; authority of, 169, 190, 193; as bound volume, 159; earlier versions of, 167–68, 244n57; embellishments, etc. in, 186; Dadu Panth and, 174, 178; *Japu Jī* in, 170; Nanak's *chāp* in, 171; rituals involving, 190, 242n18; as sovereign, 159, 190; term *dīn* in, 260n38; writing and, 86–87, 169–70. *See also* Ādi Granth; Goindval *pothīs*; Guru Harsahai *pothī*; Kartarpur *pothī*
Guru Harsahai *pothī*, 167–68, 181, 185
gurus: books as, 20, 155, 183, 190, 192, 193; books given or loaned by, 141, 146, 168; collected or transcribed words of, 35, 84, 173–75, 178; copies made for, 104, 120, 141, 144, 146, 155, 180, 187; Dadu Panthi, 182–83, 190; dialogues of disciples with, 92, 131, 140; divine, 87, 170; hagiographies of, 91–92, 175; hymns of, 175; invocations to, 183–84; Niranjani, 154–55, 187; *pothī* in performances by, 141, 144–45; recitations by, 80, 92, 109, 130, 131, 140, 183; scripture as, 159, 180, 183; Sikh, 166, 169–71, 178, 182, 185, 243n32, 262n60, 264n92; as sovereigns, 169; women, 252n31

guṭakā, xxi, 116, 177, 185, 206, 216, 224, 253n41; as briefcases, 19, 75, 101; cataloguing of, 216, 218; diverse contents of, 74–76, 98–99, 102, 104–5, 109–10, 111, 246n71, 247n85, 262n66; hagiographies' silence about, 93; Hindu, 104; Jain, 104–5; material forms of, 94–96, 104, 114, 187; orthography of, 94; performances using, 77, 94–95, 97–101, 105–6, 109, 225, 249n100; *pothī* and, 136–37, 138; religious works in, 52, 76, 104–5, 180, 224; *scriptio continua* in, 94–95; scripts used in, 95, 105, 109, 111; Sikh, 104, 146, 172, 256n74; source of name of, 96; users of, 96–97; verse order in, 99–100. *See also* notebooks

Gwalior, 36, 147; court of, 10, 85, 134

hagiographies: Dadu Panthi, 20, 91, 158, 165, 172–73, 178, 191; earliest extant copies of, 88; gurus teach in, 80; of Hindi poets, 231n14; Niranjani, 20, 88–89, 158, 165, 178–79, 230n1; *nirguṇ*, 35, 88, 108, 160, 244n43; in notebooks, 218; poetic traditions and, 88, 161; public performances in, 57, 91, 94, 109, 252n31; Pushtimargi, 161; putative illiteracy in, 18, 170, 244n46; as scripture, 180; sectarian boundaries and, 89, 244n43; Sikh, 20, 158, 165, 167–70, 178, 189, 261n40; transcriptions in, 20, 35, 173, 178; unwritten, 243n41; Vaishnava, 161, 163; writing in, 88–89, 92–93, 170

handwritten materials, xiv, xvii–xxi, 205–6, 214, 219, 224; books, xviii–xxi, 2, 20–21, 205–6, 214, 219, 224; catalogues, 209; lithography and, 56; material or paratextual aspects of, 21; notebooks (*see* notebooks); terms for, xviii–xix, 205–6

Haqā'iq-i Hindī, 37

Hargobind, Guru, 186

Haridas Niranjani, 17, 77, 249nn98–99; books or writing criticized by, 78; Didwana monastery of, 119, 130, 192; disciples or lineage of, 191–93; hagiographies of, 89, 91, 263–64n82; *melā* of, 192; notebooks including, 76, 98, 105–8; recurring terms or phrases of, 13; *samādhi* of, 192; *vāṇīs* including, 154–55, 179

Haridas Radhavallabhi, 98

Hariramdas Niranjani: *Chandaratnāvalī* by, 127, 130, 132, 134, 217, 231n1, 251n18, 263n80; colophon by, 130; copies of works by, 146–47, 256nn77–78; *Dāyal Jī Kī Pañc Paracai* by, 88; *Nāmaprakāś* by, 130, 231n1; *Paramārthasatsaī* by, 192

Harmandir Sahib, 190

Hasan, Mir, 30

hastalikhit or *hastalikhita granth*, xvii, xviii, 21, 205

heritage, xvii–xviii, 209, 230n7

Hidāyat al-Qulūb wa 'Ināyāt 'Ullam al-Ghuyūb, 29–30

hindavī, 6, 7, 30, 234n13. *See also* bhāṣā; Hindi

Hindi: book or writing culture of, xxi, 44, 54–55, 62, 120, 135; defined, 6–7, 21–22, 231n4; dialects of, 6, 10, 177, 216, 269n26; gender in, 22; history of language of, xvi, xxi, 2–4, 6–8, 21, 231n4; history of writing in, xxi, 3–6, 8–9, 17, 29–30, 43, 50, 75; innovation and, 11–12, 19, 50, 62, 123–25; Jains writing in, 16, 104, 212; lexicon of, 5–6, 22, 55; literary histories of, xiii, 2, 4–5, 8–9, 20–21, 29, 87, 110, 122, 132, 206–14, 219, 226, 233n7, 267n3, 268n22; as literary language, 2–4, 6–8, 12, 16–18, 29, 62; modern or standard, xiv, 6, 21–22; multilingual context of, 6, 9; as national language, xiii–xiv, 75, 206–7; "novelty" of, 12, 123; poetic theories in, 124–25; poetry in, 8, 62, 86, 233n7; precolonial, 2, 5–6, 20, 22–23; premodern, xiii, 3; print technology and, xviii, 56, 121, 218–19, 238n61; promotion of, xiii–xiv, 217–19, 240n2; as scholarly or intellectual language, 9, 16, 19, 119, 122–25, 132; scholars of, xiii–xiv, 4, 29, 77, 87, 98, 160, 207–8, 212–13, 221, 253n45; scripts used for, 7, 21–23, 75, 211 (*see also* Arabic script; Gurmukhi; Kaithī; Nāgari); scriptures in, 157; Sufis or Muslims writing in, 15, 30, 212, 223; terms for books, etc. in, xviii–xix, 19, 32, 160, 205–6; terms for literary activity in, 5; terms for writing in, 5–6; transliteration of, 23, 27. *See also* bhāṣā; hindavī; "Hinduki"; Urdu

Hindi Sahitya Sammelan, xiv, 216

"Hinduki," 10, 33–34, 46, 225

Hindus or Hinduism, 8, 55, 92, 156, 167, 214, 218, 223, 226, 234n13; archives or libraries of, 211–12; artists, 232n18; ascetics, 33; elites, 82, 163, 255n69; kingship in, 147, 165; manuscripts of, 44, 81, 218; Nāgarī script and, 212, 265n101; notebooks of, 104; *pothīs* of, 142; practices of, 33; religious specialists, 96; saints, 27, 57; sects or *sampradāys* of, 15, 156

hindustānī, 6, 238n61. *See also* bhāṣā; hindavī; Hindi; "Hinduki"; Urdu
Horstmann, Monika, 179, 263n68, 263n74, 263n79
hymnody, 9, 16, 36
hymns: anthologized, 172, 178; *bhajan*, 19, 89, 97, 245n67; in codices, 185, 218; communal singing of, 97, 130, 182, 187, 192, 245n67; Dadu's, 88, 92, 115, 172; fluid structure of, 99–100; genres of, 85, 182; Kabir's, 86, 88, 136; in Kaithī script, 75; *kīrtan*, 97; meters of, 85, 182; narratives and, 88–90; Niranjani, 192; *nirguṇ*, 74, 76, 98, 105; in notebooks, 74–76, 78, 94–95, 97–99, 104–9, 111, 138, 217, 225; as oral genre, 19, 77, 89–90, 95, 100, 107–9, 225; organization of, 98–99, 168, 174, 181–82; phonetic transcriptions of, 108, 138, 249n98; *pothīs* and, 136, 138; print editions of, 218, 264n83; ragas of, 99, 115, 168, 181; refrains in, 100, 108–9, 249n100; repetition in, 100; *saguṇ*, 98; Sikh, 84, 85, 167, 170–71, 178, 181–82, 189, 264n92

illiteracy, 18, 85, 86, 126, 170, 219, 244n46
illuminations, 20, 61, 155; floral, 186, 187; mark book as sacred, 186, 225; medallions, 187; in *Nal Daman*, 61, 223; palmettes, 186; in *pothīs*, 135, 138, 187; in *vāṇīs*, 155, 187
illuminators, 12, 61–62
illustrated works, xvii, xviii, 3, 122; as currency or symbolic capital, 43, 59; elite bibliophiles and, 58–59, 82; Hindu, 44, 82, 163; Jain, 44, 135; layouts of, 44–45; multilingual, 144–45; as objects of desire, 51; as objets d'art, 21, 206; in Persianate book culture, 43–45; *pothīs*, 135; reimagined, 220; separated folios of, 21, 220–23; sultanate-era, 45. *See also* Candāyan: illustrators or illustrations of; *pem-kathā:* illustrated
illustrations: as art, 21, 219–24; authors or scribes in, 50–51, 237n54; cataloguing of, 222–24; conventions or ideals of, 28, 45, 55–56, 224–25; headings link text and, 48; iconic figures in, 50, 237n53; reused, 223; text position versus, 44–45, 46, 48, 53, 144, 222, 223, 237n45, 237n52, 270n43. *See also* paintings
illustrators, 28, 34, 56, 58–59, 61, 62, 237n54; in Mughal imperial atelier, 255n69; *naqqāsh*, 44; as readers, 48–50, 237n52
ink: alternating or multiple colors of, 28, 119–20, 139, 155, 187, 198, 199, 237n49; black, 28, 41, 119, 120, 136, 184, 198, 199, 237n49; blue, 237n49; gold or silver, 28, 61; on paper, 135, 185; in poetry, 41, 74, 83–84, 86, 170; production of, 83; red, 45, 119–20, 136, 139, 144, 151, 155, 184, 187, 198, 199, 237n49, 256n74; Sikh use of, 186; smudged, 74
intellectuals: authority of, 85, 123; Brahmin, 268n14; courtly, 125, 133, 148, 226; criticism or satire of, 85; Jain, 85, 212; literary, 19, 101; monks, 19; Muslim, 92, 243n37; networks of, 19; *pothī*-reading, 19, 121; religious, 19, 101, 123; vernacular, 121–24, 132, 138, 149, 208, 250nn6–7, 260n36. *See also* pandits
Islam: art or painting in, 220, 222; esoteric diagrams in, 76, 109; influence of, 132, 164, 186–87; pedagogical lineages in, 209; profession of faith in, 33, 181; scriptures in, 32, 155, 164, 186, 257n2; writing in, 155, 164–65, 170, 257n2. *See also* Muslims

jadwal, 45–46, 53, 186
Jahangir, 239n75, 262n52
Jains or Jainism, 11, 16, 44, 76, 164; book or manuscript culture in, 16, 81, 131, 135, 136, 142, 156, 253n49; criticism of, 76, 101, 105; *granth bhaṇḍārs* of, 81, 212; intellectuals, 85, 212; linguistic ideology of, 16; literate, 96; merchants, 55, 104, 127; monks, 156, 240n8; in multireligious contexts, 76, 105, 165, 212, 218; Nagari Pracharini Sabha and, 212; notebooks of, 104–5, 110; *pem-kathās* enjoyed by, 55, 57; poets, 105; songs in, 76, 212; *tīrthaṅkars*, 76, 104, 110
Jaipur, 188, 192, 210, 216, 224; courts of, 59, 134, 148, 165, 256n82, 260n36
janam-sākhīs, 169, 244n57, 261n40
Jangopal Dadupanthi, 76, 88–89, 91–92, 109, 165, 173, 175, 243n42, 252n31, 262n67
jap, 33, 81
Jasvant Singh, 124, 134, 148, 253n38, 256n83
Jaunpur, 17, 35
Jayasi, Malik Muhammad, 37; paper in poems by, 40–42, 87, 236n31, 236n37, 243n36; self-reflection by, 38–39; on written scripture, 39–40. *See also* Padmāvat
Jiva Gosvami, xix

Jñānasamudra, 131–33, 140–41, 146
Jodhpur, 134, 165, 192, 210, 216

Kabir, 7, 36, 87, 126; in anthologies, 161, 175; background of, 77, 89; community of, 18 (*see also* Kabir Panth); in Dadu Panth, 78, 83, 86, 172, 175; date of, 236n37, 242n29; editions of, 218; hagiographies about, 89, 91, 93, 108, 172, 244n43, 244n46; ink or writing metaphor of, 83, 85, 86; language of, 108, 269n30; meters used by, 80, 249n99; in Niranjani *Vāṇī*, 154, 179; in notebooks, 76, 86, 98–99, 101, 106, 108, 246n71; *pads* by, 107, 108, 132, 248n97, 249n99; paper mentioned by, 236n37, 244n46; *pothī* reading criticized by, 78–80, 82, 136, 240n7; presumed illiteracy of, 85, 86, 170, 244n46; recurring terms or phrases of, 13; *sākhīs* by, 78, 80, 89, 101, 107, 132, 241n12, 260n38; in Sikh tradition, 166, 168, 172, 178, 240n7; speech privileged by, 80, 88, 91, 107–8; translations of, 132, 252–53n36
Kabir Panth, 15, 81, 88, 98, 172, 189, 246n69
Kabīr Paracaī, 89, 93
Kacchwahas, 59, 148, 165, 174, 260n37
kaḍavak. *See* stanzas
Kaithī, 7, 52, 71, 85, 217, 240n1; Nāgarī and, 23, 75, 95, 105, 111, 211, 239n72; in notebooks, 75, 95–96, 105, 111; *pem-kathā* in, 53, 59; *scriptio continua* for, 53
Kanhāvat, 38
Kartarpur *pothī*, 168, 171, 181–82, 189–90, 193, 261nn49–50, 262n61, 264nn91–92, 264n94
Kashmir, 11, 135, 239n69
Kavindracharya Sarasvati, 148, 164, 247n83
kāvya, 19, 251n14; cataloguing of, 217; conventions of, 134, 138; courtly, 134; Daud's *Candāyan* as, 34; devotional theory of, 125–28, 130; Pollock on, 2–3, 9–10, 29, 100; *rasa* theory of, 126; Sanskrit, 128, 129, 132, 217; *śāstra* on, 122, 129, 148; song or *gāthā* versus, 100; vernacular, 8, 19, 130, 132, 150, 225; writing and, 8, 130, 163, 225. *See also* poetry
kāyasth, 59, 97, 185, 207
Keshavdas, 123, 124, 126, 127, 134, 148, 246n71; *Kavipriyā* by, 125; *Rasikapriyā* by, 121, 125, 150, 224, 237n52, 250n9, 250n13; Sundardas and, 251n17; *Vijñānagīta* by, 164, 253n38
Khan, Dilir, 26–28, 61–62, 63, 223, 239n75
Khan, Mirza, 27, 61, 233n5
khaṛī bolī, 6, 8
Khusrau, Amir, 7, 30, 45, 56, 233n7, 234n11
kitāb, 185, 186, 226; in Akbar's library, 164; Islamicate or Persian, 44, 156–57, 186, 260n34; *qāẓīs* hold, 92, 93; scriptures, 156–57, 164, 185, 260n34; Sikh use of term, 167; as symbol, 163. *See also* ahl-i kitāb/ahl al-kitāb
kitāb-k̲h̲ānah or *kitāb-k̲h̲ānā*. *See* book ateliers
Krishna: in Braj, 16, 98, 161, 246n74; devotion to or devotees of, 15, 27, 77, 98, 133, 177, 231n14, 245n66; Keshavdas on, 250n13; works about, 38, 125, 133, 162–63, 224

Latour, Bruno, xvi, xix, 258n12
layouts, xxi, 11, 44, 48, 56, 94; calligraphic, 222; palm leaf archetypes for, 42, 135; *pem-kathā*, 55–56, 225; *pothī*, 138; print, 56; stanzaic, 52
letter or letters: Arabic (or not), 33, 46–47, 109, 235n22, 237n54; auspicious, 129; in *Candāyan*, 33; in Dadu Dayal poems, 241n12; "from the *śāstras*," 26; in Kabir poem, 79, 241n12; in magic squares, 109, 118; Manjhan on, 42, 47; mystical views of, 33–34, 170; in Ravidas poem, 86–87; ruled lines and, 95; Rupdas Niranjani's, 119; spacing of, 47, 75; superscript line (*śirorekha*) for, 138; terms *ākhara* etc. for, 33, 80
libraries: conditions of, xv–xvi, 209–10; "Hindu" or "Islamic," 211; monastic, 134; Mughal-era, xix, 58–59, 163–64
line breaks, 53, 56
literacy: cosmopolitan/vernacular binary of, 54–55; Daud's acquisition of, 32–34; discursive, 42, 96, 126, 165; elite, 92, 97; female, 233n23; graphic, 6, 42, 77, 79, 96, 126; ideology of universal, 5; Islamicate, 32; material equipment of, 242n31; modes and forms of, 23, 42, 85; monastic, 126, 144, 150; mundane, 3, 96, 150; orality versus, 87; Persian, 233n23; Persianate, 32; in Sikhism, 166–67, 170; vernacular, 12, 237n48; vocational, 14, 19, 84, 89, 96–97, 123, 126, 144, 167, 170
literature, 2–3, 6–9, 19, 29, 34, 100–101, 122, 157, 215, 223, 250n12, 250251n14; creating archive of, 206, 209–12; looking like, 138, 145; *sāhitya*, 206; vernacular, 38–39, 51, 55–56, 123–125, 225. *See also* kāvya
literization and literarization, 3, 9–10, 122, 158, 225

loose-leaf books, 13, 28; called *pothī*, 19, 52, 135; called *postak-hā*, xix; covers for, 96 (*see also* basta); numbered folios of, 139. *See also* pothī
love epics, 27. *See also* pem-kathā
love in separation (*'ishq-firāq*; *viraha*), 27, 48, 60
lyrics (*pad*), 18, 75, 97–100, 124, 132, 249nn98–100; anthologies, 177, 216, 219; cataloguing of, 216; devotional, 3, 8, 10, 77, 89, 91, 98, 101, 107, 132, 161, 166; in "Fatehpur manuscript," 142; Jain, 105; love, 233n5; manuscript types for, 94, 138; narrative-based, 101, 161; *nirguṇ*, 13, 18, 77, 101, 132, 149, 252n35; in notebooks, 18, 74–75, 94, 97–101, 105, 108, 116, 138, 142, 180, 225; performed, recited, or sung, 38–39, 74–75, 77, 89, 91, 94–95, 97, 99–101, 108, 225, 249n100; in *pothīs*, 86, 94; prosodic structure of, 95, 100; refrains to, 100, 109; as scripture, 161, 180; Sikh, 85, 166; Sufi, 30; Vaishnava, 98, 162; in *vāṇī*, 155, 179, 184; vernacular, 37–38, 162; by women, 252n31; written text versus, 39

Madhavdas, 159, 173–75, 190–91
Madhumālatī, 37–38, 43, 53, 57, 238n63, 239n72
Madhyadeshi or *madhyadeśī*, 10, 37, 45, 55, 85, 242n29
Mahābhārata, 10, 26–27, 233n1
malfuẓāt, 29–30
Malwa, 17
Mangaldas, Swami, 148, 230n1, 255n72
Manjhan, Mir Sayid Rajgiri, 37–38, 42, 47, 239n72. *See also* Madhumālatī
Mann, Gurinder Singh, 181–82, 186, 258n11, 260n38, 261n44, 262n61, 265n101
Manohardas Niranjani, 128, 133, 139, 141, 145, 148, 153, 179, 217
mantras: *bīja-*, 33; chanting, 81; graphic representations of, 184–85, 198; in notebooks, 74–75, 97, 111, 112, 218; Sikh, 168, 180–81. *See also* mūl mantar
manuscripts: as agents, xvi; books' relation to, xvii–xviii, 21; cataloguing of, xv, xvii, 206, 208, 211, 213, 214, 216–17, 222–23, 229–30n3; circulation of, xvii; damaged, xiv; data from, 13–14; defined, xviii, 21; Hindi terms for, xvii, xviii; as historical source, xvii, 20–21; illustrated, 21; interactions with, xvi; Islamic or Islamicate, 62, 143, 156, 212; as material artifacts, xviii; material aspects of, 17, 21; paratextual aspects of, 21; precolonial, xiv; print editions versus, xv; as raw materials, xvii, 21, 102, 206, 210, 219; statistics about, xv; storage of, xvii; sultanate-period, 11; value of, xvi–xvii; visual aspects of, 17, 21
Marathi, 9, 245n64, 263n70
Maru-Gujar ("Old Rajasthani"), 37
Marwar, 14, 59, 74, 134, 148, 253n38, 256n85
Marwari, 7, 74, 108, 120, 230n1, 249n98
masnavī, 31, 37, 45, 54
materiality, xv, 10, 51, 81, 180, 188, 221, 227
McLuhan, Marshall, xx, 238n59
media, xx–xxi, 12
memory or memorization, 84, 209; muscle, 75; in Persianate societies, 103; raga and, 178; of *sākhīs*, 80; writing and, xx, 18, 32, 78, 79, 81, 86, 87, 177, 243n38
merchants, 126, 133, 134, 144, 146, 150, 163; in audience, 89; authors, 91, 261n40; Bihani, 14; books circulate among, 57, 59; Dadu Panth and, 91, 93, 177; Jain, 55, 57, 104, 127; ledgers of, xvii, 96, 245n64; Niranjanis and, 14, 192; patrons, 18, 82, 146, 147; *pem-kathā* and, 18, 51–52, 55; in Persianate book culture, 43; reciters, 12; scribes, 261n41; scripts used by, 185; stamp (*nishān*) for, 84; vernacularization and, 10, 225; vocational literacy of, 123, 126, 144, 167
meters, poetic, 23, 43, 45, 80; broken, 108, 128, 132; *Chandaratnāvalī* on, 127, 130, 132, 134; *chappay*, 92, 132, 262n66; "magical" effects of, 91; mnemonic properties of, 78; organization by, 182; rubrics indicate, 140; *samān savaiyā* and *sarasī*, 85; vernacular, 26–37, 39. *See also* caupaī; dohā
Mewar, 14, 59
Miner, Allyn, 246n74
Mirgāvatī, 26, 35, 37–39, 53, 57, 71, 235n24, 237n54, 238n63
monastic orders: control of copying process by, 141, 147, 184; elites or rulers and, 147–48, 150, 256n85; governance of, 159; gurus or leaders of, 82, 104, 121, 145, 190, 191–92; hold literature of other sects, 146–47, 178, 255n72; libraries of, 134, 146–47, 178; lineages of, 130, 149, 192; *nirguṇ*, 15, 98, 102, 145, 174; north Indian, 258n16; scriptures as sovereign of, 190–91
monks: anthologies compiled by, 155, 171–72, 175–76, 178; backgrounds of, 14, 125–26, 144, 147, 150; copies made for, 81; copyists or scribes, 14, 19, 102, 119, 121, 141, 143–44,

146–47, 149, 153, 180; Gaudiya, 161–62; innovation by, 12, 129, 187; itinerant, 18, 19, 57, 101, 149, 174, 225; Jain, 81, 156, 240n8; literate, 125–26, 150; notebooks of, 18–19, 101–2, 104–5; performance practices of, 130; poets, 19, 217; *pothī*s circulate among, 141, 147–48; recruitment of, 14, 160, 258n16; rural, 2; scholars or intellectuals, 19, 121–22, 125–28, 131, 134; subaltern, 110; vocational literacy of, 144. *See also* Dadu Panth: monks of; Niranjani Sampraday: monks of; *nirguṇ* monks

Mughals or Mughal era: administrators or administration of, 84, 87, 185; bibliophilia of, 58–59, 147, 163–65, 169; book ateliers of, 59, 239n71, 255n69; in colophons, 142; court of, 26, 55, 58, 61, 123, 125, 147–48, 163, 164–65, 185–86, 239n75, 247n83, 248n88, 261n52; generals or soldiers, 18, 55, 60, 61; gurus challenged or killed by, 190, 191, 261–62n52; languages or scripts used by, 185–86, 207, 233n23, 234n12; libraries of, xix, 58, 141, 163–64, 233n23; as patrons, 18, 58, 163, 164, 165, 236n45; poet laureates, 26; political ideology of, 147, 157; portraits of, 103, 248n88; as readers, 54; Sikhs and, 190, 261–62n52; women, 233n23

mūl mantar, 168, 171, 180–81, 261n50, 262n61

munshī, 55, 59, 97, 239n69

museums, 219–23

music, 57, 121, 217, 246n74, 264n91; "written," 5, 75

Muslims, 167, 176, 223; elites (*see under* elites); musicians, 261n40; religious practices of, 33, 36; religious specialists, 76, 110 (*see also* qāẓīs); scripts used by, 34, 265n101; sultans, 8. *See also* Islam; Sufis

Nabhadas Ramanandi, 88, 188–89, 244n43, 266n113

Nafā'is al-Anfās, 29

Nāgarī: administrative use of, 185, 207, 238n61; *basmalah* in, 118; codex book format and, 52, 59; embellished folios in, 187; first print book in, 238n61; graphic literacy in, 96; in *guṭakā*s or notebooks, 75, 95–96, 105, 111; Hindi's link to (or not), 75, 207, 211; Hindu use of, 212, 265n101; Kaithī and, 53, 75, 95, 105, 111, 211, 239n72; layout or spacing of, 53, 56, 75, 138; as national script, xiii–xiv, 75, 207; in *pothī*s, 95, 144, 255n69; *śirorekhā* of, 138; in *vāṇī*s, 95, 187; variants in, 23

Nagaridas, Savant Singh, 134, 253n40

Nagari Pracharini Sabha, xiii, 267n6; archive produced by, xv, 20, 211; catalogues of, xvii, 214–16; collections of, xv, xvii–xviii, 98, 205, 211–13, 268n12; founders or officers of, xiv, xviii, 207–8, 210, 211, 213, 229n1, 268n14; geographical limits of, 211–12; headquarters of, xiii–xiv, 210–11; importance of, xiii, 206, 212, 216; library of, 208, 210; mission of, xiii, 210, 211, 267n4; Nāgarī promoted by, xiii, 207, 211; photos of, xxii, 228; publications of, xiii, xiv, 4, 20–21, 212, 218; surveys done by, 20, 206, 208, 210, 214–16

Nagaur, 148, 192

Nal Daman of Faizi, 26–27, 233n1

Nal Daman of Surdas, 26–28, 53, 60–62, 63, 214, 223–24, 233n1, 233n3, 239n75; scribal colophon on, 62. *See also* Surdas (17th cent.)

Namdev, 98, 154, 166, 172, 175, 179, 244n43, 245n66

Name (of God or *Rām*), 81, 83, 98, 107, 198, 241nn12–14

Nanak, Guru, 16, 181–82, 189, 261n50, 265n99; background of, 166–67, 185, 261n40; book (*kitāb* or *pothī*) of or as, 167–68, 190, 193, 244n57, 261n44; *chāp* of, 171; hagiographies of, 167, 169, 171, 189, 244n57, 261n40; language of, 7; merchant community of, 84, 166–67, 185; meters used by, 85; in non-Sikhs' anthologies, 172, 177–78, 262n63; *śabad* and *salok* by, 167; "seal" (*nīsān*) of, 84, 87, 171, 186; vocational literacy of, 166–67, 170; writing as theme for, 83–85, 154, 170

Naraina, 172, 191–92, 256n85, 266n124

Naths, 8, 81, 177, 179, 233n7, 247n84, 247n86

nationalists, linguistic or literary, xvi, 2, 4, 215, 220

National Mission for Manuscripts, xv, 229n3

networks: book-circulation, xv, 57, 60, 219, 225; communication, 37; of connoisseurs, 57; intellectual, xvi, 19, 121, 123, 125, 132, 149, 219, 225, 226; patronage, 82; of textual specialists, xix, 11; trade, 226; transportation, 37

Niranjani monks, 98, 102, 256n85, 257n87; authors or poets, 2, 19, 122, 127–29, 133, 148, 149, 189, 192, 230–31n1; backgrounds of, 14, 144, 147; copyists or scribes, 14, 119, 141, 144, 146–48, 150, 155, 178, 180, 184, 187, 226, 256n77; literacy of, 125–26, 144; *pothī*s of, 119, 141; scholars, 122, 125–30, 132–33; *sevā* (service) of, 121

Niranjani Sampraday: academic literature on, 2, 102, 122, 230n1; anthologies of, 186–87, 246n69; canonization of scriptures in, 20, 141; decentralized, 191–92; female ascetics in, 252n31; gurus in, 145–46, 154–55, 180, 187, 193; hagiographies in (*see* hagiographies: Niranjani); influence of, 150, 230n1; kings or queens and, 148, 150, 256n85; manuscript output of, 2, 14, 15, 25, 146; media change embraced by, xxi, 150, 158; monastic recruitment in, 14; monks of (*see* Niranjani monks); notebooks of, 76, 98, 102; religious practices in, 81, 154, 180, 192; saints of, 98, 105, 120, 154–55, 160, 170, 179, 184, 192, 244n42, 245n66, 264n82, 264n84 (*see also* Haridas Niranjani); *samādhis* of, 154, 159, 179, 192, 193, 263n81; scribes of (*see* scribes: Niranjani); scriptures of, 40, 154–55, 157–59, 163, 166, 178, 180, 187–88, 193 (*see also* Niranjani Vāṇī); Sikhs and, 16; temples of, 179, 263n81; writing practices or culture in, 20, 130, 160, 174, 184–87

Niranjani *Vāṇī*, 178–80, 183–84, 187, 193, 197, 198, 199, 263nn81–82, 265n97

nirguṇ bhakti communities: canonization of books in, 20, 141, 156, 244n57, 257–58n8, 258n15; conventional ideas about, 15, 77, 110, 132, 149, 226, 247n84, 268n16; earliest known manuscripts of, 80; gurus in, 146; hagiographies of, 35–36, 88; householders or lay devotees, 18, 101, 122; merchants and clerks in, 123, 167; monks in (*see* nirguṇ monks); north Indian, 15, 40, 85–86, 98, 172, 189, 245n66, 262n64; notebooks used by, 100–102; pedagogy in, 141; performance practices of, 130; in Rajasthan, 15, 76, 246n74, 252n31; religious practices of, 81, 101, 130, 241n14; scholasticism and, 19, 122; women in, 252n31; writing culture and, 15, 42, 85, 87

nirguṇ bhakti literature: anthologies, 101, 161, 174–77, 240n7; genres of, 18, 77, 132, 214; historiography and, 149; in language or literary histories, 149, 214, 233n7, 252n35; in notebooks, 74, 76, 98, 161; paradoxical imagery in, 91; terms or topics in, 13, 241n12, 243n33

nirguṇ bhakti saints, 13, 34, 74, 76, 98, 176–77, 242n29; criticize books and book learning, 78, 107–8, 149, 160; criticize Jains, 76; criticize pandits or intellectuals, 79, 85, 149, 240n7; criticize "superstitions," 102; criticize writing, 18, 82, 87–88, 93; emphasize experience, 79, 107; emphasize orality, 131, 176, 241n12

nirguṇ monks: authors or poets, 127, 134; intellectual networks of, 132–34; literary and scholastic writing by, 125–26, 132–35; metaphysics of sound for, 132; notebooks of, 18, 101–2, 104–5, 109–10; scholars, 122, 125–26, 131–35, 146, 148; travel by, 101

Nizamuddin Auliya, 243n38

notebooks: astrological materials in, xvii, 2, 19, 74–75, 77, 102, 109–10, 218, 247n85; auspicious syllables in, 116, 117; *bahī* features in, 97, 225; bound, 13; books versus, xx; as "briefcases," 19, 75–76; cataloguing of, 216, 218; circulation of, 104; contents in, xvii, 19; diverse materials in, 74, 76, 97–98, 110, 218; hagiographies' silence on, 93; material forms of, 95–96, 103; monks' or *sadhus*', 101–2, 110; multiple owners of, 104–5, 110; *nirguṇ*, 18, 97–98, 101–2, 104–5, 110; notational writing in, 93; orthography of, 94; performances using, 76, 94–95, 99, 102–3; personal, xvii, xx, 3, 94, 103, 135; *pothī* and, 136–37, 138, 244n57; *puja* of, 137; punctuation in, 109; rebinding or additions to, 104–5; Sanskrit in, 75, 240n3; scripts used in, 75, 85; songs in (*see* song notebooks; songs: notebooks including); *vāṇī* versus, 180; verse order in, 99–100; vocational literacy and, 14, 19, 96. *See also* guṭakā; safīnah

Novetzke, Christian, 9, 188, 249n97, 263n70

numbering: of folios, 75, 120, 139, 155, 184; of Gurus (*mahal*), 182; in reports, 214; of *sākhīs*, 101; tallies, 139, 184; of verses, 75, 99, 101, 108, 109, 115, 116, 139, 155, 254nn53–54

nuskhah, xviii–xix

O'Hanlon, Rosalind, 11, 232n17

Ollett, Andrew, 9, 61

Ong, Walter, xxi, 85

Orsini, Francesca, 4, 9, 29, 265n101, 269n28; on *pem-kathās*, 38, 55

orthography, xxi, 17, 48; Arabic-script, 42, 46; errors in, 143; for *guṭakā* notebooks, 94–95; for *pem-kathā*, 62; for *pothīs*, 137–38, 143; Sanskrit and Sanskritized, 137–38; in Sikh scriptures, 185, 261n44; variants in, 23, 46; vernacular, 30, 42, 46, 95, 143

pad. See lyrics
Padmāvat: in Kaithī script, 53–54, 68; performances of, 38; with Persian notes, 54, 72, 103, 218; print editions of, 56, 73, 238nn60–61. *See also* Jayasi, Malik Muhammad
pagination, 28, 43, 46–47, 50, 56
painters, 12, 35, 45, 50, 221, 224, 239n71; as readers, 48–50. *See also* illustrators
paintings: added later, 223–24; books in, 103, 136–37, 149, 151, 248n88; cataloguing of, 222–23; gilded, 237n55; iconic figures in, 50, 237n53; "Indic," 222; on paper, 135; Rajput, 237n52; scribes in, 237n54; stencils used for, 224. *See also* illustrations
palm leaf manuscripts, xv, xvii, 28, 206, 214, 217; as archetype, 11, 42, 120, 135–36, 143, 160; paper displaces (or not), 5, 11, 42, 44, 135, 164, 232n16, 232n18, 236n38; *pothī*, 32, 78, 135, 137, 143, 160
Pañc Vāṇī, 172, 175–76, 179, 183, 240n11, 262n63, 263n74
pandits: authority of, 123, 241n13; Brahmin, 8, 11, 78, 92, 150, 231–32n14, 240n7, 241n13; court, 123, 226; criticism or satire of, 78–79, 92, 136, 149, 154, 240n7, 241n13; libraries of, 123, 209, 210, 212; as listeners, 35; *paṇḍit* or *paṇḍita*, 19, 31, 35, 78, 119; *pothī*-reading, 78–79, 82, 92, 119, 136, 240n7; Sanskrit, 8, 133, 149; speechless, 31, 35
pāṇḍulipi, xviii, 206
paper, 5, 19, 206, 214, 215, 224, 232nn17–18, 249n2; cloth, 11, 44, 74; dimensions of, 135, 143, 232n18; early, 232n18, 236n38, 249n2; fine-grained, 61; impact of, 11, 42, 135; imported, 11, 44; indigenous, 44, 135; intellectual networks and, 122, 163; mixed types of, 96; in Mughal era, 135, 164; in notebooks, 74, 94–96; performance and, 103, 121, 232n17; poems mentioning, 41–42, 74, 82–84, 86, 170, 236n37, 244n46; religious use of, 236n37; rice, 66; rulers of or ruling lines on (*see* rulers; ruling); scraps of, 13, 72; scrolls, 28; terms for, 42, 44, 83; types of, 11; unbound folios of, 28, 32, 78, 135–36, 164; "world [earth] into," 86. *See also* palm leaf manuscripts: paper displaces; *pothī:* paper
paper makers, 12, 44, 135, 185, 186
Paramānand Prabodh, 1, 143, 145
paratexts, xxi, 9, 17, 21, 75–76, 99, 138, 225; absent or minimal, 75–76, 101, 105; in anthologies, 20, 158, 178, 183; red ink for, 120, 139; in *pem-kathās*, 44, 54, 56; in *pothīs*, 120, 138–40, 225, 256n74; Sanskrit and, 120, 139–40, 144–45, 183, 225, 256n74; in Sikh scripture, 168, 178
patronage, 58–59, 121, 206, 237n48; competition for, 15, 146, 160, 258n16; for oral performances, 91; royal, 58, 160, 162, 165; for scriptural works, 165; spiritual merit of, 91; systems of, 43, 81–82
patrons: Afghans, 37, 61, 239n75; of authors or poets, 17, 37, 236n42; book artists' choices of, 58–59, 61; of *Candāyan* copies, 43–44, 46, 51, 221, 237n55; as collaborators, 51, 232n18; colophons name (*see under* colophons); innovation and, 44; of monks, 147, 258n16; Mughal-era, 18, 58, 163, 164, 165, 236n45, 255n69; Persianized elites, 17; praised, 31–32, 35, 43, 62, 236n42; Rajputs, 36, 59, 81, 82, 163, 239n72, 270n46; of scribes, 2, 27–28, 62; women, 22; written codices and, 43, 46
pem-kathā: in archives, catalogues, or literary histories, 211, 213–14, 218, 223; audiences for, 17–18, 38; calligraphic innovations for, 45–46; characterization of reading in, 39; circulation of, 18, 57; codex book format of, 52; colonial-era, 238n60; conventions of, 27, 34, 52–53, 55–56, 60, 224; deluxe copies of, 28, 44, 46, 51, 53, 60, 223, 259n26; genre of, 17, 27–28, 43, 62, 214; illustrated, 51, 53, 55, 224–25, 219; language of, 18, 27, 55, 269n26; manuscripts of, 17–18, 28; notebook with condensed, 76, 218, 269n26; not "Hindu" or "Islamic," 55; paratextual materials in, 48, 54; patrons of, 43, 53, 59; performances of, 18, 38, 46, 55, 57, 62; popularity of, 17–18, 213; prefaces to, 17, 34, 36, 43, 48; *prem rasa* and, 39, 242n22; print editions of, 56; scripts used for, 211; stanzaic layout of, 52–53, 56, 223, 224; Sufis and, 17, 57, 62, 110, 213; unillustrated, 52, 54; written scripture in, 18, 35, 39. *See also* Candāyan; Mirgāvatī; Nal Daman of Surdas; Padmāvat
pens, 42, 74, 137; in paintings, 237n54; poems mentioning, 41, 83, 84, 86, 88, 170, 244n46
people of the book, 159, 164–65

Persian, 6, 40, 120, 136, 226, 239n74, 239n76; as administrative language, xix, 207, 234n12; *akhlāq* and *adab* genres in, 147; authors writing in, 56, 88; calligraphy in, 47, 186, 237n46; cataloguing of works in, 217; as classical language, 56, 225; in colonial era, 207; colophons or headings in, 47–48, 62, 223; commentaries in, 248n93; as cosmopolitan language, 11–12, 39, 55; critiques in, 87; esoteric works in, 28–39; in Hindi lexicon, 12, 22, 55, 207, 254n50; *kitāb*-style codices in, 44; linguistic ideology of, 11; literary conventions in, 30, 34, 36; literary culture of, 11, 170; marginalia in, 54, 103; *masnavī* in, 31, 37, 45, 54; in Mughal era, 26, 56, 164, 207, 233n23, 234n12; in multilingual contexts, 29–30, 54, 62, 103, 164, 177, 218, 234n10, 254n50; Nala/Damayanti story in, 26–27, 233n1; *pem-kathā* genre and, 18, 28, 55; people literate in, 30, 44, 167, 233n23; in performance traditions, 38; poetry in, 54, 103, 218; in *safīnah*, 103–4, 237n46, 248n90, 248n93; script used for, 22–23; in sultanate era, 56; terms for books in, xix; translations into or from, 36, 147, 164, 260n31; as "Turki," 170; writing in, 42–43, 55, 225. *See also* book cultures: Persianate
personal notebooks. *See* notebooks: personal
Plato, xx, 87
poeticians, 124–25, 127, 250n11
poetic theories (*alaṁkāra-śāstra*; *rīti granth*), 5, 123–27, 250–51n14, 253n40
poetry: in Akbar's library, 164; anthologies of, 104, 216, 248n90; audiences for, 134; *bahī*s or ledgers and, 97; in *bayāẓ* or *safīnah*, 103; book arts and, 62; Buddhist, 233n7; cataloguing of, 216–18; classifications of, 127; connoisseurs of, 142; courtly, 98, 121, 134, 206, 217, 236n42, 265n97; emotions and, 126, 250nn12–13, 251n20; erotic, 110, 252n32; formulaic phrasings in, 100; as label (or not), 29, 126, 100–101, 234n15, 235n23; languages of, 61; martial, 206; material forms of, 135; Nath, 233n7; nonsectarian manuscripts of, 86; in notebooks, 85, 97–98, 103–4, 138, 246n71, 248n92; oral composition of, 77, 89; parody in, 92; poetic or rhetorical devices in, 91, 124, 126, 251n18; in *pothī*, 244n57; recitation or singing of, 89–90, 100–101, 103, 121; *rīti*, 5, 98, 110; *saguṇ*, 110; songs versus, 100; topics of, 126; written down, 163, 187–88. *See also* devotional poetry; *nirguṇ bhakti* poetry
poets: aspiring, 103, 134, 248n92; authorial personas of, 88; *bhakti* and, 8, 18, 125; *bhāṣā* or vernacular, 7–9, 17–18, 42, 87, 123, 225, 231n14, 250n10, 250–51n14; biographies about, 104, 207, 219, 231n14; competitions of, 252n34; court or courtly, 30, 43, 62, 85, 86, 110, 123, 125–26, 134, 217, 246n71, 247n83, 250n14, 251n17; as historical actors, 16; in literary histories, 98, 207, 233n7, 267n3; monks, 19, 135, 149, 172, 217; in multilingual culture, 43, 45, 47; patronage for, 17, 37, 236n42; *rīti*, 98, 125, 126, 129, 251n14; self-identification as (or not), 19, 100, 126; women, 22, 233n23; on writing as a practice, 12, 18, 38
Pollock, Sheldon, 29, 231n10, 250n12; on "cosmopolitan vernaculars," 6; modifications of ideas of, 100, 122; vernacularization thesis of, 2–3, 8–9
*pothī*s: in art or literature, 1, 31–32, 78, 137, 151, 164, 244n57 (*see also* pothīs: pandits read); *basta*s for, 96, 136, 253nn44–45; cataloguing of, 136; circulation of, 19, 134, 141, 146–49; colophons in, 139, 141–46, 176–77; conventions of, 120, 134–37, 187, 239nn71–72; copying of, 1, 19, 139, 141, 143–44; as currency, 121, 145; defined, 19, 32; genres appearing in, 52, 135, 225, 239n72; *guṭakā*s versus, 94–96, 109, 137–38; as icon, 137, 141; Jain, 253–54n49; language(s) of, 120, 135, 137–38, 143, 144, 225; modern books versus, 121; orthography of, 94, 137–38, 143, 185; palm-leaf (*see* palm leaf manuscripts: *pothī*); pandits read, 19, 78–79, 82, 92, 119, 121, 136, 240n7; paper, 19, 32, 78, 120, 135–36, 143, 160; paratexts in, 120, 138–40, 225, 256n74; in pedagogical performances, 19, 121, 137, 140–41, 144, 149; readers or reading of, 136–37, 142; ruling elites read, 31–32, 35, 142, 147–48; ruling of lines in, 143; scholarly works in, 119, 122, 134–40, 142, 144–48, 225; Sikh, 167–68, 181–82, 185, 244n57, 256n74, 261n44 (*see also* Goindval *pothī*s; Guru Harsahai *pothī*; Kartarpur *pothī*); size of, 135, 143; unbound, 19, 32, 96, 121, 135–36, 139 (*see also* basta); use of, 19, 121, 140–41, 145, 149
Prakrit: aesthetic conventions of, 42–43; cataloguing of works in, 216; as classical language, 208; colophons in, 205; as

cosmopolitan language, 3, 8–9, 55, 96; education in, 240n8; layout conventions of, 42, 120; literacy in, 96; as literary language, 8–9, 61; loanwords from, 12, 55; manuscript conventions for, 42–43, 55, 120, 122; manuscripts in, 11, 21, 216, 255n61, 268n19; *pothī*s in, 120, 135; *śāstra* in, 129, 251n24; term *grantha* in, 160
prem-ākhyān. *See* pem-kathā
Prince of Wales Museum. *See* Chhatrapati Shivaji Maharaj Vastu Sangrahalaya
print technology, xviii, xx–xxi, 2, 56, 205
Prithi Chand, 167, 261n44
publishing, xx, 56, 103–4
punctuation, 46, 109, 138; *daṇḍa*, 99, 115
Punjab, 210, 211; Brajbhasha or Hindi in, 77, 256n75; female gurus in, 252n31; Hariramdas's *Chandaratnāvalī* in, 134, 263n80; Hindus in, 27, 214; *nirguṇ* works in, 134, 146, 150; scripts used in, 52; Sikhs in, 16, 133, 134, 146, 263n80
Punjabi, 7, 27, 60, 120, 135, 269n30; in anthologies, 177; literature in, 256n75
purān, 39–40
*purāṇa*s, 11, 108, 126, 232n17; cataloguing of, 217; commentaries on, 121, 130, 133, 134; copying of, 81, 162–63, 255n64; devotional poets on, 108, 235n25; education in, 97, 126; illustrated copies of, 163; mythic dictation of, 85; orality privileged in, 156, 158; *pem-kathā*s mention, 31, 35; in *pothī* format, 135, 137; rituals for, 81–83; in Sikh hagiographies, 169; term defined, 35; vernacular meaning of term, 35; written copies of, 162–63
Pushtimarg, 15, 133–34, 165; *Bhāgavata Purāṇa* for, 81–82, 162; *pothī*s for, 136–37; *vārtā*s of, 161, 259n19
puṣpikā, 254n60
pustak, *pustaka*, or *pustakam*, xxi, 176, 205, 241n12, 243n37, 253n41

*qāẓī*s, 92, 93, 167, 209
Qur'an, 35, 40–41, 92, 164, 181, 186, 236n38, 242n18
Qutban, Shaikh Suhravardi, 26, 35–39, 53, 237n54, 242n29

Radhavallabhi Sampraday, 16, 133
raga (*rāga*), 75, 173, 246nn73–74; notations of, 75, 99, 115, 116; organization by, 99, 155, 168, 178, 181–82; vernacularized terms for, 99
rāgamālā, 61, 168, 181, 264nn91–92
Raghavdas Dadupanthi, 88, 172, 189, 192, 244n42, 264n82
Raghunathdas Niranjani, 88–89, 91, 263–64n82
raḥl, 51, 136, 151, 155
Rajasthan, 91, 151, 212; archives or libraries in, 216–17, 230n5; book ateliers in, 59; central, 108, 249n98; courts or rulers in, 59, 133, 147, 233n23, 246n74, 249n98; monks or monk-scholars in, 134, 150; musicological writing in, 246n74; Nathdwara in, 121, 134, 151; northern, 133; notebooks from, 74–76, 217; paintings in, 137, 151; patronage in, 59, 233n23; poetic competitions in, 252n34; religious communities in, 2, 15, 76, 81–82, 137, 230n1, 240n11, 246n74, 252n31, 257n87 (*see also* Dadu Panth; Niranjani Sampraday; Pushtimarg); saint-poets in or from, 15, 77, 89; scripts used in, 240n1; Sikhs in, 16, 133; southeastern, 15; western dialects in, 10; women in, 233n23, 252n31. *See also* Marwar
Rajasthani, 7, 177; cataloguing of works in, 216–18; in notebooks, 95; romance in, 110
Rajasthani Shodh Sansthan, 216, 230n5
Rajasthan Oriental Research Institute, 2, 206, 212, 216; manuscripts held by, 75, 104, 105, 184, 217, 230n5, 263n81
Rajjabdas Dadupanthi (Rajjab), 98, 173–74, 176–78, 183, 240n11, 262n63, 263n66. *See also* Sarvāṅgīs
Rajputs, 86, 97, 142; authors, 134, 148, 253n38; bibliophiles, 51, 59, 148, 163; courts of, 59, 85, 123, 125, 133–34, 148, 165, 185, 233n23, 239n71, 260n37; Dadu Panth and, 165, 188; elites, 165, 169; libraries of, 211–12; painters, 239n71; kings or queens, 59, 134, 147–48, 150, 165, 211, 253n38; Niranjanis and, 165; patrons (*see* patrons: Rajput); political ideology of, 147, 157, 165; scripts used by, 185; Sikhs and, 165, 169, 188; written scriptures and, 163, 165
Ram (*nirguṇ*), 74, 83, 120; Name of, 154, 170, 241nn12–13
Ram (*saguṇ*; Ramachandra), 15, 77, 98, 99, 133, 177, 179, 256n85, 264n86
Rāmacaritamānas, 46, 218, 250n12, 251n20; in Arabic script, 211; editions of, 218; monks copy, 146, 150; miraculous manuscript of, 231–32n14; in *pothī* format, 121. *See also* Tulsidas

Rāmājña Rām Kathā, 146, 152
Ramanandi Sampraday, 88, 133–34, 188, 244n43
Rāmāyaṇa, 85, 144, 164, 264n86
Ramdas, Guru, 141–42, 155, 167, 168, 171
Ramdaspur, 168–69, 171–72, 190, 261
Ramsnehi Sampraday, 15, 89, 98, 102, 132, 174
rasa, 34, 38, 43, 60, 62, 91, 100, 252n35; Daud on, 234n15; Jayasi's metaphor of, 38–39; Keshavdas on, 250n13; Manjhan on, 42; in poetic theory, 126; *prem* or love, 83, 242n22
rāso genre, 8, 10, 206, 233n7, 267n2
Rathore, 147, 148, 256n85
Ravidas, 36, 77, 78, 241nn13–14, 242n29, 244n43; anthologies including, 161, 172, 175; in Dadu Panth, 86; in Fatehpur manuscript, 86; hagiographies of, 89–91; in *Guru Granth Sāhib*, 166, 266n116; meters used by, 85; in notebooks, 18, 98; *pad*s by, 82, 266n116; recurring terms or phrases of, 13; subaltern status of, 77, 82, 89, 241n13; writing for, 78, 82–83, 85–88, 126, 170, 243n33
reading: aloud or vocalized, 10, 94, 121, 138, 149, 164, 245n60, 255n61; close or distant, 12–13; as embodied practice, 10–11, 79, 136; as gendered practice, 22; illustrations and, 48–51, 220, 237n45, 237n52; as intellectual practice, 10–11, 141; material dimension of, 10–11; norms or protocols for, xix, 10–11, 37, 121, 139, 149; orality and, 10, 23, 39, 42–43, 47, 93, 94, 109, 121, 131, 143, 255n61; as performance, 35, 54, 94, 131, 139; public, 82; "for purpose of" (*paṭhanārtha*), 141, 146, 255n61; scribal cues for, 48, 139; silent or private, 121, 131, 209, 245n60; singing or speaking versus, 108, 255n61; skepticism toward, 78–80, 241n12; as social practice, 10–11, 35; term *bāṁc-* for, 35, 257n86; term *paḍh-* for, 32, 80, 130
religious orders, 141, 161. *See also* monastic orders; Sufi orders
rulers (of lines), 44, 51, 186
ruling (of lines), 13, 28, 44, 95, 120, 187; *misṭara* or pencil for, 143
Rupa Gosvami, xix
Rushd-nāma, 37

safīnah, xxi, 103–4, 237n46, 248n88, 248n90, 248nn92–93
saguṇ bhakti, 15, 77, 98–99, 110, 161, 166, 244n43, 264n86
saints. *See* nirguṇ bhakti saints
sākhīs: in anthologies, 80, 101, 155, 177, 182–84, 187, 219; Dadu Panthi, 81, 91, 173, 182–84, 241n12; *dohā* meter of, 85; exegesis of, 101, 187; Kabir's, 78, 86, 107, 244n46, 260n38; meaning of term, 80; Niranjani, 184, 187; *nirguṇ*, 101, 132, 177; in notebooks, 18, 97, 101, 109, 225; orality and, 77, 80, 89, 91–92, 108, 225; poetic theories and, 124, 126–27; as witness, 80, 173
sampradāys, 15, 172. *See also* monastic orders
Sanskrit, 28, 37, 177, 243n37, 247n83, 250n10; aesthetic domain of, 9, 43; authority or hegemony of, 8, 79, 122, 123–24; cataloguing works in, 216–18, 268n10, 268n19; collecting manuscripts in, 208, 216; conventions of, 30, 43, 122, 137; as cosmopolitan language, 2–3, 11–12, 39, 40, 55, 100; discursive literacy in, 96–97; Hindi translations or transcreations of, 104, 121, 129, 146, 260n31; lexicon of, 12–13, 207, 254n50; literary devices in, 34, 124; literary theories in, 124–28, 250n12, 251n14 (*see also* poetic theories); literature in 37, 41, 42, 56, 100, 149, 217 (*see also* kāvya); "look" of books in, 145, 225; "made into vernacular," 129; Mirza Khan on, 61; monks trained in, 126, 240n8; musicological works in, 99; in notebooks, 75, 240n3; orality and, 87–88; in paper manuscripts, 11, 121, 135; paratexts in, 120, 145, 139–40, 145, 225, 256n74; *pothī*s in, 120, 135; pseudo, pidgin, or para-, 105, 120, 144–45, 182–83, 225, 256n74, 265n97; religious works in, 119, 121, 133, 143, 161, 162–63, 255n64; revivals of, 148; *sampradāys* writing in, 15–16; scribes working in, 42, 137–38, 139, 143, 147, 254n53, 255n64, 255n68; scripts for, 23; shastric writing in 129–30, 254n50; term *granth* in, 40, 159–60; term *paṭhanārtha* in, 255n61; term *puṣpikā* in, 254n60; term *vāṇī* in, 159; vernacular mediation of, 11, 144–45, 165; as "workly" language, 8; as written language, 8, 100
Sant Guṇ Sāgar, 173, 190. *See also* Madhavdas
sant traditions, 76, 93, 98, 174, 191, 241n12, 258n15; Sikhism and, 166–67
Sarvāṅgīs, 172, 176–79, 182–83, 193, 240n11; poets included in, 178–79, 262n63. *See also* Gopaldas; Rajjabdas Dadupanthi
śāstras, 19, 122–25, 129–34, 137–41, 148, 150, 163, 225, 251n23, 251n24, 254n50, 254n57

satsaṅg, 15, 38–39, 108–9, 245n67
scribe(s): *bhāṣā* sounds transcribed by, 27–28, 42–43, 46–47, 234n10, 249n10; colophons by, 1–2, 62, 134, 141, 143, 147; complaints by, 143, 155; consciousness as a, 84; conventions followed by, 27–28, 52–53, 56, 134–38, 141–42; as copyeditors, 138; Dadu Panthi, 173–75, 184, 187; gurus or saints and, 173, 181, 263n70; headings or paratexts added by, 45, 47, 48, 54, 139–40, 254n53; illegible writing or errors by, 94, 143, 254n54; innovations by (or not), 9, 11, 12, 44–48, 50, 56, 232n18; Iranian, 234n13; *kātib*, 44; monks as (*see* monks: copyists or scribes); *munshī*, 55; *Nal Daman* (*see* Babullah bin Sayid Muhammad); Niranjani, 14, 184, 187, 193; paper used by (or not), 42, 44; Persian-literate, xix, 44–47, 97; professional, 59, 103, 135, 139, 142, 237n54; reciters and, 143, 255n64; Sikh, 167, 168, 181, 185, 190, 193, 256n74, 264n92
scriptio continua, 53, 94–95, 97, 138
scripts: calligraphic, 23, 47, 187; conventions across, 52, 53, 56; Devanāgarī, 6, 22; for Hindi, xiv, 6, 7, 21–23, 75, 211; merchant and scribal communities', 126, 185; in notebooks, 19, 75, 95, 96, 105, 111; shorthand, 7, 23, 54; for Urdu, 7, 22. *See also* Arabic script; Kaithī; Gurmukhi; Nāgarī
scriptures: anthologies, 7, 159–60, 172–75, 178–84, 225; authoritative, 166, 168–69, 172, 193; *bhakti*, 15; canonization of, 20; codex-format, 20, 159–60, 179–80; definitions of, 157–60, 258n11; deluxe copies of, 165; as gurus, 159, 183, 190; hagiographies and, 161–62, 172, 178–79, 263–64n82; lexicon for speaking about, 15, 18; literature and, 3; as metonyms, 20, 165, 193; oral origin of, 40, 156, 159, 257n2; in *pothī*, 32; ritual veneration of, 156, 160, 180, 191, 263n83; song versus, 161; term problematized, 155–56; as "things," 258n12; as transcriptions, 35–36; vernacular, 15, 155, 158; written, 15, 18, 39–40, 42, 155–60, 163, 165–66, 171, 178
Shah Jahan, Emperor, 239n75, 247n83, 248n88, 248n94
Shamā'il al-Atqiyā, 29
Shirazi, Zayn al-Din, 30
Shiva, 179, 264n86. *See also* Śivamahimnaḥ Stotram
Shukla, Ramchandra, xiv, 4, 8, 213–14, 240n2; on *bhakti* poets or poetry, 87, 98, 110, 213, 246n68, 252n35; critical edition work by, xiv, 218; on origin of Hindi literature, 8, 233n7; periodization of, 213, 268n22
Siddhas, 8
Sikhism: *bastas* used in, 136; canonization of scriptures in, 20, 158–59, 167–69, 178, 185, 187; Dadu Panth and, 16, 146–47, 171–74, 177, 178, 184, 188, 226; as distinct religion, 166, 169, 185, 260n38; Divine Court in, 189; Gurus in, 83, 159, 171, 262n60; hagiographies in (*see* hagiographies: Sikh); Hindu communities and, 16; literacy and writing in, 166–67, 169–70, 244n57; material practices for scriptures in, 160, 186, 190; monastic sects of, 146, 172; Niranjani Sampraday and, 16, 146–47, 172, 178–80, 226; *nirguṇ* traditions and, 15, 40, 133, 134, 166, 189, 244n57; scriptures of (*see* Ādi Granth; Guru Granth Sāhib); term *guṭakā* in, 104, 256n74
silsilahs. *See* Sufi orders
singers: improvisation by, 14, 99–100; notebooks of (*see* song notebooks); performances by, 12, 13–14, 46, 95, 99–100, 107, 109; repertoires of, 97–98
Singh, Pashaura, 265n99, 265n101
Śivamahimnaḥ Stotram, 41, 42, 87, 243n36
social relationships, 2, 3, 104–5, 149, 165, 248n92
Sodhis, 167–68, 261n44, 261n49
song notebooks, 7, 14, 18–19, 52, 78, 93–95, 97–101, 108, 244n57, 245n64
songs (*gīt*, *gāthā*): in bound codices, 20, 154 (*see also* vāṇi); circulation of, 85; ecumenical performances of, 161; feelings evoked by, 107; Jain, 76, 212; literature versus, 30, 37, 51, 100–101, 231n10; liturgical, xvii, 94; *nirguṇ*, 34, 85, 105, 131, 161, 175–76; notebooks including 74–76, 104 (*see also* song notebooks); performance versus paper for, 94, 158; in *pothīs*, 51, 187; of saints, 36, 85, 90, 154, 173, 175 (*see also* vāṇi); scripture versus, 161; Shia *mārṣiyah* elegies, 212
soraṭhā, 36–37
stanzas, 28, 40; headings for, 47–48, 223; illustrations and, 48–51, 53, 223, 224, 270n43; *kaḍavak*, 37, 45–46, 52; layout of, 45–46, 50, 52–53, 56, 223, 224; line breaks between, 53

Sufi orders, 15, 33, 55, 209
Sufis: authors or poets, 10, 15, 32, 33, 42–43, 46, 62, 242n22; *bhaktas* or yogis and, 37; *bhakti* and, 15, 30, 98, 247n85; Chishti, 29–30; influence of, 36; *k͟hānqah* of, 221; in literary histories, 110, 213–14; musical performances of, 30, 38; *pīrs*, saints, or teachers, 29, 57, 59, 166, 177, 189, 243n38; as readers, 39, 42–43, 54, 110; religious practices of, 33; romances of, 4, 28–29, 43–44, 226 (*see also* pem-kathā); *samā'* gatherings of, 38–39; Shattari, 42; translators, 36
Sundardas, 13, 78, 119, 147, 179, 243n32, 251n17; background and education of, 126, 127, 252n34; influence of, 191, 250n12, 252n34; *Jñānasamudra* by, 131–32, 133, 140–41, 146, 250n12, 251n20; poetic theory of, 126–28, 252n32; *pothī* in paintings of, 137; *savaiyā* poems by, 134, 146, 250n12
Surdas (17th cent.), 27, 32, 60, 214, 233n3. *See also* Nal Daman of Surdas
Surdas of Braj (16th cent.), 10, 27, 98, 101, 161, 246n71, 249n97; in Dadu Panthi scriptures, 172, 177–78; in Sikh scriptures, 166, 168, 172; *Sūrasāgar* by, 211

table of contents, 155, 168, 184
Tamil, 8, 251n24
tazkirahs, 104, 207, 248n93
ṭek, 99, 106, 109
Tibet, 11
trade, 11, 14, 57, 85, 104, 205, 226
traders. *See* merchants
Tughlaq dynasty, 30, 31, 76, 234n12
Tuhfat al-Hind, 27, 61, 233n5
Tulsidas: Name praised by, 98–99; narrative-based lyrics of, 101; on soul of poetry, 250n12, 251n20; performances of songs by, 46, 161; paintings of, 137. *See also* Rāmacaritamānas
"Turki" or "Turaki" 33–34, 39, 170, 225
Turkish, 12, 22, 55, 207, 217

unvān, 186
Upadhyay, Ayodhya Singh "Harioudh," xiv
Urdu: cataloguing of works in, 217; Hindi and, 55, 217, 223; in library collections, 211, 270n45; scripts used for, 7, 22, 211; terms for books in, xviii

Vaishnavas or Vaishnavism, 85, 101, 189; narrative-based lyrics of, 101; *nirguṇ* monks' exchanges with, 132–34; patronage of, 163, 165; poets or poetry, 98, 125, 161, 178, 179, 267n3; *saguṇ* association with, 15, 77, 98; scholars, xix, 15–16; scriptures of, 81–82, 161–63; Sikhism and, 166; spread of, 133, 163
Vallabhacharya, 137, 151, 161
Vallabha Sampraday, 15, 133, 151. *See also* Pushtimarg
vāṇī, xxi, 20, 206; Amardas's, 154–55, 187, 193, 194, 196; authority of, 190–92; conceptualization of, 155–56, 159; *guru-*, 173–75, 183, 190; other book formats and, 95, 187; as relic, 193; as scripture or sacred, 155, 225; as speech, 129, 159; table of contents in, 184, 194; used for sermonizing, 180, 187; as "utterance," 154; venerated, 155, 159, 174–75, 187, 190–91, 193, 264n83; written, 192. *See also* Dādū Vāṇī; Niranjani Vāṇī; Pañc Vāṇī
Vararuchi, 31, 235n16
Vedānta Mahāvākya Bhāṣā, 128, 133, 139–41, 145, 148, 153, 217. *See also* Manohardas Niranjani
vernacular, the, 21–22. *See also* bhāṣā; deśa bhāṣā; Hindi
vernacular book culture. *See* book cultures: vernacular
vernacularization, 2–4, 9, 17, 19, 122, 149, 156, 225
Vidyapati, 86, 233n7
Vīsaladev Rāso, 10
visarga, 99, 116, 265n96
Vishnudas, 10, 85, 242n29

women, 22, 163, 233n23, 252n31; in *Candāyan* illustrations, 49, 51
writing: criticized, 15, 18, 81–82, 85, 87–89, 93, 160, 170; defined, 5–6; gender and, 22; habit or muscle memory of, 75; history of, xxi, 3–6, 11–12, 16–17, 40, 242n27; ideologies of, 5, 16, 17, 60; Islamicate cultures, in 18, 32; literature and, 2–3, 29, 100; materials used for, xv, 12, 40–42, 214; orality and, 34–39, 87, 143, 156, 159, 257n2; practice or performance of, 5, 12, 16, 17, 40, 42, 75, 130; as religious act, 16, 170; saints' critiques of; scriptural canonization and, 156–58; social epistemology of, xx–xxi; as technology, 20, 79, 86; terms for, 5–6; of vernacular languages, 3, 17, 18, 31, 225

yogic practices, 33, 37, 76, 106, 107, 109, 118, 132, 177; eggplant recipe for, 76; Nath, 177, 247n86

Zainuddin, Shaikh, 32–33

GPSR Authorized Representative: Easy Access System Europe, Mustamäe tee 50, 10621 Tallinn, Estonia, gpsr.requests@easproject.com

www.ingramcontent.com/pod-product-compliance
Lightning Source LLC
Chambersburg PA
CBHW022032290426
44109CB00014B/831